COMPARATIVE POLITICS

Integrating Theories, Methods, and Cases

CANADIAN EDITION

COMPARATIVE POLITICS

Integrating Theories, Methods, and Cases

J. Tyler Dickovick

Jonathan Eastwood

David B. MacDonald

OXFORD
UNIVERSITY PRESS

OXFORD
UNIVERSITY PRESS

Oxford University Press is a department of the University of Oxford. It furthers the University's objective of excellence in research, scholarship, and education by publishing worldwide. Oxford is a registered trade mark of Oxford University Press in the UK and in certain other countries.

Published in Canada by
Oxford University Press
8 Sampson Mews, Suite 204,
Don Mills, Ontario M3C 0H5 Canada

www.oupcanada.com

First Edition published in 2020

Library and Archives Canada Cataloguing in Publication
Title: Comparative politics : integrating theories, methods, and cases / by J. Tyler Dickovick, Jonathan Eastwood, and David B. MacDonald.
Names: Dickovick, J. Tyler, 1973-2019, author. | Eastwood, Jonathan, author. | MacDonald, David Bruce, author.
Description: Includes bibliographical references and index.
Identifiers: Canadiana (print) 20190155876 | Canadiana (ebook) 20190155884 | ISBN 9780199026548 (softcover) | ISBN 9780199026555 (EPUB)
Subjects: LCSH: Comparative government—Textbooks. | LCGFT: Textbooks.
Classification: LCC JF51 .D53 2020 | DDC 320.3—dc23

Cover image: ©echo3005/Shutterstock.com
Cover design: Sherill Chapman
Interior design: Sherill Chapman

Oxford University Press is committed to our environment. Wherever possible, our books are printed on paper which comes from responsible sources.

Printed and bound in the United States of America

1 2 3 4 — 23 22 21 20

BRIEF CONTENTS

CONTENTS

BURKINA FASO

BOXES

INSIGHT

ONLINE CASE STUDIES

In addition to the case studies that appear in this book, you can find the following case studies online at **www.oup.com/he/DickovickCe**:

Brazil

- Brazil's Landless Movement
- Does the Global Economy Help or Hurt Developing Nations Like Brazil?
- Electoral Rules and Party (In)Discipline in Brazil's Legislature

Canada

- Should the Senate Be Reformed to Be More Accountable and Democratic?
- Why Does It Take So Long to Choose a Leader?

China

- How Did China Become a Global Economic Power?
- Is China Destined for Democracy?
- Who Governs China?

France

- Authoritarian Persistence in 19th-Century France
- Religion and Secularism in France
- The State in France

Germany

- Consensus-Based Politics in Germany
- Ethnic Boundaries of the German Nation?
- The German State: Unification and Welfare

India

- Democracy's Success in India
- Ethnicity and Political Parties in India
- Federalism and Differences in Development in India

Iran

- Constitutional Design: Theocracy in Iran
- Iran's Islamic Revolution and "Green Revolution"?
- Religion and Politics in Iran

Japan

- How Did Japan's Dominant Party Win for So Long?
- Importing National Identity in Japan?
- Resource Management in Japan
- State-Led Development in Japan

Mexico

- Industrialization, Modernity, and National Identity in Mexico
- Mexico's "Perfect Dictatorship" and Its End
- The PRI and Corporatism in Mexico

Nigeria

- The Presidency in Nigeria: Powers and Limitations
- The Nigerian Civil War or Biafran War: Nationalism and Ethno-national Conflict in a Post-colonial Society
- What Is a Weak State, and Can It Be Changed? The Case of Nigeria

Russia

- Communist Ideology in Practice: Russia and the Soviet Union
- Executives in Russia: Formal and Informal Powers

Saudi Arabia

- How Has Saudi Arabia's Welfare State Saved the Regime?

United Kingdom

- National Identity in the United Kingdom
- Political Economy of Britain
- The State in the United Kingdom

United States

- Did Free Markets Help the United States Get Rich? Will They in the Future?
- Is Judicial Activism in the United States a Problem?
- "The Most Powerful Person in the World"? Checks on American Presidents

PREFACE AND ACKNOWLEDGEMENTS

The field of comparative politics is changing, not only in how it's studied but in how it's taught. This textbook reflects the need for a new approach—one that is truly comparative, that goes beyond a litany of facts or abstract ideas. In the process, we had to rethink what a book for this course should look like. We started with a central aim: to get students to think like comparativists. Toward that end, we have integrated theories and methods with a range of country case applications to address the big questions in comparative politics today.

In this new Canadian adaption, we have also sought to reflect content of interest to Canadian students of comparative politics, most of whom are living through an era of reconciliation between Indigenous and settler peoples, and during a time when multiculturalism remains an important ideational force in Canada. This book updates the earlier US edition, with new content throughout reflecting many of the changes that have taken place since 2015. This includes the rise of global populism in Europe, Asia, Latin America, the United States, and Canada. It also includes many political changes, including the rise of Donald Trump, the re-election of Justin Trudeau's Liberal government in Canada, the machinations of the Islamic State, and the outcome of the Brexit referendum in the United Kingdom.

Many undergraduates take a course in comparative politics because they are broadly interested in world affairs. They want to understand issues such as democracy and democratization, economic and social development, transnational social movements, and the relationship between world religions and conflict around the globe. This book focuses squarely on these big issues and offers a framework for understanding through comparison.

This new adaption shifts the focus from the US version of this book, which tended to assume a certain level of knowledge of American history and politics. It also assumed a certain American-centred standpoint that needed some adjusting for students outside of the United States. Instead, this text now places Canadian students and their experiences at the centre of the analysis. Throughout, Canadian examples and data have been added to help make the concepts more accessible and engaging for students living and studying in Canada. Reflecting David's research interests, there is now considerable coverage given to Indigenous politics and issues affecting Indigenous peoples around the world. There is also additional content on pressing issues of race, gender, and sexual identities in Canada and in comparative context. In Part VI: Country Profiles and Cases, we have also expanded the number of featured countries to 14 (increased from 12), with the addition of Canada and Saudi Arabia. We have also made additional case studies available online at www.oup.com/he/DickovickCe.

Our goal is to enable students to think critically and apply these vital skills to analyze the world around them. We want our students to do more than just memorize facts and theories. Ultimately, we want them to learn how to *do* comparative politics. This course is successful if students can use the comparative method to seek out their own answers. We are successful as educators if we give them the analytical skills to do so.

An Integrative Approach

One of the distinctive features of this book is the way we have integrated theories, methods, and cases. Rather than focusing on either country information or themes of comparative politics, we have combined these approaches while emphasizing application and analysis. By providing students with the tools to begin doing their own analyses, we hope to show them how exciting this kind of work can be. These tools include theories (presented in an accessible way), the basics of the comparative method, and manageable case materials for practice, all in the context of the big questions.

We thus take an integrative approach to the relationship between big themes and country case studies. This text is a hybrid, containing 16 thematic chapters plus linked materials for 14 countries of significant interest to comparativists. This is supplemented by online case study resources. The country materials following the thematic chapters include both basic country information and a series of case studies dealing with specific thematic issues.

We link the country cases to the thematic chapters via short "call out" boxes—**"Cases in Context"**—at relevant points in the chapters. For example, a "Case in Context" box in a discussion of theory in Chapter 3, "The State," points students to a full **case study** on democratic consolidation in Brazil, included at the back of the text.

Using these short "linking" boxes has enabled us to integrate a complete set of case materials without interrupting the narrative flow of the chapters. The kind of reading we suggest with the structure of this text is similar to following hyperlinks in online text—something students do easily. This flexible design feature also caters to the diversity of teaching styles in today's political science classroom. Instructors can choose to have students follow these links to case studies as they go, using all or just some of them, or they can choose to teach thematic chapters and country materials separately.

The text integrates theories, methods, and cases in other ways as well. **"Insights"** boxes make connections by briefly summarizing important scholarly works representative of the major schools of thought.

Each chapter after the introduction closes with a **"Thinking Comparatively"** feature, which focuses on a case or set of cases to illustrate how students can apply the theories discussed in the chapter.

In these features, we highlight important methodological tools or strategies, such as the use of deviant cases and the most-similar-systems (MSS) design. We then model for students how to use these analytical tools in practice.

Organization

We have divided the 16 thematic chapters of this book into five parts:

- Part I (Chapters 1 and 2) focuses on basic methods in comparative politics, covering conceptualization, hypothesis testing, the formation of theories, and the use of evidence. The goal in these first two chapters is not to focus on the details of methodology, which can be taught in more specialized courses, but on the overarching logic of comparative inquiry.
- Part II (Chapters 3 through 7) focuses on the state (Chapter 3), political economy (Chapter 4), development (Chapter 5), democracy and democratization (Chapter 6), and the various forms of authoritarian regimes (Chapter 7).
- Part III (Chapters 8 through 11) focuses on the analysis of political institutions, giving students the tools to analyze institutional design in constitutional structures and judiciaries (Chapter 8), legislatures and elections (Chapter 9), executives (Chapter 10), and political parties and interest groups (Chapter 11).
- Part IV (Chapters 12 through 15) focuses on issues that link comparative politics to political sociology, such as the study of revolution and other forms of contention (Chapter 12), national identities and nationalism (Chapter 13), race, gender, and ethnicity (Chapter 14), and religion and ideology (Chapter 15).
- Part V consists of a single chapter, 16, which links comparative politics to international relations, emphasizing how global politics has produced new sets of problems that both comparativists *and* international relations scholars must analyze. As such, the book points to another kind of integration, pushing students to see connections between comparative politics and other courses in political science.

After Chapter 2, the thematic chapters follow a common format. They are divided into three main sections:

- **Concepts:** covers basic definitions and develops a working vocabulary.
- **Types:** discusses useful typologies, such as the major types of dramatic social change that interest political scientists.
- **Causes and Effects:** walks students through the major theories that aim to explain causes and effects, ending with the "Thinking Comparatively" feature to model analysis.

The final part of the book, Part VI, comprises country **"profiles"** and in-depth **"case studies."** We selected 14 countries after surveying instructors of comparative politics to see which they considered most crucial for inclusion. The cases are Brazil, Canada, China, France, Germany, India, Iran, Japan, Mexico, Nigeria, Russia, Saudi Arabia, the United Kingdom, and the United States. This selection offers broad coverage of every major world region, democratic and authoritarian polities, every major religious tradition, highly varying levels of economic and social development, and quite different institutional designs. In this Canadian adaption, we have added country materials on Canada and on Saudi Arabia.

For each country, we first provide a "profile": an introduction with a table of key features, a map, and pie charts of demographics; a timeline and historical overview; and brief descriptions of political institutions, political culture, and political economy.

Following each profile is a set of case studies (two or three for each country) that we reference in the thematic chapters as described earlier (via the **"Case in Context"** boxes).

The case sets end with research prompts to help students get started as comparativists, and includes a list of the online case studies that you can find at www.oup.com/he/DickovickCe.

Flexibility in Instruction: Ways of Using This Text

The chapters are arranged in a logical order yet written in such a way that instructors might easily rearrange them to custom-fit a course. Some instructors, for example, may wish to pair Chapter 3 (on the state) with Chapter 13 (on nationalism and national identity). Others might wish to assign Chapter 15 (on religion and ideology) alongside Chapters 6 and 7 (on democratic and authoritarian regimes). We have written the book with the flexibility to facilitate such pairings. Indeed, while we strongly suggest beginning with Chapters 1 and 2, students will be able to follow the text even without reading them first.

Similarly, the book's structure supports a range of options for using the country materials found at the back of the book (Part VI). Some instructors may wish to teach selected country materials at or near the beginning of a course. Some may wish to make reference to country materials as the course proceeds, assigning students to read them as they are clearly and visibly "called out" in the text. One approach could require all students in a course to familiarize themselves with only a subset of the countries detailed here rather than all 14. Another might require each student to select three or four countries, following rules or categories of countries as laid out by the instructor.

The book also works with or without supplemental materials chosen by the instructor. The "Insights" boxes throughout the text provide indications of excellent options for further readings. Many other choice readings are noted in the "References and Further Reading" section at the back of the text, organized by chapter.

Acknowledgements

We are very grateful to a number of individuals who have been helpful to us as we worked on this project. At Washington and Lee University, we thank our respective provosts, deans, and department chairs who have supported our work. This includes June Aprille, Bob Strong, Daniel Wubah, Larry Peppers, Rob Straughan, Hank Dobin, Suzanne Keen, Mark Rush, Lucas Morel, David Novack, and Krzysztof Jasiewicz. We are very grateful to the many friends and colleagues, at Washington and Lee and elsewhere, who read and commented on chapters or country profiles, including Francoise Fregnac-Clave, Rachel Beatty Riedl, Tim Lubin, Dan Kramer, Christian Jennings, Robin Leblanc, Ayşe Zarakol, Rich Bidlack, David Bello, Ken White, and Alessandra Del Conte Dickovick. We also thank Hardin Marion for his excellent close reading of the first edition and the comments he generously shared with us. We have many other colleagues and friends who have given us intellectual and moral support for which we are grateful. Numerous students have been extraordinarily helpful as well. We are particularly grateful to Miranda Galvin and Ali Greenberg. Other students to whom we wish to express our appreciation include, but are not limited to, Samara Francisco, Morten Wendelbo, Maya Reimi Wendelbo, Linnea Bond, Natasha Lerner, Amy Dawson, Justine Griffin-Churchill, David Razum, John Twomey, Grant Russell, Lauren Howard, and Kate LeMasters. We are also thankful to students in numerous iterations of Politics 105 (Global Politics), many of whom offered insightful questions on a "prototype" of this text (in early years) and on the first edition (more recently), as well as students who read the book in Eastwood's International Comparative Sociology course. We owe thanks to Washington and Lee for support for the work of some of the students mentioned previously through the Summer Research Scholar Program and our own work through the Lenfest Sabbatical Grant, the Glenn Grant, Lenfest Grant, and Hess Scholars programs for summer research.

Our families have been characteristically supportive and gracious throughout the several years that we worked on this project. Their collective patience has been extraordinary. We owe eternal gratitude to our spouses, María Emilia Nava and Alessandra Del Conte Dickovick. We are also grateful to (and for) our wonderful children: Gabriela Eastwood, Carolina Dickovick, Gabriela Dickovick, Samuel Eastwood, and Alexander Eastwood. We owe much gratitude to our parents and extended families as well, of course.

We are grateful as well to the fine editorial staff at Oxford University Press. We particularly appreciate the excellent ideas and efforts of Jennifer Carpenter, Lauren Mine, and Thom Holmes. All of them improved this text substantially with their insights and hard work over several years. We have also benefitted from the work of Jane Lee, Barbara Mathieu, David Bradley, Maegan Sherlock, and Brianna Provenzano, among others.

We owe gratitude as well to those who developed our passion for (and understanding of) comparative politics. With the standard caveat that any errors of fact or interpretation in this text are solely our own, we want to thank first our earliest teachers of comparative politics. Above, all, we wish to thank Kent Eaton and Liah Greenfeld. We also owe great thanks to Jeffrey Herbst, Deborah Yashar, Chuck Lindholm, Scott Palmer, John Stone, and Evan Lieberman, as well as Nancy Bermeo, Atul Kohli, Lynn White, and Claudio Véliz, among others.

— J. Tyler Dickovick and Jonathan Eastwood

I would like to thank my wife Dana and son Gulliver for their support, as well as the support of the University of Guelph and the Social Sciences and Humanities Research Council of Canada. I would also like to thank the many reviewers, both named and anonymous, who provided helpful feedback on the various manuscript drafts: Mark Baron, University of Calgary; Colin J. Bennett, University of Victoria; Andrea Chandler, Carleton University; Daniel L. Douek, Concordia University; Bruce Morrison, University of Western Ontario; Mariam Mufti, University of Waterloo; Bryce Offenberger, University of Manitoba; Feng Xu, University of Victoria; Yuchao Zhu, University of Regina; and Lyubov Zhyznomirska, Saint Mary's University.

I am grateful to the excellent editorial staff at Oxford University Press, including Rhiannon Wong and Leah-Ann Lymer. My thanks also to Dorothy Turnbull and Michelle Welsh. My students and colleagues have also been very supportive of this writing process, and I have trialed some of my ideas in two of my courses: 4770 International Relations and 3410 US Politics. The adaption for Canada is also based on a decade of teaching comparative politics at the MA and PhD levels at the University of Guelph. My thanks to the many wonderful graduate students I have worked with during this time.

— David B. MacDonald

FROM THE PUBLISHER

Oxford University Press is excited to introduce the first Canadian edition of *Comparative Politics: Integrating Theories, Methods, and Cases*. This first edition for Canada continues to combine thematic organization and a variety of country-specific case studies in an engaging and accessible manner. Methodological tools are introduced early in the text and integrated throughout to help students develop a systematic way of doing their own analyses of concepts and issues. These tools include theories, the basics of the comparative method, and manageable case materials for practice, all in the context of the big questions in comparative politics today.

A Guided Tour

Chapter overviews introduce the main themes of the chapter and provide a guide to the chapter.

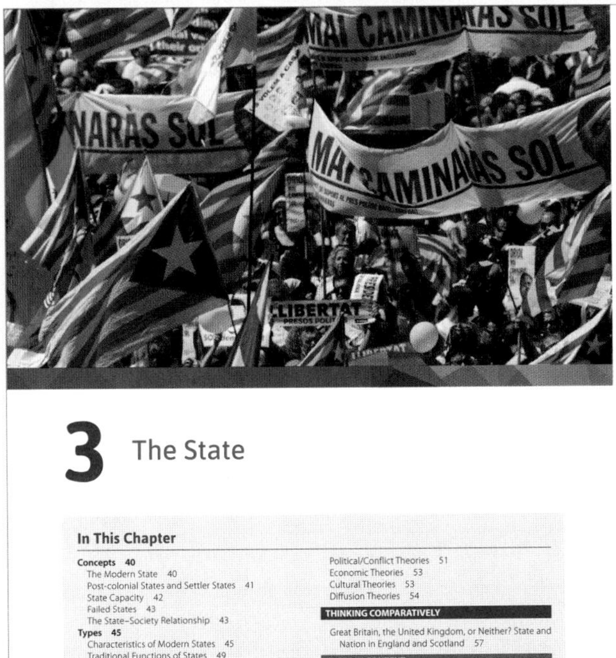

3 The State

In This Chapter

Demonstrators wave Catalonian independence flags in Barcelona, Spain in 2018. (AP Photo/Emilio Morenatti)

In the years following World War II, many observers thought of the western European state system as fairly settled. Here, the idea of modern states first developed, and this idea of what a state should look like was then duly exported to a variety of European colonies around the world, setting a template for what decolonizing peoples would also seek to implement. The consolidation of state power was high, even in cases like Germany and Italy, which unified only in the late 19th century. And despite the 1945 split of Germany into East and West, followed by its reunification in the 1990s, European states on the whole seemed likely to persist into the distant future.

But at least three recent developments have called into question the stability of the western European system of nation-states. The first has been the steady movement over the second half of the 20th century toward European integration, beginning with the European common market and culminating in the creation of the European Union (EU). For some time, many have wondered whether a European "super-state" might form, while after the failed EU constitution and the weakness of some EU economies, others have made arguments against this possibility.[1]

The second development is the presence of secessionist and sub-state nationalist movements in the region, perhaps most notably in Catalonia (an area on the Mediterranean coast of Spain) and Scotland (which is part of the United Kingdom). In the fall of 2014, Scotland held a referendum on becoming independent from the United Kingdom. The referendum failed, but some of its supporters are undaunted, especially after the majority of UK voters in mid-2016 chose to pull the UK out of the European Union. Most Scottish voters rejected Brexit and chose to remain in the EU, so now the Scottish National Party is promising a future referendum on independence. As the largest party in Scotland (third largest in the UK) and the dominant force in the Scottish Parliament, the Scottish National Party may be able to hold another referendum. Brexit will have some economically disastrous consequences for the UK, some of which might be avoided by Scotland if they seek to remain in the EU.

Similarly, many in Catalonia seek to form an independent state in the future. In October 2017, this region of Spain held a referendum on independence that resulted in an overwhelming rate of support, although many residents of the region chose not to vote. The Spanish government condemned the referendum as illegal because it violated Spain's constitution, and many political leaders involved in the referendum were imprisoned. So while a large proportion of Catalan residents may wish to leave Spain, it is unlikely they can ever do so legally. By contrast, the UK is seen as a union of different peoples, and because it was unified by the consent of its constituent people in 1707, it could similarly split apart if its people decide this is what they would like.

The third factor affecting the stability of the nation-states system in western Europe is globalization. Key manufacturing and other industries in Europe are being subjected to increasing international competition, and some classes of jobs are becoming more precarious, while the welfare state in many European countries has begun to contract. Similarly, civil instability in the Middle East, in particular Libya and Syria, has led to large influxes of refugees into Europe. This has led to questions in many European countries about how many newcomers these countries can financially afford to host. It has also led to questions of religious and cultural identity, sometimes resulting in the rise of xenophobic political parties seeking a more exclusive form of national identity. The former image of Europe as a wealthy, tolerant, multicultural, and multinational zone of prosperity and progress is now being thrown into question as right-wing, anti-immigrant parties rise to the fore in many countries.

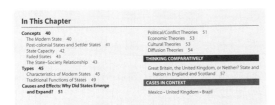

For comparativists, it is impossible to understand modern politics without understanding the state. States are the location of authoritarian or democratic governments, and states

CASE IN CONTEXT

382

The Chinese Party System

China is the most influential and important dominant-party system in the world today. The country is authoritarian and functions essentially as a single-party system. The various mechanisms for ensuring the dominance of the Communist Party are useful to understand, especially since the "Communist" in Communist Party has changed so dramatically with the many changes in China.

See the case study on the Chinese party system in Part VI, p. 382. As you read it, keep in mind the following questions:

1. How has China's Communist Party developed and maintained its dominance?
2. What are some of the mechanisms it uses to maintain this system?
3. Do you find there to be any legitimate justifications for single-party rule, and on what does the Chinese Communist Party base its legitimacy?

Kyodo via AP Images

PHOTO 11.4 President Xi Jinping (centre), Premier Li Keqiang (top right), and Li Zhanshu (top left) at the Great Hall of the People in Beijing in the annu[al] session of the Chinese People's Political Consulta[tive] Conference in March 2019. Xi Jinping is also the general secretary of the Communist Party of Chin[a]

a duopoly of power between two major parties that are seen as the main contenders for most major political offices. This duopoly usually persists over multiple elections. The two major parties present different platforms, which often correspond to one more liberal and one more conservative party in terms of economic policy, though this is not always the main political distinction. Such a model can be seen in the United States with the Democrats and Republicans, as well as in many other countries around the world, such as Spain, with its left-leaning Socialist Workers' Party (*Partido Socialista*) and right-leaning People's Party (*Partido Popular*). Canada has also traditionally had two dominant political parties, although sometimes the NDP governs provincially. As we discuss in the "Causes and Effects" section, the way elections work is a major factor in determining whether a democracy will have a two-party system. In particular, the presence of single-member districts in legislative elections (as discussed in Chapter 9) contributes to the likelihood of two-party systems for reasons we explore later.

Two-party systems are not the most common party system in a democracy, and most democracies have more than two major parties. The scholar Arend Lijphart studied 36 long-standing democracies and found that **multiparty systems** with three or more parties were the norm in about half of these countries.[7] Some multiparty systems have two parties that are strongest year in and year out, but they compete against a handful of other parties that regularly win enough seats to influence the outcomes of elections. Whereas in two-party systems one party or the other will typically win a given election by taking a majority of seats, multiparty systems quite often result in no party winning a majority because the vote is divided more ways. To recall some of the lessons of Chapters 9 and 10, a no-majority win often happens when legislative elections are based on proportional representation, and it often results in executive branches that function with a coalition of multiple parties.

multiparty system A p[...] party system consisting [...] than two significant par[...] have opportunities to g[...]

Case in Context boxes appearing within the chapters give students a taste of the corresponding full **Case Studies** provided in Part VI: Country Profiles and Cases.

CASE STUDIES

CASE STUDY

Chapter 11, Page 233

The Chinese Party System

China has the most influential and important dominant-party system in the world today. The country functions essentially as a single-party system, though some other parties are nominally allowed. China's Communist Party has held onto power for almost seven decades through a combination of factors. The various mechanisms for ensuring the dominance of the Communist Party are useful to understand, especially since the meaning of "Communist" in Communist Party has shifted so dramatically with the many changes in China over the past several decades.

The first and most obvious factor is the tight linkage between the Communist Party, the Chinese state bureaucracy, and the military. The party controls the state apparatus and can call on the military as needed to protect the regime. Through years of Communist dominance, the state and military have contributed to single-party rule. This has sometimes taken place with violent repression by the military, as in Tiananmen Square in 1989 and in purges by leader Mao Zedong in previous decades. It has also happened on an ongoing basis through the use of state organs to harass certain opposition forces that might pose a threat, imprison prominent dissidents, and control the media (including new media such as Google's China-based search engine and social media). Many of these efforts to minimize opposition have been passed by the National People's Congress (NPC), but they rely upon the state for enforcement.

A second factor is the electoral system, which provides built-in advantages for the Communist Party. The most important feature is the indirect election process by which local councils elect members of governing councils at higher levels and so on up to the NPC. For instance, national-level legislators are selected by provincial legislators, who are in turn selected by council members at lower levels. The result of this indirect election process is absolute dominance for the Communists at the national level in Beijing. While it is possible for independents and even some members of other small parties to elect a single delegate or two at the local level, it is exceedingly difficult for enough independents to be elected to get an independent or member of another party at the next level up. The well-established, well-resourced Communists are present in every local election throughout the country and dominate the indirect elections to higher levels; this means a virtual single-party state at the national level, with the only exceptions being other parties that are closely "allied" to the Communists and basically under Communist control.

A third set of factors has to do with the Communist Party's legitimacy, including its actual performance in government. China's economic growth under Communist Party rule has been remarkable. While it is difficult to get an independent view of Chinese public opinion, even international news reports suggest that many Chinese are relatively satisfied with government performance and are thus not pressing for immediate moves toward a multiparty system. This idea that a government's legitimacy can be based on economic performance has often been tested in a democracy, and it also seems to have held in some authoritarian and exclusionary systems (Epstein 1984).

CASE STUDY

Chapter 12, Page 262

The Chinese Revolution

The case of China allows us to consider two issues of concern to us in the study of contention and revolutions. First, it highlights the question considered in Chapter 12 about how to define revolutions and even subtypes like "political revolutions" and "social revolutions." Second, it focuses attention on the importance of mobilization in successful

Note: Additional case studies are provided online at www.oup.com/he/DickovickCe

Part VI features 14 **Country Profiles** along with their full **Case Studies**, and includes **Research Prompts** to help start students on their comparative analyses. The selection of countries provides broad coverage of every major world region, democratic and authoritarian systems, varying levels of economic and social development, and different institutional designs. This new edition includes two new countries profiles: Canada and Saudi Arabia.

Saudi Arabia

PROFILE

Key Features of Contemporary Saudi Arabia

Population:	33,091,113 (July 2018 est.)
Area:	2,149,690 square kilometres
Head of State:	Salman bin Abdulaziz Al Saud (King and Custodian of the Two Holy Mosques since January 2015)
Head of Government:	Salman bin Abdulaziz Al Saud (prime minister since January 2015)
Capital:	Riyadh
Year of state formation:	1932
Year of Current Constitution:	1992
Languages:	Arabic
GDP per Capita:	$54,500 (World Bank estimate 2017)
Human Development Index Ranking (2018):	39th (very high human development)
Trading Relationship with Canada (2016):	• Imports $2,022,190,583 • Exports $1,119,892,872 https://globaledge.msu.edu/countries/canada/tradestats

Sources: *CIA World Factbook 2018*; World Bank World Development Indicators; United Nations *Human Development Report 2016*

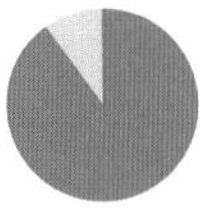

Religious Affiliation in Saudi Arabia

Ninety per cent of the population are Sunni Muslim, as is the ruling regime. Ten per cent are Shia and face some discrimination by the government. Other religious beliefs are not recognized, and there is no freedom of worship outside of officially sanctioned channels. A large and varied expatriate community comprising about 30 per cent of the population practise a range of other faiths, but only Muslims may hold Saudi citizenship.

Source: *CIA World Factbook 2018*

Introduction

Saudi Arabia is a unique country and society. First, it is an absolute monarchy, ruled by one of a succession of kings tracing their lineage to the founder of the state, Abdul Aziz bin Abdul Rahman Al Saud. The king also serves as prime minister and Custodian of the Two Holy Mosques (located in the cities of Mecca and Medina). Second, the regime is closely allied with clerics who follow the Wahhabi variant of Sunni Islam and have considerable power over civil society. Wahhabism is an extremely conservative branch of Islam that has led to repression of basic human rights. Third, Saudi Arabia is extremely rich, thanks to its enormous oil revenues, but the money has been unequally distributed and problems of corruption and mismanagement are high. Fourth, while the Arab Spring led to regime transformation throughout the Middle East region,

Saudi Arabia 473

Research Prompts

1. Despite its being an absolutist monarchy, there has been little significant internal dissent within the kingdom. What might account for Saudi Arabia continuing a strongly hierarchical system when the Arab Spring of 2011 changed the nature of many other regimes in the region?
2. Many critics of the Saudi regime in the kingdom have been calling for a constitutional monarchy for several decades. What might such a regime look like? Would it have some elements similar to constitutional monarchies in Europe?
3. Like Saudi Arabia, Qatar has a considerable number of Wahhabi followers. What accounts for their embrace of this variant of Sunni Islam? Why has it not spread to other parts of the Arab world?
4. Why does the United States continue such a close alliance with Saudi Arabia despite their human rights record and absolutist regime? Under what conditions might this alliance weaken or even end?

Online Case Studies

Go to **www.oup.com/he/DickovickCe** to find more case studies online, including:

- How Has Saudi Arabia's Welfare State Saved the Regime?

Note

1 BBC News: Middle East 2018; Bowen 2008, ix–xi; Al Jazeera News 2019a.

Insights boxes make connections among theories, methods, and cases by briefly summarizing important scholarly works representative of the major schools of thought.

14 Race, Ethnicity, and Gender 299

political and economic empowerment of African Americans, but one of its key aims was breaking down the symbolic barriers that facilitated many white Americans' support of or tolerance for discriminatory Jim Crow laws. Another example is Indigenous activism in Canada, which arose in 2012 against the federal government's plan to remove protections on lakes, rivers, streams, and other waterways. This and other legislation that was damaging for the environment and for Indigenous peoples led to the formation of Idle No More by a group of concerned educators and activists in Saskatoon. We looked at major theories of contentious action, including social movements, in Chapter 12.

Whether or not social movement activity focusing on questions of identity is novel, there is no disputing that it can be an effective strategy for empowering a group. As noted previously, one way it can work is through helping to establish and support political parties that represent the interests of a group.

Political Parties Based on Gender or Ethnicity

So how do political parties help to represent a group's interests? First, most modern electoral systems depend on political parties to organize and structure political competition. As a result of this process, parties bind political representatives together under common platforms, which can strongly influence votes and thus political decision-making. This influence varies from case to case, of course, and not all parties are equally capable of shaping the voting behaviour of party members. Another reason that parties can matter is that in some political systems, parties exist as either an official (e.g., contemporary China) or de facto (e.g., Mexico under the PRI) layer in institutional decision-making processes. As Chapters 9 through 11 demonstrate, the nature of the electoral system

INSIGHT Global Indigenous Politics: A Subtle Revolution
by Sheryl Lightfoot

Sheryl Lightfoot is an Anishinaabe scholar of Indigenous politics and international relations and a Canada Research Chair at the University of British Columbia. She is also the advisor to the president of UBC on Indigenous issues. Her book is a fascinating exploration of how global networks of Indigenous peoples were able to create and secure passage of the United Nations Declaration on the Rights of Indigenous Peoples. The Declaration was passed in 2007 by 144 states, with only four countries voting against it: Australia, Canada, Aotearoa New Zealand and the United States. *Global Indigenous Politics* explores the decades-long rise of Indigenous organization at the international level, through domestic and pan-national organizations like the International Indian Treaty Council, founded in 1974, to more international organizations like the UN Expert Mechanism on the Rights of Indigenous Peoples and the United Nations Permanent Forum on Indigenous Issues. Lightfoot suggests that Indigenous peoples are not marginal actors but potentially crucial players, helping to develop new approaches and new norms in the conduct of international relations. As she observes, "global Indigenous politics is potentially forging major changes in the international system, as the implementation of Indigenous peoples' rights requires a complete re-thinking and re-ordering of sovereignty, territoriality, liberalism, and human rights."

The book also features detailed case studies of Canada and Aotearoa New Zealand and the arduous struggles in these countries to encourage settler governments to approve the Declaration. Indigenous peoples have collective rights to self-determination. The evolution of Indigenous rights domestically and internationally will be of crucial importance for students of comparative politics.

Sheryl Lightfoot, *Global Indigenous Politics: A Subtle Revolution* (New York: Routledge, 2016).

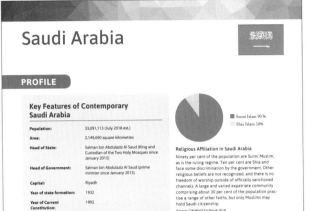

Thinking Comparatively features at the end of each chapter highlight important methodological tools or strategies, and then models for students how to use them.

THINKING COMPARATIVELY

Indicators of Gender Empowerment

KEY METHODOLOGICAL TOOL

Selecting or Creating Indicators

An indicator is a measure that indicates the presence, amount, or degree of a variable you are researching. Good indicators have to work effectively in at least two ways. First, they have to be true to the underlying concept you are researching. Second, they need to be actually measurable, meaning, among other things, that any observer using the indicator will see it in more or less the same way. Another way to say this is that indicators must comprise measures that are both "valid" and "reliable."

A useful recent indicator we have for studying women's empowerment is the GDI, or Gender Development Index, which is prominently featured in UN Development Reports. The GDI seeks to measure the extent to which women have political and economic control of their lives and environments in different societies. It is a composite indicator based on underlying measures of women's and men's shares of (1) political positions, (2) prominent economic roles, and (3) overall income.[67]

Imagine that we wanted to evaluate how well the United Kingdom and some of its former colonies are empowering women relative to Spain and its former colonies. Why would we do this? We might, for example, have looked at the Gender Development Index (formerly the Gender Empowerment Measure, or GEM) and got the impression that in the United Kingdom and formerly British Western settler states, women were better represented politically than in Spain and Latin America. The GDI on the surface is supposed to provide a measure of the political empowerment of women. Bringing together several indicators, this measure and its predecessor have been used in a number of United Nations reports in the late 2000s and for many purposes, despite criticism, was considered by many the best single measure of gender empowerment at that time.

If we look at Gender Development Index (GDI) ranks for 2016 for the former British colonies in which we are interested (see Table 14.1), we see that Australia ranks second, Canada and the United States share 10th place, New Zealand 13th, and the United Kingdom 16th. Ranks for former Spanish colonies are not this high, with only Spain at 27th place. Does this mean that former British colonies for whatever reason are sites of higher levels of political empowerment for women? This could be misleading. Since GDI is a composite measure, it captures economic empowerment as well. It may be that the strong showing of former British settler colonies (relative to former Spanish colonies) in terms of GDI is a consequence of higher levels of economic development in these societies.

Let's try a narrower indicator that can help us to better understand the *political* empowerment of women. What if we look at the percentage of women holding legislative office? This could give us a clearer indication of *political* empowerment, given that it won't include information about the relative *economic* standing of women, which we may consider to be a different question (see Table 14.2).

TABLE 14.1 | Gender Development Index (GDI) Global Ranks, Selected Countries

2	Australia
10	Canada
10	United States
13	New Zealand
16	United Kingdom
27	Spain
37	Chile
45	Argentina
54	Uruguay
68	Cuba
118	Bolivia

Source: UN, *Human Development Report, 2016*, http://hdr.undp.org/sites/default/files/2016_human_development_report.pdf.

TABLE 14.2 | Ranking of Percentage of Women in National Legislature, Selected Countries

Rank	Country	% Seats in Lower/Single House	% Seats in Upper House
2	Bolivia	53.1	47.2
4	Cuba	48.9	N/A
9	Ecuador	41.6	N/A
12	Spain	41.1	33.8
15	Nicaragua	39.1	N/A
17 (tied)	Mexico	38	33.6
22	Argentina	36.2	38.9
29	New Zealand	31.4	NA
44	Australia	26.7	38.2
49	Canada	25.2	38.6
57	United Kingdom	22.8	24.1
73 (tied)	United States	19.3	20.0

Source: Interparliamentary Union, 2015, *Women in National Parliaments*, http://www.ipu.org/wmn-e/classif.htm

Here, we see a very different pattern. In our set of comparative cases, Bolivia is on top, and the United States is on the bottom. New Zealand is the only former British settler colony in the top 30, and Bolivia, Cuba, Ecuador, Spain, Nicaragua, Mexico, and Argentina all outperform *all* the other former British settler colonies in our group (as do Costa Rica and El Salvador, though they do not rank as highly as the other Latin American countries listed in Table 14.2).[68]

Does this demonstrate that selected former Spanish colonies have higher levels of the political empowerment of women than former British colonies? Not necessarily. Can you think of some of the limitations of this indicator? One would be that legislative representation is not the only form of representation. Another might be that empowerment of a group, even political empowerment, likely extends well beyond having members of that group hold office. Both of these are concerns about the potential *validity* of this indicator as a measure of the underlying concept we are researching: political empowerment of women. What we see here is that a number of former Spanish colonies have achieved very high levels of legislative representation of women, outpacing former British settler colonies by this measure, which is interesting and deserving of comparative exploration. Using an intersectional lens, we could also ask whether these women were white or were Indigenous and/or racialized peoples as well, and we could also problematize their economic status. Perhaps white women from upper-class backgrounds have done very well in Latin American legislatures, while Indigenous women from poorer backgrounds have not.

The bottom line is that there is almost never a *perfect* indicator. (Indeed, the United Nations recently replaced the former GEM with the GDI in response to scholarly critiques.) All choices of indicators involve trade-offs. You should be mindful of these trade-offs and remember that indicators are only stand-ins for the underlying concepts you are researching. Indicators and measurements are crucial in understanding the extent to which women and ethnic and racial groups are empowered and active in politics. Conducting careful comparative research can give us greater insight into questions that matter to us on issues as profound as our very identities as people.

306 **PART IV** Politics, Society, and Culture

Chapter Summary

Concepts

- The meaning of concepts like race and ethnicity varies in relation to context. While some people think of race and sometimes ethnicity as biological, most social scientists view them as culturally constructed. As such, the term "racialized" is more often used.
- Gender is distinguished from biological sex, and most social scientists think of gender as cultural rather than biological.
- In recent years, a number of societies have grown more pluralistic and tolerant with respect to sexual orientation, although intolerance and violence remain high in many countries.

Types

- Race historically has almost always been linked to social actors' beliefs about biology, whereas ethnicity has emphasized cultural traditions. The concept of race in particular has been linked to exploitation.
- Discrimination based on both race and ethnicity is a common feature of many polities, historically and today. Discrimination has in some societies become more subtle over time but nevertheless continues. An intersectional analysis can demonstrate ways in which different forms of discrimination can converge.
- Discrimination based on gender is also a pervasive feature of polities, and gender discrimination remains a problem.
- Empowerment can be economic, symbolic, or political.

Causes and Effects

- One potential source of empowerment is social movement mobilization.
- Another is political parties, and parties tend to be more viable for ethnic groups seeking empowerment than for gender groups.
- Institutional design strategies like reserved seats and quotas can also be used in support of empowerment.

Thinking Comparatively

- A thought experiment about relative gender empowerment in the former colonies of Spain and the United Kingdom demonstrates the pros and cons of two major indicators of political empowerment.

Thinking It Through

1. The theme of empowerment is much discussed in this chapter, including dimensions of empowerment and ways in which development is conceptualized and measured by social scientists. But what *is* empowerment? Develop your own conceptualization, and link it back to the discussion in the chapter. What, if anything, is missing?
2. We discussed political, economic, and cultural or symbolic empowerment. How are these dimensions related? Is one more fundamental than the others, and, if so, why? If a group wants to improve its position, would it be best advised to begin by focusing on one or another form of empowerment?
3. Imagine now that you have been asked to consult with social movement activists who represent poor rural women of a particular ethnic group. They tell you that their ethnic, gender, and class status compound each other and that their interests really are distinct from those of other groups. They would like your technical assistance as they aim to build a social movement. In particular, they would like your advice about how to "frame" that movement. What questions do you ask them, and how do you advise them? How is this case different from organizing around "women's issues" or the interests of a particular ethnic group?
4. Imagine that you are an "empowerment consultant." You have been contacted by the representatives of a political party that represents the interests of an ethnic group that has historically faced severe discrimination, one that is largely found in a particular area of the country and that constitutes about 10 per cent of the country's population. They tell you that their country is going to write a new constitution and that they have a number of delegates in the constitutional assembly. They want your advice about what sorts of institutional designs they should push for as they aim to protect the interests of their people. What do you need to know in order to give them advice? How would your answer depend on their answers?

Supportive pedagogy also includes a running glossary, a chapter summary, **Thinking It Through** questions, and further readings to enhance understanding and promote active learning

Ancillary Resource Center

Student and Instructor Supplements for the Test

The first Canadian edition of *Comparative Politics* is accompanied by a wide range of supplementary online resources for students and instructors alike, all designed to enhance and complete the learning and teaching experiences. These resources are available at: **www.oup.com/he/DickovickCe**

For Instructors

- **An Instructor's Manual** provides learning objectives, chapter outlines, lecture suggestions, class activity suggestions, issues for discussion, internet and video resources, and sample syllabi.
- **PowerPoints slides** provide lecture outlines for each chapter.
- **Test Generator** provides multiple-choice, short-answer, and essay questions for each chapter.

For Students

- 39 **Online Case Studies** provide additional cases for the countries featured in Part VI of the text.
- **A Student Study Guide** provides key concepts, self-grading quizzes, essay questions, web activities, web links, and data assignments.
- **Flashcards** of all key terms and definitions from the text help students learn these terms and concepts.

MAPS OF THE WORLD

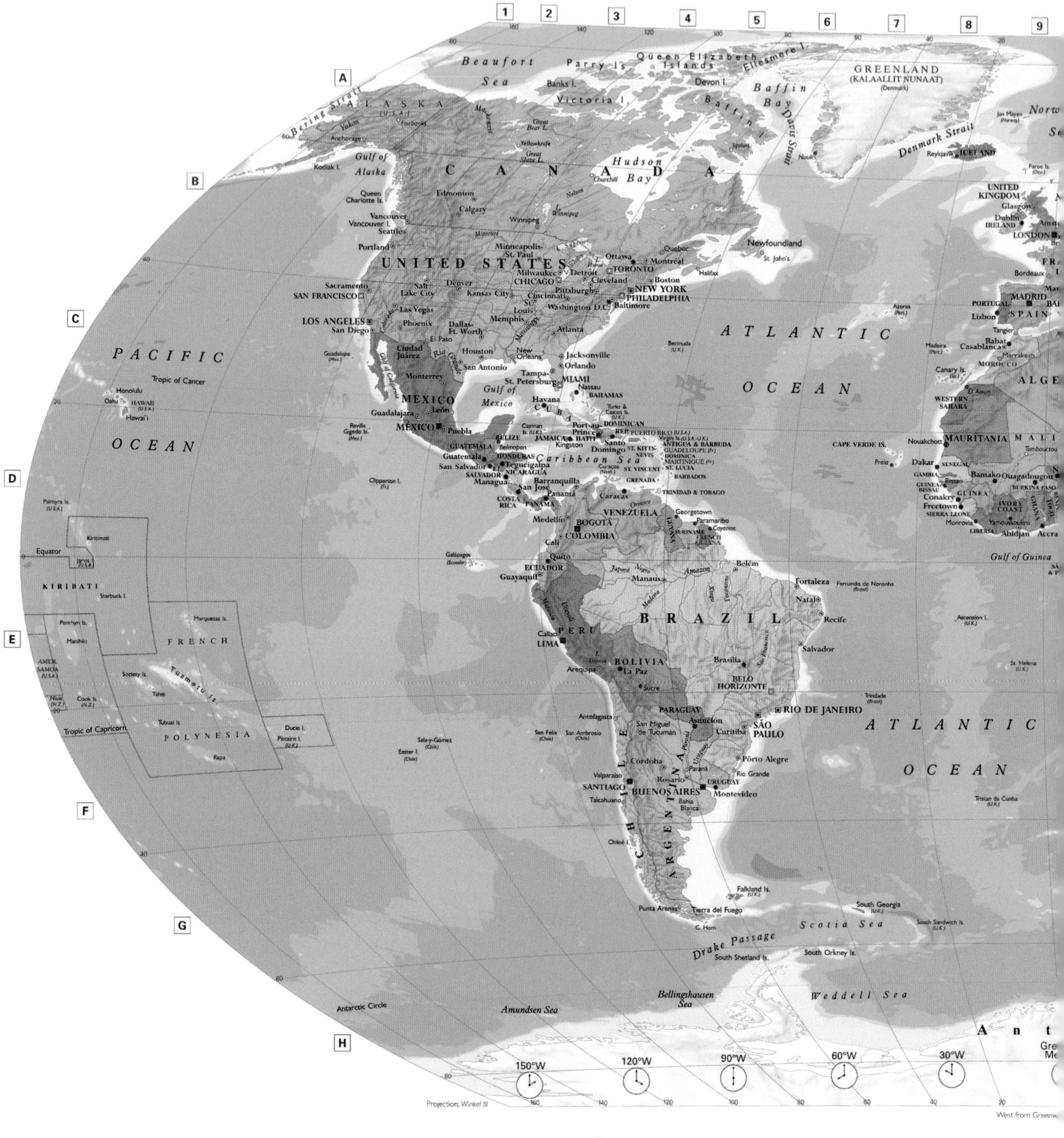

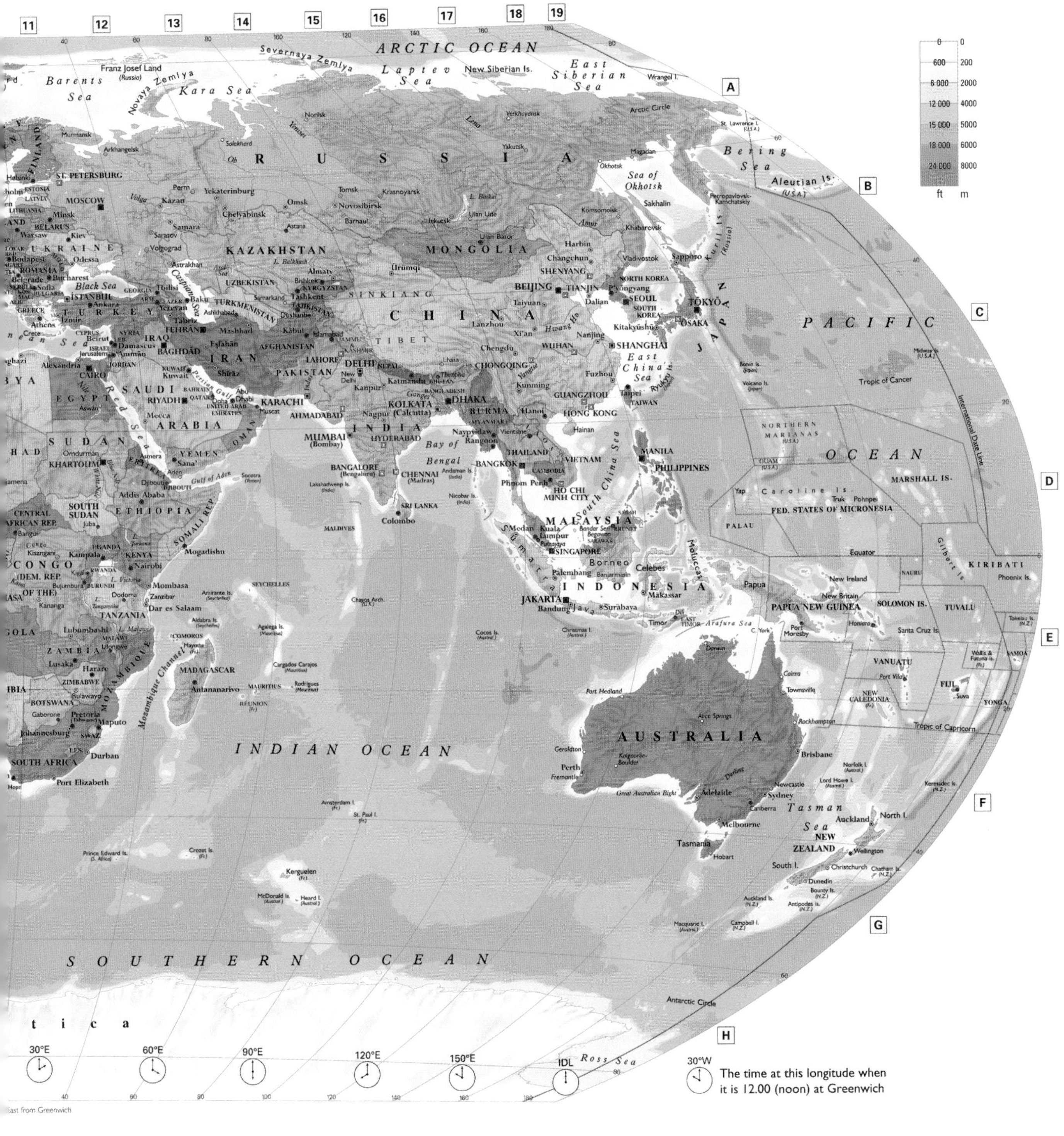

11
12
13
14
15
16
17
18
19
ARCTIC OCEAN
Severnaya Zemlya
Franz Josef Land (Russia)
Barents Sea
Novaya Zemlya
Kara Sea
Laptev Sea
New Siberian Is.
East Siberian Sea
Wrangel I.
A
B
C
D
E
F
G
H
0 0
600 200
6 000 2000
12 000 4000
15 000 5000
18 000 6000
24 000 8000
ft m
Arctic Circle
St. Lawrence I. (U.S.A.)
Bering Sea
Aleutian Is. (U.S.A.)
Murmansk
Arkhangelsk
FINLAND
ST. PETERSBURG
Helsinki
ESTONIA
LATVIA
LITHUANIA
MOSCOW
Minsk
BELARUS
Warsaw
Kiev
U K R A I N E
Bucharest
ROMANIA
Sofia
Odessa
Black Sea
ISTANBUL
Ankara
T U R K E Y
Izmir
Athens
GREECE
Crete
CYPRUS
Beirut
Damascus
Jerusalem
ISRAEL
Amman
JORDAN
Alexandria
CAIRO
E G Y P T
Aswan
R U S S I A
Norilsk
Salekhard
Ob
Yenisei
Lena
Verkhoyansk
Yakutsk
Magadan
Okhotsk
Sea of Okhotsk
Sakhalin
Petropavlovsk-Kamchatskiy
Kuril Is. (Russia)
Perm
Yekaterinburg
Kazan
Volga
Samara
Saratov
Volgograd
Astrakhan
Chelyabinsk
Omsk
Tomsk
Novosibirsk
Barnaul
Krasnoyarsk
Irkutsk
L. Baikal
Ulan Ude
Ulan Bator
Komsomolsk
Khabarovsk
Amur
Harbin
Changchun
SHENYANG
Vladivostok
Sapporo
KAZAKHSTAN
L. Balkhash
Astana
Almaty
Bishkek
KYRGYZSTAN
Tashkent
TAJIKISTAN
Dushanbe
UZBEKISTAN
TURKMENISTAN
Ashkhabad
Samarkand
Caspian Sea
Baku
Tbilisi
GEORGIA
Yerevan
Tabriz
TEHRAN
Mashhad
Esfahan
I R A N
Shiraz
IRAQ
BAGHDAD
KUWAIT
Kuwait
Persian Gulf
BAHRAIN
QATAR
Doha
Abu Dhabi
UNITED ARAB EMIRATES
Muscat
OMAN
S A U D I A R A B I A
RIYADH
Mecca
Red Sea
Nile
AFGHANISTAN
Kabul
Islamabad
PAKISTAN
LAHORE
KARACHI
Indus
DELHI
New Delhi
Kanpur
NEPAL
Katmandu
BHUTAN
Thimphu
BANGLADESH
DHAKA
Ganges
KOLKATA (Calcutta)
Nagpur
AHMADABAD
MUMBAI (Bombay)
I N D I A
HYDERABAD
BANGALORE (Bengaluru)
CHENNAI (Madras)
Lakshadweep Is. (India)
SRI LANKA
Colombo
MALDIVES
Bay of Bengal
Andaman Is. (India)
Nicobar Is. (India)
MONGOLIA
Urumqi
SINKIANG
C H I N A
TIBET
Lhasa
Chengdu
CHONGQING
Yangtze
Kunming
Lanzhou
Xi'an
Hwang Ho
WUHAN
Nanjing
SHANGHAI
Fuzhou
GUANGZHOU
HONG KONG
Hainan
BEIJING
TIANJIN
Taiyuan
Dalian
NORTH KOREA
Pyongyang
SEOUL
SOUTH KOREA
Kitakyushu
OSAKA
TOKYO
J A P A N
East China Sea
Ryukyu Is.
Taipei
TAIWAN
BURMA
MYANMAR
Naypyidaw
Rangoon
Hanoi
Vientiane
LAOS
THAILAND
BANGKOK
CAMBODIA
Phnom Penh
VIETNAM
HO CHI MINH CITY
South China Sea
MANILA
PHILIPPINES
MALAYSIA
Medan
Kuala Lumpur
Putrajaya
Sumatra
SINGAPORE
Bandar Seri Begawan
BRUNEI
SARAWAK
SABAH
Borneo
Celebes
Palembang
Banjarmasin
I N D O N E S I A
Makassar
JAKARTA
Bandung
Java
Surabaya
Moluccas
Timor
EAST TIMOR
Dili
Arafura Sea
Christmas I. (Austral.)
Cocos Is. (Austral.)
Chagos Arch. (U.K.)
P A C I F I C
O C E A N
Bonin Is. (Japan)
Volcano Is. (Japan)
Midway Is. (U.S.A.)
Tropic of Cancer
International Date Line
NORTHERN MARIANAS (U.S.A.)
GUAM (U.S.A.)
Yap
Caroline Is.
Truk
Pohnpei
FED. STATES OF MICRONESIA
MARSHALL IS.
PALAU
Equator
Gilbert Is.
KIRIBATI
NAURU
Phoenix Is.
Papua
New Ireland
New Britain
PAPUA NEW GUINEA
Port Moresby
SOLOMON IS.
Honiara
TUVALU
Tokelau Is. (N.Z.)
Santa Cruz Is.
Wallis & Futuna Is. (Fr.)
SAMOA
VANUATU
Port Vila
FIJI
Suva
TONGA
NEW CALEDONIA (Fr.)
Tropic of Capricorn
C. York
Darwin
Cairns
Townsville
Port Hedland
Alice Springs
Rockhampton
AUSTRALIA
Brisbane
Geraldton
Perth
Fremantle
Kalgoorlie-Boulder
Great Australian Bight
Darling
Adelaide
Newcastle
Sydney
Canberra
Melbourne
Tasmania
Hobart
Norfolk I. (Austral.)
Lord Howe I. (Austral.)
Kermadec Is. (N.Z.)
Tasman Sea
Auckland
North I.
NEW ZEALAND
Wellington
South I.
Christchurch
Chatham Is. (N.Z.)
Dunedin
Bounty Is. (N.Z.)
Antipodes Is. (N.Z.)
Auckland Is. (N.Z.)
Campbell I. (N.Z.)
Macquarie I. (Austral.)
SUDAN
Omdurman
KHARTOUM
SOUTH SUDAN
Juba
Asmera
ERITREA
YEMEN
Sana'
Aden
DJIBOUTI
Djibouti
Gulf of Aden
Socotra (Yemen)
ETHIOPIA
Addis Ababa
SOMALI REP.
Mogadishu
CENTRAL AFRICAN REP.
Bangui
UGANDA
Kampala
KENYA
Nairobi
L. Turkana
Kisangani
CONGO (DEM. REP. OF THE)
RWANDA
Kigali
BURUNDI
Bujumbura
L. Victoria
Mombasa
Dodoma
Zanzibar
Dar es Salaam
TANZANIA
Kananga
Lubumbashi
MALAWI
L. Malawi
Lilongwe
ZAMBIA
Lusaka
Harare
ZIMBABWE
Bulawayo
MOZAMBIQUE
BOTSWANA
Gaborone
Pretoria
Johannesburg
Maputo
SWAZ.
LES.
Durban
SOUTH AFRICA
Port Elizabeth
COMOROS
Mayotte (Fr.)
Mozambique Channel
MADAGASCAR
Antananarivo
SEYCHELLES
Amirante Is. (Seychelles)
Aldabra Is. (Seychelles)
Agalega Is. (Mauritius)
Cargados Carajos (Mauritius)
MAURITIUS
Rodrigues (Mauritius)
RÉUNION (Fr.)
INDIAN OCEAN
Amsterdam I. (Fr.)
St. Paul I. (Fr.)
Prince Edward Is. (S. Africa)
Crozet Is. (Fr.)
Kerguelen (Fr.)
McDonald Is. (Austral.)
Heard I. (Austral.)
SOUTHERN OCEAN
Antarctic Circle
t i c a
Ross Sea
30°E
60°E
90°E
120°E
150°E
IDL
30°W
The time at this longitude when it is 12.00 (noon) at Greenwich
East from Greenwich

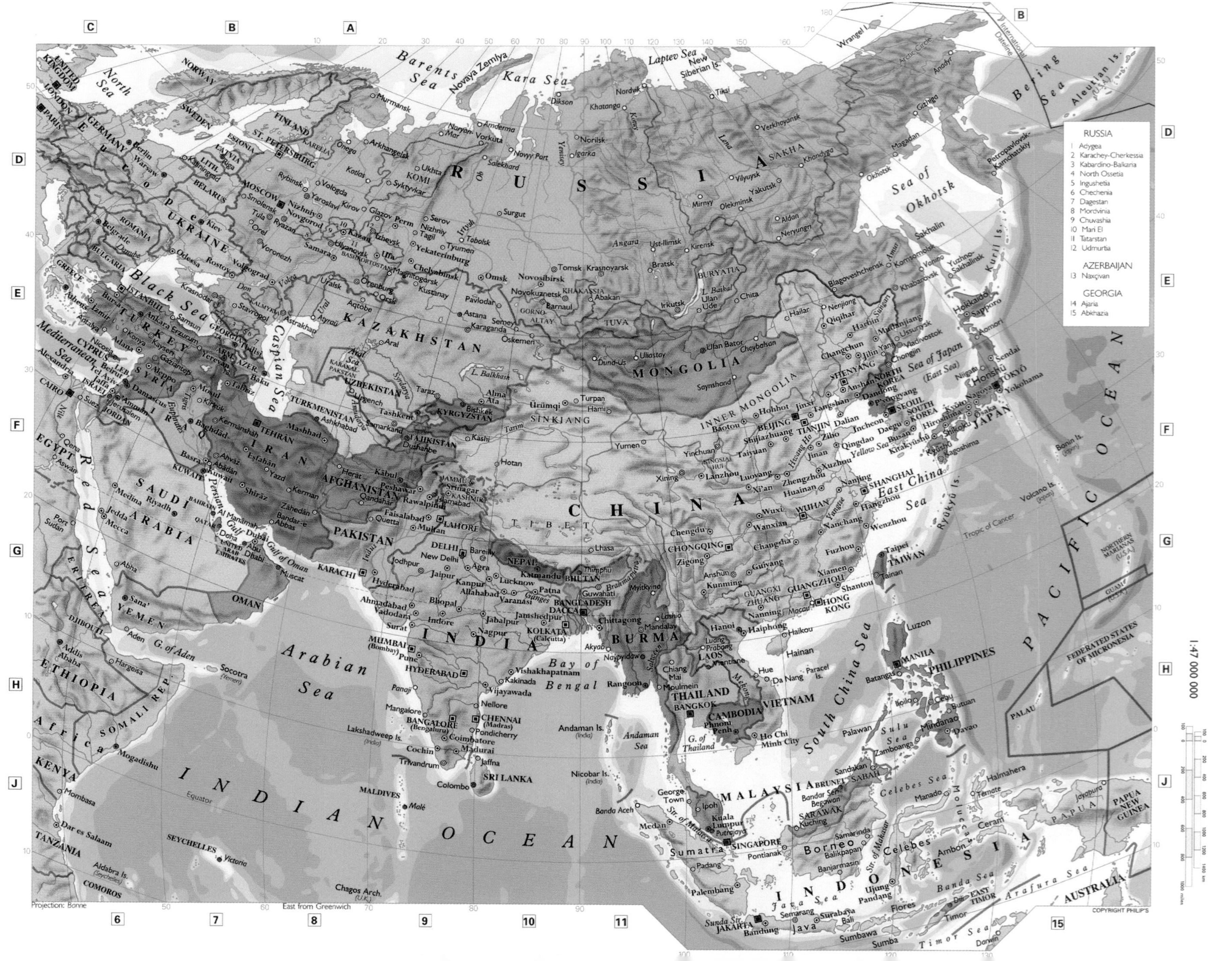
1:47 000 000
RUSSIA
1 Adygea
2 Karachey-Cherkessia
3 Kabardino-Balkaria
4 North Ossetia
5 Ingushetia
6 Chechenia
7 Dagestan
8 Mordvinia
9 Chuvashia
10 Mari El
11 Tatarstan
12 Udmurtia
AZERBAIJAN
13 Naxçıvan
GEORGIA
14 Ajaria
15 Abkhazia
R U S S I A
K A Z A K H S T A N
M O N G O L I A
C H I N A
I N D I A
T I B E T
INNER MONGOLIA
SINKIANG
SAKHA
BURYATIA
TUVA
KHAKASSIA
GORNO-ALTAY
KOMI
UKRAINE
BELARUS
TURKEY
SYRIA
IRAQ
IRAN
AFGHANISTAN
PAKISTAN
NEPAL
BHUTAN
BANGLADESH
BURMA
THAILAND
LAOS
CAMBODIA
VIETNAM
MALAYSIA
SINGAPORE
INDONESIA
PHILIPPINES
TAIWAN
JAPAN
NORTH KOREA
SOUTH KOREA
UZBEKISTAN
TURKMENISTAN
KYRGYZSTAN
TAJIKISTAN
SAUDI ARABIA
YEMEN
OMAN
UNITED ARAB EMIRATES
QATAR
KUWAIT
JORDAN
ISRAEL
LEB.
CYPRUS
EGYPT
ERITREA
DJIBOUTI
ETHIOPIA
SOMALI REP.
KENYA
TANZANIA
COMOROS
SEYCHELLES
MALDIVES
SRI LANKA
BRUNEI
SABAH
SARAWAK
EAST TIMOR
PAPUA NEW GUINEA
AUSTRALIA
PALAU
FEDERATED STATES OF MICRONESIA
NORTHERN MARIANAS (U.S.A.)
GUAM (U.S.A.)
UNITED KINGDOM
NORWAY
SWEDEN
FINLAND
ESTONIA
LATVIA
LITH.
GERMANY
ROMANIA
BULGARIA
GREECE
GEORGIA
ARMENIA
AZER.
E u r o p e
A f r i c a
Barents Sea
Kara Sea
Laptev Sea
Sea of Okhotsk
Bering Sea
Sea of Japan (East Sea)
Yellow Sea
East China Sea
South China Sea
Sulu Sea
Celebes Sea
Molucca Sea
Banda Sea
Arafura Sea
Timor Sea
Java Sea
Andaman Sea
Bay of Bengal
Arabian Sea
Red Sea
Black Sea
Caspian Sea
Aral Sea
Mediterranean Sea
North Sea
Persian Gulf
Gulf of Oman
G. of Aden
G. of Thailand
L. Balkhash
L. Baikal
I N D I A N   O C E A N
P A C I F I C   O C E A N
Arctic Circle
Tropic of Cancer
Equator
International Dateline
Projection: Bonne
East from Greenwich
COPYRIGHT PHILIP'S

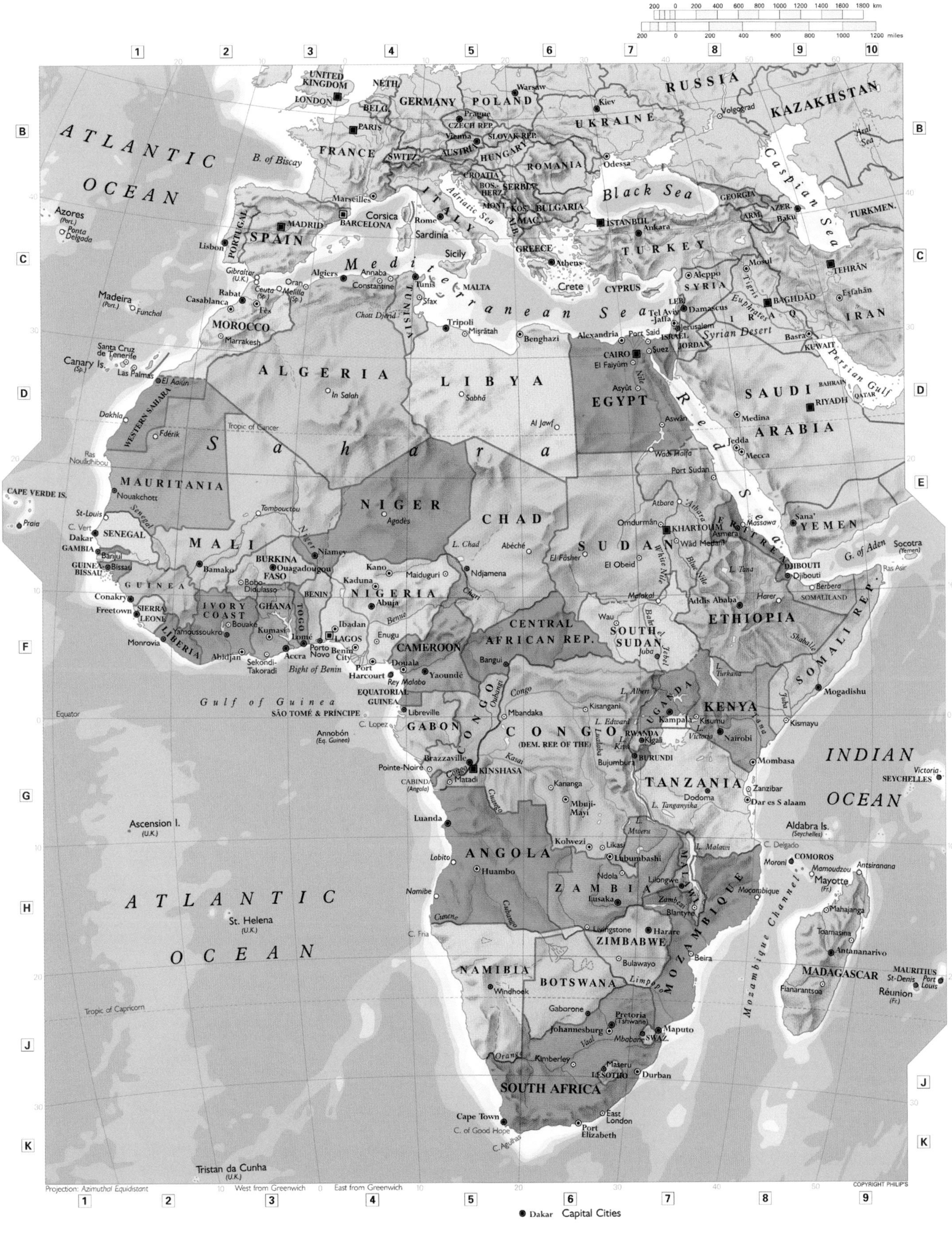

200 0 200 400 600 800 1000 1200 1400 1600 1800 km
200 0 200 400 600 800 1000 1200 miles
ATLANTIC OCEAN
Azores (Port.)
Ponta Delgada
B. of Biscay
UNITED KINGDOM
LONDON
NETH.
BELG.
GERMANY
POLAND
Warsaw
RUSSIA
KAZAKHSTAN
Kiev
UKRAINE
Volgograd
Prague
CZECH REP.
Vienna
SLOVAK REP.
AUSTRIA
HUNGARY
PARIS
FRANCE
SWITZ.
ROMANIA
Odessa
Caspian Sea
Aral Sea
CROATIA
BOS.-HERZ.
SERBIA
MONT.
KOS.
ALB.
MAC.
BULGARIA
Black Sea
GEORGIA
ARM.
AZER.
Baku
TURKMEN.
Marseilles
Corsica
ITALY
Adriatic Sea
Rome
Sardinia
Sicily
MADRID
SPAIN
PORTUGAL
Lisbon
BARCELONA
İSTANBUL
Ankara
TURKEY
GREECE
Athens
Madeira (Port.)
Funchal
Gibraltar (U.K.)
Ceuta (Sp.)
Melilla (Sp.)
Oran
Algiers
Annaba
Constantine
Tunis
Sfax
TUNISIA
MALTA
Rabat
Casablanca
Fès
MOROCCO
Marrakesh
Mediterranean Sea
Crete
CYPRUS
Mosul
Aleppo
SYRIA
Tigris
Euphrates
TEHRĀN
Esfahān
IRAN
BAGHDĀD
IRAQ
LEB.
Damascus
Tel Aviv-Jaffa
Jerusalem
ISRAEL
JORDAN
Syrian Desert
Basra
KUWAIT
Persian Gulf
Chott Djerid
Tripoli
Mişrātah
Benghazi
Alexandria
Port Said
Suez
CAIRO
El Faiyûm
Santa Cruz de Tenerife
Canary Is. (Sp.)
Las Palmas
El Aaiún
ALGERIA
In Salah
LIBYA
Sabhā
Asyût
EGYPT
Nile
Red Sea
SAUDI ARABIA
Medina
RIYADH
BAHRAIN
QATAR
Dakhla
WESTERN SAHARA
Fdérik
Tropic of Cancer
Sahara
Al Jawf
Aswân
Jedda
Mecca
Ras Nouâdhibou
Wadi Halfa
Port Sudan
MAURITANIA
Nouakchott
CAPE VERDE IS.
Praia
St-Louis
Senegal
Tombouctou
NIGER
Agadès
CHAD
Atbara
Omdurmân
KHARTOUM
Massawa
Asmera
ERITREA
Sana'
YEMEN
C. Vert
Dakar
SENEGAL
GAMBIA
Banjul
GUINEA-BISSAU
Bissau
MALI
Niger
Niamey
BURKINA FASO
Ouagadougou
L. Chad
Abéché
SUDAN
El Fâsher
Wad Medani
White Nile
Blue Nile
L. Tana
DJIBOUTI
Djibouti
G. of Aden
Socotra (Yemen)
Bamako
GUINEA
Bobo Dioulasso
Kano
Maiduguri
Kaduna
NIGERIA
Ndjamena
El Obeid
Berbera
SOMALILAND
Ras Asir
Conakry
Freetown
SIERRA LEONE
IVORY COAST
GHANA
TOGO
BENIN
Abuja
Chari
Malakal
Addis Ababa
Harer
ETHIOPIA
Yamoussoukro
Bouaké
Kumasi
Ibadan
LAGOS
Benue
CENTRAL AFRICAN REP.
Wau
SOUTH SUDAN
Bahr el Jebel
Monrovia
LIBERIA
Abidjan
Accra
Lomé
Porto Novo
Benin City
Enugu
CAMEROON
Juba
Shabelle
SOMALI REP.
Sekondi-Takoradi
Bight of Benin
Port Harcourt
Douala
Yaoundé
Bangui
L. Turkana
Rey Malabo
EQUATORIAL GUINEA
Ubangi
Congo
L. Albert
UGANDA
KENYA
Juba
Mogadishu
Gulf of Guinea
SÃO TOMÉ & PRÍNCIPE
Libreville
Mbandaka
Kisangani
Kampala
Kisumu
Tana
Equator
C. Lopez
GABON
CONGO
CONGO (DEM. REP. OF THE)
L. Edward
Lualaba
RWANDA
Kigali
L. Kivu
L. Victoria
Nairobi
Kismayu
Annobón (Eq. Guinea)
Brazzaville
Kasai
Bujumbura
BURUNDI
Mombasa
INDIAN OCEAN
Victoria
SEYCHELLES
Pointe-Noire
CABINDA (Angola)
Matadi
KINSHASA
Kananga
TANZANIA
Zanzibar
Dodoma
Dar es Salaam
Cuango
Mbuji-Mayi
L. Tanganyika
Ascension I. (U.K.)
Luanda
L. Mweru
Aldabra Is. (Seychelles)
Kolwezi
Likasi
Lubumbashi
L. Malawi
C. Delgado
Lobito
ANGOLA
Huambo
Ndola
MALAWI
Lilongwe
Moroni
COMOROS
Mamoudzou
Antsiranana
Mayotte (Fr.)
Namibe
ZAMBIA
Lusaka
Zambezi
Blantyre
Moçambique
Mahajanga
ATLANTIC OCEAN
St. Helena (U.K.)
Cunene
Cubango
C. Fria
Livingstone
Harare
ZIMBABWE
Mozambique Channel
Toamasina
Antananarivo
Bulawayo
Beira
MOZAMBIQUE
NAMIBIA
BOTSWANA
Limpopo
MADAGASCAR
MAURITIUS
St-Denis
Port Louis
Fianarantsoa
Réunion (Fr.)
Windhoek
Tropic of Capricorn
Gaborone
Pretoria (Tshwane)
Johannesburg
Vaal
Mbabane
SWAZ.
Maputo
Orange
Kimberley
Maseru
LESOTHO
Durban
SOUTH AFRICA
Cape Town
C. of Good Hope
East London
Port Elizabeth
C. Agulhas
Tristan da Cunha (U.K.)
Projection: Azimuthal Equidistant
West from Greenwich
East from Greenwich
COPYRIGHT PHILIP'S
Dakar Capital Cities

1:20 000 000
0 100 200 300 400 500 600 700 800 km
0 100 200 300 400 500 miles
Projection: Bonne
West from Greenwich
East from Greenwich
LONDON Capital Cities
COPYRIGHT PHILIP'S
Arctic Circle
ICELAND
Reykjavik
Norwegian Sea
Faroe Is. (Den.)
Tórshavn
Shetland Is.
Lerwick
Orkney Is.
Kirkwall
Stornoway
Hebrides
ATLANTIC OCEAN
UNITED KINGDOM
SCOTLAND
Aberdeen
Dundee
Glasgow
Edinburgh
Newcastle-upon-Tyne
N. IRELAND
Belfast
IRELAND
Dublin
Cork
Manchester
Leeds
Liverpool
Sheffield
WALES
ENGLAND
Birmingham
Cardiff
Bristol
LONDON
Southampton
Plymouth
English Channel
Channel Is.
Brest
Le Havre
Rouen
PARIS
Lille
FRANCE
Nantes
Loire
Bay of Biscay
Gironde
Limoges
Bordeaux
Garonne
Toulouse
Dijon
Lyons
St-Étienne
Grenoble
Rhône
Marseilles
Toulon
Nice
MONACO
Monte-Carlo
Strasbourg
Corsica
Ajaccio
North Sea
NORWAY
Bergen
Stavanger
Oslo
Trondheim
Narvik
Tromsø
Hammerfest
SWEDEN
Kiruna
Luleå
Gävle
Uppsala
Stockholm
Örebro
Vänern
Vättern
Jönköping
Gothenburg
Malmö
Gotland
Öland
Åland
G. of Bothnia
FINLAND
Vaasa
Tampere
Turku
Helsinki
Skagerrak
Kattegat
DENMARK
Aalborg
Århus
Copenhagen
Baltic Sea
Kiel
Hamburg
Bremen
Elbe
Hannover
Berlin
Magdeburg
GERMANY
Dortmund
Essen
Cologne
Bonn
Halle
Leipzig
Dresden
Chemnitz
Frankfurt am Main
Nuremberg
Stuttgart
Munich
Rhine
Amsterdam
The Hague
Rotterdam
NETHERLANDS
Antwerp
BELGIUM
Brussels
Meuse
LUX.
Luxembourg
SWITZERLAND
Zürich
Bern
Geneva
LIECH.
Vaduz
AUSTRIA
Innsbruck
Salzburg
Linz
Vienna
Graz
CZECH REP.
Prague
SLOVAK REP.
Bratislava
POLAND
Szczecin
Gdańsk
Bydgoszcz
Poznań
Łódź
Warsaw
Białystok
Oder
Vistula
Wrocław
Katowice
Kraków
Ostrava
Lublin
Kaliningrad (Russia)
LITHUANIA
Kaunas
Vilnius
LATVIA
Riga
ESTONIA
Tallinn
Saaremaa
L. Chudskoye
BELARUS
Minsk
Vitebsk
W. Dvina
Mahilyow
Gomel
Brest
Pripet
UKRAINE
Kiev
Dnieper
Chernihiv
Zhytomyr
Lvov
Dniester
Kharkov
Donetsk
Dnepropetrovsk
Zaporozhye
Krivoy Rog
Bug
Kherson
Nikolayev
Odessa
CRIMEA
Sevastopol
MOLDOVA
Kishinev
HUNGARY
Budapest
Miskolc
Debrecen
ROMANIA
Cluj-Napoca
Timişoara
Braşov
Ploieşti
Galaţi
Constanţa
Bucharest
Danube
SLOVENIA
Ljubljana
Trieste
CROATIA
Zagreb
Split
BOSNIA-HERZ.
Sarajevo
SERBIA
Belgrade
Niš
KOSOVO
Priština
MONTENEGRO
Podgorica
ALBANIA
Tirana
MACEDONIA
Skopje
BULGARIA
Sofia
Plovdiv
Varna
GREECE
Thessaloniki
Corfu
Patra
Athens
Aegean Sea
Lesbos
Khios
Crete
Rhodes
ITALY
Milan
Turin
Genoa
Venice
Bologna
San Marino
SAN MARINO
Florence
Tiber
Rome
Naples
Bari
Taranto
Adriatic Sea
Tyrrhenian Sea
Sardinia
Cagliari
Sicily
Palermo
Messina
Catania
Ionian Sea
MALTA
Valletta
Pantelleria (Italy)
PORTUGAL
Porto
Douro
Lisbon
Tagus
SPAIN
Vigo
La Coruña
Bilbao
Valladolid
Madrid
Zaragoza
Ebro
ANDORRA
Andorra-la-Vella
Barcelona
Valencia
Guadiana
Córdoba
Guadalquivir
Seville
Cádiz
Málaga
Granada
Murcia
Alicante
Gibraltar (U.K.)
Str. of Gibraltar
Ceuta (Sp.)
Tangier
Melilla (Sp.)
Balearic Is.
Majorca
Minorca
Palma
Ibiza
Mediterranean Sea
Africa
MOROCCO
ALGERIA
Algiers
Annaba
Constantine
TUNISIA
Tunis
RUSSIA
KARELIA
Murmansk
White Sea
Arkhangelsk
N. Dvina
L. Onega
L. Ladoga
Vyborg
ST. PETERSBURG
Rybinsk Res.
Vologda
Kotlas
Yaroslavl
Kostroma
Ivanovo
MOSCOW
Tula
Smolensk
Orel
Kursk
Voronezh
Tambov
Nizhniy Novgorod
MARIEL
CHUVASHIA
Kazan
TATARSTAN
UDMURTIA
Kirov
KOMI
Perm
Nizhniy Tagil
Yekaterinburg
Chelyabinsk
Ufa
BASHKORTOSTAN
Magnitogorsk
Orenburg
Samara
Ulyanovsk
MORDVINIA
Penza
Saratov
Volga
Volgograd
Don
Taganrog
Rostov
Krasnodar
ADYGEA
Stavropol
KARACHAY-CHERKESSIA
KABARDINO-BALKARIA
NORTH OSSETIA
INGUSHETIA
CHECHENIA
DAGESTAN
Makhachkala
KALMYKIA
Astrakhan
Ob
Ural
Uralsk
Atyraū
KAZAKHSTAN
Caspian Sea
Black Sea
Bosporus
ISTANBUL
GEORGIA
Tbilisi
ARMENIA
Yerevan
AZERBAIJAN
Baku
TURKEY
Bursa
Izmir
Ankara
Samsun
Erzurum
Kayseri
Konya
Antalya
Adana
Diyarbakir
Euphrates
Tigris
Araks
SYRIA
Aleppo
CYPRUS
Nicosia
IRAQ
Baghdad
IRAN
Tabriz

1:35 000 000

Projection: Bonne

■ MÉXICO Capital Cities

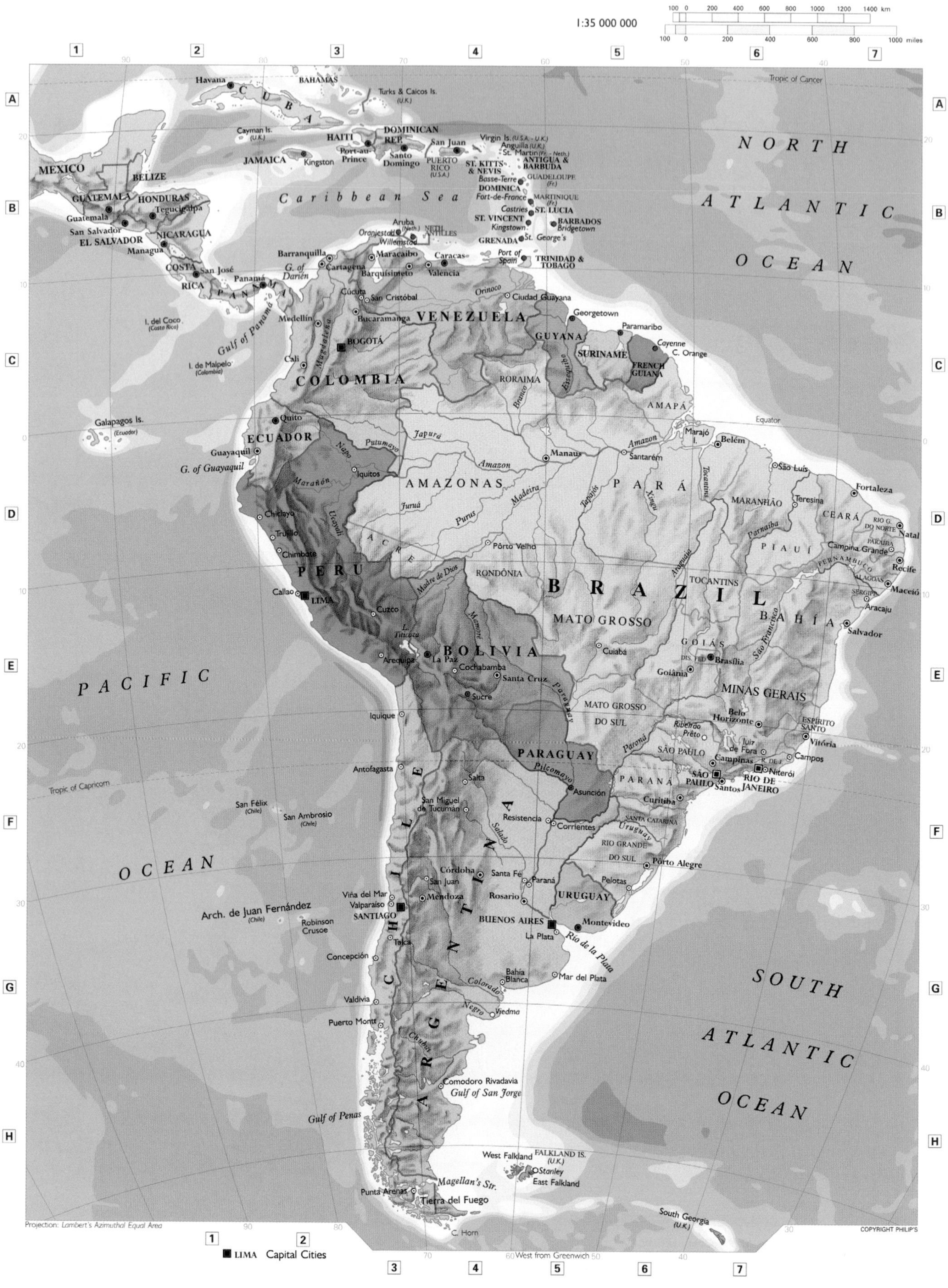
1:35 000 000
100 0 200 400 600 800 1000 1200 1400 km
100 0 200 400 600 800 1000 miles
NORTH ATLANTIC OCEAN
Caribbean Sea
PACIFIC OCEAN
SOUTH ATLANTIC OCEAN
Tropic of Cancer
Equator
Tropic of Capricorn
Havana
CUBA
BAHAMAS
Turks & Caicos Is. (U.K.)
Cayman Is. (U.K.)
HAITI
DOMINICAN REP.
Port-au-Prince
Santo Domingo
JAMAICA
Kingston
San Juan
PUERTO RICO (U.S.A.)
Virgin Is. (U.S.A. - U.K.)
Anguilla (U.K.)
St. Martin (Fr. - Neth.)
ANTIGUA & BARBUDA
ST. KITTS & NEVIS
Basse-Terre
GUADELOUPE (Fr.)
DOMINICA
Fort-de-France
MARTINIQUE (Fr.)
Castries
ST. LUCIA
ST. VINCENT
Kingstown
BARBADOS
Bridgetown
GRENADA
St. George's
Port of Spain
TRINIDAD & TOBAGO
Aruba (Neth.)
Oranjestad
NETH. ANTILLES
Willemstad
MEXICO
BELIZE
GUATEMALA
Guatemala
HONDURAS
Tegucigalpa
San Salvador
EL SALVADOR
NICARAGUA
Managua
COSTA RICA
San José
Panamá
PANAMA
I. del Coco (Costa Rica)
Gulf of Panama
I. de Malpelo (Colombia)
Galapagos Is. (Ecuador)
Barranquilla
Cartagena
G. of Darién
Maracaibo
Caracas
Barquisimeto
Valencia
Cúcuta
San Cristóbal
Orinoco
Ciudad Guayana
Medellín
Bucaramanga
VENEZUELA
Georgetown
Paramaribo
Cayenne
C. Orange
GUYANA
SURINAME
FRENCH GUIANA
Essequibo
BOGOTÁ
Magdalena
Cali
COLOMBIA
RORAIMA
Branco
AMAPÁ
Quito
ECUADOR
Guayaquil
G. of Guayaquil
Napo
Putumayo
Japurá
Amazon
Marajó I.
Belém
Manaus
Santarém
Iquitos
Marañón
AMAZONAS
PARÁ
Tocantins
São Luís
Fortaleza
Tapajós
Xingu
MARANHÃO
Teresina
CEARÁ
RIO G. DO NORTE
Natal
PARAÍBA
Campina Grande
PIAUÍ
Parnaíba
PERNAMBUCO
Recife
ALAGOAS
Maceió
SERGIPE
Aracaju
Juruá
Purus
Madeira
Chiclayo
Trujillo
Chimbote
Ucayali
ACRE
Pôrto Velho
RONDÔNIA
Araguaia
TOCANTINS
PERU
Callao
LIMA
Madre de Dios
BRAZIL
Cuzco
Mamoré
MATO GROSSO
BAHIA
São Francisco
Salvador
L. Titicaca
Arequipa
La Paz
BOLIVIA
Cuiabá
GOIÁS
DIS. FED.
Brasília
Goiânia
Cochabamba
Santa Cruz
Sucre
Paraguay
MATO GROSSO DO SUL
MINAS GERAIS
Belo Horizonte
ESPÍRITO SANTO
Vitória
Iquique
Ribeirão Prêto
Juiz de Fora
Paraná
SÃO PAULO
Campinas
R. DE J.
Niterói
Campos
PARAGUAY
Pilcomayo
SÃO PAULO
Santos
RIO DE JANEIRO
Antofagasta
Salta
Asunción
PARANÁ
Curitiba
San Miguel de Tucumán
Resistencia
Corrientes
SANTA CATARINA
Uruguay
RIO GRANDE DO SUL
Salado
Porto Alegre
San Félix (Chile)
San Ambrosio (Chile)
Córdoba
San Juan
Santa Fé
Paraná
Pelotas
URUGUAY
Viña del Mar
Valparaíso
SANTIAGO
Mendoza
Rosario
BUENOS AIRES
Montevideo
La Plata
Río de la Plata
Arch. de Juan Fernández (Chile)
Robinson Crusoe
Talca
Concepción
CHILE
ARGENTINA
Mar del Plata
Bahía Blanca
Colorado
Valdivia
Negro
Viedma
Puerto Montt
Chubut
Comodoro Rivadavia
Gulf of San Jorge
Gulf of Penas
West Falkland
FALKLAND IS. (U.K.)
Stanley
East Falkland
Magellan's Str.
Punta Arenas
Tierra del Fuego
C. Horn
South Georgia (U.K.)
Projection: Lambert's Azimuthal Equal Area
West from Greenwich
COPYRIGHT PHILIP'S
LIMA Capital Cities

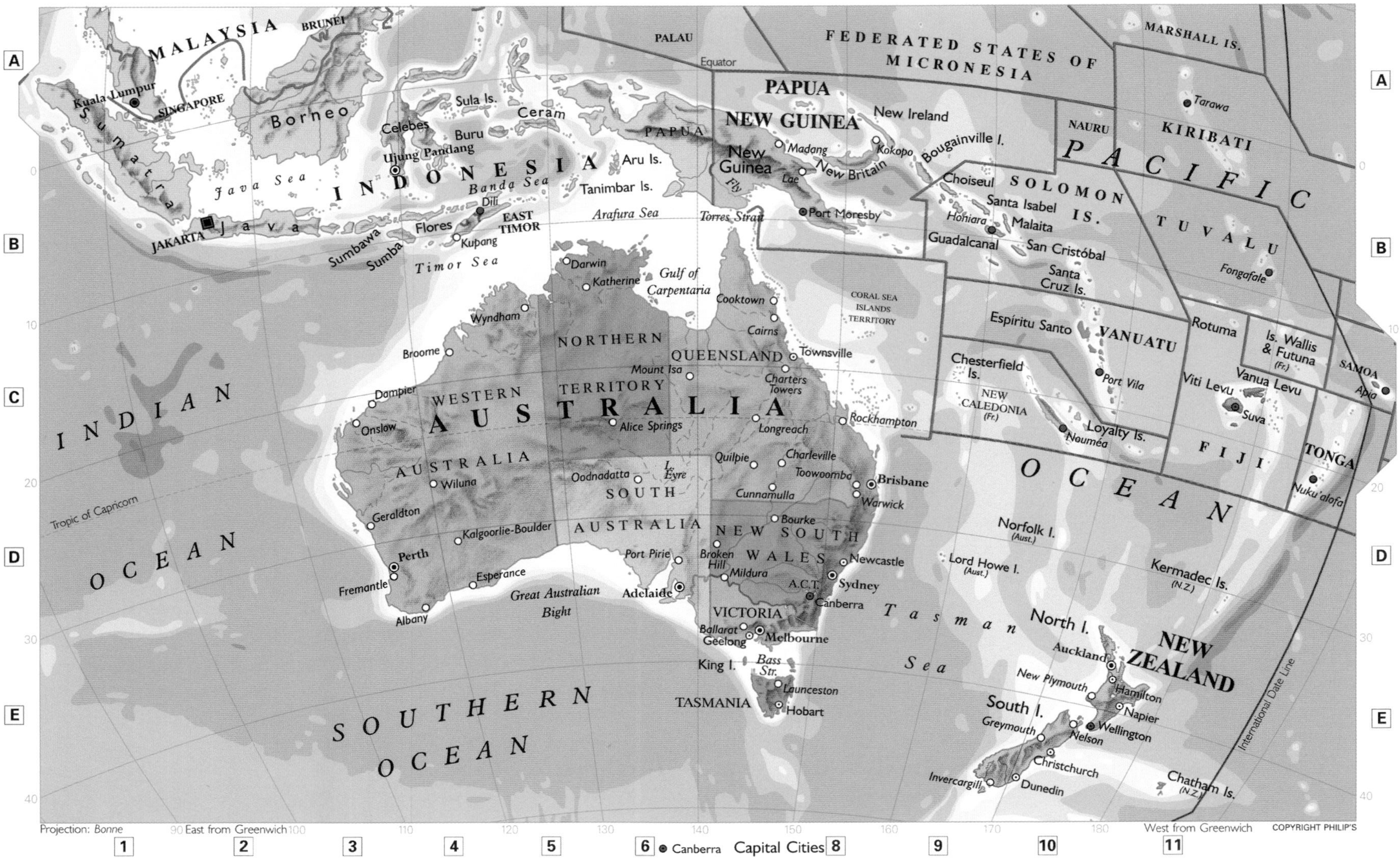
MALAYSIA
BRUNEI
Kuala Lumpur
SINGAPORE
Sumatra
Borneo
Java Sea
Java
JAKARTA
Sumbawa
Sumba
Flores
Kupang
Timor Sea
Celebes
Ujung Pandang
Sula Is.
Buru
Ceram
INDONESIA
Banda Sea
Dili
EAST TIMOR
Aru Is.
Tanimbar Is.
Arafura Sea
Torres Strait
PAPUA
PALAU
Equator
FEDERATED STATES OF MICRONESIA
MARSHALL IS.
Tarawa
KIRIBATI
NAURU
PAPUA NEW GUINEA
New Guinea
Fly
Madang
Lae
New Britain
New Ireland
Kokopo
Bougainville I.
Port Moresby
PACIFIC
SOLOMON IS.
Choiseul
Santa Isabel
Honiara
Malaita
Guadalcanal
San Cristóbal
Santa Cruz Is.
TUVALU
Fongafale
CORAL SEA ISLANDS TERRITORY
Espíritu Santo
VANUATU
Port Vila
Chesterfield Is.
NEW CALEDONIA (Fr.)
Nouméa
Loyalty Is.
Rotuma
Is. Wallis & Futuna (Fr.)
SAMOA
Apia
Viti Levu
Vanua Levu
Suva
FIJI
TONGA
Nuku'alofa
OCEAN
Darwin
Katherine
Gulf of Carpentaria
Wyndham
Broome
NORTHERN TERRITORY
QUEENSLAND
Cooktown
Cairns
Townsville
Charters Towers
Mount Isa
Dampier
Onslow
WESTERN AUSTRALIA
AUSTRALIA
Alice Springs
Longreach
Rockhampton
Wiluna
Oodnadatta
L. Eyre
SOUTH AUSTRALIA
Quilpie
Charleville
Toowoomba
Brisbane
Warwick
Cunnamulla
Geraldton
Kalgoorlie-Boulder
Bourke
NEW SOUTH WALES
Perth
Fremantle
Esperance
Albany
Great Australian Bight
Port Pirie
Adelaide
Broken Hill
Mildura
Newcastle
Sydney
A.C.T.
Canberra
VICTORIA
Ballarat
Geelong
Melbourne
King I.
Bass Str.
Launceston
Hobart
TASMANIA
INDIAN OCEAN
Tropic of Capricorn
SOUTHERN OCEAN
Tasman Sea
Norfolk I. (Aust.)
Lord Howe I. (Aust.)
Kermadec Is. (N.Z.)
North I.
NEW ZEALAND
Auckland
New Plymouth
Hamilton
Napier
Wellington
Nelson
South I.
Greymouth
Christchurch
Invercargill
Dunedin
Chatham Is. (N.Z.)
International Date Line
Projection: Bonne
East from Greenwich
West from Greenwich
COPYRIGHT PHILIP'S
Canberra Capital Cities

COMPARATIVE POLITICS

Integrating Theories, Methods, and Cases

PART I

Comparative Political Analysis

1 The Comparative Approach: An Introduction

In This Chapter

German Chancellor Angela Merkel with King Salman bin Abdulaziz Al Saud in Jeddah, Saudi Arabia in 2017. (Kay Nietfeld/picture alliance via Getty Images)

Comparing is as old as humanity, but comparative politics as a discipline is much newer. From a European perspective, the systematic comparison of politics goes back to the philosopher Aristotle, who devised a sophisticated way of comparing different forms of government. He focused on individual human citizens and then asked how much autonomy and control they had over their own lives within each system. Aristotle studied six different types of political system and divided governments into "correct" and "deviant" forms. He actively compared and made value judgments about which ones were desirable or not, based on how accountable the leadership was to the people it was supposed to serve.[1]

Much of what we take today to be the comparative method has been derived from the work of generations of European and American male theorists. This might misleadingly suggest that only one subgroup of humanity has actively and systematically compared variables in history. This is incorrect, and every culture and civilization throughout the world has had ways of comparing peoples, events, and things in order to classify what they find positive for individuals or groups or what they find negative. For example, a traditional Navajo way of evaluating whether conduct or policies should be adopted focuses on asking whether something is *hashhkeeji*, or "moving toward harmony," or *hozhooji*, "moving toward disharmony." The emphasis is on direction, movement, change. We encourage or discourage harmonious relationships by contributing positively or negatively.[2]

In this book, we examine the similarities and differences in politics within and between countries around the world, using comparisons and contrasts as our central tools. We cover more than just facts about the politics of Canada or India or France. We *analyze* politics *comparatively*.

• • •

Asking Why: Research Questions in Comparative Politics

To illustrate the type of learning we promote in our book, we can turn to a mnemonic device from elementary school:

> *Who, What, Where, When,* and *Why (And to this list we often add "How".)*

Of these "Five W's," which of these questions are the most profound and lead us to learn the most? Are we likely to gain a deep understanding of the social and political world from general questions such as "Who did this?" or "Where did this happen?" or "When did this happen?" For the most part, these relatively simple questions lead us to answers based on simple facts, such as prominent historical figures (*Who*) or places (*Where*) or dates (*When*).

Even if we don't know certain facts, we can often find them easily in modern life. Online search engines provide virtually free access to basic facts (though they can also provide inaccurate information, so it is important to always research with a critical eye). Smartphones, tablets, and other devices make basic information accessible almost anywhere. Try typing some questions using the "Five W's" into a search engine. Who is the president of Brazil? Where (or what) is the capital of Estonia? When did Tanzania become an independent state? For these questions, the correct answer is available almost instantly. Some knowledge of basic facts is obviously important, but this is not the type of question that interests us in this text. We will not focus simply on *descriptions* of *who* did *what* and *when* or on *where* things happened.

Now try searching for "*Why* did Tanzania gain independence from its colonizer?" or "*Why* was Jair Bolsonaro elected president of Brazil?" or "*Why* are aspects of globalization leading to job loss in Canada?" Your search will probably lead to an essay full of reasoning and argumentation as well as facts. Of course, the essay may or may not be reliable, and more comprehensive searching—using scholarly articles and book chapters—will provide you with other essays that offer contrary perspectives. These *why* questions lend themselves to richer discussions and debates than *who/what/when/where* questions. We cannot answer many *why* questions in one or two sentences. Answering *why* correctly requires more research, more reasoning, and more debate than the preliminary factual questions about who did what, where, and when.

argument The placement of evidence in logical form in support of a position or claim.

We can respectfully disagree on the primary cause of why something happened. We construct **arguments** by supplying evidence in a logical form in support of positions or claims, and the relative merit of our arguments depends on who has the better supporting evidence.

comparative politics The subfield of political science that aims to analyze multiple cases using the comparative method.

Questions that begin with that little word—*why*—are often answered not with a simple fact; rather, the answers begin with another deceptively powerful word: *because*. Note that the root of the word *because* is *cause*. *Why* questions give rise to answers that talk about the causes of events, and they turn basic facts (who, what, where, when, and how) into evidence supporting a claim about cause and effect.[3] This is the core pursuit of **comparative politics**: We seek to develop strong claims about cause and effect, testing various *hypotheses* (that is, possible answers to our questions) using factual evidence and developing larger theories about why the world operates the way it does. Through most of this book, we will provide some basic information necessary to speak the language of comparative scholars, but our emphasis is on asking and trying to answer *why* questions.

Few political phenomena are *monocausal*, or caused by just one thing. Often many factors combine to produce an outcome. Explaining something does not amount to simply naming one or another of these factors. Rather, we try to explain by identifying not just the *necessary* conditions to produce an effect but those that are *sufficient* to produce it. For example, when the Liberal Party of Canada won the 2015 federal election, the fact that the Liberals had a well-organized campaign team throughout the country may have been a *necessary* factor in their electoral victory. However, the perception of a weakening economy and an unpopular Conservative government also played key roles. As such, a strong campaign team is clearly not *sufficient* to produce this effect by itself. Dissatisfaction with the status quo can also play a key role. As well, Liberal leader Justin Trudeau, a younger person than Stephen Harper, may have represented a generational shift. Certainly he adopted a more positive tone. There may also have been larger international factors, such as the increasing salience of global warming and the Harper government's unwillingness to do much about reversing it. Now, what similarities and differences can we see in October 2019, when the Trudeau Liberals won a minority government with more parliamentary seats but fewer votes than Andrew Scheer's Conservatives? What variables can we use to explain this outcome?

Major Questions in Comparative Politics

In comparative politics, we focus on certain key questions that researchers have debated for years. Some important questions that we examine in this book are listed in Table 1.1. All of these are about causes and effects and can be answered, at least partly, by comparing and contrasting the politics of different countries. Some such questions, like the last two in the table, may also imply research on relations between countries as well as politics within countries.

AP Photo/Francois Mori

PHOTO 1.2 Students in Paris, France, protest the Iraq War in 2003. Why did France opt not to support the Iraq War?

The questions in the table are very general, and we would likely begin research by asking a more specific version of such questions about one or two countries. Rather than "Why do countries go to war?" we might ask, "Why did France opt not to support the Iraq War in 2003?" This question is more specific but also open-ended enough to have many possible answers. In scientific terms, this question can have several competing hypotheses we can test out using evidence, as we discuss later in this chapter and in the next. Possible answers may be based on the Bush administration's poor marshalling of evidence to support the war, France's strategic interests and calculations, its position in global affairs, French attitudes or culture with respect to war, and/or other possibilities.

Contrast this question with a more leading one, such as "How did the occupation of France in World War II lead to their decision not to support the Iraq War?" In this version, the

TABLE 1.1 | Prominent Questions in Comparative Politics

- Why are some countries democratic and others not?
- Why are some countries economically wealthy and others not?
- Why do countries have different institutions and forms of government?
- How has globalization affected North American economies?
- Which political systems better represent the interests of Indigenous peoples?
- Why do some social revolutions succeed and endure while others fail?
- Why do some countries develop a strong sense of statehood and nationhood while others do not?
- Why is there a problem of women's representation in most political systems?
- Why do countries go to war?
- How are social media changing the nature of campaigns and elections in democratic states?

questioner presumes he/she knows the answer to why France decided not to support the war. The researcher is entering the research expecting to confirm one particular answer.

Given our own human biases, this researcher may well choose evidence selectively, neglecting that which does not fit his/her assumptions and preconceptions. It is unlikely that someone asking this leading question will answer with "France's occupation in World War II had no effect." This type of question can therefore lead to a biased argument. In this particular case, we should also note that there is no easy way to measure the impact of one war on political decision-making almost six decades later.

Forming questions with *why* is a good rule of thumb, but good questions may also begin with other words, such as *how*. The questions in Table 1.2 also lead to debates about cause and effect. The first question asks about "consequences," which is just another way of asking about the effects of certain causes (in this case, the causes would be institutions). The question is also **open-ended**; that is, no expected answer is built into it, so the researcher can remain open to what the evidence reveals. The second question is just a bit more specific, identifying a certain consequence and a certain institution, but it is also open-ended. As we get more specific, we must take care not to commit the error of building the answer into the question or assume that what we are researching is the only answer. In this case, we would not want to assume that a presidential versus a parliamentary system of government is the main factor that shapes education policy.[4] The next question asks "under what conditions" democracies form, which is just another way of asking about the causes of democracy if we compare and contrast where and when and how it happens. So too does the final question ask about cause and effect, as shown by the verb *affect*. These are all valid research questions, even if they don't begin with *why*.

open-ended question A question that, in principle, is open to numerous possible answers.

Empirical Arguments versus Normative Arguments

The issue of right and wrong relates to the issue of *causal* or *empirical* arguments versus *normative* arguments. In this text, we mainly address **empirical** arguments: arguments that link cause and effect, uncovering answers to why the political world operates as it does. **Normative** arguments, by contrast, emphasize the way things should be. The following pair of questions highlights the distinction:

empirical Drawn from observations of the world.

normative Concerned with specifying which sort of practice or institution is morally or ethically justified.

- Why are some countries democratic and others authoritarian? (causal/empirical)
- Why is democracy preferable to authoritarianism? (normative)

Comparativists answer questions like the first more often than the second, though we care about the answers to both types of questions. We are not primarily concerned in this book with resolving normative arguments about what is right and wrong. This is not because comparativists are indifferent to moral concerns. To the contrary, most social scientists hold strong convictions. Most comparativists would overwhelmingly express a preference for

TABLE 1.2 | Additional Research Questions about Cause and Effect

- What are the consequences of different kinds of institutions for policy?
- What are the consequences of presidential versus parliamentary systems of government for education policy?
- Under what conditions will democracies emerge and consolidate?
- How do major social revolutions affect subsequent political developments in their respective countries?

democracy over authoritarianism if asked, though some might note the limitations of democracy and/or argue that authoritarian rule has sometimes led to economic growth.

At the same time, as social scientists we need to be aware of our biases and how our own views of the world will colour our research. Many theorists operate through what Cynthia Weber has called an "unconscious ideology," a sort of common-sense understanding that underpins how we view the world. In order to be effective social scientists, we need to explore our own biases and ask ourselves why we view the world the way we do and if that way really is better than other perspectives.[5]

While most comparativists would support democracy over authoritarianism, this does not mean that democracy is a perfect instrument or that it doesn't have problems that need to be resolved. We may need to take a step back and ask ourselves *why* we think democracy is better than other forms (if we do). What about the *type* of democracy we have in our own country? Could it be improved? What are its strengths and weaknesses? A first-past-the-post electoral system, such as we have in Canada, often results in a minority of voters getting the government they want. By contrast, a mixed member proportional system such as they have in Germany and New Zealand may be a better fit between what the voters want and what they eventually get. Comparing can help us to determine which systems have higher voter satisfaction rates or which have a better track record for representing women, Indigenous peoples, and racialized people.

As well, the way we define terms may mask what they mean for some people. Take for example the term peace—in this case we might mean the absence of war between states or at the substate level between historically antagonistic groups. However, an intersectional analysis that looks at issues of race, gender, class, and sexuality might not see a state that is not at war as being "peaceful." Rather, we might ask questions about gendered violence in the home, sexism in the workplace, racism in police forces through discriminatory carding policies, or legislation that discriminates against sexual minorities in the armed forces.

Concepts

Good scholarship seeks evidence, tests hypotheses, makes arguments, and contributes to theoretical debates. We address theories and hypotheses in greater detail in Chapter 2. First, however, we turn to the ideas of concepts, variables, and causal relationships.

Social science works with **concepts**, abstract ideas that we usually attempt to define as we ask and answer our questions. Examples of concepts are numerous and include democracy (as well as liberal democracy, electoral democracy, delegative democracy, and many other subtypes), justice, colonization, nationalism, constitutionalism, federalism, identity, gender relations, Indigenous self-determination, and social movements, among many others. Working with concepts helps us to think about the social world, which is too complex to analyze without them. We must be very careful in defining them because poorly constructed concepts make for misleading analysis.

concept An idea comparativists use to think about the processes we study.

Most concepts are categories. In some fields, such as the physical and natural sciences, certain categories are relatively clear and unchanging.[6] The elements of the periodic table are an example. Concepts like "helium" and "oxygen" describe elements that can be classified by their numbers of electrons and protons. Yet there are no such clear-cut categories in social and political life, and it would be foolish to assume we can directly apply concepts from the natural sciences to the study of politics. Concepts like "democracy" and "revolution" do not define phenomena the same way that "hydrogen" refers to an atom composed of a single proton and a single electron. Social and political concepts like democracy and revolution shade into each other by degree. Definitions do not capture exact boundaries between social and political phenomena in the real world, but we use them so that we can better understand that world and maybe make some viable predictions about what may happen if we pursue certain policy choices and not others.

Features of Good Concepts

What makes a concept worthwhile? Good concepts have several features, including clarity, coherence, consistency, and usefulness.

First, concepts must be clear and coherent.[7] Maybe you begin a research project because you are troubled by differences in levels of democratization across different countries. At the beginning, you have a common-sense understanding of democratization. To do good comparative work, however, you must make the meaning of the term explicit and clear. What do you mean by democratization? You cannot say "democratization consists of all the positive things that happen when a society changes." This is neither clear nor coherent. A clearer and more coherent statement would be "democratization is the process by which civil liberties and political rights are extended to all adult citizens in a given country." We begin with common-sense concerns about specific problems, but we need to define our key concepts precisely.

Second, concepts must be logically consistent, both internally and from one to another. For example, one cannot conceptualize democratization in terms of "expansion of liberty and equality" without addressing the likelihood that increasing liberty will likely lead to some degree of inequality. The issue here is whether our concept of democratization is *internally* consistent. Likewise, one cannot conceptualize democracy as being about a "set of institutional arrangements," such as elections, while viewing democratization as being about a "sort of political culture or set of values and norms." This is an issue of logical consistency *between* the concepts of democracy and democratization, which we presume are related but which seem to point in different directions here.

Third, concepts should be useful. They must be specific enough that they allow you to draw distinctions in analyzing examples. The concept of democratization can be useful because we can meaningfully distinguish between countries that have democratized and those that have not. Our use of concepts is pragmatic because we identify concepts based on how they help us to answer research questions.[8] For comparative analysis, concepts must allow us to identify *variations* between places, which the concept of democratization does. It allows us to differentiate and examine the variations between places that have undergone the process and those that have not. To be useful, concepts must also allow us to measure variables, a topic to which we return later.

Conceptualization

conceptualization The deliberate process through which we create and select social-scientific concepts.

Using concepts may be a creative process because social scientists need to develop their own in many cases. The process of making up and defining concepts is called **conceptualization**. It is often necessary to come up with new ideas and definitions, though we must be self-conscious and thoughtful in how we conceptualize. In comparative politics, a good practice is to look to how scholars have already conceptualized major ideas in books (including textbooks) and articles. We should not coin a new phrase just for the sake of it, and we do not want to end up with a thousand different definitions of a concept like "democracy" when there are already several good definitions available. Nonetheless, no concept is perfect, and you may need to conceptualize in novel ways on your own, depending on your specific projects, or if you feel that existing definitions tend to reproduce certain forms of bias.[9] Doing so can be part of an intellectual contribution, as long as your concepts are clear, consistent, and useful.[10]

Some questions require more general concepts and others more specific concepts. This issue is sometimes referred to as "**Sartori's ladder of abstraction**," based on the work of the Italian comparativist Giovani Sartori.[11] The ladder ranges from general concepts at the top to very specific concepts at the bottom, and the rung one stands on depends on the specific questions being asked and the cases being examined.

Sartori's ladder of abstraction The idea that we can organize concepts on the basis of their specificity or generality.

Operationalizing: From Concepts to Measures

Once we have a clear notion of a concept, we need to be able to measure it; that is, we need to **operationalize** our concept. To operationalize a concept is to make it workable, mainly by making it measurable. When a concept is operational—or we have an operational definition—we can begin to explain what we are studying. We can start to explain cause and effect only when we have clarified what we are talking about and can measure it.

operationalization The process through which we make a concept measurable.

Good Government

In Canada, we may learn in school that the country was founded on "peace, order, and good government." When we compare our system with that of the United States, we may feel we have a more transparent and egalitarian system. We may indeed think we have good government. Yet what exactly does "good government" mean? What about "order"? Does this mean stability? What if some people and some groups are dissatisfied with the status quo and wish to challenge the prevailing order because they see serious problems with it?

In settler states where countries have been created through the colonization of Indigenous lands and peoples, democracy (one adult citizen, one vote) may operate against Indigenous rights even if Indigenous peoples have the right to vote. The peace, order, and good government promised to Canadians may thus discriminate against pre-existing Indigenous traditions of government before settlers took over the land mass that we now know as Canada. As journalist Robert Jago recalled recently, Indigenous rights in Canada are often sidelined because there are not enough Indigenous peoples to have a dramatic effect on electoral outcomes. His "Canadian Problem" is a problem of population size, or numbers:

> They have them and we don't. It's not about ideology or vision; it's about math. These nomads outnumber us by sixteen-to-one. Every problem we face is an effect of their superior numbers. By weight of numbers, we are denied our democratic rights. With their majority, their control over our lands and resources seems natural and is granted democratic cover. With their pursuit of the greatest good for the greatest number, so-called democracy ensures this works against us. The greatest good is always their good; the greatest number is, by definition, them.[12]

Arguments such as Jago's suggest that the peace many Canadians take for granted may help to maintain forms of structural violence that actually prevent the types of "good government" enjoyed by Indigenous peoples before European settlement.

THE CANADIAN PRESS/Aaron Vincent Elkaim

PHOTO 1.3 Idle No More protesters demonstrate outside the British consulate in Toronto in 2013. The British Crown was the official signatory in the treaties with Indigenous nations, and there is a long history of petitioning the Crown to uphold its treaty promises.

TABLE 1.3 | Possible Operational Definitions of Democratization

A case of democratization occurs when . . .

- a country holds a free and fair multiparty election
- two turnovers of government at the ballot box have occurred in which the ruling party loses an election and peacefully steps down from power
- free and fair elections are held, and a constitutional law is in place guaranteeing the rights of freedom of speech, press, assembly, and religion to all citizens
- there is no verifiable suppression of political participation and expression
- more than two-thirds of citizens in a survey express values that reject authoritarian rule

There may be many ways to operationalize a certain concept, as shown by the example of democratization in Table 1.3. All of these may be valid ways to operationalize democratization, as long as the operational definition matches up with the concept. If we conceptualize democratization in terms of elections, we should measure it in terms of elections (not, for example, by values people hold). As we begin to measure our concepts, we move more toward the "real," or empirical, world we observe.

Empirical Evidence

Social scientists do not ask questions just to ask them but to attempt to answer them. So how do social scientists answer their questions? In short, they couple empirical evidence with theory. In comparative politics, *empirical* means those observations we can make from looking at the real world rather than using abstract theories or speculation. We look at how theory and evidence interact in Chapter 2. For the moment, we only highlight the forms of evidence most often used in comparative politics, since this is necessary for understanding the method. A key is the distinction between facts and evidence.

Facts and Evidence

evidence A set of facts or observations used to support a proposition or hypothesis.

Facts—understood here as simple statements about what is or is not the case—are abundant, but evidence is more important. **Evidence** consists of facts used in support of a proposition or hypothesis. Note, however, that the fact that someone else believes something does not mean there is evidence for it, even if that opinion has been published by a prominent scholar or public figure (such as Donald Trump's "birther" claim that Barack Obama was not born in the United States). Evidence should be available for the reader to gather as well and not be simply based on hearsay, though research sometimes requires anonymity of sources. Wherever possible, research should be replicable by someone else so that we can verify that they did not make mistakes.

To use a simple example of varying qualities of evidence, say we ask two students to make a simple claim about whether Saudi Arabia is a democracy and to back this claim with evidence. In the two examples in Table 1.4, the difference between the two students is not the correctness of the claim, which is the same. Nor is it the facts, which are true on both sides. Rather, the difference is in how well evidence is used to back the claim. Successful comparativists are known not for the correctness of their assertions but for the ways they empirically support their claims.

Strong evidence has several characteristics. Most obviously, it must be relevant to the issue at hand. If you are arguing about Saudi Arabia's democracy, the fact that the country

TABLE 1.4 | Examples of Strong and Weak Use of Evidence

Student 1	Student 2
Claim: Saudi Arabia is not democratic.	*Claim: Saudi Arabia is not democratic.*
Evidence: Saudi Arabia has not held free and fair elections for its national government. Women do not have the same political and social rights as men.	*Evidence:* Saudi Arabia is an Islamic country whose economy is based on exporting oil. It is a long-time ally of the United States and is led by a large royal family.
Claim: strong *Facts: correct* Evidence: ***strong***	*Claim: strong* *Facts: correct* Evidence: ***weak***

is Muslim, or an oil exporter, is not an indicator of democracy. The evidence should also be at the same **level of analysis** as the claim you are making—that is, at the individual, organizational, or societal level, for example. We can ask good research questions at many levels of analysis: individuals, groups within a country, whole countries and societies, regions of the world, and the world as a whole. But we need to be careful that our evidence reflects our level of analysis. Countries are made up of individuals, but individuals are not countries and there are important differences between individuals, groups, and societies at large. If you are seeking evidence about gender attitudes in Saudi Arabia, it is insufficient to note what a certain small group of men in the capital city thinks unless you can show that these men happen to be representative of the country at large. The same is true the other way around. If you are talking about an individual or a small group, you cannot assume you know everything about them just because of what country they come from; this may be ethnocentric stereotyping. Analysts risk committing logical fallacies if they do not pay attention to levels of analysis.

level of analysis The level (e.g., individual, organizational, societal) at which observations are made or at which causal processes operate.

Cases and Case Studies

Cases are the basic units of analysis in comparative politics. In many instances, our cases are countries, usually for a certain time period. We may seek, for example, to explain North Korea's lack of democracy versus the progress of democracy in South Korea; the cases here are the two countries we are comparing, and perhaps our time frame will be the period after the Korean War of the 1950s. We can also compare multiple cases in the same country. We could for example, compare every South Korean election in the 20th century to gauge the impact of the unemployment rate on voting preferences along an ideological spectrum.

case In comparative analysis, a unit or example of a phenomenon to be studied.

A case is not always a country, however. To start with, we could consider other geographical units. For example, we may be interested in the social history of the province of Saskatchewan or in comparing it with Manitoba. Or we may be interested in the state of Gujarat in India or in the city of Caracas in Venezuela. We may be interested in contrasting the European Union with the African Union or the "majority Catholic nations of southern Europe" with the "majority Protestant nations of northern Europe." In these instances, the case for study would still be a geographic area but not a nation-state.

Cases can also take other forms. They may be political groups, organizations, specific institutions, historical processes, eras, or even discrete events. The civil rights movement in the United States may be a case of a social movement. To do a comparison, one might examine the "civil rights movement of the 1960s" in juxtaposition to the "women's suffrage movement of the early 1900s." Or one might examine the rise of the labour movement in Canada promoting worker's rights by comparing Quebec, Ontario, and Saskatchewan. These are all provinces with quite different histories of labour unions and political organization. The French Revolution may be a case of a social and political revolution, and so too may the "Revolutions of 1848" (which took place across many countries in Europe) be treated as a "single case" of social and political revolution. Finally, as we discussed earlier, we may also look at comparisons over time within a single country.

Comparative politics studies vary considerably in terms of how many cases they handle. Some studies focus on a single case, providing a lot of in-depth, fine-grained analysis.[13] Most scholars feel that single cases can be illuminating but that they are not sufficient for testing all hypotheses. At the other end of the spectrum, some studies deal with *large-N* comparisons in which many cases are analyzed through statistical searches for common features (this is discussed further in Chapter 13). In between these approaches, at the heart of traditional comparative politics, we find *small-N* comparisons of two or more cases.

The Comparative Method

Comparative politics—unlike, say, the study of Canadian government or international relations—is defined by its method. It reaches conclusions about cause and effect through structured and systematic comparing and contrasting of cases.

Variables and Comparison

variable An element or factor that is likely to change, or vary, from case to case.

outcome Typically used as a synonym for "effect," something that is produced or changed in any social or political process.

The causes and the outcomes we are trying to measure are called **variables** in the social sciences because they vary from one case to another. For instance, if we were to argue that the African country of Ghana has a high level of democracy because its government is based on ancient political systems of the past (such as the powerful Ashanti Kingdom), while the neighbouring country of Togo has a low level of democracy because it did not have a long history of strong kingdoms, then both the cause and the effect vary from one country to the other. The effect (or **outcome**) is the level of democracy, which is high in one case and low in the other. The cause we would be proposing is the longevity and success of prior regime types. We can also anchor this hypothesis in other comparative studies of democracy, like Robert Putnam's landmark study *Making Democracy Work* wherein he compares the high levels of civil society and social capital in northern Italy versus a much lower level in the south.[14]

dependent variable In hypothesis testing, the dependent variable is the effect or outcome that we expect to be acted on (or have its value altered) by the independent variable.

independent variable In hypothesis testing, an independent variable is one that we expect to "act on" or change the value of the dependent variable.

We will typically be seeking to explain a certain outcome or result or consequence. In the cause-and-effect story of X Y, our research will centre on investigating the various possible causes (you might think of them as "X factors") to explain "the Y." Since outcomes depend upon the causes, a social science convention is to call the outcome the **dependent variable** while the cause(s) is (are) called the **independent variable(s)**. Many terms are used, but for our purposes, all of the expressions in each column in this table are nearly synonymous.

cause	➔	effect (or result or consequence)
independent variable	➔	dependent variable
explanatory variable	➔	outcome
X variable	➔	Y variable

variation Difference between cases in any given study of comparative politics.

If we compare or contrast two or more cases in order to make a causal argument, we will be looking for similarities and differences (also called **variations**) between the cases.

PHOTO 1.4 The city of Nogales straddles the border between Mexico (left) and the United States (right), divided by a three-mile fence completed in 2011. Why do these neighbouring countries have such striking differences?

Using just two countries for the moment (to keep it simple), we may look to explain why two countries have different outcomes, or we may look at variations in outcomes between two countries. We may ask why one country is wealthy but a neighbouring country is poor. Or, conversely, we may ask why two very different countries had very similar outcomes, such as becoming democracies around the same time.

To address such questions, we can use two simple tools as points of departure: *most-similar-systems* analyses and *most-different-systems* analyses.[15] These approaches use comparison for the same fundamental purpose: ruling out plausible explanations for certain phenomena. That is, quite similar or quite different cases are used as comparative checks to see what arguments cannot account for a certain outcome. Ruling out these other arguments allows the researcher to narrow down the research process by focusing on the possible causes that remain and testing evidence supporting these causes.

Most-Similar-Systems Design

The **most-similar-systems (MSS)** design is based on the logic that two cases (such as two countries) that are similar in a variety of ways would be expected to have very similar political outcomes. Thus, if two cases have variations in outcomes, we would look for the variations that can explain why the countries are dissimilar.

most-similar-systems (MSS) A research design in which we compare cases that are similar with respect to a number of factors but with distinct outcomes.

While Table 1.5 may make the analysis appear formal, people actually do this type of analysis informally all the time. Consider discussions you have with others about things seemingly as simple as why we like certain movies. Virtually all feature films released in cinemas are of similar length, are filmed for large screens, use professional directors and producers, have a plot with a protagonist (often a big star), use carefully chosen music as a soundtrack, and elicit emotion from the audience (or at least are intended to). Yet we all have preferences for some films over others. Amid these significant similarities among all films, we can identify—through comparison—the certain factors that lead each of us to appreciate or dislike a film.

If we can demystify the process of comparison by realizing that we use it subconsciously all the time, it is just a half-step to how this might be done in practice when analyzing political questions. Consider the presentation in Table 1.5 of two African countries.

We are wondering why one country (Ghana) is a democracy and another (Togo) is not. The table notes several similarities between the two countries, making the variation in outcomes of interest to comparativists. If we were to hypothesize a cause, we might argue that regime history (that is, the pre-colonial governmental traditions of the countries) mattered. Togo did not have a history of strong kingdoms, while Ghana had several strong kingdoms since the ninth century. As we look for the cause of variations in outcomes, we can essentially cross out the many variables on which the countries are similar because they are unlikely to cause differences.

So regime history might fit the bill, as Table 1.5 suggests. Does this mean we have proven that this is the answer? No—we would need to do several things to make this case. First, we would consider alternative hypotheses. Instead of prior regime type, we might just as easily have said that the economic performance of each country was the key factor that shaped regime type, or that the nature of the military command was the key cause, or that the ideology of the founders of each country mattered most. Only by examining and weighing these various causes could we gain real insight into why one country is democratic and the other is not. Thus, our second caveat is that we would need to find plausible evidence and have a strong argument linking the cause to the outcome.

One potential source of initial confusion is that MSS designs place a premium on identifying the differences between cases, not the similarities. You might think of it this way: If

TABLE 1.5 | Most-Similar-Systems Design

REGIME TYPES IN AFRICA

Variable	**Case 1: Togo**	**Case 2: Ghana**
Similarities		
Climate	Tropical	Tropical
Income	Low	Low
Ethnic Demography	Heterogeneous	Heterogeneous
Largest Religion	Christian	Christian
Other Religions	Islam, traditional	Islam, traditional
Outcome		
Regime Type	Authoritarian	Democratic
Cause		
Hypothesis: Regime history	Weak governments	Strong kingdom

PHOTO 1.5 People in Nakpayili, Ghana, voting in the presidential elections of 2016. Despite many similarities with its neighbour Togo, Ghana is a democracy while Togo is not. What factors account for this difference?

two cases are most similar, what is remarkable about comparing them? What is remarkable is where most-similar cases differ. Differences in outcomes between similar cases are noteworthy, and differences in possible causes are what will help us to explain them. We invert this logic when using the other tool that serves as a basic point of departure in comparative politics: most-different-systems designs.

Most-Different-Systems Design

The **most-different-systems (MDS)** design uses a logic that mirrors that of the MSS. In this approach, the researcher identifies two cases that are different in nearly all aspects yet are similar on a particular outcome. This puzzle leads the researcher to develop hypotheses to explain the peculiar similarity. See Table 1.6, which presents an example of two major revolutions in world history that happened in very different geographical and historical contexts.

most-different-systems (MDS) A research design in which we compare cases that differ with respect to multiple factors but in which the outcome is the same.

Just as MSS designs place a priority on identifying differences between cases, MDS designs place a premium on identifying the similarities that can give us analytical leverage. Again, the name is revealing: In an MDS design, what variables are noteworthy and telling? Those that are *not different*. If France in 1789 and China in 1949 are so different, what accounts for both having major social revolutions? In the interest of cultivating your habit of building comparisons, we leave it to you to insert your own hypotheses. Might both countries have had populations facing extreme deprivation at these times? Or perhaps in both countries new actors emerged at these moments in history to lead a revolution? We will not answer these questions here, but since several major variables differ between these "most-different" cases, we may surmise that similarity in revolution will be attributable to one of the relatively scarce number of other similarities we can find.

Comparative Checking

comparative checking The process of testing the conclusions from a set of comparisons against additional cases or evidence.

generalizability The quality that a given theory, hypothesis, or finding has of being applicable to a wide number of cases.

While the MSS and MDS designs are the foundation for initial comparisons, they do not complete our analysis. Analysts must constantly remain aware that one pair of cases does not "prove" a hypothesis to be true everywhere, any more than one case study can prove a hypothesis. Rather, we must constantly engage in **comparative checking**, or examining the conditions under which certain arguments hold. This checking typically involves mixing MSS and MDS designs to test our hypotheses further and to give us a sense of how **generalizable** they are, or how applicable to a wide number of cases.

Return briefly to Table 1.5, the MSS table using Togo and Ghana as examples. That MSS analysis provided us with a glimpse of the possibility that prior regime strength may affect regime type. However, a bit of comparative checking beyond these two cases will reveal that the story is not so simple. If we look at the case of Benin, for example, we see another example of a democratic country with a history of a strong government (the Kingdom of Dahomey). Does this mean strong earlier regimes translate into democracy later on? This is possible, although we can find other examples of countries with strong regimes that did not become democratic.

In looking for other possible causes, we have many strategies to pursue. We can look to a larger number of cases to see if other hypothesized arguments might still hold. We should also dig into our original cases once again to see if there are any variations or hypotheses that we may have overlooked. We can also revisit the scholarly literature—digging in to see how scholars explain the outcome that interests us. We may find new hypotheses or refine the hypothesis we have already worked with. Finally, we could use a strategy that links to the issue of how politics happens over time, called *within-case comparison*.

within-case comparison The comparative analysis of variation that takes place over time or in distinct parts of a single case.

Within-Case Comparison

Within-case comparison means looking more carefully within one's own case(s) to examine the variations there.

TABLE 1.6 | Most-Different-Systems Design

MAJOR SOCIAL REVOLUTIONS		
Variables	**Case 1: France (1780s)**	**Case 2: China (1940s)**
Differences		
Continent	Europe	Asia
Population (approx.)	< 30 million	> 500 million
Century	Eighteenth	Twentieth
Regime	Monarchy	Nationalist Party
Outcome(s)		
Social Revolution	Yes	Yes
Cause		
[Insert Your Hypothesis Here]	???	???

To use an example closer to home, consider why hopefulness about the future may have been relatively high in the province of Alberta in the 2000s but is lower today. Many variables are similar across these two periods: The basic governmental structure of the province and certainly the geography are stable, for instance. In other words, a province at an earlier period (call it Time 1) is "most similar" to the same province at Time 2. Yet some things do change over time, and those variables are good candidates to explain changing outcomes. The economy may change, for instance, or the composition of the workforce, or international events, or the political mood. In Alberta's case the falling price of oil by more than 50 per cent over a short period of time may play a key role. Here the effects of externalities from outside of the domestic context play a key role. Many other examples can also illustrate the virtues of comparing periods within a province or even a country. The takeaway point is that comparison does not end with simple charts listing attributes of different provinces or countries but instead is a way to delve systematically into the evidence case studies provide. Another key point is that the sources of change are not just from inside the country. Globalization and the behaviour of other countries can have crucial effects on politics and economics.

Is the Study of Politics a Science? The Limits of the Comparative Method

We speak of *political science* even though in comparative politics, we rarely find proof as we would in the hard sciences. Despite the scientific pretensions of some comparativists, the best we can do is show *probable* relationships between variables rather than showing general laws.[16] Most Canadian political scientists do not see themselves as conducting scientific experiments akin to their counterparts in the natural sciences. While there are quantitative researchers in Canadian political science, this is less common than in the United States. For many questions, social scientists cannot use one of the major tools that drive knowledge in the natural and physical sciences: the controlled experiment. We cannot subject individual countries to precise conditions to examine the effects in the way we can in a chemistry lab, although many social scientists do look for so-called "natural experiments" in which real-world events mimic laboratory conditions in key ways.[17] The sorts of comparative designs we have discussed in this chapter comprise one way to make up for our inability to do experiments everywhere. When we observe countries that are quite similar in the MSS design, we are approximating the controlled experiment of the laboratory: We hold many variables constant and vary one or two key variables to see if we can measure their impact.

Chapter Summary

Asking Why: Research Questions in Comparative Politics

- For scholars of comparative politics, the key questions are about *why* something happens, or about cause and effect, even though we are also interested in normative questions about right and wrong.
- Research in comparative politics addresses questions on such major issues as economic development, political regimes and institutions, and a range of social outcomes.

Concepts

- Concepts are the ideas we use to categorize the world and enable us to measure and compare observations.

- Good concepts are clear, coherent, consistent, and useful.
- Social scientists often must do their own conceptualization or develop their own concepts and must operationalize their concepts to enable measurement.

Empirical Evidence

- Comparative politics relies heavily on facts and evidence to support arguments about cause and effect.
- One of the main empirical approaches is the use of case studies and comparisons between cases.

The Comparative Method

- Variables are features that vary from one case to another and enable comparison between cases.
- Two approaches to comparison involve the most-similar-systems design and the most-different-systems design, both of which examine variations and similarities between cases to assist in testing hypotheses.
- Good comparative study requires more than just brief examination of similar and different variables; it often involves further examination through steps such as comparative checking and within-case comparison.

Is the Study of Politics a Science? The Limits of the Comparative Method

- While the study of politics aspires to scientific conclusions, it is rarely able to prove its conclusions with absolute certainty.

Thinking It Through

1. Imagine you are going to do a project that tries to explain why democracy has been relatively successful in Canada. What sort of conceptual work would you need to do before you could complete this study?
2. If you were to conceptualize democracy as a political system in which (1) certain individual rights are respected, (2) elections are periodically held, and (3) political transitions are peaceful, what would you have to do to operationalize this concept for the purposes of a comparative study?
3. What are the five most interesting *why* questions about comparative politics that you can think of? What are the main concepts they imply?
4. Take one of the questions you have formulated in response to question 3. Now think of how you could construct a most-different-systems (MDS) design to compare cases and answer your question.
5. Take one of the questions you have formulated in response to question 3. Now think of how you could construct a most-similar-systems (MSS) design to compare cases and answer your question.

2 Theories, Hypotheses, and Evidence

In This Chapter

A worker in a Honda car factory in Noida, a town on the outskirts of New Delhi, India. (MANPREET ROMANA/AFP/Getty Images)

In this chapter, we discuss how theories work. We will outline how to form *hypotheses*, or educated guesses about what will happen under certain circumstances, and how to avoid certain pitfalls in testing those hypotheses. All this will prepare you better for examining the issues of comparative politics that comprise the rest of the book.

• • •

Introduction to Theories, Hypotheses, and Evidence

Social scientists look for convincing answers to important questions about why things happen. We might be interested in asking why Quebec had two referenda on independence (1980 and 1995) but has not had another one in more than two decades. Is there a generational shift away from separatism? What does the rise in support for the Bloc Québécois in 2019 indicate about the prospects for separatism in the future? Do other demographic factors (such as religion and ethnicity) play a role? Or we might seek to understand why populism has become a salient electoral tool south of the border (with Bernie Sanders and Donald Trump) but has been less important in Canadian national politics, even when making allowance for Doug Ford's 2018 victory in Ontario or the short but ultimately doomed attempt at electoral success by Maxime Bernier's People's Party of Canada. We might also be interested in why the US political system continues to have older leaders campaigning for office (Hillary Clinton, Donald Trump, and Bernie Sanders are all in their 70s) while in Canada, New Zealand, France, and Austria, many of the leaders of major parties were under the age of 40 when first elected to high office. Or we may seek to understand the impact of the rise of Asian economies like China and India on the reduction of some types of jobs in Canada and the United States. Does the increasing globalization of manufacturing and services help explain the rise of Trump and Ford?

The first step in comparative politics is asking good research questions about the causes and effects of political events. In Chapter 1, we outlined how the comparative method can help us begin to answer those questions by comparing and contrasting cases, most often different countries or specific events in different countries. We may examine the political party systems of Germany and France or the communist revolutions in Russia and China, for instance. To do so, we juxtapose the facts of the different cases to make an argument about the similarities and differences between them.

In this chapter, we talk about the tools we need to *answer* questions, with a focus on two elements that help us to formulate possible answers: theories and hypotheses. We discuss what theories and hypotheses are and how they differ from one another. We then discuss how evidence is used to test hypotheses and theories.

Theories

theory A general set of explanatory claims about some specifiable empirical range.

Theories are general explanations of empirical phenomena, or explanations about how the world operates. A theory aims to explain more than just one or two cases or examples, and it is typically backed by a considerable number of supporting facts as empirical evidence. An explanation or framework in the social sciences will rarely earn the right to be called a theory if we cannot find considerable support for its arguments in the real world.

In political science, there are two different types of theory, typically referred to as normative theory and empirical (also known as positive) theory. Normative theory deals with questions of values and moral beliefs. An example might be the question "What is the best kind of political system we could construct?" This is a matter of morals and ethics. Empirical theory, by contrast, deals with empirical questions. An example is "Which factors are most likely to produce a preferred political system?" This is about the variables that cause things to happen. In this book, we are mostly focused on empirical theories: we discuss theory as a *general* explanation of why things happen.

Hypotheses

Hypotheses are *specific* proposed explanations for why an outcome occurs. To answer research questions, we may generate or formulate hypotheses that we hope can explain a set of facts upon further research. Hypotheses are not explanations already backed by lots of evidence. Instead, they are possible answers to a question, which we plan to test out by applying them to data, looking at specific cases to see if there is evidence to support the idea. Informally, you can think of them as hunches. If the hypothesis receives that support from the evidence, it may become a thesis in an argument.[1]

hypothesis A specific prediction, derived from a theory, that can be tested against empirical evidence.

Developing hypotheses requires us to make imaginative leaps from unanswered questions to possible explanations. Hypotheses can be generated from existing theories in a **deductive** fashion: starting with general ideas and then testing whether they work on specific examples. For example, say we are asking about why an anti-colonial revolution happened in a certain African country in the 1950s. We may begin our research with a major theory that holds that social revolutions (such as the Haitian Revolution, French Revolution, Russian Revolution, or Iranian Revolution) are caused by the social upheavals produced by modernization. We seek to apply this theory to the African country we are studying. Using the theory as our general model, we might hypothesize that the anti-colonial revolution in the African country was produced by a history of modernization. Another way to think of this sort of approach is to consider it an effort to test an *observable implication* of the starting theory.[2]

deductive reasoning The process of moving from general claims or theories to specific observations or predictions about a phenomenon or set of cases.

Associated Press/Ebrahim Noroozi

PHOTO 2.2 Iranian women in Tehran hold portraits of Supreme Leader Ayatollah Ali Khamenei at a rally in February 2019 to mark the 40th anniversary of the Iranian Revolution. What factors account for a successful revolution against the Shah in 1979 and the absence of such revolutions in neighbouring Iraq, Kuwait, and Turkey?

Not all hypotheses are deduced from general theories, of course. Some can also come from looking at a case that deviates from a particular theory. We can learn a great deal from so-called **deviant cases,** or "**outliers,**" that do not do as we might expect. For instance, in many international comparisons, the United States is a deviant case. It has both higher income inequality and greater differences in life expectancy between racial groups (to name just two variables) than one might expect based on its level of economic development. By focusing on some characteristics that make the United States different, we might sometimes understand general relationships better. For example, perhaps it is not a country's overall level of economic development that predicts the life expectancy of its people but the racialized or class identity of that person, which might then be correlated to problems of structural racism and inequality.

deviant case (outlier) A case that does not fit the pattern predicted by a given theory.

We often formulate a hypothesis with some initial knowledge of the topic at hand, but we do not want to ask questions to which we presume to already know the answer. We do not normally aim to create a hypothesis from empirical data in an **inductive** way—moving from specific observations to general claims. That is, we don't do the research, find the answer, then go back and propose our hypothesis (although sometimes our analysis does suggest new hypotheses, and inductive approaches to theory generation do exist). Instead, we approach our hypothesis with an open mind toward what answers we may find. Our hypotheses may be supported or rejected by the research we do, so there is always the possibility that they are wrong. In fact, most hypotheses are wrong, and rarely can we fully confirm or disprove a hypothesis with limited research.[3] The goal is not to pick the correct hypothesis at the outset but rather to learn something from the study we undertake. In fact, many social scientists believe that our knowledge advances more from refuting hypotheses than from defending or supporting them.

inductive reasoning The process of moving from specific observations to general claims.

Hypotheses and theories inform one another. Theories help to guide us in formulating hypotheses, and confirming hypotheses may either support or undermine theories. In general, hypotheses are more tentative and speculative than theories. A specific hypothesis is generated for each research question and is put on the line to be tested in each case. While the evidence from testing a specific hypothesis may support or oppose a particular theory, it is usually insufficient to reject or confirm a theory by itself. Generating a theory is a more elaborate, long-term process than generating and testing a single hypothesis.

After testing hypotheses for a specific study, scholars will typically offer a thesis, a claim made on the basis of evidence from research. In comparative politics, a thesis is an argument supported by the research evidence that comes from testing a hypothesis. While a thesis has evidence supporting it, that does not mean it is a full theory. Before achieving the status and prestige of being called a theory, an idea requires ample evidence to support it, typically based on research by many scholars. For the most part, students of comparative politics test hypotheses, make specific claims in the form of theses, and are expected to use evidence to argue in support of their theses, taking account of existing theories. We are informed by theory and can contribute to debates by theorizing, but we rarely craft or destroy entire theories alone.

thesis A statement for which one argues on the basis of evidence.

How Theories Emerge and Are Used

Theories have facts and evidence supporting them, but these are not proof that a theory is valid and correct in all circumstances. Often, a factually incorrect theory will hold sway for a long period of time until it is supplanted by a stronger theory backed up with better evidence. For example, the earth was long believed by many European thinkers and religious leaders to be situated at the centre of the universe, and this appeared consistent with many facts, such as the sun and moon rising and falling beyond the horizon each day. However, this theory eventually came into conflict with observations that suggested that the earth revolved around the sun. Both theories persisted for a time until it became clear that the heliocentric (sun-centred) theory best explained the structure of our solar system. Thus, competing theories may coexist, and there may simultaneously be facts and evidence that support a theory and other facts and evidence that contradict the theory. Theories may ultimately fail and be rejected, but ideally theories only "die" when replaced by new ones that better explain existing evidence.[4]

Theories in political science explain tendencies and help us to understand many cases, but there are almost always exceptions to the rules. Nothing in political science works in all cases the way the laws of physics work everywhere on earth. For example, as you will read in Chapter 6, there are several competing theories to explain why countries become democracies. There is considerable evidence that wealthier countries are likelier to be democratic than poor countries, but this does not mean every rich country will be a democracy and every low-income country will be under authoritarian rule. Rather, the theory of the link between wealth and democracy posits a tendency, much as eating healthy foods and not smoking will *tend to* increase one's life expectancy. Not everyone who eats well and avoids smoking will live to old age, and not everyone who smokes and eats junk food will die young. Cause-and-effect relationships in the social sciences are general patterns, not absolute laws. As a result, building theory is an intensive process over an extended period of formulating and testing hypotheses, gathering and examining evidence, and understanding and synthesizing debates. Theories are imperfect but can be improved over time.

Since theories compete with one another as the best explanations of social phenomena, it may be natural to think of scientists competing with one another to come up with the best theory. This is true in part, but the social sciences are also a collective endeavour. In this sense, when a theory is rejected, it represents an advance of our understanding. Even critiques of one scientist's effort by another scientist are part of the process of testing and contesting the best explanations.

Types of Evidence

For most students being introduced to comparative politics, the dominant form of evidence will be **qualitative**, meaning it comes from accounts of historical or contemporary events. For instance, if we wish to test the hypothesis that the Quebec referendum of 1980 was caused by an economic downturn, then we may look to media and other journalistic sources to get a sense of whether people were dissatisfied with the economic status quo and blamed the federal government. Qualitative evidence may come from many sources, such as written works like constitutions and laws, historical or journalistic accounts or reports, and interviews or surveys of people. Of course, it may turn out that this theory is a dead end—perhaps the referendum had little to do with perceptions of the economy at all and much more to do with other factors.

qualitative A form of analysis that aims to discern relationships between events or phenomena as described in narrative form, such as an account of a historical process.

Social scientists use **quantitative** data such as statistics and figures to complement qualitative data when they aim to make **inferences**, or conclusions based on evidence, about cause and effect. Examples include measures of average incomes or average life expectancies across countries or within countries. Such quantitative comparisons may be undertaken using national statistics from government agencies like Statistics Canada, numerical data from surveys (from, say, Environics, Nanos, or Gallup), or data collected by researcher observations. Various data sources may be used to compare and contrast outcomes in different countries. At a more advanced level, such descriptive statistics can be used to formulate and begin to test hypotheses about the causes and effects of differences between countries. Other quantitative research in comparative politics focuses on the construction of formal mathematical models of the strategic behaviour of individuals and

quantitative Quantitative analysis aims for the mathematical discernment of relationships between variables, typically involving a large number of cases or observations.

inference The process through which we aim to test observable implications (often about cause and effect) of any given theory; also refers to conclusions reached through this process.

PHOTO 2.3 Premier René Lévesque quiets the crowd in Montreal before conceding defeat in the Quebec referendum of 1980. To what extent were economic factors salient in voter decision-making? Would a more imperilled economy have produced a higher or a lower level of support for separation?

groups in political situations. Quantitative data differ from qualitative data in their presentation, but both types are used to generate and test hypotheses. While the details of statistical methodologies and formal mathematical modelling are beyond the scope of this book, we work from the premise that both qualitative and quantitative work may be used to

The Qualitative–Quantitative Debate

The increasingly sophisticated use of statistics in social science has generated considerable debate about the best methods and types of data for research. Qualitative (non-mathematical) research often closely examines a few cases. Such approaches are often called *small-N* studies, with *N* meaning the number of cases. Quantitative approaches often involve many cases, and comparativists use mathematical techniques to measure the degree of association between a set of variables that cuts across each case. Scholars who prefer quantitative work maintain that qualitative studies of one, two, or three cases are susceptible to reaching conclusions that only work for those selected cases and not a larger number of cases (some people call this the *small-N problem*).

Scholars who advocate strongly for qualitative work sometimes argue that quantitative research is unpersuasive because it neglects the context and detail needed to make arguments meaningful. From this perspective, quantitative arguments that travel too far miss the real causes in a case as they unfold over time. Despite this debate, qualitative and quantitative research are increasingly interdependent in contemporary social science, and they complement each other in important ways. The perspective of this text is that both methods have their strengths and weaknesses. In general, quantitative work has the potential to make strong empirical claims about large numbers of cases and general associations between variables, and some would argue that qualitative work has the ability to reveal causal mechanisms or processes at the case-specific level. It has been argued that a common logic underpins any good social science work.[6]

Imaginechina via AP Images

PHOTO 2.4 Customers shop for fish at a market in Shijiazhuang, China. Will China move toward democracy as its middle class grows larger? We address this question in the discussion of democratization in Chapter 6.

categorize and explain differences across cases but they can also be used to test hypotheses about the causes of those differences.[5]

In comparative politics, you will use historical accounts and data more often than you will make predictions about the future. This is because we have real evidence only for things that have happened and not for what might happen. Of course, the past may give us expectations about the future, but in terms of concrete evidence, we cannot know what has yet to happen. For this reason, we work with existing cases to develop hypotheses and theories. For instance, we may hypothesize that the People's Republic of China, which is not currently a democratic country, will move toward democracy as it grows wealthier. This hypothesis may come from observations about what has happened in other countries like South Korea or Taiwan. Well-regarded theories may strongly suggest that China will democratize, and we may hypothesize and argue that it will do so, but to test the hypothesis we will have to await future events. Evidence comes only from events that have happened.

Hypothesis Testing

The core of comparative politics is testing hypotheses about cause and effect between two or more variables. We defined variables in Chapter 1 as some measure that can vary from one observation to the next. Examples range from a country's average income or average life expectancy, to whether a revolution occurred in a given country, to the most prominent religion in a particular state, to the religion of a particular person.

In social science, cause-and-effect arguments are based on examining different variables and how those variables relate to one another and may depend on one another.

If country A is economically wealthy and country B is poor, what does country A have that country B does not that makes it so?[7] An explanation will hinge upon identifying what variable might cause A to have become rich and B to remain poor. Our goal will be to identify what other variables go alongside wealth that are lacking in countries that are poor in order to examine whether those variables made the difference. Our first key distinction here is between correlation and causation.

Correlation

correlation A relationship between two variables in which they tend to move either in the same direction (positive correlation) or in opposite directions (negative correlation).

Correlation measures the association between two variables. When two variables correlate, they are related to one another (or, to separate the words, they "co-relate"). To use a simple example, the temperature in many places will correlate with the month of the year: when it is February in Canada, the temperature will be relatively cold, whereas in July the temperature will be relatively hot. This does not mean it is impossible to have a hot day in February or a cold day in July, just that there is an association in general. There is thus a correlation between the variable "month of the year" and the variable "temperature."

If two variables have a positive correlation, they tend to increase together. One increases as the other increases. An obvious example is the income of a person and the amount the person spends on luxury goods. People with low incomes cannot afford to spend money on luxury goods, while the wealthy may spend a large amount on luxury goods. These two variables are positively correlated. A negative correlation is just the opposite and means that as one variable tends to increase, the other tends to decrease. An example might be the number of cigarettes one smokes per day and one's life expectancy.

Just as we can find a positive correlation between wealth and democracy, we can conversely find a negative correlation between another pair of variables: poverty and democracy. Consider the number of people in a country living on an income below $2 per day (call this variable the absolute poverty rate) and the level of democracy. In this case, the rich countries have relatively low levels of poverty and high levels of democracy, while many countries in Africa have high levels of poverty and low levels of democracy. When we look at the nearly 200 or so countries in the world today, these correlations are apparent, even though it should be noted that there are some countries that are rich but not democratic and some that are low-income yet are democratic.

Causation

causation The property that obtains when one thing can be shown to cause another.

Causation exists when one variable causes another. This helps us to answer the fundamental questions raised in Chapter 1, such as "Why are some countries democracies?" Recall that *why* questions are often best answered with *because* answers. As the word *because* implies, answering *why* involves explaining causes. Without causal arguments and theories, correlations are just patterns in search of an explanation. When we have causation, we usually have correlation, but the opposite is not true. Failing to distinguish between correlation and causation can lead to a variety of problems, as we will show.

Does the correlation between wealth and democracy prove that getting rich causes democracy to happen? Not necessarily. It may be that this correlation points in the direction of a causal argument, such as wealth → democracy. Or maybe the other way around: democracy → wealth. On the other hand, it may be that the correlation exists but there is no causal reason for it. It may be simply due to chance that rich countries happen to be democracies. Or there may be other factors that result in both wealth and democracy.

As it turns out, one of the central theories of comparative politics suggests that countries that grow wealthy *are* likely to become democratic for specific reasons we detail in Chapter 6. The causal argument, beginning with the positive correlation between wealth and democracy, finds that historically, countries have developed a middle class as they have grown wealthier. This middle class, rather than the elite, ends up being a central force that pushes for more rights for all citizens. In poor countries without a middle class, democracy is unlikely to succeed, but growing middle classes in countries that are growing rich have helped to bring democracy with them. While the correlation here does have a causal explanation, notice that the correlation needed an argument and logic to bring the story together and to make the fact of the correlation into evidence that supports an argument.

We cannot assume that all correlations between two variables (call them X and Y) mean that X leads to Y. We will use various examples to illustrate possible relationships between variables. The first of these is the causal argument that X leads to Y (Figure 2.1).[8]

But there are many other possibilities. Figure 2.2 shows some possible relationships between variable X and variable Y that are not the simple causal relationship where X → Y. If we assumed X → Y in each of these cases, we could run into a number of analytical problems.

We discuss each of these problems in order.

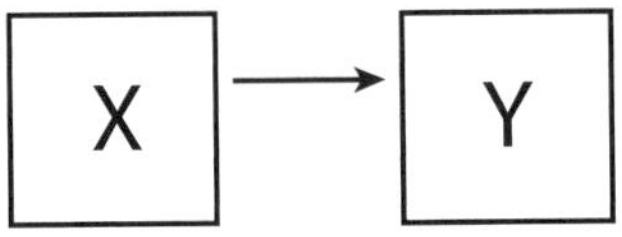

FIGURE 2.1 Causal Relationship between Correlated Variables (X and Y)

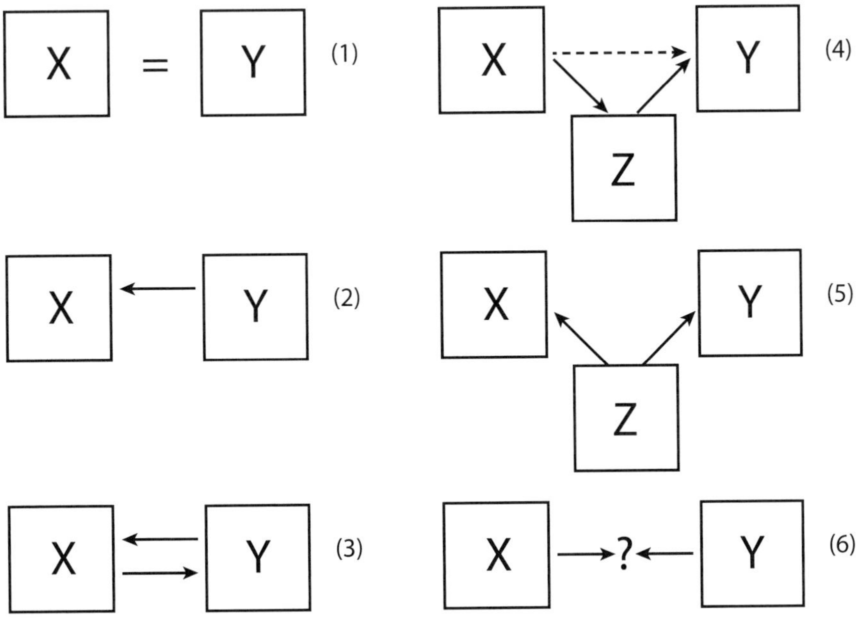

FIGURE 2.2 Possible Problems with Causal Arguments about Correlated Variables (X and Y)

(1) Definitional problems and falsifiability problem

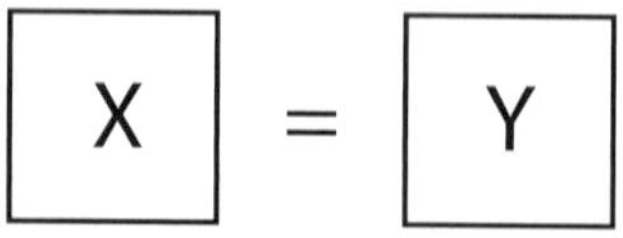

The first problem is one that is rarely noted because it apparently involves arguments that are "too correct." In reality, one common problem is confusing cause-and-effect between two variables with two variables that are the same by definition. If X is measuring the same thing as Y, they will correlate perfectly. But this is not because $X \rightarrow Y$ but rather because $X = Y$.[9] A common problem for comparativists is defining two variables that are so nearly the same that the causal argument is meaningless, or tautological. This definitional problem relates to the problem of **falsifiability**, which is the idea that for an explanation to be meaningful, it must be contestable. To argue that something is true means something only if there is a chance it could at least possibly be incorrect and could be proved wrong. For instance, say we are asked why the Toronto Blue Jays won a game and our "analysis" is that the winning team "just scored more runs" than the losing team, or "just got it done." This argument is correct in the narrow sense that it is not inaccurate, but it is also meaningless, precisely because it can never be otherwise: scoring more runs over the course of a game and winning the game are one and the same, by definition. By contrast, if we say that none of the world's democratic countries will ever again succumb to dictatorship, then that argument is falsifiable because a contrary example is possible (Turkey, for example, under Recep Tayyip Erdoğan seems to be heading down this path).

falsifiability The testability of a theory or hypothesis. A good hypothesis could be logically demonstrated to be false by evidence.

(2) Reverse causality problem

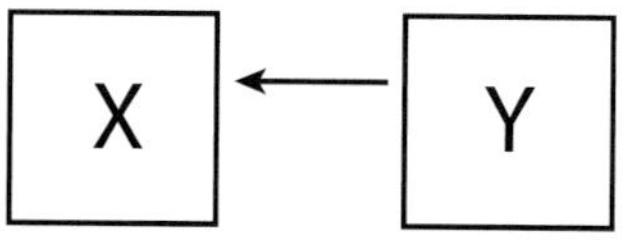

The reverse causality problem is a bit simpler to understand. To take a classic example, Ronald Inglehart outlines how some seven decades ago, electoral districts with high percentages of African Americans in the southern United States tended to elect segregationist representatives. This of course did not mean that African Americans were segregationists; the opposite was true. African Americans were often prevented from registering to vote, while white Southerners tended to vote for the segregationists. After more African Americans began to register, the voting patterns fundamentally changed.[10]

In this case, two variables are correlated, but the causal argument linking the two may be the opposite of what we anticipate. Instead of X leading to Y, perhaps Y leads to X. Getting the "causal arrow" pointed in the right direction is essential, and reversing causality has the potential to lead to disastrous consequences.

(3) Endogeneity problem

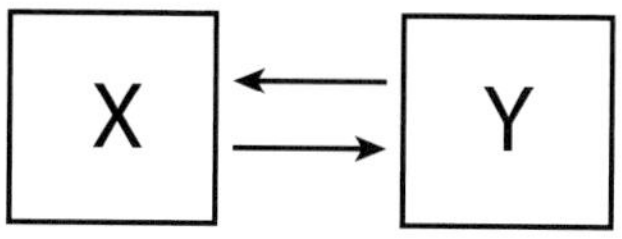

endogeneity The name given to any circumstance in which two variables exhibit mutual or reciprocal effects.

The **endogeneity** problem is about circularity: It happens when two variables exhibit mutual or reciprocal effects. You may know of a simple expression such as "the chicken and the egg" problem, though endogeneity arises any time variables mutually affect one another. If X and Y correlate and seem to go together, we may be left trying to figure out whether X caused Y to happen or Y caused X to happen. Reasonable people may disagree about which direction the causal arrow goes.[11] Endogeneity problems are common in the real world. When we talk of vicious circles (of, say, poverty and dictatorship) or virtuous circles (of, say, economic growth and human development), we are describing a situation in which many important variables are endogenous. Indeed, endogeneity as such is not a problem but a feature of many social and political phenomena. It becomes a problem when we mistakenly claim one variable causes another when the two variables are, in fact, endogenously linked. Even so, social scientists don't want simply to identify multiple variables as endogenous but to understand more precisely the *ways* endogenously linked variables interact over time. One of the leading strategies for resolving this dilemma in qualitative research is closely tracing the historical sequence. When we have good information about when and where things happened, who did them, or how events unfolded, we may be able to determine whether $X \rightarrow Y$ or $Y \rightarrow X$. If we can identify clearly whether the chicken came before the egg (or vice versa), we may be able to address this problem. This is not, however, always possible, as the box on education and health shows.

In addition, there are statistical strategies for dealing with this problem that we cannot explore here, but you could learn about them by taking a more advanced social science methods course.

(4) Intervening variable problem

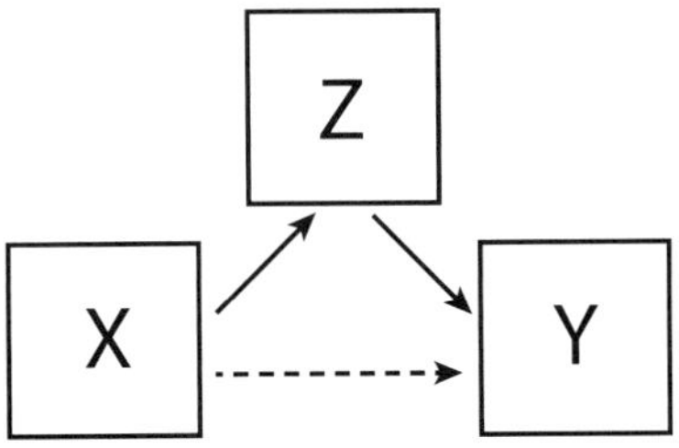

Intervening variables are another potential problem, though they are not always problematic. The situation here is that X leads to Y, but indirectly: The effect of X on Y is mediated through another variable, Z. This is not always a problem. We may make the argument that children from economically disadvantaged families statistically do not do as well in school as children from economically advantaged families. Thus, being poorer may reduce

Endogeneity: Education and Health

Children's health and children's education seem to correlate positively: When one improves, so does the other. So, do improvements in education lead to better health, or do improvements in health lead to better education? Both are plausible. Healthier students will be more likely to have good attendance at school and will be better able to thrive in their work there, making improved health a cause of improved educational outcomes. Conversely, better education may lead to more knowledge about healthy practices, including nutrition and sanitation. So education may make for less frequent visits to the doctor. In this case, the two variables are endogenous.

the chances of a child to achieve high grades in school. Historically, a range of spurious explanations were used to explain this problem—such as children of poorer families were less intelligent, which was not the case.

The potential problem arises when we miss an intervening variable and this leads us to a wrong interpretation. For example, the issue described above may have more to do with poorer children not having breakfast or lunch while at school than having lower levels of intelligence. In other words, there may be an intervening link between nutrition and attention span and the ability to concentrate and work effectively. Aware of this link, in 1992 a group of people in Ontario began the charity "Breakfast for Learning," providing breakfasts to children. They now provide funding across the country, benefitting more than 260,000 children annually.[12] In this case, it's not a lack of intelligence that may be resulting in a lower level of academic success but rather poverty and the lack of good food to enable a child to have enough vitamins, carbohydrates, and other nutrients to focus on their studies.

(5) Omitted variable problem

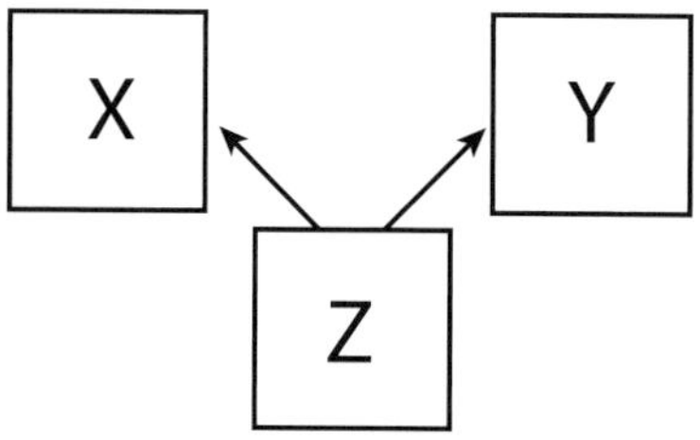

We frequently miss or omit variables that should be in our analysis. We observe an empirical relationship between X and Y and assume this means that one creates the other when in fact both are attributable to a third factor, sometimes also called a confounding or "lurking" variable because though it is there in the background, we might not see it. If X and Y are positively correlated, it may not be that X → Y or Y → X at all. Instead, some factor Z may lead to both X and Y, thus giving rise to the correlation between them. That is, Z → X and Z → Y.

(6) Spurious correlation problem

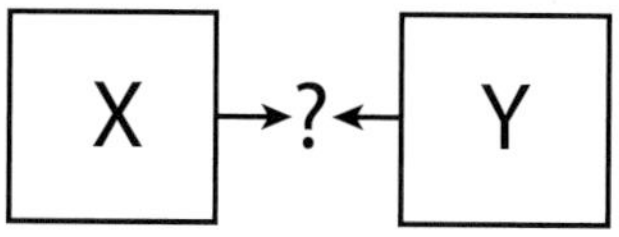

Finally, there are many variables out there, and some are bound to correlate with one another even in the absence of any causal relationship. Many problems that seem to be of this sort will actually be omitted variable problems upon further investigation, but there are examples of correlations where simply no meaningful causal relationship exists. Lucky superstitions are examples where two variables seem to correlate but there is no plausible relationship between them. Perhaps your university's soccer team always seems to win when you put your lucky hat on for the game. This correlation may continue for some time, but there is no reasonable scientific explanation linking your hat-wearing tendencies to victory and no reason to expect that you putting on your hat will lead your team to win the next game. Though the variables "hat-wearing" and "victory" may correlate, there is no causation.

Omitted Variables: Ice Cream Sales and Murders

There is a peculiar correlation between ice cream and murder rates, often cited in methodology textbooks.[13] Let's say a study gives convincing evidence of a positive correlation between increases in ice cream sales and increases in murder rates. What's more, the analyst plausibly claims to have a causal argument. What could such a causal argument be? Does eating ice cream lead people to murder? This is unlikely. Might murdering someone give one a craving for ice cream? Again, this is unlikely. A more plausible answer is a missing variable: the hot temperature outside. This omitted variable affects both ice cream sales and murder rates, both of which increase in the summertime. Failing to account for omitted variables can lead to dangerously flawed causal arguments.

Critiques: Using Theories and Evidence

Evidence can be used to support an argument, but it can also help us to counter an argument, and this too is a meaningful contribution to advancing our understanding and knowledge. It is clear that we often want to use evidence to support our own arguments. Less obviously, however, evidence can be used to enhance a theory or an argument by providing a helpful critique of the conventional wisdom. Accordingly, empirical critiques have a prominent place in comparative politics, as do the theoretical critiques they enable.

Empirical Critiques: Using Deviant Cases

In testing hypotheses, we often hope to find evidence that supports a particular theory. Specifically, we want to find cases that confirm or reaffirm our theory or support our hypothesis. But many interesting advances come from empirical evidence that does not fit a theory well. Deviant cases—those that do not fit a theory or are exceptions or outliers—are very important in advancing social science theory. These cases help us to test out why a theory doesn't work and understand what improvements need to be made to our knowledge. They allow us to make an **empirical** critique of a theory because they do not support it. Much like getting a bad result on a certain test can encourage us to do better where we fell short, so too a deviant case forces us to think about how to improve our arguments.

empirical critique An effort to point to important evidence that does not support a conventional version of any given theory.

Theoretical Critiques: Improving Theories and Hypotheses

Theoretical critiques are new ideas that improve upon the logic or reasoning of existing theories. Theory and empirical evidence constantly interact, and when deviant cases help to provide an empirical critique, they can help us to improve our theories. They often provide the impetus for improvement of the theory. Empirical critiques allow us to advance social science by pointing out anomalies, inconsistencies, and deviations from a theory. Theoretical advances can also come from critiques of the theory itself through re-examinations of the logic, assumptions, or arguments underpinning it. The following box gives an example of how a theoretical critique emerged from empirical evidence that didn't fit a theory.

theoretical critique An effort to show that a given theory has logical limitations.

Empirical Critique: Ghana and Modernization Theory (see Chapter 6)

Ghana is a low-income West African country that defies many Western preconceived assumptions by having a robust democracy. This presents an intriguing challenge to the theory of modernization, which we present further in Chapter 6. Modernization theory, which can tend towards ethnocentrism (and Eurocentrism), holds that democracy can be expected as a consequence of economic development, industrialization, education, and urbanization, all of which contribute to the emergence of a middle class.[14] While Ghana is advancing on some of these criteria, the country clearly is economically poor with a limited industrial base, low levels of education, and only some recent urbanization. Yet it is a rather successful democracy, with free and fair elections and protections for citizens' rights and liberties. Ghana thus becomes a very interesting case to examine, precisely because it facilitates an empirical critique of a prominent theory about democratization.

Of course, theories can also receive theoretical critiques from other scholars who are not looking to refine and better them but rather to offer an entirely different theoretical perspective. This is certainly the case with the dependency theory example, which has been challenged in many ways. For the comparative analyst's purposes, theoretical critiques can be favourable amendments to a theory or they can oppose a theory entirely.

scope conditions The conditions or range of cases for which an argument works.

Critiques help us to craft better arguments and theories. First, they can improve our understanding of **scope conditions**, or the conditions under which an argument works. Identifying and examining cases that do not fit an argument is a good potential avenue for further research. Second, critiques based on empirical evidence can help to improve our concepts and lead to clearer understanding of what exactly we are studying. For instance, the tiny, oil-rich country of Equatorial Guinea has grown rapidly to become one of the wealthiest countries in Africa, but much of its wealth goes just to the dictator's family. Studying this empirical example might give us more insight into what exactly a country's "economic development" means. By identifying weaknesses in arguments and offering alternative explanations, critiques give us better understandings of why things happen.

Theoretical Critique: Dependency Theory in Latin America (see Chapter 5)

From the 1940s to the 1960s, many leading scholars of Latin America argued that the continent suffered from economic dependency relative to the world's industrial powers. This "dependency theory" suggested that poor Latin American countries lost money, resources, and power to the wealthy and powerful countries of the world. The image was of exploitation of the poor countries on the world's periphery by the rich "core" countries. However, some empirical evidence after World War II challenged this theory as countries such as Brazil managed to grow, develop, and industrialize with some success. As a result, dependency theory received a theoretical critique from other scholars, including Peter Evans and Fernando Henrique Cardoso and Enzo Faletto. (Cardoso, incidentally, later became president of Brazil in the 1990s.) This next generation of dependency theorists characterized the relationship between Latin America and the core countries as one of "dependent development" in which the continent could develop and grow but still in a subordinate position that furthered its dependence on capital from the wealthy countries. This theoretical critique came from the recognition that the original dependency theory had a weakness: It could not explain or account for growth or progress in Latin America.

The Challenges of Measurement: Biases, Errors, and Validity

The challenges of garnering and wielding evidence are multifaceted. Beyond determining how to gather evidence and which pieces to use, we must pay attention to measures and **indicators** (elements or features suggesting underlying factors). Without careful and thoughtful measurement, we may accidentally introduce biases and errors into an analysis. **Bias** is a preference for one idea or perspective over another, especially a preference that may result in unbalanced use of evidence or in analytical error.

indicator An element or feature that indicates the presence of an underlying factor.

bias A preference for one idea or perspective over another, especially a preference that may result in unbalanced use of evidence or in analytical error.

Bias aside, it is possible to simply make **measurement errors**, such as by typing the wrong number in a spreadsheet. This kind of error happens more often than you might expect and sometimes in consequential ways. As a well-known example, a spreadsheet data error in work done by Harvard economists Carmen Reinhart and Kenneth Rogoff produced erroneous results in highly influential research about government debt and economic growth (note that this error was discovered by a graduate student).[15]

measurement error Either an episodic error, such as improperly recording data, or a systematic error, meaning that a measurement does not fully reflect what it is designed to measure.

A second measurement problem is **measurement bias**. One example of bias comes from respondents in a survey who are untruthful, whether consciously or subconsciously.[16] Another would be if the questions we ask people are interpreted differently by different groups of respondents. Perhaps the most serious form of bias for beginning researchers is seeking to confirm one's favoured hypothesis. This can include a tendency to believe things are a certain way that we want to see them. Imagine that a right-of-centre student wants to show that countries with free markets have performed better economically than countries that have more active government involvement in the economy. The eager student knows that the United States performed better than the USSR in economic growth rates in the 1980s and uses these cases to "prove" the hypothesis that less government involvement in the economy is better for the economy. Subconsciously, the student may have chosen those cases because they knew what they would find and that it would support their preference. But looking at the same question in other cases (say, Scandinavia or Canada vs African countries) might show very different results. The point is not that the student is wrong, but that the student's preconceptions biased the research. We must ask research questions and test hypotheses fairly by ensuring the answer is not predetermined.

measurement bias A measure is biased if it will not produce comparable results for all observations.

Even when researchers are careful not to bias their measures, we must consider the problem of **measurement validity**—that is, whether a given measure effectively captures or represents what is being researched. Indicators that are valid accurately reflect our concept. Informally, validity means measuring what we claim we are measuring. In some cases, this is straightforward, and our measures may be perfectly valid. To measure the "total number of political parties represented in a legislature," we may simply find a record of every member of the legislature, note which party each member is from, then count the number of distinct parties to which legislators belong. On the other hand, consider the challenge of trying to measure overall health outcomes of a given country. Is life expectancy the right measure for this? Or infant mortality rates (e.g., the percentage of infants who die before the age of two)? Or rates of asthma, malaria, or HIV/AIDS? In truth, each of these is a valid measure of something specific, but none precisely measures "overall health."

measurement validity Whether a given measure effectively captures or represents what we are researching.

Several guidelines can help here. We should strive for valid measurement to the greatest extent possible, but sometimes, when dealing with certain questions and sets of data, we will have to work with imperfect indicators of the concepts that interest us. We should explicitly state our reservations about our measures when we present our work. This allows others to make their own judgments. In addition, we should be mindful of how our measured variables relate to our concepts and questions. In your own research, you should ask yourself the following two questions. First, can this actually be measured? Second, does this measure actually correspond to the concept we are trying to study?

Thinking Comparatively

Qualities of Good Analysis and Argumentation

Comparative politics tests hypotheses and builds theories by using evidence and identifying causal relationships. Careful use of theory and evidence allows a researcher to give a hypothesis a good test. The results of that test and that research will lead to a thesis that can be well substantiated and compelling. Good argumentation will avoid, or at least address, the problems of causal inference and measurement shown in this chapter. We conclude the chapter with some guidance for high-quality analysis in comparative politics.

Step 1: Asking Good Questions: Why?

Good arguments are generally good answers to good questions. Good questions have a number of characteristics, among them the following. First, good questions can be answered with evidence. The question of why human beings form political societies is not a bad question for political philosophers, but it is not an especially good question for comparative politics because it is virtually impossible to answer using empirical evidence. Second, good questions are interesting. Questions can be interesting in several ways. They may produce knowledge that is relevant to making policies and laws, for example. But especially important is that they somehow contribute to existing theories. Related to this, they should provoke curiosity, both from a potential audience and from you, the analyst. Third, good questions can be answered, at least in a preliminary but meaningful fashion, given the time and resources at your disposal. Finally, good questions ask for causal explanations. They do not just ask for descriptive accounts of processes, but they push us to explain why some phenomenon or phenomena has (or have) come to pass.

Step 2: Hypothesis Testing: Generating Good Hypotheses and Testing Them Fairly

The second set of issues for beginning comparative political analysis is formulating an appropriate hypothesis and testing it with as little bias as possible. A hypothesis should be based upon clearly defined variables and concepts. To explain why country X became a democracy, for example, we need a good definition of democracy and how we know country X is a democracy. A good hypothesis will typically be rooted in some existing theory from comparative politics. For example, can modernization theory (see Chapters 5 and 6) offer a hypothesis for why country X democratized? Good hypothesis testing often involves reading theories and arguments about cases other than the one we are interested in. Generating a hypothesis about democratization in country X may require us to read theories and arguments not just about country X itself but also about other countries. Good hypothesis testing does not mean the researcher goes looking to prove her/his own pet argument, picking and choosing evidence to make the point. Once a hypothesis is formulated, it should receive a fair test from the researcher, who can and should use the available evidence to weigh the proposed argument and how well it works or does not.

Step 3: Balancing Argumentation: Evidence, Originality, and Meaningfulness

A final key to good comparative analysis is making meaningful claims and avoiding trivial arguments. If you are developing your own argument, you should offer your own distinct hypothesis and then your own original claim based upon your research. Self-evident and obvious arguments contribute much less to social science than arguments that are memorable. You do not want to replicate, copy, or transcribe others' ideas; you want to generate and defend your own.

Originality matters, but it must be balanced with a respect for existing knowledge. Originality does not mean developing implausible arguments or ignoring previous research. Serious evaluation of existing evidence is as important in formulating one's argument as it is in testing the hypothesis. Good comparative analysis means more argumentation than pure description and more attention to evidence than pure opinion. It is neither an opinion piece nor a book report about a country. It represents a middle ground in which you have an argument in which original claims and interpretations are backed by evidence. Basing your argument on significant reading and research will be the likeliest route to success. There is no substitute for this research work. Indeed, original research is original precisely because it contributes in helpful ways to an existing research tradition.

Normally, you can expect to find that there will frequently be multiple variables that have some impact on a particular outcome. For instance, a country's economic growth may be shown to depend upon the following: geographic location, relationship to the dominant powers in the world economy, policies, leadership, culture, institutions, history of colonialism, chance and luck, and many other variables. It is important, however, to do more than make a "laundry list" and simply say "all of these matter." The challenge is to prioritize the variables that have the most significant and substantive impact on the outcome. In the jargon, we call this being parsimonious, selecting the most important variables and giving them pride of place in the argument.

Doing all of this will enable a researcher to engage with the larger scholarly literature and the central debates in comparative politics. The strongest works of comparative politics—the major books and articles in the field—are the product of years of research work and refined thinking, but the basic process can be emulated by those new to the field. The best student work comes from analyses that draw on diverse sources, including theoretical sources, to weigh the validity of different claims, show competent understanding of relevant literature, build on relevant concepts and theories, and highlight the individual's unique synthesis and contribution. This asks a great deal, and it requires practice, but our guidance boils down to the suggestions in Table 2.1.

Comparative research requires considerable thought and planning, but it is also best learned by doing. This comes from reading in the field to see how scholars analyze politics and by conducting one's own research for papers, presentations, exams, or other outputs. The remainder of the book will help to provide you with this practice. In the next chapters, we turn to the major themes of comparative politics and use them to work on the process of formulating and generating questions, hypotheses, arguments, and theories. We provide some of the requisite knowledge of these topics and examples of quality research, while pushing you to analyze comparative politics on your own.

TABLE 2.1 | Guidelines for Comparative Research

Guideline	Step 1: Ask Good Questions	Step 2: Test Hypotheses	Step 3: Write Your Argument
Do the basics	Ask open-ended *why* questions about cause and effect.	Define concepts and variables clearly.	Read and use the scholarly literature on your topic.
Be original and informed	Ask questions you do not know the answer to before starting your research.	Use theories from scholarly books and articles to help form hypotheses.	Aim for meaningful, original claims, and avoid laundry lists of factors that just "matter."
Consider the evidence	Ask questions for which evidence is available to test a hypothesis.	Be aware of your biases, and work from the evidence, not assumptions.	Use evidence and not opinion to make your claims.

Chapter Summary

Introduction to Theories, Hypotheses, and Evidence

- Social scientists use theories, hypotheses, and evidence to build arguments about how the world operates. Theories are general explanations of how empirical phenomena operate across a range of cases. They are typically backed by some evidence. Hypotheses are potential explanations of cause and effect for specific cases. They are designed to be tested using evidence and are often derived from theories.

Hypothesis Testing

- The central practice in comparative politics is testing hypotheses about causal questions using empirical evidence. This involves measuring variables and seeing how variables correlate across cases.
- Variables that correlate with one another may have a causal relationship, but not necessarily.
- There are several fallacies and logical traps to avoid when making causal arguments about correlated variables, including reverse causation, omitted variables, intervening variables, and spurious correlation.

Critiques: Using Theories and Evidence

- Political science can advance by developing critiques of existing theories and arguments. Critiques can be empirical, based on demonstrating cases that do not fit a theory, or they can be more purely theoretical by using reason and logic to show problems with a theory.

The Challenge of Measurement: Errors, Biases, and Validity

- Measurement is a leading challenge facing comparative political scientists. Comparativists aim to avoid measurement errors and biases and seek to ensure that measures are valid, or measure what they claim to measure.

Thinking Comparatively

- Good practices in comparative politics include asking causal "Why" questions, developing unbiased hypothesis tests, and making arguments that are original yet informed by an understanding of existing theories and findings.

Thinking It Through

1. Considering the examples of problems with causal arguments in Figures 2.1 and 2.2, come up with your own examples of omitted-variable problems in the real world.
2. Considering the theory of modernization, which holds (among other things) that wealth is likely to lead to democracy, what sorts of countries would you seek out if you wanted to test the theory on deviant cases? Think of some examples, or do some preliminary research online that will help you to identify some.
3. What are some examples of measurement problems that you could foresee if you were to conduct a study of how a country's culture affects its wealth?
4. What beliefs do you have about politics that you think are rooted in a theory? For example, do you have beliefs about how politicians tend to behave, the media's role in politics, or the likelihood that student activists can "change the world"? If so, consider what you think the theory is, and contemplate it in light of this chapter. What are the achievements and shortcomings of the theory?
5. Ask yourself what puzzles you about politics or social life in a certain country. Now try to develop a hypothesis for a possible answer that would explain the puzzle. How could you develop a research plan that would allow you to gather evidence and test your hypothesis?

PART II

The State, Development, Democracy, and Authoritarianism

3 The State

In This Chapter

Demonstrators wave Catalonian independence flags in Barcelona, Spain in 2018. (AP Photo/Emilio Morenatti)

In the years following World War II, many observers thought of the western European state system as fairly settled. Here, the idea of modern states first developed, and this idea of what a state should look like was then duly exported to a variety of European colonies around the world, setting a template for what decolonizing peoples would also seek to implement. The consolidation of state power was high, even in cases like Germany and Italy, which unified only in the late 19th century. And despite the 1945 split of Germany into East and West, followed by its reunification in the 1990s, European states on the whole seemed likely to persist into the distant future.

But at least three recent developments have called into question the stability of the western European system of nation-states. The first has been the steady movement over the second half of the 20th century toward European integration, beginning with the European common market and culminating in the creation of the European Union (EU). For some time, many have wondered whether a European "super-state" might form, while after the failed EU constitution and the weakness of some EU economies, others have made arguments against this possibility.[1]

The second development is the presence of secessionist and sub-state nationalist movements in the region, perhaps most notably in Catalonia (an area on the Mediterranean coast of Spain) and Scotland (which is part of the United Kingdom). In the fall of 2014, Scotland held a referendum on becoming independent from the United Kingdom. The referendum failed, but some of its supporters are undaunted, especially after the majority of UK voters in mid-2016 chose to pull the UK out of the European Union. Most Scottish voters rejected Brexit and chose to remain in the EU, so now the Scottish National Party is promising a future referendum on independence. As the largest party in Scotland (third largest in the UK) and the dominant force in the Scottish Parliament, the Scottish National Party may be able to hold another referendum. Brexit will have some economically disastrous consequences for the UK, some of which might be avoided by Scotland if they seek to remain in the EU.

Similarly, many in Catalonia seek to form an independent state in the future. In October 2017, this region of Spain held a referendum on independence that resulted in an overwhelming rate of support, although many residents of the region chose not to vote. The Spanish government condemned the referendum as illegal because it violated Spain's constitution, and many political leaders involved in the referendum were imprisoned. So while a large proportion of Catalan residents may wish to leave Spain, it is unlikely they can ever do so legally. By contrast, the UK is seen as a union of different peoples, and because it was unified by the consent of its constituent people in 1707, it could similarly split apart if its people decide this is what they would like.

The third factor affecting the stability of the nation-states system in western Europe is globalization. Key manufacturing and other industries in Europe are being subjected to increasing international competition, and some classes of jobs are becoming more precarious, while the welfare state in many European countries has begun to contract. Similarly, civil instability in the Middle East, in particular Libya and Syria, has led to large influxes of refugees into Europe. This has led to questions in many European countries about how many newcomers these countries can financially afford to host. It has also led to questions of religious and cultural identity, sometimes resulting in the rise of xenophobic political parties seeking a more exclusive form of national identity. The former image of Europe as a wealthy, tolerant, multicultural, and multinational zone of prosperity and progress is now being thrown into question as right-wing, anti-immigrant parties rise to the fore in many countries.

For comparativists, it is impossible to understand modern politics without understanding the state. States are the location of authoritarian or democratic governments, and states exhibit the institutional features such as executives and legislatures that we discuss later in this book. States are what ethnic, political, business, and other groups aim to influence and control and that social movements and revolutions seek to transform. States are also the collection of institutions that have colonized Indigenous peoples and either inhibit or help to enable Indigenous forms of self-determination on their traditional lands. States are key factors in economic development, and they shape the experiences of citizens, residents, and still other individuals. Finally, states are the central characters in the story of international politics: Even in this rapidly globalizing world in which nonstate and transnational actors are increasingly important, the state remains the most important and powerful force.

But what *is* the state? Where do states come from, and what does this tell us about their character and likely future? What do states do? How do they differ from one another, and why are some strong and others weak or even failed states? These are the questions we begin to answer in this chapter.

• • •

Concepts

Analysts of comparative politics do not always agree completely on the definitions of words such as *state* or *development* or *democracy*. Often, though, there is a sort of lowest common denominator, an agreed-on general idea about what a concept covers. With respect to the state—and here we focus on the modern state that evolved over the past several centuries[2]—this lowest common denominator is the classic definition posited almost a century ago by the German social theorist Max Weber: The state is the central political institution that exerts a "monopoly on the legitimate use of physical force within a given territory."[3]

What does Weber's definition mean? Definitions work, in part, by telling us what something is *not*. What is a state not? Well, it is clear from this definition that a political arena with many distinct actors using legitimate force would not be a **state**. If a society has no central authority that can use force, then perhaps anyone can. In such a society (sometimes called a failed state), individuals need to either acquire the ability to use force themselves or make an arrangement with someone who can. If they do not, they remain vulnerable to the threat that someone else could harm them, and without some higher authority, they have no one to turn to. Yet the diversity of political societies is not limited to the extremes of failed states and modern states. Indeed, there are many intermediary types.

state The most important form of political organization in modern politics, which, in its ideal form, is characterized by centralized control of the use of force, bureaucratic organization, and the provision of a number of public goods.

The Modern State

We begin by comparing the modern state to *another* sort of political society that was not anarchic but in which a nonstate order was present: European feudalism in the medieval era.[4] In the feudal political order, hierarchical ties linked peasants at the bottom to kings, who at least nominally sat at the top (in a tenuous balance with the church), with a nobility mediating between them. In the feudal order, however, kings or queens were understood to be the greatest among nobles, and their rule over the population of their kingdoms was mostly indirect. There was little standardized taxation, there were few standing armies, and the monarch's administration did not provide meaningful public services. Peasants in such a system were unlikely to find recourse against local nobles by petitioning the monarch.[5] Achieving such recourse was not impossible in principle, but the organizational capacity of the system typically made it unfeasible. Most people travelled very little, and the authority to which they were subjected was local and often arbitrary. Law was present, but **rule of law**,

rule of law A system that imposes regularized rules in a polity, with key criteria including equal rights, the regular enforcement of laws, and the relative independence of the judiciary.

referring to a political system in which the law is consistently applied equally to all, was not. No single, centralized authority could claim to control the legitimate use of force.[6] Indeed, it was considered legitimate for a variety of actors to exert force and not just because such authority had been delegated to them.[7] The king's authority was rivalled by both the authority of the church and the nobility.

Now think about where you live in Canada. Imagine a violent incident taking place. Is that violence considered legitimate or illegitimate? This will depend on who is doing it and why. If it is your neighbour and he or she holds no official position, chances are the violence is illegitimate and would be considered some form of assault. What about a police officer subduing what seems to be a violent suspect? What is critical here is that all of the use of force considered legitimate in a society ultimately traces its legitimacy back to the state. In other words, in a society with a state, violence is tremendously concentrated in the military and law enforcement agencies.[8] This means that in well-functioning states, interpersonal violence is likely lower than in other systems.

States with high capacity can limit and control interpersonal violence to the extent that citizens of well-functioning states are often able to ignore what little interpersonal violence is present. This does not mean, though, that states with high levels of capacity are nonviolent. Rather, they represent the greatest concentration of the capacity to exert force that the world has ever known.[9] A state's legitimate use of violence is also based on whether it uses violence arbitrarily and whether there are forms of racial or other bias in how the police and military carry out their work. Those who are not singled out in biased policing (those who are not subject to profiling) may feel the system is fair and legitimate. Those who are frequent targets of the police (often racialized and Indigenous peoples) may feel the opposite. This is especially true if the police engage in carding and profiling, practices that assume that some people are potentially violating the law based on their skin colour, their clothing, or other indicia that they belong to a marginalized group. In late 2018, the Ontario Human Rights Commission reported that Toronto police officers were far more likely to target black people than white people and that black people were consequently more likely to be injured or killed by the police.[10]

Beyond this fairly minimal definition of the state, it is worth noting that there are other important features of **modern states**, which we discuss further later in the chapter. This includes their bureaucratic type of organization, their impersonality, and above all the fact that they claim sovereignty. Moreover, states aim to *do* many things, and as time passes these actions of the state get incorporated into our idea of what a state is.

modern state A concept used to distinguish states in the modern world from earlier forms of political centralization; it includes features such as extensive bureaucracy, centralization of violence, and impersonality.

Post-colonial States and Settler States

The institutional structures and borders of many modern states have been based on former European colonies. Some states were formed after peoples struggled to gain their independence from European colonizers. Sometimes the transitions were peaceful, but they were often the product of organized resistance and mobilization, which sometimes involved violence. Many colonial powers, fearing a loss of power and prestige as well as cheap labour and resources, violently suppressed popular aspirations for independence.

From the 1960s onward, many former colonies gained their independence during decolonization struggles. Today, a large proportion of the world's countries are formed from former colonies, especially in Africa, Asia, the Caribbean, and the Pacific. We might call these post-colonial states, and in these cases, the local pre-colonial populations outnumbered the colonizers, making independence seem attractive for anyone believing in democracy. After all, why should not the majority of the population decide on their system of government and type of state they should have? There were some holdovers from the colonial period, namely South Africa and Rhodesia, where the white minority used violence and its structural power to keep control for many decades.

In another group of countries, known as settler states, Indigenous lands and peoples were colonized by Europeans, who came to live, work, and establish institutions in many parts of the world. During the waves of decolonization in the 20th century, these former colonies did not decolonize, and Indigenous peoples did not gain their independence. Why not? In most cases this had to do with the relative size of the Indigenous populations. In settler colonial states like Canada, Australia, New Zealand, and the United States (sometimes abbreviated as CANZUS) settlers outnumbered Indigenous peoples, and so settler institutions, laws, cultures, and languages have become dominant, while Indigenous peoples and their interests have been marginalized. Their traditional lands were also taken away such that the vast majority of former Indigenous land is now held by the state or in private hands by settlers. Decolonizing movements of the 1960s, such as "Red Power" in the US and Canada and "Brown Power" in NZ, sought to promote Indigenous self-determination. These movements operated alongside civil rights and decolonization movements in other contexts. There was a global nature to these struggles as many Indigenous activists made connections and trained with decolonizing movements in other parts of the world.

When we look at issues of state capacity and failed states (discussed below), a history of past or ongoing colonization is important to take into consideration. This is because many of the hierarchical relationships and networks established during colonial times continue to influence the way some states conduct both domestic and international affairs.

State Capacity

state capacity The ability of the state to achieve its objectives, especially the abilities to control violence, effectively tax the population, and maintain well-functioning institutions and the rule of law.

State capacity is the measurement of a state's ability to accomplish its goals.[11] In general, today we would say that a state has high capacity when (1) it has established a monopoly on the use of force; (2) it has a smoothly functioning bureaucracy with relatively low levels of corruption and irregularity, accomplishing tasks such as coordinating defence, maintaining infrastructure, and managing projects in education and public health; and (3) rule of law is maintained, producing a predictable and manageable environment for citizens as they go about their business. To do this it must successfully generate revenue, usually by taxing its population, a task that can be challenging.[12]

As we will see later, state goals have increased over time as its capabilities have commensurately increased.[13] Because the list of states' necessary activities is a moving target, so too is the definition of "state capacity." A state that would have been considered to have high capacity in the late 17th century, such as the English or French state of that time, would today be considered weak or low-capacity. For example, 17th-century France—unquestionably a strong state with high capacity in its own time—did not provide (or aim to provide) public education, but today this is considered a key function of states. A state that fails at doing so is now considered to have lower capacity than a state that succeeds.

Another way to think about this would be to see states as moving along a continuum of stateness.[14] In other words, rather than thinking of state or nonstate as a dichotomous ("yes" or "no") variable, we could think of stateness as a quality of a given political order: State capacity, from this point of view, is the degree to which a political order has achieved stateness. For political theorist Francis Fukuyama, a successful modern state is based on three key pillars of political order: a modern bureaucratic system capable of collective taxes and administering for the needs of the state; the rule of law; and an accountable government that is responsive to the needs of the people. If these pillars are in balance, a state can ensure stability and even prosperity.[15]

Failed States

As with many other concepts, scholars do not always agree about how to precisely define and measure **failed states**, but, put simply, states fail when their capacity declines below a certain point. A failed state is one that cannot or does not do what states are conventionally supposed to do. Perhaps the clearest example in recent years has been Somalia, where the state as such is just one actor among many. Rival groups, essentially large gangs, control their own territory and battle over it at the margins. Public service provision is minimal, where it exists at all.

failed state A state that cannot or does not perform its expected functions.

The State–Society Relationship

The state is fundamental to understanding modern politics, but it does not exist alone. The state is very much a part of the society in which it is embedded. By "society" we mean the set of webs of ties that connect people to each other. In other words, it can be thought of as a space created by lots of different overlapping social networks—webs of friendships, professional linkages, voluntary groups and religious organizations, media ties, and many other structured systems of relationships. In these patterns of overlapping networks, power is distributed. In modern societies, formally organized power is, as we have seen, concentrated in the state. But in most modern societies, despite the state's concentration of *formal* power, there is a great deal of political activity that is not controlled by state actors. We need to be able to take this activity into account because these other actors are the ones who often bring about changes to the nature of the status quo, such as New Zealand adopting nuclear-free policies during the 1980s because of the work of the Campaign for Nuclear Disarmament or the weakness of gun laws in the United States as the result of the influence of the National Rifle Association and other lobby groups. The New Zealand movement was also influenced by anti-nuclear organizations in Australia, the Pacific, Europe, and North America. Few movements for change happen only domestically.

When political scientists speak of state–society relationships, they imply that the modern state is partially autonomous and is situated in relationships with other actors and that these relationships are important to study. Why is this? Sets of relationships with other actors affect the state's goals and constrain its policy options and, thus, its actions. These relationships also have implications for those other actors and especially for participants in "civil society," which we discuss further later in the chapter.

Many scholars think that countries have different degrees and types of civil society with different organizations, networks of social actors, media, and customs and habits of organizing, talking, and meeting. Scholars do not all agree about how precisely to define civil society, but most use this term to mean something like a space that is relatively autonomous from state coercion within which people can deliberate and strategize about matters that have political implications. Organizationally, civil society can be thought of as housed in labour unions, in social clubs and other voluntary groups, in churches, mosques, and synagogues, and in many other such sites. In settler states, there are often Indigenous governments with their own institutions, cultures, and ways of conducting their own affairs. Some of them are represented by local Indigenous governments, such as the Six Nations of the Grand River (to name just one in Ontario) and nationally through organizations such as the Assembly of First Nations in Canada or the Iwi Chairs Forum in New Zealand.

Globalization is changing the focus and scope of these movements, increasing the scope for people and movements in other countries to influence change. Forms of virtual civil society are growing through social media like Facebook and Twitter. The Indigenous-led

Christopher Katsarov/THE CANADIAN PRESS

PHOTO 3.2 Assembly of First Nations Chief Perry Bellegarde participating in discussions regarding the renegotiation of the North American Free Trade Agreement in September 2017. Chief Bellegarde sought to have an Indigenous chapter added to this trade agreement in order to recognize and protect Indigenous inherent and treaty rights. In the end, the chapter was not added, but Justin Trudeau claimed that "its ideals were 'woven throughout' the fabric of the final deal" (https://www.cbc.ca/news/indigenous/usmca-trade-deal-indigenous-rights-1.4846073).

movement Idle No More (INM) relied heavily on social media to build up civil society networks. INM was formed in 2012 to protect lands and waters from further resource exploitation by federal and provincial governments and corporations. In particular, the movement was formed to protest federal government legislation by the Harper administration, which removed federal protection from many bodies of water and waterways. INM made widespread use of Facebook and Twitter to organize demonstrations across the country. Their Facebook page had more than 63,000 photos and likes within two months of its formation at the end of November 2012. On one well-known day of protest, 10 December 2012, there were more than 11,000 tweets in support.[16] Globally, they also connected to similar movements in other countries, and Indigenous peoples as far away as New Zealand and Indonesia staged their own demonstrations in support.

Overall, we can say that civil society depends on the possibility of many people being able to know and communicate with each other without those exchanges being predominantly coordinated (or limited) by state actors.

These civil society organizations and networks allow groups of citizens to analyze politics and make claims on the state.[17] Tied to civil society are racial and ethnic groups, which may create their own organizations and political parties. Ethnically based political parties are found in many countries, such as Trinidad and Tobago and New Zealand. However, they are not found in many other countries, such as the United States and Mexico. (See "Case in Context: Why Aren't There Major Ethnic Parties in Mexico?")

CASE IN CONTEXT

441

Why Aren't There Major Ethnic Parties in Mexico?

Mexico, like many countries, has had a long history of ethnic discrimination. As in the United States, we might expect to find a history of political parties forming there on the basis of ethnic cleavages. Yet again, as in the United States, we find little such history. This outcome, however, seems likely to be due to a different set of conditions, thus facilitating an interesting comparison.

For more on ethnic cleavages and political parties in Mexico, see the case study in Part VI, p. 441. As you read it, keep in mind the following questions:

1. Why might one expect to find ethnic parties in Mexico?
2. What major features of Mexican political development might help us to account for their absence?
3. How does this interesting case compare with the cases of the United States and India (discussed later)?

According to many scholars, strong civil society accompanies strong states with well-institutionalized democracies, but it is more problematic for authoritarian states, which will often seek to co-opt or even eliminate citizen activities of this sort.[18] An authoritarian state's position is strengthened to the extent that potential rivals do not have the organizational capacity to challenge it. For this reason, many political scientists believe that proponents of democratization would do well to invest in civil society: for example, by subsidizing a diverse array of organizations or by trying to help lay the infrastructure for dense and transitive networks to form.

In general, we could say that strong, democratic states tend to be relatively autonomous from civil society but nevertheless responsive to citizens. Paradoxically, many of the strongest states might be those that are self-limiting in a lot of key ways. Weak states are often simultaneously less autonomous and less responsive to the broader citizenry. Weak states do not necessarily refrain from intervening in the economy and society: rather, they tend to intervene often but irregularly and unpredictably. And strong states sometimes help societies to solve problems of collective action, providing "public goods" that would be impossible for individuals in large-scale societies to produce on their own.[19] Nonetheless, a debate continues about whether having a "strong society" that is influential and wields political power correlates with a "strong state" or a "weak state."[20]

Types

As noted earlier, states have many other characteristics besides exerting a monopoly on the legitimate use of force. In the discussion that follows, we focus first on several key characteristics of states and next on state functions.

Characteristics of Modern States

States are defined in part by characteristics such as a bureaucratic mode of organization, impersonality, and the claim of sovereignty. Here we discuss each of these in turn.

Bureaucracy

Canada, like most other developed countries, has a wide range of different bureaucracies, as do provinces, territories, cities, and municipalities. Organizations are bureaucratic when they have a rational, universally applicable system, administered on the basis of rules and by office-holders.[21] Bureaucracies are, in their ideal form, impersonal and transparent. In other words, in a well-functioning bureaucracy, those rules are available for all to see. Think about the ministry of transportation or the equivalent in your province or territory. You would hope that getting your driver's licence was not dependent on, for example, who you are related to, the whims of your examiner, or the paying of a bribe. Instead, there is a clearly stipulated set of rules governing who can and who cannot receive licences and also governing who can and who cannot make judgments about who has satisfied the appropriate conditions.

When we say that bureaucracies are efficient, we mean that they are the most efficient way to *organize collective action in pursuit of common projects*. Think of the military as an example. Wars are not conducted on the basis of the whims of individual troops but rather through their bureaucratically organized action. A well-functioning bureaucracy is like a system of levers linking a leader or group at the top of an organizational hierarchy to a large number of individual actors lower down (see Figure 3.1). Bureaucracies turn the people who hold offices into *instruments* for the realization of goals set higher up in the organization. If this mode of organizing collective action still seems inefficient to you, imagine administering a welfare program or a health care system or waging a war through non-bureaucratic channels.

Modern states are much more bureaucratic than other, older political organizations. This feature of modern states—combined with their unprecedented abilities to extract resources (in the form of taxes) from the populations subject to their control—helps to explain their efficacy and power. Note that states with less functional bureaucracies necessarily have far lower state capacity.

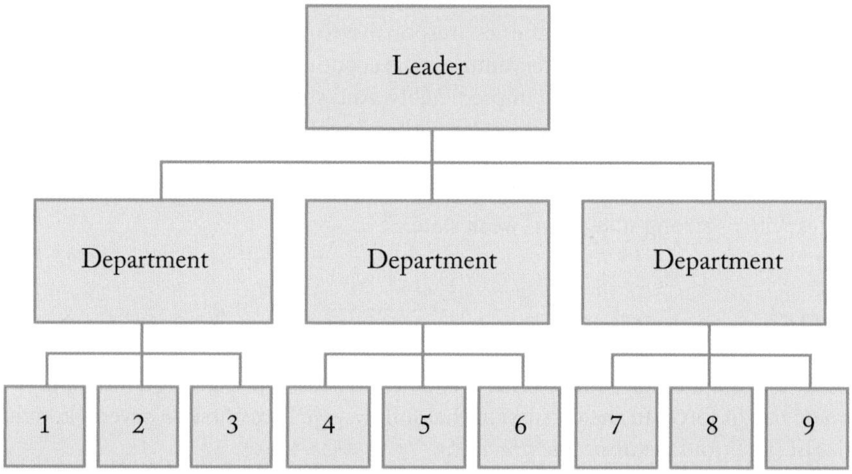

FIGURE 3.1 This is a simplified model of how a bureaucratic structure can achieve the coordination of complex tasks carried out by individual office-holders. Imagine that this organization's mission requires the coordinated performance of nine complex tasks. How difficult might it be to accomplish these tasks in the absence of bureaucratic organization?

Impersonality

Modern states are also more **impersonal** than many other political organizations.[22] This feature is related to their bureaucratic character but not reducible to it. When we say that they are impersonal, we mean that they are not closely identified with the personality of an individual.

impersonality A quality attributed by some scholars to modern states, which are presumed to be less likely to be identified with the personalities of their leaders.

You might find this a bit confusing. Don't we pay a lot of attention to our presidents and prime ministers? Doesn't it make a difference if Justin Trudeau is in power and not Stephen Harper? Or Donald Trump and not Barack Obama? And haven't there been some societies with modern states in which cults of personality centre on individual dictators, such as Kim Jong-un of North Korea? Indeed, all of these points are true, and the impersonal character of the modern state is a matter of degree. Think of the difference, though, between the type of legitimacy accorded a president of the United States and that accorded a king in a pre-modern kingdom. Imagine what would happen if President Trump were to declare that the Constitution is just a manifestation of his will or that the country is his personal possession. President Trump is constrained by the US Constitution, by Congress, by the Supreme Court, and by operating only one branch of government within a federal system that also has important powers delegated to states.

This same impersonality is extended to the treatment of the general population. The ideal-typical modern state treats members of the population as **citizens**, meaning that it regards them as essentially equal in terms of their political role and rights. Modern states tend to offer fewer special privileges to individuals based on *who they are*. Of course, there are still dominant elites in every modern state, and the mere fact that these states formally treat citizens impersonally does not eradicate preference or discrimination. Indeed, an illusion of impartiality may mask serious problems of institutionalized sexism, structural racism, and other problems. A goal of the "Black Lives Matter" movement is to show publicly that in US and Canadian society, black lives matter for less and are less respected than the lives of white people. The focus is on clearly identifying the ways in which racism is manifest in society and in exploring ways to stop that racism and its negative effects on black people.

citizenship A form of relationship between the state and individuals subject to its control in which citizens have certain basic rights and are in some way represented in the state.

Sovereignty

The third key dimension of modern states is **sovereignty**, a concept with several overlapping meanings. The two most important, though, are (1) sovereignty as the control over some territory and (2) sovereignty as the *source* of legitimate authority.[23] Of course, these two meanings are related, and they derive partly from the basic feature of the state—that it exerts a monopoly on the use of force. Further, sovereignty can be seen in the external recognition of sovereignty provided by other states and international organizations. When a state declares its independence, one of the first things it will do is seek recognition from larger states and then ultimately from the United Nations. This is what Slovenia and Croatia both did in 1991 when they declared their independence from Yugoslavia. Both countries canvassed a range of states to recognize their borders and sovereignty. Ukraine, also newly independent, was the first country to recognize these two newly sovereign states, followed by other European countries that helped both Slovenia and Croatia to lobby for UN recognition.

sovereignty The key way the authority of the modern state is conceptualized: states are understood to be the ultimate authority within their specifically demarcated territories.

As states developed, the relationship between political organizations and territory changed in important ways. Before modern statehood, boundaries tended to be permeable. For example, the Pyrenees Mountains (which separate France and Spain) were once a kind of informal division, a shared space across which people easily moved back and forth, blurring the differences between subjects of the French and Spanish kings. After the rise of modern states, however, the frontier was redefined as a formal boundary, and the population became fixed as citizens of either France or Spain.[24]

Historically, within the British imperial system, dominions like Canada were not considered independent states. As historian Duncan Bell puts it: "All those born in territories ruled over by the monarch were classified as 'British subjects,'" although there were clear divisions between "'civilised' and 'uncivilised' populations" based on race.[25] In his overview of Canadian history, Douglas Belshaw puts it that for Canada's founders like John A. Macdonald, the core of Canadian identity was "British subjecthood." He observes that in 1867, "being part of the biggest imperial chain on the planet was something to boast about."[26] Canada went through a process of gaining more and more independence, through the 1931 Statute of Westminster and later, in 1982, by the patriation of its own Constitution. Canada remains part of the Commonwealth, and we share our head of state, Queen Elizabeth II, with the United Kingdom and many other former dominions and colonies. However, Canada, like the other settler states, has permanent, internationally recognized borders and institutions.

Today, the boundaries between state territories are generally better delineated. Related to this territorial distinction is the notion that the state holds ultimate authority within its territorial zone. States are sovereign not only because they can exercise force but because they can act in other ways as well. They can tax, organize the citizenry, and produce a variety of public services. Territoriality is a key principle in doing so, and territorial disputes have been quite common in the history of the state system. Sometimes such disputes are settled by violence and other times by diplomacy. As we mentioned earlier, international recognition is typically a key feature of sovereignty. That is, it is difficult for a state to maintain claims about its sovereignty over a given territory if other states do not recognize its

Jason Lee/Pool Photo via AP

PHOTO 3.3 Chinese foreign minister Wang Yi (centre) and representatives of the United Nations Security Council pose in the Great Hall of the People in Beijing before a meeting in November 2018.

sovereignty. Take Taiwan, for example, which is still claimed by the People's Republic of China as part of its territory. Because of China's seat on the UN Security Council and its growing economic and military power, Taiwan is not recognized as a UN member state and is not officially recognized as a sovereign state by most countries. Many countries like Canada and the US informally recognize that there are "two Chinas" and toe a very careful diplomatic line.

As we have said, states have a tendency to acquire more roles and functions over time, and so it is ultimately impossible to construct an exhaustive list of the state's activities. But in the contemporary world, we can observe a number of particularly important ones, several of which we discuss next.

Traditional Functions of States

States provide defence against external threats, police internal threats, tax their citizens, and document and sort populations, in addition to managing the economy. (We discuss additional key functions of modern states in the domain of political economy in the next chapter.)

Defence

A first key function of states is the coordination of military action, ostensibly, at least, to protect the citizenry from potential foreign threats, although domestic threats like terrorism are equally important. As we shall see later, this feature of states, like taxation, was a key component in their emergence. Moreover, it is one of the most visible tasks of states. Modern states tend to have highly organized, bureaucratized, permanent military organizations. How the military is positioned within the state varies. In some instances, military officials are key players in state decision-making. In others, civilian control is well institutionalized.[27] This is often very important because if civilian control is not well institutionalized, one often sees a higher incidence of coups d'état. The political instability generated by such events can have important short- and long-term effects. Even in societies with relatively well-established civilian control of the army, however, the military remains a potentially important actor. The United States is a good example in that some of President Trump's key advisors are former generals. So too were those of former President Obama.

Policing

States do not just establish and maintain militaries for use in conducting foreign policy. They also establish organizations to police their societies internally. States that do this effectively have well-institutionalized rule of law and transparent judicial procedures.[28] Again, this characteristic of states is related to the core aspect of their definition discussed previously: Policing is one of the key mechanisms through which the monopoly on force is maintained. Sometimes this role is shared with the military. More generally, the organizational and administrative arrangement of policing varies a lot, and how these functions are organized has much to do with how a country's specific political institutions are structured, as we discuss in later chapters.

States also create and maintain systems of punishment linked to the police and judicial systems. Some states continue to use physically violent forms of punishment, such as the death penalty. States typically use incarceration as a key strategy, though they vary quite considerably in the frequency and extent of imprisonment. The United States, for example, incarcerates an astonishingly high percentage of its population, a very large number of them African Americans.[29] And while Canada, Australia, and New Zealand imprison far lower percentages of their citizens, these countries disproportionally imprison Indigenous peoples. States also vary considerably in the quality of their prison systems. Some scholars have emphasized the centrality of systems of policing and incarceration in creating the modern state.[30]

Taxation

To perform the basic functions just discussed (defence and policing) among other responsibilities, states need money. Taxation is thus among the key roles of states. The state's very existence is dependent on taxation, and strong states tend to be those that tax their citizenry successfully and efficiently.[31]

Although funding their own activities is crucial for states, efficient taxation serves other purposes as well. States with high levels of capacity often encourage citizens to feel that they are contributors to the state's collective projects via paying taxes.

The processes through which the earliest modern states established systems of effective taxation were arduous and often violent. A number of early social and political revolutions were, at least in part, responses to centralizing states' efforts to extract more resources.[32] Today, many societies in the developing world continue to experience taxation difficulties, and the situation is often a catch-22: Weak states have trouble taxing their citizenry, but they cannot become stronger until they do. These problems are sometimes exacerbated in developing states that are rich in natural resources. In such instances, leaders may avoid the political conflicts involved in trying to increase taxes because they can instead rely on revenues from exports of those resources. This situation, sometimes called the "resource curse," is seldom good for the long-term development of state *or* society.[33]

Order, Administration, and "Legibility"

Modern states also carry out some less obvious ordering practices. Given the challenges of administering complex societies, most states gather considerable information about their territory and about their population. Both state and private actors invest heavily in maps and in the demarcation of different types of territory. For example, public lands might be administered by the state, private lands regulated, and other forms of land ownership (e.g., communal land ownership in a number of historical and contemporary cases) transformed into one or the other. The use of private property is often subjected to considerable regulation. Sales and purchases of lands, houses, and businesses are tracked, and zoning laws proscribe certain uses of each.

States also go to great expense to learn about their populations. Public services are often contingent on government registration, and states often try to bestow services on some and withhold them from others (this includes access not just to the state's resources but, in the case of migrant populations, to its territory). In the process, various statuses (e.g., citizen, legal resident, migrant, and so forth) are bestowed on different individuals. Population surveys and censuses enumerate residents, document their characteristics, and sometimes even catalogue their beliefs and values. James Scott has referred to this as the process through which states render their populations "legible," by which they mean knowable and, as such, amenable to centralized administration.[34] Some scholars emphasize that these efforts to render populations "legible" sometimes lead to the creation and perpetuation of social and political categories, for better and worse.[35] On the one hand, being able to categorize and know about the populace may make it possible to deliver needed public services more efficiently. On the other hand, the process of viewing society through certain categories (which Scott called "seeing like a state") can lead to states micro-managing society in ways that are intrusive and counterproductive. This can also lead to citizens being subject to unnecessary forms of surveillance and control, a problem that was exacerbated in many countries following the 9/11 terrorist attacks in 2001.

Causes and Effects: Why Did States Emerge and Expand?

In this section, we consider a core explanatory question about the rise of the modern state: Why did states emerge in the first place and become the dominant form of political organization around the world? In other words, why do we live in a world dominated by states? In 1500, there were few strong states and none that had the capabilities of contemporary states. Today, all large-scale societies *try* to have states and therefore at least nominally do. This is perhaps the most important change in modern global politics and is in need of causal explanation.

Several major theories of the modern state concentrate on trying to explain the rise of states as such, while others seek to explain the rise of the **state system** and its global diffusion from early modern Europe to the rest of the world. We begin with the first set of theories, which includes political/conflict theories, economic theories, and cultural theories of the state.

state system The condition that many of the most important actors in international relations are states, which can be understood as systemically linked to one another.

Political/Conflict Theories

Political or conflict theories argue that the state's rise was a consequence of conflict. One set of such explanations, rooted in classical political theory, tries to explain the state as essentially a compromise between warring factions.[36] These theories tend to be abstract, and they may be influenced by their close linkage to political theories that aim to *justify* the state. Some scholars see the state as having developed as a sort of predatory institution through which stronger actors asserted their dominance and extracted resources from others.[37] Some, in turn, focus on predation as a case of state failure: In these cases, what we need to explain in the rise of strong states is how predation is minimized or restrained.[38]

The authors of some of these theories of the state have tried to trace the actual historical development of the state as an organization. A much-cited version of this theory is the "**bellicist theory** of the state," which holds that states are created by war.[39] The core idea is that for states to rise, they have to figure out how to do three things. First, political administration had to be at least partly centralized. In the first states that emerged in Europe, feudalism (a very decentralized form of rule) had to be dismantled. Second, extraction of revenues from the underlying population had to be dramatically enhanced. Administering a modern state costs lots of money, and until the state gets good at taxing its citizenry, it cannot do very much. Third, the state had to develop the ability to mobilize the population in collective endeavours such as infrastructure projects and defence.

bellicist theory Theory associated with scholars such as Charles Tilly who argue that interstate wars were decisive in the creation of the modern state.

According to proponents of the bellicist theory, warfare is particularly useful for all three tasks, particularly once innovations in military technology changed conflict so as to make large armies necessary.[40] If frequent foreign warfare takes place, states need to increase their revenue generation and to mobilize important elements of their populations in order to win. The threat posed by total warfare also presumably helps to convince otherwise unwilling individuals to make these sorts of sacrifices. In the process, such warfare undermines the power of nonstate actors like a military nobility. In medieval Europe, where knights were the main combatants, the upper nobility's control of related resources ensured them great power. But military innovations like advanced archery and gunpowder "democratized" warfare in a certain sense, also rendering it far more costly, requiring large-scale collective efforts and revenue extraction.[41]

Photo by Imagno/Getty Images

PHOTO 3.4 *The Arrival of Napoleon Bonaparte at Schloss Schönbrunn*, engraved by Aubertin, ca. 1820. According to conflict theories of the state, under certain conditions war-making can help states grow stronger. It encourages the state's ability to extract revenue, its ability to mobilize the population, and its capacity to exert the Weberian monopoly on legitimate force.

Essentially, the bellicist theory argues that warfare forges strong states. One of the virtues of the theory is that it seems able to account for the particular historical trajectory of Europe. For many scholars, the fact that strong states developed first in Europe is a mystery, precisely because of the relative backwardness of Europe in preceding centuries when you compare it to great civilizations like China, India, or the Islamic, African, and Meso-American worlds.[42] Indeed, these other civilizations had developed complex, bureaucratic, imperial structures that in many respects looked like modern states. But according to the bellicist theory, the very dominance of these organizations helps to explain why strong modern states did not first develop in Asia or the Middle East: These large empires did not face frequent interstate "total wars" against their rivals, though they did face plenty of conflicts. Europe's backwardness—the fact that it was internally divided with small, petty kingdoms endlessly fighting each other—meant that for several centuries European states were constantly at war. As a result, the states that survived were the ones that developed into powerful war-fighting machines, and their rulers effectively established the ability to tax and mobilize the population, marginalizing their rivals in the process. Some proponents of this theory have used it to try to explain relatively weak state structures elsewhere. For example, one has argued that the allegedly weak states of Latin America may be due to the fact that Latin American states almost never fight foreign wars.[43] The theory has also been used to try to explain Africa's relatively weak states.[44]

Bellicist theory also helps to explain the formation of many settler states. While treaties and trade agreements were often used to colonize what were once Indigenous lands, wars over land were also deployed to expand and consolidate settler colonies. We can see this clearly in the United States where military expansion in the 18th and 19th centuries through a series of infamously named "Indian Wars", which were instigated against the Indigenous peoples and not by them, greatly increased the size of the country. Settler governments in Canada, Australia, and New Zealand also deployed military force against Indigenous peoples to expand and consolidate their control over lands and resources.

INSIGHTS Coercion, Capital, and European States
by Charles Tilly

Tilly is the most famous exemplar of the bellicist theory of the state, as epitomized by his phrase from an earlier book: "War made the state and the state made war."[45] He explains why modern states replaced previous structures as well as why the form of this change differed across cases. Tilly argues that warfare is the critical driver of state-building because war demands extraction of resources from the population and requires complex administrative systems. Modern state development took three forms. "Coercion-intensive" formation came in Russia, an agrarian society with little commercial development and little concentrated capital where the tsars used coercion to force their population to fund wars by producing agricultural surplus. "Capital-intensive" state-building in the Netherlands and some Italian city-states came as monarchs borrowed funds from merchants and paid for mercenary armies. "Capitalized coercion" came in Britain and France and was based on capital accumulation in large towns like London and Paris, combined with large rural populations that could also be coerced to produce rents. According to Tilly, this last model produced the strongest modern states.[46] Competition eventually produced modern states in all of these cases because states proved better at fighting wars than other forms of government. Not discussed in Tilly but also of tremendous importance was British and French success at developing resource extractive empires, able to transfer vast amounts of resources from the colonies to the imperial centre.

Charles Tilly, *Coercion, Capital, and European States, AD 990–1992* (Oxford: Blackwell, 1992).

Economic Theories

Economic theories of the state don't ignore the role of geopolitical conflict, but their proponents think that economic modernization is the fundamental cause of the rise of modern states. Karl Marx was an influential proponent of this idea. For Marx, the modern state primarily represents the interests of the bourgeoisie, the owners of capital.[47] These capitalists create the state as an organization so that they can manipulate the circumstances that will maximize their profits, which ultimately means exploiting labour. Of course, the actual historical processes through which this happened, according to Marxist scholars, is more complex than this formulation suggests and requires understanding the specific mechanisms through which these changes happen in given places at given moments in time.

Not all proponents of economic theories of the state have a Marxist or left-leaning perspective, however. Others see states as products of elite coalitions responding to new economic circumstances. From this point of view, the best way to explain the rise of any given state is to trace the process through which elite coalitions were formed and maintained.

Critics of economic theories of the state note that they often treat the state merely as a reflection of underlying interests rather than an autonomous actor.[48] You might think about whether this criticism applies equally well to both Marxist and non-Marxist versions of this theory. And how might proponents of economic theories answer such criticisms?

Cultural Theories

Some scholars argue that structural factors like geopolitical conflict and economic change are not enough to explain the rise of states. For these scholars, we must include cultural factors such as changing beliefs and values in the explanation.[49] Among the most persuasive reasons for including such factors is the notion that state-building involved a dramatic disciplining in the daily life of individuals.[50] Could state-building really have been coerced from the centre of society? Or, perhaps, did cultural changes increase people's willingness to do things like accept state scrutiny, pay taxes, comply with regulations, face periodic conscription, and accept more extensive policing?

How could such "cultural factors" have played a role in the rise of states? One possibility is that nationalism and national identity (discussed further in Chapter 13) may have contributed to the willingness to accept these impositions in emerging states.[51] The core idea here is that national identity is closely bound to the state. If I consider myself a member of a nation, I might see the state as the expression of that nation, and I might accept its legitimacy. Moreover, nationalists might have been able to justify projects of state expansion on the grounds of national interest or national pride. A second idea is that religion might have played a role in early modern state formation. While few analysts of comparative politics view cultural factors such as religion or nationalism as the *sole* explanation for the emergence of states, they do recognize that these are often important factors, which *interact* with the economic or political processes discussed previously.

Indeed, all major theories of the state's emergence focus on both political/conflict and economic factors, and most acknowledge the importance of culture. As you will see in later chapters, theoretical advances in comparative politics are often made not by replacing old theories with completely new ones but by synthesizing existing theories, considering them against new evidence, and adding new dimensions or features to them.

Diffusion Theories

diffusion The process through which a practice or idea spreads locally, nationally, and globally.

Not all theories of the state begin by trying to explain the rise of states in western Europe. Indeed, some theories are more interested in explaining **diffusion**, or the global spread of the state as a form of organization. Why and how, these theories ask, did the state come to be the dominant way of doing politics *everywhere*? Of course, such theories are not incompatible with those that we have considered so far. Indeed, often they are based on implicit or even explicit answers to that prior question.

CASE IN CONTEXT

481

No Constitution? No Supreme Court? Constitutionality in the United Kingdom

The United Kingdom has no single document that counts as its written constitution, and it also has no process of judicial review to interpret the constitution on most matters. It is the archetypal case of parliamentary sovereignty. The British constitution is thus one of the most flexible in the world. Yet there is considerable continuity in the system: The country has a long-standing set of traditions and values that seems to transmit the meaning of the constitution from one generation to the next. How does this system work, and what are its consequences?

For more on this case, see the case study in Part VI, p. 481. As you read it, keep in mind the following questions:

1. In what ways does the doctrine of parliamentary sovereignty link together the various themes of this chapter: a flexible constitution, federalism versus unitarism, and judicial review?
2. Would this sort of constitution be feasible in a new country today, or is it feasible only in the relatively unique circumstances of Britain's history?
3. In what ways could one make a case that the UK system is more or less democratic than the Canadian system? What about the US system?

When a social or political form like the state appears to spread, there are at least three logical explanations. One is that its development is purely coincidental. Given the extent of the spread of the state, however, this seems unlikely. The second is that common underlying features present in all cases explain each individual case. For example, maybe over the course of the 20th century—when many modern states were created—we merely saw a repeat of the same processes from early modern Europe, such as increasing interstate warfare. But the evidence does not seem to fully fit this picture. A third logical possibility is that the spread of the state had *systemic* qualities.[52] In other words, there is some sort of international system through which it diffused globally. Here we will try to distinguish three basic models for how this might have happened. Note that these are not necessarily incompatible or mutually exclusive.

The first version of this theory has an affinity with the bellicist theory of the state's emergence. Once states are formed as war-making machines, we might expect them to rapidly out-compete rivals because of their skill in making war. Proponents of this sort of theory would point to the extent to which state forms were bound up with colonialism: The European states, over just a couple of centuries, extended political control over most of the world, bringing state forms of organization with them. Their military and technological capacity allowed them frequently to achieve victories over less militarily advanced and less warlike civilizations. Because of a long history of warfare, European colonizers often had a low regard for the lives of those they considered culturally or racially inferior to themselves. During waves of decolonization, newly independent regions sought to form states in order to guarantee some degree of order, stability, and prosperity.

CASE IN CONTEXT

360

Democratic Consolidation in Brazil

For years, Brazil alternated between authoritarianism and transitory attempts at democracy. In recent decades, though, its democracy has achieved consolidation. This is despite the recent impeachment of president Dilma Rousseff in 2016 and the election of Jair Bolsonaro in 2018. Given that Brazil is one of the world's largest countries and an increasingly influential one, this is generally a positive development. But how did it happen?

For more on this case, see the case study in Part VI, p. 360. As you read it, keep in mind the following questions:

1. How does Brazil's economic performance relate to its democratic consolidation?
2. How, and to what extent, has Brazilian democracy come to include poorer Brazilians?
3. How has the Bolsonaro government changed some of these perspectives?

Associated Press/Eraldo Peres

PHOTO 3.5 Shirts with the image of Jair Bolsonaro are displayed at a shop in Brasília, Brazil, during his presidential campaign in September 2018. He was stabbed during a rally that month but recovered from emergency surgery and went on to win the election and become president.

Not all versions of this theory focus exclusively on the state's military prowess, however. Instead, some variations note that the state can produce social and economic gains that, in turn, reinforce it (see the "Insights" box on Spruyt's *Sovereign State and Its Competitors*).

The second version of this theory has a still greater affinity with economic theories of the state. This version says that states spread to serve the interests of the international capitalist class. Building on the Marxian idea that the state represents capital's interests and Lenin's idea that capitalism turned to imperialism in order to protect itself from internal "contradictions,"[53] proponents of this version argue that colonialism aimed to create new markets for European goods and also sources of raw materials and exploitable labour of certain kinds. From this point of view, colonial subjugation was one way to achieve capitalism's desired ends but not the only one: Indeed, ongoing neo-colonial exploitation can take place perfectly well via a division of core and peripheral states in the international system.[54]

Yet there is a third strategy in which some scholars try to explain the spread of the state, one that has more of an affinity with cultural theories of the state's emergence. Here the notion is that organizational forms like the state are cultural phenomena or ideas and that ideas about how organizations should be structured play an important role in determining the organizational forms adopted by others.

organization Institutionalized group such as a state, corporation, political party, social movement, or international body.

isomorphism In institutional theory, the quality that two or more organizations have by virtue of being structurally very similar.

Organizations in a given field very often take on the same or at least a very similar structure, a phenomenon known as **isomorphism**.[55] For example, it used to be that universities did not have specific registrar's offices, financial aid offices, and so forth, just like political organizations once did not have professional, standing armies. When organizational forms spread, there seem to be two main sources of their spread: efficiency with respect to the organization's chosen ends *and* fit with cultural models and expectations for how such organizations are *supposed* to be organized.[56] In the first case, a university might develop a registrar's office because increasing complexity requires an office to coordinate classrooms, meeting times, and so forth. In the second case, anyone who starts a university already "knows" that a university is "supposed to" have such an office: A cognitive map or template

INSIGHTS

The Sovereign State and Its Competitors
by Hendrik Spruyt

Spruyt focuses on the development of states in early modern Europe, but his theory is about the spread of the state as an organizational form and the resulting emergence of the *state system*. The state had several rival types of organizations, including the feudal order, city-states, and leagues of merchant cities like Germany's "Hanseatic League," yet the modern state survived while these other forms essentially disappeared. Why? Spruyt argues that the state rose up as a product of both economic changes and political conflict. States became formidable fighting machines, so their relative success might be partly explained through a kind of "survival of the fittest." However, Spruyt says this is not a sufficient explanation because other formations (such as city-states) were often as good at fighting wars. Rather, states acted in ways that helped them to out-compete their rivals. In particular, states did things that were good for their long-term economic development, such as standardizing currencies and measures and establishing clearer territorial boundaries. Spruyt also notes that states won out in part by "mutual empowerment," since they preferred to deal with other states and encouraged the emergence of one another's organizational and institutional forms.

Hendrik Spruyt, *The Sovereign State and Its Competitors* (Princeton, NJ: Princeton University Press, 1996).

for the organization already exists. According to **world society theory** (sometimes called "world polity theory"), the state is very much like this: It became an institutionalized part of modern politics and is therefore replicated culturally even when causes that might have been operative in its initial emergence are not present.[57]

world society theory A theory associated with scholars such as John Meyer who argue that basic organizational features of the state system are cultural and have diffused globally.

THINKING COMPARATIVELY

Great Britain, the United Kingdom, or Neither? State and Nation in England and Scotland

KEY METHODOLOGICAL TOOL

Thinking through Case Studies

Political scientists use case studies for a variety of purposes. In later chapters, we will formally specify hypotheses and methods for testing against them, but here we begin by using a basic case study to think about general theories. In this example, we consider three of the major theories of state-building discussed in this chapter and then ask what each would say about the development of the state (and nation) in the United Kingdom. Although all three theories seem capable of explaining the general outlines of this case, they are not necessarily equal. Political scientists concerned with these problems must come up with strategies to get leverage over the competing theories.

Perhaps the simplest tool in comparative politics is the single case study (often a country, as noted in Chapter 2). Through this type of examination, we can gather information to develop hypotheses that cut across other cases. Case analysis can help us to identify key mechanisms and define general relationships. Debates in comparative politics are seldom ended on the basis of a single case study, but this approach nonetheless has much to contribute. Here we will consider how looking at the single case of the United Kingdom (from England to Great Britain) might help us to think about theories of state formation.

The island now known as Great Britain was long made up of distinct kingdoms (Map 3.1). For much of their political history, state-building projects were specific to these kingdoms. The most influential of these in political history has been England, which comprises a large share of the island's territory (with Wales to the west and Scotland to the north).

A number of scholars have considered the *English* state-building project a paradigmatic case. To some extent, the nobility's power to rule over the inhabitants of the countryside was curbed as early as the 800s, but with the Magna Carta of 1215, the Crown also took on some limitations. After King Henry VIII in the 16th century, the state was independent of the Roman Catholic Church, having separated from Rome and created its own church with the monarch at its head. Over the course of the 17th century, despite—and perhaps because of—civil conflict, parliamentary power grew, and nationalism and national identity were further developed. By the close of the century, a "constitutional monarchy" was established. Slowly, England evolved the characteristics of a full-fledged modern state: effective local administration developed[58] into a centralized bureaucracy, which resulted in a standing army and the authority to collect taxes regularly after 1688.[59] The country went through many fluctuations in royal power, but the rough balance of power between the Crown and the parliament progressively shifted toward the latter.

MAP 3.1 The land that became the United Kingdom, circa 900.

England's political history merged into a single state with the other parts of the modern United Kingdom. At different stages, this took place in different ways. English kings conquered Wales and governed it from the 13th century. Dynastic ties often meant partially shared governance between England and Scotland. With the Act of Union (1707), Great Britain was born from a merger of the kingdoms of England and Scotland. Thereafter (at least until our day), many state institutions were consolidated, and efforts were undertaken to create a "British" rather than "English" or "Scottish" national identity.[60] Interestingly, this did not mean that English or Scottish (or Welsh) identities disappeared. Rather, they coexisted with an overarching sense of Britishness. Meanwhile, over the course of centuries Ireland had been incorporated by force; even after the secession of the Republic of Ireland in 1922, Northern Ireland remained part of the "United Kingdom of Great Britain and Northern Ireland."

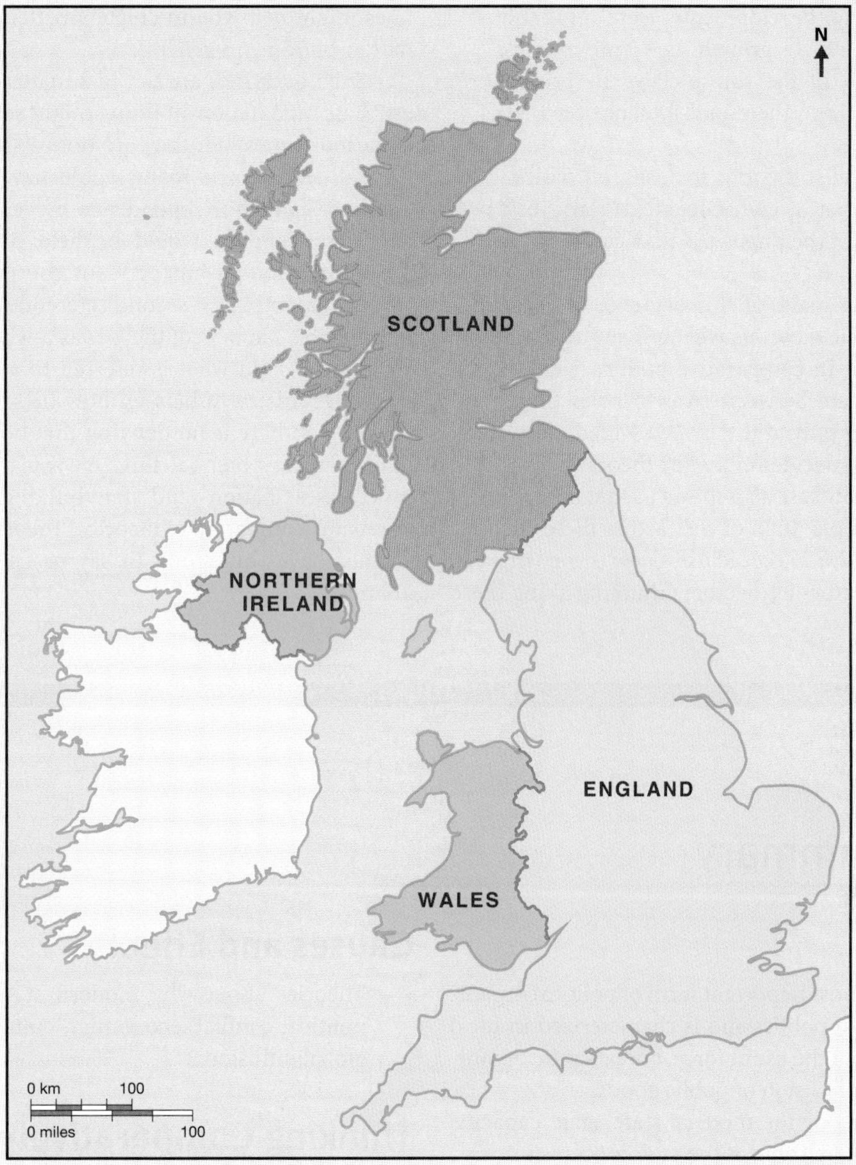

MAP 3.2 The United Kingdom today.

We can find evidence in this case study for all of our major theories of state-building—bellicist, economic, and cultural. Let's consider briefly how each of these theories might view this single case:

Bellicist: In the early modern period, like the rest of Europe, the British Isles were often involved in interstate war. The imperatives of war and continental alliances meant that the state had to be prepared for conflict, which meant taxation and, as time went on, greater investment in the military.[61] There is little doubt that this military preparation contributed to state-building.

Economic: At the same time, the giving up of privileges in exchange for the rule of law (as analyzed by North, Wallis, and Weingast) probably saw its earliest expression in England. And it was Britain that, according to institutional economists, first saw the emergence of sustained economic growth. Proponents of the economic state-building theory argue that these developments were probably linked. They see state growth as a consequence of the extension of the rule of law, the protection of property, and the establishment of a well-functioning state.

Cultural: Culturalist theories focusing on nationalism (such as that of Liah Greenfeld)[62] also find ample evidence in the English/British case.

What should we make of this evidence? It shows us several things. First, it shows us what a case study can and cannot do. Typically, in comparative politics a case study cannot fully adjudicate between rival theories of general processes. In looking only at the United Kingdom, we will probably be unable to decide among the theories considered in this chapter. But this case also shows us that existing theories may be too simple. If all of the factors these theories emphasize are operative, we could use a new theory that addresses how those factors fit together. Thinking along these lines might help you to create a better model of state- and nation-building in general.

Such questions are not just matters of historical interest. State- and nation-building might settle into equilibrium at various times, but they are not really static phenomena. Several decades ago, many would have been skeptical that a strong Scottish independence movement would emerge, that a referendum would be held on whether Scotland should become an independent country, or that Scotland would contemplate a second referendum after the virtually unthinkable happened: the UK as a whole voted in 2016 to leave the EU (in what is referred to as the Brexit referendum). It remains to be seen how these issues might be resolved, but there is no denying that both the state and the nation are in potential flux. As you think about ongoing processes of nation- and state-building, consider whether the major comparative-historical theories discussed in this chapter have something to say to us about 21st-century politics.

Chapter Summary

Concepts

- The state is the most important form of political organization in modern politics and is characterized in ideal form by control of the use of force, bureaucratic organization, and the provision of public goods.
- The related ideas of the modern state, state capacity, and failed states are some of the core concepts in comparative politics.

Types

- Major features of modern states include bureaucracy, impersonality, and sovereignty.
- States are coordinators of collective projects, such as taxation, defence, and policing.

Causes and Effects

- Theories about why modern states emerge focus on political conflict, economics, culture, and processes of global diffusion.

Thinking Comparatively

- We considered some of the uses of the single "case study," noting that the case of the United Kingdom seems to offer some support for several of the major theories of state-building discussed in the chapter.

Thinking It Through

1. In the "Causes and Effects" section of this chapter, we considered the causes of state formation. Since the map of the world is now covered with states, do you think these theories are of purely historical interest? Or do they still matter today? Think in particular of countries recently in the news—such as Afghanistan, Iraq, Somalia, or Syria—where commentators and policy-makers still talk about a need for "state-building." Do theories of state formation have any relevance today in those countries?
2. Test the theories of state formation considered here against your knowledge of Canadian history. Which of the theories seems to explain the formation of the Canadian federal state best, and why? What were the major steps in state formation in the state, and how well can each theory address these stages?
3. Consider whether you think the presence of a strong civil society will tend to make a state relatively strong or relatively weak in the sense of the state being a powerful decision-maker that affects lots of social and political activity. Do civil society and the state compete and divide a fixed amount of power, or do they reinforce each other, each making the other more powerful? Think of a case study that might help you to examine this question.
4. Return to the opening paragraphs of this chapter, which discussed the possibility of the formation of new states in contemporary western Europe. After reading the chapter, what do you now think about the likelihood of this happening? Ground your answer in the theories of state formation you have learned.
5. Many people agree that our world is rapidly "globalizing." This globalization can be economic, can involve social norms, customs, and institutions, or it can involve organized force (e.g., international organized crime, terrorist groups, and imperial powers). If the globalization of organized force gets carried very far, what implications, if any, might this have for the utility of the Weberian definition of the state? Would a radically (politically) globalized world be one in which new types of states were observable? Or would it be a world of weak states?

4 Political Economy

In This Chapter

The Shibuya shopping district in Tokyo, Japan. (visualspace/Getty Images)

The subject of this chapter is **political economy**, which can be loosely defined as the ways politics and economics interrelate and affect one another. In the past, the focus was more on comparing domestic economic and political strategies. However, as the world becomes more globalized and interdependent, external pressures and opportunities are of central importance to many analyses.[1]

political economy The interaction or interrelationship between politics and the economy in a given country or internationally, including how politics affects economies and how economies affect politics.

Our emphasis here is on politics and public institutions that affect the economy, though we will also highlight ways that economic change affects politics. In the next chapter, we will consider the political economies of developing countries (especially those in Africa, Asia, and Latin America), while the emphasis in this chapter is on what are sometimes called the "advanced, industrialized countries."

As a subject area, political economy has a rich heritage. You may be reading this textbook for a course in a department called "political science," or possibly "government," or "international relations." The official organization of those dedicated to studying the field is the Canadian Political Science Association, and its official publication is *The Canadian Journal of Political Science*. But 200 years ago, the academic study of "political science" in its modern sense didn't really exist. Prominent philosophers and thinkers who considered questions of political organization and public action had another name for their area of study: *political economy*. Implicit in this name was the idea that politics and economics were deeply intertwined. To political thinkers of the 18th and 19th centuries, including Adam Smith, Friedrich List, and Karl Marx, what happened in the economy would affect politics in almost any country and vice versa.

Later on, the disciplines of "politics" and "economics" became separate (along with sociology, among other fields) as the social sciences underwent a division of labour. Political scientists focused especially on issues such as the state (see Chapter 3), types of governing regimes (Chapters 6 and 7), and government institutions (Chapters 8 through 11). Yet the study of politics has remained deeply concerned with questions about society and the economy. Many chapters in this text address these intertwined issues. In Chapters 12 through 15, for instance, we examine questions related to social institutions, identification, organization, and action. In this chapter, we explore the enduring linkages between politics and economics. Our particular emphasis here is on the political economy of so-called "advanced, industrialized countries," such as those in most of Europe plus other economically powerful countries like Canada, Japan, South Korea, Australia, and the United States.

• • •

Concepts

To better understand political economy, we should first define several of the key measures and indicators that help characterize a country's economy. Which statistics can tell us something about its overall level—that is, its sophistication and advancement? Is it a large economy, is it wealthy on average, and how is the wealth distributed? Apart from the level of a country's economy, how is it performing? A country may be rich and successful, but its economy may be declining and performing poorly, while conversely, a country may be relatively poor but performing well. (We examine this question of performance in low-income countries in Chapter 5.)

gross domestic product (GDP) The total value of goods and services produced in a given country or territory; per capita GDP is divided by the population.

gross national income (GNI) A measure of the total income of all of a country's citizens, whether living in their home country or abroad.

The most common ways of measuring a country's economy involve the **gross domestic product (GDP)** or similar measures such as **gross national income (GNI)**. Each of these provides a composite measure of a country's total economy, but each measures it slightly differently. GDP is the total market value of all goods and services produced within a country's borders, usually in a year's time. In other words, the gross domestic product is the total (or gross) amount of goods and services produced (i.e., the product) in a given country (hence, domestic) in a given year. GNI is the total income from all goods and services earned by a country's producers, regardless of where they operate. In practice, an Indian company operating in Canada that earns profits would be counted both in the GDP of Canada and in the GNI of India. We will refer to GDP as our most common basic measure of a country's economic activity.

We often wish to compare the average wealth of individuals in different countries, not just the total wealth of each country. Economists therefore turn to *per capita* measurements of GDP, which represent average income per person. Relatively wealthy countries (such as Canada, Japan, and many in western Europe) may have annual GDP levels of $40,000 per capita or more, while the poorest countries have GDPs per capita of less than $500 per year and "middle-income" countries are in the range of a few thousand dollars per year. One benefit of this approach is that it standardizes GDP across countries of different sizes, dividing production by the population size. Otherwise, it would be very difficult to compare the economic performance of large and small countries.

The overall GDP and GDP per capita measure the overall size and income level of an economy, and *GDP growth* from year to year is the simplest measure of economic performance. Very high GDP growth, such as in China and India over the past 20 years, is in the neighborhood of 7 per cent to 10 per cent. Such rates of growth are possible in lower-income countries that are starting from a low economic base where many people are not employed to their full potential. In advanced industrialized countries, however, which tend to be wealthier, 5 per cent growth would be very strong, and a growth rate of about 3 per cent a year or lower is more typical. Some countries also have negative GDP growth rates. This happens in times of recession in advanced economies, and it has happened frequently in poorer countries, such as many in Africa.

GDP is a simple concept, but the value of a person's income also depends on how much their money can buy. That is, the cost of living matters. An income of $30,000 per year goes much further in a country where rent is $250 a month and a week's groceries cost $50 than it would in a country where rent is $1500 a month and a week's groceries cost $300. Because prices are frequently lower in low-income countries, a dollar (or other local currency) can go further. The adjusted measure scholars often use is income based on **purchasing power parity (PPP)**. In many instances, in countries where average incomes are very low (such as in Liberia or the Central African Republic), a GDP/capita of about $400 may correspond to a GDP/capita at PPP of more than $1000. Conversely, in countries where prices are very high (such as Japan or Switzerland), a GDP/capita may be *reduced* by adjusting for PPP; for instance, someone earning $50,000 in one of these countries may only be able to buy as much as an average person earning $40,000 in the United States (see Table 4.1).

purchasing power parity (PPP) An adjustment made to income measures to account for differences in cost of living.

Just comparing countries to one another assumes that the average income buys roughly the same amount throughout the country. This is rarely true, and there are often great differences in income and affordability from one part of a country to another. This is certainly true of Canada, which has great diversity in terms of income and affordability. The highest levels of inequality can be found in some of the largest cities—Toronto, Vancouver, and Calgary.[2]

The measurement of economic performance may extend beyond the economic indicators discussed previously. Measures also include a range of social outcomes, including such factors as standards of living, quality of life, and cultural change. The section on "Types" outlines several important ways of measuring development besides economic growth.

TABLE 4.1 | Economic Measures around the World

Country	GDP/Capita (PPP$)	Consumer Inflation (%)	Absolute Poverty Rate*	Gini Index**
Brazil	15,600	3.4	3.4	49.0
Canada	48,300	1.6	0.5	32.1
China	16,700	1.6	0.7	46.5
France	43,800	1.2	< 2	29.3
Germany	50,400	1.7	< 2	27.0
India	7,200	3.6	21.2	35.2
Iran	20,200	9.9	< 2	44.5
Japan	42,800	.5	< 2	37.9
Mexico	19,900	6.0	2.5	48.2
Nigeria	5,900	16.5	53.5	48.8
Russia	27,800	3.7	< 2	41.2
South Korea	39,400	1.9	< 2	35.7
United Kingdom	44,100	2.7	< 2	32.4
United States	59,500	2.1	< 2	45.0

* Note: Poverty rate is measured as per cent of the population living on less than $1.90/day (PPP) with statistics collected between 2011 and 2018. https://databank.worldbank.org/data/reports.aspx?source=2&series=SI.POV.DDAY&country=WLD).

** Note: Estimates for the Gini index are from 2013 or the most recent year available from the World Bank, with years available varying by country.

Sources: World Bank, *World Development Report* data 2017; World Bank, *GDP per Capita* (https://data.worldbank.org/indicator/ny.gdp.pcap.cd); CIA, *The World Factbook 2018* (https://www.cia.gov/library/publications/the-world-factbook/rankorder/2004rank.html); CIA, *The World Factbook 2018* (https://www.cia.gov/library/publications/the-world-factbook/rankorder/2172rank.html); Consumer Inflation: CIA, *The World Factbook* (https://www.cia.gov/library/publications/the-world-factbook/rankorder/2092rank.html)

Inequality

Measures of income such as GDP do not give us much information about how income is distributed among people. An average GDP per capita of $30,000 can result in a country where half the people earn $60,000 and half earn nothing, or it can happen in a country where everyone earns $30,000 exactly. The first country would obviously have a more unequal distribution of income and would see half of its population in grave poverty. Measuring poverty and inequality is thus important to many who study development.

inequality In the social sciences, the differential distribution of access to goods like power, status, and material resources.

Inequality measures how income is distributed. Some societies have incomes that are distributed very equally across people, while other countries have incomes that vary dramatically between different people. Imagine two societies. In the first, the average income for someone in the richest 10 per cent is $150,000, and the average income for someone in the bottom 10 per cent is $12,000. In the second, the average income for someone in the top 10 per cent is less (say, $75,000), and the average income for someone in the bottom 10 per cent is higher (say, $16,000). We might say the first country is more unequal because the ratio of the incomes between those at the top and those at the bottom is much larger.

To use specific examples, the United States has a more unequal distribution of income than the countries of Scandinavia, and this has been getting worse over time. As *CNN Money* reported recently: "the top 1%—earn an average of $1.3 million a year. It's more than three times as much as the 1980s . . . Meanwhile, the bottom 50% of the American population earned an average of $16,000 in pre-tax income in 1980. That hasn't changed in over three decades."[3]

Canada's economic structure is quite different from that of its neighbour to the south, but Canada has undergone significant changes to its economic structure according to recent data compiled by Statistics Canada. One major change has been the loss of manufacturing industries and jobs, with losses felt most keenly in Ontario and Quebec. By contrast, there has been a boom in the past decade in resource extractive industries, which at least temporarily boosted economies in Alberta, Saskatchewan, Nunavut, and other resource-rich regions. In the past decade, while median incomes have risen throughout the country, income inequality has grown, and as one recent study revealed: "The top 20 per cent of Canadian earners took home 44.7 per cent of all income in 2015, up from 43.9 per cent in 2006."[4] After the 2019 election, a movement against Ottawa and federalism known as Wexit, grew in Alberta and Saskatchewan, calling for the separation of the oil-rich prairie provinces from the rest of Canada. The movement had support on social media, but had little ability to operationalise its political goals.

Gini coefficient The most common measure of income inequality in any given population, usually expressed as a number between 0 and 1, with 0 being total equality and 1 being maximal inequality.

The most commonly used measure of inequality across an entire population is the **Gini coefficient**, which measures how much of a society's wealth or income is held by which percentage of the population. The number ranges between 0 and 1, with 0 being absolute equality with everyone having the same amount of wealth or income and 1 being a scenario in which a single person owns all wealth.[5] Rough Gini coefficients can be calculated using deciles or quintiles of the population (each tenth or fifth). There are quicker

Larry MacDougal via AP

PHOTO 4.2 An oilfield pumpjack works to pump crude in front of a chemical plant and a gas extraction plant at Joffre, Alberta, in 2016. A boom in resource extractive industries in the past decade temporarily boosted economies in resource-rich regions in Canada, such as Alberta, Saskatchewan, and Nunavut.

measures of inequality one can calculate as well. As we noted previously, one may simply examine the incomes of the top 10 per cent versus the bottom 10 per cent of the income range. Inequality is a pressing concern in most countries, from the United States to Brazil. Information about Gini coefficients and other measures of inequality and economic performance of this sort can be easily found online. See, for example, the Human Development Reports provided by the United Nations.

Some studies of inequality can sometimes combine both country and province studies, such as one study done by the Conference Board of Canada in mid-2017. This study concluded with the following statement, which compares Canada to other countries in terms of inequality but then also compares individual provinces and territories to get a stronger sense of regional disparities across the country:

> New Brunswick (Gini coefficient of 0.285) and PEI (0.287) have the lowest income inequality among the provinces, ranking 8th and 9th respectively among the 26 comparator regions and scoring "A" grades. The Nordic countries Denmark (0.254), Finland (0.257), and Norway (0.257) have the lowest income inequality among all the comparator regions, with Gini coefficients below 0.26. Quebec ranks just behind PEI (0.290) in 10th place and gets a "B" grade. Five other provinces are "B" performers and do better than the national average: Manitoba (0.298), Nova Scotia (0.303), Newfoundland and Labrador (0.306), Saskatchewan (0.308), and Alberta (0.320). Overall, Canada (0.322) gets a "B" and ranks 13th among the 16 peer countries. The provinces that rank the lowest on the income inequality report card are B.C. (0.323) and Ontario (0.331). Both provinces get "C" grades and place ahead only of worst-ranked peer countries Australia (0.337) and the United States (0.391).[6]

Employment and Inflation

Other economic measures relate to how people experience the economy on a daily basis. **Employment** and **unemployment** are especially important because of their impact on people's well-being and on a country's overall economic health. Employment can be measured by the total number of jobs created or lost or as a percentage of the population with or without paid employment. **Underemployment** is another factor being tracked, signifying the degree to which members of the labour force are part-time instead of full-time, are poorly paid, or are in jobs "below their skill level." In many developing countries, analysts draw a distinction between formal and informal employment as well, and most consider formal employment preferable because it tends to offer more benefits, rights, and support. In developed economies, far fewer people are informally employed (say, as unofficial and unlicensed street vendors) than in much of the developing world.

Tied to these concepts is **precarious work** in which workers do not have the rights of permanent employees. As the International Labour Rights Forum describes it:

> Globally, these workers are subject to unstable employment, lower wages and more dangerous working conditions. They rarely receive social benefits and are often denied the right to join a union. Even when they have the right to unionize, workers are scared to organize if they know they are easily replaceable. Women, minorities and migrant workers are much more likely to fill these kinds of jobs.[7]

employment Ongoing, regular access to paid work.

unemployment The lack of ongoing, regular access to paid work.

underemployment When workers are employed less than they wish to be or below their skill level or are not earning sufficient wages to support themselves and their dependants.

precarious work Where workers are denied the same rights given to permanent employees. This can mean lower wages, more dangerous working conditions, lack of union protection, a higher possibility of being fired, and reduced social benefits. Women, racialized peoples, and migrants comprise the majority of such workers.

iStock.com/Kritchanut

PHOTO 4.3 Precarious workers do not have the same rights as permanent employees. They typically are paid less and do not have the right to unionize.

This is very important to understand. Some groups in a country, because of their race, gender, sexual orientation, indigeneity, or other reasons, may be systematically excluded from secure, well-paying jobs. Additional statistical measures are needed to assess which people are most affected by inequality.

inflation Increase in the prices of goods and services.

Inflation is a measure of how quickly prices are rising. Prices affect the cost of living, and people find it more difficult to plan for the future when they are uncertain what prices will be in the future. Inflation can ruin people's savings by making the amount they have saved worth less in terms of what it can buy—in this case it makes no logical sense to save. As a result, high levels of inflation have brought about the collapse of many regimes. In the worst cases, countries have slipped into **hyperinflation** in which prices rise by as much as several thousand per cent per year, or more. Conversely, **deflation** (or declining prices) is also a significant problem that arises in economic crises as people stop buying to await lower prices in the future and the values of homes and other assets decline. Finally, it is worth noting that inflation and employment, though distinct, are related in ways that you might find surprising. Indeed, central banks and other policy-makers often face trade-offs when they try to keep both unemployment and inflation low. An emphasis on keeping inflation low at all costs is associated by many with higher levels of unemployment.

hyperinflation Exceedingly high inflation, which dramatically erodes the value of money over time.

deflation Decline in the prices of goods and services, often associated with depressions or serious slowdowns in economic activity.

fiscal measures Measures of a government's revenues and/or expenditures.

Fiscal measures—that is, measures of the government's revenues and expenditures—of a country's economic health, such as total indebtedness, may also be taken as indicators of a country's economic well-being. In many circumstances, poor fiscal indicators imply economic challenges in the future as debts come due. By the same token, some argue that an excessive focus on fiscal balance sheets can hamper a government's ability to engage in counter-cyclical spending, which means evening out the business cycle and avoiding recessions. Indeed, one of the great debates of political economy pits those who favour fiscal conservatism versus "Keynesians," who favour higher levels of government spending. This distinction often aligns with another that pits those who favour policies designed to reduce inflation with those who favour policies conducive to "full employment."

Types

In this section, we will think about the roles of the market and the state in modern economies. We first look at market-led and state-led economies as two main types, and we consider the intellectual arguments for why each might enhance economic performance. We then consider the types of state activities in an economy.

Markets and States in Modern Economies

Perhaps the most meaningful way to consider the different types of political economies around the world is to think about how the role of the state plays out differently across countries. We addressed the concept of the state in Chapter 3, focusing on how it originated and on the basic features of a functioning state, especially with respect to national defence and the administrative ordering of the polity. However, it is clear that modern states do far more today than simply exercise a "monopoly on the legitimate use of force in a given territory." In the process of governing in the modern world, states act in ways that affect the political economy. States provide a range of public services and **public goods**, perhaps with a view toward creating opportunities for the citizenry and toward protecting the vulnerable. The role of the state in the economy is counterbalanced in many countries by the role of private actors (from individuals to corporations). State actors have been involved in economic activity from the moment states were formed. After all, if we accept Tilly's bellicist theory, the state developed because powerful interests sought to expand their power and used the formation of the modern state as a means of increasing their power, wealth, and influence.

public goods Goods or services, often provided by a government, for use by all members of a society and for which theoretically one person's use of the good does not compromise anyone else's use of the good. Examples include public health care, education, national defence, infrastructure, and a healthy environment.

Markets and Economic Performance

A central debate in political economy in recent years, then, has been over which actors should take the lead in promoting national economic advancement: private markets or the state. The most significant debate in political economy has to do with the role of the market and the role of the state in guiding economic decision-making. We will first consider the argument that a country with a market-led economy will perform well and will then follow this by considering how an economy with significant state intervention might perform well.

A leading ideological view in American political economy has been that free markets are the basis for creating wealth. This argument has a long history, harkening back to the Scottish economist Adam Smith's publication of *The Wealth of Nations* in 1776. This perspective spawned the field of economics, whose market-oriented thought is often called **neoliberalism**. In an obscure passage, Smith's idea of the "invisible hand" concluded that through the individual efforts of people seeking only their own well-being, society as a whole is made better off. This logic of the market is expected to promote economic advancement within any given country, and it also extends to the world economy as a whole, with the idea that free trade between countries makes all countries better off.[8]

neoliberalism An ideological tendency that favours liberal democracy and market-led development and a reduction of state influence over economic activity.

Advocates of free market economics are influential in some countries today (certainly in the United States) and argue that the "invisible hand" should operate largely unrestrained, without government interference. At the same time it is also clear that this theory is intellectually dubious. This notion has demonstrably caused more economic problems than it has solved, which is one reason why the *Harvard Business Review* has concluded: "One of the best-kept secrets in economics is that there is no case for the invisible hand."[9]

Neoliberal approaches can generate wealth for the economy as a whole, but this may be very unequal wealth, which favours a small number of economically influential actors at the expense of the rest of the population—the so-called 1 per cent. Market-driven approaches such as these also tend not to have much regard for the natural environment or long-term policy or infrastructure planning. The notion of the invisible hand has been rejected by many leading economists as being little more than simplistic mythology.[10]

A major problem for the longevity of this market-first economic model is that markets can and do fail. Markets after all are composed of individual actors seeking profits. They may work collaboratively if it suits their interests, or they may undermine the system if that, too, works to better their own interests. The 2008 economic crisis in the United States, which spread to Canada and many other countries of the world, was the result of too little state regulation of the US economy. Corporate greed and a focus on very risky short-term profits prompted banks and investment firms to invest in subprime mortgages and other dubious financial investments. Had the state taken its role over the economy more seriously and sought to regulate the growing housing bubble, many of the worst problems could have been mitigated. As *The Economist* has argued, "bankers were not the only people to blame. Central bankers and other regulators bear responsibility too, for mishandling the crisis, for failing to keep economic imbalances in check and for failing to exercise proper oversight of financial institutions."[11] Canada, with a much stronger regulatory system, was able to weather the financial crisis without major economic disruption internally. Of course, the Canadian economy did feel major shocks from the economic crisis in the US, but the government through the Bank of Canada was able to coordinate policy to mitigate much of the damage.

States and Economic Performance

As a central institution in public life, the state takes a very active role in economic life in many countries, and many scholars argue that state intervention can be instrumental in supporting good economic outcomes while also ensuring that workers and more vulnerable

Associated Press/Richard Drew

PHOTO 4.4 President-elect Barack Obama appears on a television screen on the floor of the New York Stock Exchange in November 2008. Obama was elected just a few weeks after the collapse of the Lehman Brothers investment bank, which resulted in the biggest financial crisis in the United States since the Great Depression.

people in society are protected. The German economic theorist Friedrich List proposed what he called "national economics," in part as a critique of Smith. The argument here was that while individuals could profit from certain types of industries (for example the slave trade), some forms of economic activity hurt the state and many people within it. List argued that governments should prioritize future generations and should not just encourage short-term economic growth. Not only was List in favour of state intervention into its own economy, he also advanced the case for governments cooperating internationally to regulate international economic relationships.[12]

Proponents of **state interventionism** hold that markets are unlikely to generate national wealth on their own. Where states function well, they have an ability to coordinate the behaviour of various economic actors, stimulate needed investment, and promote human capital and advanced industrial production. Many state policies can promote successful industry and can see that it is in the interests of the country to have a strong economy that keeps its people employed and comfortable. These policies may include various ways of protecting local businesses from foreign competition, especially in the early stages of development when a country is trying to build up its "infant industries." Japan and South Korea are excellent examples of strong, state-led growth that favoured domestic industry. They may also involve direct state investment in important industries (such as steel) or incentives or advantages provided to private businesses (such as low-interest loans to build factories). Governments may also actively intervene to make their currency cheaper and their exports thus more desirable to foreign consumers.

state interventionism An approach to economic management in which the state plays a central role, not just through enforcing contracts and property rights but through active interventions such as coordinating investment, supplying credit, and, in many instances, the establishment and running of state-owned enterprises.

Advocacy for state interventionism in economic management grew in the 20th century, with governments taking on much larger economic roles. Around the mid- to late 1800s, European countries such as Germany and Italy unified and consolidated into nation-states. Some new government roles came in terms of social welfare provision. An important change was the establishment of social insurance programs (such as a state-supported old-age pension and disability insurance) in Germany in the late 1800s. Soon thereafter, the world went through major events that led to increased central state power: countries mobilized militaries in the lead-up to the horrors of World War I (1914–18), and the subsequent Great Depression (mainly in the 1930s) gave rise to much more active state involvement in the economy. Pushes for more government involvement in economic and social life ranged from William Lyon Mackenzie King's social policies of the 1930s in Canada to Adolf Hitler's National Socialism (Nazism) in Germany. Each of these resulted in states that took on larger roles in societies and their economies, in very different ways that ranged from simply increased social services in liberal democracies to state-dominated overhauls of the economy in totalitarian systems.

As states took on more prominent roles in the economy, a major debate emerged about the best institutions to promote economic performance, with views reflecting pro-market and pro-state perspectives. To represent this debate, consider Table 4.2. As Table 4.2 shows, the statist argument is not simply the opposite of neoliberalism or market-led approaches. The neoliberal approach generally expects that states hinder economic performance when they intervene, but statism does not expect states to promote the economy in every possible way. Rather, success depends upon the *quality* of states and the decisions they make. Actions by states may promote or may hinder the economy, depending on whether the state is strong or weak and makes good or bad decisions. In the next chapter, we will see that this argument has continued application to developing countries when considering regions such as East Asia (note South Korea in Table 4.2) and much of Africa.

State-led growth was at the heart of the rise of many Asian economies during the 1960s and after. In 1950s Japan, because of a large and willing labour force and extensive government investment and planning through the Ministry of Economy, Trade and Industry, the

TABLE 4.2 | The Market–State Debate: An Overview

Perspective	Market	State
Does policy matter?	Yes	Yes
What causes economic success?	Free markets	Strong states / Quality state interventions
What causes poor performance?	Too much state involvement	Weak or low-quality state / Poor state interventions
Testing the theory: What countries provide good evidence?	United Kingdom Canada	South Korea Canada
Testing the Theory: Why has China been successful? (see Chapter 5)	After 1979, opening up the market has led to economic success.	Even after 1979, strong state remains active in managing economy.
Main policy recommendation	*Reduce* the size of the state and its role in economy.	*Build* the capacity of the state to intervene well.

state worked with private companies to invest in manufacturing. Inexpensive manufactured products were produced for export, mainly to Western countries. Japan also took advantage of a favourable free trade environment during the Cold War. This strategy led to high rates of growth from the 1960s, and other Asian countries (known as the Asian Tigers) also began promoting state-led, export-oriented growth. South Korea, Singapore, Hong Kong, and Taiwan are clear examples of this type of growth strategy. By the 1970s and 1980s, a series of emerging tigers, or "Tiger Cubs," also came on the scene, using similar strategies. They included Indonesia, Malaysia, Vietnam, Thailand, and the Philippines. China also began pursuing similar strategies during this time, especially during the 1980s. Asian economic growth, in short, has been the result of careful direction by governments working with private and public industry partners. Of course, the histories and strategies are more complicated than what we have outlined here, and there have been problems with aspects of growth. Corruption and poor planning in some cases have been serious problems, and Asia suffered an "Asian crisis" in 1997 when speculators lost confidence in some of the Asian economies.

The Chinese and Indian economies have both surged ahead in recent years, sometimes recording annual growth rates in the double digits. In China, the state has taken an extremely important role in directing the economy through a series of five-year plans to intervene and manage almost every sector. This strong state-led growth has resulted in a high level of economic success for China. It has also, interestingly, encouraged very high rates of entrepreneurship and creativity. In a paradoxical situation, the Chinese Communist Party has now allowed business owners to become Party members and take part in the country's decision-making processes. The state has become an active promoter of entrepreneurship, and it sees the growth of new business as a key driver of the economy. Writing in *Forbes*, Edward Tse describes the growing mixed nature of the Chinese economy, which began as state-led but is now increasingly reliant on entrepreneurial spirit and forms of private enterprise:

> In 2000, total revenues earned by Chinese state-owned industrial enterprises and those in the non-state-owned sector Chinese private enterprises were roughly the same at about 4 trillion yuan each. By 2013, while total revenues at state-owned companies had risen just over six fold, revenues in the non-state sector had risen

by more than 18 times. Profits in the same period showed an even more remarkable difference, with state-owned companies showing a sevenfold increase but profits at non-state-owned ones increasing nearly 23 times.[13]

Nevertheless, China remains under the control of a tight-knit Communist Party that dominates mass communications and exerts a high level of influence over its population. Massive industrialization has also brought growing gaps between rich and poor, urban and rural populations, as well as serious problems of pollution.

Social scientists recognize that both the market and the state can play important roles in promoting and facilitating economic performance, but the experiences of individual countries suggest that there is no one-size-fits-all model.

Economic Functions of Modern States

States commonly engage in economic management, serve the welfare goals of their citizens such as education and health care, and build infrastructure. They also intervene in the economy to support those who might be vulnerable, such as the poor or the elderly, who may no longer be able to engage in as much economically productive work. This last category of state action can be called the provision of a welfare state, as in ensuring a degree of social well-being.

States and Economic Management

Citizens also typically hold their states responsible for **economic management**. This does not mean that all modern states play the same economic role: Some states intervene greatly in the economy, holding ownership of firms in key economic sectors, for example, while others intervene less. The Canadian state, for example, owns a large number of Crown corporations, as do individual provinces and territories. These corporations generate income for the governments, which they can then use to reinvest in the economy, pay down government debt, or fund a range of social programs.

economic management States' efforts to shape the economic performance of their societies, especially in fiscal and monetary policy.

States endeavour to manage the economy in several main ways. Additionally, all states regulate the economy. They perform basic functions such as enforcing contracts. They establish and enforce rules about the banking system, helping to structure the ways in which capital is accumulated and invested. States create rules that govern labour and its contractual relationships with employers, codifying rules about strikes, collective bargaining, and minimal conditions, such as safety protections, work hours, and, in some cases, wages. States often regulate commercial products: for example, regulating the nature of advertising claims, banning toxic products such as lead paint, and imposing controls on pollution from factories.

Equally important, modern states carry out economic management through attempts to influence the business cycle. States try to engender economic growth and to avoid or at least mitigate periodic economic downturns. The two main tools states have in this connection are fiscal policy and monetary policy.

Fiscal policy essentially involves taxing and spending. States can attempt to produce economic growth during downturns by increasing their spending (or by cutting certain taxes), which essentially adds to existing demand in the economy. This practice is often called fiscal stimulus or counter-cyclical spending because it aims to counter the business cycle, evening out economic performance and producing steady growth over time. Equally important to fiscal policy is the management of the state's balance sheets: A certain amount of debt is normal, but excessive debt can produce crises that can threaten economic performance and the political viability of regimes holding power.

fiscal policy Budget setting, which is dependent on generating revenue followed by government spending.

monetary policy States' efforts to shape the value of a society's currency, often through the use of a central bank in the case of a modern state.

Monetary policy involves the government's efforts to shape how much money is in circulation and the value of a state's currency relative to other currencies. Governments have a variety of specific tools to help them manage how the prices of goods and services rise and fall. Some states will try to reduce the value of their currency in relation to other countries' because this policy will increase demand for their exports (which will now be cheaper for consumers in countries with a higher value currency). Others will aim to establish and maintain a strong currency. Inflation (or rising prices) and deflation (or falling prices) are frequent worries, and while governments cannot completely control the rising and falling value of prices and currencies, modern states are typically considered responsible for this sort of economic management.

Investments in Human Welfare: Education and Health

The modern state has often taken on new roles over the course of its history. One such role is coordinating the provision of education, public health, and welfare commitments. In most instances, the state is tasked with establishing and funding educational institutions. This might be done also by provinces, states, territories, and other substate units within a federal system.

Historical research shows that states initially endeavoured to use public education to help create citizens and instill loyalty to the state.[14] This is still an important function of educational systems, which teach people about the rights and duties attached to their status as members of the society subject to the state's authority. An educated workforce has more skills than an uneducated one and as a result becomes more attractive to prospective employers while also helping people to develop creativity and innovation. Higher education has expanded globally as states develop and subsidize higher education, both because they hope to educate their workforce and because they view institutions of higher education as sources of technological innovation.

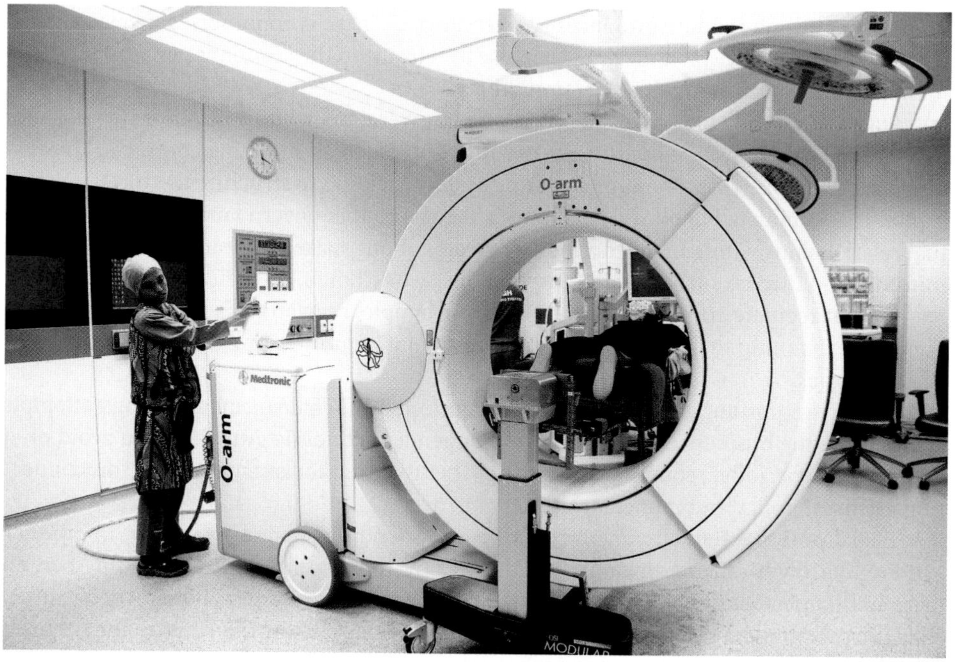

Singapore Press via AP Images

PHOTO 4.5 A demonstration of the O-arm surgical imaging system at Changi General Hospital in Simei, Singapore, in 2017. This technology provides a real-time, 3-dimensional view of the patient's spine, allowing surgeons to perform minimally invasive spinal surgery.

CASE IN CONTEXT

Online

State-Led Development in Japan (online case)

Japan's modern state began to develop in the late 19th century and grew in the 20th and 21st alongside the country's rapid economic development. For this reason it is often cited as a rapid modernizer. This case also shows that states can play a key role in successful economic performance, as we discuss further in Chapter 5.

For more on state-led development in Japan, go to **www.oup.com/he/DickovickCe** to see the case study. As you read it, keep in mind the following questions:

1. How, historically, has the Japanese state been involved in the economy?
2. How has this involvement changed in recent years?

The modern state is also responsible for many aspects of public health, such as coordinating and regulating vaccination, overseeing food distribution and safety, and managing infectious diseases. Many states like Canada, Australia, and New Zealand create and fund extensive publicly funded health care systems, including doctors' offices, specialist laboratories, hospitals, and so on. This is also true of most European countries, the Caribbean, much of Latin America, and many Asian countries such as South Korea, Singapore, Taiwan, India, and Japan. The United States, with its lack of coherent publicly funded health care, is an outlier by the standards of the modern industrial state. States have come to provide these services because important constituencies have demanded that they do so, bolstered by the expanding perception over several decades that this is simply part of what states do.

Infrastructure and Other Public Goods

States are also typically responsible for the establishment and maintenance of a variety of forms of infrastructure. States license and regulate media infrastructure, controlling, for example, radio, television, phone, and Internet systems. States typically create and maintain civil engineering infrastructure, particularly highways, railway lines, airports, and waterways. Commerce depends on reliable and efficient transportation, and states that neglect investment in these areas often handicap their societies' economic performance, and, therefore, ultimately their own strength.

Welfare State Functions

In the period after the Second World War, advanced industrial societies converged on the idea that the state should serve certain broad economic and social functions, and they were to some extent followed in this, where possible, by developing-world states. The model that was constructed is often referred to as the **welfare state**, meaning that the state should have as a key task the maintenance of its population's welfare.

welfare state A state that provides a basic safety net for its population, often accomplished through social insurance, public health care, public education, and poverty relief.

While welfare states do many different things, their key tasks include providing social insurance or pensions that protect the elderly and the physically and mentally challenged, unemployment insurance that protects those who cannot find work, health care for their citizens, and education. They vary widely in their ambition in this respect and in their efficacy. Many have argued that the United States shows an insufficient commitment to the welfare state model, whereas the Scandinavian countries are often held up as exemplars of strong and successful commitments to welfare state goals.

While most advanced industrial and post-industrial societies have welfare states, they vary in terms of how they collect most of their taxes, how much tax they collect, and the extent and form of their social spending. Today, many welfare states currently face fiscal challenges, in part because of demographic trends. As "Baby Boomers" age, social insurance and health care provision will grow more costly. At the same time, fiscal problems have often been exacerbated or even caused by tax cuts and other actions carried out by the welfare state's opponents. The question of what will happen to the welfare state will be one of the most important issues in global politics in the coming years. Certainly, there is little indication that a more market-oriented deregulated system would do a better job helping society to care for the elderly, the ill, and the poor.

Causes and Effects: Why Do Welfare States Emerge?

One of the leading questions raised in this chapter is "What explains economic performance?" with the role of the market and that of the state being important hypotheses to explain variations in outcomes across countries. These hypotheses shape the debate in both advanced, industrial economies (the subject of this chapter) and lower-income, developing countries (the subject of the next chapter). We address these hypotheses in the next chapter on development. We turn now to another important (and related) question about the political economy in advanced, industrialized societies: *Why are states as economically active as they are?* In a sense, this section bridges the various discussions about the state and the economy, as seen in the key causal question in Chapter 3 (Why did states emerge?) to the key causal question in Chapter 5 (Why do economies perform as they have?). We ask here why states have gone from having been relatively minimal economic actors in the 19th century to having larger roles as more robust "welfare states" in the world's most advanced economies in the 21st century.

As we noted earlier, the modern welfare state began to develop in the 19th century when a number of states, notably France and Germany, developed "social insurance" programs.[15] The major causal question we address here is why the economic functions of the state have changed over time. In particular, we consider the expansion of the state's role in regulating or even providing for the welfare of its citizens. In other words, why have states increasingly taken on tasks like providing health care, social insurance, and other social safety–net features over the course of decades?

Note that this question should not imply that all movement is in one direction on this issue. Some countries have often moved toward implementing neoliberal reductions in providing social welfare services. Prominent examples include the United Kingdom under Margaret Thatcher in the 1980s, the Mulroney government in Canada from 1984 to 1993, the US under Ronald Reagan from 1981 to 1989, and the former communist countries of central and eastern Europe after 1989. However, under Reagan, state spending on defence rose dramatically along with America's debt. A major research question has been why states have generally gone from entities with limited economic functions to ones that have larger roles over time. To address this question, we look at several prominent theories about the emergence of welfare states.

Cultural Changes

Some scholars have argued that welfare states emerge because of changing values and norms.[16] From this extremely myopic point of view, earlier states did not develop a social safety net because citizens did not ask for them. The argument here is that other institutions were regarded as more suitable to the provision of welfare: for example, religious organizations or workhouses before the late 19th century. Another argument is that something in the post-Enlightenment world made people start to think that formerly intractable social problems could be solved and that the state should play a role in solving them.[17] One classic theory of the welfare state focuses on changing ideas of *citizenship* in this connection, as argued most influentially by T.H. Marshall. The argument can be made that those who were marginalized and needed welfare states had little voice in politics and were simply unable to articulate their interests against those who controlled the economic and political life of the country.

Industrial Capitalism

Another important theory, though, has been that industrial capitalism creates welfare states. Industrial capitalism has, without doubt, led to massive economic growth, but it has also generated social and economic changes that have proved dislocating to many people and many societies. At a very fundamental level, capitalist societies (with their more advanced economies) have more complex divisions of labour in the economy. For example, a few centuries ago the vast majority of working people in the world were farmers, but today only a small fraction are in the most industrialized nations. This economic change—however much opportunity and growth it brought—disrupted long-standing social institutions. Thus, in "traditional" agrarian societies, families played many roles in providing what we may think of today as government social services: support to the elderly and some form of education to the young (with the latter often coming in the form of experience in farming practices or a trade learned from a family member or close associate). Meanwhile, religious institutions and norms about charity or alms-giving were the primary means of providing protection to the more vulnerable people; self-organized mutual-aid associations and community institutions might have supported poorer people rather than "the state." In more complex economies, as the prospects for growth took off, things changed: More people went to factories or offices to work, families became more nuclear, and so on. In this process, institutions such as the family and the church lost some of their roles to a state that emerged as an important agent in managing the complexity of the economy.

There are several very distinct theories about how capitalism leads to welfare states. Some are more Marxist and emphasize a *critique* of capitalism. Some of these theories see the welfare state as essentially reactionary. Marx thought that capitalism would inevitably undermine itself because it would produce larger groups of impoverished, suffering workers who would eventually overthrow the state. However, some Marxists argue that welfare states involved the co-optation of workers by the state and the owners of capital such that "immiseration" did not proceed as Marx had predicted. In general, the position most closely associated with Marx on these questions has been that the welfare state as such cannot, in the end, do away with exploitation, which can only happen with a revolution.[18] At the same time, though, many self-described Marxists and others on the left have been strong proponents of expanding the welfare state on humanitarian grounds.

Neoliberal theorists have tended to view the welfare state as "creeping socialism," an argument often found on the right of the American political spectrum.[19] The welfare state is, from this point of view, the creation of social actors disaffected with capitalism and who would end capitalist development if they could, which would result in less wealth being created in a society and thus the impoverishment of everyone.

Finally, another view holds that the welfare state is primarily a response to the social dislocations that industrialization generates. Some scholars argue that industrial capitalism more generally produced such dramatic changes that a new sense of order was needed.

CASE IN CONTEXT

371

How Does Canada Compare in Terms of Gender Equality?

In terms of female representation in political institutions, Canada ranks 50th behind Rwanda, Cuba, Bolivia, and Sweden. Political scientists have often asked: *Why are there not more women in politics?* The reasons for low female representation are often divided into supply and demand factors. On the supply side, explanations often involve a lack of financial resources for women, gendered social roles, a low number of female political role models, and women self-selecting themselves to not run for office. On the demand side, political cultures at the municipal, provincial, and federal levels may be unwelcoming to women, and party gate-keepers (usually men) can block women from running or can simply avoid recruiting them. Proposed solutions include improving the political climate and creating a more equal economic playing field, as well as changing the electoral system to one that is more proportional.

For more on gender and representation in Canada, see the case study in Part VI, p. 371. As you read it, keep in mind the following questions:

1. Would a proportional representation system enhance the representation of women?
2. Will having more women in power lead to a political culture that is more attractive for women?
3. What role has sexism played in discouraging women from participating in the political process?

It is very important to recognize that while different theories might have ideological implications (or policy implications), as comparative political analysts we should not let these implications drive our research. In other words, the fundamental causal question here is not "What should we do about the welfare state?" but "Why did it emerge?" We may be motivated by policy outcomes or ideology, but we benefit from being able to distinguish these from our causal analysis.

Mobilization and Political Action

A number of scholars who are interested in the welfare state are critical of both sorts of theories mentioned so far (cultural changes and industrial capitalism). The first focuses on ideas in the creation of welfare states, the second on the impact of social structures. Where, one might ask, are the actors in these theories? Those searching for an alternative approach might focus on trying to identify the key actors in the creation of welfare states and seeing how they are interested. The main relevant ones to consider would, in the opinion of many scholars, be more concrete groups that claim to represent economic classes, such as labour unions and business groups, and the state itself.

In essence, this third theory sees the state as a product of negotiation and contestation among different interest groups.[20] Imagine, for example, an industrial society with a minimal state. In this society, business leaders exert strong influence on politics, using that influence to ensure that the state does not regulate their employment practices. In such a situation, workers would be poorly paid and have few rights or benefits. Imagine also that a strong labour movement develops. Further, some members of the labour movement are proponents of the state nationalizing industries and introducing further regulations on how businesses treat their workers and produce their products. Finally, imagine that some political leaders, or perhaps a political party, declare themselves the representatives of labour. Think about the strategic position of the different actors we have identified in this simplified story. In narrow terms, the labourers want basic rights, higher pay, safer conditions, and perhaps access to certain jobs. The business leaders wish to continue to make and if possible increase their profits. Political leaders wish to acquire office or stay in office.

To oversimplify a bit, we could say that labourers have two options: to push for radical social change or to compromise. Business owners face the same sort of choice: either compromise and accept a moderately redistributive and regulatory state or push to keep state regulations low. It is not hard to see how such a situation could present at least the possibility of a welfare state compromise.

One of the advantages of this general theoretical approach is that it can potentially explain variation in types of welfare regimes.[21] Not all welfare states are the same. Scandinavian welfare states have been very robust and have retained high popularity with their citizens. Welfare states in France and Germany have been somewhat more modest, and Canada has developed a comprehensive but also (by Scandinavian standards) fairly modest social safety net. The United States stands out for having a weak welfare state in comparative terms,[22] with less generous transfers and a more individualistic orientation. Retrenchment has been strong in the United States and has been getting stronger.[23] Moreover, much of the state's welfare functioning targets the middle class and has been "submerged" in the sense that its action is partly hidden from the view of the average citizen.[24]

Any satisfactory theory of the emergence of the welfare state should be able to account for these sorts of variations. The theories just discussed can *try*, if they can show that the independent variables they are interested in vary in ways that match the pattern. For example, such a theory could potentially explain the varied paths of welfare states by talking about different forms of capitalism or different timing of industrialization. But actor-centred theories are poised to offer detailed accounts of variation in welfare state regimes. They can

INSIGHTS

The Three Worlds of Welfare Capitalism

by Gøsta Esping-Andersen

Esping-Andersen's classic study is best known for two of its many features. First, it emphasizes "de-commodification" as the key goal of welfare states. This draws upon Polanyi's ideas and certain arguments of Karl Marx: Under capitalism the individual becomes "commodified"—because workers sell their labour for wages in the labour market—and this is thought to be dehumanizing. Esping-Andersen argues that welfare regimes, through providing for basic human needs, push back against the commodification of people.

Esping-Andersen's second contribution is to argue that three main types of welfare regimes developed in the 20th century: (1) liberal regimes in places like the United Kingdom and the United States, (2) corporatist regimes as developed in continental Europe, and (3) social democratic regimes as developed in Scandinavia. They vary in the extent to which they successfully resist the commodification of citizens, with social democratic regimes being the most successful. Further, he tries to explain *why* these different regimes developed and focuses on "the nature of class mobilization" as well as "class-political coalition structures" and "the historical legacy of regime institutionalization."[25] Early welfare state development, he argues, depends in part on the class position of farmers. In Scandinavia, small farmers developed a coalition with urban workers. In mature welfare state development in the postwar period, the position of the middle class is key. In Scandinavia, the middle class emerged as part of the welfare state coalition. In some other societies, it was more ambivalent. Moreover, these processes are path-dependent. The type of welfare state created in Scandinavia not only owed its success to middle-class support, but it was structured in such a way as to retain that support. Other welfare states might have been institutionally designed in ways that would later produce political weaknesses.

Gøsta Esping-Andersen, *The Three Worlds of Welfare Capitalism* (Princeton, NJ: Princeton University Press, 1990).

point to differences in, for example, (1) the relative power, size, and interests of actors such as labour and business interests; (2) different institutional features of the state that can facilitate or impede certain types of compromise; or (3) different organizational methods for aggregating interests, such as parties or labour unions, with varying capacity to mobilize.

Another advantage of actor-centred theories is that they seem more capable of handling contingencies and exogenous shocks to political development. A critical juncture in the creation of European welfare states was the dual shock of the Great Depression and the Second World War. Think about how these events might have changed (1) the willingness of key groups, such as the middle class, to participate in a welfare-state-supporting coalition and (2) the ability of the welfare state, once created, to maintain such a coalition by maximizing middle-class interests. Note that structural factors from industrial capitalism are not missing from this account and that ideas can be brought into such theories as well. For example, many analysts see Keynesian economics and its focus on government management of the business cycle as having an affinity with the welfare state. The rise of Keynesian policies in the post-Depression world also likely contributed to the welfare state's institutionalization.

International Learning Effects

From the beginnings of the welfare state in the late 1800s, countries have looked to other countries' experiences, sometimes emulating them, sometimes avoiding them, and sometimes adapting international experiences to local realities. At present, states in Asia are rapidly taking on many of the functions performed by welfare states in the world's wealthiest regions such as Europe; in so doing, the Asian states are building in a matter of perhaps a decade what took "Western" countries many decades to build.[26]

This idea that countries "learn" from one another is not to imply that late-developing welfare states simply mimic others. First, countries adapt the form and functioning of the welfare state to local realities. For instance, there is evidence that Japan's welfare state gave a greater role to the family than was the case in western Europe and that Asian countries attempted to adapt the welfare state to respond to the decline in the size of families and households (given the importance of these foundational social units in Asia, as elsewhere) during a period of rapid industrialization after World War II.[27] Similarly, international "learning" can flow from successful experiments in lower-income developing countries; it is not simply a matter of the poor countries learning from the rich. A recent example is seen in the experiences with so-called conditional cash transfers in Latin America, which are cash payouts to citizens (often low-income citizens) that are conditional on the citizen undertaking certain actions. In Brazil, a program known as *Bolsa Familia* provides cash to low-income Brazilians as long as they keep their children in school and up-to-date on vaccinations. Such policies have also flourished in Mexico, among other countries. In addition to some evidence of poverty reduction, initial experiences with these programs have generated policy interest in other countries across Latin America and in other regions of the world as well that have considered "learning" from existing programs.

As is the case with many theories, this one about international learning effects can be combined with other theories discussed in this chapter. For instance, the rapid emergence of welfare states in Asia in recent years may be linked to the rise of industrial capitalism in that region, or it may be a response to the mobilization of important political actors or changing notions of citizenship in that part of the world. The emphasis is not on one theory to the exclusion of others but on understanding how each might contribute to our overall understanding of the emergence of the variety of welfare state programs observed around the world today.

THINKING COMPARATIVELY

Welfare States in the Nordic Countries: What Can We Learn, and How?

KEY METHODOLOGICAL TOOL

Formulating Hypotheses

Formulating a hypothesis is one of the most important steps in comparative analysis. Usually, analysts generate hypotheses *deductively* from a theory. This means teasing out specific and testable claims that logically follow from the theory and that can be judged in relation to empirical evidence. Sometimes, though, analysts proceed *inductively*. This means thinking about how a theory could potentially account for observable features of a case or set of cases. But the method of formulating a hypothesis is less important than the rigour of efforts to objectively test that hypothesis.

For many social scientists, the goal of a research project is to test a hypothesis and, using evidence (often from case studies), to reach a conclusion. Ideally, that conclusion will help to inform more general theories about the way the world works. However, not every good piece of research will result in a clean test of a hypothesis. In many instances, good research will delve into the particular experience of a case study, noting factors that seem relevant in understanding that case. This process may generate a hypothesis for future use rather than be a full hypothesis test itself.

In formulating hypotheses about causation, it is important to keep your focus on the evidence from the cases you examine. As an example, let's consider what we might learn from investigating Nordic countries such as Denmark, Norway, and Sweden. The welfare state is reasonably large and sophisticated in these countries. We will consider how to move from that basic empirical observation toward hypothesis generation, hypothesis-testing, and theory-building. Let's say you read Esping-Andersen's account (see the "Insights" box on *The Three Worlds of Welfare Capitalism*) and focus on Sweden. You learn that Sweden has a relatively robust welfare state of the "social democratic" variety; according to existing theory, this is due to the nature of class coalitions at certain key moments in the country's history. Consider a few options for how one might develop a research project from this observation, and think about which add the most value.

Option 1: You discover that a different country Esping-Andersen didn't consider (say, Finland) has a robust welfare state that seems consistent with the "Scandinavian" model. You consider the author's argument ("class coalitions help explain welfare states") and seek evidence to test the hypothesis about the role of class coalitions in this new case of Finland.

Option 2: You study Sweden further, reading the entirety of Esping-Andersen's analysis. You follow the footnotes and bibliographic resources. Through this considerable work, you discover ample confirming evidence for the author's argument. You then declare that you have rigorously tested Esping-Andersen's hypothesis using the Swedish case.

Option 3: You discover that another country (say, Brazil) has a growing welfare state, but you notice that a major factor in its creation seems to be a desire to promote rapid economic growth. You treat this as a hypothesis that could be tested in Sweden (and other countries) to rival Esping-Andersen's "class coalitions" hypothesis.

Do any of these options make more or less sense to you as a research agenda? Each may be a good learning exercise. Certainly option 1 appears to be a good opportunity to use a case study to test a hypothesis you have drawn from the academic literature. Now look at option 2 more carefully, and see what is limited about it. Are you really "testing the hypothesis"? It sounds as if you generated a hypothesis based on the case of Sweden and then proceeded to test that hypothesis using the case of Sweden. You are really using the same evidence to replicate the analysis that Esping-Andersen did. (To be sure, being able to "replicate" existing studies is important, but option 2 is quite different from rigorously testing a hypothesis or examining a case afresh using *new* evidence.) To contribute toward building a theory of the causes of the welfare state, it might be more helpful to see if hypotheses generated from the Swedish case work in other cases (option 1).

Conversely, you might see if hypotheses generated from other cases can help to explain the Swedish case. This latter possibility leads us to option 3—a good and promising avenue for research. By looking at Brazil, you might discover a new factor that seemed to contribute to welfare state development in that country. This in turn might help you in re-examining or rethinking the original Swedish case, which could help to build a better theory of the welfare state overall.

Let's look at option 3 a bit more. Ask yourself: Would it be fair to say you "tested the hypothesis" that the desire to promote economic growth leads to the growth of the welfare state, using Brazil as your case? Not really. This is the same logic behind what limits option 2: you can't really say you are *testing* a hypothesis using the same evidence from which the hypothesis is *generated*. If one case study leads you to a certain argument, that can *generate* a hypothesis for testing on future cases. That is different from a true hypothesis test, in which you make a prediction before knowing the empirical realities of the case.

We want to emphasize here that generating hypotheses can itself be a contribution to the advancement of political science. That is, not every contribution in the discipline takes the form of hypothesis-testing or theory-building; it is sometimes useful to make empirical observations that generate hypotheses for future testing (perhaps helping us to redefine our terms as well). One or more well-done case studies that generate hypotheses for future testing can represent an important contribution and step forward.

Chapter Summary

Concepts

- Key concepts and measures from political economy include gross domestic product (GDP), gross national income (GNI), inequality and the Gini coefficient, employment, unemployment, underemployment, inflation, deflation, hyperinflation, and fiscal measures.

Types

- Many scholars argue that a balance between both markets and well-coordinated state action are the keys to political economic success. There are, however, disagreements as to where the balance lies and what strategies work best to achieve it.
- Concepts such as the "invisible hand," popular among some neoliberal thinkers, have been roundly disproved in practice. One outcome of a lack of adequate government regulation of the economy was the 2008 financial crisis.
- States perform a number of key functions in the economy, including but not limited to economic management, investment in education and health, and welfare state provision.

Causes and Effects

- Three main theories of the rise of welfare states emphasize (a) cultural changes, (b) industrial capitalism, and (c) mobilization and political action.

Thinking Comparatively

- We considered the Nordic welfare state model in thinking about how to develop a research agenda.

Thinking It Through

1. Consider the various political economy indicators offered in the "Types" section of the chapter. Do you think some of them are more relevant than others? If you were "ranking" countries' political economies, which of them would take precedence for you in evaluating how countries are performing? Noting that GDP per capita and GDP growth are the most commonly used indicators, are there any reasons to argue for an alternative indicator on economic, political, or moral grounds?
2. One of the central debates in political economy and development (as seen in the next chapter) is about the relative roles of the "market" and the "state" in promoting growth and economic performance. Which of those arguments is the more intuitive to you? What evidence supports that argument, and what evidence have you seen that challenges it?
3. Test the theories of the establishment of welfare states against your knowledge of Canadian history. Which theory best explains the development of the welfare state in Canada, and why? What, if any, are the special features of welfare state development in Canada that need to be explained, and how well can each theory address these features? Why do you think the welfare state developed more quickly and robustly in some provinces and much later in others?
4. Many argue that the welfare state is now in crisis. What would each of the theories of the welfare state's emergence suggest about the likelihood of the *survival* of welfare states?
5. Given that welfare state functions became common in advanced industrial societies in the middle of the 20th century, do you think that these functions ought to be incorporated into the concept of strong states? In other words, can a contemporary state be strong without performing welfare state functions, or does failure to provide welfare benefits make a state relatively weak by definition?

5 Development

In This Chapter

North Korean leader Kim Jong-un (left) and South Korean president Moon Jae-in (right) visit Mt. Paektu, the highest peak on the Korean Peninsula in 2018. (Kyodo via AP Images)

Since the 1950s, North and South Korea have been separated by a "Military Demarcation Line" that is heavily fortified. Yet the people of these two states are separated by more than this: there are dramatic differences in health, life expectancy, infant mortality, levels of education, prospects for advancement, access to information, and the freedom to participate in political life. North of the line, the indicators are very poor and below them, extremely good. What makes this comparison still more interesting is how recently this profound divergence occurred.

The comparison of North and South Korea is potentially instructive in its own right, but it is just one example of a general situation of interest to scholars of comparative politics who focus on development. Some countries are incredibly rich, and citizens have a high "capability" to achieve the ends they set for themselves,[1] while others are poor and citizens have far fewer resources and opportunities. Many comparative political analysts hope to help explain why and in doing so to help citizens and policy-makers maximize their own chances.

North and South Korea are clearly different on various indicators, ranging from economic growth to poverty levels to citizens' opportunities. In this chapter, we examine the differing ways development can be understood. We begin by looking at the concept of "development," focusing on the most commonly used definition of the term, which is overall income. The subsequent section, "Types," highlights the many other forms and definitions of development, including other economic outcomes, more social indicators, and even measures of cultural values and ecological sustainability. The "Causes and Effects" section then explores the various theories that seek to explain why development happens. In the "Thinking Comparatively" section at the end, we return to the two Koreas to illustrate how we might use comparative case studies to test hypotheses for why development happens.

• • •

Concepts

development A process by which a society changes or advances, often measured in terms of economic growth, but also sometimes measured in terms of quality of life, standard of living, access to freedoms and opportunities, or other indicators.

Development is a complex concept, and there is heated disagreement about what counts as development and what does not. For example, would you say an oil-rich country such as Saudi Arabia is experiencing development if its economy is growing rapidly but nearly all of the benefits of that growth are going to a small number of elites and women have very few political and social rights? Would you say that a country is developing if people are not getting wealthier but are living longer, healthier lives? What about a country like China, where wealth is increasing for many people and poverty is declining fast, but the environment is being damaged severely? The indicators of development outlined in this section range from narrow macroeconomic indicators, such as economic growth, to social indicators, such as cultural development, that are more difficult to measure. As you read them, consider which best captures for you the idea of development.

The first and most straightforward sort of development to consider is economic growth, or increases in a country's overall level of economic activity. Beyond growth of the overall economy, we can also evaluate development using other economic and social indicators, including income inequality, poverty levels, and the standard of living. We could even define development in political terms, saying a country is more developed when it becomes more democratic, although we will leave this topic to the next chapter.

The simplest indicator of a country's economic development is how much the economy produces, or how much income its people earn. As we noted in Chapter 4, this can be measured using such indicators as gross domestic product (GDP) or gross national income (GNI). Here we will not discuss all of the various economic indicators that could be used to evaluate development, since several were explored in the "Concepts" section of Chapter 4. However, in the next section we consider some major ways that development has been evaluated in lower-income countries beyond the economic indicators already examined. These include questions of poverty and inequality, such as whether people of different races and genders have comparable access to economic and social opportunities, and overall well-being. We consider social indicators (such as health and education) and how or whether development can be compatible with environmental sustainability and respect for distinct cultural values in an age of global interactions.

Types

As we noted previously, there are many ways of understanding and measuring development beyond income per capita, and we examine some of them here. We still consider some economic measures related to how income is distributed in a population. Yet we also look at other possible ways of understanding development. One is to focus on more social indicators, such as those based on health, education, and other measurements of quality of life or standard of living. Another is to think about whether a society treats different groups equally (such as men and women or majority and minority ethnic groups). Finally, we will consider the relationship between development and issues such as environmental sustainability and cultural autonomy.

Poverty

poverty The state of being poor, as measured by low income, deprivation, lack of access to resources, or limited economic opportunities.

poverty line A specified threshold below which individuals or groups are judged to be in poverty.

extreme poverty A conception of poverty defined by the United Nations and the World Bank that involves setting a certain line below which people will be defined as poor, typically understood in terms of the inability to purchase a certain set of basic goods or services.

Poverty is usually measured with respect to an established **poverty line**, a basic level of income needed to maintain a reasonable standard of living in a given country. Traditionally, major international agencies such as the World Bank and the United Nations Development Programme have used about $1.90–$2.07 per day (per person) as the **extreme poverty** threshold worldwide, although this rises along with inflation and as the price of goods and services changes. There has also been an effort to expand the criteria for measuring poverty, taking into account additional indicators such as access to public services and public goods. Poverty may be understood as an income measure but also as a measure of whether people have access to health care and education.[2] The number of people facing extreme poverty is about 1.3 billion worldwide, with another 3 billion living on less than $2.50 per day.[3]

Poverty lines may also be measured by individual countries, and each country may do so in different ways.[4]

In Canada, for example, the poverty threshold (or "low income measure (LIM)") is defined by Statistics Canada for households and families of different sizes and is recalculated on a regular basis to reflect the cost of living. The LIM in 2017 was $22,133 for one person or $38,335 for a family of three people. Looking at only the poverty line, however, does not indicate poverty *depth*, or how far someone is below the poverty line. It is simple just to count the number of people living below the line, but this means a person with an income of $22,100 will be counted the same way as someone with $10,000 or less, even though there is clearly a difference in how deeply someone is in poverty in the two cases.[5]

Social Outcomes and Human Development

Several indicators of an individual's overall well-being and standard of living are not based only on income and macroeconomic performance. They may be termed *human capital* because they represent the accumulated skills and investments people have made

CASE IN CONTEXT

412

What Explains India's Recent Growth?

India in recent years has achieved strong economic growth but nevertheless still has a large population suffering from extreme poverty. In many ways, India's development story has not fallen within Western political science predictions, above all because it became the world's biggest democracy in 1947, decades before achieving strong growth. As we discuss in Chapter 6, comparativists have traditionally predicted that economic development commonly precedes democratization.

For more on Indian development, see the case study in Part VI, p. 412. As you read it, keep in mind the following questions:

1. Why was India's economic performance so weak for so long, and why did it finally take off?
2. Was democracy a help or a hindrance to India's economic development?
3. What are the prospects for those living in extreme poverty?

in their own capacities. Health is perhaps the most fundamental aspect of human capital. It can be measured by a number of instruments. One is **life expectancy**, or the age to which a given person may expect to live, depending on the circumstances into which they were born. Another is **infant mortality**, often measured as the percentage of children who do not survive to the age of one. Other health measures include infection and morbidity rates for different diseases and accessibility of health care. Education is a second major aspect of human capital. The most significant measures are **literacy rates** and school enrolment and completion. The quality of education is important as well, since the standardized scores of youth on math and science tests are often compared across countries, for example.

life expectancy The average age until which members of a society (or some group within society) live.

infant mortality A major public health indicator, which typically measures the number of infants per 1000 born who do not survive until the age of one year.

literacy rate The percentage of a population who can read.

Some analysts who want to define development broadly have aimed to capture the "standard of living." They often use some of the indicators just discussed. One of the most commonly used measures of standard of living around the world is the United Nations' annual **Human Development Index (HDI)**. It combines income, life expectancy, and educational measures (literacy and school enrolments) in a single index to give a broad view of development and well-being.

Human Development Index (HDI) A composite measure developed by the United Nations to provide a broad view of annual development and well-being around the world, based on income, life expectancy, and literacy and school enrolments.

Standards of living often go along with (or are positively correlated with) other indicators of development. Yet the evidence suggests that inequality actually *increases* as income increases at certain stages of economic development, specifically in moving from low-income stages of development (where nearly everyone is poor) to middle-income stages (where a fraction of the population grows wealthier and the remainder does not see much increase). Conversely, some societies (such as Cuba and the state of Kerala in India) have aimed to increase access to education and health *without* necessarily doing so via increasing the personal incomes of their citizens.[6] There are many routes to improving standards of living and reducing poverty, but many countries continue to face major challenges. In many African countries, such as Nigeria, standards of living and human development remain lower than in wealthier countries. In 2017, all of the world's poorest countries in economic terms were located in Africa, with Malawi as the poorest.[7]

Associated Press/Kike Calvo

PHOTO 5.2 Children at a school in Las Terrazas community in Cuba in 2012. Literary rates and school enrolment and completion are important measures of education, which is a major aspect of human capital.

Gender Relations and Racial and Ethnic Identities

In recent years, scholars have begun to break down statistics by groups, and a leading focus of analysis is gender. We now recognize that a society with large differences in life expectancies between men and women, for instance, may be seen as a less developed society than one where life chances are more equitable. Those who are transgender, or who otherwise fall outside of the traditional binary gender norms, often face an even greater challenge. The number of terms to fully describe the range of gender identities is continuing to grow

CASE IN CONTEXT 431

Gender Empowerment in Japan?

Centuries ago, Japan was noteworthy, among other reasons, because it was sometimes governed by empresses. Yet contemporary Japanese politics has been regarded as a case in which gender discrimination against women is high. How and why is this the case?

For more on the subject, see the case study in Part VI, p. 431. As you read it, keep in mind the following questions:

1. On what grounds could someone claim that gender discrimination in Japanese politics is relatively high?
2. What are the major factors that have contributed to this tendency?

as mainstream society becomes more open to understanding and accepting. We examine gender and politics in depth in a later chapter but reinforce the point here that gender matters for development in two major ways: It is both a *means* to development and one of the *ends* of development.[8] In terms of *ends*, we might define development to say it occurs when economic and social opportunities are equally available to both women and men (while also recognizing gender fluidity). Regardless of how well a country's economy does, that society might not be considered developed if women are not allowed to own property, or hold jobs outside the home, or voice their opinions.[9] In terms of *means*, gender also matters because empowering women helps to advance other aspects of development. Well-known examples include the benefits of extending education and small business loans (sometimes as little as $25 or less) to women in low-income countries. These small changes often have the effect of increasing women's incomes, which in turn typically results in households making more resources available for nutrition, family health care, and children's education. Indeed, evidence suggests that women, on average, are more likely than men to invest scarce resources in their families. Similar issues also apply to those with non-binary gender identities, who often lack state protection and also face high levels of discrimination both officially and unofficially.

Major differences in development levels of other population groups may also be an indicator of development (see Table 5.1). If certain racial or ethnic minorities are systematically deprived of the opportunity to participate equally in the economy, we can argue that development is incomplete. This gap between groups may not always be captured by economic statistics like GDP, inequality, and poverty, and it may go beyond political rights as well. South Africa under the official racism of *Apartheid* (1948–94) was one example.

iStock.com/2511photos

PHOTO 5.3 A microfinance loan recipient sells dried fish in a market in Burundi. Empowering women by giving them access to education and small business loans often helps them to increase their incomes, which in turn helps them to improve the health and education of their children.

CASE IN CONTEXT 470

The Rise of Mohammed bin Salman (MBS): Reform or Repression?

Saudi Arabia is a highly developed economy but has a reputation of being oligarchic, ruled by a small group of elite princes descended from the founder of the country. Different princes control key ministries and large corporations, which some have described as fiefdoms and "multiple kingdoms." There is a lack of transparency and accountability in decision-making. However, a new generation of ruler has emerged. In 2017, King Salman's son Prince Muhammad bin Salman (known as MBS) took control as crown prince, deputy prime minister, minister of defence, and the heir presumptive to the throne. Bin Salman has sought to break up much of the old factionalized system and has centralized political, economic, and military power. He has also introduced a wide range of reforms, outlined in his blueprint for change, Vision 2030. This includes diversifying the economy away from just oil and attracting more tourism and foreign investment. Many argue, however, that bin Salman is not seeking to reform the country but merely to rebrand it as more progressive. In short, the reforms conceal continued repression, particularly against women.

For more on bin Salman and reform in Saudi Arabia, see the case study in Part VI, p. 470. As you read it, keep in mind the following questions:

1. How is bin Salman perceived differently among the older and younger generations?
2. Will the centralization of power improve the Saudi economy or lead to more infighting and corruption?
3. How much is bin Salman a reformer, and how much is this window dressing for the continued repression of much of the population?

Blacks certainly had lower incomes than whites and no political rights to speak of, but they also suffered from separate and inferior systems of education, health care, and housing. Under *Apartheid*, South Africa had higher average social indicators than most other African countries (because of whites profiting from the system), but its inequalities were especially shocking. Furthermore, many aspects of inequality have continued even after the dismantling of this racist system. Unfortunately, however, disparities in development based on discrimination on the basis of race, ethnicity, and gender are not only found in extreme cases like *Apartheid*-era South Africa. Indeed, Canada too faces major disparities between the majority settler populations and Indigenous peoples. Overall, the life expectancy of an Indigenous person is considerably lower, as are household incomes, levels of Western education, and funding for education and access to health care.[10] James Anaya, the former United Nations special rapporteur on the rights of Indigenous peoples, was not exaggerating in 2013 when he stated: "Canada faces a crisis when it comes to the situation of indigenous peoples of the country."[11] For many Indigenous peoples, poverty is an important aspect of internal colonization, a topic we explore further in the text box "Internal Colonization and Indigenous Underdevelopment" on page 97 later in this chapter.

Satisfaction and Happiness

For many people, development is really about each person's satisfaction or happiness in life. Understanding development in these terms recognizes that income is a means to an end and not an end in itself. People usually seek higher incomes because it gives them access to other things they desire or the opportunity to consume things they like, such as good food, or better housing, or access to higher education, or luxury items, or a vacation. The most

TABLE 5.1 | Measures of Human Welfare

Country	Life Expectancy (at birth) (in years)	Infant Mortality (per 1000 live births)	Literacy Rate (%)	Human Development Index (HDI) Rank
Brazil	75.7	13.5	90.4	79
Canada	82.5	4.3	99	12
China	76.4	8.5	95.1	86
France	82.7	3.2	> 99	23
Germany	81.2	3.2	> 99	4
India	68.8	34.6	62.8	129
Iran	76.2	13	85.0	61
Japan	83.9	2	> 99	19
Mexico	77.3	12.6	93.5	74
Nigeria	53.9	66.9	51.1	156
Russia	71.2	6.6	> 99	49
South Korea	82.4	2.9	> 99	22
United Kingdom	81.7	3.7	> 99	14
United States	79.5	5.6	> 99	12

Source: United Nations Human Development Report 2018; life expectancy data from 2017; infant mortality data from 2016; HDI rank from 2016

fundamental concept in economics for measuring people's ability to fulfill their preferences is not income but **utility**. Utility gives a notion of the value people derive from consuming or having access to that which pleases them.

utility The value that people derive from resources to which they have access.

Happiness comes from more than just consuming goods and services. It may come from having free time, or social status, or strong ties to family and friends, or living a spiritually fulfilling life. Social scientists face major challenges in trying to measure human happiness, but they continue to make efforts. In recent years, the mountainous nation of Bhutan (in the Himalayas) made a splash internationally by publishing its own measures of "Gross National Happiness." Increasingly, other countries such as China, Canada, France, and the United Kingdom have recently begun to think about how to measure their people's happiness. Indeed, there is even a World Happiness Report, which is compiled annually. In recent years, Norway has ranked first of 155 countries analyzed, with Denmark, Iceland, Switzerland, and Finland following closely after. In 2017, Canada ranked seventh (a relatively low score for us in comparison to previous years) but much better than the US, which fell to 14th place.[12]

Cultural Development

For many people around the world, development might mean retaining and deepening one's own culture(s). In this view, economic modernization does not necessarily improve a society: If economic growth brings commercialization and cultural disintegration, some people(s) will wish to have none of it and will prefer to define development as exercising the right to self-determination, living autonomously from the rest of the world, and enjoying the rich cultural traditions they hold dear. For many people, "development" might not even be a positive word but might instead signify a push by outsiders—intentional or unintentional—to undermine local practices.[13] Increasingly, many researchers, sensitive to these concerns, argue that citizens of the countries we study should play a central role in defining development goals. The desire to protect traditional cultures is not limited to small and remote Indigenous groups but can also be seen in many modern nations wrestling with questions of growth and development, such as France.

Sustainability

environmental sustainability The quality that one or another practice has with being compatible with the long-term health of the environment.

Finally, **environmental sustainability** is an important aspect of development. With increasing attention to the issue of climate change, many development scholars are attempting to understand development as that which is sustainable. Sustainable development can be defined as development that conserves the environment to respect the needs of future generations. Only by stewarding natural resources effectively and not depleting them too rapidly will any society remain viable over the long run. To incorporate sustainability into development discussions, some scholars have proposed replacing GDP with new measures that account for the use of resources. They note that cutting down a tree increases GDP, as does polluting, thus promoting short-term gain for some at the expense of the health and well-being of future generations.[14]

For many Indigenous peoples around the world, the natural world has its own right to exist and to be protected. Waters, lands, air, plants, and animals should be respected because they are part of us and we are part of them. The well-known legal theorist John Borrows provides an Anishinaabe perspective on political community, based not on citizenship relations between humans but as citizens of the land:

> Our loyalties, allegiance, and affection are related to the land. The water, wind, sun, and stars are part of this federation. The fish, birds, plants, and animals also share this union. Our teachings and stories form the constitution of this relationship and direct and nourish the obligations it requires.[15]

What will be clear is that among the main political challenges in promoting sustainable development are the difficulties of securing collective action between many countries when each country has incentives to "free ride" on the efforts of others.

Causes and Effects: Why Does Development Happen?

To examine the causes of development, we focus mainly on GDP growth per capita, for two reasons. First, as noted earlier, these measures are the most commonly used in studies of development. Second, GDP growth per capita often goes hand in hand with several other indicators of development listed previously. In particular, countries that grow in terms of GDP per capita often also advance on other social indicators, with improved health, more education, higher levels of happiness, and reductions in poverty. Of course, this is not true in all cases, and rising GDP is not the only determinant of these other indicators, but it is true quite often. For this reason, and since it is more comprehensive than many of those other indicators, development scholars often use it when they are seeking a single indicator. That said, there can be trade-offs between GDP growth and other indicators, such as inequality, as we have noted, and GDP per capita certainly does not capture every dimension of development. These strengths and limitations of the measure should be kept in mind.

The central question here is why economies grow, diversify, and become more productive and successful. What allows countries to move people from their small farming plots to work in cities, factories, law offices, research labs, banks, and hospitals? Why have people and societies been able to foster more productive economic activity? The answers to these questions are debated extensively, and several theories have arisen to explain them. We group the focal points of these theories into four categories:

1. the role of the market and the state in promoting development, a topic we explored in the previous chapter in the context of "developed" countries;
2. institutions such as legal rules and social norms that shape the behaviour of economic actors;
3. cultural values; and
4. the domestic and international structures that condition development, including a country's place in the international system.

market-led development An approach to economic management in which the state aims to control private economic behaviour as little as possible.

state-led development An approach to economic management in which the state plays a prominent role in coordinating the behaviour of economic actors and intervening in the economy.

Institutions: The Market–State Debate, Revisited

A leading institutional argument about the causes of development reflects a major debate in political economy, which we emphasized in Chapter 4. The issue is the relative merits of **market-led development** versus **state-led development**. According to pro-market argu-

Associated Press/Anupam Nath

PHOTO 5.4 Farmers in India irrigate a paddy field using a traditional system on the outskirts of Gauhati, India, in 2019. The Indian government's interim budget in early 2019 had announced cash handouts for small farmers, a pension scheme for informal workers, and a doubling of tax relief for the lower middle class. This included a plan to pay farmers 6000 rupees ($116 CAD) annually, which would benefit as many as 120 million households.

ments (some of which, it has to be said, are quite self-serving), a low level of state restriction on economic activity will lead to a more efficient allocation of resources and economic prosperity.

By contrast, advocates for state-led approaches argue that development requires an actor capable of coordinating disparate agents, planning for the long term, and supplying capital for big development pushes in low-income countries. The state is uniquely suited to performing this task. This perspective was especially prominent immediately after World War II when Europe was reconstructed and new states emerged from colonialism around the globe. Development scholars envisioned a "big push" in development in the world's poorer countries, where state-led investment would generate a virtuous circle of self-sustaining growth.[16]

In subsequent years, East Asia was the most rapidly growing region in the world. Statist scholars argued that the success in that region was due to timely and constructive state involvement in the economy. As we briefly outlined in the previous chapter, beginning with Japan immediately after World War II—and then extending to South Korea, Taiwan, and elsewhere into East and Southeast Asia—the "Asian Tigers" offered compelling evidence. In these cases, active involvement by well-organized and capable states helped to direct investment to productive enterprises. Effective states helped to propel these economies to growth rates that sometimes exceeded 8 per cent to 10 per cent per year. Similarly, statists might attribute China's current growth to a state that maintains a steady hand in the economy.

For several decades after World War II, the state played a leading role in the economies of many developing countries, from Japan to India to Brazil to much of Africa. In some countries, this role was inspired or encouraged by the apparent economic, military, and technological success of the Soviet Union in the 1950s and 1960s and by the easy availability of loans in the 1970s. In the early 1980s, however, many Latin American countries in particular suffered from economic crises driven by accumulated debts. Less than a decade later, communism collapsed in central Europe, and the Soviet Union broke apart (see the country profile on Russia).

At this time, many institutions advocated for economic liberalization in developing countries, or moves toward free-market economics, often to help create a favourable climate for the spread of Western corporations. Major proponents of this approach included the International Monetary Fund (IMF) and the World Bank, based in Washington, DC. These organizations arranged loans to many developing countries facing economic difficulties. The loans were conditional upon those countries reducing control of their own borders, opening up to freer trade and flows of capital, and often reductions in the role of the government in the economy. The 1980s and the 1990s were times when many developing countries moved toward more free-market systems.

Reducing the role of the state in the economy often led to increases in unemployment and underemployment, a rise in inequality, and crises such as hyperinflation. Toby Carroll raises serious objections to the bank's influence in developing countries and observes in his book *Delusions of Development*:

> [T]he Bank, frustrated by the earlier politics of development, has used various political technologies (such as participatory approaches) and delivery devices (new programme and project instruments) in its attempt to establish market societies. These political technologies and delivery devices often appear to be about increasing participation and inclusion in policy-making processes. However, in practice (using a combination of co-option, functionalist consensus building, opposition marginalisation and via maintaining a monopoly on what constitutes development

CASE IN CONTEXT

Online

How Did China Become a Global Economic Power? (online case)

China's development has been dizzyingly rapid in the past 40 years, manufacturing everything from bathmats to iPhones. The country's economic performance was weak through most of the 20th century, but after a series of reforms beginning in 1978 and 1979, the Chinese economy took off. The country is now often referred to as the "global factory," and it rivals the United States for the title of the world's largest economy.

For more on Chinese development, go to **www.oup.com/he/DickovickCe** to see the case study. As you read it, keep in mind the following questions:

1. What factors—political, institutional, and cultural—likely contributed to poor growth in China in the years when Mao Zedong held power?
2. Is China's recent success due to strong government intervention in the economy, or the reverse, or a mix of factors?
3. How might we explain the emergence of the reforms that began in 1978 and 1979? In other words, *why* did China reform?
4. What sorts of challenges does the Chinese economy face in the medium-term future?

> "knowledge") these elements actually do the reverse—they attempt to narrow and constrain politics in the interests of establishing market society (which itself is seen as requiring the insulation of particular institutions from politics in the interest of the market). *In short, the Bank promotes illiberal politics in its promotion of liberal economics.*[17]

Evidence accumulated that "state-led" or "state-directed" development had worked effectively in certain places, namely where the quality and professionalism of the state was high. Thus, a theory emerged that the *quality* of the state might matter more than the *quantity* of the state in determining how an economy develops. High levels of performance in several East Asian countries over several decades—and in China in the 2000s and 2010s—showed that some of the strongest performing economies may exhibit relatively high levels of state involvement.

Institutions: Beyond the Market–State Debate

Development takes place over long periods of time, and the state and the market are not the only things that make it happen. Other institutions also matter. By **institutions**, political scientists mean the many features of a society that shape people's behaviour and actions, as discussed in the previous chapter and later chapters. The **new institutional** framework focuses on a broader set of institutions.

The institution-based approach to comparative politics, or **institutionalism**, has several strains. **Rational institutionalism** holds that political and economic outcomes are functions of individuals' responses to their institutional environments. Rational institutionalists emphasize economic logics, and many of these scholars would be found engaging in the debate about states and markets mentioned previously. **Historical institutionalism** also finds that institutions matter but traces these consequences through time, showing how historical changes shape future events. For historical institutionalists, the timing and sequencing of events matter, as do specific circumstances that may arise at "critical junctures"

institution A regularized or patterned activity that shapes the behaviour of individuals and groups, including formal organizations like the state or political parties as well as more informal institutions such as norms and values.

new institutionalism The name given to the turn to institutional theory in the past several decades in economics, political science, and sociology.

institutionalism An approach to theorizing in comparative politics and related fields that places emphasis on the power of institutions to shape the behaviour of individuals.

rational institutionalism An approach to theorizing in comparative politics and related fields that places emphasis on the power of institutions to shape the behaviour of individuals, one that often focuses on implications of institutions for individuals' strategic choices.

historical institutionalism An approach to theorizing that places emphasis on the power of institutions to shape the behaviour of individuals and how this operates over time.

path-dependent The name given to historical processes in which future developments are shaped or partially determined by events at previous stages in those processes.

in time when a country may take any number of different paths.[18] The reason historical trajectories are so important is that changes are **path-dependent**: The more a society goes down a certain path, the less and less likely it is to diverge from that path.

Historical institutionalists also tend to focus on how institutions produce collective actors and organize interests, in contrast to the individualist tendency of rational institutionalism. Institutionalists argue that development is shaped by the institutions in place, by how institutions are created, and by how they evolve over the long run.

Culture and Development

The approaches just discussed characterize institutional actors as the protagonists of development, yet there are other approaches to development that emphasize deeper features of a society itself—features that reflect commonly held customs, norms, habits, and values. That is to say, for many trying to understand development, culture matters. Many scholars are interested in *both* culture and institutions as predictors of development, and the links between these factors are not always clear.

Civil Society and Social Capital: Who Is Included and Who Is Excluded?

A society in which people can cooperate and work together is more likely to thrive than one filled with distrust and poor organization. Such a society is not easy to build and can take time, and some groups will tend to benefit more than others unless great care is taken to create a society that benefits everyone. French aristocrat and theorist Alexis de Tocqueville, in his classic *Democracy in America*, engaged in a comparative analysis of the many groups in the newly independent America, noting both positive and negative features. On the plus side, de Tocqueville attributed the success of America's white settlers (and their "Anglo-American union") to a variety of cultural characteristics (including inventiveness), reserving special mention for the degree to which the settlers constructed an active civic life, noting famously that "Americans of all ages, all stations of life, and all types of disposition are forever forming associations."[19]

On the negative side, however, it was clearly understood in de Tocqueville's era that the "Americans" were white colonists who were actively displacing Indigenous peoples and stealing their lands while also promoting the exploitation of enslaved Africans throughout the country. De Tocqueville lamented how the colonists exploited these two groups: "Both of them occupy an equally inferior position in the country they inhabit; both suffer from tyranny; and if their wrongs are not the same, they originate from the same authors [i.e., the white settlers]." He noted that settler success in colonizing the continent would come at a severe price: "I believe that the Indian nations of North America are doomed to perish, and that whenever the Europeans shall be established on the shores of the Pacific Ocean, that race of men will have ceased to exist."[20] Regarding the settlers' treatment of enslaved Africans, de Tocqueville wrote, "[the settler] makes them subservient to his use, and when he cannot subdue he destroys them. Oppression has, at one stroke, deprived the descendants of the Africans of almost all the privileges of humanity."[21]

In short, the American settler example shows how a culture can develop strong forms of social capital within its own group, but it can also develop systems that oppress others in order to make that system economically viable. To what extent was white American success dependent on the dispossession and exploitation of Indigenous peoples and enslaved Africans? Could America have succeeded without African labour and Indigenous lands and resources?

As you go through this book, we encourage you to ask questions about our cases and dig deeper:

1. In the political arrangements we describe and analyze, who is brought into the institutions of governance and who is excluded?
2. Are these inclusions and exclusions deliberate, or are they inadvertent?
3. Once these exclusions were made obvious, what was done to correct them? What sorts of policies have been pursued?
4. Have these policies made a difference? Are these societies more equal and more just than they were originally?
5. If not, what could be done to improve that society?

Civil society in the US continues to encounter major problems along racial and social lines. However, there are many positives too, such as a diverse, extremely wealthy, and vibrant economy. The same holds true for Canada, which is also a wealthy country with a strong and diverse economy. However, also like the US, Canada has problems of inequality, especially with regard to Indigenous peoples, many of whom remain at the margins of settler society yet in most cases do not have the economic and territorial capacity to fully exercise their rights to self-determination.

It is very difficult to imagine a modern economy without complex organizations, such as corporations or cooperatives, that either are relatively large or have rich linkages to many other organizations. Researchers find that civil society—the public space or zone of social life—links directly to economic outcomes. Societies with extensive social networks in political and economic life are said to have the virtue of high levels of **social capital**, advantages held by virtue of relationships. The key for a harmonious and vibrant civil society is to

social capital Advantage that individuals or groups hold by virtue of their social relationships.

Internal Colonization and Indigenous Underdevelopment

Internal colonization and underdevelopment can occur when a dominant settler government creates structures that undermine Indigenous peoples and prevent them from exercising self-determination over their own lives and territories. Without the return of lands taken during colonization, economic development is not viable for most Indigenous peoples. The late Arthur Manuel articulated a vision of how Indigenous self-determination might look.

> These land-bases need to be large enough to protect our languages, cultures, laws and economies. Canadians must accept that the existing 0.2 per cent model does not work. That fundamental increase must be made to accommodate Aboriginal and treaty rights to land. These larger land-bases will ultimately be part of Canada's economy. It will provide Indigenous Peoples with the right to make and influence economic development choices because of our increased governance over our larger land base.[22]

Much of this land could come from the larger lands beyond the reserves, lands that Indigenous treaty signatories supposedly "surrendered" to the Crown but that, according to treaty, could also be used for traditional activities, such as harvesting, fishing, hunting, and ceremonies. Legal scholar Shin Imai calls these "treaty lands." However, such rights have been unilaterally reduced by provincial governments, or the "provincial Crown," which have been given the power by the federal government to "take up" Indigenous lands for mining, logging, pipelines, and other extractive and industrial activity. Federal and provincial agreements with industries are often undertaken without the consent of First Nations.[23] Ideally, development must benefit Indigenous peoples as well as settlers, and those responsible should bear in mind the long-term costs of any action to the environment that we all share.

ensure that all groups and individuals have equal access to that society and that the institutions and norms in place are such that everyone can feel free to provide input and to benefit.

trust The extent to which an individual has confidence in the reliability or good conduct of others.

Social capital can build on itself and help to reinforce a society's development. It is said to work in several ways. First, density of network ties may generate **trust**, or confidence in the reliability or good conduct of others. This is because shared ties help people to build and maintain reputations, and in dense networks characterized by high transitivity (i.e., the people you know also know each other), people have a lot to lose from behaving in untrustworthy ways. It is also because in dense networks, information tends to flow rapidly, which has many economic benefits. The notion of "bonding capital" is based on density of ties and the idea that deepening these ties will benefit the economy. Another form of social capital is sometimes called "bridging capital," which is the set of benefits that come from networks extending out to reach new people and places.[24] Sometimes, these benefits are beneficial for the group, such as when trade between previously disconnected subgroups becomes possible. Sometimes benefits accrue mainly to the relatively small number of people who are themselves the "bridges" and who can act and profit as "brokers" (of information or contacts, for example). It is also important to understand that groups who are excluded, either deliberately or inadvertently, from these "bonding" and capital generation projects will not benefit from any positive developments.

Religion and Values

Some argue that religious differences between groups and between nations may also explain differences in economic development, while also positing that religion and values are closely tied together.[25] Theories of this kind gained prominence early in the 20th century and have remained part of the discourse about economic and social change ever since. In contemporary development studies, scholars have attempted to explain the relative success of different world regions on the basis of religious beliefs. Many arguments linking religion and development operate through *intervening* or *mediating* variables. That is, religious

INSIGHTS

The Colonial Origins of Comparative Development
by Daron Acemoglu, Simon Johnson, and James A. Robinson

This article traces differences in economic development around the world today to the varying historical paths of different world regions. Colonialism and geography played especially important roles, with the impacts playing out over more than a century. Colonizers such as Britain established different types of states in the different regions of the world. Where mass settlement was not possible (for reasons of geography and endemic disease), colonizers set up exploitative systems that worked primarily to extract resources with little investment. This happened in tropical Africa, for instance. Places that were easier to "settle," such as Canada, the United States, Australia, and New Zealand, ended up with stronger state structures. Over time, these institutions evolved into colonial dominions and later into independent states in the 18th, 19th, and 20th centuries. States that were originally designed to extract resources tend to continue that way today (with negative consequences), whereas countries actively settled by white colonizers tended to develop into systems more capable of promoting development. The historical development of the state as an institution (from decades or centuries ago) still casts a long shadow over development today.

Daron Acemoglu, Simon Johnson, and James A. Robinson, "The Colonial Origins of Comparative Development: An Empirical Investigation," *American Economic Review* 91 (2001): 1369–401.

beliefs affect certain behaviours or institutions that in turn affect economics, perhaps with several steps in between. This was one of the original lines of thinking pioneered by Max Weber, a founder of modern sociology and political science, in his book *The Protestant Ethic and the Spirit of Capitalism* ([1905] 1958). Later conservative theorists like Francis Fukuyama and Samuel Huntington described American-style individualism as a key to economic success, while others, such as Jeremy Rifkin in *The European Dream* (2004), argued instead that too much individualism could be corrosive for any society. Rather, the key to a stable and well-developed society was a focus on community, social connections, and respect for diversity and human rights.[26]

Religion, culture, and economics often travel together. Confucianism, with its traditional focus on hierarchy, harmony, and working together, is interpreted by many Asian scholars as a key ingredient in the economic rise of Japan, the Asian Tigers, the "Cubs," and China. This is the case whether the regime is democratic or authoritarian.[27] Zhang and Zhu's analysis of "Confucian capitalism" outlines what they call the "Three Guides," and they relate these guides to the growing success of the Chinese economy: "ruler guides subject, father guides son, and husband guides wife—and 'Five Constant Virtues'—benevolence (ren), righteousness (yi), rites (li), wisdom (zhi) and honesty (xin)." Their 2012 study includes interviews with Chinese CEOs, who describe how these Confucian virtues are central to their management styles and relationships with employees. They also argue that "Confucianism encouraged free trade," and they credit Confucian views of trade for influencing the much later work of Adam Smith.[28]

CASE IN CONTEXT

421

Gender in Post-Revolutionary Iranian Politics

Many people think of post-revolutionary Iran as a country where discrimination against women is widespread. Indeed, this is accurate. However, as is so often the case with this country, the reality is more complex than many know. Iranian society is one in which women—despite structural and institutional obstacles and inequalities—do find ways to assert their agency.

For more on these issues, see the case study in Part VI, p. 421. As you read it, keep in mind the following questions:

1. What conditions did women face in Iran before the revolution?
2. How has the revolution affected women's position in Iranian society?
3. How do some Iranian women resist coercion?

Associated Press/Ebrahim Noroozi

PHOTO 5.5 An Iranian woman prays at the grave of Ayatollah Ruhollah Khomeini at his shrine just outside of Tehran, Iran, in January 2019. Khomeini was the face of Iran's Islamic Revolution.

Prominent candidates for values that favour development are those that allow people to orient their behaviour toward the future rather than toward the present, to engage in long-term planning rather than the day-to-day. The virtue of thrift, or a propensity to save, can matter here because economically successful societies are those in which people can defer gratification from today into the future in the hope of using savings to invest and build more wealth. Work ethic is also important, which links back to religious values but also finds its roots elsewhere in a culture.

Systems and Structures: Domestic and International

Institutionalist approaches generally hold that development is determined largely by the actions and decisions of individuals as shaped by institutions and the incentives and constraints they create. Culturalist approaches generally see people's behaviour in the economy as shaped and constrained by beliefs, values, norms, and habits. In the case of statist and neoliberal approaches, the domestic forces that matter are the extent and nature of states and their involvement in the economy. But there are other approaches as well. Some scholars—most notably Marxists—have traced economic outcomes to fundamental underlying structures in an economy, such as the basic form of economic production and the system of social classes generated by these forms of production.

Domestic Economic Structures and Class Interests

Several schools of development scholarship emphasize the impediments and traps confronting societies as they attempt to promote development. In this view, certain powerful groups may block development by seeking to perpetuate their own advantages at the expense of the populace at large. Even where the institutions of democracy seem to be functioning well, interest groups or lobbies may demand special treatment from the government that prevents the reforms needed for economic growth. Scholars on both the right and the left of the political spectrum may adopt this view regarding the importance of domestic structures and vested interests. On the right, some scholars have argued that democracy itself can undermine capitalism because in democracies, special interests will often seek preferential treatment from the government.[29] The most important scholar on the left was the intellectual founder of one of the 20th century's most important ideologies: Karl Marx.

International Economic Structures and Class Interests

Karl Marx's ideas were made the official ideology in the Soviet Union (USSR), an empire that emerged after the Russian Revolution of 1917. Many early Marxists hoped for a "permanent revolution" around the world and diagnosed the global inequalities that capitalism had engendered. (Vladimir Lenin, leader of the Russian Revolution and the USSR's first head of state, led the charge with a book entitled *Imperialism: The Highest Stage of Capitalism.*)[30] Over time, however, many Marxist approaches in social science shifted from emphasizing prospects for global socialist revolution to offering critiques of how politics operates within capitalist economies.

According to Marxist arguments, the structure of the international economy will place some powerful countries in the favourable position of capitalist accumulation. Meanwhile, other countries and world regions are subjected to serving the role of providing low-cost labour and resources, though a small number of elites residing in the low-income countries may be complicit with the interests of the rich countries.

Many scholars adopted such perspectives to account for underdevelopment in the "global south," the "Third World," or the "lesser developed countries." In the views of many of these scholars, the international economy has involved both economic winners and economic losers. In order for some to be rich, others in the world must be poor. While the poorer countries may gain a degree of wealth as a result of trade with other countries, the wealthier countries will benefit far more.[31] One of the leading concepts has been **dependency**, which holds that low-income countries will remain in a subordinate economic position relative to wealthy countries, depending on markets in the rich world as a place to sell their low-value goods while importing high-value goods from those rich countries. In its earliest versions, dependency theory held that low-income countries faced deteriorating terms of trade relative to the capitalist countries at the centre of the world economy, which would make the goods from the dependent countries ever less valuable.[32] The theory was revised when it became clear that some developing countries experienced "partial" development, moving from the world's "periphery" to its "semi-periphery." [33] The revised version of dependency theory thus acknowledges that development is possible for low-income countries but that their circumstances necessitate the state's active involvement in the economy to promote industrialization.[34] The early version of dependency theory that argues that developing countries will always be disadvantaged has been discarded, but this revised version of the theory continues to inform the debate about development today through its discussion of the state's role.[35]

dependency A theory that argues that developing countries cannot simply embrace free trade because this will lead to ever-increasing wealth disparities between them and the advanced economies.

Geography

Another set of structural variables that may condition development is geography. The location that a country or region inhabits is largely unchangeable and may shape economic opportunities. One major geographic factor is whether a country has access to the sea; landlocked countries rely more on relations with their neighbours if they want to trade with the rest of the globe, and the distances to global markets and logistical challenges associated with being landlocked might hinder growth.[36] By a similar logic, development might be favoured in areas with good natural harbours or in countries that have oceans as barriers to would-be attackers. One might say, then, that the United Kingdom was relatively *favoured* by geography because as an island state it was hard to invade. More controversially, location in the tropics has long been posited as a hindrance to development, relying on sometime blatantly racist theories to account for the "backwardness" of non-European peoples.[37] Geography's impact on development may not be constant over time. In other words, geographic factors may prove advantageous or disadvantageous only when coupled with certain technologies or institutions.

INSIGHTS

The Modern World-System
by Immanuel Wallerstein

Wallerstein developed a theory of international politics in which each place on the globe would fit into a certain role in the global economy. Known as world systems theory, this approach broke the world into categories of states: core, periphery, and semi-periphery. The core countries constitute the economic and technological centre, accumulating the preponderance of profits from global production. The peripheral areas are those poor locations destined to supply basic inputs to the world capitalist system, mainly raw materials (including minerals and foodstuffs) and cheap labour. Semi-peripheral areas—roughly the "middle-income" countries—would have their own particular structural role as well, "allowed" or "encouraged" to industrialize to a certain degree in order to keep the global system functioning.

Immanuel Wallerstein, *The Modern World-System*, vol. 1: *Capitalist Agriculture and the Origins of the European World-Economy in the Sixteenth Century* (New York: Academic Press, 1974; rpt. Berkeley: University of California Press, 2011).

When the World Values Survey, a massive, ongoing project being carried out by an international network of social scientists, polled more than 80,000 people in more than 80 countries about the most important issues they face, the topic of economic growth and development stood out above all others.[38] A strong economy can lead to a better quality of life and greater satisfaction for most people, while a weak economy can severely restrict social improvements and make politics more divisive. Since people care so much about this issue, development is not exclusively an academic concern. It matters to policy-makers and everyday citizens as well. For instance, imagine you are the top economic official in a poor African country and you want to know how best to raise people out of poverty in your country. Comparing South Korea to Brazil, you may examine why **export-led growth** (an economic strategy based on selling natural resources or products in foreign markets) seemed to work in South Korea and import-substitution worked for a time in Brazil, and may ask under what conditions each can work.[39] Brazil, for example, is a geographically large and populous country, while South Korea is much smaller. Whether a policy-maker or a citizen, can you draw practical lessons for Canada from development successes and failures?

export-led growth A strategy for achieving economic growth dependent on sending natural resources or agricultural or industrial products for sale in foreign markets.

THINKING COMPARATIVELY

Explaining the Development of North and South Korea

KEY METHODOLOGICAL TOOL

Most-Similar-Systems (MSS) Design

As noted in the first chapter, one way to set up a useful comparison is to choose two cases that are very similar on several criteria yet different on a key outcome. The comparison of the two Koreas and their differences in economic development is an example. Choosing two countries that have much in common allows the analyst to isolate the variables that are likely to cause the different outcomes. In this case, geography and many aspects of culture are similar, which means these variables are unlikely to explain the major differences in outcomes. Comparative political scientists do not have laboratories to work in the way natural scientists do, so "most similar" cases are as close as one can get to controlling for many variables the way one does in a laboratory. In fact, some MSS designs come from what is called a "natural experiment" such as when a country is divided into smaller parts and analysts can observe the subsequent outcomes across the different parts of the country. Examples include comparisons of East and West Germany after the country was divided after 1945 or comparisons of India and Pakistan after the partition of British India in 1947. Another pair of countries with similarities is the Dominican Republic and Haiti, which are located on two halves of the same island. Of course, in each of these instances, the two cases will have developed quite differently over time. Setting up MSS design is not enough to definitively demonstrate which variables cause an outcome because that requires exploring the evidence, but it can help to rule out unlikely causes of variations in outcomes.

At the beginning of this chapter, we noted that the neighbouring countries of North and South Korea have had radically different experiences with development. South Korea went from being one of the poorest countries on earth in the late 1950s to one of the richest by the 1990s. It has seen its incomes skyrocket and its economy transform into an industrial powerhouse, while the population has gone from having a majority illiterate and in poverty to one in which less than five per cent of people fit in those categories. North Korea started in roughly the same position as the south yet remains extremely poor. It experiences periodic famines and frequently depends on foreign aid that its leadership extorts through creating international crises. As shown in the following table, if we use the 2013 estimates, South Korea's per capita GDP is almost 34 times North Korea's.[40] Explaining such differences over time between economically successful and unsuccessful countries is one of the classic questions in development studies. In fact, a major book in this area (*Why Nations Fail*, by Daron Acemoglu and James A. Robinson) addresses this precise divergence between the Koreas and others like it.

Country	**Per capita GDP (CIA, *The World Factbook*)**
North Korea	$1700 (estimate as of 2015)
South Korea	$39,500 (estimate as of 2017)

Here we walk through how a comparative analyst might try to explain this difference. We would note right away that we don't aim to offer a definitive "answer" to this question that focuses on one theory over another, though some might argue that this is a relatively straightforward comparison with an obvious answer, as we note a bit later. We want to emphasize that we use simple thought experiments here for the sake of simplicity; these are not full hypothesis tests using substantial amounts of evidence. As you read this section, focus on the *logic* of hypothesis-testing and the general strategy we use to apply theories to these real-world cases. Note that for more definitive results, we would need to consider much more evidence and carefully measure each of the variables we consider.

One reason this is an interesting comparison is that North and South Korea are very similar in terms of several variables we might expect to affect development, including culture and geography, but these countries vary dramatically in terms of the dependent variable (development). Table 5.2 summarizes some similarities and differences between the two cases, noting how much or how little variation there is on the key variables.

South Korea's political and economic institutions are based much more than North Korea's on capitalism and the use of domestic and global markets, as well as democracy in more recent decades. (In fact, for Acemoglu and Robinson, the comparison of the Koreas is a prime example of the importance of political institutions in shaping economic outcomes. You might see this as the "leading candidate" theory to explain the divergence, though we would emphasize the logic of considering different theoretical perspectives). In terms of external influences, the country followed a model established by Japan, in two ways. First, Korea was a Japanese colony before World War II and was subject to very harsh treatment. At the same time, Japanese colonialism brought economic linkages to Japan and a powerful state, along with an emphasis on educating the workforce.[41] Second, Japan's economic success served as a model in terms of policy. South Korea's state adopted a pro-business strategy that included some state intervention, but with strict

TABLE 5.2 | Possible Explanations for Variations in Development

SOUTH KOREA AND NORTH KOREA

Variable	Case 1: South Korea	Case 2: North Korea	Extent of Variation
Independent Variables for Hypothesis Testing			
Culture	Korean heritage (with minority Christian population)	Korean heritage (with tiny Christian population)	Limited
Geography	Korean peninsula Coal and mining resources	Korean peninsula Coal and mining resources	Limited
Economic and Political Institutions	Mixed state/market economy Capitalist orientation influenced by Japan, United States Export-led growth for decades Use of markets Democracy (in recent years)	Command economy Communist rule influenced by China, USSR Inward-looking economy Almost no use of markets Autocracy for decades	Major
Dependent Variable			
Development	High development and growth Advanced economy	Low development and growth Poor economy, major poverty	Major

rules: Companies receiving state support had to meet targets for production and exports or they would be cut off.[42] Thus, the South Korean case was interpreted by some as a constructive form of state intervention and by others as a country where the state did right by "emulating" the rules of the market.

Even the East Asian financial crisis of the late 1990s and the global economic crisis that began in 2008 did little to dent South Korea's long-term achievements. In fact, South Korea has served as a model for other Asian economies, much as Japan had served as a model for South Korea during the 1960s and 1970s.[43] Indeed, several features of China's current economic approach appear to have drawn from South Korea's experience in promoting export-led growth. This has had interesting implications for the different theories mentioned previously: The focus here is on political and economic institutions, but there is also renewed interest in cultural theories of development because development has spread so convincingly across East Asian countries in particular.

North Korea differs quite dramatically from South Korea in its political and economic institutions, while it shares a similar geography and a common cultural background from the period before Korea was divided. The country was pulled into the Soviet orbit after the end of World War II, while South Korea was aligned with the United States. Eventually, a major conflict broke out, the Korean War, in which the North was supported by China under Mao Zedong and South Korea was supported by the United States (with numerous American troops) and its allies. Eventually, the conflict was halted without satisfactory resolution for either side, and as a result we are left with the two countries, each of which claims to be the legitimate government of all of Korea. North Korea still employs a Soviet-style "planned economy." This means that all key decisions about production and funding are made by the state, and to the extent that market forces govern exchange, they do so only informally.

How would each of our theories explain the relative economic fortunes of North and South Korea in recent decades? (See Table 5.3.) Notice that the institutional arguments are promising for the reasons noted previously. At the same time, while we note that the cultural arguments might not work at first glance, that does not mean "culture" is irrelevant. A scholar doing a deeper exploration of the two countries might find ways to show that political

TABLE 5.3 | Hypothesis Testing: North Korea and South Korea

Theory	Hypothesis: What Explains Variation?	Thought Experiment and Hypothesis Test	Next Steps for Theory
Institutions (market institutions)	Different enforcement of property rights and contracts South: Strong enforcement North: Weak enforcement	Promising	Bring in additional cases, and examine these cases further. Consider how to account for South Korea's practice of state-led development.
Institutions (states and state policy)	Different qualities of state and state policy South: High quality (with robust industrial policy) North: Low quality	Promising	Account for why North Korea has failed with statist strategy. Examine South Korea's mix of state involvement and market forces in state-led development.
Culture	Different cultural backgrounds, including values, religion, and habits	Not promising (despite some differences, countries have similar cultural backgrounds).	Adapt hypothesis to include values and habits along with other variables. Develop more complex hypothesis on how institutions change national economic cultures over time, for example.
The World System	Different positions in "world system" South Korea: American and Japanese influence North Korea: Soviet and Chinese influence	Somewhat promising but incomplete (positioning in the global system likely mattered by influencing institutions).	Adapt hypothesis to include world system along with other variables. Develop more complex hypothesis that also draws on institutional theories, for example.

cultures changed over time between the two countries in ways that affected the economy as well. In short, both countries may be culturally "Korean," but that does not mean they are identical on that variable: The North Korean political culture is certainly different from the South Korean political culture after decades of separation and such different experiences.

As you can see here, our thought experiment does not definitively establish that one of these theories is right, but it demonstrates how we would initially proceed in applying these general theories of development to the basic outlines of these two cases. This helps us to think about what types of arguments might work and which might not in explaining variations in outcomes by country.

Chapter Summary

Concepts

- Development is a topic of pressing interest to billions of people around the world, and it can be measured in many different ways.
- The most common ways of measuring development are economic, most notably the level and growth of per capita GDP but also the extent of poverty and economic inequality.

Types

- Development can be measured by social indicators (such as health and education), standard of living, satisfaction and happiness, equity across societal groups, cultural change, and environmental sustainability.
- Cases from around the world show that many of the indicators of development positively correlate with one another but not always.

Causes and Effects

- Using economic growth as an outcome, scholars have theorized about many important factors that lead to development. An important debate is about whether the economy should be led by the market or by the state. The current consensus is that both market and state play important roles in a modern economy.
- Culture shapes development as well. It may be manifested in levels of trust and social capital or in norms, ethics, and cultural tendencies that emerge in different places at different points in time.
- Colonization can result in the underdevelopment of some peoples, such as Indigenous peoples who, without a viable land base, may find it difficult to self-determine their own futures.
- A final category of explanations for development can be found in "structural" or "systemic" factors whereby the backdrop of the world economic and political order can either support or hinder economic advancement.

Thinking It Through

1. The "Causes and Effects" section of this chapter focused on growth, but can you use at least one theory from that section to propose why some developing countries have more or less inequality (as defined in Chapter 4) than others?
2. The so-called "BRIC" countries—**B**razil, **R**ussia, **I**ndia, and **C**hina—all boomed at points in the 2000s. Does this correlation suggest they are all following similar development patterns? Does this timing provide evidence to support one theory about the causes of development more than others? Does it mean something "global" was causing growth and not something specific to each country? Why have some stopped booming while in other cases growth continues?
3. Many countries have more and less successful economic periods over time. Which of the theories in this chapter

does this fluctuation support? Does it "disprove" any theory based on culture because a country's culture is relatively "stable"? Does it "prove" that development depends on things that change over time, like a government's policies?

4. Many prominent developing countries are (or have been) major exporters of oil. Why have the resource-rich countries not benefitted from consistent, rapid growth? To what extent are natural resources beneficial for development, and to what extent are they a "curse"?
5. Why do countries go through economic boom and bust cycles in their development? If countries are "most similar" (see Chapter 2) to themselves, should economic performance be relatively consistent over time unless there are major changes in policy (as was the case in China)?

6 Democracy and Democratization

In This Chapter

Roch Marc Kaboré (pictured here at the African Union summit in 2019) became president of Burkina Faso in the country's first free elections in 2015. (ISSOUF SANOGO/AFP/Getty Images)

Imagine a country where less than half of the population can vote, half have very limited basic rights, and social roles are allocated on the basis of ethnic or racial affiliation so that members of some groups have virtually *no* rights and are the property of other people. Imagine still further that elections are periodically held but that to stand any chance of election one must be from the elite class, meaning (1) a wealthy landowner; (2) a wealthy businessman; or (3) a doctor, lawyer, clergyman, or other professional whose social networks intersect with those of wealthy landowners or businessmen. If we told you that this situation were true of a given developing country, would you consider it fully democratic? Probably not, and yet the country we are describing is the United States of America in the years after its founding.

Ironically, the US was, at the time, one of the most democratic large-scale societies the world had ever known. Deciding whether a given country is democratic is more complicated than it appears at first glance. Democracy changes over time, meaning that its benchmarks and criteria are moving targets. Moreover, the line between more and less democratic regimes is somewhat grey.

Democracy is, for much of the Western world, part of the backdrop of politics: It is simply assumed to be present (yet, as the preceding example demonstrates, this has not always been the case, and there are democratic deficits in all countries, including the US and Canada). Ideally, where regimes are democratic, individuals and groups can freely contest their ideas and try to shape political life, with the winners of fair elections having greater opportunity to craft their preferred policies and laws through the democratic process. The losers typically accept the principle that in a democracy it is possible one will lose a political battle, a debate, or an election; they continue to support the system or the *regime*, even if they oppose the particular government administration of the moment.

In much of the world, however, authoritarianism is normalized, and the very existence of democracy itself is a fundamental political issue. Only in recent decades has the world reached the point where more than half of its people live under democracy. Understanding whether a country is democratic is thus a prerequisite for further discussions about politics, whether we are interested in legislatures and executives, or the power of interest groups and political parties, or religious politics and gender politics. While the precise definition of democracy is debated—and many will disagree on which countries are democratic—most political scientists will concur that prominent countries, such as China, Iran, Saudi Arabia, and North Korea, are not democracies and that many more countries, such as Russia, fall far short of full democratic practice, even if elections are held on schedule. We discuss authoritarian regimes in the next chapter.

In this chapter, we begin by addressing the concepts of two major categories of regime type: democracy (or democratic regime) and democratization, the process through which authoritarian polities become (more) democratic. We then discuss subtypes of democratic regimes, using a number of our case studies to exemplify them. Finally, we turn to political science debates about the causes of democratization and democratic consolidation. Why do they happen where they do, in some places and not others? And why do they happen when they do, at some times and not others? We present several possible explanations. We close with a critical examination of whether Canada should be treated by political scientists as a model for democracy elsewhere.

• • •

Concepts

democracy A form of regime associated with "rule by the people" that signifies rights and liberties for citizens, including political rights to participate in elections and civil liberties such as freedom of speech.

Democracy is one of the most fundamental concepts in politics, and given its importance, scholars have contested and reworked the concept and causes of democracy over the years.[1] As with many constructive debates in political science, contestation over the definition is an important part of the study of democracy.

Democracy and Democratic Regimes

political rights Rights of individuals to participate in political life, including the right to political speech, the right to vote, and the right to join political associations.

civil rights Rights of individuals to participate in civic life, including freedoms of assembly and speech, access to information, and equal access to institutions, among others.

Despite disagreement over exactly what democracy means, there is broad agreement on two salient points. First, many political scientists would share an intuitive sense of which geographic units in the world are relatively more or less democratic. Second, even in the midst of some disagreement, political scientists commonly accept definitions of democracy that emphasize two main types of rights, which we discuss further a bit later in the chapter: **political rights** to participate in electoral processes and **civil rights** and related freedoms. The non-governmental organization Freedom House, which monitors democracy in countries around the world, explicitly builds both elements into its assessment (Map 6.1). Leading works in recent years emphasize the distinction between mere electoral democracy and a more genuine democracy that also includes civil rights protections. To define democracy, most scholars use what is called a procedural, or minimal, definition. This approach

MAP 6.1 Democracy in the World, 2018

Source: Courtesy FreedomHouse.org

emphasizes the minimal standards that a country should have in place—procedures or rules that govern political life—as contrasted with a variety of *substantive* issues noted later.[2]

Freedom House rates countries as either free or unfree (see Map 6.1). Is this binary useful in comparative analysis? Would a sliding scale be better? How many categories would you use to define states along a scale from fully democratic to fully authoritarian? The Economist Intelligence Unit, based in the United Kingdom, instead uses a four-category system, starting with full democracies, then flawed democracies, hybrid regimes, and authoritarian regimes.

Procedural (Minimal) Definitions of Democracy

procedural definition of democracy A conception of democracy, contrasted with a substantive definition, that emphasizes the minimal standards, procedures, or rules that a country should have in place to govern political life.

Procedural definitions of democracy claim that what makes a country democratic is that it follows certain procedures, or rules and methods. Yet most leading procedural definitions of democracy view it as more than just elections every few years; they also include the civil rights and civil liberties that should be guaranteed to every citizen on an ongoing basis. Thus, even when political scientists speak of minimal, or procedural, definitions of what democracy is, they mean more than elections. Consider the following lists of political rights and civil liberties, which many political scientists agree are central to democracy[3]:

Political Rights:
- Elections are free and fair, and most adults can vote.
- Elections are regularly scheduled or held periodically.
- Elections have multiple political parties, or some choice.
- Elections are open to most adults to run for office.

Civil Liberties:
- Freedom of speech and expression
- Freedom to access sources of information/freedom of the press
- Freedom of assembly/to join interest groups and parties

Note that all of these are essentially measures of whether certain rules or procedures are followed. Also, note that the first four may be seen as directly related to electoral processes and they presume that peaceful transfers of power do take place in accord with electoral decisions. The latter three are about political action outside of the realm of electoral processes and centre on the rights of the public not to be harassed by the state. Important civil liberties can be found in the US Constitution's first 10 amendments. Passed together in 1791, this Bill of Rights set an international standard for civil liberties.

To illustrate the importance of both categories of freedoms, consider a thought experiment in which a country has regular free and fair elections but allows no protest, controls the press, and represses free speech. This would be less a true democracy and more a competitive authoritarian or electoral authoritarian regime.[4] Conversely, a system in which people have relative freedoms to voice their grievances but no right to elect their government officials would also be non-democratic. Only by fulfilling the basic requirements on both counts will a country earn a reputation for democracy.

Other criteria could conceivably be added. For instance, some leading scholars have proposed adding the following two additional criteria in determining whether a country is democratic:[5]

- Democracies are not overruled by an outside power (such as a colonizer).
- Democracies must maintain a clear distinction between civilian and military rule.

These two additional features further clarify the requirements for a democracy, ruling out the likes of countries that look like democracies internally but that systematically overrule the will of the populace. These countries may include locations such as the so-called "independent" homelands under South Africa's *Apartheid* government before 1994.

Substantive Definitions of Democracy

While procedural definitions long dominated the debates about democracy, recent years have seen an increasing turn to more **substantive definitions of democracy**. This range of definitions examines the notion of democratic depth and quality, suggesting that democracy is not just about certain rule-governed procedures being followed but rather about certain outcomes, in particular the coordination of a certain kind of collective action. Proponents of a substantive definition often argue that countries can always undergo further democratization and that the question of democracy is not restricted to whether countries meet a minimum threshold.

substantive definition of democracy A conception of democracy, contrasted with a procedural definition, that views a polity's democratic status as dependent on the satisfaction of certain substantive ends, such as the extension of broad rights or the reduction of income inequality.

Elements of a substantive definition may include the following:

- Participation, social inclusion, and civil society involvement
- Equity/equality by gender, race, ethnicity, indigeneity, or other
- Accountability (including lack of corruption) and institutional performance
- Public knowledge and awareness
- Poverty, inequality, and other economic outcomes

Obviously, these criteria rarely lend themselves to yes/no evaluations. Even the more established democracies can always make progress toward greater democratic depth or quality. In the United States, for instance, the percentage of citizens who vote in Congressional elections ranges from about 40 per cent in years without a presidential election to about 60 per cent in years when a presidential election is held. This contrasts with much higher voter turnout in most of Europe, leading some to suggest that the United States falls short on certain substantive aspects of democracy. Canada also compares favourably with the US, with 66.1 per cent voter turnout in the 2015 federal election.[6]

Questions of substantive democracy lend themselves to some of the most intriguing research questions in comparative politics. In fact, as the number of democracies in the world has risen in the democratic wave since 1989,[7] questions of substantive democracy have taken an increasingly important position in comparative politics relative to procedural democracy. Certainly, studying procedural democracy and studying substantive democracy are not mutually exclusive, since reaching the procedural/minimal threshold may be related to improvements in a country's substantive elements. For students interested in researching democracy, either or both of these definitions may be useful, but it is important to distinguish between them.

regime change Any major change of regime type, including democratization, democratic breakdown, or certain types of authoritarian persistence in which one type of authoritarian regime gives way to another.

Regime Change and Democratization

The history of democracy and authoritarianism is one of change from one **regime type** to another. **Democratization** is the process that leads from authoritarianism to democracy, while changes in the opposite direction are commonly called **democratic breakdown** (and not "authoritarianization").[8] We discuss the latter in the next chapter.

regime type The form of a political regime, such as democratic versus authoritarian, as well as subtypes, such as personalistic dictatorships or totalitarian regimes.

democratization The process of a regime becoming more democratic, including both democratic transition and democratic consolidation.

democratic breakdown The process through which a democratic regime partially or completely loses its democratic status.

Democratization may be seen as a process that a country completes once it transitions from authoritarianism to a basic minimum democratic threshold, or it may be a more indefinite, ongoing process that continues to consolidate even after a country has reached a basic level of political and civil freedoms. Democratization itself can thus be a rich and diverse area for study. Three additional concepts that are central in the literature on democratization highlight the different stages of the process: transition and consolidation.

CLAUDIO REYES/AFP/Getty Images

PHOTO 6.2 Chilean presidents Michelle Bachelet and Sebastián Piñera in 2017. Some view the peaceful and democratic alternation in power of these two ideologically very different leaders as a sign of the consolidation of Chilean democracy.

transition The movement from an authoritarian regime to a democratic one.

Transition is the movement from an authoritarian regime to a democratic one. This can happen through revolutionary means. For example, the Arab Spring uprisings of 2011 *might have* led to successful democratization, and some of the countries involved clearly took steps in this direction, but in some respects this democratization seems to have stalled in a number of the affected countries. Transition can also happen through more gradual and negotiated means, such as the transition from the Augusto Pinochet dictatorship to Chilean democracy in 1990.

consolidation The process through which a new democratic order becomes institutionalized and therefore more likely to endure.

Consolidation refers to the process through which the new democratic order becomes institutionalized and therefore becomes more likely to endure. For example, in the Chilean case, many thought the election and peaceful transfer of power from the very popular, left-leaning president Michelle Bachelet to the right-leaning Sebastián Piñera in 2010 and back again to Bachelet in 2014, then to Piñera in 2017 was a sign of just how successfully consolidated Chilean democracy was after only two decades.

Regression, by contrast, refers to the opposite trend of a country moving away from democratization. This could mean a country that was on the path to democratization moving more into the authoritarian category (such as Turkey) or a consolidated democracy becoming less democratically accountable, such as we have seen in the United States according to the 2018 Economist Intelligence Unit's "Democracy Index."[9]

Types

As noted earlier, not only are there varying ways to define both democracy and authoritarianism (as we shall see further in the next chapter), but democratic and authoritarian regimes come in a variety of forms, with major implications for life in political society. Here we discuss representative versus direct forms of democracy before moving on to consider major forms or elements of transition to democracy.

Types of Democracy

Democracies—and ideas about democracy—come in multiple forms, with one of the most important contrasts being that between less direct (or representative) democracy and direct democracy. The heart of the difference lies in the degree and form of *mediation* between voters and the state.

Representative Democracy

Much of what we consider democracy is actually a representative form of government that is either a **constitutional republic** or a **constitutional monarchy**. Democracy, in the original sense of the term, signified direct rule by the people through mass assemblies or legislation by direct vote of the masses. Because of their sheer size, modern nation-states do not typically govern on this basis, but democracies instead rely on elected representatives who vote for legislation on behalf of the populace as a whole. This form of government has come to be called **representative democracy** when it meets several criteria that show government is based on the people.

constitutional republic A polity without a monarch in which the basic rules of politics are laid out in a constitution.

constitutional monarchy A political system in which a monarch such as a king, queen, or emperor plays a role as a head of state but has powers limited by a constitution and/or a legislature.

representative democracy A conception of democracy in which politicians and institutions are understood to represent the electorate, who nevertheless can constrain their behaviour through periodic elections and other forms of participation.

Foremost among the criteria for being considered a representative democracy is constitutionality, which guarantees rights to citizens. Constitutional rights limit the powers of government and also limit the power of the political majority so that those who lose an election need not fear that their rights will be "alienated" by the "tyranny of the majority." The United States is a constitutional republic, while Canada is a constitutional monarchy in which our monarch (represented by Governor General Julie Payette) is little more than a national figurehead and elected officials do the business of governing. Both can be considered representative democracies. We will refer to representative democracies to identify these modern nation-states where citizens elect representatives democratically and are guaranteed constitutional rights. These regimes are thus characterized by the citizenry having two broad categories of rights, both of which are necessary for a country to merit being called a democracy: political or electoral rights and civil rights or civil liberties.

Political rights relate directly to electoral processes and include what is often considered the most fundamental of all democratic rights: the freedom to vote in free and fair elections. Also understood in the definition of political rights are various features that underpin and extend this simple consideration of electoral freedom. All citizens who have reached the age of majority (such as 18 years) should have the right to vote; the franchise should not be restricted to one sex, one race, one ethnicity, or one religion. Elections should be held with some reasonable frequency (and not, say, every 50 years). Citizens should also have the right to present themselves as candidates for office and should be allowed to join different political parties in their running for office; they should not be required to join an official single party. Democracies may differ on many criteria, but we would argue that all that are worthy of the name **multiparty democracies** should fulfill the preceding.

multiparty democracy A democracy in which at least two parties compete for power.

Civil rights or civil liberties are those that guarantee citizens the ability to participate in civic life *outside* of elections. They are coequal with political rights in determining whether a country is democratic. Some of the key civil rights are usefully summarized in the second section of the Canadian Charter of Rights and Freedoms (1982), entitled Fundamental Freedoms: "Everyone has the following fundamental freedoms: (a) freedom of conscience and religion; (b) freedom of thought, belief, opinion and expression, including freedom of the press and other media of communication; (c) freedom of peaceful assembly; and

Sean Kilpatrick/THE CANADIAN PRESS

PHOTO 6.3 Canada's 29th Governor General Julie Payette approaches the steps of Parliament with Prime Minister Justin Trudeau to attend her installation ceremony in Ottawa in October 2017.

(d) freedom of association." All elements here suggest the freedom of an individual's conscience with respect to his/her own beliefs.

Of course, democracies differ in both political rights and civil liberties, and these rights are rarely absolutes. To take the case of the civil liberties surrounding free opinion and expression, the oft-cited example is that "freedom of speech does not give you the right to yell 'fire' in a crowded theatre." More formally, we may consider that freedom of expression may be bounded by the need to protect others' freedoms as well. Hence, even democracies that stand firmly on the principle of free expression will wrestle with questions of what sorts of speech may be illegal, including libel and slander and hate speech or provocations to violence.

Similarly, other civil liberties have reasonable limits that are shaped by interpretation of constitutions and the law. For instance, a democratic free press may not be allowed to report secrets that could compromise national security, and freedom of religion may not extend to allowing murderous cults to engage in human sacrifice. In the United States, the right to bear arms, found in the Constitution's Second Amendment, has been interpreted in various ways, including giving individuals the right to possess a range of firearms. The actual wording of the amendment is important: "A well-regulated Militia, being necessary to the security of a free State, the right of the people to keep and bear Arms, shall not be infringed." We might see this more as the right of Americans to organize into militia groups rather than the right to individually stockpile unlimited numbers and types of weapons.

Political rights are also shaped differently in different countries, and variations reflect the number of possible ways of crafting democratic institutions. Elections may come at fixed intervals (maybe every three years as in New Zealand or four as in the US) or on a slightly more flexible schedule, as in Canada. While the Canada Elections Act provides a fixed date for federal elections, the prime minister can request that the governor general issue the writs of election earlier. Exercising the vote may be mandatory (as in Australia) or optional (as in Canada). Elected officials may switch parties freely when in office, or they may be required to resign their seat if they change parties.

Some arrangements are touted as democratic but seem to call the process into question. For instance, many systems with (sometimes highly) questionable democratic credentials have made the case that all political discourse can be contained within one single unifying national party, such as China's Communist Party.[10] While this clearly violates the principle of multiparty democracy, it nonetheless seems clear that some single-party countries are more democratic than others. An example that shows the complexity of the debate is the African nation of Uganda from the 1980s to 2005, which maintained a "Movement system" under Yoweri Museveni. There, a generally popular president maintained that the best system for governance in Africa was "no-party democracy" because in too many African countries political parties tended to reflect and reinforce volatile ethnic divisions. Without any political parties, the state itself (and its president) may wield control that looks rather anti-democratic. After a referendum in 2005, Uganda returned to a multiparty system.

In short, representative democracies include a range of debates about the specific nature and extent of civil liberties, and there are numerous ways to set up the political institutions of such systems. As is often said, not all democracies follow the American model, or the British model, or any other. They do, however, share in common the basic features discussed in this section.

Associated Press/Ben Curtis, File

PHOTO 6.4 Uganda's long-time President Yoweri Museveni waves to supporters from the sunroof of his vehicle as he arrives for an election rally at Kololo Airstrip in Kampala, Uganda, in 2016. Museveni is one of Africa's longest-serving presidents.

Direct Democracy

The challenges of understanding democracy do not end with reaching the democratic threshold. As noted previously, many of the world's most powerful democracies today continue to deal with the challenges of deepening democratization. Among the controversial issues in these polities are some options that may be seen as taking democracy closer to the people yet sidestepping elected representatives. **Referenda** (or plebiscites)—in which specific issues are put to popular vote—are prominent here. They feature in individual countries in the European Union, as well as in American states, most notably California, where citizens can place initiatives and propositions on the statewide ballot and recall elected officials. This has some positive features but can also allow extremely rich individuals or well-organized groups to dominate a particular agenda issue.

referendum A popular vote on a specific issue.

The increasing use of referenda, plebiscites, or ballot initiatives may be considered an increasing use of **direct democracy**. (At least the votes themselves are direct democracy, though there are questions and debates about which items should be placed before the people in these forms and who should place them there.) While democracies may be increasingly using direct democratic initiatives, they are not a necessary feature of representative democracy.

direct democracy A conception of democracy that places great emphasis on direct citizen involvement in politics, especially involving plebiscites and/or citizen assemblies.

Direct democracy can also take the form of citizen assemblies, community councils, and similar forms of association. Often, proponents of direct democracy also favour representative democratic institutions, seeing them as complementary. Some people, though, see direct or "participatory" democracy as an alternative to representative forms. Many traditional Indigenous forms of government operated through consensus politics, active deliberation, and debate, which had some similarities with Western systems.

Types of Democratization

In this section, we discuss two different aspects or stages in the process of democratization. You can think of them as types of democratization but only in a certain sense. A fully successful case of democratization will involve *both* **democratic transition** and then the consolidation of the emergent democracy.

democratic transition The process through which a non-democratic regime becomes democratic.

Democratic Transitions

Democratic transitions are changes from one regime type (authoritarianism) to another (democratic rule). In some countries, these transitions may be relatively rapid processes, taking only several days. By contrast, some countries go through long, slow transitions from authoritarian rule to democracy. Brazil in the 1980s and Mexico in the 1990s are examples of slower-motion transitions in which it became increasingly clear over time that the authoritarian system was being replaced by a democratic regime.

Transitions are also diverse in their causes and impacts. Some are relatively controlled by authoritarian leaders who are on their way out of power, while others come from the collapse of the previous power structure. In Latin America in the 1980s, many countries (such as Brazil and Chile) had slow transitions to democracy in which the military built in advantages for itself to ensure that its policies and preferences would influence democratic politics for some time. Other democratic transitions have happened in more revolutionary fashion in countries ranging from the Philippines to the West African nation of Benin.

Democratic Consolidation

democratic consolidation The process through which, after a transition from authoritarianism, a polity strengthens its democracy.

Democratic consolidation is typically a longer-term process than transition.[11] It may be seen as the process by which democracy and its political and civil rights become normal or habitual for citizens. The term "consolidation" has been characterized as happening when democracy is "the only game in town."[12] That is, a democracy may be seen as consolidated when there are no major political groups advocating for a return to authoritarianism or for the overthrow of the democratic system. Related to this, consolidation may have happened when the populace as a whole has rejected the idea of authoritarianism and supports the democratic regime. Compared with these ideas or values, a more mechanical indicator of consolidation may be when a country has "turned over" its government two or more times; that is, the people who used to govern lose an election and step aside, and then the people who replaced them eventually lose and step aside. When and where this happens, it is a good sign that democracy is accepted by all the major political actors and has become routine.

Consolidation is challenging even in leading democracies. Many countries that have made the transition to free and fair elections and civil liberties face difficulties in guaranteeing them for the citizenry. Even the world's longest-standing democracies, such as the United States, have not fulfilled all of the promises often associated with democracy. Consolidation is a long-term endeavour because delivering full democratic rights to all citizens (and indeed developing a full notion of who is a citizen) is a historically complex process and regression is always possible.

Causes and Effects: What Causes Democratization?

Uncovering what causes and sustains democracy is a central challenge facing political scientists. Here, we combine the debates about democracy and democratization to ask why democracy varies both across countries and over time. In other words, we consider both *where* democracy happens and *when* it occurs. Note that both of these considerations get at the underlying question of *why* regime types emerge, consolidate, and shift. While we cannot capture the entire debate, we highlight five prominent lines of theory:

1. *modernization theory*, which traces democracy to broad social changes, especially economic development and the changes that accompany it;[13]
2. *cultural theories*, which attribute democratization and democratic consolidation to cultural variables that predispose some countries to democracy and prevent or hinder democracy in other places;[14]
3. *systemic or structural theories*, which situate countries in an international environment where major powers or global trends may condition whether democracy emerges or not;[15]
4. *domestic institutional theories*, which posit that the advent and success of democracy depend on the forms of political institutions within a country (such as political parties and interest groups or the ways branches of government are shaped);[16] and
5. *agency-based theories*, which argue that individual actors, or small groups of actors, are the drivers of changes in regime types (whether democratic or authoritarian).[17]

We will consider these five perspectives in the sections below.

As we noted in the previous chapters, different theoretical perspectives are not entirely mutually exclusive, but they do offer different arguments about political behaviour and what causes it. While good arguments may draw from multiple perspectives, it is important that comparative political scientists understand both what they are arguing for and how they might be arguing *against* some other perspective. Fundamentally, arguments are based on efforts to test specific hypotheses—derived from theories—against empirical evidence.

CASE IN CONTEXT 372

What Is the Future of Reconciliation between Indigenous Peoples and the Canadian Settler State?

One of the most important questions as Canada advances a reconciliation agenda with Indigenous peoples is what form Indigenous governments will take in future years. Many traditional governments were forcibly disbanded, while spiritual practices were outlawed and children were sent away to residential schools. For many Indigenous leaders, a key issue is the return of lands taken by the federal and provincial governments, which currently control more than 90 per cent of Canada's land mass. Indigenous reserves constitute a mere 0.2 per cent of the total lands, which is insufficient for Indigenous nations to exercise their rights to self-determination.

For more on settler colonialism in Canada, see the case study in Part VI, p. 372. As you read it, keep in mind the following questions:

1. How does land reform factor into Indigenous goals of self-determination?
2. How might Canada be different if Indigenous peoples with status had been able to vote in federal elections from the 19th century instead of from 1960?
3. How have the legacies of the Indian Residential Schools affected First Nations communities?

Modernization

modernization theory A theory that traces democracy to broad social changes, especially economic development and the changes that accompany it.

Perhaps the most central debate in modern comparative study of democracy centres on elements of **modernization theory**. Advocates of a modernization approach examine the relationship between economic development and democratization. An extensive literature finds changes in economic structure to be a key to democratic change; in these analyses, economics drives much of politics. Modernization scholars argue that economic change drove democratization through the emergence of such factors as a middle class (or *bourgeoisie*) and a literate population. Urbanization over decades and centuries was key in turning former lords and peasants into small business people who demanded greater political say. More recently, the link between modernization and democratization finds new support (with modifications and revisions) for the idea that democracies become more stable and secure when they are relatively wealthy.

Conversely, poor countries that lack the stabilizing force of a robust middle class may tend toward authoritarianism. Societies divided between a small, wealthy elite and impoverished masses will be prone to non-inclusive politics.

Modernization theory includes a variety of different approaches. According to some versions, the economic and social forces of modernization that shape democracy do not only occur at one point that triggers a democratic transition. Rather, economic development may also support the persistence of democracy once democracy is established.

Modernization theory faces the challenge that there are exceptions it has trouble explaining. For example, India is the world's largest democracy, and it remains quite poor. Moreover, it democratized well before its recent years of economic growth. Can modernization theory explain India's democratic success? And how can modernization theory explain the fact that democratization often happens rapidly and in waves?

Different versions of this theory specify different hypothetical mechanisms linking economic development to democracy. Remember, what we mean by "causal mechanism"

CASE IN CONTEXT

Online

Democracy's Success in India (online case)

India is a major anomaly (in a positive way) for modernization theories of development. In essence, the relationship between its political and economic development has been the inverse of what modernization theory would predict. India is the world's second-largest society and its largest democracy. This has been the case since independence in 1947 and presents an interesting contrast to Pakistan, which has been subject to several military coups during the same time period. The two countries were formed at the same time by the partition of British-ruled India.

For more on democratization in India, go to **www.oup.com/he/DickovickCe** to see the case study. As you read it, keep in mind the following questions:

1. What, if anything, does Indian anti-colonial resistance have to do with the country's democratization?
2. What, if anything, does Indian democratization suggest about the importance of individual actors, leadership, and institutional design?
3. How is India's democracy different from that in other parts of the world, given the sheer size of the electorate?

is the process through which something produces something else, according to a theory.[18] Scholars can agree that two variables—like economic development and democracy—are related without necessarily agreeing about how they are linked. As we have seen, classic versions of modernization theories of democracy point to the intervening variable of a strong middle class.[19] Some more recent versions of modernization theory suggest a different intervening variable: Economic development might produce democratic values such as the value of "self-expression."[20] We return to this issue later in the chapter.

Culture and Democracy

Economic development is just one of many conceivable causes of democratization. Cultural arguments may be able to provide substantial leverage on understanding political trajectories in different countries.[21]

One prominent cultural argument from the 1990s was the "Asian values" thesis, as articulated by certain leaders in Asia (such as Singapore's Lee Kuan Yew) who argued that Asia had different values and would not readily embrace Western-style democracy.[22] According to this argument, based on Confucianism, Asian cultures value stability and harmonious social relations over individual rights and are comfortable with respect for authority and deference to the state. Accordingly, democracy is not a priority but is secondary to order, hard work, and social progress. These arguments were critiqued by others who suggested that the assertion by a Malaysian or Singaporean prime minister (or anyone else, for that matter) generalizing about their country's culture should not be taken as the definitive word on the subject. Indeed, political cultures may be deliberately shaped by states and governments—especially in non-democratic countries—for a number of purposes. Many Malaysians and Singaporeans may differ with the former prime ministers Lee Kuan Yew or Mahathir Mohamed about their own societies' compatibility with democracy.

Generally, cultural scholars recognize that values, norms, and customs are shaped and reshaped, defined and redefined over time. Culture is dynamic rather than static. While cultural differences among countries may help to explain some continuities over the years,

Associated Press/Wong Maye-E

PHOTO 6.5 Singapore's Prime Minister Lee Hsien Loong (centre) is seated next to an empty chair belonging to the late Lee Kuan Yew at a remembrance ceremony in 2016 marking the first anniversary of the former prime minister's death. Lee Kuan Yew was Singapore's first prime minister and is recognized as the country's founder.

ideas and values are also constantly shifting. For instance, culturalists may note that Latin America was long deemed to have male-dominated polities but may also note the increasing empowerment of women in many countries in Latin America that may have played a role in the processes of democratization there, as with the case of the Mothers of the Disappeared (*Madres de [la] Plaza de Mayo*) in Argentina. As *The Guardian* has observed, Latin America has had a much better track record of elected women leaders than does North America:

> Argentina's Isabel Peron was the first woman to become president in the region in 1974, and between 1990 to 2014, a record number of women were elected as political leaders. After Violeta Chamorro in Nicaragua, Panama elected Mireya Moscoso in 1999; in Chile, [Michelle] Bachelet in 2006 and 2014; Argentina elected Cristina Fernández de Kirchner in 2007 and 2011; Brazil elected Dilma Rousseff in 2010 and, in the same year, Costa Rica elected Laura Chinchilla.[23]

It should be noted that Rousseff was impeached and removed from office in 2016 and that by 2018, none of these countries had female leaders.

While some cultural theorists see aspects of a country's culture as an impediment to democracy, other scholars have noted cultural aspects that may play a role in democratization. When it comes to culture and democracy, it is also important to understand that Western-style democracy is the product of certain European ways of thinking about reality. This brings us to a discussion of colonization. While most European colonizing powers pulled out of Africa, the Caribbean, and Asia during the 1960s and 1970s, forms of settler colonialism remain in Latin America, North America, and the Antipodes. In these cases, settler governments were imposed on Indigenous peoples. For many decades, Indigenous peoples had no say in the establishment and functioning of these systems yet were subject to laws passed by settler colonial legislatures and parliaments. What does democracy mean when it is imposed by a colonizing power on Indigenous peoples to the extent that these people are rendered voiceless in government?

New Zealand Māori lawyer and activist Moana Jackson, who helped to draft the United Nations Declaration on the Rights of Indigenous Peoples in 2007, notes clearly that Māori, alongside all Indigenous peoples, had their own political systems before colonization and their own ways of self-determining and exercising their capacity for governance. However, during colonization "those different systems were dismissed as inferior and even anti-democratic while those in Europe were regarded as universal constructs which needed to be imposed on so-called primitive peoples in order to civilise and bring them to the light of true democracy." Jackson posits: "There is a kind of verbal gymnastics in that assertion because colonisation, with its violent and racist need to dispossess, is itself inherently undemocratic. The imposition of the Westminster system denied the will of those being dispossessed except on its own terms." Unfortunately, as he observes, "the Westminster system could be imposed even though iwi and hapū [national and subnational units] already had their own political institutions."[24] Jackson leads us to ask fundamental questions about whether Western-style democracy is really the best system for everyone. His analysis demonstrates the need to understand that this type of democracy has weaknesses as well as strengths.

The International System

For any country, the prevailing tendencies in the international system are likely to affect the prospects for democracy, and stable countries may get caught up in the affairs of the unstable. To use the 20th century as an example, it may seem sensible to suggest that the periods between the two world wars (including the Great Depression), the Cold War, and the post–Cold War era were three very different time periods with respect to the spread of democracy. Looking at snapshots of the global situation at certain moments in time can convey the importance of the international environment.

During the Cold War, for example, the countries of eastern and central Europe (the so-called "Second World") were kept under authoritarian rule by the power of the Soviet Union. Similarly, the poorest countries of the developing world also languished under dictatorships sponsored by both the Soviet Union and the United States. At a time when the major international powers prioritized security and influence over democratic rights in Asia, Africa, and Latin America, military leaders found it relatively easy to retain power over civilians. To use a slightly earlier example, colonial rule was fundamentally non-democratic. For many of the peoples of the world, the political and economic systems of the colonial era—when Britain, France, Spain, Portugal, and the Netherlands dominated much of the globe—were non-democratic and exploitative.

As seen in the examples of postwar Japan and Germany, the international system can promote democracy as well as hinder it. After the collapse of communism from 1989 to 1991, democratic ideas were transmitted and propagated around the world. Some theorists observed that countries effectively learned from one another as populations worldwide witnessed democratization in other countries and, in effect, concluded that "if they can do it, so can we."[25] The positive "demonstration effects" of watching neighbouring countries change may have helped to propel a wave of democratization that spread globally.

While it seems apparent that global patterns of democratization are real, an important puzzle for comparativists is what causes those patterns. One possible answer is that democratization waves are caused in part by shared or global economic development. Another answer is that as important *structural* features of the global system change, rates of democracy rise or fall. A third approach combines the international system and cultural perspectives, such as ideas of democratic learning and "demonstration effects"[26] or the notion that certain prestigious ways of organizing politics diffuse globally and exert cultural influence because they are perceived by "world society" as legitimate.[27]

Domestic Institutions

Whether a democracy is sustained or collapses, whether transitions to or from democracy happen, and how well a given democracy functions may depend on the institutions in a given society. To reiterate: *institutions* are those features of a political system that shape the behaviours of actors. They can include organizations and groups, rules and patterns, norms and values. We will address arguments about the effects of domestic institutions in later chapters: Does federalism or unitarism work better to hold countries together (Chapter 8);[28] do parliamentary and presidential forms of government affect the likelihood of democracy (Chapters 9 and 10);[29] and so on. But the possible impacts on democracy are noteworthy here.

To use an example familiar to many students of Canadian history, the basis of the country we know today was formed in 1867 after a series of conferences and negotiations between the united province of Canada (formerly Upper and Lower Canada or Ontario and Quebec), New Brunswick, and Nova Scotia. While the early Canadian colonies had weak legislatures, power was primarily held by British-appointed governors and colonial elites. This changed to a more democratic system after Confederation, and democratic institutions further developed as Canada expanded—with the addition of Manitoba, Prince Edward Island, British Columbia, and the Northwest Territories and Yukon during the 1870s. Important in creating Canada was laying out a coherent country that would go from the Atlantic to the Pacific. The first Canadian governments offered representative institutions to some white male property owners, a national railway to bind the provinces together, coherent national symbols, and a military force capable of preventing American invasion.

Poorly functioning political institutions can also undermine a regime, whether it is democratic or authoritarian. Chile's long-standing democracy collapsed in 1973. At least some problems were electoral; in elections in 1970, electoral rules split the centre and right parties, allowing leftists to obtain the presidency with the support of only about one-third of the country. This likely contributed to some middle-class support for the overthrow of the democratically elected regime by the military. The Weimar Republic in Germany between the two world wars was hobbled by similar institutional issues in the electoral system, as well as by an unclear division of power between the president as head of state and the chancellor as head of government. The economic weakness of the state, mass unemployment, and hyperinflation also contributed to dissatisfaction with this new democratic regime. So too can authoritarian regimes fail partly for lack of functional institutions, as when Mexico's PRI finally lost power in 2000 after 71 years; again, the reasons were numerous, but institutional factors range from the fragmentation of the leading party, to the development of opposition at local and state levels, to increasingly competitive elections, to the increasing recognition of the government's inability to provide services.

Agents and Actors: The Role of Individuals and Groups

Many political outcomes are ultimately traceable to actions by major individual decision-makers—that is, powerful individuals in positions of leadership. The question is whether these decisions are shaped and conditioned by other factors—such as economic development or institutions—or must be understood primarily in terms of individual choices.[30] A prominent example is from South Africa in the 1990s, where national hero Nelson Mandela had a leading role in the process of democratization. Mandela seemed "uniquely" capable of making difficult decisions and compromises, leaving open the question about what would have happened in his absence. In the South African case, there were many other individuals—both prominent political figures and lesser-known negotiators—who also had significant individual roles. For example, Archbishop Desmond Tutu also played a key role in peaceful activism and laid the basis for the country's Truth and Reconciliation Commission (TRC). This commission, created in 1994 (two years after the end of *Apartheid*), was designed to help society transition from a white-dominated regime to a representative modern democracy. The TRC heard testimony about *Apartheid*-era crimes and had the ability to both imprison and grant amnesties to those who committed crimes during this lengthy era.

The emphasis on specific individuals and groups tends to be focused more on specific transitions in certain countries than on broad patterns of democracy around the world. Analytically, we might *expect* individuals and other actors to matter more when the question at hand is about specific changes at a certain historical moment. Looking broadly at the world map and trying to understand where democracies are found might naturally lead us to consider broad forces, such as geography and the large sweep of world history, or perhaps cultures. Looking more closely at a single country at its particular moment of democratization might push us in the direction of more "proper names."[31] Much as looking through a telescope gives a sense of large-scale natural and environmental forces and looking under a microscope gives a sense of the detailed actions of individual organisms, so too might looking "cross-nationally" give a sense of broad scope and looking "within a country at a given moment in time" give a sense of individual action.

This approach is about more than just great individuals—the Mahatma Gandhis and Nelson Mandelas of history. Groups and coalitions matter. For instance, the transitions in the 1970s and 1980s (which included southern Europe, Latin America, and central-eastern Europe, as well as some countries elsewhere) highlighted the importance of divisions within authoritarian leadership as a cause of democratization. In particular, some leading scholars (discussed further in the following "Insights" box on *Transitions from Authoritarian Rule: Prospects for Democracy*) argued that democracy comes about when splits within an authoritarian regime lead to "softliners."[32] These softliners interact with pragmatists in the opposition to form a powerful coalition for moving toward democracy. This movement comes at the expense of hardline authoritarians and to the disappointment of those "maximalists," or radicals, in the pro-democracy movement who oppose any cooperation or negotiation with elements of the authoritarian regime.

Important interest groups or pressure groups can exercise their collective power in ways that facilitate democratization or democratic breakdown. Trade or labour unions might call a strike and immobilize a country and its economy, helping to bring down a

TABLE 6.1 | Actors in Democratic Transition

	Authoritarian Regime	Pro-democratic Forces
Extreme	Hardliners	Maximalists/radicals
Moderate	Softliners	Minimalists/pragmatists

regime. Or business groups or investors may boycott a regime, refusing to invest and ruining the economy to push politics to the breaking point. Powerful religious movements and representatives of the clergy might help to bring down a regime from their positions within their churches, mosques, or temples. And many other mobilized groups in civil society—from human rights campaigns, to ethnic solidarity movements, to university students (yes, you), to revolutionaries—have helped to keep regimes in place and helped to bring them down.

Combining Arguments and Theories: Multiple Causes

It is not always necessary to pick one and only one of the preceding categories to explain why democratization succeeds or fails. Many scholars of democratization will acknowledge the importance of multiple causal factors. Arguments can recognize complex causality (or causal complexity): Most important outcomes, like democracy, will be the result of multiple factors.

Cultural change and economic development can affect one another, and both can condition democracy. In addition to *economic modernization* came the *declining legitimacy of authoritarian regimes*, the role of the *Catholic Church*, and two external factors: *demonstration effects* (or the effect of watching your neighbours become democracies) and *greater international support for democracy* from the United States and other large powers.

INSIGHTS

Transitions from Authoritarian Rule: Prospects for Democracy

by Guillermo O'Donnell, Philippe C. Schmitter, and Laurence Whitehead

Unlike the accounts produced by modernization theorists, *Transitions from Authoritarian Rule* stresses the uncertainty of democratic transitions. According to these scholars, transitions are extremely complex and indeterminate, meaning that producing a general theory of transitions is a challenging if not impossible task. Nevertheless, they draw some important general conclusions. First, they judge international systemic factors to be important but *less* important than the jostling of domestic actors. Second, they stress that the uncertainty in question is above all the uncertainty faced by those very domestic actors. In other words, they frame the question from the perspective of actors *within* transitioning societies.

O'Donnell, Schmitter, and Whitehead, in their summary of the project's conclusions, note that governing coalitions in authoritarian regimes tend to divide into two camps: "softliners" and "hardliners" (see Table 6.1). At the same time, one tends to see a division in the opposition between "radicals" who want no compromise with the existing regime and "pragmatists" who are willing to work with the existing regime if they see the chance for a democratic transition. Successful transitions tend to involve collaboration between softliners in the authoritarian regime and pragmatists. Critical here is that these softliners need to feel as if they are able to initiate and partially control the process: In other words, they are unlikely to cooperate if they expect to be persecuted in the aftermath of a transition. Likewise, the dynamics internal to the opposition is important. Pragmatists must be able to ensure sufficient buy-in on the part of other opposition actors such that agreements can be honoured.

Guillermo O'Donnell, Philippe C. Schmitter, and Laurence Whitehead, eds., *Transitions from Authoritarian Rule: Prospects for Democracy*, 4 vols. (Baltimore, MD: Johns Hopkins University Press, 1986).

CASE IN CONTEXT

491

Is American Democracy in Trouble?

There is no doubting that the United States has been one of the most important and influential democracies in the world. However, many scholars have long expressed concerns about declining levels of public trust and civic association, along with increasing levels of income inequality.[33] The 2016 presidential, congressional, and gubernatorial elections highlighted many worries about the state of American society, and the election of Donald Trump, many argue, has further eroded democracy. With President Trump and the popularity of Democratic presidential primary candidate Bernie Sanders, there are strong populist movements across the country.

For more on the question of whether American democracy may be in trouble, see the case in Part VI, p. 491. As you read it, keep in mind the following questions:

1. What are the implications of this issue for the major theories of democracy and democratization discussed in this chapter?
2. How does this question relate to procedural versus substantive definitions of democracy?
3. How do populism and democracy go together? Is it *more* democratic if leaders can emotionally connect with voters the way Trump and Sanders seemed to have done?
4. If, indeed, income inequality and declining trust (in institutions and in others) suggest that we have reason to be concerned, what could be done about it?
5. Is authoritarianism rising under the Trump administration?

THINKING COMPARATIVELY

Is Canadian Democracy a Model?

KEY METHODOLOGICAL TOOL

Within-Case Analysis

Not all comparison in comparative politics is about comparing multiple, distinct countries as cases. That is, sometimes we make comparisons and conduct analyses *within* cases. When we compare multiple cases, we are often trying to get "leverage" on some key variation.

Within-case analysis, in contrast, is often used for the purpose of tracing causal processes.[34] In the case at hand, we are interested in comparing different junctures in the process of democratization in Canada. This is useful precisely because comparing different aspects or stages of that process might reveal a more complex and realistic pattern of causality.

So when would you use within-case analysis? Ideally, it is used in the context of broader, comparative analysis.[35] A comparative politics researcher might use the within-case analysis that we describe in this section as part of a broader comparative project that looks at long-run democratization in Canada in comparison with other cases.

A central question in the study of democratization is why democratization happens or does not happen. This necessarily involves an understanding of the dates and time periods at which democratization may occur. If we take Canada as our example, this may initially seem like a relatively straightforward proposition, but that is an illusion. Consider the following multiple-choice question:

In what year did Canada achieve democracy?

a. 1867
b. 1918
c. 1931
d. 1948
e. 1960
f. 1969
g. None of the above

At first glance, the most obvious answer might appear to be A, the year that four provinces joined together in Confederation. Similarly, one may argue that 1918, the year women gained the right to vote, was the crucial moment. The year 1931 was when Canada under the Statute of Westminster achieved self-governing status as a dominion; before this time Canada was legally under the authority of the British Empire, and voting didn't matter as much as it did later.

The remaining three dates have to do with voting, race, and Indigeneity. In 1948, the franchise was finally extended to Japanese Canadians, who, as many students may know, were stripped of many of their rights and interned during World War II. 1960 and 1969 are both dates of importance for Indigenous peoples. In 1960, Indigenous peoples with status under the Indian Act finally gained the right to both vote in federal elections and keep their Indian status. This federal legislation, however, did not bind the provinces, and it was not until 1969 that Indigenous peoples in Quebec could vote in provincial elections.

Yet one may also argue with some validity that "none of the above" is the best response to the question of when Canada achieved democracy. This would be true particularly for Indigenous peoples, who were often stripped of their traditional forms of government under the Indian Act. Indigenous nations did not ask for this European form of government (as echoed in the Māori experience) yet are forced to live under its provisions. While some Indigenous leaders have been elected at all levels of government, this does not mean that democracy is the "only game in town" or the preferred way of making decisions. Recall Robert Jago's "Canadian Problem" that we outlined in Chapter 1. Democracy is a problem of math—whoever has the superior numbers can always argue that their wants and preferences constitute the well-being of the greatest number. As such: "With their majority, their control over our lands and resources seems natural and is granted democratic cover."[36]

At another level, we can explore the disenfranchisement of permanent residents. Permanent residents live in Canada, pay taxes, work, send their children (if they have any) to school. Yet they cannot vote for school board officials, police commissioners, MLAs, MPPs, or MPs. Is this fair? A large proportion of the electorate who make valuable contributions to Canadian society is frozen out of the political process. In other countries like New Zealand, permanent residents can vote, although they cannot stand for office.

Canada is not perfect and constitutes one example of an evolving democratic system. There is no ideal system, and democracy and democratic norms are often the product of certain political cultures, and changes are often the product of mobilization and collective action.

Table 6.2 demonstrates how different theoretical approaches might be used to explain a variety of democratizing moments in Canadian history. These are not definitive statements but are simply illustrative of how scholars in different theoretical "schools" or "traditions" might approach the same question. We choose three different moments in Canada's democratic evolution: Confederation in 1867 and the extension of political rights to women and to Indigenous peoples with Indian Act status in the 20th century. Notice the research question and the outcome at the top, and then consider the cells of the table as possible ways different scholars might address these questions and explain these outcomes.

Regarding our earlier point about why you might use within-case analysis, note that it is perfectly possible that the best explanation of the 19th-century sequence is derived from the theory that focuses on structures/the world system; that the early 20th-century sequence is best explained by the theory that focuses on culture; and that the later 20th-century sequence is best explained by modernization theory. Or some other such combination may be the strongest. The payoff here is that if we were to find this, it would bring nuance to our general theory in a useful way, and we could bring this insight back to comparative analysis.

TABLE 6.2 | Causal Interpretations of Canadian Democracy and Democratization across Time Periods

	19th Century	Early 20th Century	Later 20th Century
Dependent Variable	Confederation	Suffrage for Women	Suffrage for Indigenous peoples with status
Research Question	Why did British colonists push for a federal state?	How did women attain voting rights?	How did registered Indigenous peoples gain the right to vote?
Modernization (Economic/ Social Change)	Merchants and small businesses of colonial economy seek protection from the Americans and a larger trading area.	Women are key to the economy in World War I when men are fighting overseas.	After World War II, Parliament recognizes Indigenous peoples as the most neglected group with major health and economic problems.
Culture	Settler groups seek more control over domestic affairs; Quebec is unhappy with British assimilationist policies in the united "Canadian" province.	Declining tolerance for overt prejudice on the basis of sex; recognition of discrimination in employment and education.	Reaction against crimes in World War II; formation of welfare state; and Bill of Rights legislation (1958).
Structures/ Systems (International)	Violence of US civil war and fears of US invasion and annexation.	International suffragette movement and early examples from British dominions: New Zealand (1893), Australia (1902).	Waves of decolonization in Africa, Asia, and the Caribbean.
Institutions (Domestic)	Divided colonies worry about American invasion and see protection in a united country.	Voting rights provincially (Manitoba and Saskatchewan).	Government wants to make it clear that Indigenous peoples are Canadian citizens and have no legal relationship with the British Crown.
Agency/Actor	"Fathers of Confederation" have formative role in shaping country's institutions.	Provincial governments first, followed by federal government.	Federal government, followed by provincial governments.

Chapter Summary

Concepts

- The word *democracy* has numerous meanings.
- One major distinction is between procedural and substantive definitions of democracy.
- Regime change can include both the development of democracy and also the breakdown of an existing democratic regime.

Types

- Types of democracy include both representative and direct forms.
- Democratization can be thought of in terms of both democratic transition and consolidation.

Causes and Effects

- Scholars have developed a number of theories to explain why democratization takes place when and where it does. Perhaps the most famous is modernization theory, which predicts that economic development increases the likelihood of democratization.
- Another theory is that political culture shapes the possibilities for democracy and democratization and that some political cultures increase the possibility of the

establishment and persistence of authoritarian regimes as well.

- Western-style democracy is not perfect and may conflict with Indigenous and other forms of governance. Indigenous critiques are valid and constitute important standpoints through which to engage with the weaknesses of democratic theory and practice.
- Systemic and structural theories say that democratization is more a function of factors operative at the level of the international system than things happening within societies. They focus, among other things, on waves of democratization and also of democratic breakdown.
- Some theories place more emphasis on contingency, agents, and institutional *design*.

Thinking Comparatively

- We looked at several key sequences in the history of democratization in Canada, and we introduced the concept of within-case analysis.

Thinking It Through

1. As we have noted, India achieved a robust democracy *before* achieving economic modernization. What would modernization, cultural, structural, institutional, and actor-centred theories say about this case? Which of these theories do you think could make most sense of the Indian case? Why?
2. Democracy can take a variety of forms, with one major distinction being between "representative" and "direct" democracy. But what is the relationship between these forms? Are they ultimately compatible? Do gains in one involve trade-offs in the other? Think about this question in relation to case examples.
3. In recent years, there has been much discussion among politicians and public intellectuals about whether democracy can be engineered or even imposed. Some think that if the appropriate conditions are established, democracy can flourish anywhere. Others think that societies need to come to democratization organically and on their own. What would each of the theories we have considered have to say about this question?
4. "American Exceptionalism" has long held that the United States is different from Europe and the British settler states. We have seen notable trends that bear on democratic practice in the United States: (a) increasing levels of income inequality; (b) declining public trust in major institutions; (c) the rise of populist leaders and an "America First" strategy. What are the implications of these trends for the future of American democracy? What would each of the major theories of democratization and democratic consolidation say about these issues?
5. Imagine that the leader of a poor country with low levels of rule of law and dysfunctional political institutions asks you to help design a new democratic system for their polity. What would each of the theories considered in this chapter say about the possibility of your doing so? Now imagine that you were asked to help institutionally engineer increasing democratization in Canada. Ask the same question of this project. Are the implications the same? Different? Why?

7 Authoritarian Regimes and Democratic Breakdown

In This Chapter

Zimbabwean president Emmerson Mnangagwa receives the chain and sash of office as he is officially sworn-in during a ceremony in Harare in 2017. (JEKESAI NJIKIZANA/AFP/Getty Images)

In 1965, the white settlers of a former British colony in Africa, called Southern Rhodesia, asserted their "independence" from British rule. The settlers created a white-dominated government and renamed the country Rhodesia. They forcibly withheld rights from the black African majority and hoarded economic and political power in their own hands. By the 1970s, an African resistance movement emerged to overthrow the white regime, led by a charismatic leader who vowed to bring democracy to the majority. After a long struggle, this movement for democracy finally overthrew the repressive white regime in 1979, and a negotiated settlement gave rise to a freer society in 1980. The transition even set in motion some much-needed land reform that would reshape the terrible inequalities between poor blacks and rich white farmers, and the new president set to work.

The name of the charismatic liberation hero was Robert Mugabe, and his party, the Zimbabwe African National Union-Patriotic Front (ZANU-PF) took control of the country, which was soon renamed Zimbabwe, reflecting centuries of impressive history. The Shona-speaking civilization had dominated this part of Africa since the 13th century. They had constructed a massive capital city known as Great Zimbabwe, which housed as many as 18,000 people. This civilization created the largest pre-colonial state in southern Africa, and so choosing this name helped Mugabe stress a return to the greatness of the past.[1]

After an initial burst of enthusiasm with Mugabe's rule (as he invested in causes such as girls' education, a policy and idea well ahead of its time), however, things regressed quickly. Beginning in the 1980s, his regime was responsible for massacres of opponents and innocent victims in the region known as Matabeleland. By the 2000s, he presided over a brutal and repressive regime that encouraged so-called "war veterans" from the liberation war to occupy white-owned farms and frequently kill the owners and anyone loyal to them. In the midst of the killing and disorder, Zimbabwe's economy collapsed into hyperinflation, and the agriculturally rich country once known as "the bread basket of Africa" saw extreme economic problems. Mugabe came to be widely reviled around the world and by many Zimbabweans as one of the most abusive and despotic dictators in Africa.

Mugabe was eventually forced to resign after a military takeover in November 2017, and Emmerson Mnangagwa assumed control as the country's new president. Mnangagwa had served as Mugabe's vice-president for three years before being dismissed by Mugabe in 2017; Mnangagwa led the coup against Mugabe within the same month. In early 2018, Mnangagwa announced that elections would take place in the first half of the year, the first free elections in more than 37 years. Many critics and opposition politicians in Zimbabwe point out, however, that Mnangagwa has awarded key positions to the military and his other political allies, which casts doubt on how democratic this transition will actually be.[2] Mugabe died in the summer of 2019.

What gives rise to such brutal regimes, and what allows them to persist even as they preside over ruination? While the previous chapter sought to explain democracy and democratization, this chapter turns the question around to look at authoritarian regimes. These sorts of regimes were for a long time the majority of all governments.

It can be very complicated for outside observers to know what to do about authoritarian regimes, especially when the average people living under those regimes are still in need of trade with the outside world to support themselves. Canada, for example, began formal relations with Zimbabwe in 1980 and maintained an embassy in the capital Harare during the entire Mugabe era, while a Zimbabwean embassy was located in Ottawa. Canada maintained a small amount of two-way trade (about $11 million in 2013) but also engaged in targeted economic measures to freeze the assets of Mugabe's advisors and supporters as well as several economic entities. Canadians were also banned from engaging in any trading of or assistance related to arms. In dealing with authoritarian regimes, countries ideally work to carefully target those in power while still allowing the average people to engage in trade or to travel (several hundred Zimbabwean students, for example, have studied in Canada).[3] It is always extremely challenging to achieve a balance.

• • •

Concepts

In the previous chapter, we looked at democratic regimes and transitions to democracy. In this chapter, we focus on two main concepts: authoritarianism (along with authoritarian regimes) and authoritarian transitions.

Authoritarianism and Authoritarian Regimes

Defining **authoritarianism** is not as straightforward as it might seem. It can be thought of as a characteristic of some ideologies (e.g., fascism and some varieties of socialism) or even as a behavioural tendency, as in so-called "authoritarian personalities," and can thus also be found in democratic countries.[4] In general, we can characterize an ideology or behavioural tendency as authoritarian to the extent that it is favourable to hierarchy and to closed, concentrated processes of decision-making.

authoritarianism A form of government or regime that is non-democratic.

Authoritarian regimes are those that exemplify, to one degree or another, this authoritarian ideal. While many of us have grown up in democratic societies such as Canada (although Canada too has its problems), we should recognize that in many places and times authoritarian regimes have been the norm and democracies have tended toward the authoritarian, given that decision-making has often been in the hands of a small number of (mostly white male) people. Indeed, if we take a historical view of political regimes, we would see that most different subtypes (e.g., oligarchies, empires, monarchies, and sultanates) fall into the general authoritarian category.[5]

authoritarian regime A non-democratic regime.

While we are interested in modern regimes here, there is still a lot of variation to explore. Modern authoritarian regimes vary in several respects. One is the extent to which the regime centres on an individual as opposed to a ruling elite clique, *junta* (which means a small political or military group), or bureaucracy. Personalistic regimes may invoke the names of history's greatest villains: Adolf Hitler, Joseph Stalin, Pol Pot, Papa Doc Duvalier, Shah Reza Pahlavi, and even as far back as Caligula in the Roman Empire. Of course, these personalistic rulers relied on institutions such as political parties, militaries, or secret police to support their rule, but their rule was quite different from that of the nondescript generals and admirals who ruled Brazil or Argentina in the 1970s. Another distinction is the degree to which the regime expounds an overarching ideology, such as communism or fascism, as opposed to governing without attempting to socialize the citizenry in such ways. A third major difference is the extent to which the regime constrains or violates human rights. Most theorists would recognize all authoritarian regimes in the contemporary world as violating some basic rights, such as the right to self-determination and basic political freedoms. However, some authoritarian regimes are willing to leave individuals alone, in relative freedom, as long as they accept the regime's authority and stay away from politics. Others aim to control almost every aspect of their citizens' lives. The subtypes of authoritarian regimes described in the "Types" section express some of these distinctions.

Transitions to Authoritarian Regimes

Regime change is not a one-way street from authoritarianism to democracy; on the contrary, democracies can break down and collapse, and authoritarian regimes can persist and solidify their rule. Although the end of the 20th century witnessed a wave of democratization in central and eastern Europe, Latin America, Asia, and Africa, authoritarianism persists and even grows in some places.[6] Reversion to authoritarianism in democratic countries has a long history, from the breakdown of the Weimar Republic and the rise of Nazi Germany in the 1930s to the many coups in Latin America and Africa in the 1960s and 1970s. Consolidation may stop or be reversed. Transition may fail, or a country may retransition from democracy back below the threshold to authoritarianism. Democratic states may also become less democratic while not ever becoming authoritarian. Political scientists examine these processes of democratic breakdown and **authoritarian persistence**.[7] We also consider the various paths to the establishment of **hybrid regimes** (which combine authoritarian and some democratic elements).[8]

authoritarian persistence The ongoing continuation of an authoritarian regime such that democratic transition does not take place.

hybrid regime A class of regime that appears to be neither fully democratic nor fully authoritarian, such as electoral authoritarianism, delegative democracy, and illiberal democracy.

Types

As noted previously, authoritarian regimes vary in important ways. In this section, we discuss what we see as the key subtypes of authoritarianism as well the more common variable forms that transitions to authoritarian regimes can take.

Types of Authoritarianism

Some of the most important types of authoritarian regimes are totalitarian regimes, theocracies, personalistic dictatorships, and bureaucratic-authoritarian regimes. We discuss each of these in more detail here.

Totalitarian Regimes

Totalitarian regimes represent the most notorious form of authoritarian rule, epitomized by the communist and fascist regimes of the 20th century that sent tens of millions of people to their deaths, especially in Nazi Germany and the Stalinist era of the Soviet Union. Many consider today's North Korea to be another example of a totalitarian regime, although on a much smaller scale. Totalitarian regimes deny most civil rights to citizens and do not hold free and fair elections, but their manipulations and machinations go far beyond those of many other authoritarian regimes.

totalitarian regime A form of authoritarian regime that aims to control everything about the lives of its subject population, such as in the Soviet Union under Stalin and Germany under the Nazi Party.

Totalitarianism gets its name from the attempt to control the totality of a society, most notably through an official governing ideology to which all people are expected to conform.[9] Totalitarian regimes will go to great lengths to stop freedom of thought and conscience, often using secret police, spies, and informants to report on suspected dissidents. Such regimes also deploy a full range of technology to conduct surveillance, gather and transmit intelligence, and coordinate repressive state activities. Freedom of thought is antithetical to the ambitions of totalitarian leadership.

There is usually one official governing party, often led by a dominant figure who is the subject of hero worship or a cult of personality. State control over the economy is common and prevents any economic actors from building up a power base that might be used to challenge the total domination the state has over public life. Many totalitarian regimes use prisons, work camps, and mass executions in an attempt to re-educate society and to eliminate supposedly undesirable elements, especially ethnic minorities.[10]

Associated Press/Pavel Golovkin

PHOTO 7.2 Communist Party supporters carry red flags and portraits of Joseph Stalin as they walk to place flowers at his grave in Red Square in Moscow, Russia, in March 2019 to mark the 66th anniversary of his death. Joseph Stalin led the totalitarian regime in the Soviet Union from the late 1920s until his death in 1953.

Totalitarianism can be seen as a modern phenomenon. There certainly are precedents for totalitarianism in historical societies, such as ancient Sparta. But for the most part, the relative weakness of pre-modern states and their lack of technology precluded the possibility of true totalitarian regimes, despite *efforts* that look quite totalitarian, such as medieval European states' efforts to censor literature and to enforce Christian orthodoxy by force.

Some analysts argue that the concept of totalitarianism was an artifact of the Cold War or even a propaganda tool for the liberal-democratic West, used to demonize the Soviet Union and its allies.[11] Totalitarianism was most associated with the atrocities committed by both the Nazis and the Soviets, but it can be used to describe and better understand other regimes. It is important as a concept, however, because it allows us to describe important variations between forms of authoritarianism that aim to control everything in the lives of their people and those that allow greater latitude.

Theocracies

Some authoritarian regimes are closely linked to religious institutions. If religious leaders control an authoritarian state, or if a state imposes very strict religious restrictions and uses religion as its main mode of legitimation, we refer to it as a **theocratic** regime. In the pre-modern world, many if not most states were theocratic, and the monarchies of western Europe, for example, had strong theocratic features, including the British imperial system in which the monarch was also head of the Church of England. Today there are fewer theocratic regimes, but some stand out as particularly noteworthy, such as Iran. Many states, though, continue to involve religion or to impose religious restrictions, a subject to which we return in Chapter 15.

theocracy An authoritarian state controlled by religious leaders or a state with very strict religious restrictions that uses religion as its main mode of legitimation.

Personalistic Dictatorships

personalistic dictatorship A form of authoritarianism in which the personality of the dictator is highlighted.

Not all authoritarian regimes are totalitarian or theocratic. Indeed, many contemporary authoritarian regimes are not. Some simply allow little role for the population in political decision-making, but the state does not aim to control every aspect of their lives. Among more limited authoritarian regimes we find the classic forms of dictatorship that have been particularly common in modern political history. The terms **personalistic dictatorship** and the more antiquated "sultanism" refer to domination of a political system by a single individual.[12] This individual concentrates power and governs as he (or she) sees fit. Autocracy, despotism, dictatorship, or tyranny can be used to express similar ideas, though some of these terms can sometimes refer to domination by a clique of more than one leader. As distinct from totalitarian rule, the autocrat/despot may not aim to establish an overarching ideology. In other cases, an ideology may be promoted but does not come to be implemented to the extent that it would be in a totalitarian regime. As distinct from theocratic rule, while a personalistic dictator might support religion, repress religious minorities, and use religion as a tool of the state, it is the dictator—and not the religious system in question—that is the highest authority.

The justification for rule in personalistic dictatorships may be based on the assertion of the public interest, such as the ability to promote economic success or the need to combat subversives. Sometimes, dictatorships are explicitly framed as temporary. On other occasions, they have been presented as likely "necessary" for a long time.

CASE IN CONTEXT

422

Democratic Features of Authoritarian Systems? The Case of Iran

In 1979, Iran underwent a social revolution that brought a radical and religious government into power. This regime overthrew Mohammad Reza Pahlavi, the self-styled Shah (or king) of Iran, who was allied with the United States and promoted an autocratic, personalistic, and corrupt form of rule that practised widespread torture and other human rights abuses. Many of the excesses of the revolutionary movement were reactions to the Shah's own repressive policies, and their anti-American stance reflected US support for Pahlavi rule. Some regard Iran's Islamic republic as authoritarian, since it imposes strict controls on public expression, religion, and issues of "morality." Journalism is tightly controlled, and torture and the death penalty are widely applied. Religious leaders have ultimate control over policy-making, and thus we would be justified in considering it theocratic. However, Iran still has some quasi-democratic features as well. Elections are still regularly held for local governments, the national legislature (Majlis), and an "Assembly of Experts." They are contested by a range of political parties, although not always fairly and not in a particularly transparent manner. Much of the power is concentrated in the hands of both the Revolutionary Guard and the Guardian Council.[13] In short, there is some debate within the Iranian state but within a rather narrow band policed by religious authorities and within a broader context that most would regard as authoritarian.

For more on authoritarianism and democracy in Iran, see the case study in Part VI, p. 422. As you read it, keep in mind the following questions:

1. On what grounds does Iran claim to be democratic? What criteria do social scientists use in judging it not to be so despite some clearly democratic features?
2. What are the implications of Iran's authoritarian and theocratic approach for the long-term viability of its regime? Does authoritarianism help the regime to stay in power or create vulnerabilities?
3. Compared to other regimes in the region like Iraq, Saudi Arabia, and Yemen, is Iran comparatively better or worse in terms of its governance practices?
4. Assess the prospects for genuine democratic reform in Iran.

Conveniently, though, such self-appointed leaders are often slow to judge the countries they rule to be *actually* ready for democracy. Some authoritarian rulers of this sort argue that democracy is not right for all countries, and some hold that a country needs a strong leader to keep people in line. There have been a number of personalistic dictators in Africa, among other regions of the world, and several of them are unfortunately memorable. They include Mobutu Sese Seko of the former Zaire (now the Democratic Republic of the Congo), Jean-Bedel Bokassa of the Central African Republic (who declared himself emperor), and Idi Amin of Uganda.[14]

There were also a number of personalistic regimes in communist countries. Nicolae Ceausescu in Romania promoted a personalistic cult of personality both for himself and his wife Elena. Nicolae ascended to power in 1965 and was only ousted in 1989 when he and Elena were assassinated by members of his own security forces. Enver Hoxha of Albania maintained a similar style of personalized rule to Ceausescu, holding tight control over state power until his death. Josip Broz Tito in Yugoslavia also maintained a highly personalized form of rule, although his regime was more liberal and open to the West. Many of these leaders modelled themselves on Joseph Stalin in the Soviet Union as well as Chairman Mao in China. Ceausescu is said to have really advanced his own form of personalism after visiting Kim Il Sung in North Korea.

Associated Press

PHOTO 7.3 Nicolae Ceausescu, accompanied by his wife Elena, receives applause at the last convention of the Communist Party in Bucharest, Romania, in November 1989. He was overthrown the next month, and he and his wife were executed on Christmas Day.

Bureaucratic-Authoritarian Regimes

bureaucratic-authoritarian regime A type of authoritarian regime, common in Latin America and elsewhere in the mid- to late 20th century, that was associated with control of the state more by a group of elites (often military) than by a single individual leader.

Personalistic dictatorships and related forms of autocracy shade into a form of authoritarian regime that became very common in parts of the developing world in the mid- to late 20th century: the **bureaucratic-authoritarian regime**. These regimes are usually focused less on a single individual than personalistic dictatorships, instead relying on an organized bureaucracy (often, though not always, the military) to run the country.

Though less often associated with particular historical figures, such regimes are not necessarily less brutal than personalistic regimes. The Argentine military in the 1970s was infamous for torture and for methods of execution that included throwing dissenters out of helicopters into the Atlantic Ocean.[15] Bureaucratic-authoritarian regimes in Asia and Latin America used a range of justifications for assuming rule, including the political impasses and economic failures of civilian regimes in their countries.[16]

Like most personalistic dictatorships, bureaucratic-authoritarian regimes tend to be less ideological than totalitarian regimes, or more pragmatic. They can be right-wing or left-wing, but the fundamental rationale they typically use in trying to garner legitimacy is the alleged need to establish order or economic progress. They tell their societies they can achieve full modernity only through a strong hand and technical administration. Yet these regimes, which were very common in the 1960s and 1970s, typically viewed their role not as displacing civilian regimes in order to call new elections but as governing their countries for extended periods. In other words, bureaucratic-authoritarian regimes seldom view themselves as merely brief caretakers.

Hybrid and Semi-Authoritarian Regimes

Sometimes regimes are hard to classify as either democratic or authoritarian. Indeed, this seems to be a growing problem. This was especially true after the third wave of democratization (see our discussion in the previous chapter), which led to stronger democratic international norms with which regimes wished to appear compliant.[17] Accordingly, regimes developed techniques and learned from one another about how to appear to comply with these norms while nevertheless remaining in power. Over the years, the range of variations among different types of regimes has led to a proliferation of names for regimes that fit somewhere between full democracy and complete authoritarianism. Some scholars have urged caution about coming up with new names, noting that while there are many subtypes of democratic or authoritarian regimes, we want more than simply "democracy with adjectives."[18] Nonetheless, these terms have resonance and have become prominent.

illiberal democracy A polity with some democratic features but in which political and civil rights are not all guaranteed or protected.

delegative democracy A hybrid form of regime that is democratic but involves the electorate "delegating" significant authority to a government.

electoral authoritarianism A name applied to situations in which authoritarian regimes nominally compete in elections.

competitive authoritarianism A form of government or regime that allows some political competition but not enough for it to qualify as fully democratic.

The notion of **illiberal democracy** emerges from the many experiences whereby countries have reasonably fair elections but then do little to hold elected leaders to account.[19] While these countries are described as democracies, largely because of reasonably fair elections, they may have more in common with authoritarian regimes. Several regimes in Latin America have been characterized as **delegative democracies**,[20] while the term **electoral authoritarianism** has been used to describe hybrid regimes elsewhere.[21] More recently, some of these regimes have been labelled as **competitive authoritarian**, meaning that they do allow some political competition but not enough for them to qualify as fully democratic.[22] Note that these terms are not perfect synonyms. A delegative democracy is considered at least partially democratic. **Competitive authoritarianism** blurs the line in this connection, the key idea being that the regime is not truly democratic but that it exerts control through elections that are at least nominally competitive.

Types of Transition (or Nontransition) to Authoritarianism

Many forms of regime change can end in authoritarianism. They include the replacement of one form of authoritarian regime with another, as well as democratic breakdown and transitions to hybrid regimes. We discuss these forms here, but first we will take a look at authoritarian persistence.

Authoritarian Persistence

Authoritarian persistence is a pressing issue in light of the many non-democratic regimes in the world today that seem enduring. In discussing democratic transition and consolidation in the previous chapter, we noted that these processes may not always be completed. Such a case may suggest partial democratization, but the flip side of the coin is the persistence (and therefore apparent "success") of an authoritarian regime. At some level, this distinction may seem to be merely semantic, but we must take care not to assume that all countries are destined to become democracies in the end.[23] Indeed, questions about the persistence of authoritarianism become more interesting if an authoritarian regime persists despite predictions that it should not.

Authoritarian regimes have their own characteristics and attributes, which may contribute to their stability. For instance, the Chinese Communist Party—which was an

Associated Press/Esteban Felix

PHOTO 7.4 Daniel Ortega, president of Nicaragua, as he is sworn into the presidency for his third term in 2012. He was subsequently re-elected in 2016. Ortega's supporters claim that his policies aim to reduce inequalities and poverty, while his critics charge that his government is not fully democratic.

economic failure for its first 30 years in power—has very successfully presided over decades of economic growth since it undertook reforms in 1979. This economic success is undoubtedly part of why the regime has endured and democratization has not gained steam after the brutal crackdown on protestors in Tiananmen Square in 1989. In short, to understand regime types and regime changes, we must recognize that they depend not only on the details of how a transition goes but also on the features of authoritarian regimes.

Moreover, it is worth noting that there are at least two main kinds of authoritarian persistence. The first is the persistence of a single authoritarian regime, as suggested earlier. Often this persistence is accompanied by major internal changes to the regime. An example, again, is the rule of the Chinese Communist Party. Today's Communist Party embraces very different policies and a different style of rule from what it did, say, under Mao Zedong in the 1960s and even includes many business people and entrepreneurs. Yet the same party and the same basic state have remained in place, and thus most political scientists would consider this a case of a single authoritarian regime's persistence. In other words, the reforms of Deng Xiaoping and his successors, while radical, did not constitute an institutional break in regime type but rather a slower transition that leaves the regime firmly in the authoritarian category.

Let's consider a different sort of pattern: the substitution of one authoritarian regime for another. Whereas the first type of authoritarian persistence that we considered has no punctuated regime change, this type does. Some authoritarian regimes give way to other authoritarian regimes, often of very different types. One example is modern Iran. In 1979, millions of protestors backing the Islamic Revolution succeeded in overthrowing Shah Reza Pahlavi, a US-supported authoritarian leader (see extended discussion in the Country Profile and Case Studies for Iran in Part VI). The result was a very different type of regime: The Islamic Revolution was theocratic (i.e., led by religious clerics), conservative, and nationalistic as opposed to the secular and pro-Western rule of the Shah. Yet both were authoritarian, and both opposed liberal democracy. Indeed, what is particularly interesting about this case is the question of which of the two authoritarian Iranian regimes in question is *less* democratic, a subject Iran scholars debate.

Authoritarian regimes use a number of techniques and strategies in their efforts to persist. They are sometimes called strategies of "regime maintenance." One such strategy is to produce economic benefits for citizens. This can take the form of efforts to produce growth or the form of patronage and clientelism, which involve the state using its own resources to benefit supporters.[24] Authoritarian regimes also often use repression. This can take the form of using police to stifle protest activities and, in its most egregious cases, the use of large-scale violence against civilians.

Post-Communist Transition, Authoritarianism, and Illiberal Democracy

From the period 1989 to 1991, the states of central and eastern Europe underwent major changes as the Soviet Union fell apart, leading to the emergence of a hybrid regime under Boris Yeltsin. Yeltsin presided over the fragmentation of the USSR and the formation of the Russian Federation. Other, smaller units that had some autonomy within the Soviet system as administrative units gained their independence as separate states. In total, 14 former "Soviet Republics" gained independence: three Baltic states, five in Central Asia, three in Uzbekistan, and three in Transcaucasia. This was perceived by Russia as a great loss of prestige and power. In the Russian Federation, a period of economic and political instability followed until Vladimir Putin, aided by an oil boom, began to impose political order. He did this, in part, by developing a hybrid of electoral politics with strong authoritarian features, considered a classic case of competitive authoritarianism.[25]

In former Soviet republics like Kazakhstan, Belarus, Azerbaijan, and Uzbekistan, a series of authoritarian leaders maintained power for decades, sometimes with support from Moscow. For example, Belarus's Alexander Lukashenko has been in power since 1994. In Azerbaijan, Ilham Aliyev took over as president from his father in 2003, who had ruled for the first decade of the country's independence. Similarly, Nursultan Nazarbayev has had a lengthy time as president of Kazakhstan, having gained power in 1990. Uzbekistan's Islam Karimov took power in the same year, dying in office in 2016.[26]

The Baltic states of Latvia, Lithuania, and Estonia have all managed the transition to regular democratic elections and have all become members of the European Union and the Eurozone. They are all recognized as high-income countries with a high standard of living. All are also members of the Organisation for Economic Co-operation and Development.

Central European states such as Hungary, Poland, and the Czech and Slovak republics transitioned to forms of illiberal and then fully functioning liberal democratic societies. The carrot of membership in the European Union was a major draw card for these states to abandon single-party communist rule and to adopt free market policies. The EU's 1993 "Copenhagen criteria" outlined criteria for membership, including "stable institutions guaranteeing democracy, the rule of law, human rights and respect for and protection of minorities." Equally important was a "functioning market economy and the capacity to cope with competition and market forces in the EU."[27] However, after more than two decades of democracy, Hungary under Viktor Orban and Poland under the rule of the Law and Justice Party have slipped into illiberal rule. Albania, Bulgaria, and Romania all had difficult periods of transition. The same also holds true for former Yugoslav republic Slovenia. Croatia and Serbia (also former Yugoslav republics) encountered difficulties with corruption and authoritarianism during the 1990s, with Croatia reforming its system to court EU membership. Serbia will have much further to go before it overcomes its illiberal system.

Democratic Breakdown

The decline of democratic regimes may be the most iconic type of regime change leading to authoritarianism. Examples abound, such as the collapse of Germany's Weimar Republic in the 1920s leading to the rise of the Nazis (see box on "Democracy and Authoritarianism in Germany") and the coup d'état against the Allende government in Chile in the 1970s that led to the Pinochet dictatorship. Democratic reversals and returns to authoritarian rule are

CASE IN CONTEXT 442

The Mexican State and Rule of Law

Mexico is a country that has had varying success in terms of state-building. In recent years, rule-of-law issues have been of special concern. The Mexican government has made an effort to crack down on organized crime, leading to high levels of violence. The causes of this violence, and the policies that might reduce it, are subject to much debate.

For more on rule of law in Mexico, see the case study in Part VI, p. 442. As you read it, keep in mind the following questions:

1. Is Mexico really likely to become a failed state, as some have worried, or is this fear hyperbole? Why or why not?
2. Does the United States play a role in Mexico's recent difficulties in maintaining rule of law? If so, how?

also diverse in form, much like democratization and authoritarian persistence. Some countries may "authoritarianize" (that is, witness a democratic breakdown) in fits and starts, perhaps with partial losses of freedom and increasingly suspect elections interspersed with moments of continued political participation by the citizenry. One could argue whether this applies to Russia under Vladimir Putin. Other democratic breakdowns may be abrupt and dramatic, with a military force overthrowing a democratic regime in a coup or an elected ruler declaring a state of emergency and martial law; examples are numerous in the history of the developing countries of Africa, Asia, and Latin America.

As is the case with democratization, these democratic breakdowns may also reverse (in this case with a return to democracy), sometimes indefinitely and other times only temporarily, or stop somewhere in between democracy and authoritarianism. One democratic breakdown that stopped, for instance, was in Ukraine in 2004 when hundreds of thousands of citizens took to the streets in the Orange Revolution to protest a fraudulent and manipulated election. While Ukraine was a flawed and partial democracy before the Orange Revolution, the movement undoubtedly prevented further movement in the direction of authoritarianism at that time. Sadly, weak institutions contributed to a renewed crisis in Ukraine in 2014, leading to violence, further weakened institutions, and the loss of some of the country's territory to Russia.

Several patterns of democratic decay and collapse are worth special attention. First, democratic regimes sometimes collapse because voters elect authoritarians. This may sound surprising. Why would people vote for an authoritarian when they have democracy? One reason is that they may not know they are voting for an authoritarian. A political candidate who promises law and order, economic development, and the end of corruption may give no indication that he or she intends to close the parliament and the court system and to declare martial law as means to this end. Another reason is that in some societies where democratic consolidation is incomplete, democracy may appear to have weaknesses as well as strengths, and voters might have different trade-offs to calculate than do citizens in well-institutionalized democracies.

Second, democratic regimes sometimes collapse because organized actors in society move against them. Organized labour can strike; middle-class individuals can demonstrate, marching, setting up barricades, or banging pots (a form of protest common in Latin America called the "cacerolazo"); businesses can withdraw capital; and, perhaps most dangerous, the state bureaucracy itself can refuse to comply with the orders of civilian leaders. This is most dangerous when the military, or segments of the military, lose faith in democracy or in the given democratic regime. When this happens, a coup d'état becomes more likely. In the view of most analysts, coups d'état are intrinsically anti-democratic when brought against democratic regimes. They can, however, issue in different sorts of outcomes, including democratizing effects. Indeed, coups against authoritarian regimes sometimes happen and sometimes for the sake of establishing democracy. Many coups, though, involve the military acting against a civilian (and often democratic) regime and substituting an authoritarian regime in its place.

Third, sometimes regime change takes the form of revolution. These revolutions can in some instances be democratizing, but in many other instances they actually lead to greater concentration of power under an authoritarian regime.

Transition to Hybrid or Semi-authoritarian Regime

Hybrid regimes can emerge out of either democratic or authoritarian regimes, as we discuss in further detail in the "Causes and Effects" section later in the chapter. Partial democratic breakdown can lead a formerly democratic polity to fall into semi-authoritarian status, as has been the case in Turkey. A traditionally authoritarian regime can enter into the same

CASE IN CONTEXT

402

Democracy and Authoritarianism in Germany

Germany is a country that has seen a number of major regime changes over the course of its modern history. As such, it is a sort of laboratory for scholars interested in questions of democracy, democratization, and democratic breakdown. It has seen failed democratic consolidation, emergent authoritarianism, the splitting of the country after military defeat, with parallel authoritarian (East Germany) and democratic (West Germany) polities and, finally, successful reunification with a very well-consolidated democracy.

For more on this case, see Part VI, p. 402. As you read it, keep in mind the following questions:

1. Why did Germany see so many transitions in the 20th century?
2. Does the German case help us to understand why transitions happen more generally, or is it idiosyncratic?
3. These transitions occurred back and forth in the same country. What are this fact's implications for theories about why regime change happens?

hybrid status as a result of partial and limited democratization—or else superficial efforts to appear compliant with international norms and expectations.

Here we will sketch a fictitious but roughly representative example of each scenario. Polity A involves a transition from a more democratic regime to a hybrid regime, and Polity B involves a transition from a more authoritarian regime to a hybrid regime.

The citizens of Polity A achieved democratization several decades ago against the odds. Similar countries in their region remained authoritarian or reverted to authoritarianism in subsequent years, but Polity A remained democratic. Of course, there were problems. Ongoing poverty and inequality were major issues. Political parties became bureaucratic and prone more to elite corruption than to representing the populace. Those parties came to dominate political life: You could not access state resources or services without going through the parties. Then, a major regional crisis struck. The country's debt expanded dramatically, and as a result it had to make major cuts in public spending. Polity A's state could no longer do the kinds of things its citizens expected the state to do, such as (more or less) effectively policing, providing some minimal health care and food and housing assistance, and managing the business cycle through effective government spending when times were tough. A political candidate came along promising to change all of that by throwing the corrupt elites out of office. Once elected, this leader began to argue that the very institutions of representative democracy were part of the problem because they were inherently elitist and that the existing legislature and judiciary were full of representatives of the old parties. The leader used this argument to justify the constitutionally questionable transformation of these institutions. Soon, the legislature and judiciary were filled with loyalists of the new leader, as were the electoral authority and the military. Elections continued, but in many ways the deck was stacked against the regime's opponents.

The citizens of Polity B lived for many decades under an authoritarian regime. That authoritarian regime collapsed, however, and savvy politicians rushed to fill the political vacuum. These political entrepreneurs quickly (maybe even recklessly) embarked on major political and economic reforms, creating a brief and limited democracy. The result was that the publicly owned resources the state had amassed during its many decades of authoritarianism quickly fell into the private hands of a small, highly concentrated group. At the same time, living standards for the majority of the population fell dramatically, and social problems such as crime and drug addiction soared. Within a few years, a leader arose promising to restore the country's glory and the people's old standard of living, blaming the new elites for Polity B's problems. This leader, like the leader in Polity A, continued to allow regular elections to be held but practised intimidation of the press, selective prosecution, and occasional fraud to remain in power.

Both Polity A and Polity B underwent transitions to hybrid or semi-authoritarian regime status. You may call them "Venezuela" and "Russia," if you like, though with those two countries, there will be disagreement about whether they are hybrid or authoritarian regimes.[28] The first started from a position of relatively robust democracy and the second from long-standing authoritarianism. These are only two of numerous possible patterns through which such regimes can emerge.

Causes and Effects: What Causes Authoritarian Regimes to Emerge and Persist?

In this section, we consider four major theories of the emergence of authoritarian regimes: those that focus on class coalitions at critical junctures, those that focus on poverty and inequality, those that focus on weak states, and those that focus on political culture. We also discuss some special causal circumstances surrounding hybrid regimes.

Historical Institutionalist Theories

As discussed in Chapter 5, historical institutionalist theories look for critical junctures in which institutional patterns become set.[29] In explaining the emergence of authoritarian regimes, these theories look for junctures when either authoritarian institutions are formed or coalitions supportive of authoritarian rule are established. Why might these events happen at certain key moments in the development of a polity? First of all, there are in many societies at many times certain groups that would be better off without democratization or believe that they would be. Such groups might include (1) representatives of organizations who receive special treatment under an existing authoritarian state—perhaps religious organizations or military actors; (2) economic actors who want to control the state to use it as a tool against those who wish to redistribute wealth or to expand economic rights; or (3) individuals or groups who fear that democratization will lead to the confiscation of their wealth or the reduction of their privileges—possibly wealthy economic actors such as landlords or business owners and/or nobles, depending on the circumstances. If elite actors have reason to fear democratization, they may try to form and maintain nondemocratic institutions and to assemble a coalition supportive of such institutions.

A historical institutionalist theory tries to explain how institutions get set in a particular pattern and then explains subsequent development as a consequence of the institutional path that has been established. Such a theory would thus mainly try to explain why authoritarian institutions were established in the first place. It may further argue that the coalitions of actors supporting the institutional arrangements must remain present to account for the persistence of those arrangements.[30]

Let's imagine another fictitious society. It undergoes a transition from one type of authoritarian regime—an absolutist monarchy with an agrarian economy and an economy based on estates—to a more modern dictatorship. The following actors are present at the transition:

- the existing authoritarian state;
- the representatives of the old nobility, who fear revolutionary change;
- landowners, some of whom are noble and some not, who make their living from collecting rents from peasants on their land;
- a relatively small but increasingly powerful group of industrial entrepreneurs;
- a relatively small but growing group of industrial workers;
- a large religious organization that has exerted a monopoly with the support of the old state; and
- a large population of peasants.

The old state had bankrupted itself and then had begun imposing heavy taxes on the rents acquired by agricultural elites (including the dominant church, which owned a lot of land). It had also taxed its own exporters heavily, arguing that manufacturing should serve the interests of the crown by producing goods for sale only to the king's subjects. It had cut all military spending. Under such circumstances, a coalition has formed among four elite groups: landowners, the military, the church, and the industrial entrepreneurs. While these groups' interests are not identical, they all are being hurt by existing policy. If this coalition brings about regime transition, though, that regime might be authoritarian because each of these groups wants to protect its existing privileges. Now let's imagine further that this coalition successfully creates new institutions: We might expect those institutions to endure and for authoritarianism to persist until some new crisis emerges later in the country's history. The importance of such coalitions is central to the classic argument by Barrington Moore about why authoritarian and democratic regimes emerge (see the "Insights" box on *The Social Origins of Dictatorship and Democracy*).

Some would argue that Moore's argument is not really historical institutionalist because he places so much emphasis on class relations and democratic or authoritarian outcomes. A key question here is the extent to which the persistence of a given democratic or authoritarian regime is a consequence of (1) ongoing class coalitions or (2) institutional inertia. Moore, despite being criticized for not being sufficiently state-centric,[31] seems to have assumed that once the conditions for democratic or authoritarian regimes are established, they are largely set for the foreseeable future. Some other, rational-choice institutionalist accounts differ in this respect.

Poverty and Inequality

If we accept modernization theory's explanation of democratization—that economic development causes societies to become more democratic—we would expect the obverse to be true as well. Economic collapse, increasing poverty, and increasing income inequality likely predict a turn toward authoritarianism, and ongoing economic stagnation and poverty likely predict authoritarian persistence.

This theory may make sense for some people at an intuitive level. If you are worried about where your next meal is going to come from or how to access health care, you are probably less likely to devote your energy to demanding the right to vote, engaging in political speech, protesting, reading political newspapers, and the like. As a result, all else being equal, we would expect pressures in poorer societies to link more directly to the satisfaction of basic economic and social needs than to political liberties. This certainly does *not* mean that poorer people do not value political rights and liberties but rather that

INSIGHTS

The Social Origins of Dictatorship and Democracy: Lord and Peasant in the Making of the Modern World

by Barrington Moore

Moore is essentially the intellectual grandfather of one variety of contemporary historical institutionalism. He offers a modified Marxist account of why some societies ended up with liberal democratic, fascist, or communist/socialist regimes by the 20th century, and he finds his answer in the class structures of the societies he studied as they made the passage to modernity. While Moore's book is nuanced, the *key* variable he notes is the presence or absence of a "bourgeoisie" or "middle class." If a strong middle class was present when a society passed to political modernity, it was likely to end up a liberal democracy.

Conversely, countries without a strong and large middle class present during the passage to modernity were likely to result in coalitions averse to democracy. There are lots of ways that this can happen. An existing agrarian elite might join forces with the small middle class to outcompete peasants, or the middle class might form an alliance with the peasants themselves, producing a revolution that tends toward authoritarianism. Moore argued that the first scenario tends to produce right-wing authoritarianism and the second, left-wing authoritarianism.

Barrington Moore, *The Social Origins of Dictatorship and Democracy: Lord and Peasant in the Making of the Modern World* (Boston: Beacon Press, 1966).

some needs will tend to strike us as more immediate than others, depending on our circumstances.[32] International survey research that tracks political attitudes supports this finding: As economic development increases, prioritization of political freedoms tends to increase, whereas in poorer societies, "survival values" score more highly.[33] Again, people in poorer societies would, all else being equal, likely *prefer* democratic regimes in many instances, but they may be less likely to successfully *press* for democratization and/or the maintenance of democratic institutions.

Economic factors of this sort might matter not just in how they affect citizens' attitudes but also in how they shape the institutional environment. While historical institutionalists argue that paths are set at critical junctures, determining long-run outcomes, rational-choice institutionalists are more interested in how institutions relate to the ongoing interests of groups and individuals in the polity. Further, rational-choice institutionalists look at how shifting configurations of interests and institutions change the bargaining positions of those groups and individuals.

Income inequality, in addition to absolute poverty, is another likely factor contributing to the establishment of authoritarian regimes. Societies with high levels of income inequality seem more likely to be authoritarian than those with low levels of income inequality. The relationship between these variables is complex, however. One source of the association between authoritarianism and inequality may be that authoritarian regimes sometimes promote social and economic inequality in addition to obvious political inequality. In an authoritarian regime, there is not open access to the state.[34] Rather, some elites are privileged, and other citizens are excluded from connections and decision-making power. This discrepancy is clearest in cases in which dictators amass property for themselves and their associates, such as the infamous Somoza family, which held power in Nicaragua from 1936 to 1979 and came to hold an absurdly high percentage of Nicaraguan territory as its personal property.[35] If a large segment of the population has limited access to resources, we might expect that segment to be less involved in democratic participation or in pressing for democratization.

Income inequality may help to favour authoritarianism in another way as well: It may engender envy and social division of the sort that potential authoritarian leaders can exploit. Many authoritarian regimes will present themselves as avengers of injustice. Populist leaders who tend toward authoritarianism can claim to represent disenfranchised poor people and can promise to redress visible inequalities. Interestingly, this seems to be a characteristic of both left- and right-wing populism.[36]

State Weakness and Failure

Another theory focuses on state structures, arguing that weak or failing states are more likely to yield authoritarian politics.[37] This may be related to economic theories of authoritarianism. While some forms of authoritarianism go with strong states (e.g., totalitarian forms), many tend to be linked to weak states or to those shading toward state failure. Even the major totalitarian polities emerged from states that faced serious difficulties, such as late-Tsarist Russia in the 1900s or Weimar Germany in the 1930s.

As noted in Chapters 3 and 4, one of the key features of strong states is that they are well institutionalized. Well-institutionalized states tend to be less personalistic and more resistant to the efforts of private actors to co-opt them for their own gain. "Predatory states" or regimes, however, are those in which one group in society is able to capture the state and use it for the group's own benefit.[38] In some of the worst cases, the boundary between the private property of the ruler's family and that of the state is unclear, and ruling elites use the military instrumentally against their opponents within society.[39] So we seem to have a kind of paradox. On one hand, well-institutionalized, strong states with high capacity may be less likely to fall into authoritarianism, but when they do, there is a higher chance that they will develop totalitarian forms of authoritarianism, which requires a strong state to begin with. Just the same, authoritarianism in weak states with predatory regimes can be very destructive as well.

Of course, state failure or state weakness can be an independent variable that causes authoritarianism, but it in turn is caused by something else. State failure or state weakness happens for a reason, as discussed in earlier chapters. It may be that low economic development leads to weak states, which in turn leaves a polity vulnerable to authoritarianism. If this is the case, low economic development can be thought to indirectly encourage authoritarianism *through* its impact on state weakness. In other words, causal sequences like the following simplified model are possible, with the arrows understood to represent *probabilistic* causality:

Low economic development → *Weak state* → *Authoritarianism*

An alternative theory might look like the following, also treating a weak state as a variable that intervenes between a more distanced cause and authoritarian politics:

Unstable class coalitions → *Weak/poorly institutionalized state* → *Authoritarianism*

This theoretical causal sequence rests on the assumption that strong states might be products of stable class coalitions. If this is true, and if weak states breed authoritarianism, then unstable class coalitions might be thought to indirectly raise the likelihood of authoritarian outcomes.

Political Culture Theories of Authoritarian Persistence

Other theories of authoritarian regimes hold that the beliefs, norms, and values of a country's citizens determine its regime type. The idea here is that people in societies that are culturally authoritarian are more likely to have and keep authoritarian regimes. Theorists have identified different types of authoritarian cultures, and some argue that certain countries or regions have inherently different values.

Which values are hypothesized to matter depends very much on the theory in question. Some scholars have argued that certain types of national identity might be more conducive to authoritarianism than others.[40] Others have suggested that certain countries or cultural regions, like Latin America, have a generalized "centralist" disposition that increases the likelihood of accepting authoritarian regimes.[41] Others have noted that some societies establish "traditions" of authoritarianism and that the weight of tradition predicts a higher probability of future authoritarianism.[42] Still others have argued that what matters are not general cultural dispositions of this sort but rather the variation, observed through extensive survey research, in attitudes toward civic participation.[43]

Even those who are skeptical of the claim that political culture strongly predicts authoritarianism will often be more receptive to the idea that political-cultural variables can, under certain circumstances, increase the likelihood that certain *types* of authoritarianism will develop. This idea might be clearest in the case of modern totalitarian regimes. It is very difficult to explain the *path* taken by Soviet or Nazi totalitarianism without paying some attention to the ideas of Marxist and fascist thinkers and the ways in which these ideas influenced the thinking and strategic behaviour of key actors in the establishment of those regimes.

Barriers to Collective Action

collective action Action undertaken by individuals and groups to pursue their ends in formally or informally coordinated ways, often in pursuit of some common or public good such as expanded civil rights or sustainable use of common resources.

Rational-choice and game-theoretical approaches constitute an alternative to political culture theories in attempting to explain authoritarian persistence. These approaches are especially popular in the United States. Such approaches try to model the rational processes of decision-making in which citizens and politicians engage.[44] They tend to presume that these actors know their own interests (or preferences) and have imperfect information about the likely behaviour of others. According to these approaches, actors are unlikely to engage in **collective action** unless it becomes rational for them to

INSIGHTS

Now Out of Never: The Element of Surprise in the East European Revolution of 1989

by Timur Kuran

Kuran tries to explain how rapid transitions from authoritarian rule could take place when previous data indicate support for the old regime. He is particularly interested in the revolutions that took place in 1989 in countries like Poland, Czechoslovakia, and East Germany. His key insight is that under certain circumstances *preference falsification* may be quite common. If it is risky or socially unacceptable to publicly state your preference for more democracy, you are unlikely to do so. In such an environment, people are likely to overstate their support for authoritarianism. This preference falsification is costly: It is psychologically unpleasant to have to pretend to like things that you do not like. Some people most opposed to the regime are least willing to falsify their preferences and are the first to make their voices known. If they do so without major repercussions, more people begin expressing their true preferences. A cascading pattern then develops as it becomes safer for more people to speak out against the regime.

Many authoritarian states seem to implicitly understand this, which is why so many of them devote such resources to controlling discourse and public gatherings. Barriers to the collective expression of preferences for democracy are barriers to mobilization against authoritarian regimes.

Timur Kuran, "Now Out of Never: The Element of Surprise in the East European Revolution of 1989," *World Politics* 44 (1, October 1991): 7–48.

do so, meaning the chances of success seem high, their contribution seems important to the desired outcome, and they are unlikely to face major costs for participating in such action.[45] These approaches constitute alternatives to political cultural theories of authoritarian persistence because they assume that most people want more democratization (regardless of their culture) but that sometimes there are major barriers to democratic transition such that it would be *irrational* for any individual actor to take the necessary steps to provoke a transition.

These factors can interact with political culture. Part of the information that a rational actor takes into account is the likely behaviour of his or her peers. This information is largely gleaned from their public expression of their beliefs and attitudes (the same things students of political culture are studying), and sometimes populations under authoritarian regimes might appear to be more supportive of the regime than they really are. We return to these themes in later chapters on political parties, social movements, and revolutions (Chapters 11 and 12).

Special Causal Circumstances Surrounding Hybrid and Semi-authoritarian Regimes

In contemporary politics, we have witnessed an increase in the number of hybrid regimes, a pattern of political change that has given rise to a good deal of new and productive theorizing. According to the Economist Intelligence Unit (EIU), hybrid democracies can be defined by the following criteria:

> Elections have substantial irregularities that often prevent them from being both free and fair. Government pressure on opposition parties and candidates may be common. Serious weaknesses are more prevalent than in flawed democracies—in political culture, functioning of government and political participation. Corruption tends to be widespread and the rule of law is weak. Civil society is weak. Typically, there is harassment of and pressure on journalists, and the judiciary is not independent.[46]

To some extent, explanations for the emergence of hybrid regimes differ from those for the emergence of more traditional forms of authoritarianism, though we would not want to exaggerate these differences. Equally important, if we are interested in transitions *from* or persistence *of* hybrid or semi-authoritarian regimes, we need to be attentive to their special characteristics.

We should not draw the conclusion that the factors cited earlier to explain the rise of authoritarian regimes or authoritarian persistence are irrelevant to hybrid regimes, but we should note that a particularly important variety of hybrid regimes—the competitive authoritarian regimes of recent decades—seem to show their own, historically specific, causal factors of importance.

The EIU reports that there were 39 hybrid regimes in 2018, representing 23.4 per cent of countries and 16.7 per cent of global population. Turkey is a good example of a country that has regressed from a functioning if flawed democracy to something quite different now. Changes to the nature of the political system have come under Turkish president Recep Tayyip Erdoğan, who was elected in 2002 with 34 per cent of the popular vote. Since that time, he has worked to instill his Justice and Development Party (Adalet ve Kalkınma Partisi, AKP)

Press Presidency Press Service via AP, Pool

PHOTO 7.5 **Turkey's President Recep Tayyip Erdoğan (centre), surrounded by his entourage and security detail, talks to people gathered after Friday prayers at a mosque in Ankara, Turkey, in July 2016. After an attempted military coup in 2016, Turkish lawmakers declared a state of emergency that continued to 2018, which allowed the government to extend detention times and issue decrees without parliamentary approval.**

as the only party capable of ruling the country. After an attempted military coup in 2016, a state of emergency was declared, which continued until 2018. In 2017, a referendum was held to approve 18 constitutional changes, moving Turkey from a parliamentary to a presidential system. The referendum (which was extremely close and fraught with irregularities) allowed Erdoğan to dissolve the office of prime minister, to tighten control over the military, to increase his influence over the judiciary, and to ensure that elections would be non-competitive, dramatically reducing the legal channels for opposition parties to compete for political power. Turkey imprisons large numbers of people opposed to the regime, including political figures, journalists, teachers, activists, and others. Charges of terrorism are lavishly used to support imprisonment.[47]

Turkey joins other countries in the region that were also classified as hybrid in 2018: Albania, Armenia, Bosnia-Hercegovina, Georgia, Kyrgyz Republic, Macedonia, Moldova, Montenegro, and Ukraine. Some countries, like Armenia and Bosnia-Hercegovina, saw their EIU-generated scores improve while others, like Georgia, plummeted during the same period. Georgia is controlled by billionaire former prime minister Bidzina Ivanishvili, who exerts tremendous influence over the electoral system, including widespread corruption. In 2018, he signally influenced the government to intervene "in the second-round presidential election, offering a debt write-off to 600,000 citizens two weeks after election day."[48] Hybrid regimes can be found throughout the world.

THINKING COMPARATIVELY

Why Did Zimbabwe Become Authoritarian?

KEY METHODOLOGICAL TOOL

Evidence and Empirical Critiques

One reason that many theories continue to endure in different areas of comparative politics is that most of the major theories have some empirical support. This makes it challenging to determine which theory is the most accurate. In reality, most theories will not be accurate under all circumstances, but rather each will explain some outcomes better than others. So how do you avoid simply making "laundry lists" (as noted earlier) and saying, "Everything matters"? In preparing to make theoretical arguments, it is of course important for any particular question to examine how the empirical evidence lines up with the theoretical predictions and the specific hypotheses you might offer. One very useful tool can be evidence that allows you to critique a particular argument.

In aiming to build arguments, there is one very important misconception: that the only valuable type of evidence is that which supports a hypothesis or theory. In fact, some of the most valuable evidence is that which allows you to critique or challenge one particular argument. This is useful especially when you are trying to determine the strongest argument among many that have some supporting evidence.

Authoritarian regimes come in many varieties, and they come from many different origins. We have emphasized that there is no single thing called "authoritarianism" that one theory can explain. Rather, authoritarian regimes have distinct features and exhibit many different types of transitions (and nontransitions). Scholars have developed a number of explanatory models to account for them. Some of the main general factors in most cases, though, include (1) historical relationships between contending groups, (2) the strength and form of existing institutions, (3) a country's level of economic development, (4) political-cultural traditions and tendencies, and (5) the strategic situations and choices of key actors. Of course, as we have seen in other chapters, it is not enough to merely list such contributing factors; we must figure out how such factors interact and which are the most important. What do you think? And how could we test your ideas empirically?

As we noted at the outset of the chapter, modern-day Zimbabwe has until recently had the characteristics of an authoritarian regime. It was "personalist," characterized by repression, a lack of secure political rights, seemingly arbitrary rule, and so on. Not everywhere in Africa is like this, and Zimbabwe itself has not always been like this and may not be in the future, so our research question might be: "Why was Zimbabwe authoritarian? Why did it become so, and why did it remain so for almost four decades?"

We should expect theories of authoritarian rule to be able to account for an authoritarian regime like the late Robert Mugabe's. Looking at the various causal theories of authoritarianism, we can consider how each might propose an explanation for the emergence and/or longevity of the regime. In the section on "Causes and Effects" in this chapter, we looked at several such theories. We list them in Table 7.1, along with what the theory might explain was the cause of Zimbabwe's authoritarianism. We also list in the third column an example of evidence that we might find supports this theoretical proposition. Note that the examples of supporting evidence here are not proven but are simply plausible for this particular case.

Looking at the theoretical prediction and the examples of evidence to support the theory, we may see a problem: We can find some plausible evidence to support all of these theories. We can go right down the column and come up with decent evidence. Robert Mugabe's authoritarian regime did indeed receive the support of some key coalition actors, it appealed to many of the poor in a populist fashion, it was a poorly institutionalized predatory state, it represented itself as a quintessentially African unit resisting Western influence, and it saw many hundreds of thousands of its opponents flee the country rather than risk repression. Indeed, this discussion illustrates something often experienced in the study of comparative politics. Sometimes, at

TABLE 7.1 | Authoritarianism in Zimbabwe: Theories, Explanations, and Examples of Supporting Evidence

Theory	Theoretical Explanation	Example of Supporting Evidence
Historical Institutionalist	Coalitions of powerful political actors emerged that favoured elite domination.	Mugabe received support of the military and key economic actors.
Poverty and Inequality	Poorer citizens sought economic security and allowed authoritarian rule.	Mugabe appealed to some poorer citizens as populist.
State Weakness	Weak, poorly institutionalized, predatory state will be authoritarian.	Mugabe engaged in predatory behaviour and undermined institutions.
Political Culture	Cultural values shaped the type of authoritarian regime that emerged.	Mugabe worked within bounds of some top-down traditional cultures and the ways they were co-opted under British rule.
Collective Action	Disapproval of the regime was impeded by repression.	Mugabe's regime created large numbers of exiles.

a certain stage in the development of research on a topic or question, we do not know *which* theory truly offers the best explanation for a given phenomenon, and multiple explanations seem promising.

Does this mean we are stuck? Or that we should assume that all theories work equally well and that we should list them all as the answers to our research question? No. On the contrary, it is common for many good research questions to have multiple possible answers. Indeed, it is often a sign of a good question that it can have many possible answers: It suggests that the question is open-ended and not one with a foregone conclusion that is self-evident and therefore uninteresting. In the parlance of comparative politics from Chapters 1 and 2, a good theory must be falsifiable, and the fact that multiple possible theories can address a question is often a sign that the question is well-conceived. Furthermore, theories in comparative politics will not last if they get no empirical support, so we should not be surprised if more than one theory has evidence working for it. But the job of the comparativist is to analyze the relative merits of these different arguments and to find ways to adjudicate among them.

What can you do if several different theories each have some evidence going for them? Our most important tool here is looking for evidence that works *against* one theory or another. This disconfirming evidence that allows you to critique one or more theories can sometimes help you to identify which theory stands strongest. In fact, evidence that works against one theory can be just as valuable as an extra bit of evidence that supports a theory. It may be *more* valuable, since the implications of truly disconfirming evidence are stronger than the implications of some evidence that is simply consistent with a theory.

What might be examples of disconfirming evidence for the theories in our Zimbabwe example? Table 7.2 has the same theories and theoretical explanations as Table 7.1, except that this time we consider evidence that might show that Mugabe and Zimbabwe did not follow what the different theories predict. Notice that we can actually come up with at least plausible examples of disconfirming evidence as well for any of the theories we noted previously.

Here we see examples of how each theory could have some evidence against it, just as each theory had some evidence for it. Comparativists can use evidence both to support and to critique different theories as they try to identify which theory is strongest. We should be particularly attentive to evidence that would post a strong challenge to a theory. For example, in Table 7.2 the evidence presented for the "political culture" and "collective action" theories might suggest real weaknesses in their ability to explain Zimbabwe's long history of authoritarianism. We cannot say, for instance, that traditional Zimbabwean political culture was the source of Mugabe's authoritarianism if Zimbabwean political culture was not actually authoritarian. Likewise, we cannot say that the source of his authoritarianism was that dissidents could not organize or speak if, in fact, dissent was widespread and organized.

On the other hand, some theories can be defended in the face of potentially challenging evidence, either because the evidence is being interpreted wrongly or because the theory has been construed in a limited or wrong way. Imagine proponents of the historical institutionalist theory trying to make their argument. They might acknowledge the evidence that Mugabe alienated many elite economic actors and that this had negative implications for the argument attributed to historical institutionalism in the table: "Coalitions of powerful

TABLE 7.2 | Authoritarianism in Zimbabwe: Theories, Explanations, and Examples of Contrary Evidence

Theory	Theoretical Explanation	Example of Contrary Evidence
Historical Institutionalist	Coalitions of powerful political actors emerged that favoured elite domination.	Mugabe's economic policy alienated key economic actors, including industry and commercial farmers.
Poverty and Inequality	Poorer citizens sought economic security and allowed authoritarian rule.	Mugabe was relatively unpopular among peasants and poor urban dwellers.
State Weakness	Weak, poorly institutionalized, predatory state will be authoritarian.	Zimbabwe's state and Mugabe's party and military exhibited considerable capacity in the past.
Political Culture	Cultural values shaped the type of authoritarian regime that emerged.	Zimbabwe's deep cultural values through traditional tribal principles have deep emphasis on human rights.
Collective Action	Disapproval of the regime was impeded by repression.	Zimbabwe's people were relatively open to expressing dissatisfaction with the regime.

political actors emerged that favoured elite domination." They could point out, though, that commercial and farming elites were not the only important actors among whom coalitions could form and that the Zimbabwean state under Mugabe created a *new* coalition of powerful actors from the military and masses of unemployed men. Theories cannot proceed by being adapted to deal with each individual case, but if a theory has been misconstrued or its implications not fully built into tested hypotheses, seemingly disconfirming evidence might still be compatible with the theory.

Authoritarianism remains one of the most analytically and morally pressing questions in comparative politics today. As it has become clear that democracy was not simply going to predominate all over the world after the Cold War, scholars have re-engaged on the question of authoritarian rule. The types and causes of authoritarianism are numerous and complex, but young scholars who develop the analytical skills of comparativists will be in a position to shed real light on these issues in the years to come. And as we discuss throughout this book, all democratic states have authoritarian tendencies within them and among some actors and institutions at certain times. Democratic states can slide into authoritarian modes of governing while remaining democratic. Some scholars have argued that the United States is becoming increasingly authoritarian while still remaining democratic. Former president Jimmy Carter argued in 2017 that the proliferation of big money in US politics was making his country more of an "oligarchy than a democracy."[49] President Trump is routinely criticized in the mainstream media for his authoritarian tendencies.

Chapter Summary

Concepts

- Authoritarianism refers to political systems that are hierarchically ordered and have relatively closed decision-making processes.

Types

- There are many different types of authoritarian regimes, including totalitarian regimes that attempt to control entire societies through ideology, personalist dictatorships centred around individual autocrats, and bureaucratic-authoritarian regimes centred around groups such as the military.
- There are also many different possible transitions (or lack of transitions) between regime types other than democratization: Authoritarian regimes can persist, they can give way to other authoritarian regimes, or they can turn into hybrid regimes, while democracies too can break down and move toward authoritarianism or hybrid regimes or become more authoritarian while remaining nominally democratic.

Causes and Effects

- There are many theories about the causes of authoritarianism and its persistence, including theories based on: historical institutional factors; poverty and inequality; state weakness; political culture; and impediments to collective action.

Thinking Comparatively

- Theories about the causes of authoritarianism (like theories in other areas) may all find some supporting evidence, and a useful strategy for judging the power of theories for specific research questions is also to consider how evidence may disconfirm a theory.

Thinking It Through

1. We have discussed the distinction often drawn by political scientists between democratic regimes and "hybrid" or "competitive authoritarian" regimes. Where is the line between these sorts of regimes? Consider any two cases of democratic regimes, and try to work out what combination of developments would lead you to reclassify them as "hybrid."
2. We discussed a number of different theories of authoritarianism. Note that the historical institutionalist theories, the economic theories, and the political culture theories all aim to explain both the emergence and the persistence of authoritarian regimes. Can these theories explain the emergence and persistence of hybrid regimes equally well? If so, demonstrate how. If not, what sorts of modifications might help them to do so?
3. Is authoritarianism simply the opposite of democracy? Is it best thought of as an absence of democratic freedoms and rights? Or is democracy best thought of as an absence of authoritarianism? Why?
4. Is the United States becoming more authoritarian? How might we measure increasing or decreasing levels of authoritarianism over time?
5. Why has the Economist Intelligence Unit classified the United States as a flawed democracy and Canada as a full democracy? What differences account for these classifications?
6. Identify your preferred theory to account for the persistence of authoritarianism in Russia, North Korea, Iran, or another country of your choosing. Consider yourself a theorist associated with this preferred theory. Now imagine you have been called in to consult with Global Affairs Canada about the best way to deal with authoritarian regimes the government deems dangerous, such as North Korea, Syria, or Russia. What would your theory imply as a policy recommendation for how to deal with authoritarian regimes?

PART III

Institutions of Government

8 Constitutions and Constitutional Design

In This Chapter

From left to right, F.W. de Klerk, Cyril Ramaphosa, Nelson Mandela, Leon Wessels, Thabo Mbeki, and Kobie Coetzee outside the Parliament of South Africa on the day the new constitution was adopted in May 1996. (Oryx Media Archive/Gallo Images/Getty Images)

Consider the following passage:

We, the people of South Africa,
Recognise the injustices of our past;
Honour those who suffered for justice and freedom in our land;
Respect those who have worked to build and develop our country; and
Believe that South Africa belongs to all who live in it, united in our diversity.

We therefore, through our freely elected representatives, adopt this Constitution as the supreme law of the Republic so as to

Heal the divisions of the past and establish a society based on democratic values, social justice and fundamental human rights;

Lay the foundations for a democratic and open society in which government is based on the will of the people and every citizen is equally protected by law;

Improve the quality of life of all citizens and free the potential of each person; and

Build a united and democratic South Africa able to take its rightful place as a sovereign state in the family of nations.

May God protect our people.
Nkosi Sikelel' iAfrika. Morena boloka setjhaba sa heso.
God seën Suid-Afrika. God bless South Africa.
Mudzimu fhatutshedza Afurika. Hosi katekisa Afrika.

This passage is the preamble to the South African Constitution passed in 1996, which established the foundational laws and the basis for democracy after decades of racial discrimination and white-only rule known as *Apartheid.* A key function of a constitution can be to express the values of a society, especially those relating to the unity and aspirations of the people. The South African charter was a major step in creating a "New South Africa" based on equality and respect for the dignity of the country's peoples (even if it certainly did not solve all the country's racial problems). The preamble addresses this aspiration and notably concludes with an expression translated into six of the country's major languages. These aspirations may vary from place to place: The lengthy introductions to China's and Iran's constitutions, for example, document the history of the revolutionary movements that gave rise to the regimes currently in power.

The Constitution of the Republic of South Africa, and most others like it, also does more than express the country's ideals in writing. It is a very specific legal document that creates a design for the country's formal political institutions, including the legislative, executive, and judicial branches. It also addresses the division of power between a central government and the provinces. With regard to judiciaries in particular, the South African Constitution established a very important power of constitutional interpretation: judicial review. Judges were given the authority to determine which laws are consistent with the Constitution and which are not. The South African judiciary even ruled on whether the Constitution itself was constitutional, evaluating the text, determining what was adequate and proper and what was not. It accepted much of the text submitted in 1994 but sent the Constitution back to its drafting body, the Constituent National Assembly, to clarify some issues and rewrite others.

In this chapter, we examine constitutions, the questions of whether and how they separate power between levels of government, and whether they are interpreted by judiciaries. We leave the discussion of the constitutional roles of legislatures and executives to the subsequent two chapters, in which we treat those two branches of government individually. The issues related to constitutions and constitutional interpretation matter because, in most modern societies, constitutions establish many of the formal organizational features of the state and thus are keys to understanding politics.

This chapter begins our examination of formal government institutions, which are the structures and organizations that shape political behaviour. The most obvious among these are the branches of government, two of which we explore in depth in later chapters (the legislative and executive branches[1]), and we also include the study of political parties and interest groups that are a regular part of political life. Because the very foundation of political institutions is usually located in constitutions, we focus on these basic charters in this chapter and on the question of constitutional interpretation. Who helped create the constitution, and were all groups involved? Who was included, and who was excluded? How is political power divided among different governing institutions? Who decides whether a law is constitutional? We take a close look at these issues and discuss both federalism and judiciaries, which are key elements of what constitutions say and what they do.

• • •

Concepts

We look first at concepts and definitions, outlining what we mean by constitutions, federalism and unitarism, and judiciaries. We then turn to types across different countries to show how constitutions, constitutional design, and constitutional interpretation may vary from place to place.

Constitutions

constitution Fundamental and supreme laws, usually written in a charter, that establish the basis of a political system and the basis for other laws.

Constitutions are the foundational charters and fundamental laws of most modern states. They elaborate the structure of government and express founding principles. They are usually written documents passed by some sort of constitutional convention or constituent assembly that brings together many of a country's dominant political figures to hammer out the rules, laws, and structures needed to establish the basis for political life. This may occur at the founding of a country, as in the case of the United States, or as part of a very long transition to full judicial independence, such as when Canada patriated its Constitution in 1982, fully 115 years after Confederation.

While the US gained its independence immediately through force of arms, Canada pursued an evolutionary rather than revolutionary course. The 1867 British North America Act created Canada, not so much as a separate country but as "One Dominion under the Crown of the United Kingdom of Great Britain and Ireland, with a Constitution similar in Principle to that of the United Kingdom."[2] Britain continued to decide most of Canada's foreign policy, and Canada was part of the British imperial system.[3] Various other pieces of legislation changed the nature of Canada's ties to Britain. The 1931 Statute of Westminster created a Crown which was effectively "split," meaning that Canada as a self-governing dominion had the right to create its own laws independent of Britain, although Britain still had the right to amend the Canadian Constitution. Treaties with Indigenous peoples signed by the British Crown (guaranteeing protection against encroachment by settlers) were now handed over to the governments elected by and representing settlers.[4] In 1948, Canadian citizenship was created, whereas before, Canadians were still technically British subjects. In 1982, the Liberal government of Pierre Trudeau succeeded in patriating the Constitution, which meant that Canada now had full control over its ability to amend its Constitution, something that only Britain had the power to do before 1982. Canada thus became fully sovereign at that time, which is within the living memory of most Canadians over the age of 40.[5]

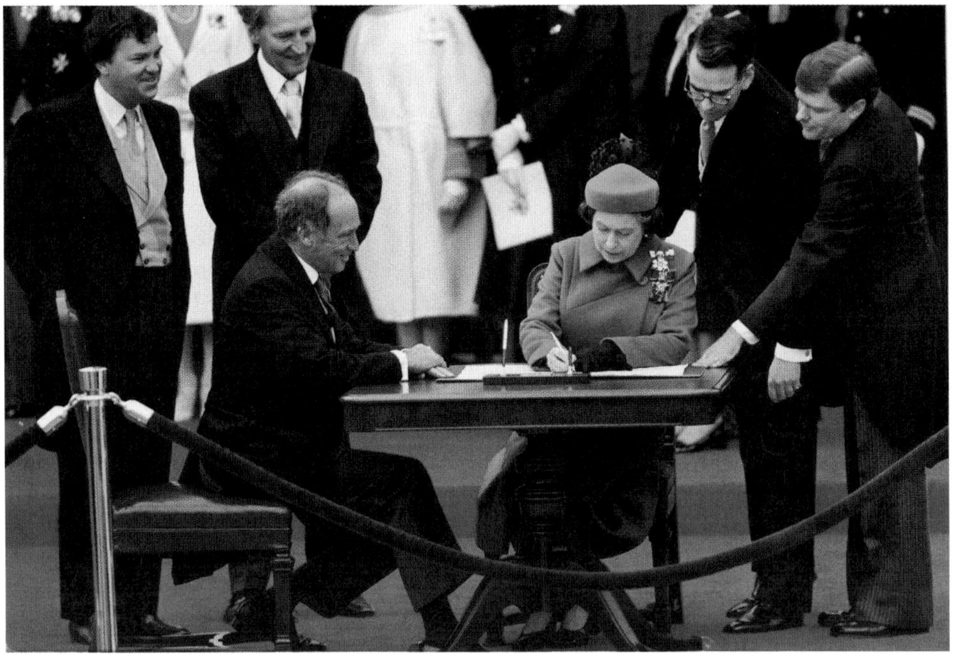

Stf-Ron Poling/THE CANADIAN PRESS

PHOTO 8.2 Queen Elizabeth II signs the Proclamation of the Constitution Act, 1982, in Ottawa on 17 April 1982 as Prime Minister Pierre Trudeau (seated) looks on. This patriation of the Constitution transferred the British North America Act from Britain to Canada, meaning that Canada now could amend its Constitution without needing approval from Britain.

Constitutions may be short, like the US Constitution (just over 4500 words; more than 7500 words with its 27 amendments) or long, like the failed European Union constitution, which contained 70,000 words, often of a very dense bureaucratic prose. It helps if a constitution can be clear and accessible to the population. James Madison, the main architect of the US Constitution, observed that "It will be of little avail to the people that the laws are made by men of their own choice if the laws be so voluminous that they cannot be read, or so incoherent that they cannot be understood."[6]

Constitutions have come to symbolize the social contracts that societies make to "constitute" themselves in which "the people" confer authority on political actors in exchange for the establishment of order and a rule of law. This can be a problem if certain groups (such as Indigenous peoples or enslaved Africans) were deliberately excluded from the process of founding the society and the laws to which they are subject. What happens when a society constitutes itself without the consent of many of the groups that comprise that society? This question has still to be answered in most settler states, as we discuss later.

The history of constitutions links closely to the idea of **constitutionalism**, or limited government, and is thus part and parcel of the story of the evolution of modern governance and especially the emergence of democracy itself.

constitutionalism The limitation of government through a constitution.

As the basic founding laws of a society, constitutions are the set of rules and norms on which all other laws are based. In Canada, the Constitution is the ultimate point of political reference and the key focus of legal cases at the federal level. One unique aspect is Section 35, which both recognizes and affirms the existing Indigenous and treaty rights of Indigenous peoples. Another unique aspect is the Charter of Rights and Freedoms (1982), which sets out the limits of the federal and provincial governments and the extent to which they can encroach into the lives of their citizens. This is in some respects similar to the first 10 amendments to the US Constitution, known collectively as the Bill of Rights. Unlike the US amendments, Canada's Charter of Rights and Freedoms does not include a guaranteed right to purchase and use firearms and does not have an absolute right to freedom of speech. The Charter provides protections for Canadians but does not guarantee any absolute rights.

Generally, constitutions can be seen as sets of laws outlining the basic structure of the state and its patterns of governance, noting which branches of government have which powers and which responsibilities. In many cases, constitutions recognize or grant the basic rights of a country's citizens, though these rights are not always guaranteed in every case. Indeed, even highly authoritarian regimes (like Iran, North Korea, and the former Soviet Union) often make use of constitutions, regardless of whether rights are infringed in practice. In most cases, constitutions are written down in a single document that is subject to change by a process of amendment.

We should note that in many former British colonies, new citizens and elected officials take an oath to the head of state rather than to the constitution. This is true of Canada and some other Commonwealth countries. Those taking the oath "swear (or affirm) That I will be faithful And bear true allegiance To Her Majesty Queen Elizabeth the Second Queen of Canada Her Heirs and Successors And that I will faithfully observe The laws of Canada And fulfil my duties As a Canadian citizen."[7] An oath like this reminds Canadians that their country is not a republic like the US but rather, as we noted in Chapter 6, a constitutional monarchy still governed by settlers and steeped in British traditions of governance.

Constitutional Design: Including Some, Excluding Others

constitutional design Features of constitutions that shape the basic features of the political system, such as separation of powers and responsibilities between levels of government and branches of government.

Constitutional design refers to the features of the constitution that shape the powers of different political institutions. These features vary, though all constitutions define the basic structure of government. Constitutional design is important because it gives countries the chance to set up effective institutions. Consider the examples of the United States, Australia, and Canada. America's founding after its revolt against Great Britain depended on its writing a constitution that would make one country out of 13 former colonies. One of the central issues in the American Constitution was how to divide powers between the central government and the states. Its early history was largely about creating a constitution that would allow 13 quite different settler colonies to come together as a political unit. Who was involved in creating the Constitution? In the American case, well-educated, white, property-owning males were the decision-makers. In a sense, they acted for some of the other peoples in their society (namely, women and children), but the Constitution was designed to promote the rights of those within what Alexis de Tocqueville called the "Anglo-American union." So what about everyone else?

Charles Mills's book *The Racial Contract* argues that the contractarian basis of the American republic was inequality because without Indigenous lands and African-American slave labour, the social system could not have functioned effectively. The state was always constructed on the basis that some peoples (namely, white men and to a lesser extent white women) would be in control and benefit the most from the social, political, and economic goods generated by the state. Conversely, other groups (namely, Indigenous peoples and racialized peoples, particularly African Americans) would be in a permanent state of exploitation. Inequality was thus a central part of the political system from the very beginning.[8]

As America was founded, Indigenous peoples were included only as a threat to the colonists, necessitating independence from Britain. The Declaration of Independence (1776) listed a series of charges against King George III, who "endeavored to bring on the inhabitants of our frontiers, the merciless Indian savages, whose known rule of warfare, is undistinguished destruction of all ages, sexes and conditions."[9] The Constitution was created by white settlers seeking to form a settler-based government to the exclusion of Indigenous peoples, whose lands the new state would take over. Enslaved Africans were also excluded from any constitutional deliberations. This creates some fundamental problems at the heart of many constitutions, and political elites have subsequently tried to expand constitutions to create more inclusive polities.

In the Australian colonies, because Aboriginal lands were not cultivated, used for grazing, or used for urban development, the British declared Australia *Terra Nullius*, "belonging to no one, empty, a wasteland that could be claimed without having to acknowledge the native title of the Aborigines."[10] Australia's Indigenous peoples were not recognized in the 1901 Constitution as political actors and continue to struggle to have their rights recognized. Many Australians seek constitutional reform to properly recognize Aboriginal prior ownership, occupancy, and rights over the lands, at least in the preamble to the Constitution.

Canada's British North America Act of 1867, as we discussed earlier, set out the duties of the provincial and federal governments. However, Canada was not fully independent at that time. Rather, the creation of the country was premised on having dual benefits, both for "the Welfare of the Provinces" and "the Interests of the British Empire."[11] Indigenous peoples were not recognized or included in this process. This exclusion had some very negative implications for Indigenous peoples, who had most of their lands taken by the government and were stripped of the ability to govern themselves as they had done for thousands of years.

Associated Press/John Pye

PHOTO 8.3 A group of Indigenous protesters block a road, bringing a temporary halt to the Queen's Baton Relay before the opening ceremony for the 2018 Commonwealth Games on the Gold Coast, Australia, in April 2018. The protesters termed the games the "Stolenwealth Games," referring to the injustices suffered by their communities.

That Indigenous peoples were self-determining, sovereign, political actors was affirmed by the British Crown through the 1763 Royal Proclamation and the 1764 Treaty of Niagara. In 1763, some 2000 Indigenous representatives met with Crown officials, establishing a system of relationships for sharing lands and going forward together using the language of kinship. The treaty was crucial in establishing Canada because it recognized Indigenous ownership of the land and premised European settlement on Indigenous consent.[12] The treaty established clear lines of authority and gave the British Crown responsibility for ensuring that local colonial administrations would not bother Indigenous peoples in the exercise of their rights, in the practice of their government, and in their use of resources and lands.[13] At Niagara, Two Row Wampum belts were exchanged, conveying for Indigenous peoples an "understanding of a mutual relationship of peace and non-interference in each other's way of life." The treaty's oral implications were a recognition of Indigenous self-government and a recognition of "an alliance between sovereign nations."[14] The Covenant Chain belt, also part of the treaty, depicting two individuals holding hands, represented distinct peoples who were also interdependent, participating in mutual aid while also respecting the differences of each.[15]

The treaties, however, were violated, and the Canadian government proceeded to do everything in its power to take control of Indigenous lands and peoples. One of the most negative legacies of settler colonization was the creation of Indian Residential Schools. These schools were funded by the federal government and run by the main Christian churches in Canada, mainly the Catholic, Anglican, Presbyterian, and United churches. Starting in the 1880s, seven generations of Indigenous children were forcibly taken from their families and communities so that they could be assimilated in a network of more than 130 residential schools. Verbal, physical, and sexual abuse were widespread aspects of this system. Survivors of the residential schools system launched a series of class action suits against the federal government and the churches, culminating in an agreement in 2007 providing compensations and other benefits to formally recognize the crimes that had been committed against Indigenous peoples. In 2009, a Truth and Reconciliation Commission (TRC) was formed, funded by survivors, to gather testimony about what these children had endured in the schools and also to document the often painful legacies of their experiences. The TRC operated under a six-year mandate and concluded its work in 2015. The commission issued a two-million-word report, which included 94 Calls to Action to bring about reconciliation.

The TRC observed that given that the Canadian state was established against the interests of Indigenous peoples and actually went against early agreements between the British Crown and Indigenous leaders, fundamental changes were needed. In recognition of the fact that the state did not include Indigenous consent, the TRC's 45th Call to Action recommends that the federal government work with Indigenous peoples to jointly create:

a Royal Proclamation of Reconciliation to be issued by the Crown. The proclamation would build on the Royal Proclamation of 1763 and the Treaty of Niagara of 1764, and reaffirm the nation-to-nation relationship between Aboriginal peoples and the Crown. The proclamation would include, but not be limited to, the following commitments:

i. Repudiate concepts used to justify European sovereignty over Indigenous lands and peoples such as the Doctrine of Discovery and terra nullius.
ii. Adopt and implement the United Nations Declaration on the Rights of Indigenous Peoples as the framework for reconciliation.
iii. Renew or establish Treaty relationships based on principles of mutual recognition, mutual respect, and shared responsibility for maintaining those relationships into the future.

v. Reconcile Aboriginal and Crown constitutional and legal orders to ensure that Aboriginal peoples are full partners in Confederation, including the recognition and integration of Indigenous laws and legal traditions in negotiation and implementation processes involving Treaties, land claims, and other constructive agreements.[16]

These recommendations would help make the Canadian polity a more respectful and just regime for Indigenous peoples. While Section 35 of the Canadian Constitution of 1982 guarantees that "The existing aboriginal and treaty rights of the aboriginal peoples of Canada are hereby recognized and affirmed," it's not obvious what this means in practice. A new royal proclamation could repudiate the exclusionary founding concepts of the state and might help Canadians usher in a new era of reconciliation. It could also pave the way for further aspects of Indigenous self-determination, which could include political control by Indigenous nations over the traditional lands and perhaps a House of First Peoples as part of a "third order of government." There are precedents in other countries. The indigenous Sami people in Finland, Norway, and Sweden all have parliaments where they exercise a range of rights through their representatives and negotiate with national and municipal governments.[17]

The Separation of Powers?

Federalism is a political system in which multiple levels of government have some degree of autonomy in the same territory. This system is often developed in very large or very populous countries where it would be very difficult to administer all policies and social programs from one central capital. Rather, administration and the duties of government are divided, reflecting regional, demographic, and other differences in the country's population.

federalism System of government with constitutional design of separation of powers between the central government and subnational governments.

Only in some countries do subnational governments (such as provinces, territories, states, or regions) have constitutional protection or authority and a guarantee of autonomy from the central government. These may be called federal systems. For instance, the 10 provinces of Canada, the 50 states of the United States, and the nine provinces of South Africa have constitutional guarantees of their authority to govern and establish laws in their respective regions, even as the central government also has the right to do so.

By contrast, the absence of federalism is unitary government, or **unitarism**, in which the institutions and branches of the central government effectively wield political power. Most countries in the world are unitary. In these countries, local governments (such as towns, cities, or villages) have some authority to shape local rules, but the laws made by these local governments are subject to central authority. As we shall see, federalism is not necessarily more or less democratic than unitarism, but its implications for how government works are numerous.

unitarism System of government in which the central government is predominant and the powers of subnational governments are limited to those delegated by the centre.

Constitutional design usually also involves establishing a **separation of powers** among distinct branches, each with its own responsibilities and duties. Constitutions frequently begin by establishing a legislative branch responsible for formulating and passing laws. This may be called a parliament, a congress, or an assembly or may be given any number of other names, as we examine in the chapter on legislatures (Chapter 9). The executive branch (Chapter 10) is the other portion of the government that is usually elected, at least in democratic regimes, and the powers and functions of the executive branch are routinely outlined in a constitution as well. For both of these branches, constitutions often outline the procedure by which representatives are chosen, in addition to the powers they hold and duties they must perform. Constitutions also often address the structure and power of the judicial branch as well as the structure of the administrative apparatus.[18] This delineates the

separation of powers The division of powers in a government system between branches of government or between levels of government.

separation of powers between the three "branches" of government: legislatures, executives, and judiciaries. We discuss legislatures and executives in full in Chapters 9 and 10, respectively, though they are also clearly elements of constitutional design.

judiciary The branch of government responsible for the interpretation of laws in courts.

Judiciaries functioning together as a system form the legal branch of government, and they have particular importance in how constitutions are interpreted. The principal duty of the judiciary is to preside over cases in courts. This implies the power to interpret the laws put into effect by the other branches of government, but the extent of the judiciary's power to interpret (and even strike down) laws varies from one country to another. In some countries, judiciaries have considerable powers of constitutional interpretation (Canada and the US are obvious examples), while in other countries, they do not rule on whether laws are constitutional. The principal distinction is the strength of **judicial review**, which refers to the power of constitutional courts to determine the legality of laws.

judicial review System of constitutional interpretation in which judges rule on the constitutionality of laws passed by legislature and executive.

These two features—the extent of federalism and the respective roles of the branches of government—are central to both constitutional design and constitutional interpretation. For the remainder of this chapter, we will discuss variations in constitutions themselves, as well as the different ways constitutions are designed and interpreted. These variations are considerable, as we will see in the section that follows.

Types

There are several ways countries differ in how their constitutions are designed and interpreted. In general, constitutions can be designed to be flexible and easily changed or rigid and difficult to change. A second issue is how the constitution is interpreted and specifically whether the judiciary has the power to interpret the constitution. A third element is the degree of federalism in a constitution. Finally, we note that both democratic and authoritarian regimes have constitutions, and they may differ in some ways but may also look quite similar on paper.

Flexible and Rigid Constitutions

One of the central distinctions among different types of constitutions is how easily they can be changed. Many constitutions are designed to be relatively difficult to change. Amending them may require supermajorities in each chamber of the legislature (i.e., more than just a simple majority of votes) or approval by a number of the units of the federation—the states, provinces, or regions. Some constitutions, such as that of the United States, are even harder to change. An amendment to the US Constitution requires a two-thirds vote in each of the two houses of Congress, followed by approval of three-fourths of the states' legislatures. It has been amended only 27 times since its passage and only 17 times since 1791.

At the other end of the spectrum are highly flexible constitutions that are easy to change, at least nominally. The most obvious case is those that can be changed by a simple majority of the legislature. The Constitution of the United Kingdom is one of the most flexible, at least according to the law. This is because in the British system, the Parliament is sovereign: If a majority of the legislature passes a law, that law is by definition constitutional.

This flexibility relates to another feature of the British Constitution. Today, most countries have a single written document (which can be amended) that defines the parameters of the political system. The United Kingdom does not have a single constitutional text, but rather several documents are deemed to have constitutional significance as the country developed its political system over the course of many centuries. The major constitutional documents include the Magna Carta of 1215 but also a range of other laws of great significance and stature, such as the Bill of Rights of 1689, which emphasized certain limitations on the power of the monarchy, and the Acts of Settlement of 1701, which established patterns of succession to the throne. In this sense, it may be said that the United Kingdom has a "written" Constitution but one that relies on a range of documents rather than on a single one. What is considered constitutional is also determined by acts of Parliament and precedents in common law. New Zealand, a former British colony, similarly relies on a set of major acts of Parliament that established the constitutional basis for the country's governance. This does not mean that the United Kingdom has no constitution; in fact, it has one of the longest traditions of constitutional government in the world.

As societies have grown more complex, constitutions in more recent years have often grown longer and more intricate as they attempt to balance a range of different interests, institutions, and ideas. The South African Constitution, mentioned at the top of the chapter, is an example. So too is the Brazilian constitution of 1988, as noted in the concluding "Thinking Comparatively" section of this chapter.

Constitutions regularly recognize the rights of citizens or grant rights to the citizenry. In the case of the US Constitution, many fundamental rights were passed as a set of amendments, known as the Bill of Rights. Since then, many contemporary constitutions (including the South African and Brazilian examples) have incorporated significant rights into the main text from the very beginning, which is likely one cause of constitutions becoming much lengthier over time. That is, articles in the original constitutional texts of many countries specify civil rights and civil liberties, political rights, and social rights (such as access to certain public services).

PHOTO 8.4 Delegates to Brazil's Constituent Assembly celebrate the passage of the country's constitution in 1988.

Separation of Powers: Judicial Review and Parliamentary Sovereignty

In many (but not all) countries, courts have the power to decide some constitutional issues and rule on whether a law passed by the legislature is constitutional. If constitutional courts find that the law is not consistent with the constitution or basic laws of a society, they may strike down the law. In these countries, constitutional courts are usually separated from the civil and criminal court systems. In systems with separation of powers, this is the "check" that the judiciary has on the legislature. Constitutional courts are not the only type of courts. Local courts are for local disputes and for claims involving local laws, including arrangements over property (such as buying and selling houses), issues of marriage and divorce, traffic violations, and some criminal offences.[19] Constitutional courts are reserved for major constitutional issues about whether a law passed by the government is valid.

The process by which national courts examine the constitutionality of law is called judicial review. Most constitutions provide for a process of judicial review in which constitutional courts have judges who rule on the constitutionality of law. Judicial review is the central political power of the judiciary, and it occurs when judges examine the constitutionality of a law passed by the legislature. In countries with judicial review, the constitution is seen as the supreme law of the land, and it is the role of the courts to verify that laws passed by the legislature are consistent with the constitution.

Judicial review generally operates with a high court or "supreme court" at the pinnacle of the judicial system that serves as the final arbiter of constitutional law. The Supreme Court of Canada was founded in 1875 and became the final court of appeal in 1949. Supreme courts may be built on top of a system that has "lower courts" in different states, provinces, or localities around the country.[20] The high court is composed of a select number of established jurists or justices. In the United States, there are nine justices on the Supreme Court, nominated by the president and approved by the Senate for life terms. In Canada, the Supreme Court also has nine justices, appointed by the prime minister and serving until the age of 75. In systems with judicial review, the decisions of such courts are often final and can be overturned only by subsequent judicial decisions or by legislatures amending the constitution itself. This system of constitutional interpretation by judges is regularly a source of debate and disagreement in the United States and in other countries, as discussed in the "Causes and Effects" section later in the chapter.

The most prominent examples of countries without constitutional courts and judicial review are those where the constitutionality of law is determined by parliament. In such cases, the judicial system is composed of courts that rule on the merits of specific cases in accordance with the laws that exist, without questioning the legitimacy of those laws. Of course, here too there may be some interpretation of what the laws mean, but the court is not empowered to strike down or alter laws passed by the legislature. The United Kingdom is the most noteworthy example. Here, there is no high court empowered to rule on most matters of law; the few minor exceptions relate to the question of how some powers have been decentralized to the regions of Scotland, Wales, and Northern Ireland, and this has been true only since 2009.[21]

Constitutional interpretation in the United Kingdom generally follows the doctrine known as **parliamentary sovereignty**. This means that if the legislature—often called the Parliament—passes a law, that law is constitutional by definition. The legislating body is the highest political and legal authority in the land.

parliamentary sovereignty System in which the constitutionality of laws passed by legislature and executive are not subject to constitutional interpretation by judiciary.

Federalism and Unitarism

The distinction between federal and unitary countries (and countries in between) is a fundamental difference in the way power is divided in a society. Federal countries have a system in which power is separated between the central government and some subnational governments that are partly autonomous. In unitary systems, power is located at the centre. In unitary states, the centre may delegate certain powers to local, regional, state, or provincial governments, but it retains the constitutional or legal authority to reverse its decision at virtually any time.

Federalism

The question of ruling large, complex territories is perennial, but the idea of federalism as a solution came more recently.[22] The United States was an early leader in establishing federalism, along with Switzerland, Canada, and Australia. Today, many federal countries around the world have intricate sets of interacting institutions. Originally designed to unify diverse territories while preserving subnational autonomy, federal institutions now do more than simply offer a way to ensure that nations do not fall apart: They divide governing power and allow some laws and policies to vary from place to place within a country, even as some national laws (and the national constitution) take precedence everywhere inside the borders.[23] Federalism is now seen by some as a strategy to ensure more than stability and protection, since it may also promote democratic inclusion. For these reasons, many of the world's largest countries either are federal or have prominent features that resemble federalism.

Although only about 20 of the nearly 200 countries in the world are considered federal, these 20 countries account for a large portion of the world's population. Many of the largest and most populous countries are federal, including the world's four most populous countries after China: India, the United States, Indonesia, and Brazil. Other federal countries include Nigeria, which has the largest population of any African country, and Canada, Australia, Pakistan, Russia, Mexico, and Germany, which are some of the largest countries in their respective regions of the world. Using a relatively inclusive definition designed to capture virtually any country that *might* be considered federal, we have constructed Map 8.1.

There are debates about whether many of the countries shaded in Map 8.1 are reliably federal (such as Spain and Pakistan). Several institutional elements and historical features may suggest otherwise, and federal countries do not always respect real autonomy for subnational units. Conversely, other countries may have some federal features yet remain unitary states, as is the case with China, where provinces have gained economic and political autonomy relative to the central government in recent years. China shows that some countries can seek the benefits of decentralized government without necessarily establishing federalism.

Federal systems may be defined as those where subnational governments have constitutional guarantees of some power and autonomy in their own jurisdictions, as well as constitutional protections from infringement on the part of the central government. In practical terms, virtually all federal countries share other characteristics: an upper legislative chamber defined in the constitution with territorial representation for the states/provinces/regions that provides them with political protection and full legislative and executive branches at the subnational level.[24] While the specific definitions may vary, it is clear that federalism is intended to ensure representation for the subnational level in national decision-making.

Unitarism

Most countries in the world are unitary states in which the central government is the only level of government specified in the constitutional charter. In unitary states, power is not constitutionally divided between layers of government but resides exclusively in the central

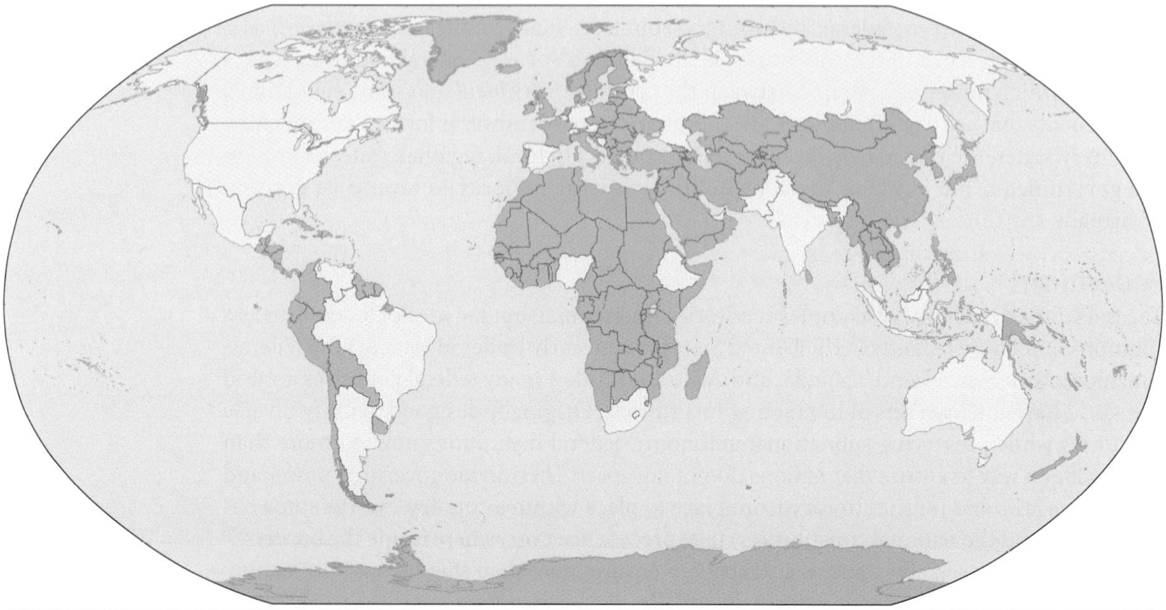

CONTINENT	AFRICA	ASIA	EUROPE	NORTH AMERICA	SOUTH AMERICA	OCEANIA
FEDERAL COUNTRIES	Comoros Ethiopia Nigeria South Africa	India Indonesia Malaysia Pakistan Russia United Arab Emirates	Austria Belgium Bosnia & Herzegovina Germany Spain Switzerland	Canada Mexico United States	Argentina Brazil Venezuela	Australia Micronesia

MAP 8.1 Federal systems around the world (in yellow).

government. This central government may then create (or allow for the creation of) more local levels of government, but these lower levels are dependent on the centre and often accountable to the centre. Municipalities, prefectures, counties, or other local governments may elect officials locally, but they generally have little power. To use a translation from the French, the republic is "one and indivisible." Local governments may be able to elect officials, but the national government makes most significant policy. For instance, the centre may establish the national school curriculum and may staff the offices of the health service, with relatively little scope for discretion at the local level.

Unitarism is especially prevalent in countries with certain characteristics. One is small size, as contrasted with the large size of most federal states. Most countries that are small are also unitary, with the exceptions being a handful of federal countries composed of a cluster of small islands.[25] Another tendency is for unitarism to hold in places where the population is ethnically, linguistically, and culturally homogeneous. Federalism seems to take root more where populations are linguistically diverse, as in Belgium and Switzerland, which are divided into different linguistic communities. Finally, unitarism may vary at least in part on colonial heritage. For example, former French colonies in Africa have long tended to follow the highly unitary features of France itself, while former Spanish and British colonies have varied in their structures. Some countries have tried out one system before switching to another. For example, New Zealand had a federal system in 1841 as six planned settlements from around the country joined together. The initial six then rose to nine—each with its own provincial capital and legislature. This was done primarily for reasons of convenience because the settlements were geographically isolated one from the other. By 1876, a strong central government was created as the population grew, and the federal system was officially abolished.[26]

Authoritarian and Democratic Constitutions

Historically, making government constitutional meant eliminating the divine right or absolute power of monarchs, such as kings, queens, princes, or emperors. Constitutionalism, as established in western Europe progressively over the centuries, meant preventing such rulers from exercising power in an arbitrary fashion and holding them at least partially accountable to the will of at least some of the people. As the power of monarchs faded in many countries, the drafting of constitutions became one way to limit the power of government, to divide and separate power such that a single person or family could no longer dominate. In parts of Europe, for example, constitutional monarchy was seen as distinct from divine right monarchy or absolute monarchy because executive power came to be derived by a mandate from the consent of the governed.[27]

Still, not all countries with constitutions exhibit the characteristics of democracy and limited government. In fact, the actors that demanded constitutionalism and the end of absolute monarchy were in many cases elites, nobles, revolutionaries, or military leaders. They were not always interested in political rights and civil liberties for all, and they did not always represent the people. For many centuries, the rights established in constitutions were often restricted to a small subset of the population, such as property-owning males of a certain racial or ethnic background, as Charles Mills has discussed in the case of the United States.[28]

Even today, not all political systems are perfectly constitutional, nor are all systems legitimate, fair, and just. Writing down a set of basic laws and rights on paper does not guarantee that those laws and rights will take effect or be enforced in practice; some countries that have constitutions fail to protect rights. Authoritarian regimes usually have constitutions, even where they deny political rights and civil liberties to their people. Such regimes may seek to establish their legitimacy on the basis of claims made in the constitution. For instance, a revolutionary socialist government may draft a constitution holding that the Communist Party is the sole entity capable of expressing the general will of the people. This would not seem "democratic" or "constitutional" to the minds of people who value individual rights and liberties, but the document itself could nonetheless be recognized as a constitution. Other authoritarian regimes may place less importance on political parties (or may outlaw parties entirely) and instead vest the ruler(s) with the authority to determine what the population as a whole requires.[29]

Authoritarian constitutions do not typically declare dictatorial rule, however, and in fact may appear quite progressive in terms of the rights and powers they list. Even totalitarian regimes may formulate extensive sets of rights in their constitutions, at least on paper, whether they defend them in practice or not.[30] In some instances, authoritarian regimes may even outline some rights that a democratic constitution may not contemplate. For instance, the constitution of the Soviet Union established rights such as guarantees of education, access to health care and housing, and a pension in old age. Some authoritarian regimes simply continue to govern under the constitutional charter of a previous democratic regime but suspend or override certain elements of the constitution. Military regimes have been known to establish martial law or states of emergency, which sometimes extend for long periods of time and during which normal constitutional principles do not apply. This is often done using the justification that national security requires exceptional measures.

Some countries also base part of their judicial and legal system on another authority: official religious law. This tendency is most noteworthy in the Islamic world, where *sharia* law plays an important role in many countries, though the use of religious law is not limited to Muslim countries. *Sharia* law is based on the Qur'an (Koran), the Holy Book of Islam, and to a lesser extent on other core Islamic texts such as the Hadith (or the sayings and practices of the prophet Muhammad). Countries that follow *sharia* have judges and clerics that rule in conjunction with their interpretations of the Qur'an. Judiciaries in both Saudi Arabia and Iran are linked to the state religions, and they rule on the basis of religious law in many areas. Even interpretations of issues not treated directly in the Qur'an are reasoned by analogy with reference to the Holy Book or to the words and deeds (known as the *sunnah* and the *hadith*) attributed to the prophet Muhammad.

Religious law is not necessarily authoritarian, nor does it characterize all Muslim countries. For instance, Turkey is a majority Muslim country that is politically secular although it has become a hybrid regime and is no longer considered a democracy, as we discussed in Chapter 7. Other countries, such as India and Indonesia, make partial use of Islamic law, such as applying it in certain kinds of legal cases between Muslims (such as family law about marriage, divorce, and parenthood). Israel, the United Kingdom, and other countries make provisions for the use of religious law by Orthodox Jews and others, largely as an option for use by populations who wish to resolve such matters in religious courts. In fact, one leading scholar has argued that recent years have seen a rise in "constitutional theocracy" in which constitutional law is combined with recognition of an official state religion and some use of religious beliefs or texts as a foundation for law.[31]

Causes and Effects: What Are the Effects of Federal Constitutions?

Two essential questions in the study of political institutions are (1) whether a given design is better than others (and if so, how) and (2) whether the ideal institution depends on country contexts. Political scientists engage in extensive debate over the relative merits of different forms of institutions, whose foundations may lie in constitutions, as we've discussed. We can consider at least three substantial questions about the consequences of federal constitutions: (1) Are they good for social stability? (2) Are they good for protecting democratic rights? and (3) Are they good for the economy? We consider these questions here, as well as whether judicial review is necessary in protecting rights and upholding the law.

Are Federal Constitutions Good for Social Stability?

To help answer the question of stability, we can start by looking at the origins of federalism and unitarism in different societies. A long-standing argument held that federalism was the result of disparate political units coming together for the purpose of security, with the post-revolutionary United States being the classic example. Canada is another obvious example, although ironically, the original provinces joined together in part because of the threat of a militarily expansionist America, which threatened to annex the British North American colonies.[32] It may also be, however, that countries go federal in order to hold together; that is, they may devolve authorities to regions to prevent secession or division and increase economic potential, such as we see in Australia.[33] As for unitarism, here too the causes may be found in deep historical legacies, including efforts by monarchs long ago to

CASE IN CONTEXT

Online

Constitutional Design: Theocracy in Iran (online case)

In Iran, clerics have considerable power, both at the pinnacle of the political system and at lower levels of government. Some analysts may see this power as emerging from a dominant cultural feature and thus reflective of the norms of the people. Some may also see it as fitting that different societies have different systems reflecting cultural differences. For others, basing law on a single religion (and a single religious text, as interpreted by clerics) constrains, by definition, the rights and liberties of those who are not Muslim or otherwise religious.

For more on theocracy in Iran, go to **www.oup.com/he/DickovickCe** to see the case study. As you read it, keep in mind the following questions:

1. How is the judiciary an especially powerful branch of government in Iran, and what are its powers?
2. Are there checks on the judiciary's power, and if so, what are they? Or should the country be seen as a case of "judicial sovereignty" as opposed to parliamentary sovereignty?
3. Is it possible to conceive of religious law that is compatible with democracy—and if so, how? Or is separation of religion and the state a necessary feature of democracy—and if so, why?

consolidate power or to unify authority. As noted in Chapter 3, the modern nation-states of Europe were created from the merging of much smaller units, such as principalities, as well as the splintering of large empires.

From one perspective, federalism may be an institution uniquely capable of holding together a large and diverse polity. By conferring powers on levels of government below the national, federalism may give more people a stake in the political system. If certain regions or groups feel they have greater autonomy, then they may be more willing to participate instead of demanding independence. Movements demanding separatism, secession, or break-up of a country will gain less traction in countries where these groups have powers reserved to them by a federal constitution. One such approach has been taken by Ethiopia, where the constitution actually gives different regional groups the right to secede (though it is unclear how this would work in practice). The expectation is that by giving autonomy and power to the ethnic groups, and by offering an out, the constitution will encourage compromise and enhance the recognition of the merits of unified government. By this logic, federalism enhances stability.

On the flip side, federalism might lead to exacerbating differences and undermining stability. By drawing significant lines (almost literally) between different groups, federal systems may end up encouraging different regions of the country to develop independent identities. This question emerges in Canada, with Quebec "sovereignists" seeking to separate and form their own independent country. After two failed referenda on independence (1980 and 1995) and generational and demographic changes, this era may be drawing to a close . . . or not. In other countries with more precarious economies and more fragile societies, such as Nigeria, ethnic minorities or regions that feel they are being treated unfairly by the central government are often critical of the federal system. In some such cases, they may increase demands for secession or separation, which may even explode into ethnic violence.

CASE IN CONTEXT

373

Is Quebec Independence Now off the Agenda?

Canada is one of the most interesting cases for the study of how federalism relates to secession. Quebec is the only province that is predominantly French-speaking and was one of the key founding provinces of the country in 1867. During the 1960s, a movement for Quebec independence developed as the province became more urbanized. In 1980 and 1995, the Parti Québécois held two referenda on independence. The first failed by a wide margin, the second by barely one per cent of the vote.

For more on this case, see the case study in Part VI, p. 373. As you read it, keep in mind the following questions:

1. What are the links between the urbanization and modernization of Quebec in the 1960s and the demand for independence?
2. Why is independence much less likely now than in previous decades? What is the role of immigration?
3. Have Pierre Trudeau's bilingual policies helped to reduce Quebec's interest in becoming an independent state?

Are Federal Constitutions Good for Democratic Rights?

Federalism may have an impact on democracy in ways similar to those discussed earlier: Federal institutions may make government more stable and may facilitate the democratic incorporation of the demands of many groups, or federalism may reinforce divisions. Beyond the question of whether federalism is likely to make democracy persist, we may also find the question of democratic rights.

Consider a very heated cultural debate, such as over abortion in the United States, and how it relates to the question of federalism. The pro-life position holds that embryos and fetuses are people and therefore have a right to live (usually starting from the time of conception), implying that the biological mother may not choose to abort a pregnancy. The pro-choice position holds that a woman has a right to have control over her own body with respect to reproduction and that the government may not dictate to her what she must do in terms of the decision to terminate a pregnancy.

There are many ethical, moral, and legal aspects to such a debate, but for the moment we ask only a question about federalism. One perspective on abortion has been a "states' rights" perspective, which maintains that different states (say, Vermont and Alabama) should be allowed to have different laws governing abortion, which would reflect the different sets of values and beliefs of the majorities in each place. This structure would allow different parts of a federal country to express their own views on rights and would be consistent with some of the perceived advantages of federalism. Basically, states would exercise choice over whether to legally restrict abortion.

It's worth taking a minute to point out that Canada is quite different with respect to this issue and that there have been no legal restrictions on abortion since the Supreme Court decision *R. v. Morgentaler* in 1988 ruled that restrictions on abortion were unconstitutional. While there are both pro-life and pro-choice positions in Canada, 57 per cent of respondents in a 2016 survey favoured a woman's right to choose "under any circumstances," with only 3 per cent arguing it "should never be permitted."[34] While this is not a major issue in Canada, Americans see it as an extremely important litmus test of political ideology and identity. It is also a central question about the nature of federalism: Should people have different fundamental rights in a country depending on where they happen to be born or live?

Let's say that Vermont adopted a more pro-choice set of policies and Alabama a more pro-life set of policies. If you favour the pro-life argument, should a human embryo or fetus in Vermont have fewer rights than one in Alabama? Should Vermont be allowed to adopt its set of policies because of federalism? If you favour the pro-choice argument, should a woman in Alabama have fewer reproductive rights and less choice than one in Vermont? Should Alabama be allowed to adopt its set of policies because of federalism?

This question is fundamentally about what is in a constitution and what federalism should be. The question about democracy and rights under federal constitutions is not straightforward, as this example shows. Ultimately, as in Canada, this question was settled by the Supreme Court. In their well-known *Roe v. Wade* (1973) decision, the court mandated that abortions are legal until such time as the fetus is medically "viable" outside the womb. Viability changes as medical technology becomes more advanced. This overrides state laws and makes the restriction of abortions before this time illegal. The current Trump administration has taken a strong stand against *Roe*. He has appointed two pro-life justices to the Supreme Court who may exercise their powers to overturn *Roe*; this is something that concerns many pro-choice advocates.

Are Federal Constitutions Good for the Economy and Society?

Federalism may be good or bad for an economy, depending on one's point of view and on circumstances. On one hand, some see federalism as generating healthy competition among states or regions, which can be good for the economy. If province or state A sees that businesses are relocating to province B next door (maybe for reasons of lower taxes or better public services, for example), then province A may do its best to govern in a way more like province B (say, by providing better services). On the negative side, provinces may perform differently from one another, which may lead to significant differences in development and opportunities within a federal country, as the case of India shows (see "Case in Context: Federalism and Differences in Development in India"). In the Canadian context, some provinces have emerged as major industrial or resource extractive centres, while others have not. With its smaller, aging population and low endowments of mineral wealth, the Maritime Provinces have not done as well economically.

For Indigenous peoples, dealing with multiple levels of government can become problematic. In Canada, the federal government (as the Crown) is supposed to be the primary point of contact for Indigenous nations. The BNA Act of 1867 supposedly gave the federal government exclusive responsibility for "Indians and lands reserved for the Indians," which means it, as the Crown, is meant to provide education, social services, health care, and infrastructure such as houses, roads, community-building, and waste disposal. For non-status Indians and other Canadians, these functions are normally provided by provincial and municipal authorities. Some Indigenous theorists, however, point out that since the treaties had two signatories—the leaders of First Nations and representatives of the Crown—one signatory cannot change its identity without the consent of the other. That is, the treaties should still be guaranteed by the British Crown and not the "Canadian Crown," which has a direct conflict of interest in that it wants to control Indigenous lands for its own benefit.

CASE IN CONTEXT

Online

Federalism and Differences in Development in India (online case)

India is one of the world's fast-growing economic powerhouses, but it is also the country with the largest number of people living in extreme poverty. Some of the dramatic differences in development in India can be understood by looking at differences across states. Some states have performed very well, while others have performed quite poorly. The country retains a politics that has a very regional flavour despite decades of efforts at political centralization.

For more on this case, go to **www.oup.com/he/DickovickCe** to see the case study. As you read it, keep in mind the following questions:

1. What are the positive and negative examples of development in India's states, and what lessons does each of them offer?
2. What factors can account for the variations in the performance of Indian states?
3. What lessons do you draw from the Indian case about whether federalism might contribute to poverty reduction or perhaps worsen poverty?

The shift from the British to the Canadian Crown was further complicated when the Canadian Crown devolved many of its responsibilities to the provinces from the 1950s. This devolution created problems for Indigenous peoples with status, who saw many of their rights eroded by the splitting of the authority of the Crown. Devolution led to provincial encroachment into child welfare, which has led to massive numbers of Indigenous children being taken "into care" by provincial social welfare agencies. There have also been splits over who should be funding education and health care on reserves, disputes that have led to grossly substandard care in many cases. In 2013, the auditor general noted that "Services available on reserves are often not comparable to those provided off reserves by provinces and municipalities." In early 2016, the Canadian Human Rights Tribunal criticized the federal government for inadequately funding social services on reserves, arguing that this was a form of discrimination and funding should be equalized.[35] Is this a "passing of the buck"? How has it resulted in substandard services for Indigenous peoples? How can these problems be resolved?

Judicial Review and Democracy

Along with the division of power between levels of government implied by the issue of federalism versus unitarism, another prominent feature of most constitutions is the division of power among branches of government. In particular, one major question is who is responsible for interpreting the constitution, as we noted earlier in our section on judiciaries. A judiciary with constitutional powers of review can engage in an interpretation of the laws, and a question for many observers is whether this is appropriate and to what extent. In the United States, one of the biggest debates about the judicial system is over **judicial activism**, a term that has a negative connotation for many observers.[36] Judicial activism is a key issue in the United States, and the phenomenon is also recognized and debated in other countries as well. According to critics, unelected judges and justices may take advantage of the power of judicial review to essentially legislate from the bench as opposed to situating lawmaking power with the representatives in the legislature. This practice may take some of the most heated and controversial debates out of the democratic process by

judicial activism Term used, often pejoratively, to characterize judicial actions that actively reinterpret legislation and thus imply exercising powers typically reserved for the legislative branch.

removing them from the arena of elections, public debates, and protests and placing them in the arena of lawsuits, legal challenges, and the rulings of a small number of unelected judges in robes.

For some, judicial review is crucial to protecting rights and upholding the law.[37] By this argument, judges have the role of interpreting laws to ensure compliance with the letter of the constitution and legal precedent. Proponents of an active judiciary may argue that courts have often led legislatures (rather than followed them) in the recognition and expansion of fundamental rights. For this reason, proponents might argue, a judicial system has the task of interpreting laws and guaranteeing that they are consistent with rights and obligations laid out in constitutions.

As a term, "judicial activism" is susceptible to unclear definition. For instance, critics of judicial activism in the United States have often been conservative critics of justices' rulings on social and cultural issues, such as *Roe v. Wade* and recent judicial decisions at the state level over marriage equality involving the extension of civil union benefits and marriage rights to same-sex couples. Canada legalized same-sex marriage in 2005, and the majority of Canadians approve of this move. From a more left-of-centre perspective, many were dismayed in 2000 when the Supreme Court, in the case of *Bush v. Gore*, ended the recount of the Florida presidential vote and more or less declared George W. Bush president. Equally troubling was the 2010 Supreme Court decision in *Citizens United v. Federal Election Commission*, which ruled that organizations could spend virtually unlimited amounts of money in support of candidates in elections because a limit on spending was a restriction on free speech. While those on the right accuse the court of dictating morality, those on the left accuse the court of sabotaging the democratic process.

Sipa via AP Images

PHOTO 8.5 Protesters gather to demonstrate against Supreme Court nominee Brett Kavanaugh in late October 2018 in Washington, DC. Kavanaugh, a conservative, was President Trump's choice, and many on the left worried that he would be an activist judge and help to overturn liberal court decisions such as *Roe v. Wade*.

There is one clear way to end judicial activism: End judicial review. This is not merely a thought experiment or hypothetical exercise. In fact, as noted earlier, one can look to the United Kingdom as a model. One argument against extensive use of judicial review is that judiciaries remove contentious issues from the public arena. According to this argument, debates about the most fundamental issues in a democracy are fought out by the strongest ideologically committed advocates in front of unelected judges. These issues are thus examined and decided on by small groups and powerful individuals, and they may not be reflective of broader public opinion. Those arguing against judicial activism would often prefer to have society's most contentious issues decided in legislatures rather than in courts. The United Kingdom prevents judicial activism by granting the legislative branch of government an unambiguously higher power than the judicial branch. One way to view opposition to judicial activism is to ask about the extent to which one would sacrifice judicial review. Put another way, judicial review and some degree of judicial activism are the flip side of the checks and balances between branches of government.

Most countries with written constitutions do have a constitutional court that is responsible for judicial review. By some accounts, the power of judiciaries has increased around the world over time. Canadians too have debated whether judicial review is conducive to the public good, although the courts have not faced the same level of criticism as they do south of the border because they have tended to be less activist and do not have the same broad powers of review.

THINKING COMPARATIVELY

What Explains the Similarities between the Brazilian and South African Constitutions?

Key Methodological Tool

Most-Different-Systems Design

As noted in Chapters 1 and 2, comparison can be based on two cases that are quite *different* in many ways, not just based on countries that are similar in many ways. Countries that are "most different" can make for very compelling comparisons whereby one finds a common outcome between them. Since the commonalities come from such different cases, it can give some confidence that they are attributable to some of the few similarities between dissimilar countries. In some cases, such as the prevalence of written constitutions discussed in this chapter, the reasons for the common outcome may be that lots of countries follow a similar logic. For the example here, the two countries of Brazil and South Africa established constitutions with several similar features, including strong judicial review and institutions to support federalism. This happened despite the fact that the two constitutions were created on different continents and in different social circumstances by rather different groups of actors. The fact that the countries are "most different" in many ways yet similar in outcomes makes it an intriguing pair of cases for hypotheses about why constitutions take the forms they do.

Contemporary Brazil and South Africa were quite different places in many ways when they both convened constituent assemblies to write new constitutions in the late 1980s (in Brazil) and early 1990s (in South Africa). South Africa was emerging from a long history of racial injustice and segregation in the system known as *Apartheid* from 1948 to 1994. Conflict in the society was centred on the state's oppression of the black majority and the responses of black South Africans to that oppression, though violence also erupted among and between ethnic groups. In South Africa, the transition to democracy in the early 1990s took place against the backdrop of attempts to move beyond a racially charged past, with the white-led National Party and the black-majority African National Congress (nominally headed by Nelson Mandela) taking the lead roles in negotiation. Brazil, by contrast, had no such legacy of legal, formal discrimination (though it certainly has a long history of "unofficial" racism and discrimination) in the 20th century. It was a country coming out of two decades of military rule, with the military seeking a peaceable exit from power. We might thus expect them to come up with very different constitutions as their leaders formed conventions to establish a common framework for governance.

Yet the two countries' constitutions share many fundamental similarities. Most obviously, they both are based on a written constitution. Both constitutions expressed aspirational goals for the countries, but more important, they established basic political institutions, and the countries featured many similarities in their constitutional designs. Both established constitutional courts that would become powerful in interpreting the constitutions. Both also established a principle of shared power between the central government and state or provincial governments; that is, both had a degree of federalism.

Perhaps most noteworthy, however, is the sheer length of the constitutions. As of its adoption, Brazil's constitution of 1988 had 245 articles and filled a small book with all of its provisions. South Africa's (approved in 1996) had a very similar 243 articles and took on a comparably huge number of issues: It instituted large numbers of rights beyond the freedoms of speech and liberty, specified rules for issues such as funding for political parties, introduced a variety of municipal structures, created a formal role for traditional leaders, established procedures for the division of revenue between the levels of government, and described the design of the national flag.

Why might such different countries have such similarly extensive constitutions, with features of judicial review and of federalism? The reasons for the resulting similarities may be numerous. We might propose several hypotheses. Hypothesis 1 could be a matter of historical timing in that both countries adopted their constitutions at a similar moment in history; this may have mattered more than geographic distance between them. Simply put, constitutions written in an era (like the 1980s and 1990s) may be extensive because countries have grown compelled to address more sets of rights and issues when drafting a new constitution (for a "new country"). Perhaps socially complex societies (whether because of multiethnic identities or complex economic systems, as both Brazil and South Africa have) require more negotiations between conflicting parties. This may result in extensive constitutions detailing the compromise. The American Constitution and the original Canadian Constitution did not envision all the issues that would emerge in modern societies (and ignored women and non-white ethnic groups), but those writing constitutions today may write more thorough contracts. For example, a constitution that receives input from both men and women of different races, social classes, and ethnic or linguistic backgrounds may involve more written agreements than one written by a homogenous dominant group operating on a shared set of assumptions.

Other hypotheses might also explain the extensive nature of these two constitutions. Hypothesis 2 might be less focused on historical background and more on the powerful actors in the constitution-writing process, with an emphasis on the economic and political interests of the negotiators. The political parties in South Africa, and the politicians and military in Brazil, might have thought it necessary to make clear statements about the rights of all parties in the constitutional convention, with guarantees for both the new democratic governments and provisions that would provide some protection to the departing (non-democratic) government. Hypothesis 3 could be that the cases are not completely independent but are actually linked in that the South African and Brazilian constitutions may have been modelled on certain aspects of other constitutions (whether in Germany or Mexico). Insofar as countries do not exist in vacuums, the South African and Brazilian constitutions may have been modelled in part on experiences elsewhere. If research turns up evidence (as is the case) that South African and Brazilian constitution writers did explicitly look to other constitutions as models when writing their own, that would provide some support for Hypothesis 3.

Hypothesis 4 might identify other key similarities amid the differences between the countries, much as was discussed in Chapter 1. South Africa and Brazil may have many differences, but there are also some key political and social similarities that may affect constitutional design. For instance, both are racially and ethnically diverse, and both have high levels of economic inequality. The constitutions were certainly attentive to potential inequities, which may be construed as evidence for this hypothesis. They are also relatively large countries with various identity groups living in different locations; this may favour a degree of federalism (which itself requires more extensive constitutional language than is necessary in smaller, unitary states).

We will not explore the causality in detail, but as with previous chapters we can simply think about what sort of evidence would support each hypothesis. Research can help to determine which of the preceding hypotheses has the strongest support from the empirical evidence, and the findings from a specific comparison of these two cases will then have implications for broader research questions and other countries. Why do constitutions take similar forms in such different countries? Why do very different countries adopt federalism under disparate circumstances? These questions can be asked with respect to comparisons across many countries. Someone with expertise on the Brazil–South African comparison (or a similar comparison) will not have the final word on this for all countries but can contribute to thinking comparatively about important political questions such as constitutional design. The comparison can point to fruitful avenues for further research on the design and interpretation of constitutions. The comparative method we outlined in the beginning chapters and used in the previous chapters—including its use of the most-similar-systems design and most-different-systems design—can help us in the area of institutions as well.

Of course, we should note that these two constitutions are not completely similar. They have many differences that can also be the subject of further research. For one, the Brazilian constitution established a system with a president elected by popular vote, while in South Africa, the legislative chamber known as the National Assembly elects the president. The range of questions one could ask about these constitutions is thus considerable, and the same holds for the other major institutions explored in this chapter. Much as we can ask questions about federalism, we might look at seemingly similar countries and ask why one ends up being federal and the other unitary. Both Germany and Italy formed into coherent nation-states in the second half of the 19th century, and both have major regional differences internally, so why is one federal and the other unitary? Or, with regard to judiciaries, why have courts become so significant in constitutional interpretation even in former British colonies, given that Britain is the home of parliamentary sovereignty? These sorts of questions serve to show that institutions can be examined using the same comparative perspective developed and used in the earlier chapters. The possibilities of comparing institutions continue as we look at the branches of government in the next chapters.

Chapter Summary

Concepts

- Constitutions are the basic charters of modern states, and they are written documents in most countries.
- Constitutions lay out the basic framework for government institutions in a country, and they are the foundational laws of that country.
- Constitutions have tended to include some groups and individuals and exclude others. A challenge for marginalized peoples is how to use the constitution effectively to represent their rights. This includes Indigenous peoples and members of racialized communities.
- Two of the leading elements of constitutional design are federalism versus unitarism and the power of the judiciary to review for constitutionality laws passed by legislatures.

Types

- Federal countries are those in which subnational units such as states or provinces have some constitutional protection and political autonomy from the national government.
- Unitary countries are those in which the central government is sovereign and any subnational administrative units are subordinate to the national government. Some countries start with one system and move to another, like New Zealand.
- Countries with judicial review like Canada and the United States have constitutional courts that rule on whether laws passed by the legislature are in accordance with the constitution, and these courts have the power to strike down legislation as unconstitutional.
- Countries with parliamentary sovereignty do not have judiciaries that review the constitutionality of legislation.

Causes and Effects

- Federalism has been associated with enhancing national stability and democracy under some circumstances and with conflict in other cases.

- Federalism has also been linked with improvements in economic growth and development, as well as economic difficulties.
- There is a long-standing debate about whether judicial review contributes to the protection of democratic rights or not.

Thinking Comparatively

- While many countries have written constitutions, they differ in many ways, and it is an open question whether one country's constitution is suited to other circumstances.

Thinking It Through

1. What might a federal system that includes an Indigenous order of government look like? How well have the Sami parliaments in Nordic countries worked for representing Sami interests? Could such a system work in Canada or the United States?
2. Imagine a country that has just achieved a ceasefire in a decades-long civil war. You have been asked by the government to accompany several constitutional experts to the country to advise the new "constituent assembly," whose job it is to write a new constitution that will ensure "stability, democracy, and prosperity." Under what circumstances would you advocate that the country adopt a federal structure?
3. Why has the US Constitution survived for more than two centuries? Do you believe it is because of the design of the document itself or because it happened to be implemented in a place with a certain history, geography, and cultural backdrop?
4. The United Kingdom is a country where a wide range of individual rights are respected. Given that many major rights are well protected, what are the problems with parliamentary sovereignty and a lack of judicial review? Are there any disadvantages to eliminating judicial review (and the potential for judicial activism) in well-established democratic societies?

9 Legislatures and Legislative Elections

In This Chapter

The Parliament Buildings in Wellington, New Zealand. The Executive Wing on the left is also called the Beehive. (Jill Ferry/Getty Images)

E Te Atua Kaha Rawa, Ka tuku
whakamoemiti atu mātou, mō ngā karakia
kua waihotia mai ki runga o Aotearoa.
Ka waiho nei I ō mātou pānga whaiaro
katoa ki te taha, nei rā ēnei e īnoi atu ana
mō Tō ārahitanga, I roto i ō mātou
whakaaroarohanga, ā, kia whakahaere ai
e mātou ngā take o Te Whare nei, I runga
i te mōhio, me te whakaiti mō te oranga,
te maungārongo, o te tūmatanui o Aotearoa.
Amene.

Source: Non-sectarian prayer in Te Reo Māori for the opening of the New Zealand House of Representatives (2017)[1]

What can New Zealand teach other countries about how to run a democracy? The island nation has four and a half million people, and its greatest claim to fame may be its world-class rugby team the All Blacks or that it was the setting for *The Lord of the Rings* movie trilogy. Its capital, Wellington, is the southernmost of any country on earth. This former British colony has an electoral system for its legislature that many countries might wish to consider. This includes Canada, where several provinces over the years have held referenda on electoral reform (most recently British Columbia in 2018), citing New Zealand as a model of how their system could change.

New Zealand voters actually have two votes in their parliamentary elections. They have one for a specific individual to represent their district and one for their preferred party (a constituency vote and a party vote). When all the votes are tallied and computed, the winners in each district go to Parliament, just as in many countries around the world, including the United States. But there's more: Along with these representatives go additional members chosen from lists made by the political parties. These "at-large" members of Parliament are allotted to each party in a way that makes the overall composition of the Parliament proportional to the vote each *party* received. The idea is to give each New Zealander his or her own representative for the local constituency while making Parliament more generally reflective of party preferences in the country as a whole. Additionally, there are seven separate electoral seats for the Indigenous Māori population, and Māori voters may choose to go on the general or the Māori electoral rolls.

New Zealand is not the only country to use this innovative approach to electing its legislature. In fact, other than the Māori seats, which are unique, New Zealand drew inspiration from Germany's similar model, as we discuss later in the chapter. Whether the system is ideal or not depends on how each individual believes representation and legislatures should work, which we also discuss in this chapter. Considering the relative merits of models like New Zealand's and Germany's, as contrasted with other models in countries ranging from Canada to Japan to Brazil, will provide insight into both representation and the legislatures that are designed to ensure it.

This chapter offers an introduction to the study of legislatures, with specific attention to the electoral rules and systems that shape them. Of importance here is the similarity between legislative systems in many former British colonies. The Westminster system was spread far and wide, from New Zealand and Fiji in the south to Trinidad and Tobago and Canada in the north. Many countries did not independently adopt a system from scratch but incorporated norms and institutions from the colonial systems that preceded independence.

In this chapter, we discuss how legislators are elected to represent the citizenry. In the two subsequent chapters, we elaborate on many aspects of representation and elections. Chapter 10 discusses the executive branch, but it must be noted that a discussion of executives cannot always be separated from that of legislatures. As a result, we discuss briefly in this chapter the relationships between legislatures and executives but leave to the next chapter the way in which many of the issues play out in parliamentary and presidential systems. Similarly, in talking about legislative representation in this chapter, we discuss political parties, but a fuller treatment of those important institutions is left to Chapter 11.

• • •

Concepts

A key aspect of politics involves making laws to govern people, and legislatures are the most important bodies that shape the process of making and changing laws. Legislators legislate. While heads of state and heads of government in the executive branch may be the first *individuals* that come to mind when we think of *politicians*, the legislatures of the world are often what we will think of when we view politics as a whole process of governing.

What Legislatures Are

legislature Assembly or body of representatives with the authority to make laws.

Legislatures can be defined as deliberative bodies composed of the decision-makers who represent the population at large. Legislatures make laws and many political decisions, especially in democracies but also even in personalistic dictatorships, which may rely on legislatures to seem legitimate or to create the appearance of deliberative decision-making. Legislatures are where debates take place about the fundamental values and preferences of voters. They are where interest groups and lobbyists often turn when they seek to influence the political process. They are where presidents and prime ministers often start their careers, and they are also typically the institution in government with the greatest responsibility for overseeing the conduct of the executive (an institution discussed in greater detail in the next chapter). In these bodies, legislators are of course important political figures, being leaders in major debates, whether in actual face-to-face settings in the legislature itself or through the use of the media.

The rise of legislatures, as opposed to executives, is part and parcel of the story of the emergence of constitutional and democratic regimes. For centuries, the history of representative government was the history of elected legislatures increasingly taking political authority from unelected executives. Parliaments, assemblies, congresses, and other legislative bodies asserted their rights to represent the populace, usually critiquing the unaccountable power of monarchs, such as kings, queens, or emperors. Of course, the earliest legislatures were not truly representative in most cases. The Parliament that asserted its authority over King John of England with the drafting of the Magna Carta in 1215 were not elected "commoners" but rather nobles in their own right. The French Estates-General revealed its inegalitarian character in its basic structure, with separate meetings for nobles, clergy, and commoners (the "third estate"). Even earlier, in the republics of ancient Rome, membership in the Senate was generally restricted to male property-holders or upper-class patricians. In many forms of colonial rule as well, legislatures were initially chosen not by the people at large but rather by an elite subset of the population.

This existence of less-than-democratic legislatures can be found in authoritarian regimes today. In authoritarian systems, legislatures may be selected in a number of ways that exclude a free and open vote. For instance, the legislature may be comprised only of a subset of the population, such as members of a certain dominant political party. This would be the case in communist regimes such as China where only members of the official Communist Party (or their close allies) are elected to office in practice. In other authoritarian regimes, legislators may be appointed by unelected executives. These are legislatures, even if the quality of representation is suspect. Despite these non-democratic instances, many countries have moved toward more democracy over time, with more regular elections and the extension of the franchise to more people, most notably women, racialized peoples, and men of lower social and economic status.

What Legislatures Do

Representatives generally make laws by proposing legislation and then organizing votes and bringing them to the floor of the legislature. Legislators who propose or favour a piece of legislation often undertake the necessary compromises and "horse-trading" that enable laws to get passed. The necessary trading and compromises may take place among the multiple parties in a governing coalition (as discussed in the chapter on executives) or within parties as different legislators make specific demands of one another in exchange for "yea" or "nay" votes. Depending on the power of party leaders to control the legislators, it may be necessary to make many concessions to specific legislators.

The specific process of legislation will vary from one legislature to the next. In some instances, a strong executive cabinet may be comprised of members of the legislature itself, and the rules governing legislative elections may make passage of the executive's favoured proposals almost "automatic." In other circumstances, legislation may have to pass through multiple houses, or may have to work its way through votes of multiple committees, just to get to the "floor" for a vote. Indeed, in some systems, the legislative process requires both these and more. In the United States, for instance, proposed legislation must often pass through committees in each of the two chambers of the legislature, then must pass votes in the whole body, then through a conference committee that reconciles any differences between the two chambers' bills before going to the president for a signature.

The powers of legislatures are considerable in most democracies. In many countries, one of the main powers of the legislative branch is the power to decide what gets funded and to what extent. Legislatures typically have control over government budgets and are empowered to disburse funds to the executive branch and to the administrative agencies or to cut off funding for certain initiatives that are unpopular or that it deems to be mismanaged. This power to allocate resources is one of the reasons executives must be attentive to the needs of legislatures, even in the absence of new laws being passed.

Legislatures often debate as part of the functions of representing the electorate and making legislation, and in doing so they also serve the function of focusing national discussion. Legislatures are where many public debates play out. The halls of the legislatures are designed for speechmaking, discussion, and debate, but this does not only happen in the chamber itself. Legislators also engage in less formal debate by shaping and responding to public opinion in the media and through interactions with citizens who have requests, complaints, arguments, suggestions, ideas, and new perspectives. Of course, not all such debate will be meaningful. Especially in authoritarian regimes, legislative debates may be reduced to displays of loyalty to the executive. In North Korea, legislators' most apparent role is to serve as an applauding audience for a dictator. In democracies too, not all legislators clarify and improve political discussion: they may also obfuscate or muddy the waters of political discussion or may be beholden to special interests acting against the public good (though many such examples are matters of opinion). And they may—perhaps deliberately—spread misinformation or misleading information. In principle, however, elected legislators at the national level are expected to be opinion leaders who contribute to national discussions and propose solutions to public problems.

There are also several overlooked roles of legislatures. One is "socializing" politicians. Legislatures can be a "training ground" for future presidents and prime ministers.[2] Another role is constituent service: Citizens often contact their representatives' offices for assistance with a variety of concerns specific to local individuals or groups. Last but definitely not least, legislators often try to get re-elected.[3] Indeed, some scholars believe that the fundamental force driving legislative action is the push for electoral success.[4] Getting re-elected may not be part of the "job description" of being a legislator, but it is certainly understood as one of the key aspects of the job in many countries. This may involve extensive campaigning and fundraising in candidate-centred elections or working to retain a spot on the political party's list of favoured representatives in systems in which electors vote by party.

Types

Legislative bodies may take a number of forms. They may have one or more houses or chambers, for example. In addition, the electoral processes that give rise to the legislators are numerous. Elections may involve voting for specific candidates, for political parties generally, or both. These different forms of legislatures and legislative elections give rise to different patterns of representation, as we shall see.

Unicameral and Bicameral Legislatures

bicameral legislature Legislature with two chambers, which may have equal or unequal powers.

chamber An assembly or body of a legislature, often referring to one of two such bodies in a bicameral legislature.

lower chamber In a bicameral legislature, the house that typically has a larger number of legislators than the upper chamber and often represents the national vote either more proportionally or through smaller geographic constituencies.

upper chamber The chamber in a bicameral legislature that is usually smaller in number of legislators, often representing larger geographic constituencies such as states or provinces.

Legislatures consist of one or more houses of assembly. **Bicameral legislatures**—those with two **chambers**, or houses—are common in democracies, especially in relatively large countries. This is the case in Canada, Australia, the United States, and many nations in Latin America, for instance, where there are two legislative chambers, with each having its own name (such as House of Representatives or Chamber of Deputies). Many other countries exhibit a similar structure, using different names to signify the two chambers. For example, India has a lower chamber, the Lok Sabha (or House of the People) and an upper chamber, the Rajya Sabha (or Council of States).

In bicameral countries, the **lower chamber** is usually the one whose composition most closely reflects the population at large. Examples are the House of Representatives in the United States and the House of Commons in Canada. The **upper chamber** is usually smaller in size, and its composition is often less directly reflective of the population at large; it may represent territories such as states or provinces, as in the case of the senate in many countries, or specific groups, such as the House of Lords in the United Kingdom. The lower chamber has greater authority than the upper chamber in many countries. In countries such as Germany, the upper chamber is limited to voting on certain items that pertain to the states, and in other countries such as the United Kingdom, the upper chamber has even more limited (largely vestigial) powers. Here again, the United States is a bit of an exception in that its upper chamber—the Senate—has at least as much power as the lower chamber. At the provincial and territorial levels in Canada, there are unicameral legislatures that are subject to regular elections. The United States has a slightly different system, with a bicameral system in most states (except Nebraska), with both a lower house and an upper house, usually called a state senate.

Press Association via AP Images

PHOTO 9.2 The House of Lords is the upper chamber in the United Kingdom.

unicameral legislature Legislature with a single chamber.

Unicameral legislatures are quite common in countries with small populations. For instance, unicameral parliaments are used in Scandinavia and are common in sub-Saharan Africa and some parts of the Middle East. Unicameral representation is usually most appropriate in unitary states and in countries that have relatively homogeneous populations; conversely, unicameral legislatures are uncommon where there are histories of different regional population groups with their own identities or in which regional minorities may demand special representation on the basis of territory. Interestingly, New Zealand had a bicameral system from 1852 to 1951, with an appointed Legislative Council. The upper chamber was seen as ineffectual and unnecessary in such a small country and was eventually abolished.

In addition to working in small, unitary democracies, unicameralism is also common in systems in many authoritarian regimes where a single political party dominates. In these cases, the governing regime may seek to minimize the "separation of powers" between national and regional interests that is implicit in bicameralism and prefer to channel all political demands through a single body dominated by the single party. The world's most populous country, China, fits the bill here because it also has a unicameral legislature despite its size.

Beyond the basic unicameral or bicameral structure, legislatures vary in another simple way: They have many different names, as noted earlier. For example, a legislature may be called a *congress* or *parliament*, an *assembly*, a *house*, or a *chamber*. Some of these terms have relatively specific meanings or are most commonly used in certain ways to designate whether a legislative body constitutes the entire legislative branch or merely one part of it. Congresses and parliaments generally refer to the entirety of a legislative branch, which may include more than one chamber. Houses and chambers often refer to one of the component parts of the legislature, especially in the many countries with a bicameral (two-chamber) legislature, as noted later. Assemblies may refer to either a legislature as a whole or one particular house or chamber within it.

TABLE 9.1 | Common Attributes of Congresses and Parliaments

Type of Legislature	Congress	Parliament
Example	United States	Canada
Head of Government	President	Prime Minister
Election of Head of Government	Separately elected by voters	Selected by Parliament
Independence of Head of Government	Executive does not depend on confidence of Congress	Executive depends on confidence of Parliament
Separation vs Fusion of Powers	Separation of powers between Congress and executive	Executive fused with Parliament
Checks vs Supremacy	Checks and balances between branches in constitution	Parliament supreme by constitution (but see next row)
Strong vs Limited Executive	Executive limited by separation and checks	Executive *may* dominate lawmaking in practice
Bicameral vs Unicameral	Either, but usually bicameral	Either

congress A form of legislature, typically associated with a presidential system in which there is a separation of powers.

parliament A type of legislature, often associated with systems in which the legislators vote on the leadership of the executive branch and the formation of a government.

Congresses and parliaments also have different connotations, as shown in Table 9.1. **Congresses** are typically branches in a system with a separately elected head of government, while **parliaments** are often the name used for legislatures that choose their own head of government. In most congresses, the separately elected head of government—often called a president—does not depend on the congress for his or her position but rather is accountable to the populace at large and to the constitution generally. These are usually systems designed with separations of powers and checks and balances between the legislative and executive branches. By contrast, parliamentary systems have executives that depend on parliament to legislate and even to retain their position. While the parliament is often the supreme lawmaking body, this does not mean the executive is weak: These systems may actually feature strong executive powers in practice, depending on whether the executive can control his or her political party and its allies in parliament. We elaborate on this basic distinction further in Chapter 10 when we discuss presidential and parliamentary executives, and we look at party systems in Chapter 11.

Electoral Systems

Different legislative systems vary in how they organize elections. Among the various options, there are two basic categories of electoral systems used for legislatures and any number of combinations of these two systems. The first is the constituency-based electoral system, and the second is proportional representation.

constituency system An electoral system in which voters select representatives from specific-geographic constituencies.

constituency A group of voters or a geographic district that legislators or other elected officials represent.

Constituency Systems

Constituency systems allocate one or more seats in the legislature to each of a number of districts in the country. These constituencies are usually territorial, with different geographic regions representing the different districts. They may be known as districts, and in most such systems, the **constituency** will have a single representative. The most common version is the single-member district (SMD).

Single-member constituency systems divide up a country into a number of territorial constituencies, with each constituency having the right to elect one legislator. This person is then expected to represent the interests of that constituency in the legislature while also balancing this with the interests of the party of which the legislator is a member. In most circumstances, political parties run candidates for the seat in the legislature, and those representing major, well-known parties will have an advantage over those without such a party affiliation. Parties often have considerable discretion in how they choose their own candidates. In some countries, party leaders may exercise considerable control over who the candidates will be in each constituency. Another procedure involves openly contested "primary" elections in which members of the same party run against one another for the party's nomination to a seat. While major parties have an advantage in name recognition and in communicating to voters what their candidates probably believe, "independent" candidates may also run if they meet the qualifications for getting their names on the ballot.[5] Ballot access is challenging in some countries but famously easy for candidates in others, especially for small local elections.

single-member constituency (SMC) Electoral system in which voters choose a candidate and the winner is elected by earning the most votes or by winning a runoff vote.

Elections in SMC systems can have different features. A common approach is the **first-past-the-post**, or "plurality," system in which the constituency holds elections and the candidate with the most votes wins. This may sound obvious, but note that in such a system, it may be common to have a winner with less than 50 per cent of the vote if there are many candidates who split up the vote between them. This can lead to surprising outcomes in some cases. For instance, consider a Canadian federal election in a relatively left-of-centre constituency in which a Liberal and a New Democratic Party candidate run alongside a Conservative one. The Conservative may get only 40 per cent of the vote but still win the seat if the two other candidates split the remaining 60 per cent. Accordingly, many SMD systems adopt other electoral rules, with a popular version being a **runoff** system between the top two candidates that ensures that the eventual winner will have received a "mandate" by winning a majority of the valid votes cast.

first-past-the-post Electoral system in which the candidate with the most number of votes is elected, regardless of whether a majority has been attained.

runoff Electoral system in which the top candidates after a first round of voting compete in one or more additional rounds of voting until a candidate receives a majority.

In general, first-past-the-post systems often disproportionately favour larger parties that can gain a winning number of votes in many constituencies even if these parties cannot win an outright majority of the votes cast. It can also disfavour slightly smaller parties that might get a solid fraction of the vote but not enough to gain a plurality in many constituencies. A well-known example of this is Canada where the Conservative and Liberal parties have often won majorities of parliamentary seats without winning a majority of votes cast. The third-largest party, such as the New Democratic Party, usually wins a smaller proportion of seats than votes, although this is not always true. For example, in the 2006 federal election, the NDP received 17.48 per cent of the vote but won only 9.4 per cent of the seats—a major disparity. The situation was less pronounced in the 2015 elections but involved a similar dynamic, with 19.7 per cent of the vote translating into only 13 per cent of the seats. Interestingly, in 2011 the NDP won 30.63 per cent of the vote and gained 33 per cent of the seats. In that year, the Liberals were the big losers and while garnering almost 19 per cent of the popular vote were only able to translate this into 11 per cent of the seats. This meant that for the first time in Canadian history, the NDP served as the official opposition at the federal level. In 2019, the Conservatives got 34.41 per cent of the votes and 121 seats in Parliament, while the Liberals got 33.07 per cent of the vote and 157 seats. The Conservative vote was regionally concentrated in the prairie provinces while the Liberal vote was more spread out. While many Conservative supporters were unhappy with the result, the Conservative Party has long stood against proportional representation, which would in 2019 have favoured their electoral prospects.

Not all district systems are single-member constituencies. There are also **multi-member constituencies (MMCs)** in which more than one representative is elected from each district. These arrangements are less "winner-take-all" because they allow for multiple representatives and also multiple parties to have representatives in the same constituency.

multi-member constituencies (MMC) Electoral system in which constituencies have more than one representative.

What happens in these MMC systems often depends on the size of the constituencies and the number of representatives in each. Imagine if Canada had a system for its House of Commons with two representatives in each constituency. Since the Liberal and Conservative parties are usually the two leading parties in each constituency and are usually fairly close in polling, most reasonable calculations would result in the two parties each getting one seat in most districts around the country. But if districts were to have, say, 10 representatives, the results might be significantly different. The two leading parties may split the seats between them. Or perhaps the two leading parties would each take four seats, and then a couple of smaller parties—say, one on the far left and one on the far right—would win one seat each. This would change the composition of the legislature, encouraging more small parties to have representatives. It might also encourage more minority and Indigenous voices. How about women's representation? In 2014, Canada's former Prime Minister Kim Campbell developed the idea for gender parity in elections by having a male and female MP from each constituency. While this idea has not succeeded in practice, gender quotas within political parties are common around the world. In New Zealand, both the Māori Party and the Green Party have had male and female co-leaders and ensure that they have gender parity when constructing their party lists.

Proportional Representation (PR)

In October 2017, British Columbia's coalition provincial government announced an upcoming referendum on changing the electoral system. In late 2018, mail-in ballots were sent to all BC voters so that they could choose whether to keep their current first-past-the-post system or switch to a **proportional representation system** (PR). The threshold for change

proportional representation (PR) In its pure form, an electoral system in which voters choose a preferred party and seats are allocated to parties according to the percentage of the vote the party wins.

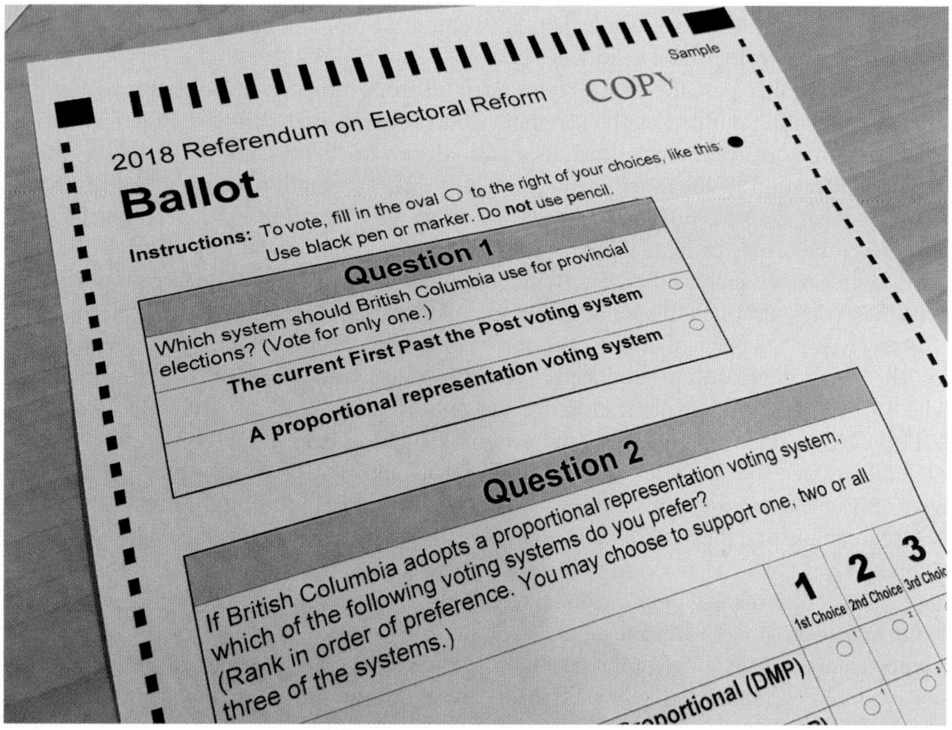

Dirk Meissner/THE CANADIAN PRESS

PHOTO 9.3 A sample copy of the mail-in ballot used for the proportional representation referendum in British Columbia in late 2018. Voters were asked if they wanted to keep the first-past-the-post voting system or if they wanted to switch to proportional representation. Sixty-one per cent of voters said they wanted to stay with the first-past-the post system.

was 51 per cent. In a previous referendum in 2005, the threshold was 60 per cent, so even though 57 per cent favoured electoral change, it was not forthcoming.[6] Many hoped this electoral innovation in BC would set the stage for change in other provinces and ultimately at the federal level. However, the referendum was unsuccessful in that 61 per cent of voters wanted to keep the first-past-the-post system.

Many countries maintain that the most important factor in representation is not the constituency or geographic territory one represents or having an individual candidate to represent certain people but rather the distribution of seats between parties. The logic is simple: If party X wins 44 per cent of the vote in the country, party Y 33 per cent, party Z 22 per cent, and all other parties 1 per cent, then party X should have about 44 per cent of the seats in the legislature, party Y about 33 per cent, and party Z about 22 per cent. Proportional representation can do a better job than SMC of making this happen.

Systems featuring an element of PR still face the challenge of allocating seats once the votes are tallied. There are many ways to allocate seats, but certain rules are common. First, in many PR systems a threshold is often required to earn seats in the legislature. This may be 5 per cent, for instance. With that threshold, any party with less than 5 per cent of the vote would not earn a seat in the legislature because their vote totals were insufficient. This would prevent PR systems from being dominated by lots of small parties—which would make complex coalitions necessary and likely not be conducive to stability—and could help to ensure governability by restricting power to a handful of substantial parties. Second, the number of seats for each party cannot perfectly reflect the vote because there are always fewer seats than there are voters and there will be some "remainders." In general, the number of votes a party gets is rounded off to a certain number of seats. For instance, if three parties contest an election for 12 seats and all the votes for party A would suggest it earned 6.7 seats, party B earned 3.1 seats, and party C earned 2.2 seats, then one actual distribution might be 7 seats for party A, 3 for party B, and 2 for party C. A variety of calculation methods exists for sorting out the seats from votes in proportional representation systems.[7]

PR is designed (by definition) to offer proportionality in the vote for different parties, as we explore further in the "Causes and Effects" section. A leading example of a relatively "pure" PR system, albeit one where democracy is very suspect, is now found in Russia. South Africa also uses a model that features the classic form of PR for its lower house, the National Assembly. However, most countries using PR do not use it in its purest form. Rather, they blend it with district-based systems or make other modifications, as discussed in the section on hybrid systems later in the chapter.

Proportional representation may work in different ways, with different details. For instance, in the variant of PR known as **open-list proportional representation** (used in Brazil and many European countries), voters choose individual candidates, but the candidates' votes are combined together with the other members of their party, and then seats are allocated based on the parties' performances. This makes the legislature proportionally representative, yet the votes for candidates still influence which individuals are elected to the legislature: The candidates with the most votes within their party will have the highest priority for earning a seat. The system attempts to combine some of the features of PR with the right to vote for individual candidates (hence, "open list" rather than a "closed list" controlled by the party). It encourages candidates to seek individual support and can leave parties "less disciplined" than under forms of PR in which the party exerts greater control over its slate of candidates.

open-list proportional representation Electoral system in which voters choose a candidate but votes are aggregated by political party to determine the allocation of seats across parties.

Even with the distinction between PR and SMC and the diversity of rules and mechanisms for each, there is additional variety in the types of electoral systems around the world. As suggested previously, many countries attempt to find a balance between the perceived advantages of PR systems and SMC systems. We might call these "mixed" or "hybrid" systems.

Mixed or Hybrid

Many countries have sought to balance the advantages of SMC and PR systems and have invented a number of seemingly ingenious mechanisms for doing so, though these generally make the electoral system more complicated. These systems—which represent a hybrid between the two sets of systems already discussed—may have individual elected representatives but attempt to retain (or create) the proportionality among parties that PR systems provide. We return to the cases of Germany and New Zealand at the end of the chapter but note here that it is possible in theory to elect representatives from constituencies and then ensure proportionality of party representation in the legislature, mainly through the addition of supplemental "at large" seats to the legislature.

Other mechanisms ask voters to do more than choose their preferred candidate: They ask voters to *rank* candidates. The electoral system then uses this information about ranked preferences to determine winners. The **alternative vote**, also called the instant-runoff vote or preferential vote, is a simple version. All votes are counted to see voters' first choices. If no candidate wins a majority, the candidate with the lowest total is eliminated, and the votes for this last-place candidate are redistributed according to those voters' second-choice picks. If there is still no majority, then the candidate with the next-lowest total is eliminated, and their votes are redistributed as well and so on until one candidate has a majority of the vote.

alternative vote Voting system in which voters rank candidates and the votes of low-ranking candidates are reallocated until a winner is determined.

A similar system is the **single transferable vote (STV)**, which is used in some MMC systems where more than one candidate is elected. Under STV, the voter ranks candidates, just as in the alternative vote. But some winning candidates will have more than enough votes to win a seat, with some votes left over. The "surplus" votes for winning candidates are redistributed to voters' second choices (and third choices as necessary and so on) until a slate of candidates is elected. STV was the system British Columbia put out to a referendum in 2005. Table 9.2 presents voting procedures under different electoral systems.

single transferable vote (STV) Electoral system in which voters rank candidates and the winners' surplus votes are reallocated to other, lower-ranking candidates until a slate of representatives is chosen.

These ranking systems have a major advantage: They encourage voters to pick their most preferred candidate, thus reducing the need for strategic voting. Under strategic voting, many citizens may not vote for their favourite candidate because they fear he/she will not win, preferring instead to vote for a favourite (or a "least bad" option) among those who have a reasonable chance of winning. Ranking systems are used in Australia and for some local elections in the United States. And the applicability of these voting models is not limited to traditional politics: This vote procedure is also used to select the winners of the Academy Awards, or Oscars.

TABLE 9.2 | Voting Procedures under Different Electoral Systems

Electoral System	Procedure for Voter
Single-Member Constituency (SMC)	Choose candidate; top candidate is elected by most votes or runoff.
Proportional Representation (PR)	Choose preferred party; seats allocated to parties by vote percentage.
Open-List PR	Choose candidate; votes aggregated by party for allocation of seats.
Mixed Systems/Hybrid Systems	Choose candidate and party (two votes) or other combination with above.
Single Transferable Vote (STV)	Rank candidates; winners' surplus votes reallocated until slate chosen.
Alternative	Rank candidates; votes of losers reallocated until winner found.

Axel Schmidt/dapd/AP Images

PHOTO 9.4 The German Bundesrat, which represents German states, or "Länder."

indirect election Electoral system in which representatives are chosen by other elected officials rather than directly by the citizenry at large.

Indirect election is also a possibility for choosing legislators and is used most often for the upper chambers of bicameral parliaments. Legislators in the lower chamber (which in reality is the more powerful chamber in most bicameral countries) choose the members of the upper chamber in some countries. Alternatively, the members of the upper chamber may be chosen by the states/provinces/regions of a federation. In Germany, for instance, the members of the *Bundesrat*, the upper chamber of the legislature, are chosen by Germany's state legislatures.

There is a virtually limitless number of conceivable electoral systems around the world. While certain trends predominate, this small selection of possible formats serves to illustrate the variety of options. The preferences for one system over another owes a great deal to national traditions and habits, as well as to the structure of the polity, to include population size and the importance of group identities and the extent of homogeneity in the population. Moreover, they are presumably "sticky" in the sense that parties and groups that do well within a given electoral system, and who therefore can potentially block changes, typically have an interest in preserving the system from which they benefit. For this reason, one seldom hears calls from the Republican and Democratic parties for the adoption of an alternative framework.

Executive–Legislative Relations

Legislatures routinely have responsibility for oversight of the executive branch. A classic example might be legislatures requiring testimony by military leaders on the conduct of a war, since the military may come under the authority of the executive branch yet may be required to report to the legislature. In February 2019, President Trump declared a state of emergency on the US border with Mexico in order to deploy federal funds to build a southern wall to keep out illegal immigrants. Claimed the president: "We have an invasion of drugs and criminals coming into our country." By declaring an emergency, the

CASE IN CONTEXT

432

The Hybrid Electoral System of the Japanese Diet

The Japanese Diet uses a mix of proportional representation and single-member constituencies. For much of the period after World War II, the country was dominated by the Liberal Democratic Party (LDP), but it now has a more competitive legislature. In the House of Representatives, 300 members are chosen in their districts and 180 by proportional representation. The upper chamber, known as the House of Councillors, is also elected by a mixture of district-based systems and PR but with subtly different rules. This is a simple example of a hybrid electoral system.

See the case study on the Japanese Diet in Part VI, p. 432. As you read it, keep in mind the following questions:

1. What might be the reasons for developing a hybrid system such as this?
2. What would be the expected consequences of this arrangement for the size and success of political parties?
3. Would there be advantages to adopting such a system in countries such as the United States that rely exclusively on districts?

White House could potentially divert almost $6 billion from military construction projects, counter-narcotics programs, and an asset forfeiture fund from the Treasury Department.

Building a southern wall was one of Trump's key election promises, but he was stymied by Congress, which under the Constitution is in charge of funding federal agencies and programs. Democrats, who controlled the House of Representatives, called this an unconstitutional abuse of presidential authority. The president was roundly criticized for this move, especially when he conceded that there was no emergency and that he "didn't need to do this . . . I just want to get it done faster, that's all."[8]

Less dramatic examples of such legislative oversight can occur in any number of policy areas, with cabinet ministers and executive officials regularly being required to submit reports and to undergo legislative questioning. This may entail the right to review executive appointees to major political positions (including those to the judicial branch in some instances, as well as appointees to some high-ranking executive offices in the administration). Oversight may also, in especially discordant situations, result in a motion of censure in which the legislature sanctions or scolds the executive for actions it deems inappropriate.

Beyond simply providing oversight, the legislature may be empowered to remove the executive from office if the executive "loses the confidence" of the people (or its elected representatives in the legislature). In parliamentary systems, the relationship between the executive and the legislature is relatively close because of the fusion of the two branches of government. The executive consists of a government elected by the members of the legislature, including a cabinet of ministers led by a prime minister (or equivalent). In these systems, the executive is "responsible" to the legislature and relies on the backing of the legislature for its continuation as a government. This fact confers power to the legislature to remove the executive from office, according to rules that vary from country to country. For instance, in many countries a majority of the legislature voting "no confidence" in the executive will result in the government being disbanded and new elections being called. In Germany, however, bringing down the government requires a "constructive vote of no confidence" in which the vote of no confidence must be accompanied by a specific proposal for a new government that will take effect upon the completion of the confidence vote.

CASE IN CONTEXT

402

Institutional Design: Germany's Bundestag and Bundesrat

The elections for the German *Bundestag* have constituencies but also aim to ensure overall proportionality to make the lower chamber reflective of voters' party preferences. The system is known as a mixed-member proportional system, and it allows (or requires) voters to vote twice: once for an individual and once for a party. Members of the Bundesrat, meanwhile, are selected by assemblies in the states (*Länder*).

See the case study on the German parliament in Part VI, p. 402. As you read it, keep in mind the following questions:

1. What are the mechanics of how the size of the Bundestag is calculated?
2. Which sorts of political actors in Germany would be expected to like this system, and which would not?
3. Does the structure of representation in the Bundesrat affect the way one views the electoral system in the Bundestag?

The parliamentary model allows the legislature to remove the government—making a call for new elections—without necessarily leading to a major constitutional crisis. In presidential systems, the procedure for removing a member of the executive is usually more elaborate, at least for the highest-ranking officials in the government. Legislatures can use processes of impeachment (or of demanding resignation) to remove the executive from office under relatively stringent conditions. In parliamentary systems, legislatures can remove executives at almost any time for a lack of confidence in governing ability. In presidential systems, their power to do so is more limited by the fixed term of office given to the president.

Causes and Effects: What Explains Patterns of Representation?

Many heated debates centre on the systems that elect legislative representatives. At question is how representation is structured and particularly how votes are translated into seats. Earlier in the chapter, we outlined the district-based representation and proportional representation approaches to legislative elections as well as hybrid forms. In general, district-based systems are more centred on the election of individual candidates and the latter more centred on the election of political parties, though we discuss a few caveats to that rule. A question for further consideration is "Which type of election is more representative?"

This, of course, depends on what "representative" means. When you consider what it means to have a legislature represent the people, what is essential? Is it necessary to have a single politician representing your district? If so, how do those who voted against that politician feel "represented"? Advocates of PR or party-based elections argue that political systems should come as close as possible to making sure each person's vote "counts" in representation. If you wish to vote for a smallish (but non-trivial) party because that party matches your beliefs, your vote should not be "wasted" simply because that party does not win a district seat. Rather, your vote should be reflected in the proportion of seats allocated to that party in the legislature.

Patterns of Representation

representation In legislatures, the process by which elected legislators reflect the interests and preferences of voters in their constituencies.

The first challenge with a causal argument about "what types of legislatures are more representative" is having an understanding of what **representation** means. In the terms of Chapters 1 and 2, we have to define the dependent variable. It may be that no single, easily quantifiable indicator of "representativeness" exists, but this should not stop us from engaging in comparative analysis. In fact, the study of the consequences of different legislative forms is a leading example of how comparativists debate challenging concepts that are difficult to define.

The central function of legislatures is to represent citizens; a relatively small number of legislators represents the population at large, and individual legislators can never exactly represent the views of each and every citizen, but the process of election is seen to approximate the idea of "rule by the many." Electoral representation may take place on the basis of geography, identity group, or political party. In many countries, people in local or regional districts may choose one or more area residents to represent their constituency. In some other countries, specific seats may be set aside for women (as in the case of local assemblies known as the *panchayati raj* in India), racial or ethnic groups, or specific under-represented castes or social groups, as discussed further in Chapter 14. Yet not all representation is based on individual representatives, since PR systems offer representation by political party, with citizens voting for parties instead of individual candidates. In this case, representatives appointed by the political parties staff the legislature, voting generally in accordance with the policy directives of the party as a whole.

Implicit in democratic elections is the fact that many citizens will not agree with their representatives some of the time. One may vote for a losing party or candidate, or one may be disappointed with a position taken by a representative one voted for. This raises the question of whether representatives should follow the public opinion of their constituents or their own consciences.

Ask yourself if you believe elected legislators should reflect the opinion of the public that elects them. It may seem obvious that legislators should follow public opinion. After all, representatives are there to represent the people who elected them and can reasonably be expected to reflect the preferences and values of their voting constituents. However, if legislators primarily make it to parliament because they represent a political party with a clear set of policies, voters may expect them to support their party above the views of constituents. In the Westminster system, legislators are there primarily to represent the party line. Party whips ensure that MPs and provincial legislators vote as the party leaders wish. If not, legislators might be ejected from the party caucus. For this reason, many excellent prospective candidates for office will choose not to run. In other words, many professional people do not want to end up blindly toeing a party line with which they may at times disagree.

Alternatively, voters may want their legislator to exercise independence, demonstrating their own thoughtfulness and reason, their own ability to foresee the consequences of legislative choices, and their own skill at compromise. In other words, the electorate may expect their legislator to exercise discretion and to "make the tough choices," even if the populace does not favour these choices.

Clearly, elections are the leading accountability mechanisms for legislators in democracies. If representatives vote in ways that are too far removed from the interests and preferences of their constituents, they can expect forceful challenges from political opponents (whether in other parties or in their own), and they can probably expect not to win re-election if they get too far "out of line." On the other hand, public opinion may be fickle, and representatives need to cast votes not just on what is popular at a given moment in time but also with a view toward the future, both at the time of the next election and beyond.

INSIGHTS

The Concept of Representation
by Hanna F. Pitkin

In this classic work, Pitkin elaborates the concept of representation that is so central to the study of legislatures and legislative politics and does so through an examination of the term, its origins in political theory, and even its etymology. One of the key elements of Pitkin's analysis is the distinction between representation that entails following the will of a constituency's voters and representation that involves individuals exercising their own discretion and judgment once they are elected. Calling this the "mandate–independence controversy," Pitkin argues that no clear rule can be established for whether representatives should follow the general wishes of the electorate or should follow their own counsel if they find these views incorrect. Rather, the essence of representation is acting on behalf of others, which implies that representatives should habitually be in harmony with the wishes of their electors but are also justified in voting independently when there are compelling reasons to do so on behalf of that same group. The rule for mandate versus independence must be examined on a case-by-case basis.

Hanna F. Pitkin, *The Concept of Representation* (Berkeley: University of California Press, 1967; rpt. 1972).

Electoral Systems and Representation

Some of the most fundamental questions about representation come from the electoral systems outlined previously: SMD, PR, and hybrid systems imply different forms of representation. Each has advantages in providing for a certain form of representation, and each faces challenges in providing representation by other definitions.

In any electoral system, the question of how to divide up legislative seats is crucial, and SMD systems face challenges of **apportionment** and **districting** of seats. In lower chambers of most legislatures with district systems, the districts are often expected to be discrete geographic areas, but they are also expected to have comparable numbers of voters for the lower chambers of most legislatures. Of course, precise ratios of seats to the population of each district are not possible. The American electoral system is very decentralized, and unlike Canada, where Elections Canada plays a key role in marking out electoral districts and supervising elections, much of this work in the US is done at the state level by partisan legislators.

apportionment The process by which legislative seats are distributed among geographic constituencies.

districting The process by which districts or other geographic constituencies are created for the purposes of elections.

The potential for partisan politics emerges when populations of different areas change. Keeping districts at roughly the same population size requires changing boundaries. This leads to processes of redistricting, as described in the "Case in Context: The United States Congress: Dysfunctional or Functioning by Design?" box on page 195. One of the challenges of redistricting is that legislators themselves often have a role in the districting process, whether directly or through officials they have nominated, and this creates incentives for legislators to shape districts that favour them or their party. One consequence is **gerrymandering**, in which districts are created in irregular shapes or of odd composition in order to achieve a desired political outcome.

gerrymandering Creation of districts of irregular shape or composition in order to achieve a desired political result.

Malapportionment comes with imbalances in allocating seats to different districts. The extent of malapportionment varies tremendously from one country to another, but it is generally more common in upper chambers of bicameral parliaments, which are often designed to protect the territorial interests of states or provinces. Malapportionment can be defined as the extent to which a system gives some regions a higher ratio of representatives to voters than others. This is very common in federal systems like Canada, Australia, and

malapportionment Apportionment in which voters are unequally represented in a legislature, such as through relatively greater numbers of legislators per capita for low-population areas and lesser numbers of legislators per capita for high-population areas.

the United States, where each subunit, such as a province or state, has equal representation in the upper house. This of course leads to a situation where tiny Prince Edward Island has the same representation in the Canadian Senate as Ontario, echoing the American system where Rhode Island and Wyoming have the same number of Senate seats as California and Texas. Wyoming has one senator for approximately every quarter of a million people, while California has one senator for about every 18 million residents.

Federal countries that wish to guarantee representation for smaller, less populous regions will—almost by definition—create seats in the legislature that disproportionately favour those regions. In Brazil, the smallest state (Roraima) has three senators for about 400,000 residents, while the largest state (São Paulo) also has three senators but for more than 41 million people. The relevant ratios are that Roraima has one vote in the senate for every 133,000 residents, while São Paulo has one vote only for about every 14 million people.

The consequences of apportionment and malapportionment are significant. In a theoretical sense, the question of apportionment is about nothing less than the basic principle of "one person, one vote." Put another way, malapportionment could be viewed as the degree to which an electoral system deviates from the "one-person, one-vote" principle: Even if everyone has the right to vote, not everyone's vote "counts the same" if seats are malapportioned. For example, the residents of America's 25 lowest-population states comprise about 16 per cent of the population and represent half of the Senate. In theory, these 50 senators voting as a bloc could (with a vice-presidential tiebreak) stop a policy favoured in states representing 84 per cent of the American population.

The advantage of small states in representation may have consequences that translate into political outcomes as well. The most obvious examples are those policies that favour low-population regions that are "overrepresented" by malapportionment, especially rural regions. In many instances, malapportionment may serve to prevent or impede implementation of a policy that will favour a majority of the population. In France, the Senate (*Sénat*) has long been known as the "agricultural chamber" because it provides an institutional bulwark to protect the interests of French farmers. The same may be said of farm policy in the United States. In Brazil, the military created additional new states at the end of authoritarian rule in the 1980s, and this was interpreted by some as a deliberate effort to ensure a larger number of senators from pro-military regions of the country.

By contrast with SMD, elections in PR systems are often party-centred rather than candidate-centred. For proponents of PR, one advantage of these systems is precisely the emphasis on parties, their platforms, and their policy proposals rather than the particular ideas and charisma of individual candidates. In candidate-based elections, charismatic and/or thoughtful individuals may communicate well with voters, leading to successful election campaigns, yet these skills may matter less in the job of legislating and making policy decisions. Instead, what matters is which party has a majority or which parties are in the coalition that makes up the governing majority. By ensuring that the whole of the legislature reflects the interests or preferences of the whole country, PR entrusts government to the largest party or leading parties that can make up a governing coalition. In theory, this can make government more capable of passing laws and enacting policies that "the people as a whole" want.

PR also tends to support multiple smaller parties, as contrasted with SMD systems, which favour large parties and accentuate the tendency toward two-party systems instead of multiparty systems. We explore the impacts of these electoral systems on party systems in Chapter 11.[9]

Under SMD, smaller parties may earn a healthy minority of the vote (say, 10–15 per cent) in many districts across a country yet still be largely shut out of the political process.

CASE IN CONTEXT

492

The United States Congress: Dysfunctional or Functioning by Design?

In the United States, apportionment in the Senate and the pattern of districting in the House of Representatives are both areas that have been subject to criticism. That each state gets two senators means that residents of smaller states have more representatives per capita than residents of larger states. In the House of Representatives, a big question is how decisions are made to reshape districts because the state legislatures can decide how to change Congressional districts after each census, which occurs every 10 years. At the state level, whichever party controls the government gets to determine the electoral boundaries, and that can lead to the problem of gerrymandering—the redrawing of districts to suit party needs while undermining democratic representation.

See the case study of the US Congress in Part VI, p. 492. As you read it, keep in mind the following questions:

1. If virtually all adults are allowed to vote, then in what sense could one say the US electoral system is less "one-person, one-vote" than other possible systems? Is this characterization fair, and why or why not?
2. What is it about the US electoral system that favours the status quo, whether in terms of policy or in terms of who gets elected?
3. What features of the US system, if any, would you alter?

Let's say the two largest parties—call them the Progressive and the Industrial parties—get an average of 40 per cent of the vote each, ranging from about 30 per cent to about 50 per cent in each district, depending on the district's political leanings. Say also that two smaller parties (the Libertarians and the Greens) get about 10 per cent of the vote in every district. Even if the country had 500 districts (each with one seat in the legislature), it is very possible that the Progressives and the Industrials would split all the seats between themselves, while the Libertarians and the Greens would have zero seats under the district system because the Progressives and the Industrialists would outpoll them in every single district. Under PR, the Libertarians and the Greens would not be shut out: In a 500-seat legislature, they would each get about 50 seats, reflecting their support by 10 per cent of the population each. PR would give these smaller parties leverage in political debate because they may be able to swing to and from the larger parties, making the difference between the Progressives or the Industrials having a majority or not.

On the other hand, PR does not provide voters with a single identifiable legislator who "represents them." This can be troubling for several reasons. First, it can mean that voters do not know to whom they should direct their demands. It may be more challenging to participate and feel represented when one must contact an office of a political party rather than the office of one's district representative. This is especially true for voters who voted for a losing party and must go through a period of government in which they feel it will be very difficult to have someone who can speak on their behalf. Second, and related to this, PR can break the geographic link between citizens and their legislators. While political parties may have local offices and look to attend to local issues, they tend to respond to the overall national constituency in PR systems. By contrast, in district systems, the adage goes that "all politics is local," and citizens may feel more represented when it comes to getting political attention for local issues such as a need for bridge repair, sanitation, or other local issues.

Legislative Decision-Making and Representation

committee In a legislature, a body composed of a group of legislators convened to perform a certain set of tasks.

Another source of questions about the quality of representation comes from how exactly decisions are made within the legislatures. For some time, a particular emphasis was placed not on individual members but on **committees** and their roles.[10] These organizations can take on the role of "legislatures within the legislatures" because a select group of parliamentarians or congresspersons shapes a policy and then presents it to the larger body with the expectation that it will be passed in the larger house. As politics has grown more complex and technical over time, legislators have tended to specialize in certain committees and defer to their party colleagues on others. If committees are powerful, then representation is less about each individual vote in the assembly and more about who is assigned to what committee and how this sets or shapes the agenda.

Political parties are some of the key actors in legislatures and are often more important than individuals. In terms of representation, parties are considered "disciplined" if their members vote together and less disciplined if their members vote differently from the party line. This party line is usually determined by the way the national party leadership would like the members to vote. Legislatures vary dramatically in the extent to which their parties exhibit discipline. One of the key factors in determining party discipline is the degree to which party leaders control the electoral fates of their members.[11] Dominance by party leaders may seem to be "less representative" than systems in which legislators vote more independently, but many systems—whether SMD, PR, or hybrid—rely on party discipline to get legislation passed.

Assume for the moment that most politicians would like to get re-elected or to continue their political careers. This implies that politicians will be attentive to the people who nominate and select them. Now notice that who chooses the nominees and the representatives will differ from one electoral system to the next. In many party-centred systems, voters select parties, and the party itself chooses who will be the representatives to the parliament. In practice, this gives a great deal of power to the leaders of the party, who can "set the lists" to determine who will become a member of the legislature. Where individual party members depend on party leaders for their nomination, they will typically adhere to the wishes of the leadership, currying favour with those who set the party list. On the other hand, many candidate-centred systems allow voters to choose party nominees, as is the case with party primary elections in the United States. In these instances, party leaders' leverage declines.

Differences in electoral rules should imply variations in the discipline of the political parties. Electoral systems that give more power to party leaders should lead to systems in which parties vote in a disciplined fashion. Systems that encourage candidates to focus on district constituencies should lead to less-disciplined parties, with more representatives who have an "independent" streak or vote like "mavericks." Of course, these representatives will often be bucking the trend of their parties in order to conform to the preferences of the districts they represent. Even in such cases, parties have tools that they can use in their efforts to keep their representatives "in line." We examine these issues further in Chapter 11 on political parties and party systems, but note its significance here for understanding how legislatures operate.

Legislative decisions may be shaped by committees or by political parties (and their leaders), but in both instances it is clear that decisions are not simply a function of adding up the preferences and the single vote cast by each representative. Other institutions within the legislature shape what issues get on the agenda and how they are presented to the legislature as a whole. These institutions ensure that legislatures have "structure" in how decisions are made: This is a view of representation different from what is suggested by public and open debate on the floor of the voting chamber.

Executive–Legislative Relations and Representation

In most countries today, the power of legislatures and the nature of representation depend heavily on executive–legislative relations. At times, legislatures have considerable powers over executives—some of which are noted in the next chapter, such as "votes of no confidence." On other occasions, legislatures are relatively less powerful than executives. The balance of power between these two branches says a great deal about how politics plays out in any given country.

Executive–legislative relations are shaped by a number of underlying powers these institutions have vis-à-vis one another. A national constitution may be the ultimate source of *formal power* for legislatures and executives. Legislatures with formal powers to recall or bring down the government may see their leverage over the executive enhanced. This may be expected to make the executive more accountable to the legislature and to make it more attentive to the legislature's demands. As important as these formal powers are *partisan powers*. Where party leaders in the executive have considerable powers to control the political fates of their fellow party members, they will be able to influence the so-called "rank-and-file" members of the legislature. This refers to the party discipline criterion mentioned previously. Where executives have control over party lists, executives will have considerable control in executive–legislative relations.

Executive–legislative relations are more complex than simple rules on paper of who has constitutional power. In many parliamentary democracies, legislatures have the nominal authority to remove the executive at any time with a vote of "no confidence" in the

JACK GUEZ/AFP/Getty Images

PHOTO 9.5 Israeli Prime Minister Benjamin Netanyahu applauds with members of his Likud Party. In 2015, Netanyahu called a parliamentary election more than two years before it was required in an attempt to re-establish and manage his governing coalition.

executive, but this does not necessarily mean that there will be constant turnover in the executive branch.[12] Similarly, in presidential systems, where executives are directly elected, there is most often a formally established balance of powers between the branches, but this can vary from time to time as the political fortunes of presidents fluctuates. Forms of executive–legislative relations shape the quality of representation as much as electoral systems and the internal functioning of legislatures; the exact ways it does so vary tremendously.

Altogether, many factors shape the nature and quality of representation. Electoral systems can give rise to candidate-centred politics, party-centred politics, or a mix of the two. How legislatures themselves operate then also shapes representation: Sometimes parties and their leaders wield considerable control, sometimes certain committees wield power, and sometimes power is more open to all members of the legislature. Finally, the relationship between the legislature and the executive gives rise to different patterns of representation. All of these affect representation, as do many other factors. Representation itself is a hard concept to measure, but it is at the crux of most comparative questions about how legislatures matter.

THINKING COMPARATIVELY

Representation in New Zealand and Beyond

KEY METHODOLOGICAL TOOL

Hypotheticals and Counterfactuals

The approach to the question of representation here is designed to stimulate debate on the best model for an electoral system and whether countries might change them. This question involves taking political lessons from one country case, comparing them with those of another case, and then making a proposal based upon an expectation of what would happen if an institution were changed. Of necessity, this means a degree of prediction and speculation but based on inferences. Hypotheticals are questions designed to get at what likely *might happen* in a scenario under certain circumstances; notice that the root of the word is the same as "hypothesis." Counterfactuals are ways of considering what *would have* happened in a given case under different circumstances; two classic examples, which are staples of alternative fiction, are "what would history have been like if the American colonies had lost their war against the British?" and "What if Hitler and the Nazis had won World War II?" Of course, it cannot be known with certainty what would have happened. In fact, this is why the comparative method—with its most-similar- and most-different-systems designs—is so helpful. But these thought experiments can help us to think through the implications of changes in variables such as electoral systems.

Careful analysts will not be cavalier about using hypotheticals and counterfactuals. Predictions and policy recommendations are only valuable if based on considerable, careful study and thoughtful consideration of possible consequences. In the case here, there could be unintended consequences of any country switching its electoral system, and it is the duty of the analyst to think them through. Good comparative analysis should be based on evidence of things that have happened, not simply guesses about "what might happen if." Nonetheless, hypotheticals, counterfactuals, and thought experiments are used all the time by comparativists eager to play out the logic of how outcomes might be different in countries with different institutions, social structures, and cultures.

Can any electoral system plausibly claim to have the "best of both worlds" when it comes to representing the electorate? The debate between PR and district-based electoral systems often comes down to one common debate: Is representation choosing a political party and its platform or voting for a specific candidate closest to one's views? It is likely that an observer will have a "gut reaction" to the advantages of one or the other while acknowledging that the opposing side "has a point."

Party-based elections allow the electorate to focus on the issues and platforms that most interest them and then to hold the elected government accountable for acting on such issues. They also give a sense, of course, that the overall representation in the legislature actually reflects the will of the overall population rather than the will of specific segments of the population. Candidate-centred elections, on the other hand, give voters the sense that they have one or more people who represent their interests, and this allows the voters to hold their specified representative accountable for providing services to their constituency. On the downside, district-based elections may result in disproportionate influence for certain parties—especially large parties at the expense of small parties—and proportional representation elections may sacrifice the identifiability of a specific legislator for a specific constituency. It may seem ideal if a country could have a political system that would have both of these characteristics: individual representatives for different districts of the country and also a legislature whose overall composition reflects the partisan preferences of the country.

So an ideal might be a system in which each citizen would have a representative for their district and the overall composition of the legislature could be guaranteed to be proportional. As noted before, countries such as Germany and New Zealand have done this. In fact, New Zealand switched its electoral system by national referendum in 1993, and the change brought about a German-style model that was explicitly intended to bring greater proportionality into what was previously a first-past-the-post system. This makes the country an especially compelling case that illustrates how electoral systems change the proportionality of seats. In both Germany and New Zealand today, each voter has two votes: a vote for a candidate to represent the district in the parliament and then a vote for one's preferred party. Voters may vote for their favourite party and the local candidate from the same party, but no one is required to do so: One can "split" the ticket, picking one's favoured candidate and then voting for another party. In each district, the candidate with the most votes is elected to the legislature, and there are a fixed number of such seats. The electoral commission also tallies all the votes for the parties and figures out how to make the legislature accurately reflect the proportion each party received.

For example, the New Zealand House of Representatives has approximately 120 seats, of which 71 are elected from districts and 49 are available for allocation to the parties according to the party vote. In the 2017 elections, the National Party secured 44.4 per cent of the party vote and constituencies, followed by Labour with 36.9 per cent of the party vote and constituencies. New Zealand First came third with 7.2 per cent of the party vote (and no constituencies), followed by the Greens with 6.3 per cent of the party vote. As a centrist party with policies reflecting both Labour and National appeal, NZ First became the deciding factor in creating a coalition government. In October 2017, a Labour-led government emerged under Jacinda Ardern in formal coalition with NZ First and with support from the Greens. United Future and the Māori Party, both of whom were long-term coalition partners with the previous National governments, were electorally wiped out after failing to reach the five per cent threshold and failing to gain any constituencies. Other parties such as Mana, the Opportunities Party, the Conservatives, and the Internet Party failed to make much electoral inroads.

Meanwhile, the parties that win more seats in the constituencies than their party vote are allowed to keep the extra seats they have won; these are called overhang seats. A consequence of this is that the exact number of seats in the legislature is not constant. Germany's system is similar, and, for example, the lower house of their legislature (the Bundestag) does not have a fixed number of seats; while the parliament elected in 2009 had 622 legislators, the parliament elected in 2013 had 631, and following the 2017 elections, the parliament had 709 seats.

The intended result is both identifiable representatives for each district and overall PR. A sample of a ballot from such a system can be seen in Figure 9.1, which is from the 2017 election in New Zealand. Notice that the candidates in the right-hand column represent some of the parties listed in the left-hand column.

Why might some argue for countries like Canada to adopt this sort of approach? One major challenge is a willingness to accept a totally new view of representation as both district-based and proportional, which is not how the country has operated historically. It would also require accepting that a computer will make the necessary adjustments to make the legislature proportional. But this process and its decision-making criteria would be quite transparent, being determined before the elections and visible to any and all observers. If you are living in a country that does not use this model, how would you attempt to explain to a German why your country should *not* change to such a model? The idea of representation varies from country to country, with different countries having different patterns of representation and different ways that representatives are chosen.

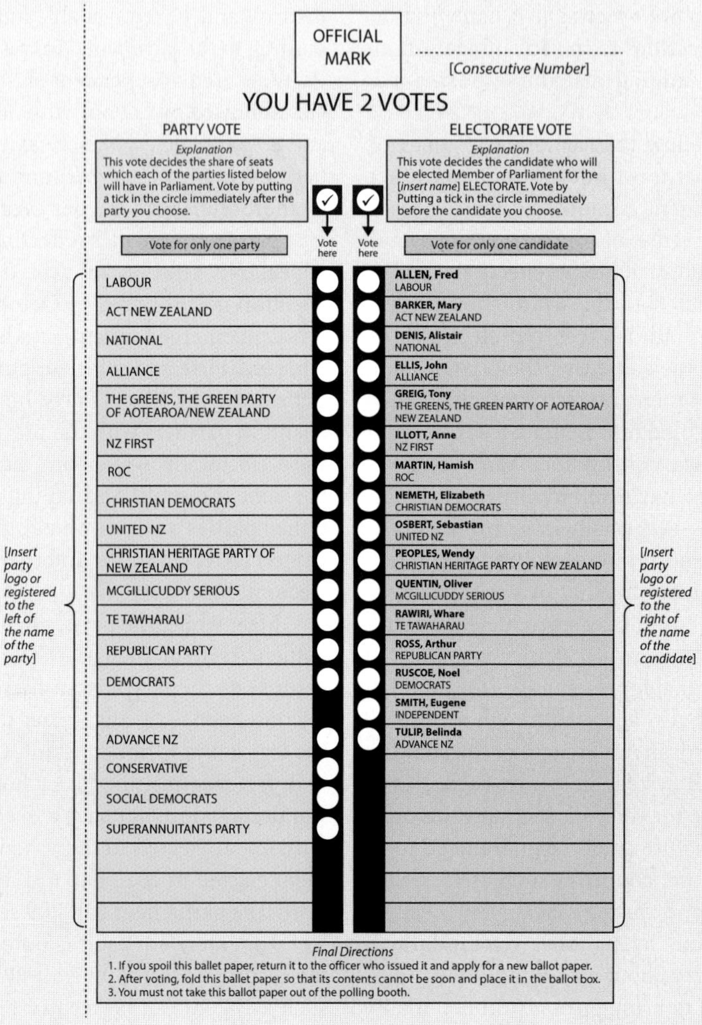

OFFICIAL MARK

[*Consecutive Number*]

YOU HAVE 2 VOTES

PARTY VOTE	ELECTORATE VOTE
Explanation This vote decides the share of seats which each of the parties listed below will have in Parliament. Vote by putting a tick in the circle immediately after the party you choose.	*Explanation* This vote decides the candidate who will be elected Member of Parliament for the [*insert name*] ELECTORATE. Vote by Putting a tick in the circle immediately before the candidate you choose.
Vote for only one party (Vote here)	(Vote here) Vote for only one candidate
LABOUR	**ALLEN, Fred** LABOUR
ACT NEW ZEALAND	**BARKER, Mary** ACT NEW ZEALAND
NATIONAL	**DENIS, Alistair** NATIONAL
ALLIANCE	**ELLIS, John** ALLIANCE
THE GREENS, THE GREEN PARTY OF AOTEAROA/NEW ZEALAND	**GREIG, Tony** THE GREENS, THE GREEN PARTY OF AOTEAROA/NEW ZEALAND
NZ FIRST	**ILLOTT, Anne** NZ FIRST
ROC	**MARTIN, Hamish** ROC
CHRISTIAN DEMOCRATS	**NEMETH, Elizabeth** CHRISTIAN DEMOCRATS
UNITED NZ	**OSBERT, Sebastian** UNITED NZ
CHRISTIAN HERITAGE PARTY OF NEW ZEALAND	**PEOPLES, Wendy** CHRISTIAN HERITAGE PARTY OF NEW ZEALAND
MCGILLICUDDY SERIOUS	**QUENTIN, Oliver** MCGILLICUDDY SERIOUS
TE TAWHARAU	**RAWIRI, Whare** TE TAWAHARAU
REPUBLICAN PARTY	**ROSS, Arthur** REPUBLICAN PARTY
DEMOCRATS	**RUSCOE, Noel** DEMOCRATS
	SMITH, Eugene INDEPENDENT
ADVANCE NZ	**TULIP, Belinda** ADVANCE NZ
CONSERVATIVE	
SOCIAL DEMOCRATS	
SUPERANNUITANTS PARTY	

[*Insert party logo or registered to the left of the name of the party*]

[*Insert party logo or registered to the right of the name of the candidate*]

Final Directions
1. If you spoil this ballet paper, return it to the officer who issued it and apply for a new ballot paper.
2. After voting, fold this ballet paper so that its contents cannot be soon and place it in the ballot box.
3. You must not take this ballot paper out of the polling booth.

FIGURE 9.1 Sample Ballot from New Zealand, 2017.

Source: Historic Collection / Alamy Stock Photo

Chapter Summary

Concepts

- Legislatures are deliberative bodies that are the foundation of modern governments.
- Legislatures pass laws and make policy, but they also lead public debate and have responsibilities for overseeing the executive, among other functions.

Types

- Legislatures can be bicameral (with two chambers) or unicameral (one chamber).
- Legislatures are elected by many different methods, including single-member constituencies (SMC), proportional representation (PR), and mixed or hybrid systems.
- There are several different patterns of interaction between legislatures and executives.

Causes and Effects

- A function of legislatures is representation, which can be conceptualized in different ways, and the nature and quality of representation are affected by several factors.
- Electoral systems can result in representation based on individuals, parties, or some mix of the two.
- Legislatures vary in the ways they function internally, and this too affects how they represent the populace.
- Executive–legislative relations also affect patterns of representation.

Thinking It Through

1. Imagine you are the leader of the Monster Raving Loony Party, a small party in the United Kingdom whose manifesto is posted at the following link: http://www.loonyparty.com/about/policy-proposals. You are a big believer in the cause and are eager to win some seats in Parliament. Currently, you are at 6 per cent in most opinion polls, but elections are not due for another couple of years. However, the government has called for public comment on a commission considering changing the electoral system in the United Kingdom. What would you propose the system should be for House of Commons elections? Considering political incentives, what do you expect would be the reaction of Members of Parliament from the three leading parties there: the Conservatives, the Liberal Democrats, and Labour?
2. Imagine that as a Canadian, accustomed to (and approving of) the first-past-the-post system for electing MPs, you are debating with a European who lives in a system that has always had PR. This European argues that the PR system offers chances to more political actors, saying that this enlivens debate and forces the legislature to take into account the interests of a broader range of people. Can you convince your interlocutor that the Canadian system is preferable to the European one?
3. What are the disadvantages, if any, of a system that requires ranking candidates and then calculates winners on the basis of voters' second or third choices?
4. Would you expect changes in institutional structures (such as a legislature or legislative elections) in a given country to reshape the political outcomes and policy decisions, or would these fundamental outcomes likely be shaped by cultures and other structures and thus be mostly independent of the institutional design? How could you find evidence or arguments to support your claim?

10 Executives

In This Chapter

Boris Johnson greets Queen Elizabeth in London, England in 2016, when he was the mayor of London. Johnson became the prime minister of the UK in July 2019. (Max Mumby/Indigo/Getty Images)

In 1776, a group of influential male landowners from 13 American colonies signed a Declaration of Independence from Great Britain. Most of the document listed claims of abuse perpetrated by King George III, Britain's monarch and head of state, including the now infamous charge that the King had provoked "merciless Indian savages" against the colonists. Following the American Revolution, which ended in 1783, the former British colonists established a system of government with several notable differences from that of Britain. Known as a republic, the United States had a written Constitution, no monarch, powerful state governments, and several branches of government that were independent and designed to balance one another. The new republic arranged for an elected president as both head of state and head of government.

Over the next two centuries, as both the United States and Great Britain became more mature democracies, the American presidential system and the British parliamentary system became two defining models for how governments could function. With its executive branch led by a prime minister and a monarch who increasingly became a figurehead in a ceremonial position, Britain became the "Mother of Parliaments" around the world, emulated in Canada, New Zealand, Australia, India, Fiji, Trinidad and Tobago, and many other countries. Meanwhile, other states came to adopt aspects of the American system of a presidency with checks and balances. Canada and Australia both have British-style parliamentary systems, although both copied the American model in calling their upper house the Senate. Canada's Senate is appointed like the British House of Lords, while Australia's Senate is decided by regular elections, as in the US.

In the United States and Great Britain, the executives have kept their same basic form over time, though their powers have shifted somewhat. Parliament formally retains political power and sovereignty in Britain, and the prime minister's continued power rests on retaining the legislature's confidence. The American president has become more influential over time as the United States has grown but still remains deeply entrenched in the same basic system of checks and balances that endures to this day.

• • •

Concepts

Executives earn their name because they *execute* or administer policies and laws. In most countries, executives implement and administer the laws passed by legislatures, though in some authoritarian regimes the executive may act without a functioning legislature. Executives also contribute to the making of law. Legislatures (as examined in Chapter 9) are usually authorized to initiate and pass laws in representative democracies, but executives play a major role in the public debate and decision-making that leads to new laws. For example, executives may send budget requests to the legislature, or they may work with legislators to formulate a policy that the executive branch desires.

executive The branch of government, or the individual(s) at the top of that branch, that executes or administers policies and laws in a country.

In most cases, executives have a substantial role in determining which laws and policies pass. In the United States, the president usually signs final bills as they become laws and has the power to veto (disapprove) bills, though the legislature can override the veto with a strong enough majority. In parliamentary systems like Canada's, the executive shapes the agenda of the parliament to decide which initiatives will come to the floor for debate and also pressures parliamentarians to pass its desired policies. The relative power of the executive and legislative branches is one of the leading issues that determine how political decisions are made, and the relationship between the branches is a major theme running through this chapter.

bureaucracy The organization of unelected officials, often considered part of the executive branch, that implements, executes, and enforces laws and policies.

The executive is the branch of government that runs the government **bureaucracy**, such as the Department of Defense or Department of Education in the United States or the Ministry of Health or Ministry of Agriculture in Canada. These departments or ministries include large numbers of officials and civil servants who work for the executive branch. For this reason, the executive branch is often held to be responsible for the quality of government actions. When social services improve, executives may successfully claim credit, or when a war policy fails, the executive may take the blame. Legislatures have their portion of responsibility, since they typically pass the laws authorizing executive action and also expenditures, but executives are responsible for executing the laws on the books. In Canada and other Westminster systems, the House of Commons has elements of both the executive and legislative branches. The prime minister and cabinet (who are all elected MPs and members of the House of Commons) comprise the executive branch (alongside the governor general and the monarch). At the same time, however, the prime minister and cabinet are also part of the legislative branch, alongside all other MPs. In the US, the executive branch and legislative branch are separate—the president and cabinet represent the executive branch, while the legislative branch is comprised of both houses of Congress.

head of state A person with executive functions who is a country's symbolic representative, including elected presidents and unelected monarchs.

head of government The top executive official responsible for forming governments and formulating and implementing policies.

prime minister A chief executive in a parliamentary system of government.

president An executive leader who typically combines the functions of head of state and head of government and is not directly responsible to a legislature.

monarch A head of state in a monarchy, who usually inherits a position for life and may have either substantial political powers or very limited ceremonial powers.

The executive can also refer to specific individuals who lead this branch of government. These "chief executives" are heads of state or heads of government. The distinction between these two—head of state and head of government—is significant. In brief, the **head of state** is a country's symbolic national representative, while the **head of government** is responsible for forming governments and formulating and implementing policies. **Prime ministers** are examples of heads of government. **Presidents** often combine the powers of head of state and head of government.

Monarchs such as kings, queens, and emperors are classic examples of heads of state. Traditional monarchs still wield political influence and power as heads of state in some contemporary societies, such as the sultanates and emirates in some countries of the Middle East and some small nations such as Swaziland. In Europe, traditional monarchies persist but are essentially figureheads with only symbolic power; there are 12 such monarchies in Europe. In some other countries—usually where the nation-state is of more recent origin, such as India and Israel—a ceremonial president may be the nominal head of state, with political power again reserved for the head of government in the form of a prime minister.

The responsibilities and powers of the executive branch are extensive. By most measures, the executive could be the most powerful and dominant branch of government: It commands the bureaucracy and maintains nominal control over the military, and it is responsible for spending the budget approved by the legislature. Indeed, when democracies break down into authoritarian regimes, a typical result is the dissolution of the legislative branch and the loss of independence for the judiciary; it is often the executive's domination over other branches that distinguishes authoritarianism from the more balanced institutional arrangements of a democracy.

government In the context of executives, the set of top elected executive officials and high-level political appointees that shapes and orients policy; also refers to the broader administrative apparatus of the state.

Executive branches of **government** consist of both a set of elected politicians and a more permanent bureaucracy or civil service. Elected officials generally have discretion to make only a limited number of political appointments to allies, supporters, and co-partisans. In Canada, these appointments are centred in the Prime Minister's Office (or PMO), where key staffers are hired to provide advice on political appointments, media relations, how best to pitch new legislation, and other issues of importance to the prime minister. Beyond these, most of the bureaucracy is expected to remain neutral, executing the law regardless of election results. In 1908, the Public Service Commission

PHOTO 10.2 Saudi Crown Prince Mohammed bin Salman (left) speaks to his father, King Salman, at a meeting of the Gulf Cooperation Council in Riyadh, Saudi Arabia, in December 2018. Saudi Arabia is an absolute monarchy ruled by a succession of kings tracing their lineage to the founder of the state, Abdul Aziz bin Abdul Rahman Al Saud. The king serves as prime minister and Custodian of the Two Holy Mosques (located in the cities of Mecca and Medina).

was created in Canada to safeguard the non-partisan nature of the civil service. This was further reinforced in 2003 when the Public Service Employment Act was passed to provide oversight over government appointments with a view to preventing political patronage.[1] In many countries, this ideal is not always upheld in practice, but bureaucrats are generally expected to implement and administer policies rather than to promote a political vision of what government should do.[2]

In parliamentary systems, when a "new government" is formed, this does not mean that the state bureaucracy changes, except perhaps at the highest level. Similarly, in the United States, the word **administration** can be used to refer to the top elected officials in the executive or to the broader bureaucracy that executes policy. This falls under the purview of the president and their advisors, and it can be a time-consuming process.

administration The bureaucracy of state officials, usually considered part of the executive branch, that executes policy.

Understanding politics requires understanding how executives are selected. In turn, understanding executives depends on understanding legislatures, which we discussed in the previous chapter. Especially in representative democracies (but also even in some authoritarian regimes), executives rely on legislatures or assemblies to pass laws that the executive will then implement or "execute." In this chapter, we begin by identifying what executives are and what they do. We then discuss the consequences of different patterns of executives. One of the main distinctions we draw is between presidential and parliamentary forms of government. We use our cases to examine executives comparatively and discuss which forms are most likely to support democracy.

Types

There are two basic ways to structure the executive branch of government: presidential and parliamentary. The United States is an example of presidentialism, while Canada is an example of parliamentarism. Some countries, such as France, have executive systems that combine features of presidentialism and parliamentarism, as do some less democratic countries, such as Iran. The relative power of the executive depends upon the constitution as well as a range of formal and informal powers, including the ability of the chief executive to discipline and manage their party and any other parties needed to comprise a governing coalition. Presidential and parliamentary systems thus have different kinds of **executive–legislative relations**. We discuss these variations throughout this section (and a summary view of types can be found in Table 10.1).

executive–legislative relations The set of political relationships between the executive branch of government, which executes laws/policies, and the legislative branch, which often has the authority to pass those laws/policies.

presidentialism A system of government in which a president serves as chief executive, being independent of the legislature and often combining the functions of head of state and head of government.

direct election With regard to executives, an electoral system in which voters cast a vote directly for the head of government or head of state.

Executive Structures: Presidential and Parliamentary

Under **presidentialism**, the populace at large votes in elections for a chief executive, usually called a president, in a nationwide election.[3] This president is usually elected for a fixed term of several years and depends on the voting populace for their position, though the legislature or courts may have the power to remove the president in serious cases of criminal behaviour, unconstitutional action, or other impeachable offences. Most presidential systems in democracies feature **direct elections** in a nationwide popular vote, with particular electoral rules varying by country. In many countries (such as Mexico), the top vote-getter among all candidates wins, with or without a majority; in others (such as France, as seen in the "Case in Context: Electing the French President" box on page 207), there is a first round between all candidates and then a runoff between the top two vote-getters, unless one candidate receives an outright majority in the first round. The United States is actually an exception in its presidential electoral process, since election depends on winning a majority of the electoral votes allotted to the various states.

Presidential systems also have legislatures as another "branch" of government, and the issue of executive–legislative relations is important. In nearly all presidential systems, both the executive and the legislature are expected to abide by the rules of a written constitution,

TABLE 10.1 | Executive Structures

Form of Executive	Features
Presidential	President is directly elected by population at large. President is ceremonial head of state and chief executive. Legislature is elected independently of executive.
Parliamentary	Prime minister is indirectly elected by parliament/legislature. Prime minister is head of government. Ceremonial monarch, government appointed representative, or president may be head of state.
Semi-presidential (hybrid)	President is directly elected by population at large. Prime minister or chief minister is responsible to parliament. President may have power to appoint prime minister, dissolve legislature, etc.

CASE IN CONTEXT

392

Electing the French President: What Do Runoffs Do?

The French presidential election contrasts with the American presidential election with which most Canadian students will be familiar. In France, the election is based on the nation-wide vote and usually features two rounds. The first round is between a large number of candidates, while the second round is a "runoff" between the top two candidates from the first round. These electoral systems can produce different results because of the ways they encourage people to vote for or discourage them from voting for compromise candidates.

See the case study on the French executive in Part VI, p. 392. As you read it, keep in mind the following questions:

1. What are the advantages and disadvantages of the French runoff system?
2. Would the 2016 American elections have turned out differently if the electoral system were changed to follow the French model?
3. Would a change to such a system have any implications for smaller parties, or would the overall effect be not much change?

Sipa via AP Images

PHOTO 10.3 Emmanuel Macron delivers his victory speech at the Louvre in Paris after winning the "runoff" round in the French presidential election in May 2017.

though these rules may be flouted by powerful presidents in less-democratic countries. Each branch of government has certain powers, rights, and responsibilities, with the legislature generally having the power to make most law. Presidents have the power to execute these laws, but they cannot make most laws themselves. They typically have the right to assent to a law proposed by the legislature or to veto it; specific rules for what happens in case of a veto vary by country, but the legislature can often overturn the president's veto with an ample majority. The interplay that results between the executive and legislature is known in the American system as a set of "checks and balances" between different political actors. Judiciaries also have a role in this set of checks and balances, since they have some authority to interpret the law and rule out provisions that conflict with the constitution or legal code.

parliamentarism A system of government in which the head of government is elected by and accountable to a parliament or legislature.

Parliamentarism works differently from presidentialism. The first step is when political parties select candidates to run in various constituencies around the country. Large mainstream parties will choose candidates for all constituencies, while smaller parties (like the Green Party) may choose strategic ridings instead, given that they have fewer potential candidates. The second step is an election of members of parliament (MPs) in which voters vote for a political party and/or elect a specific representative of a political party from their district. The third step is when these MPs select an individual as head of government and chief executive. This is an indirect election in which most voters never vote directly for the individual who becomes head of government. In most cases, each major party participating

CASE IN CONTEXT

Online

"The Most Powerful Person in the World"? (online case)

The President of the United States is both the ceremonial head of state and the titular head of government, as well as the Commander-in-Chief of the country's armed forces. Presidents are part of a system of checks and balances between executives and the other branches. The nature of these American-style checks and balances is the subject of much of the study of executives.

For more on the US presidency, go to **www.oup.com/he/DickovickCe** to see the case study. As you read it, keep in mind the following questions:

1. Why might the founders of the American Constitution have insisted on checks and balances between the branches of government?
2. Are there negative consequences of checks and balances for making laws and making governments work, and are there examples in which these consequences have played out?
3. Other than parliamentarism, can you conceive of other ways to protect democracy that would not involve this style of checks and balances?

in the election has a prominent standard-bearer known to the public, so while individuals may not get to vote for this individual, there is often a leading face associated with the party. The leader of the party that wins the most votes is often selected by the parliament as the head of government, though not always. Since many parliamentary systems have a quite a few large parties with none large enough to claim a majority of seats, the selection of the head of government depends on negotiations between the parties to see who can form a coalition big enough to govern; we discuss this later in the chapter. What heads of government are called in parliamentary systems varies by country and by language and include prime minister, premier, and chancellor.[4]

An indirectly elected head of government wields a form of executive power that is *fused* with legislative power. The fact that the executive and legislature come out of the same body gives rise to a kind of executive–legislative relations different from that in presidential systems. On one hand, parliamentary systems often feature a high degree of party unity, with executives who can count on the "backbench" legislators in their party to support executive proposals. This is in part because legislators who do not vote along with the executive may create conditions for "no confidence" in the government, which can put legislators' seats at risk, as we discuss later. On the other hand, executives in parliamentary systems depend on the continued "confidence" of the legislature, since the legislature selected them and generally has the power to vote out the government. This is much easier to do in most parliamentary systems than in presidential systems that require complicated procedures to impeach presidents or force resignations. Parliamentary systems thus have back-and-forth exchanges between executives and legislatures, but "checks and balances" have different meanings from those in presidential systems.

Other countries combine features of presidentialism and parliamentarism. These systems typically feature both a directly elected president as the head of state and a prime minister chosen separately as the head of government. In these **semi-presidential systems**, the prime minister and other government ministers or cabinet officials may be appointed by the president, but they are responsible to the legislature (or parliament) and can be dismissed by the legislature. France is a useful example of this system, as can be seen in the discussion of the political regime in that country (see the France Country Profile in Part VI, p. 385).

semi-presidential system A mixed or hybrid system combining aspects of presidentialism and parliamentarism.

Many other configurations of executive power are possible besides the preceding three democratic examples. In Iran, for instance, the president may have some power in executive–legislative relations but is relatively powerless compared with the religious clerics. Whether the Supreme Leader in Iran is best seen as a judicial or executive authority (or both) is open to debate, but it shows that many executives often operate in an intricate web of institutions and cannot simply make decisions unilaterally.

Formal Powers

What executives can do depends on the **formal powers** they have, which are usually outlined in a country's constitutional charter or basic laws. One important formal power is the ability of some presidents to **veto** laws passed by the legislature. Depending on the country, the legislature may be able to override the veto with a majority or supermajority of greater than 50 per cent. Veto power gives executives a chance to react to the legislature, but executives may also have more proactive formal powers.

formal powers The powers possessed by a political actor, such as a chief executive, as a function of their constitutional or legal position.

veto An act of executive power in which an executive rejects a law passed by a legislature.

dissolving the legislature The practice of a chief executive disbanding the legislature, often accompanied in a democratic regime by the calling for new elections.

An example of a proactive executive power is the ability in many countries to **dissolve the legislature**. In some countries, this may be exercised only on rare occasions or perhaps a limited number of times per presidential administration, while in others it may be exercised frequently when the executive deems it will improve governance or perhaps give the government a larger majority. In Canada, for instance, elections must be held at least every four years, but a prime minister and the government are entitled to call an early election—sometimes called a "snap election"—at a moment that may be most advantageous for the governing party. In some countries, this can be a major advantage to the incumbent because governments can schedule elections at their convenience after big boosts of government spending, a phenomenon known as the political business cycle.[5] Governments can also choose to hold elections when the opposition parties are in disarray. In Canada, the Harper government called elections during periods when the Liberal Party of Canada struggled with a succession of politically unpopular leaders.

In Canada, political parties often elect their own leaders by holding very lengthy leadership contests that can take a year or more in which prospective party leaders travel across the country, debate other would-be party leaders, and seek to fundraise and sign up new party members. During this process, parties have an interim leader, but there is no permanent leader to articulate a new vision for the party. The Liberal Party went through a series of unpopular leaders: Stéphane Dion, Michael Ignatieff, and then Bob Rae (who served as interim leader). The lengthy period between leaders provided the Harper government with a tremendous advantage. Some other Westminster systems, notably Australia, New Zealand, and the UK, don't engage in this lengthy leadership selection process because any drawn-out leadership process almost guarantees a reduction in public support for the party during this period. In August 2017, the Labour Party of New Zealand encouraged the resignation of an unpopular Andrew Little as party leader (and leader of the opposition), and Jacinda Ardern became leader soon after. Ardern campaigned vigorously and managed to gain enough votes to form a government with the support of two other parties.

Other formal powers in some countries include the power to pass certain laws or orders without the intervention of the legislature. For example, presidents may have the ability to issue **decrees**, which are orders that have the power of law despite not being passed through a legislature. They have been used extensively in more authoritarian regimes to limit political mobilization. Decrees have also been used by assertive presidents in relatively democratic countries, such as Brazil in the 1990s, when a president sought to halt an economic crisis. They may go into effect immediately and, in some instances, may only

decree An executive-made order that has the force of law despite not being passed through a legislature.

PHOTO 10.4 New Zealand's Labour Party leader Jacinda Ardern talks to supporters after election results are announced in Auckland, New Zealand, in September 2017. The next month she became prime minister when the Labour Party and New Zealand First Party entered a deal to form a coalition government with the backing of the Green Party.

be overturned by restrictive votes in the legislature or by expiring after a certain period of time. Executives can also issue **executive orders** to the bureaucracy that shape the way the bureaucracy enacts and interprets the law. This can affect whether and how important regulations are enforced. In some situations, presidents may be empowered to declare a nationwide **state of emergency** that confers extraordinary powers on the president (and often on the military) to govern with less input from the legislature. The case of Russia shows that it is possible to centralize a great deal of decision-making power in the executive branch, whether as president or as prime minister.

executive order An order made by a chief executive or top official to the bureaucracy that determines how the bureaucracy should enact or interpret the law.

state of emergency A condition allowed by some constitutions in which guarantees, rights, or provisions are temporarily limited, to be justified by emergencies or exceptional circumstances.

It is important to know what executives *cannot* do because all democracies (by definition) have numerous checks on executive power. The first and most obvious restraints on executives are periodic *elections* for new governments. These elections ensure that an executive cannot remain in power indefinitely without popular support. Second are *constitutional limitations* on executive power, such as rights guaranteed to all citizens that the executive may not infringe. Third are *separations of powers*. This may include separating powers between levels of government, such as between central governments and state and local governments in a federal system. It also includes the ways the judicial and legislative branches check executive power and ensure oversight of the executive. Strict **term limits** on time in office may also be seen as a restriction on executive powers, as is the case with the American president, who serves a maximum of two terms and a total of eight years. In most parliamentary systems, there are no precise limits on prime ministers, although there are often term limits for governor generals.

term limit Restriction on the number of times or total amount of time a political official can serve in a given position.

The other branches of government are responsible for ensuring that executives do not overstep their limits. Constitutional courts may rule that an executive has acted unconstitutionally or illegally. Legislatures may have even stronger mechanisms. One is public rebuke, such as the ability to censure or reprimand the executive. Legislatures may also be able to prevent executive action by withholding funds from executive agencies. In many instances, the legislature can also remove executives from office. In presidential systems, for example, this can occur after an **impeachment process**.

impeachment A process by which a legislature initiates proceedings to determine whether an official, often a top-ranking executive official, should be removed from office.

In parliamentary systems, the legislature chooses the executives, and the executive formally depends on the support of the legislature to retain office. The legislature has the power to dismiss the executive if it no longer deems that the government is functioning adequately. This mechanism, the **vote of no confidence**, makes removing an executive much easier than in a presidential system. The vote of no confidence comes in many forms. In its simplest form, a confidence vote is simply called by members of parliament, and the government is voted out if a majority votes no confidence. The head of state then calls new elections for a new government. In Germany, on the other hand, there is a so-called "constructive vote of no confidence," which is designed to ensure that there will always be a government in place. There, the legislative majority voting no confidence in a government simultaneously proposes a new government that will take its place.

vote of no confidence A vote taken by a legislature that expresses a lack of support for the government or executive, which, if successful, often results in the dissolution of the government and the calling of new legislative elections.

More formal powers for the executive leads to greater influence over legislatures, while more checks on executive powers gives greater authority to legislatures.[7] Weaker formal powers may limit executives in their ability to promote their initiatives or agendas. It is relatively obvious that the ability to veto legislation enhances a president's power, for example, or that a legislature that can easily override a veto weakens the executive's power. However, as noted before, formal rules do not fully determine an executive's power, and it

CASE IN CONTEXT

460

Oligarchy, Democracy, and Authoritarianism in Russia

For decades, Russia was the centre of the Soviet Union, which, like virtually every modern state, claimed to be democratic, though in this instance quite dubiously. Then, between 1989 and 1991, the Soviet Union fell apart, more quickly than almost anyone had anticipated, leading to the emergence of a hybrid regime under Boris Yeltsin. A period of economic and political instability followed until Vladimir Putin, aided by an oil boom, began to impose political order. He did this, in part, by developing a hybrid of electoral politics with strong authoritarian features, considered a classic case of competitive authoritarianism.[6] The state has been used to repress his opponents, and his 2012 re-election to the presidency has been denounced by many for its irregularities and has been the source of much popular protest. Putin could conceivably alternate between holding the presidency and governing indirectly through others in the coming years, though his ability to hold onto power over the long term remains to be seen.

For more on Russia as a competitive authoritarian regime, see the case study in Part VI, p. 460. As you read it, keep in mind the following questions:

1. If Russia is a competitive authoritarian regime rather than a democracy or a fully authoritarian regime, when did it become one? What does the case suggest about how we can distinguish hybrid from democratic and authoritarian regimes?
2. How much of Russia's authoritarian character is a function of the state's ability to make use of oil wealth? If there is a prolonged downturn in the market for oil, will the hybrid regime model be likely to continue to work indefinitely? Why or why not?

is not always clear how formal rules themselves matter. For example, Brazil's president used decrees a great deal in the 1990s, but most legislation of any significance ultimately had to be passed through the legislature.

In parliamentary systems, one of the main issues with regard to formal powers is how confidence votes work. Where they are used, confidence votes are examples of the legislature exerting its control over the executive, but the existence of votes of non-confidence is not proof of legislative power. In fact, legislatures can be powerful even without using confidence votes. Often, the mere threat of a confidence vote will be enough to force the executive to do the legislature's bidding. Actual votes of non-confidence may rarely come to the floor of a legislature or parliament and may succeed even more rarely, even when executives are weak. They do happen sometimes, however. In June 2017, the British Columbia Liberal government, led by Premier Christy Clark (who had served as premier and party leader for six years), suffered a vote of non-confidence 52 days after a very close provincial election. The NDP and Green MLAs stood together to form a voting block of 44 members who opposed the 43-member Liberal government. Soon after, a coalition NDP-Green government was formed.[8]

Parliamentary countries are not all destined to have a merry-go-round of failed governments that last only a brief time before being voted down in confidence votes. Some countries have notoriously unstable systems, while other countries rarely witness a confidence vote. Because prime ministers usually represent one of the largest parties in parliament, the executive in a parliamentary system will often have substantial support in the parliament. Parliamentarians who call for a no confidence vote place their own careers on the line, since these votes usually trigger new elections or shake-ups within the party.

Partisan Powers

partisan powers The powers accruing to a government official, such as a chief executive, by virtue of the official's leverage or power over members of a political party.

The formal powers of an executive are not the only factor that determines whether an executive has leverage over legislation. Formal powers are often less important than the **partisan powers** of the executive—that is, the president's leverage over same-party legislators and over parties in the governing coalition. Chief executives who can exercise such authority and can thus control the careers of other politicians will typically be able to pass a great deal of legislation.

The balance of power between the executive and the legislature depends partly on whether executive leaders can control the electoral fortunes of legislators. One of the most important forms of control is over the party's list of candidates for elections, as noted in the previous chapter. If the executive leaders can choose who will be on party's list of candidates, then those would-be candidates will be responsive to the needs of the executive. On the other hand, the executive's partisan powers are lessened if party leaders do not control the electoral fortunes of co-partisans. When party candidates are chosen by voters in primary elections, for instance, they will tend to be more loyal to their constituents than to their party leadership. This may result in legislators who vote against the wishes of their party leaders in the executive.

Coalitions

coalition A group of two or more political parties that governs by sharing executive power and responsibilities.

The power of executive leaders also depends on whether a party governs alone or is part of a **coalition** of two or more parties. Governing coalitions form among parties in the legislature, but they determine the composition of the executive and the government, so we consider them in this chapter. Coalitions usually arise when there are several major parties in a country and the party that won the most legislative seats in an election does not have the majority needed to pass legislation on its own. In parliamentary systems, where the executive depends on the confidence of the legislature, heads of government frequently need to hold together a coalition in order not to be voted out of office. This is especially common under systems of proportional representation (see Chapter 9) in which small parties are more likely to emerge and remain in existence. On some occasions, a governing party may have a majority but choose to form an alliance with another party for other reasons.[9] Coalitions are somewhat less common in presidential systems, in which an election is held for a single chief executive who represents a certain party. Yet even in presidential countries like Brazil, presidents sometimes need to form a cabinet that represents various parties in order to have a coalition of parties that can get legislation passed.

In parliamentary systems, the largest party in the legislature by convention normally forms a government and is usually the one from which the head of government emerges.[10] Parties with fewer seats are the "junior" members of the coalition but will demand some political reward for agreeing to participate in government. This comes from **cabinet** appointments to control ministerial **portfolios**. By controlling certain ministries, coalition members can reward their supporters with the ability to shape policy in the area where they control the cabinet position and can help some of their top partisans with high-ranking appointments in the bureaucracy.[11]

cabinet The group of senior officials in the executive branch, including ministers, who advise the head of government or head of state.

portfolio The set of duties and tasks that correspond to a given ministerial office.

Forming governing coalitions is a political art, especially in countries with many parties in the legislature. Not all coalitions are based on the largest party in parliament, for example. If a group of smaller parties gets together as in New Zealand, they may be able to exclude the largest party or parties from the government. This occurred in 2017 when the National Party, which had the most seats in Parliament, did not form the government. Instead, the Labour Party joined in coalition with New Zealand First Party (NZF) and also made an agreement for support with the Green Party. Substantial bargaining often takes place over how cabinet positions will be distributed among the parties. Smaller parties can gain considerable leverage that can translate into political power. In the New Zealand case, the coalition agreement provided NZF with a large (one might even say oversized) number of cabinet portfolios. While NZF had only nine MPs elected, their MPs gained the following ministerial positions: Foreign Affairs, Defence, Deputy Prime Minister, Racing, State Owned Enterprises, Veterans, Children, Internal Affairs, Seniors, Associate Education, Forestry, Infrastructure, and Regional Economic Development.

Provincially, coalition governments can also form. In the 2017 British Columbia elections, the NDP formed a confidence and supply agreement with the Green Party, which won three seats. This allowed the NDP to form a razor-thin government, which was precarious, given that there was also one independent legislator and one vacant seat at the time. The referendum on electoral reform, which we discussed in Chapter 9, was one of the conditions outlined in the coalition agreement.

There are several types of governing coalitions. Consider the following hypothetical example of the fictional country of Tapawera (Table 10.2). There are 100 seats in the parliament, and the parties are arrayed along the political spectrum from far left (XL) and left (L) through the centre (C) to right (R) and far right (XR). Imagine that each seat represents 1 per cent of the vote so that party R got 27 per cent of the vote and therefore 27 seats.[12] Many possible kinds of coalitions can be formed after this election. We give one example for several types of coalitions, listing the largest party first in each case, and encourage you to figure out other possible examples that fit each type of coalition. What different coalitions might form, and which parties might be represented in the executive branch?

A **minimum winning coalition** has no "surplus" parties beyond those required to form a government. So, for instance, a coalition of the four parties C, R, L, and XR would not be "minimum winning" because parties C, R, and L could still have more than 50 per cent of

minimum winning coalition A governing coalition that contains no surplus parties beyond those required to form a government.

TABLE 10.2 | Hypothetical Distribution of Seats in Parliament of Tapawera

Party	XL	L	C	R	XR
Seats	30	7	21	27	15

the seats even without the seats of XR. However, removing any one of the parties from the C-R-L coalition would give the coalition less than the 50 per cent of seats needed. C-R-L is thus an example of a minimum winning coalition. There are several other possibilities in this election, such as an XL-XR-L coalition. A more restrictive version of a minimum winning coalition is **minimum connected winning**; this arrangement occurs when all parties in the coalition are "connected" to one another on the political spectrum. This prevents the example of the parties XL (far left) and L (left) forming a coalition with the party XR (far right), which would be improbable because there is no realistic "connection" linking these parties. There are other parties in between, namely R and C. The logic is to include policy preferences as a factor in coalition formation. This rules out several minimum winning coalitions, but C-R-L is an example of a minimum connected coalition.

minimum connected winning coalition A minimum winning coalition in which all parties in the coalition are "connected" or adjacent to one another on the political spectrum.

The **minimum size coalition** goes a step further and says the coalition that governs will be that closest to the threshold needed, usually 50 per cent plus one seat. A coalition that includes only 51 per cent of the seats is preferred to a coalition that includes a larger percentage of seats because the participating parties will maximize their relative power within the coalition by not dispersing power. There will often be only one possible minimum size coalition, even when there are many possible "minimum winning coalitions." In Tapawera, XL-C is the minimum size coalition.

minimum size coalition A governing coalition that is closest to the threshold needed to govern, typically 50 per cent of the legislative seats plus one seat.

Other logics can also shape the types of coalition that emerge (Table 10.3). One logic is to minimize the number of parties involved: two-party coalitions will be preferred to three- or four-party coalitions, even if the two-party coalition means more seats. Another option is that coalitions should contain the party holding the median seat in parliament, or the "middle" parliamentarian on the political spectrum, because this echoes the will of the "median voter" or average citizen. In this case, party C is the median party. The median party coalition may or may not be "minimum winning." A final type of majority coalition will minimize the range or number of "spaces" on the political spectrum between parties. Between C and XR, for instance, there are two "spaces" (C to R and R to XR). The same is true for L and R, while XL and R would have three spaces. Such coalitions prefer parties that are not too far apart, but there is no requirement that parties need to be "connected" or adjacent to one another. In Tapawera, two spaces is the minimum possible. Sometimes this includes three parties connected to one another and sometimes two parties with a space in between them.

These coalitions all have a governing majority, and all share a logic in which participating parties attempt to minimize the size or scope of the coalition. However, there are also two other major possibilities in coalition formation. A **grand coalition** may be made up of two or more parties that represent well over half of the electorate and hold well over half the seats. One motivation for a grand coalition is national unity among the largest parties in a time of crisis. An example was the national unity government in Britain during World War II when Conservatives, Liberals, and Labour all joined to support the war effort. Canadian politicians have generally avoided such governments. In both World Wars I and II, the Conservatives made efforts to create unity governments, only to be rebuffed by the Liberals. In 1917, Liberal Party leader Wilfrid Laurier rejected Conservative Prime Minister Robert Borden's invitation to form a united government. In 1940, the Conservatives ran

grand coalition A governing coalition composed of two or more major parties that hold a supermajority of legislative seats and represent a supermajority of the electorate.

TABLE 10.3 | Types of Coalition

Type of Coalition	Definition of Coalition	Example	Seats (#)
Minimum Winning	No extra or surplus parties that are not needed to govern	XL – XR – L	52
Minimum Connected Winning	Minimum winning and parties are connected on policy spectrum.	C – R – L	55
Minimum Size	As close as possible to minimum number of seats needed (often 50 per cent)	XL – C	51
Minimum Number of Parties[10]	Fewest number of parties needed to form majority	XL – R	57
Median Party[11]	Includes the median party in the middle of the political spectrum	XL – C	51
Minimum Range	Minimum number of spaces between parties on policy spectrum	R – C – XR	63

in the federal election under a banner of national unity, but the Liberals under William Lyon Mackenzie King secured a majority of the vote and governed alone. More recently, Chancellor Merkel has formed a series of grand coalitions in Germany that emerged after several closely contested elections. These grand coalitions were formed in 2005 and 2013, both times in an effort to keep the former East German communist party (in its present incarnation the Party of Democratic Socialism) out of power.

Certainly, not all governments have a majority of the seats in the legislature. In some parliamentary systems, the largest party (or a group of parties) may be able to form a government even with less than 50 per cent of the seats. This happens when there are three

Associated Press/Michael Sohn

PHOTO 10.5 German Chancellor Angela Merkel of the Christian Democratic Union (centre) talks with then–Foreign Minister Guido Westerwelle of the Free Democratic Party (right) and others as they negotiate to form a governing coalition in October 2009.

or more major parties represented in parliament and no party gains a majority of seats. The government's ability to remain in power is tenuous in these cases, lasting until a vote of no confidence occurs or the next election is held. In Canada from 2008 to 2011, the Conservative government of Stephen Harper governed with only 46 per cent of the seats in Parliament, since the next largest party was the Liberals (25 per cent of seats), followed by the New Democratic Party and the Bloc Québécois, with whom neither the Conservatives nor the Liberals could form a majority coalition. The Conservatives formed a government, which fell in 2011 when the other three parties agreed to vote no confidence and call new elections; the Conservatives then won an outright majority in the ensuing election.

Informal Powers

informal powers Those powers possessed by an office holder that are not "official" but rather based on custom, convention, or other sources of influence.

Apart from formal and partisan powers, executives can have others that we simply call "**informal powers**" (see Table 10.4). They include the ability to influence public debate and public opinion. For instance, if President Macron of France wishes to force a public debate on immigration, he may bring up the issue in speeches and talk about it in the media. There is nothing in most democratic constitutions giving the president legal authority to shape public opinion, but the president is clearly free to use the podium and public position to shape politics. Indeed, one prominent scholar has referred to the most essential power of the American president as the "power to persuade," since formal authority alone will not work to control the legislature or the bureaucracy.[13] Since 2017, President Trump has made widespread use of Twitter to directly reach tens of millions of "followers" (the exact number is contested because of trolling, and it changes constantly). In many countries, presidents can also use the government as a source of **patronage** or for the purposes of **clientelism**. This means providing jobs or other benefits to supporters, with the executive known as the patron and the recipients of this support known as the clients. Patron–client politics is generally seen as poor governance, but it is clearly a power that some presidents have.

patronage The use of govern-

clientelism The practice of exchanging political favours, often in the form of government employment or services, for political support.

Causes and Effects: What Explains Executive Stability?

One big question in the study of executives has been whether parliamentary forms of government are better for protecting democracy than presidential forms of government. The debate has generally had presidentialism "on the defensive," and advocates of parliamentary

TABLE 10.4 | Presidential Powers

Type of Power	Definition	Examples (Not in All Countries)
Formal Powers	Powers assigned to the office of the president by constitutional authority or by law	Dissolve the legislature Issue decrees and executive orders Veto legislation
Partisan Powers	Powers to control decisions and votes of legislators and other politicians through control of political party	Control lists of candidates for office Appoint party members to executive office Affect career paths of party members
Informal Powers	Powers of the president that are not official but come from informal ability to influence public policy	Influence public opinion and public debate Campaign for individuals or causes Patronage and clientelism

CASE IN CONTEXT

450

Federalism and the States in Nigeria: Holding Together or Tearing Apart?

Nigeria is one of the most interesting cases in the world for the study of how federalism relates to secession and violence. The country began with three regions around the time of independence in 1960, and after a civil war broke out among the regions in the late 1960s, governments have created new states in an attempt to defuse conflict. Federalism is thus explicitly linked to the question of stability.

See the case study on Nigeria in Part VI, p. 450. As you read it, keep in mind the following questions:

1. What is the nature of regional divisions in Nigeria, and along what lines are people in the country divided?
2. In what ways could expanding the number of states be expected to address the challenge of stability and violence between regions?
3. To what extent have the attempts to further federalism contributed to reducing conflict, and to what extent can we know how successful they have been?

government have argued that parliamentarism better protects democracy. They point to evidence from Europe and several former British colonies around the world. These countries have a long history of parliamentarism and a stronger record of democracy than many presidential systems.

Stable and Unstable Regimes: Presidentialism, Parliamentarism, and Democracy

The debate has been whether presidentialism or parliamentarism affects the stability of democracy, not about whether parliamentarism is preferable to presidentialism in every respect. Presidential systems may have other advantages over parliamentarism, such as allowing voters to identify clearly with an individual candidate, giving voters a greater range of electoral choices, and providing the opportunity to "split a ticket" and cast a vote for one party in legislative elections and another party in the executive election.

Consider what is likely to happen in each type of system and how it will affect democracy. According to the argument in favour of parliamentarism, a parliamentary regime makes governments more likely to reach compromise and share power. There can be multiple parties represented in a parliamentary cabinet, although this is not always the case. Presidential regimes, on the other hand, generally have only one party represented in the cabinet and are less willing to compromise and share power. Moreover, if a parliamentary executive becomes unpopular, it can be easily removed by a no confidence vote. This means that a crisis in a particular government does not become a crisis of the whole political regime, whereas removing an unpopular elected president from office creates more of a constitutional crisis. (See the "Insights" box on the work of Juan Linz.)

To put it another way, correlation is not causation. Just because parliamentary Germany is more democratic than Iran, and Iran has an elected president, does not mean that parliamentarism *causes* Germany's democracy to succeed or that directly electing a president *causes* Iran's democracy to fail. The challenge is to document cause and effect rather than to

INSIGHTS

The Perils of Presidentialism *and* The Virtues of Parliamentarism

by Juan Linz

Juan Linz argues that parliamentary systems are better for democracy than presidencies, for five reasons:

1. *Competing vs Clear Legitimacy.* Presidentialism divides power between the legislature and executive, which makes it unclear who is responsible for public action. Parliamentarism makes clear that the executive heads the government.
2. *Fixed vs Flexible Terms.* Presidential systems have rigid terms for presidents (such as four years), which makes changing an unpopular government difficult. Parliamentary governments may be replaced at any time upon losing the confidence of parliament.
3. *Winner-Take-All vs Power-Sharing.* Presidentialism allows a single party to lead the executive branch. Parliamentarism leads to more power-sharing (via coalitions). This helps democracy by including more participants in decision-making.
4. *Presidential vs Prime Ministerial "Style."* Presidencies lead to more authoritarian, bombastic style than is found with the negotiating tendencies of prime ministers.
5. *Outsider vs Insider Executives.* Presidents are more likely to be outsiders than prime ministers because parliamentary leaders may have been in politics for decades.

Linz argues that these factors in the long run increase the likelihood that presidential systems will be taken over by authoritarians.

Juan Linz, "The Perils of Presidentialism," *Journal of Democracy* 1(1, 1990): 51–69; and "The Virtues of Parliamentarism," *Journal of Democracy* 1(4, 1990): 84–91.

assume it. This means that we need to try to anticipate and control for other, confounding variables—such as rich versus poor societies—when we look for causal relationships between outcomes such as parliamentarism and successful democracy.

Stable and Unstable Executives: Styles of Presidential Rule

Looking beyond whether a democratic regime persists, there is also the question of how executives govern. Popularly elected leaders in a democracy are expected to work within a society that has rules and other institutions. For example, the legislature is expected to have some say as well as the president, and the president is not expected to be above the law. However, chief executives govern in very different ways, and there are some circumstances in which elected executives wield considerable power. In many cases, even if a regime is formally a democracy, the president may assert more authority and centralize power considerably. One such type of regime is "delegative democracy," which confers substantial power on presidents. While the concept of delegative democracy was originally conceived for Latin American countries, you might consider whether the case of Russia under Vladimir Putin fits with the model.

Executives influence the economy as well as politics, and they may contribute either to good or to poor economic performance. Executive powers in the economy include proposing budgets for the legislature to approve, collecting taxes, and regulating the economy. Executives also make decisions about staffing key economic institutions, such as the central bank that controls the money supply. Finally, the executive in some cases make major interventions in the economy. Examples include nationalizing companies or privatizing them and perhaps bailing out important industries such as banks in a financial crisis. Altogether, these economic responsibilities mean that the executive branch has a great deal of leverage over the economy.

So how does a strong executive benefit or hurt the economy? One argument is that powerful executives can damage the economy through **populism**, a political approach in which leaders make appeals to "the people" and seek to develop direct political ties with the masses. With populist approaches, presidents often use the resources of the government to reinforce their personal power, making themselves into the symbolic embodiment of the nation and working to undermine other institutions. In many cases, such leaders literally hand out money as they go, spending large sums of government revenue to help their supporters and increase their own popularity. This propensity for populism has the potential to hurt the economy over the long run if it results in excessive and misdirected government spending. In a similar vein, executives can control patronage, and they may use control over government as a way to distribute favours to certain groups; this too can prove detrimental to the economy in the long run.[14] (For more on populism, see Chapter 15, "Thinking Comparatively: Is 21st-Century Populism an Ideology?" on page 323.)

populism A political approach in which leaders, often heads of government and top executive branch officials, make direct appeals to "the people" and seek to develop direct political ties with the masses.

On the other hand, strong executives may also make for a strong state, which is often associated with good economic performance, as seen in Chapters 3 and 4. This may include decisive national leaders, such as strong presidents, or strong bureaucracies in the executive branch. Examples would include ministries and government economic councils in East Asia that were responsible for major decisions that promoted economic development. To use a contemporary example, it is difficult to understand China's recent development without talking about the importance of decisions made by executive officials and leaders, from the president and premier to top officials at the central bank.

Stable and Unstable Executives: Patterns of Parliamentary Rule

A final set of causal questions about executives is what makes their *governments* endure or collapse. The case of Italy shows that governments in some countries are unstable while others endure. Italy has changed prime ministers nearly 40 times since the end of World War II; during that time, Canada has had 14 if we include Mackenzie King, who was in office from 1935 to 1948. This means a change of government has happened in Italy more than once every two years, although elections are only required to be held every five years. The turnover in the executive is even more dramatic if one counts a government as new every time a cabinet is reshuffled to accommodate various parties. By this criterion, Italy has had more than 60 governments since World War II, leaving the average duration of a government at just about one year. This gives Italy perhaps the most unstable government among advanced democracies, though the constitution and the basic structure of government have persisted for some time. That is, Italy has seen unstable governing coalitions in a stable regime.

Despite the frequent turnover of governments, there are some ways in which Italian politics exhibits continuity. There are not necessarily new faces leading Italian politics every year or so. In fact, the very first postwar prime minister, Alcide de Gasperi of the Christian Democrats, led eight different cabinets in his eight years in office before finally losing the prime minister's chair. Several prime ministers, including Silvio Berlusconi, were in the post three or more times. Moreover, there have been some time periods when prime ministers have been relatively secure, including Berlusconi from 2001 to 2006. Nonetheless, many governments have lasted less than a year, and very few last more than three.

A flip side of instability is the fact that many parliamentary systems are relatively inclusive of different parties and interests. This can be as a result of the electoral rules that favour multiparty systems (as discussed in Chapters 7 and 9) or because cooperation happens when different groups in society have reasons to share power and build trust. For example, if countries are divided into different ethnic groups, elites and leaders may attempt to find mechanisms that will help them to govern without worsening conflict. However, these incentives are not limited to divided societies. In many European countries, political parties and interest groups have developed political systems that strive for consensus and inclusion of major actors in all big government decisions. These mechanisms are sometimes known as **consociational** arrangements, as discussed in the next "Insights" box.

consociational Systems that use formal mechanisms to coordinate different groups sharing access to power.

The debate about whether presidentialism or parliamentarism is "better" enters into this discussion of unstable coalitions and consociational arrangements. Note that in the upcoming "Insights" box, the parliamentary systems are quite stable, while the presidential systems in Colombia and Lebanon have struggled more to prevent conflict. An argument in favour of parliamentarism holds that the flexible terms of office mean that a "crisis of government" does not become a "crisis of regime." That is, a government that fails and falls does not imperil the whole constitutional system. In a sense, Italy shows that. On the other hand, it is not clear that such instability in governments is desirable either. Certainly, the fixed terms of presidential systems at least theoretically provide the possibility that a government will adapt and respond to unpopular moves in time. Moreover, extreme instability in governments is likely to place many politicians in "permanent campaign" mode, which may compromise their focus on governing.

Of course, whether a country has stability or instability in its governments depends on several features of political institutions: political parties and how they operate; electoral rules; rules about votes of no confidence; and whether party leaders can "discipline" the members of a party's rank and file. In addition, history and social realities contribute to these outcomes, and only further comparative research can point to the factors that cause these different outcomes.

INSIGHTS

Consociational Democracy

by Arend Lijphart

This classic article shows that there are many ways for different groups and parties to share power in the executive branch, whether the system is parliamentary or presidential. In societies where reaching consensus is a priority and there are many political parties, one leading form of power-sharing is the grand coalition cabinet that includes multiple parties. Another way to share power is for leading political elites to appoint powerful advisory councils and committees that reflect the interests of many major actors. Efforts such as these have featured in countries in central and northern Europe, such as the Netherlands, Austria, and Denmark. Presidential systems can find mechanisms for sharing power as well as parliamentary systems. At the time of Lijphart's writing, examples included agreements by the two leading parties to alternate the presidency in Colombia and between different religious groups to divide executive posts in Lebanon. This idea of consociational democracy suggests that executives need not be "winner-take-all" if there are other factors that push toward social consensus.

Arend Lijphart, "Consociational Democracy," *World Politics* 21(2, 1969): 207–25.

THINKING COMPARATIVELY

Beyond the American and British Models

KEY METHODOLOGICAL TOOL

Case Selection

One main lesson from the debate over presidentialism versus parliamentarism is the importance of case selection for comparisons. Cases are often (but not necessarily) countries that we select to study, and selecting the right ones is key. The disadvantages of presidentialism for democracy certainly appear to be greater in countries that are lower-income and have been democracies for only a short time. To make a causal argument, it is important to understand the background conditions that shape the likelihood of democracy.

Would it be reasonable to compare a low-income presidential country in Africa with a long-established parliamentary regime in northern Europe and make inferences about how presidentialism affects democracy? Or would a comparison of the United States and a European country be more appropriate? Conversely, is the United States a representative example of all presidentialist countries around the world, or is it a special case? After all, many Americans like to think of themselves as "exceptional." The right selection depends on the specific question the researcher is asking and the argument one hopes to make.

Several rules of thumb are useful for beginning comparativists in selecting cases. The first is to select cases that make possible a comparison on the basis of most-similar-systems (MSS) or most-different-systems (MDS) analysis. This choice will help to prevent "selection on the dependent variable" in which a researcher looks only at countries with similar outcomes and makes faulty inferences based on limited information.[15] A second general rule is to select cases for which the researcher does not have a preconception or bias that will complicate the honest assessment of the evidence.

As the chapter suggests, looking only at these two cases will tell us little about the variety of types of executives, much less give us a full understanding of the merits of different systems. Apart from executives that follow the two basic forms—presidential and parliamentary—there are hybrids and other models that combine features of both. From France to India to Switzerland to Uruguay, countries around the world have a huge variety of executive structures beyond the American and British archetypes.

In fact, the United Kingdom and the United States themselves are not static in how executive power works. The United Kingdom's form of parliamentarism has usually been winner-take-all for the winning party, but a coalition between two parties governed from 2010 to 2015. Comparative research can help us to explain how executive power can change over time within a country and not just in the United Kingdom. Why do some Italian coalition governments last longer than others, if the rules that shape elections of the legislature and the executive remain the same? Similarly, presidentialism is expected by some to lead to more "winner-takes-all" politics, but these systems also divide and share power in different ways over time. Some American presidents have asserted greater executive control over other branches.

Consider Table 10.5, which includes a basic summary of the executive structure for the 14 countries profiled in this book. You will note a diverse array of executive structures, with some countries sharing certain features in common. You may detect patterns in the presidential and parliamentary experiences of the countries, and you can select cases for further comparison. The comparative method allows researchers to analyze why countries developed the executive structures they did or what the consequences of these structures have been. It is also possible to do a comparison over time within one country, along the lines suggested previously for the United Kingdom or the United States. Why have executive structures changed or remained static over time? This question could be asked for any number of countries, including Canada, France, Iran, Nigeria, or Russia. Considering what you may know about these countries from this table and from other chapters, can you suggest what might be good test cases for studying the causes and effects of executive structures?

TABLE 10.5 | Comparing Cases

Case	Executive Structure
Brazil	Directly elected president chosen by national popular vote. Runoff election held between top two vote-getters if none receives a majority in first round. President has weak partisan powers but can issue decrees.
Canada	Prime minister is leader of the largest party or group of parties in the House of Commons, the lower chamber of Parliament. Executive has strong powers to set agenda and pass legislation, largely because of partisan powers. Monarch, represented by the governor general, is ceremonial head of state, with no real political power.
China	Executive structure includes president as head of state and chief executive. Two other top positions—often held by president—are head of the single (Communist) party and head of military. Premier is head of government in legislature.
France	Semi-presidential system combines presidentialism and parliamentarism. President is directly elected and appoints prime minister, but this appointment must be approved by legislature and government depends on confidence of National Assembly. President has power to dissolve legislature.
Germany	Parliamentary system with chancellor as the chief minister chosen by lower house of parliament (Bundestag), often at the head of a governing coalition of multiple parties. Ceremonial president has relatively limited powers.
India	Parliamentary system in which prime minister is head of government chosen by lower house of parliament (Lok Sabha) and depends on confidence of this body. President is also chosen by legislature but has relatively minor powers.
Iran	President is elected and has authority vis-à-vis legislature, but real power lies with Guardian Council of top clerics and Supreme Leader, also a cleric (ayatollah). Other councils (Expediency Council, Assembly of Experts) also wield power.
Japan	Parliamentary system in which prime minister is head of government chosen by parliament (Diet) and depends on confidence of lower chamber (House of Representatives). Emperor is ceremonial head of state.
Mexico	President is directly elected by popular vote; top vote-getter wins even if no majority is attained. No re-election is allowed. For decades up to 2000, presidents in the dominant PRI party picked successors by "pointing the finger" (dedazo).
Nigeria	President is directly elected in national popular vote, separate from legislature. Prior to 1999, military leaders often led executive after coups. Largest party prior to 2015 elections (PDP) attempted to alternate northern Muslims and southern Christians in executive posts.
Russia	President is directly elected head of state. President appoints prime minister (chairman) as head of government, subject to approval of the legislature (State Duma). Vladimir Putin has exerted considerable authority both as president and as prime minister.
Saudi Arabia	The head of state and head of government is a hereditary monarch (king, prime minister, and Custodian of the Two Holy Mosques). Under the king are three appointed bodies: the Council of Ministers, a Consultative Council, and the Council of Senior Ulama (comprised of religious leaders). The monarch's legitimacy rests on his following Sharia, or Islamic, law. Aside from this, he has near absolute political power within the state.
United Kingdom	Prime minister is elected by House of Commons, the lower chamber of Parliament. Executive has strong powers to set agenda and pass legislation, largely because of partisan powers. Monarch is ceremonial head of state, with no real political power.
United States	Directly elected president chosen by electoral college. Executive powers are separate from and checked by legislature. President has veto power but cannot dissolve legislature. President has relatively weak partisan powers over legislature.

Selecting the right cases for comparative study can make the difference between an effective analysis and a weaker one. While we have referred to the United Kingdom and the United States as emblematic examples of parliamentary and presidential systems, the selection of cases for further study only begins with acknowledging these two models. The best cases to select will depend on the question being asked. Considering Table 10.5, a question about why ceremonial presidents have lost some of their powers over time might best be addressed by looking at countries such as Germany, India, Japan, or the United Kingdom. On the other hand, a question about the partisan powers of directly elected presidents might be well suited to a comparison of countries in the Americas, such as Brazil, Mexico, and/or the United States. A question about the informal powers of heads of state or chief executives might be able to draw on any number of the countries in the table. Russia and France might make for a useful analysis of the causes or consequences of semi-presidential systems.

Executives do not operate in a vacuum. They are affected by other structures and institutions. The legislative branch of government is a most important example, but the institutions of federalism and constitutional authority discussed in the previous chapters matter as well. Political parties (discussed in the next chapter) are equally important. Moreover, features of certain executives, such as populism, are partially shaped by factors that lie beyond political institutions, such as high income inequality, low levels of public trust, and perhaps even culturally rooted styles of leadership. Much of the discussion in this chapter cannot be isolated from how legislatures, political parties, and other institutions operate and, ultimately, from political society more broadly. The ways all of these features interact will shape how executives perform.

With the concepts and arguments developed here, you should be able to investigate other executive structures around the world and form your own hypotheses and comparative arguments about them. There is much research to be done about the relative powers of executives in political systems and the consequences of these powers. This suggests that executive power will for a long time demand further study in countries around the world.

Chapter Summary

Concepts

- Executive branches execute and administer the laws proposed by legislatures in representative democracies.
- In non-democratic or authoritarian regimes, executives often have a great deal of power.
- Executives have formal powers outlined in the law, partisan powers that come from influence over a political party, and other informal powers associated with the prominence and position of the executive.

Types

- Executives can be structured in two main ways— parliamentary and presidential—though there are also executives that combine features of both.
- The United Kingdom is the original example of a parliamentary system, and the British model is known as the Westminster model. Canada's political system is closely modelled on that of the UK, as are those of New Zealand and Australia.
- Presidential regimes predominate in the Americas and in Africa, including the United States.
- Like many other countries, France, Russia, and China combine some aspects of parliamentarism and some aspects of presidentialism.

Causes and Effects

- There is a debate about whether parliamentarism is better for democracy than presidentialism because parliamentarism should lead to fewer outsiders and less radicalism and it allows legislatures to remove unpopular executives.
- Presidential systems are most prevalent in lower-income regions and parliamentarism in Europe, so the advantage of parliamentarism may be due to other factors.
- Powerful executives have been associated with both centralization and populism but also with promoting economic development.
- Parliamentary systems can operate in many ways and may have relatively stable or unstable governments.

Thinking It Through

1. Considering the experiences of other countries described in this chapter and in Part VI, are there any institutional features you would advocate the United States to adopt? Why?
2. Do you think populism is possible under parliamentary rule? Why or why not?
3. To what extent is presidential power in the United States limited by convention rather than the Constitution? How has the Trump presidency demonstrated what happens when conventions are challenged?
4. Why has the Canadian political system largely rejected coalition governments and power-sharing between parties while this practice is common in western Europe, Australia, and New Zealand? Is it because Canada has been influenced by the American presidential system and its political culture? Or are there other, more important factors?
5. We reproduce Table 10.2 here. Imagine yourself as the leader of each of the different parties and that you are interested in having an influence on government policy. What other parties would you approach in an attempt to form a coalition, and what would be your ideal coalition in each case? Why?

TABLE 10.2 | Hypothetical Distribution of Seats in Parliament of Tapawera

Party	XL	L	C	R	XR
Seats	30	7	21	27	15

6. Consider Table 10.2 again. Identify the possible coalitions following the various criteria for coalition formation:
   a. Minimum winning
   b. Minimum connected winning
   c. Minimum size
   d. Minimum number of parties
   e. Median party
   f. Minimum range

11 Political Parties, Party Systems, and Interest Groups

In This Chapter

Statues symbolizing the two political parties of the United States: the Democratic donkey and Republican elephant, in front of Willard Hotel in Washington, DC. (Visions of America/Universal Images Group via Getty Images)

Throughout the Cold War (1945 to 1991), the United States and the Soviet Union (or USSR) were presented as political opposites in many ways, with Canada, western European countries, and others sort of sandwiched ideologically in the middle. More in between was a group of non-aligned states such as India, Yugoslavia, and Egypt, who together with other like-minded countries formed the Non-Aligned Movement. At its height, there were some 120 member states of the NAM.

One of the key differences between the superpowers (on the surface at least) was between the capitalist and communist economic systems, but some of the other major differences lay in how politics operated. The United States was a constitutional democracy in which political parties—the Democrats and Republicans—competed for votes and in which citizens could join interest groups to express their beliefs and opinions. The USSR was dominated by a single party and state that claimed to be the sole legitimate representative of all the country's people. In political terms, the United States was a multiparty democracy, while the USSR was a single-party authoritarian regime. While most Americans believed that the right to freedom of association and to vote for multiple parties was based on individual rights, the leaders of the Soviet Union argued that the Communist Party alone—in collaboration with the state—could speak for the rights of workers.

Both countries, however, shared a strong interest in developing and expanding nuclear technology, as well as devoting an outsized proportion of their country's GDP to military expenditure, even at the expense of social programs closer to home. Both came to also adopt a Manichean (good versus evil) view of the world in the conduct of their respective foreign policies. Surveillance in both countries and the punishment for dissent also became extreme at various periods of the Cold War. Those in the middle managed to maintain some form of balance between military preparedness and a coherent social welfare state.

The USSR and its eventual collapse seemed to show that single-party rule was less legitimate, as were systems where citizens had little voice in politics. Yet many countries today remain dominated by a single party, as Map 11.1 shows. The United States has only two major and decentralized parties, far fewer than some other democracies in Canada, Europe, the Asia-Pacific, and elsewhere that may have five or six major parties represented in the legislature. The number of major parties in a given country thus continues to vary in the post–Cold War world.

Countries also vary in how the state interacts with interest groups. The US model—in which different groups compete for influence in a "marketplace of ideas"—is not the only way a democracy can work. Indeed, such a system can lead to undue influence by large corporations and wealthy individuals to the detriment of less wealthy, less organized voters. In most other democracies, there are fewer opportunities for interest groups and wealthy individuals and corporations to so overtly influence the political system. Canada too has had its share of undue influence, as the Pacific railway scandal of the 19th century and the 2006 sponsorship scandal attest. The nature of democracy—and how and who should have influence—is the subject of this chapter.

• • •

Concepts

In considering institutions in the last several chapters, we have focused on the branches and structures of government itself: elected legislators and executives, as well as judges that may be elected or appointed. Yet many of the most important institutions that shape politics and policy-making in different countries are composed of groups of individuals who are not

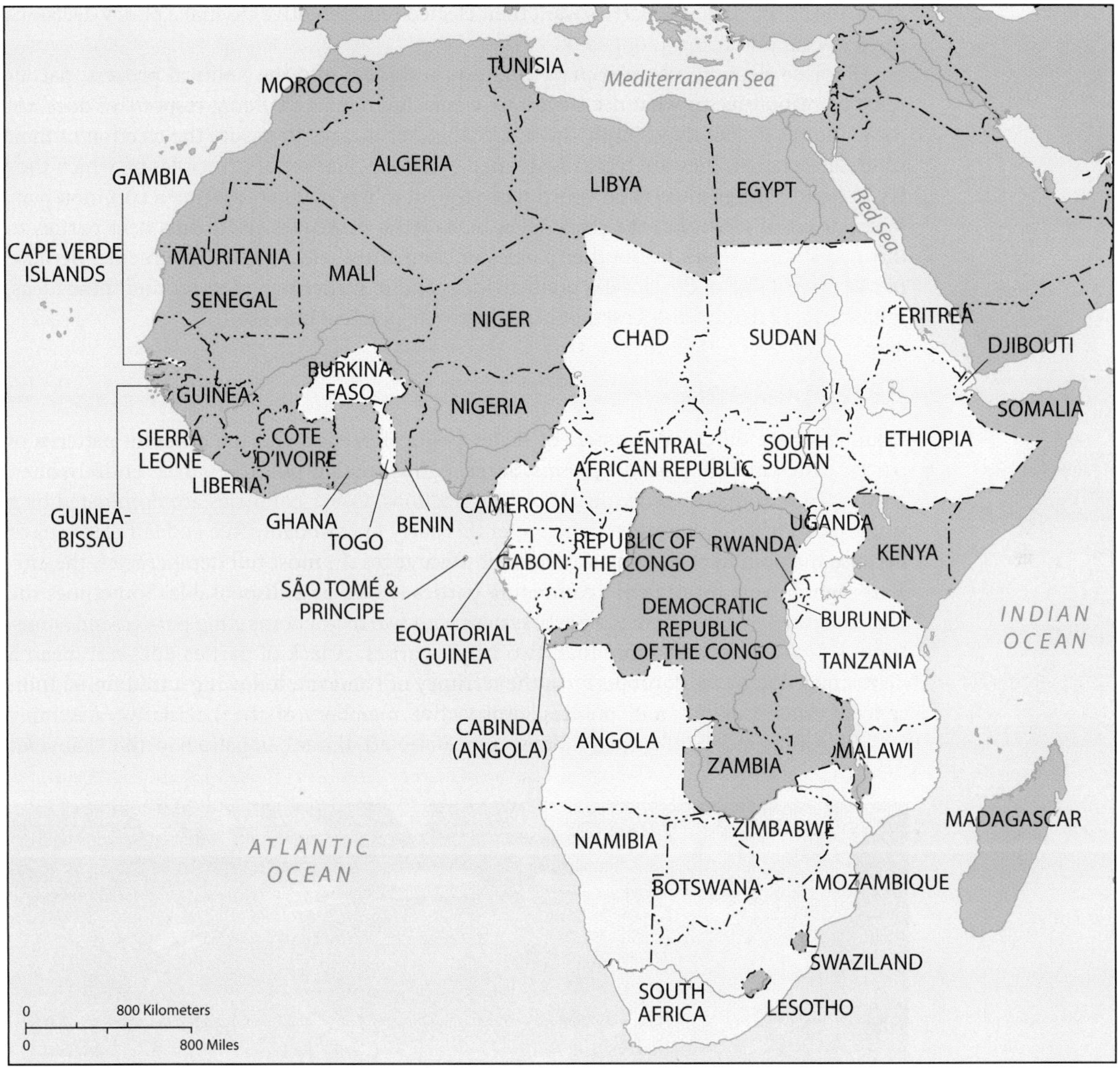

MAP 11.1 Dominant-party states in Africa (in yellow).

necessarily politicians themselves. Citizens can work in groups to change political life. They support their preferred candidates for public office and may join a political party to do so, and then they may volunteer time or contribute money to those parties. They also form interest groups that share common ideas or goals, and they may volunteer time or contribute money to those groups as well. In so doing, they bring together people with common interests in attempts to influence politics, policy, and the lawmaking process.

Political Parties

political party A political organization that seeks to influence policy, typically by getting candidates and members elected or appointed to public office.

We consider **political parties** first because they are closely linked to the institutions of government we have examined so far. The main goal of political parties is the election of their candidates to public office. This goal is not only pragmatic but also ideological (related to ideas, ideals, and beliefs): Parties want their elected representatives to make policy decisions the party supports.

Because elections channel party interests and ideas into the political process, parties must be responsive to what the electorate wants and demands. Being responsive does not mean, however, that they simply do or say whatever it takes to ensure the election of their candidates; rather, they are typically defined by a particular set of principles by which they try to stand. Parties must often coordinate large numbers of voters around a common platform, or set of ideas that the party takes as its basic principles. Platforms help parties to distinguish themselves from other parties in competitive electoral environments. Because parties have a role in developing political ideas and in gathering voters around these ideas, it is often said that parties articulate and aggregate political interests.

Party Systems

party system Patterns of party politics characterized by the number of relevant parties in a country.

Countries have different numbers of major political parties, and the different patterns of party politics are called **party systems**. Some regimes outlaw political parties entirely, often on the grounds that they divide people into factions. Other countries are dominated by a single party, whether because voters prefer this party in reasonably free and fair elections or because the dominant party has systematic advantages. In most full democracies, the citizens' right to vote for different competing parties is seen as indispensable. Sometimes the result of exercising this right is a party system with two major competing parties, and sometimes it is a system with more than two major parties. A lack of parties does not mean a democracy doesn't work properly. In the territory of Nunavut, following a traditional Inuit style of consensus-oriented politics, prospective members of the Legislative Assembly (MLAs) run as independent candidates. Once elected, the MLAs gather in the "Nunavut

Nathan Denette/THE CANADIAN PRESS

PHOTO 11.2 The Nunavut legislature in Iqaluit. There are no political parties in Nunavut's consensus government system. Once elected, MLAs gather in a leadership forum to choose the premier, ministers, and the speaker using a secret ballot system.

Leadership Forum" to choose the premier, the ministers, and the speaker, using a secret ballot system. There are no parties in this "consensus government" system, and MLAs are expected to work together to deliberate on policies.[1]

Interest Groups

The other main type of organization that can potentially play an important role is an **interest group**. Their level of influence depends on their size, funding, appeal among voters, and whether their particular issue is popular at the time. These organizations make any number of demands on behalf of their constituents and members; such groups often have an active membership that pays dues to participate in and support the organization. Interest groups generally advocate for some policy position or political perspective, though they may not always seek to support specific candidates in elections. Like political parties, interest groups may endorse politicians in the hope of getting support for their causes, may contribute to or support campaigns, and so on, but they may also focus on petitioning or lobbying politicians to pass certain policies or laws. Interest groups want to see laws and policies that reflect their interests or views on the issues, so these groups often make public expressions of their political views.

interest groups Organizations that make demands in the political system on behalf of their constituents and members.

Examples of interest groups are numerous and show the range of what such groups are and do. In some circumstances, interest groups may be huge, such as confederations of labour unions in some countries that may represent a large proportion of all workers or households. However, in most Western countries, labour union influence is substantially declining. Interest groups can also reflect the interests of a relatively smaller group of people and may serve different demographic groups. In Canada, examples include the Fraser Institute, the Council of Canadians, the Canadian Manufacturers' Association, and the Ukrainian Canadian Congress. While the Fraser Institute promotes neoliberal policies and increased deregulation, the Council for Canadians promotes protection for the environment and the shielding of domestic industry from foreign (often American) pressure. One of Canada's most influential organizations is the Canadian Association of Petroleum Producers, which advocates for the oil and natural gas industries. South of the border, the National Rifle Association (NRA), which represents the interests of many gun owners, has long maintained a strong affiliation with the Republican Party. It has a close relationship with the current US president, Donald Trump.

Some interest groups advocate on behalf of their members and also provide certain services or products to their members. For example, CARP (formerly the Canadian Association of Retired Persons, founded in 1985) estimates that it has approximately 400,000 members, mostly senior citizens and people in or approaching retirement, although anyone over the age of 45 can join. The Canadian Automobile Association (CAA) was founded in 1913 and advocates on behalf of motorists. It provides members with tour books and guides, travel discounts, and access to tow truck services. For our purposes, interest groups are broadly defined but can include any organization that advocates on behalf of a particular cause or in favour of certain legislation or policy.

The concept of interest groups is closely linked to the concepts of civil society and social movements. The first of these, **civil society**, is made up of many types of civic associations and social organizations, including volunteer organizations, neighbourhood associations, and the like. Many of them are interest groups, though some may not take a political stand or advocate for a specific policy position, instead preferring to mobilize group members to take action on their own for improvement of their community, for instance. In the next chapter, we discuss another set of actors and organizations known as social movements, which are often distinct from interest groups in the ways they make their demands and the conditions under which they operate.

civil society The set of organizations in civic life outside the state through which inhabitants (citizens but also residents) associate and articulate and advance their interests; includes civic associations, interest groups, and volunteer organizations.

interest articulation The process by which political actors express their demands, needs, or wants in a political system, often through interest groups.

interest aggregation The process by which individuals' preferences are brought together to make collective decisions, often through political parties and the party system.

Interest groups and political parties are responsible for the functions of **interest articulation** and **interest aggregation**. Interest articulation is the process by which individuals and groups express their demands, needs, or wants in a political system. This is especially associated with interest groups, which publicly express their viewpoints, though parties do some interest articulation as well. Interest aggregation is especially associated with political parties and is the process by which individuals' preferences are brought together to make collective decisions. In most modern countries, it is not possible for those in government to govern by knowing each individual and taking his or her unique perspective into account. Rather, governments theoretically rely on citizens to express themselves collectively through mechanisms such as parties and interest groups. Citizens take on the responsibilities of making demands of their government, and doing so regularly involves the collective action of many people.

Types

Political parties can take on a variety of different forms, and political systems can have different numbers of parties. The number of different examples and types of interest groups are too numerous to mention, but we can outline how interest groups work in different countries by looking at something of great political importance: the structures of interest group representation.

Political Parties: Elite, Mass, and Catch-All Parties

For the average observer, the most distinguishing features of different political parties are the views they champion. For example, the New Democratic Party and the Conservative Party in Canada can be distinguished by their policies, ranging from Indigenous issues to immigration to health care, to taxes and foreign policy. Some parties are on the left of the economic spectrum, and others are on the right. In the United Kingdom, for instance, the Labour Party has historically been associated with workers and unions, and the Conservative Party is tied to business. Some parties—such as the Green Party in many countries—support environmental groups and are in turn supported by environmentalists. In many countries, there are parties that represent specific ethnic and racial groups, such as the Inkatha Freedom Party in South Africa that is strongly identified with the Zulu people or the Māori Party in New Zealand, which before its electoral demise in 2017 advocated for Indigenous Māori. There are single-issue parties—such as those specifically opposed to immigration (Australia's One Nation party) or favouring the legalization of marijuana (New Zealand's Aotearoa Legalise Cannabis Party)—and there are parties with no identifiable ideology whatsoever. Some obvious distinctions thus exist between political parties in the people they represent and the basis of their platforms.

Alongside differences in what policies parties want, there are differences in how parties are structured. By most accounts, political parties first emerged as coalitions between individual legislators and politicians who shared common political interests and/or common beliefs; they formed their parties together to promote these common interests. These parties were known as **elite parties** because their membership and scope were largely restricted to a small number of political elites, mainly white, male property owners. By contrast, the 20th century saw the massive political mobilization of large numbers of citizens in larger parties. Communist and socialist parties, for example, emerged as powerful groups in many countries, and they envisioned their structures as containing millions of workers and labourers who would pay dues, have membership cards, and become part of a broad movement.

elite parties Political parties in which membership and scope were largely restricted to a small number of political elites.

These came to be known as **mass parties**. More recently, some major political parties have shifted to become brokerage or **catch-all parties**, which are flexible on their ideological positions as they aim to attract support from a broad range of interest groups and voters.[2] Proponents of the catch-all thesis have argued that when one party becomes successful as a catch-all party, it puts pressure on other parties to adopt the same approach and become more catch-all themselves.[3]

mass parties Parties consisting of large numbers of citizens as members and that undertake massive political mobilization.

catch-all parties Political parties that are flexible on their ideological positions and aim to attract support from a broad range of interest groups and voters.

Other categories may exist as well, but this change over time describes many of the major shifts in the types of parties that exist. For some scholars, however, the distinctions between elite, mass, and catch-all parties can be overstated because all of these types are subject to common problems. One of the leading critiques of how parties operate—which we explore further in the next chapter—was made by Robert Michels: It is that they tend to operate from the top down, having "oligarchical tendencies," regardless of their ideology and rhetoric.[4]

Party Systems: Dominant-Party, Two-Party, and Multiparty Systems

The many forms and structures of political parties shape the politics of different countries. But as important as the parties themselves is the party system in which they operate. How politics plays out in a given country depends on which parties can get enough seats to have a strong voice and make a difference. A Green Party may be relatively inconsequential in policy-making if it never gains legislative seats because one or two other parties dominate, but it may affect policy more if it is a partner in a governing coalition. This is currently the case in New Zealand, where the government is composed of an alliance between the Labour Party and New Zealand First, with support from the Greens.

The most basic characteristic of party systems is how many major parties can be expected to compete meaningfully in elections to participate in government. Some countries have one party that is dominant, others have two, and yet others have more than two major parties that compete and jockey for position. Countries with only a single large party can be referred to as **dominant-party systems**. These systems occur in both authoritarian and democratic countries. Among democracies, South Africa is an example of a democratic country with a dominant party, the African National Congress (ANC). Many authoritarian regimes have dominant-party systems in which the governing party is in charge of politics. One particular type of system with a dominant party is the authoritarian **single-party system** in which parties besides the dominant one are banned or disallowed. Examples have come from around the world, including many communist regimes—especially during the Cold War, but also in countries such as China, North Korea, and Cuba today—as well as right-wing dictatorships such as Nazi Germany, right-leaning regimes in Asia, and many regimes with less clear ideologies in Africa up to the 1990s.[5]

dominant-party system Party system in which a country contains only one large political party that predominates politically, often controlling the legislative and executive branches of government.

single-party system An authoritarian system in which parties besides the single dominant party are banned or disallowed.

Single-party regimes are often authoritarian, but they do have their defenders. Proponents may say they are better suited to the needs of some countries. One such argument has been that liberal democracy is not equally well adapted to all cultures and regions of the world. This perspective was associated with, among others, the late Lee Kuan Yew (1923–2015), the long-time prime minister of Singapore. Lee's argument in favour of single parties was based on a concept of "Asian values" that were argued to be distinct from "Western values," as we noted in Chapter 6.[6] This included an emphasis on community and deference to authority, as opposed to a foremost emphasis on individual rights. A cultural acceptance of dominant parties, the theory argued, was capable of delivering strong

Associated Press/Themba Hadebe

PHOTO 11.3 Cyril Ramaphosa was elected leader of the African National Congress in South Africa in 2017 and became president in 2018.

economic performance. A similar argument has been made more recently by the Chinese Communist Party.

Another argument has held that multiparty systems can be too divisive. This has featured prominently among leading parties in ethnically divided countries in Africa and countries divided along sectarian lines in the Middle East. In the African country of Uganda, for example, President Yoweri Museveni—who has been in power since 1986—long argued for "no-party" democracy on the grounds that political parties in Africa would simply split the vote along ethnic lines and give rise to conflict. These lines of argument have been contested by many scholars, including African and Asian scholars who see the argument for dominant parties or restrictions on multiparty systems as an effort by elites to justify their own regime's continuation in power. Nonetheless, these examples feature prominently in discussions about whether dominant parties are appropriate or not.

While many single-party systems are not democratic, some democracies have single dominant parties as well. Examples include several countries in Africa today, such as South Africa, which is dominated by the ANC. The major distinctions from the authoritarian regimes just discussed are that voting is relatively free and fair and civil liberties are protected: It just happens that people elect and continue to re-elect the same party to govern, even though they could potentially make other choices. Some regimes have made the case that a single political party can encompass the many political debates in a country, but most observers in Western democracies argue that the right to choose from different parties (with their advocacy of different policies) is essential to democratic governance. A characteristic of dominant-party systems is a lack of competitiveness in national elections and, hence, a relatively certain outcome of those elections.

two-party system A political party system consisting of two significant parties that have a duopoly on opportunities to govern.

To many people living in advanced, industrialized democracies, the **two-party system** is more common and familiar than the dominant-party system. In two-party systems, there is

CASE IN CONTEXT

382

The Chinese Party System

China is the most influential and important dominant-party system in the world today. The country is authoritarian and functions essentially as a single-party system. The various mechanisms for ensuring the dominance of the Communist Party are useful to understand, especially since the "Communist" in Communist Party has changed so dramatically with the many changes in China.

See the case study on the Chinese party system in Part VI, p. 382. As you read it, keep in mind the following questions:

1. How has China's Communist Party developed and maintained its dominance?
2. What are some of the mechanisms it uses to maintain this system?
3. Do you find there to be any legitimate justifications for single-party rule, and on what does the Chinese Communist Party base its legitimacy?

Kyodo via AP Images

PHOTO 11.4 President Xi Jinping (centre), Premier Li Keqiang (top right), and Li Zhanshu (top left) at the Great Hall of the People in Beijing in the annual session of the Chinese People's Political Consultative Conference in March 2019. Xi Jinping is also the general secretary of the Communist Party of China.

a duopoly of power between two major parties that are seen as the main contenders for most major political offices. This duopoly usually persists over multiple elections. The two major parties present different platforms, which often correspond to one more liberal and one more conservative party in terms of economic policy, though this is not always the main political distinction. Such a model can be seen in the United States with the Democrats and Republicans, as well as in many other countries around the world, such as Spain, with its left-leaning Socialist Workers' Party (*Partido Socialista*) and right-leaning People's Party (*Partido Popular*). Canada has also traditionally had two dominant political parties, although sometimes the NDP governs provincially. As we discuss in the "Causes and Effects" section, the way elections work is a major factor in determining whether a democracy will have a two-party system. In particular, the presence of single-member districts in legislative elections (as discussed in Chapter 9) contributes to the likelihood of two-party systems for reasons we explore later.

Two-party systems are not the most common party system in a democracy, and most democracies have more than two major parties. The scholar Arend Lijphart studied 36 long-standing democracies and found that **multiparty systems** with three or more parties were the norm in about half of these countries.[7] Some multiparty systems have two parties that are strongest year in and year out, but they compete against a handful of other parties that regularly win enough seats to influence the outcomes of elections. Whereas in two-party systems one party or the other will typically win a given election by taking a majority of seats, multiparty systems quite often result in no party winning a majority because the vote is divided more ways. To recall some of the lessons of Chapters 9 and 10, a no-majority win often happens when legislative elections are based on proportional representation, and it often results in executive branches that function with a coalition of multiple parties.

multiparty system A political party system consisting of more than two significant parties that have opportunities to govern.

fragmentation (of party system) Contrasting with concentration, the extent to which political power and representation in a party system are characterized by relatively large numbers of relatively small parties.

concentration (of party system) Contrasting with fragmentation, the extent to which political power and representation in a party system are characterized by relatively small numbers of relatively large parties.

Within these different categories—dominant-party, two-party, and multiparty systems—the specific nature of the party system can still vary from case to case. For instance, a multiparty system can be considered relatively **fragmented**, with many small parties, or relatively coherent or **concentrated**, with a small number of larger parties.[8] Two-party systems may see frequent alternation of power between the two or may see one party that is stronger and wins more often for an extended period. Dominant-party systems may feature different degrees of dominance by the leading party, ranging from single-party regimes with 100 per cent of the seats in a legislature to systems where a dominant party wins elections routinely but narrowly.

Counting the actual number of parties that matter is more challenging than it might sound. To determine the nature of a party system, assume one wants to consider only relatively serious parties that have a chance of winning a reasonable number of seats. As a hypothetical example, take the United States House of Representatives with its 435 members. If 434 were from the Republicans and Democrats while one representative was a member of the Socialist Party or Libertarian Party, would it be reasonable to call this a multiparty system? Most would say it would remain a two-party system. What about the United Kingdom, where the Conservative and Labour parties have long been the two largest but the Liberal Democrats regularly command a substantial fraction of the seats that is enough to prevent either of the other two from winning a majority? In 2012, the Liberal Democrats were in a position where they were a necessary part of the Conservative-led governing coalition. Or we could look at New Zealand, where in 2017 neither the Labour nor the National parties had a majority of the seats and thus relied on New Zealand First to choose with which party it would enter into coalition to form the government. Are these two-party or multiparty systems? Could we call them "two-and-a-half"-party systems?

effective number of parties A measure designed to capture the number of meaningful parties in a party system that weights the number of parties represented by their size.

Perhaps surprisingly, the answer for many political scientists is yes, we can say a country has "two-and-a-half" major parties. There are a number of metrics used to measure the **effective number of parties**, and they are designed to get at how many major parties of consequence a system contains.[9] Another way to look at this issue is how fractionalized or fragmented a party system is on a range between a perfectly concentrated dominant-party system to a perfectly fragmented system in which each seat goes to a different party.[10]

We will not explore the formulas in great detail here, but a simple example can illustrate the difference between a more fragmented and a more concentrated party system. Table 11.1 gives some fictional countries for which any resemblance to actual countries is coincidental. The middle columns reflect the proportion of legislative seats won by each of the five largest parties in descending order. So P1 is the largest party, and P5 is the smallest (if there is a P5; these systems have different numbers of parties). The formula for the effective number of parties takes the proportion of seats held by each party, squares each one, and adds these squares together. The result is a fraction, and the calculation then takes the inverse. So a system with two parties each having 50 per cent of the seats would have $1/[(0.50)^2 + (0.50)^2] = 2$ as the effective number of parties. And a system with three parties each having 33.3 per cent of the seats would have $1/[(0.333)^2 + (0.333)^2 + (0.333)^2] = 3$ as the effective number of parties. This formula generates the results in Table 11.1 for less clear-cut cases.

The effective number of parties calculated by this formula should be close to what one might expect from the proportions of seats won. There is a clear dominant-party system and a clear two-party system, even if other tiny parties compete in those two countries. In Duopolia, the two small parties matter more than the small one in Monopolia because they can tip the balance of power from P1 to P2 or vice versa. The United Realm looks like it should have about "two-and-a-half" or three parties: The third-largest is only half as powerful as the two largest parties, but it is also big enough to tip the balance of power once again. Fragmentia, meanwhile, has close to five meaningful parties, but we probably would not think of P3, P4, or P5 as being quite as important as P1 or P2. By contrast, New Coalitania

TABLE 11.1 | Number of Parties

	Proportion of Legislative Seats Won (%)					
Country	**P1**	**P2**	**P3**	**P4**	**P5**	**Effective No. of Parties**
People's Republic of Monopolia	99	1				1.02
United States of Duopolia	49	48	2	1		2.12
United Realm	40	40	20			2.78
Federation of Fragmentia	27	25	17	16	15	4.71
New Coalitania	38	35	9	9	9	3.43

Note: P = Party

has two clear leading parties, and it looks more concentrated than Fragmentia, so it has a smaller effective number of parties but will also require governing coalitions for as long as this distribution of parties stands. As a result, it is more than just a two-party system. In fact, P3, P4, and P5 are all important, and either of the big parties would need at least two of them to make a coalition government; the effective number of parties is more than three.

A final aspect of party systems to consider is **party system institutionalization**, or the extent to which a party system is stable and remains so over time. It has several aspects.[11] One is the persistence and electoral success of parties over time. Do parties endure for a long time once they are established, or do they come and go, with old ones fading away and new parties emerging constantly? A more volatile party system is less institutionalized. Another aspect is the degree to which parties have stable ideologies, programs, or platforms. This relates to the question of whether a party is coherent and cohesive or not.[12] A final aspect is the degree to which parties operate as institutions as opposed to being focused on certain individuals. Where a party system is more institutionalized, a party's name has significance: It is likely to be associated with a certain set of ideas. By contrast, in less institutionalized party systems, a party's name (or brand) is less meaningful and more often subject to the whims of personalistic leaders.

party system institutionalization The degree to which a party system is stable and remains so over time, as measured by such characteristics as the persistence of parties, the stability of their ideologies, and the degree to which they are distinct from the specific individuals who lead them.

Party systems are often more institutionalized in long-standing democracies and less institutionalized in less-established democracies, but this is not always the case. In France's well-established democracy, for example, the main party of the centre-right has gone through many changes in name and structure in recent years, even as the right has won the presidency regularly for nearly 20 years. Conversely, other countries, such as Chile and Ghana, developed institutionalized party systems soon after becoming democracies in the 1990s.[13] Despite these exceptions, the tendency persists: Substantial breakdowns of party system institutionalization are more common in fragile democracies, as the case of Russia showed from the 1990s to the current authoritarian era dominated by President Vladimir Putin (see "Case in Context: Personalism and the Party System in Russia").

Interest Groups: Pluralism and Corporatism

Like political parties, interest groups are distinguished from one another by the specific ideas they hold as well as by their structure. Apart from the forms and functions of specific groups, there are also different patterns of how interest group representation works in politics. The most fundamental distinction is between countries where interest groups compete openly to influence government decision-making—a pattern known as pluralism—and countries where there is a formal, established relationship between certain interest groups and state power—a pattern known as corporatism. The distinctions between the two forms of interest group representation can be summarized in terms of whether specific interest groups are identified as having a monopoly on the representation of a specific interest; both forms are ideal types, and many countries have had some mixture of the two forms.

pluralism A system of interest group representation in which groups compete openly to influence government decisions and public policy and in which specific groups do not have official preferential access to decision-making.

Pluralism (a popular American political science theory of the 1960s) reflects the idea that interest groups compete in a "marketplace of ideas." Countries that have pluralist politics will often have large numbers of competing groups that strive to affect policy. Under a theoretically pure form of pluralism (which has yet to exist), none of these groups would have privileged access to the government or receive preferential treatment, even if they would sometimes win and sometimes lose arguments about what the government should do. In reality, corporate interests usually predominate and tend to exert a disproportionate share of influence over the economy and political system. In the 2016 US primary processes, both Bernie Sanders and Donald Trump in their own ways pledged to reduce the power of large corporate interests in US politics, whether it was taking aim against the "billionaire class" or "draining the swamp." As president, however, Trump's tax cuts for the wealthy and some of his other policies appeared to be increasing elite privilege.

corporatism A system of interest group representation in which certain major groups are officially designated as representatives of certain interests and have a more structured interaction with the government in power and with the state's administration.

Under **corporatism**, certain major groups are designated as representatives of certain interests, and these groups have a more structured interaction with the government in power and with the state's administration (or bureaucracy). Advocates of corporatism sometimes assert that people "naturally" belong to certain interest groups—such as workers belonging to labour unions and business owners belonging to business organizations—and that organizing on this basis is thus important for political representation. Rather than an open competition among all interest groups, corporatist arrangements seek consensus based on regular interactions between designated groups and the state. Using the same root word as corporatism, one way to understand the phenomenon is that there is "incorporation" of specific interest groups into the decision-making structures of the state.[14]

Since many of the major decisions made in politics are about economics and economic policy, the most important interest groups in corporatist countries are usually organizations representative of business and those representative of labour. Business and organized labour confer with the state on issues such as wages, benefits, taxes, and policy toward foreign capital and international competition. At the national level, the bargaining between groups often involves **peak organizations**, which are top-level associations that bring together many like-minded organizations. Examples include national labour federations made up of many different unions or business organizations representing many different companies or industries.

peak organization Top associations, such as labour federations and large business organizations, that bring together many like-minded organizations.

Corporatism has been a major force in contemporary history. In fact, some have argued that the 20th century was the "century of corporatism."[15] Over the course of the 20th century, corporatism was influential across much of Europe and Latin America and in many parts of Asia and Africa. The geographic and historical reach of this phenomenon has led to many variants: Some are more social and some more pro-market liberal in Europe, while some forms in Latin America have been more state-led, others more led by labour, and yet others more inclusive of the peasantry.[16] Some analysts have advocated corporatism as a relatively successful and harmonious way to promote economic growth and development, while others have criticized it as favouring specific groups over individual rights and lending itself to exclusionary politics. Countries such as Mexico may provide evidence for either perspective.

It is possible to distinguish between more authoritarian and more democratic forms of corporatism.[17] In some cases, corporatism has overlapped with dominant-party systems,

CASE IN CONTEXT

461

Personalism and the Party System in Russia

Russia illustrates the challenge and importance of party system institutionalization. The country has seen some major parties come and go, while a single individual, Vladimir Putin, has accumulated more power over many decades. Even in the absence of single-party rule, a poorly institutionalized party system can facilitate authoritarian tendencies.

See the case study on the Russian party system in Part VI, pp. 461. As you read it, keep in mind the following questions:

1. Building on the observations of previous chapters, how do weak institutions in Russia facilitate the rise of a "strong man" like Putin?
2. What might account for the poorly institutionalized party system in Russia?
3. Which seems to have come first, the weak party system or the personalism of Putin?

Associated Press/Alexander Zemlianichenko, Pool, File

PHOTO 11.5 Vladimir Putin enters to take the oath during his inauguration ceremony as Russia's re-elected president in the Grand Kremlin Palace in Moscow, Russia, in May 2018.

and a single leading party undertakes the coordination of different interest groups. This has often been an authoritarian form of corporatism in which interest-group participation is highly regulated by the state. Versions of these circumstances can be seen in many single-party countries. Indeed, corporatism was especially noteworthy for part of the 20th century as a strategy by which central governments could co-opt different groups, bringing them into the political system on terms set by the state or the leading party. Incorporated groups included workers and unions, business elites, peasants or farmers, and even students.

Corporatism happened under authoritarian regimes and dominant-party regimes in many cases, but it is not limited to dominant- or single-party systems and in fact has featured prominently in many of Europe's multiparty systems, especially in social-democratic countries of northern Europe. This can be seen as a more democratic form of corporatism. Many of the political systems of northern Europe are consensus-based and have been multiparty regimes in which corporatism has played a major role. We now examine the pros and cons of pluralism and corporatism.

Causes and Effects: Why Do Party Systems Emerge, and What Effects Do They Have?

Why do different party systems emerge? Why do some countries have greater party system institutionalization than others? Why do certain types of parties—such as communist parties, social-democratic parties, conservative pro-business parties, or fascist parties—emerge in some countries and not in others? Why do some interest groups have greater impact in some places than others? We cannot address all of these questions here, but we encourage you to do further research on them. We will focus on three questions: the causes of the emergence of party systems, the consequences of party systems on the quality of representation, and the consequences of different patterns of interest-group representation.

Party Systems and Representation

Party systems are closely related to how political representation works. In some senses, party systems are both a consequence of how representation works and a cause of how representation takes shape. We examine both sides briefly.

What Factors Shape Party Systems?

Looking first at what causes different types of party systems to emerge, one main factor is the type of electoral system, as we discussed in Chapter 9. Recall that a basic distinction among types of electoral systems is between first-past-the-post (FPP) and proportional representation systems. In their simplest forms, the first has legislative elections within the geographic subdivisions of a country, while the second allocates legislative seats according to the overall proportions of seats parties win in an election.[18] What would these different types of systems imply for whether two-party or multiparty systems will emerge?

In democracies that have single-member district systems, there is a pronounced tendency for two-party systems to emerge and persist (e.g., Canada and US), while multiparty systems are quite common in countries that use proportional representation (such as Germany, New Zealand, Italy, and Israel). For many analysts, the electoral system itself seems to have an impact on the number of viable parties that emerge. The logic behind this is intuitive. Proportional representation, for example, is designed to accurately reflect the overall distribution of preferences for different parties, and the result often is many different parties winning legislative seats. District-based representation, by contrast, often favours relatively large parties that can win a plurality of votes and tends to result in fewer seats for

INSIGHTS

Les Partis politiques [Political Parties]

by Maurice Duverger

Duverger's work in this book and related articles discusses numerous features of political parties and party systems, but it is most renowned for its establishment of "Duverger's Law." The core result of this finding was that two-party systems tend to emerge where elections are based on a simple plurality vote. The logic is that parties on each side of the political spectrum (left and right) will recognize that they cannot afford to split the vote in a plurality system. To use an example, if six parties on the right each got 10 per cent of the vote, their combined total would be 60 per cent, but individually they would lose to the Communists if the Communists had 40 per cent of the vote. The parties on the right would therefore work together—to collaborate on selecting candidates and even to merge—in order to compete with the parties on the other side. The left would do this as well, leading to a two-party system. By contrast, Duverger finds that proportional representation is conducive to multiparty systems because it encourages small parties, and other systems such as runoff elections have effects in between these two extremes. Duverger suggests that this is a virtual law of political life and is true in so many cases that it is often seen as one of the strongest findings in political science, though he and others do note occasional exceptions.

Maurice Duverger, *Les Partis politiques* [*Political Parties*] (Paris: A. Colin, 1951).

small parties. The consequence of FPP systems as opposed to proportional representation was most famously associated with Maurice Duverger (see the "Insights" box on his book *Les Partis politiques*).

A leading argument linking social and other political factors to the party system holds that which parties emerge and where parties stand depend largely on ideology and the beliefs of the citizens. This may sound obvious, but it is quite distinct from the argument that the electoral rules and other institutions determine what party systems will look like. Parties often have deep roots in an ideology or in a social base, and party systems will be shaped by the parties that emerge. A prominent example would be communist parties around the world, which traditionally have had a strong ideological basis in Marxism and strong support among members of the working class and labour unions (as well as some intellectuals). Even in the US, among millennials and people critical of the Trump administration, socialism has moved from being an insult to being a label many people are happy to adopt. As PBS observed in mid-2017: "The Party of Socialism and Liberation's meetings have tripled in size at the group's New York headquarters in the months since Trump won the election. And the Democratic Socialists of America's membership has more than doubled to 19,000 activists since Sanders, a self-described Democratic socialist, launched his first presidential campaign in 2015."[19]

How Do Party Systems Shape Political Outcomes?

In addition to being caused by various factors, party systems are themselves causes of political outcomes. In particular, they may shape whether politics are very moderate or more extreme or even what those terms mean in the context of a particular country. For example, one consequence of a two-party system under many circumstances is the tendency of the major parties to try to attract the hypothetical **median voter**, or the voter who is theoretically in the middle of the distribution of voters in a certain geographic area. If we assume for the moment that voters in a given district can be put on a spectrum from most liberal on the left to most conservative on the right, as in Figure 11.1, then the voter in the exact centre is shown by the vertical line. In this example, the Conservative Party will generally capture the votes to the right of centre, and the Liberal Party will capture the votes to the left of centre. If both the Liberals and the Conservatives are strategic and rational, they will each do what they must to capture the entire half of the electorate that is on their side—plus a little more. Since the Liberals know that people on the far left are unlikely to vote Conservative and the Conservatives know that people on the far right are unlikely to vote Liberal, the best strategy becomes trying to capture those represented by the median voter—the person right in the middle. In this case, the median voter is the swing voter (i.e., one

median voter The voter who is theoretically exactly in the middle of the distribution of voters.

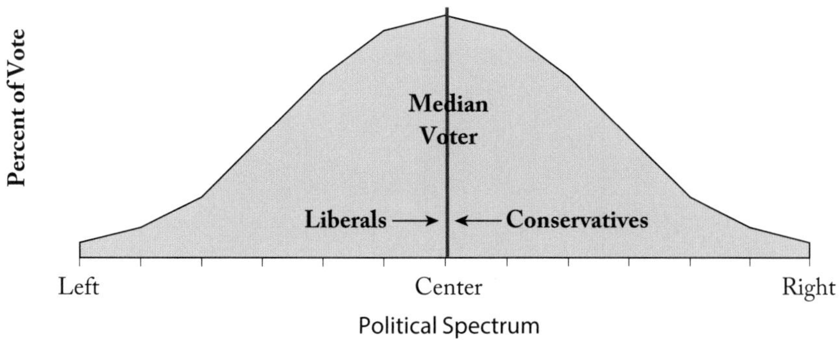

FIGURE 11.1 Voter Distribution and Political Party Strategy with Median Voter

who could go either way), and winning the swing vote is the key to getting a majority: 50 per cent of the vote plus at least one person. The major parties will therefore propose policies that appeal to the median voter. Visually, you can think of this as the parties positioning their platforms where the vertical line is: Both become relatively moderate and centrist. However, this does not always happen, and we are seeing a populist turn in many Western democracies in which the centre seems to be shifting to the right, even what we would have taken for the extreme right one or two decades ago. This has been the case in the United States, where the traditional median voter has changed greatly from the 1970s and 1980s, moving further to the right. Austria, Australia, France, and Hungary are also seeing rightward turns.

Of course, parties must try to attract the median voter while still retaining the votes of the ideologues at their respective ends of the political spectrum. Yet those more extreme voters on the far left and far right also make their own rational calculations. They know that not voting for the large party on their side (when there are multiple parties on a side) may help to tip the election to the other side. A very conservative voter, for example, has a reason to vote for a moderate Conservative Party if doing so helps to prevent the Liberal Party from winning instead. This thinking discourages relatively extreme voters from voting for smaller and more extreme parties. Voters thus engage in **strategic voting**, or voting in ways that do not reflect their ideal position in order to prevent outcomes they think are even worse. Since swing voters are often the deciding factor in winning or losing an election, some analysts suggest that single-member districts and two-party systems draw candidates and voters alike toward the middle, in the direction of the median voter, therefore having a moderating impact on representation.

strategic voting The practice of voting in a way that does not reflect one's ideal preference in order to prevent electoral outcomes one thinks are worse, such as voting for a second-best candidate one thinks can reasonably win.

There are several reasons why a system with two dominant parties might not lead to moderation, however. In particular, one could imagine that the distribution of voters does not always look like what is shown in Figure 11.1. Perhaps it looks more like that in Figure 11.2, which is known as a bimodal distribution because it has two peaks: many voters who are fairly liberal and many voters who are fairly conservative but not many in the centre or at either extreme. In this case, the Liberals might try to maximize their vote by offering platforms that appeal to voters on the left, about where the vertical line is shown. The Conservatives will do the same on the right. If they failed to do this, they would open themselves up to defeat by another new party that could claim more of the vote by

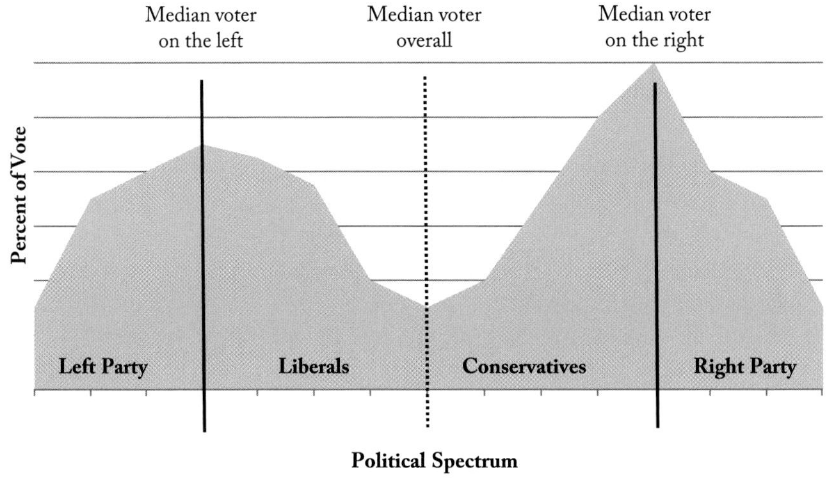

FIGURE 11.2 Bimodal Voter Distribution

positioning themselves strategically. For instance, if this country had exactly 100 people and the Liberals went for the centre, then another party—call them the Left Party—could position themselves just to the left of the Liberals, and the Conservatives would position themselves just to the right of the Liberals. The Conservatives would sweep the vote on the right, and the Left would take the vote to the left. The Liberals would thus be committing political suicide. More likely is that the Liberals and Conservatives would each go for the vertical line to capture the votes on their respective sides. In this case, a system with two dominant parties leads to polarization, not moderation.

We return to this example in questions at the end of the chapter. For now, though, you can imagine how such a political system might develop into a more competitive multiparty system because new parties might emerge in an attempt to position themselves strategically. The key point is that this distribution of voters within this party system does not result in the two big parties going for the median voter if the parties are strategic and rational.

There are other reasons, too, why parties might not attempt to appeal to the median voter. Imagine a case in which voters cannot simply be arrayed along a spectrum from right to left, and you will see that predicting their voting is much more complex.[20] Since people care about many different issues, such as religious or moral issues or Indigenous rights, it is not always clear what the left and the right will mean. Finally, in many Western democracies like Canada, the US, and the UK, there are essentially "safe seats" in many electorates because certain parts of the country are quite liberal or quite conservative; parties as a whole are therefore less likely to move toward the centre because each legislator responds to his or her own electorate's voters.[21]

It should be noted that the ways dominant-party and single-party regimes shape political outcomes is not as straightforward as it might seem; even in these systems, there are debates about the quality of representation. For more than a century, many communists claimed that only a communist party could truly represent and speak on behalf of workers,[22] but the collapse of communist governments around the world seemed to discredit this alternative to the multiparty democracy.[23] Similarly, single-party fascist regimes—including Nazi Germany—led to an association of single-party regimes with authoritarian and even totalitarian rule. The result was that prominent theories about democracy often assume multiparty competition to be the best form of political representation.[24] This did not, however, mean that all multiparty systems extend the principle of competition in the same way in the realm of interest groups. In multiparty democracies, interest groups may operate in relatively open competition under pluralism or in a more structured fashion using corporatist arrangements, as we discuss next.

Interest Groups and Representation

Pluralism and corporatism are each advocated by their respective proponents on the basis that they provide better and more effective representation. To start with pluralism, this theory describes how interest groups work in some countries, but it is primarily a theory about how interests *should* operate. Some theorists called "pluralists" openly advocate that this is the best approach for a government system: The government "should" listen to the competing arguments laid out by different social interests and mediate between them. In the case of pluralism, an emphasis is on the equal opportunity for different groups to influence politics, with guarantees of rights to organize and assemble to petition the government.

There are major critiques of the pluralist model, given that there is often a gap (and sometimes a large one) between theoretical idealism and reality. A key problem in the United States is that the system remains dominated by large corporate interests to the extent that one former president, Jimmy Carter, has argued that the political system functions more like an "oligarchy than a democracy."[25] Central to this critique are several recent court decisions that have uncapped the amount of money big donors can spend on elections. This has meant that the differential access to political power enjoyed by elites has increased tremendously in the past three decades. In Canada, many argued that the oil and gas industries were far too close to Stephen Harper's Conservative government, a level of influence that had a negative impact on protection for the environment. There is more debate about how the Trudeau Liberals will navigate oil and gas in their second term. The Liberal government purchased the Trans Mountain pipeline but faces resistance from many Indigenous peoples and others, while the purchase has not pacified Albertan anger against the Liberals for their other policies, such as the carbon tax.

collective action The pursuit of political or social goals by members of a group.

Another of the main challenges to assumptions about pluralism is the existence of the **collective action** problem. People do not necessarily participate in interest groups for all the beliefs they support. Rather, they consider the benefits of their own action and the costs of undertaking the action. This is especially true with public goods whereby if a benefit for a certain person is small, then joining an interest group may not be worth the effort. The same is true if costs to the individual of joining the group are high. Achieving a desired result is rarely due to one more person's action, so people have an incentive to be free riders: Let others do the work and hope to participate in the collective reward.

The other critique of pluralism comes from the perspective that corporatism does a better job at integrating interests and ensuring the structured representation of major groups in society. The argument draws upon a variety of empirical examples, ranging from economic growth successes in East Asia to harmonious social policies in Europe. In terms of economic growth, the likes of Japan and South Korea from the 1950s to 1980s were countries where scholars found that close linkages between the state and top business organizations (as well as labour) were important in setting national goals and reaching high levels of economic performance.[26] Meanwhile, in the context of long-established democracies in Europe, corporatist arrangements were argued to be a political solution that gave rise to consensus-based decision-making. This was reputed to be useful in reducing social tensions and in ensuring a relative political harmony between business and labour, since both were regularly integrated into political decision-making.

INSIGHTS

The Logic of Collective Action: Public Goods and the Theory of Groups *and* The Rise and Decline of Nations: Economic Growth, Stagflation, and Social Rigidities

by Mancur Olson

Olson's early book, *The Logic of Collective Action*, is the basis of the field of study in how collective action occurs, as outlined previously. The logic of collective action applies to interest groups as well as to other actors we discuss in the next chapter. Rather than assuming people will easily form interest groups to press for public demands, Olson noted the free rider dilemma and the tendency of interest groups to function better when they provide specific benefits for their members. This is a critique of pluralism in the sense that interest groups cannot be assumed to form to represent diverse interests. Olson extended this critique in his later work, *The Rise and Decline of Nations*, in which he argued that the accumulation of special interests over time slows down economic growth because governments respond to politically powerful actors rather than to the needs of the economy. One empirical example is striking: The United Kingdom, a victor in World War II, did worse economically for several decades than Germany and Japan, which lost the war. Olson attributes this to the continuity of special interests in the United Kingdom as contrasted with the elimination of many of those interests for the defeated countries.

Mancur Olson, *The Logic of Collective Action: Public Goods and the Theory of Groups* (Cambridge, MA: Harvard University Press, 1965), and *The Rise and Decline of Nations: Economic Growth, Stagflation, and Social Rigidities* (New Haven, CT: Yale University Press, 1982).

Corporatism can also have major disadvantages, given its lack of an "arm's-length" relationship between interest groups and the state. Certainly, what seems like useful collaboration at certain moments can seem like "crony capitalism" and favouritism at others. How can one differentiate between the two? In addition, the structured relationships may favour some of the institutions that are powerful in the status quo. For example, who is more truly representative of American industry, Amazon, Google, or General Motors? Corporatism may tend to "calcify" relations between the state and certain actors. If the automobile industry and autoworkers have had close relationships with the state for decades, will they combine to support the General Motors of the world rather than the Googles? We must also remember that Google emerged from an extremely competitive field that included AltaVista, Netscape, Lycos, and other search engines that are now unfamiliar to most younger people. In its own time too, GM grew large by swallowing or crushing many of its competitors.

Corporatism also tends to result in decision-making by a relatively small number of elites, specifically those in government, business, and labour. In a more severe form, corporatism has been highly exclusionary and authoritarian. The idea of corporatism even contributed to totalitarian ideologies such as the early years of German Nazism in the 1930s and the period of Italian fascism under Benito Mussolini from the 1920s to the 1940s. For many, this association with totalitarian regimes discredited corporatism because corporatist arrangements infringed individual rights in favour of groups and the state; totalitarian regimes provide the worst examples of this. The debate between pluralism and corporatism may never be resolved, given the changing contours of both models, and the reality that political systems are adapting on a regular basis.

THINKING COMPARATIVELY

Party Systems in Sub-Saharan Africa

KEY METHODOLOGICAL TOOL

Comparative Checking

Comparative politics is often based on the examination of a small number of case studies. This allows the analyst to dig into the case in depth, but it also has the disadvantage of giving a "small sample size" of just a couple of cases. Unless one uses quantitative and statistical methods, one often does not subject the hypothesis to full testing across all the possible cases. A danger of this can be making inferences too quickly without keeping sight of whether the argument applies beyond the cases in the study. Ideally, we would like to make arguments that apply to more than just the cases we examine. A partial solution to this challenge is comparative checking, or relatively brief glances at other cases to see if the argument holds up or has obvious flaws. This does not mean doing a full study of more and more cases but rather briefly reviewing other cases to see if one's conclusions seem to work at a glance. If so, one has greater confidence in the argument; if not, the comparative check can be useful in forcing the analyst to revisit the argument to see if it can be modified to make it more applicable to other cases.

Different political party systems have flourished at different times and in different places around the world. Some countries in western Europe have often had multiparty regimes in which parties that perform the best in elections often do not win a majority and thus need to make coalitions with other parties to govern. At the federal level in Canada, the Liberals and the Conservatives jockey for power in a stable two-party system, while at the provincial level there is more variety such that the New Democratic Party is also a major contender and has formed governments in British Columbia, Alberta, Saskatchewan, Manitoba, Ontario, Nova Scotia, and Yukon.

Meanwhile, single-party and dominant-party regimes have rarely been found in western Europe since the end of World War II but have been much more common in Asia, in the Middle East, occasionally in Latin America, and in eastern Europe under Soviet rule. Africa is a final region of the world that has seen many single-party and dominant-party regimes. One may be tempted to reach some relatively straightforward conclusions about what shapes party systems: Poorer regions and developing countries are likelier to have single-party systems. Leaders in Africa and scholars alike have at different times offered justifications and explanations for single-party dominance. The same has held in countries from Syria to Singapore. One might even hear (or make) arguments that these regions are culturally or politically unprepared for multiparty democracy.

However, one should not jump to such a conclusion. To take Africa as an example, the continent also has a number of other types of party systems, from multiparty competition in the tiny country of Benin to a stable two-party system in Ghana. Moreover, there is a major distinction between the quite democratic dominant-party systems in countries like Botswana or South Africa and the more authoritarian dominant-party systems in countries like Cameroon or Ethiopia.

This illustrates the importance of avoiding excessive generalizations that do not match up with the evidence. In particular, it is advisable to engage in a bit of "comparative checking" so as not to generalize from one or two cases. Indeed, the particular cases that do not fit the generalization would be useful ones to examine further if they are "deviant cases" as noted in Chapters 2 and 5.

There are several causes and consequences of different party systems and patterns of interest-group representation, and this area is still the subject of considerable research and debate. While it seems that electoral institutions do help to shape party systems, these systems are also influenced by ideologies, cultures, economics, histories, and many other factors. Similar factors also shape how pluralist or corporatist the state's relationship to interest groups is. In turn, the patterns that emerge in party systems and interest group representation affect what citizens do and how they vote and participate in politics. This chapter has thus begun to give a bigger role in politics to those citizens who may never consider themselves politicians. This focus on the actions and behaviours of groups of citizens will continue into our next chapters, in which we look at the many ways people identify politically and express their interests and beliefs through different kinds of action.

Chapter Summary

Concepts

- Political parties are organizations that have the aim of nominating candidates and electing representatives to public office.
- Political party systems are different patterns in the number of major political parties and in the patterns of party politics.
- Interest groups are organizations that advocate for some policy perspective or political goal, and they may or may not support specific candidates.

Types

- Political parties have taken forms that include elite parties, mass parties, and catch-all parties.
- Political party systems can be divided into dominant-party systems, two-party systems, and multiparty systems.
- Interest groups can compete with one another for political influence in a system known as pluralism, or they may have more structured interactions with the state under corporatism.

Causes and Effects

- Political party systems are shaped by electoral rules as well as other factors such as ideology and social and historical influences.
- The political party system itself also affects politics by helping to determine whether major parties tend toward the centre of the political spectrum or not.
- Pluralism and corporatism have both been argued by their respective advocates to result in stronger democracy.

Thinking Comparatively

- Certain types of party systems may be more prevalent in some regions of the world, but it is important to engage in comparative checking to avoid over-generalizing.

Thinking It Through

1. Look back at the voter distributions in Figures 11.1 and 11.2. Imagine you are trying to start a third party called the Citizens Progressive Party to compete with the Liberals and Conservatives in a country that those two parties have dominated politically. You believe that the Liberals are too moderate and would ideally like to position yourself as far to the left as possible. Strategically, what would be your best position on the political spectrum, keeping in mind that the height of the peaks in the figures reflects how many voters there are on that part of the spectrum? Would your strategy be different for Figure 11.1 as opposed to Figure 11.2?
2. Building on the last question, now place yourself in the position of the Liberals. What would prevent parties from beating you? If the Citizens Progressive Party comes along, how could you prevent this other party from taking your place? What argument would you make to voters about why they should vote for you rather than a party that is farther out on the political spectrum?
3. Thinking back to some of the comparative strategies from previous chapters, how would you determine whether a certain country's party system is shaped more by its electoral rules or by other factors? How can comparison help you to answer this question, and what sorts of comparisons might you set up to distinguish between different causal factors?
4. This chapter has addressed both party systems and interest groups. Do you find one of these sorts of groups responds to the other more? Which set of organizations do you find more important in shaping how politics operates and what governments do? If you were given $500 that you were required to donate to either a party or an interest group, which would you donate to, and why?

PART IV

Politics, Society, and Culture

12 Revolutions and Contention

In This Chapter

A youth waves Egyptian flags from a lamp post in Tahrir Square in Cairo, Egypt in February 2011. (Peter Macdiarmid/Getty Images)

In late 2010, in a small town in Tunisia, a police officer insulted a street vendor and toppled his produce cart. This would normally have been an event of limited consequence, but what happened next made history. The vendor, Mohamed Bouazizi, went to the municipal offices to register his complaint. Rebuffed there, he set himself on fire in the street. He is believed to have done so to protest his humiliation and his lack of opportunity. His act galvanized protesters, seeming to indicate to many that "enough is enough" when it came to poor governance and a lack of social opportunities. The symbolic tactic of self-immolation would be repeated in Tunisia and elsewhere. Faced with continuous street protests, the Tunisian government fell by mid-January, not long after Bouazizi died of his injuries. By the end of the month, protests had spread to other Arab countries, notably Egypt. There, the state began to make strong efforts to quell protests. On one hand, it repressed protesters, in among other places the famous gathering point of Tahrir Square in Cairo. On the other hand, it became clear that there were limits to the army's willingness to repress the population. By mid-February 2011, the government of Hosni Mubarak had fallen. The uprisings then spread to other parts of the Arab world. In response, the Canadian government froze more than $4 billion of assets owned by Middle East dictators, much of it related to Libyan leader Moammar Qadhafi and, to a lesser extent, regimes in Tunisia, Syria, and Egypt.[1]

Like the Americans and Europeans, as well as people from the region, the Spring was a big surprise. Canada's Department of National Defence released a report two years after the Spring, admitting that "the study found that the wave of protests and regime changes that swept the Middle East in 2011 had not been anticipated."[2]

For years, many analysts and citizens had been skeptical about democratic opening and regime change in this region, and yet suddenly the air was full of excitement and a sense of opportunity. Outcomes have varied dramatically. Tunisia and Egypt ousted their old governments largely as a result of protests. The former case seemed like a democratic success story. In the latter case, post-revolutionary elections led to Mohammed Morsi and the Muslim Brotherhood briefly holding power before they were displaced by a military coup in July 2013. Libya witnessed a NATO-supported insurgency that eventually dislodged the Qadhafi regime. Syria harshly cracked down on protesters, followed by insurgency, partial state failure, and the de facto control of some parts of its territory by ISIS, precipitating a civil war and mass killings. Saudi Arabia cracked down on dissent too, imprisoning human rights activists like Raif Badawi in 2012. In 2018, they imprisoned his sister Samar, which led to a major outcry by the Canadian government and a diplomatic standoff involving Saudi threats, cuts to investment, and the cancelling of flights to and from Canada.

The varied outcomes from the Arab Spring need explanation. Why did these events happen? Why did they occur in a "wave"?[3] Finally, why was coordinated citizen action against the government successful in some places, less successful in others, and non-existent in still others? Revolutions and related efforts remain an important part of the contemporary world, and they are among the most interesting subjects in comparative politics.

• • •

Concepts

Students of comparative politics ask many questions about dramatic events like social movements and **revolutions**. Why do some instances of collective action achieve their apparent objectives while others do not? How do individuals and groups select different strategies

revolution A form of collective action in which some large-scale, structural change is either attempted or accomplished.

and tactics for the pursuit of their interests? Why are some conflicts "reformist" and others "revolutionary"? Why are some violent and others peaceful? In shedding light on these and other questions, comparative political analysis can help to influence policy choices for governments and social movement organizers.

Conflict is a near constant of political life because politics involves disputes over resources. These include not only material resources, such as housing, food, consumer goods, and access to services like medical care but also less tangible goods like *status* and *power*.[4] All modern societies distribute resources unequally, though they vary considerably in the extent and form of this inequality. Politics can be viewed as an arena in which resources are distributed and one in which conflict takes place over *how* they are distributed. In this chapter, we consider some of the many forms that such conflicts take. Social scientists interested in studying conflict often refer to it as "**contention**."[5] They refer to the joint efforts of individuals to bring about a preferred outcome as "collective action."

contention The name, most associated with scholars like Sidney Tarrow and Charles Tilly, referring to the pursuit of collective goods largely outside of formal political institutions.

What Is "Contention"?

formal institutions Institutions that are governed by formal rules and typically linked to complex organizations like the state or corporations.

Conflict can be peaceful or violent and can happen inside **formal institutions** or outside of them. In democratic societies, conflict can theoretically be channelled through participation in electoral politics via the institutions we discussed in Chapters 8 through 11. For example, people can theoretically organize themselves into political parties and try to use these parties to gain office and work through the executive or legislative branches of the state. Constitutions, discussed in Chapter 8, can from this perspective be viewed as the formal rules in terms of which conflicts in a society will be resolved. Of course, this is not always the case, and many groups can be informally frozen out of a political system.

Indigenous peoples in settler states, for example, may have treaty rights guaranteeing their own forms of government on their own lands through rights to self-determination yet may be marginalized by the state. This is true in settler states such as Canada, the US, Australia, and New Zealand. Consensus-based (often matrilineal) systems were dismantled by settler governments in the 19th and 20th centuries and replaced with state-controlled governance systems that had little relation to the traditions and desires of Indigenous peoples.

The Idle No More movement in Canada is a good example of Indigenous peoples and others working together to protest against a lack of government accountability and the exploitation of natural resources. This movement developed in late 2012 in reaction to Canadian Prime Minister Stephen Harper's attempts to reduce Indigenous rights through a range of omnibus bills. It gained the support of Indigenous organizations as well as environmental groups and international actors. Indigenous contentious politics can occur in ostensibly democratic countries because Indigenous governance systems are not properly recognized by settler states. In Australia, there are no treaties with Indigenous peoples and thus no legal standard by which Indigenous peoples can achieve recognition of their self-determining rights. Similarly, some groups may be marginalized because of systemic racism, such as African Americans in the US, and often have much less access to political power.

Contention can often develop in non-democratic societies, although they sometimes have formal channels through which some conflict can be negotiated. For example, local councils or committees, as well as governmental organizations like the police, might be responsive to citizen inquiries in some such societies. No political system is perfect, and when people are marginalized and excluded from the level of influence they feel they deserve, forms of contention can result.

Revolutionary and Non-revolutionary Contention

What political scientists call "contention" is behaviour that occurs mostly outside of formal political channels.[6] The category includes **social movements**, **social revolutions**, **insurgencies** and **civil wars**, and even **terrorism**, as well as so-called "**everyday forms of resistance**"[7] in which people without the resources needed to organize themselves for ongoing mobilization nevertheless resist power. Scholars try to understand both the nature of these different sorts of conflict and their *causes*.

Perhaps the most fundamental difference is between forms of contention thought of as "revolutionary" and those that are not. Social scientists debate the exact definition of revolutions, as we will see, but most agree that they either attempt to or succeed in *radically transforming* social, political, and economic relationships. Of course, other forms of contention also involve efforts to make change but often more gradually or less radically.

social movements Ongoing, organized collective action oriented toward a goal of social change.

social revolutions Revolutions that dramatically change social structures.

insurgencies Contention with formalized military conflict.

civil wars Sustained military conflict between domestic actors.

terrorism In the context of revolutions or insurgencies, a tactic used by some participants that involves violence directed at non-military targets.

everyday forms of resistance Efforts to resist or obstruct authority that are not clearly organized over time, such as work stoppages, slowdowns, and sabotage.

Types

Not all forms of contention are as transformative as the "great social revolutions" of France, Russia, and China. As we shall see in this section, scholars have defined several distinct *types* of revolution according to actors' aims or accomplishments, and there are many important but non-revolutionary forms of social change.

Social Movements

Social movements are in some ways the most normal of the major forms of contentious action and are considered a healthy part of civil society, at least in democracies.[8] As discussed in Chapter 3, "civil society" can mean different things, but the main idea is that modern, democratic polities should allow for citizens to come together and debate questions of value and policy, ideally free from state coercion.[9] Thus, civil society can be found in media sources like newspapers and the Internet but also in public gatherings and interactions between citizens and above all in the social networks that make this kind of deliberation sustainable. Social movement organizing takes place in this space: That is, social movements have a kind of *autonomy* from the state.[10]

Social movements take place when citizens *organize over time* in the pursuit of common purposes. For example, movements have sought the expansion of suffrage rights to women or members of minority groups. In contrast, regardless of its goals, we would not typically characterize a spontaneous protest like a riot or a mob as a social movement. However, social movements might use public demonstrations as a *tactic*. What would make a string of public demonstrations a social movement, then, would be their common underlying coordination.[11] Some group or connected groups of people, linked via **social networks**, work together on common goals and use protest activity as a way of achieving those goals. Other tactics might include community organizing, "consciousness-raising," educational or propagandistic work, and political lobbying. Since social movement activity is the most "normal" of the major forms of contentious action, most modern democratic societies have essentially reserved a place for it alongside formal politics. Former social movement leaders often enter into formal politics, perhaps most famously the African-American Congressman John Lewis, who was the chairman of the Student Nonviolent Coordinating Committee in the civil rights movement in the 1960s. Increasingly, social movement activity of this sort is becoming *transnational*, crossing the boundaries of the nation-state and taking place in what some call global civil society.[12] Think, for example, of protests against globalization

social networks Structures of social ties and connections among individuals.

like the World Social Forum, the Occupy Movement, and the more recent yellow vest movement in France. These sorts of protests often deliberately seek to cross national borders and to protest forces that do so as well.[13]

social movement organization An organization that has been created to help maintain and lead social movement activity over time.

Social movements organize, or coordinate collective action, in many different ways. Organizations created to serve the purposes of social movements are called **social movement organizations**. While we must be careful to remember that movements do not reduce to such organizations, social movement organizations are often very important. Some are more elite-led and others more grassroots.

For example, the Solidarity movement in Poland that eventually triumphed over the communist government had clear leadership directing its activities during the 1980s. By contrast, social-movement organizing against the authoritarian regime in Iran in 2009–10 was more decentralized, communicating via technology like texting, Twitter, and Facebook and even involving activists literally calling to one another from rooftops. Some are highly unified, meaning that most activists agree and that there is not a lot of competition among different groups with their own aims. Others are more factious and divided. What seems to be true in most cases is that for social movement activity to endure, *some* organizing must take place and this often means that some individuals will be set off from other participants as *leaders*. Some argue that social movement activity (like party organizing) eventually runs up against the "**iron law of oligarchy**."[14] According to this theory, organizational leadership necessarily creates its own interests, and every movement creates a new elite. It is worth noting that these concerns apply not just to social movements but also to other forms of contention discussed later.

iron law of oligarchy The idea, developed by Robert Michels, that collective action always produces new elites.

Associated Press/Czarek Sokolowski

PHOTO 12.2 A sculpture made out of bicycles at the Gdansk Shipyard during the 30th anniversary celebrations of the Solidarity movement in Poland in 2010. Bicycles were the most common mode of transportation for shipyard workers. Solidarity began as a non-governmental trade union that became a non-violent movement against communism in the 1980s. In 1989, Solidarity formed part of a coalition government, and one of its leaders, Lech Walesa, was elected president of Poland in 1990.

Imagine that you and your fellow students create a social movement. Your goal is to organize in favour of changes in your city—such as an end to racially motivated profiling of black and Indigenous peoples by the police, sometimes called "carding." If there is broad consensus among the supporters, there are clear and available mechanisms for communication (maybe on social media), and, most important, if your goals are clear and minimal and do not encounter sharp resistance, relatively little organization and complex coordination will be necessary. But what if the goals are less clear, or can only be accomplished in stages, or meet with strong resistance by the city? Then the movement will need to achieve ongoing **mobilization**. In *this* instance, some individuals are going to have to assume positions of leadership, making decisions about what sorts of statements to issue, how to frame arguments and goals, and when to call for demonstrations. Otherwise, individual protest actions will be easily dispersed.

mobilization The engagement of individuals and groups in sustained contention.

If goals are fairly narrow and focused, positive results can sometimes be achieved. Take for example the "Fight for $15 and Fairness" campaign at York University (Toronto) in early 2017. Here, students, workers, campus unions, and others joined together to protest the very low wages paid to campus food service workers and their often-poor working conditions. Discrimination against racialized peoples, Muslims, and women were also a focus of contention.[15] In this case, the movement, which went well beyond York University, achieved some degree of success. The former Liberal government in Ontario introduced legislation in November 2017 to raise the minimum wage to $15 by 2019, as well as increasing a range of protections for workers. The incoming Progressive Conservative government in 2018 refused to carry this out and kept the minimum wage at $14 per hour.

Typically, some individuals form groups and present themselves as strategic leaders. Once such groups are formed, the groups themselves, as well as the leaders within them, often get a vested interest in the group and the movement.

Moreover, in most major social movements, alternative groups claim the mantle of leadership. This can be seen clearly in the most famous social movement in US history, the civil rights movement of the 1950s and 1960s, in which there were periods of tension and cooperation between the Southern Christian Leadership Conference (SCLC) and the Student Nonviolent Coordinating Committee (SNCC) as well as pre-existing organizations like the National Association for the Advancement of Colored People (NAACP) and more militant organizations like the Nation of Islam and the Black Panther Party.[16] The point is not that the leaders of these different groups pursued only their own interests—they were all clearly devoted to the expansion of civil rights, and each played an important role in the movement's achievements—but that the interests of organizations and their leaders *matter* in social movements.

At the same time, the American civil rights movement offers cautionary evidence against simply associating social movements with their most visible leaders and leading organizations. Grassroots participation and organization and on-the-ground improvising were common. To take just one example, the Montgomery Bus Boycott of 1955–6 depended heavily on the ingenious improvisational work of hundreds or even thousands of black citizens not identified as social movement "leaders" in the conventional sense.[17] While social movement organization depends on official leaders, it also depends on the initiative of grassroots activists.

Most important, movements are dependent on ongoing mobilization. A great deal of work in recent years has been devoted to tracing and explaining different patterns of mobilization. Two of the most important political scientists in this area stress several key "mechanisms of mobilization," including "diffusion, brokerage, and new coordination."[18] This means that when mobilization happens successfully, it spreads, often "shifting scales" (moving from the local to the state, national, or global level or else moving in the other

PHOTO 12.3 **Leaders and activists involved in the Montgomery Bus Boycott, which took place in 1955 and 1956 in the southern US state of Alabama.**

direction from more macro levels to local activism). It involves individuals, groups, and organizations bringing previously disconnected actors together in pursuit of common goals, and it involves novel efforts on the part of those actors to work together.[19] We can think of this as an effort to break down some of the elements of what is happening when a social movement achieves mobilization. An important part of explaining any social movement is explaining how such steps are traversed.

Since social movement activity has been normalized in contemporary democracies,[20] it can influence electoral politics and sometimes even revolutions. We can distinguish revolutions from social movements based on differences in *goals* or in *consequences*, though there is perhaps no single clear line separating the two categories. Social movements tend to be viewed as reformist. They aim to make a society live up to some of its idealized values or to extend rights associated with citizenship to groups to which those rights were previously denied. In other words, social movements aim to affect important social change but not dramatic *structural transformation*. Revolutions, in contrast, aim at the latter.[21]

Revolutions

Most commentators agree that revolutions must be relatively sudden and must achieve dramatic social and political change. Beyond this, revolutions are challenging to define.[22] They must be *transformative*, at least in intent, and, depending on how narrowly we want to define "revolutions," in their actual consequences.[23] Thus, a reform program is not a revolution, though failed reforms can help produce revolutions.[24] They must involve, like social movements, some level of popular *mobilization*.[25] Given the difficulty in defining "revolution," one common strategy has been to enumerate different *types* of revolutions. One basic distinction is between so-called social revolutions and more limited political revolutions.[26]

Social revolutions transform social and political structures. In other words, they make *major* changes in how power and other resources are distributed in society. For thinkers like Karl Marx, social revolutions more specifically transform the distribution of material resources among groups. Contentious action, according to this line of thinking, is only a social revolution if the **class structure** is transformed. Thus, the Russian Revolution of 1917 would be considered a social revolution because it used the power of the state to transform the basis of economic activity by "nationalizing" industries, redistributing land from wealthy landowners to collectives comprised of peasants, etc. The same is true of the French Revolution, which essentially dismantled France's nobility and the social system on which it rested.

class structure The ongoing and patterned relationships between "classes," typically understood as groups of individuals linked together by economic interest or activity.

Political revolutions are probably more common than social revolutions. A political revolution changes *political institutions* like the state rather than transforming social structures like a class system or an economy. It is important to distinguish political revolutions from other kinds of political change, however. Electoral transference of power between parties or groups would not be considered a political revolution (despite what Bernie Sanders may have promised) because it would not actually change political *structures*. While Americans often argue that they brought about a social revolution in 1776, this is not entirely true, since the elite—the white, male British property owners who launched the revolution—also continued to benefit by it. There was no major shift in wealth, property ownership, or leadership. The social and institutional structures were not really overturned. The creation of a constitutional republic was innovative, as was the concept of equality of citizens, but society did not fundamentally change as a result of the US political revolution, not in ways comparable to changes after the French or Russian revolutions.

political revolutions Revolutions, the main effect of which is to alter political institutions rather than social and economic structures.

We might also like to distinguish coups d'état, which often present themselves as "revolutions," from revolutions themselves. For some scholars, what would distinguish a **coup d'état** from a revolution is that the former is elite-driven (typically by the military and sometimes in alliance with civilian actors), whereas revolutions necessarily involve the mobilization of some other important groups besides elite actors holding formal power. However, sometimes military leaders respond to ongoing public mobilization by staging a coup. In such instances, depending on the outcome, scholars are more likely to consider the event a revolution.[27]

coup d'état The use of force or threat of force, typically by the military or a coalition involving the military, to impose a non-electoral change of government.

Other examples of political revolutions might include some of the Latin American wars of independence in the early 19th century and the wave of anti-Soviet revolutions in central and eastern Europe in the late 1980s and early 1990s. In these latter cases, far-reaching political transformations took place, and the satellite states of the Soviet Union were replaced with nominally democratic republics (although some transformed into new forms of authoritarian government). These changes, in turn, gave rise to economic changes that affected the class structure in these societies. Most political scientists would still consider these "political revolutions," however, since such changes were not *direct* aims or consequences of the revolutions in question.

A third possible type is **anti-colonial revolutions**.[28] Most of the social and political revolutions discussed so far in this chapter are made against the state and/or the groups controlling the state before the revolution. But sometimes groups are subject to the domination of powers beyond their own nations and states. In such cases, those powers are sometimes the ultimate targets of the revolution. One of the earliest of these types is the Haitian Revolution, which began in August 1791 and ended with this former French colony's independence in 1804. Led by the former enslaved African Toussaint L'Ouverture, the

anti-colonial revolutions Revolutions brought by subjugated populations against colonial powers, typically with the purpose of removing them so that the society in question can achieve independence.

revolution brought together many racial and linguistic groups, resulting in the first example of enslaved peoples rising up and successfully forming their own independent state.

In the middle of the 20th century, numerous anti-colonial revolutions, typically motivated by *nationalism*, were made against colonial powers as well as local interests perceived to serve them. Their articulated goal was the *removal* of these powers so that the nation could gain independence. Whether anti-colonial revolutions should be considered a type of political revolution or their own category is open to academic debate. In such revolutions, the colonizing power is typically located at some distance from the colony. It becomes more complicated when Indigenous peoples in settler states seek a revolution because in such cases the settlers often outnumber the Indigenous peoples. This can paradoxically make settler-dominated democracy a major impediment to decolonization.

A good example of this problem can be seen in Canada with the actions of Pierre Trudeau's government in 1969. In that year, the government promoted a "White Paper"—a policy document proposing that Canada should do away with the treaties signed between the Crown and Indigenous peoples. Trudeau argued that the treaties were outdated and that all people in Canada should be treated the same way under Canadian law. The White Paper proposed the assimilation of Indigenous peoples and preventing them from exercising their treaty rights. The result of this proposal was major Indigenous organization and activism throughout the country, including a well known "Red Paper" being published, which led to the White Paper being dropped.

Third World Revolutions A concept developed by John Foran holding that revolutions in the developing world have special characteristics.

While traditional forms of colonialism are now relatively rare, some scholars treat "**Third World Revolutions**" as a distinct type.[30] According to these theorists, inequalities in the developing world depend for their enforcement not just on the states, armies, and police of those states themselves but on *international* networks of powerful states (e.g., the United States, Canada, western Europe, Japan, China) and international organizations (e.g., the World Bank and the International Monetary Fund). "Third World Revolutions," these scholars argue, therefore have distinct dynamics and should be analyzed separately. Just the same, this category overlaps with the broader distinction between social and political revolutions. A given case might, for certain purposes, be classified as both a political revolution and a "Third World" or anti-colonial one.

subaltern Marginalized groups and individuals in a hierarchical system where other groups are dominant.

Revolutions may take place "from below" or "from above." All revolutions involve elite and **subaltern** actors (those lower down the social hierarchy or with less power and status before the revolution), but some are more and some less elite-driven than others. This

CASE IN CONTEXT

392

The French Revolution

The French Revolution is the most iconic and probably the best-studied revolution, and leaders of other revolutions have often looked to its history.[29] While not all scholars consider it the first modern revolution, most agree that it was seen as novel and that it dramatically influenced and still shapes revolutionary patterns.

For more on the French Revolution, see the case study in Part VI, p. 392. As you read it, keep in mind the following questions:

1. Why would the French aristocracy help to bring about reforms that ended up undermining its group interests?
2. Why do some scholars see this as a "bourgeois revolution"?
3. How do causal factors like state weakness, status-order problems, and new, potentially revolutionary ideologies like nationalism interact in this case?

PHOTO 12.4 The French Revolution has been a model for many revolutionaries ever since it took place, and it is a case that has been considered by virtually all theorists of revolution.

distinction is complicated by the fact that, as we will see in the "Causes and Effects" section, different *theories* of revolution place greater or lesser emphasis on elite and popular participation in *explaining* revolutions. In any case, the categories of revolutions "from below" or "from above" cut across some of the other types of revolutions discussed in this section. For example, India's independence movement included both elite and subaltern actors.

Insurgencies and Civil Wars

Insurgencies can be thought of as enduring, organized, armed actors contesting the power of the state. Insurgencies in some instances shade into revolutions, and many insurgencies claim to be *making* revolutions. Insurgencies also sometimes look like social movements, and they can often be tied to social movements carried out by civilians. We might distinguish insurgencies from revolutions and social movements, however, by the degree of *formalization* of military conflict.[31] One recent work defines insurgents as "nonstate armed actors that use violence to reformulate or destroy the foundations of politics in a given country."[32] Often, conflicts between groups of insurgents or between insurgents and the state are classified as "civil wars."

Sometimes it is difficult to distinguish revolutions from the civil conflicts to which they give rise.[33] For example, consider the wars of independence in Latin America in the early 19th century. They were considered revolutions, although they did not achieve major social-structural change and so would best be seen as political revolutions. Not unlike the United States, they were led primarily by European land-owning civilians who aimed to create independent republics and to make citizens where there was before only the monarchy and its subjects. However, because Spain used its army to attempt to put down these revolutions, the conflict took military form. Different actors in these societies took sides. A number of groups were loyal to the crown and fought *against* the revolutionaries, and thus we might even think of these conflicts as "civil wars."[34]

Insurgencies might develop when several conditions occur. First, a government that oppresses the residents of a given region, class, or group, or one that otherwise seriously fails to fulfil their expectations, is likely to generate the desire for insurgent activity. Second, a political system that does not allow for other avenues for the expression and resolution of grievances increases the likelihood of insurgency. Third, a weak state increases the chances of an insurgency developing. For an insurgency to endure, neither the insurgents nor the state can be strong enough to decisively win. **Guerrilla tactics** are designed to produce just this sort of situation.[35] This often leads to protracted conflicts spanning years or even decades.

guerrilla tactics Military techniques designed to produce ongoing stalemate, usually employed in situations of asymmetric military capability.

Terrorism

Definitions of terrorism have been controversial. We can define it as broadly as the use or threat of violence for political ends or as narrowly as the use of violence by nonstate actors against civilians for the purpose of reducing civilian support for one or another official policy. Some would argue that terrorism should be seen as a tactic or strategy rather than a distinctive type of contentious action.[36] If we view terrorism in this way, then it really is nothing more than a potential tool of individuals and groups participating in the other forms of contention discussed in this chapter. Yet terrorism is a concept that appears more complex upon examination. It necessarily involves violence or at least the threat of violence. Definitions of terrorism must all take into account the following issues: (1) who or what is perpetrating the violence; (2) who or what is the target of the violence; and (3) the goals, purposes, or consequences of the violence. Not all definitions give the same answer to each of these questions.

The broadest definitions of terrorism say that it makes little difference who or what is carrying it out.[37] Most important, they accept that *states* can be terrorist actors. This was the original meaning of the concept, which derives from descriptions of the violence of the French Revolution.[38] States like the former Soviet Union, Nazi Germany, or Chile under Pinochet (1973–90) were doing essentially the same thing as nonstate actors like al Qaeda or would-be state actors like the Islamic State (also known by the acronyms ISIS or ISIL). Western countries are also accused of engaging in state terrorism when they kill civilians in the conduct of wars outside of their own borders. The United States, in various military forays during the 20th century, killed large numbers of civilians, especially during World War II and also during the Vietnam wars.[39] Britain and France likewise have been responsible for atrocities against civilians during periods when they maintained empires in Asia, Africa, and the Caribbean. Narrower definitions seek to exclude state-led terrorism or at least to designate a separate category ("state terrorism") for it.[40] The rationale for this is that the causes of organized violence perpetrated by a state and by a group of clandestine civilians are likely to be very different even if, for the victims, the effects are the same.

Broad definitions of terrorism highlight that whether a given case of violence is terrorism does not depend on the status or identity of its victims. Narrower definitions tend to exclude violence directed toward certain classes of victims. For example, some would not consider violence directed at military installations or at military personnel, particularly in wartime, to be terrorism.[41] The question gets a bit fuzzier when we consider other functionaries of the state: Is violence carried out against the police terrorism? What about bombing a government building, such as a post office, when it is closed after working hours? The narrowest definitions assert that a distinctive feature of terrorism is that its victims are themselves civilians.[42] Broad definitions, again, say that the "purposes" of the violence are unimportant or that they cannot even be reliably known.[43] Narrower definitions claim that to be terrorism, violence must be intended to instil fear in a population.[44] Still narrower definitions assert that this intended fear must be part of a calculated strategy to bring about some major political change.[45]

"Everyday Resistance"

Some groups resist when they *don't* have the organizational resources to mobilize into social movements or revolutions. Banditry and other forms of resistance defined by the broader society as "crime" can often be understood in this way.[46] Subaltern groups employ what the political scientist James Scott has called "weapons of the weak" to practise "everyday resistance."[47] For example, they might struggle *symbolically* against inequality by telling stories that challenge prevailing power relations. They might struggle against it *materially* by engaging in tactics like work stoppage, slowdowns, boycotts, or even sabotage (some of these behaviours can be used as *tactics* in social movement organizing as well, of course). As Scott describes such efforts, "they require little or no coordination or planning; they make use of implicit understandings and informal networks; they often represent a form of individual self-help; they typically avoid any direct, symbolic confrontation with authority."[48]

Subaltern groups likely to engage in "everyday resistance" are also likely to be excluded from formal politics. This may because of an autocratic state or simply a matter of their distance from formal political life. For example, a centralized authoritarian state might deliberately not extend *any* political voice to the rural poor. Or political parties in an established democracy may discover that there are few gains to be made in catering to marginalized constituencies, either because their numbers aren't sufficient, or because they aren't perceived to be likely to vote, or because no other parties are competing for their support. In Canada and the United States, this had often been true of major parties and Indigenous peoples, although in Canada this may be changing.

At first glance, it may seem harder to understand why someone would engage in "everyday resistance" rather than other forms of contentious politics. Here we need to step back and think about what makes mobilization *possible*. In the case of resistance against totalitarian regimes like Nazi Germany, the answer is clear: A repressive state makes organizing too dangerous. But what about other circumstances?

Thinking about Contention: Summary

Scholars have a variety of views on how distinct these different types of contentious action are. Some decades ago, most of them were placed under the general category of **collective behaviour**.[49] Now we often try to treat them separately, although many social scientists continue to focus on common features of different types of collective action. For example, some scholars specialize in explaining social revolutions and others social movements, assuming that they are distinct phenomena with distinct causes. Some argue, though, that we can treat them as existing on a *continuum* of contentious action.[50] These phenomena—and their causes—can overlap. We divide them here—as ideal types—for the sake of clarity, but in reality the lines separating different forms of contention are not always so clear.[51] Moreover, an instance of collective action can change form, moving, say, from everyday resistance to social movement organizing to social revolution.

collective behaviour A paradigm for understanding various forms of contention, popular for part of the 20th century, which emphasized the irrational, social-psychological dynamics of protest.

Causes and Effects: Why Do Revolutions Happen?

There are a number of theories to explain contentious action. For the sake of clarity, we focus on explanations of *revolutions* specifically. It is worth noting, however, that each of the explanatory strategies have been applied (with differing levels of success) to many of the forms of contentious action discussed previously. As you go over these theories, think about how they might be modified and applied to other forms of conflict. Note that some theories try to explain why revolutions and other forms of contention are attempted and others try to explain why they are successful, a subtle but important difference.

Relative Deprivation

According to our first theory, relative deprivation can change people's psychology and increase the demand for social transformation. This family of theories attempts to explain revolutions as abnormal *deviations* from a normal status quo. The theory assumes that societies tend toward a kind of "equilibrium" in which conflict is normalized or settled through formal political channels. However, sometimes certain conditions—for example, rapid economic growth, efforts to reform the state, or the intervention of a foreign power—produce *disequilibrium* to which revolution serves as a response. This theory goes by different names (as it has been presented in different forms) such as **strain theory**,[52] "collective behaviour theory,"[53] and "social psychological theories."[54] Most theories of this kind specify a *social psychological* mechanism linking changes in the social order to the desire for rapid social transformation. People's lives are disrupted, this produces tension, and they resolve that tension through reconstructing society and its political institutions.

strain theory A theory suggesting that major social change causes social "strain" or conflict, which increases demand for revolution.

There are certain surprising things about many revolutions that "disequilibrium theory" can help to explain. Some major revolutions have taken place during or just after periods of economic *growth* or some other sort of improvement in the lives of one or another group.[55] We might intuitively expect groups that are *suffering* to be more inclined to revolutionary behaviour (and sometimes they are). However, this theory suggests that dramatic upward *and* downward mobility raise the possibility of revolutions because they upset established conventions and status relationships and open up the possibility of a potentially revolutionary group experiencing **relative deprivation**.[56]

relative deprivation The state of having or feeling that one has less than other members of one's reference group (including one's own group over time).

Resource Mobilization and Political Opportunities

Theories of relative deprivation focus on explaining *demand* for revolution. By contrast, "resource mobilization" theories assume frequent or even constant demand for social change, often treating it as a consequence of **absolute deprivation** rather than relative deprivation. Proponents of this theory argue that what matters in producing a revolution are **political opportunities** or events that allow potential revolutionaries to "mobilize resources."[57] The most important political opportunity for revolutions is **state breakdown**, when a state loses its ability to carry out its core functions and to stifle dissent.[58] Other political opportunities that might facilitate contentious action would include elite conflict, military or other coercive forces becoming discontented with the prevailing order, the opening of a political system, or the creation of new groups or communication technologies that facilitate organizing.[59]

absolute deprivation A condition of being deprived of resources below some given threshold, as distinguished from *relative* deprivation.

political opportunities The availability of political options to redress grievances.

state breakdown Dramatic decline in state capacity.

Another set of resources for would-be revolutionaries are pre-existing patterns of mobilization. For example, in a heavily industrialized society factory workers labour closely

CASE IN CONTEXT

461

The Russian Revolution

You may have already learned about the Russian Revolution of 1917, sometimes called the Bolshevik Revolution. This was one of the most consequential revolutions in history, in part because its success contributed to the polarization of global politics throughout much of the 20th century. The Russian Revolution is interesting, though, not just because of its consequences but because of how it stands in relation to revolutionary theory. It was a Marxist revolution that didn't strictly follow Marx's template, in particular because of innovations made by Russian Marxists, especially Vladimir Lenin. Among other things, Lenin emphasized that revolution was possible in Russia even though it had not experienced robust capitalist modernization and remained a primarily rural, peasant-based economy. He also emphasized that a small "vanguard" of organizers could lead a revolution, which some think contradicts Marx's idea that major structural forces, rather than leaders and groups, produce revolution (an idea with which Lenin did not entirely disagree).

To learn more about this process, see the case study in the Russian country profile in Part VI, p. 461. As you read it, keep in mind the following questions:

1. What were the major factors that increased the probability of revolution in Russia?
2. What is a "Leninist party," and how important were Lenin and the sort of organization he championed to the revolution's success? More generally, what does the Russian case tell us about how much individuals and leaders matter?
3. Could the Russian Revolution have produced a different outcome, or was Soviet authoritarianism inevitable given the conditions of Russian society at the time?

together and may have a history of mobilization via union organizing. In this instance, there is a pre-existing pattern of mobilization, as well as potential *organizational resources*, which can be put to new uses.

In an industrial setting, the relevant organizational resources would be the labour unions themselves. However, organizational resources can take many forms. What is key to all of them is that organizational resources allow some central coordination, which can be important in early mobilization: It is very difficult for any given leadership to remain in control of a revolutionary process for long. Along similar lines, social networks and media access are important resources facilitating contentious action.

Finally, political opportunity and resource mobilization theorists are interested in access to *material* resources. Revolutions, like any other collective behaviour, need to be financed, which means revolutionary actors need access to weapons, meeting places, and supplies for the combatants.

Rational Choice

The rational choice theory of revolutions says that to understand revolutions we need to understand the conditions under which it becomes rational for people to engage in collective action.[61] Proponents of the rational choice theory of contentious action, including revolution, sometimes present it as a complement to resource mobilization/political opportunity theory.[62] It shares the general assumption that conflict is endemic to society and that individuals rationally pursue their own interests. However, it pushes these assumptions much further.

CASE IN CONTEXT

382

The Chinese Revolution

In some ways, the Chinese Revolution emulated aspects of the Russian Revolution, as described in the previous case in context. Like the Russian Revolution, it was based on Marxism, and many of its leaders hoped to create a world of equality and social harmony. Some also trained for revolution in Moscow. However, it evidenced some major differences, perhaps the most important being the centrality of peasant participation (Marx thought that peasants were not revolutionary, but Mao Zedong felt that peasants were the most important revolutionary class in the Chinese context).

This revolution raises two key questions that interest us, and you can consider them further by looking at the case study in the China country profile in Part VI, p. 382. Those questions are the following:

1. When did the Chinese Revolution begin or end? Was the overthrow of the Qing Dynasty in 1911 and the establishment of the republic its own revolution or just a part of the broader revolution that led to the establishment of the (Communist) People's Republic of China in 1949?
2. Why did the communists, rather than their opponents, the "nationalists," triumph in the Chinese Revolution? Does this case show us that organizational resources and practices are key to successful revolutions?

Associated Press/Mark Schiefelbein

PHOTO 12.5 **A Chinese honour guard marches out beneath a large portrait of Chinese leader Mao Zedong at Tiananmen Square in Beijing.**

This approach focuses on individuals' rational analysis of costs and benefits for participation in contentious action. According to this theory, states hold together when they prevent individuals from making the choice to pursue dissenting interests through alternative organizations.[63] When states are successful in doing this, they hold together because the majority of individuals—even if they do not like the state or the regime that controls it—judge that it would not be in their own interests to engage in protest activity or revolution. Indeed, according to this theory, this is the state of affairs most of the time: It is seldom rational for the individual to join organized protest activity. This is so because it is extremely difficult to predict if your sacrifices for a cause will result in actual benefits for you as an individual. It is more likely as you rationally weigh the options, for example, that you might lose your part-time or full-time job and other things you have if you try to push too far for changes in your society.

INSIGHTS

States and Social Revolutions: A Comparative Analysis of France, Russia, and China

by Theda Skocpol

Skocpol's theory is a ***structuralist*** account of revolutions. This means that she aims to explain social revolutions by focusing on the behaviour of social structures (most importantly, states and social classes) rather than individuals and their beliefs, goals, and strategies. In concentrating on her three main cases of France, Russia, and China, Skocpol found two necessary conditions that, she argued, together *cause* social revolution. First, state collapse, provoked by foreign conflict, creates the possibility of revolt, dividing elites. Second, certain conditions facilitate revolt among the rural poor. According to this theory, if the potential for peasant mobilization accompanies "state breakdown," successful revolution will take place. Skocpol's emphasis on state breakdown was anticipated by scholars like Alexis de Tocqueville and Crane Brinton and has been carried forward by Jack Goldstone and others.

Critics of this theory worry that it is too mechanistic, that it leaves out human agency, and that it pays little attention to culture and ideology.[60] Others suggest that it only applies to a limited range of cases.

Theda Skocpol, *States and Social Revolutions: A Comparative Analysis of France, Russia, and China* (New York: Cambridge University Press, 1979).

For many people considering radical action to demand major changes to the existing system, the rational thing to do is to be a **free rider**: not join and hope that others do the job for you. This is how rational choice theory explains the relative strength of states and the weakness and infrequency of revolutions despite the fact that they believe conflict is endemic to society. Most people make the rational choice to *not* participate in revolutions most of the time, *often because* they have no conception of actually being in a revolution. This is an important point drawn out by Skocpol in her book. People don't participate in a revolution—they have much more local, immediate interests, which ultimately feed into a larger revolutionary movement.

free rider Someone who benefits from a collective or public good without contributing to it.

Efforts to explain revolution and related activities, from this point of view, should focus on conditions that alter the rational calculus of interest of potential revolutionaries, as illustrated in Table 12.1.

If a situation becomes so polarized that there will likely be costs brought to bear on individuals by *both* sides (the state and a revolutionary group), this increases the cost of abstention. If this is coupled with a perceived weakness of the state, it will likely increase

TABLE 12.1 | One Scenario in Which Many Actors May Judge It Rational to Join a Revolution

	Participate	Do Not Participate
Revolution Succeeds	Share in collective benefits but also receive personal favours and special access to resources because I am a "revolutionary"	Share in collective benefits but no personal favours or special access to resources
Revolution Fails	Low likelihood of personal costs because the state is weak and so many people are participating in the revolution	My group may be targeted for reprisal, so I may face personal costs even though I didn't participate. My family might also be punished.

the willingness of a number of individuals to join the revolution. Another example: If the revolution's success seems fairly likely, and its current participants can plausibly promise rewards to participants, this will also likely increase participation.

Cultural or "Framing" Explanations

Proponents of cultural or "framing" theories argue that previous theories like resource mobilization or political opportunity theory pay insufficient attention to variation in how social movement and revolutionary actors think about their participation and the *causal* impact of differences in how movements' and revolutions' targets are "framed."[64] Others argue that contention itself has changed, becoming more focused on cultural issues like "identity."[65] Many are interested in "new social movements" like global feminist movements or movements that mobilize around ethnic identities, a subject to which we turn in Chapter 14.[66]

framing The way in which a given problem or situation is described and understood, with implications for how it might be addressed.

The core idea of **framing** is that every type of social action takes place via "discourse" or "stories" that we tell about ourselves, our behaviour, and its context.[67] Participants in all kinds of social behaviour aim to construct narratives that make sense of their behaviour in the social environment. Your act of reading this textbook might be "framed" in relation to a basic narrative about how you are a student enrolled in a university. Your long-term horizon probably includes advanced study and a career. Your act of reading is likely framed in relation to your role. As a student, you want or are expected to *learn*, and your act of reading the text is understood in this light. Note that these "frames" are more or less *collective* in character. In other words, you can reject them privately if you want to, but it is very difficult to do so publicly—say, by standing up in class and telling your instructor that you don't *want* to learn—without facing consequences.

Where do frames come from? Some theorists argue that they are part of *culture*. Different communities, practices, and walks of life exhibit shifting "frames" through which social problems and appropriate responses are constantly interpreted. The idea is the same, however: Contentious action like revolution can only take place when participants have a frame for conceiving of it and talking about it. In many, if not most, modern social revolutions this language is provided by nationalism.[68] Some scholars have even argued that the very idea of revolution (sometimes called "revolutionism") is itself a prerequisite for revolutionary activity.[69] From this point of view, revolution cannot take place simply whenever there is inequality, anger, and frustration. Rather, revolution is only possible when the *idea* of revolution already exists as a model for addressing that discontent. Scholars increasingly emphasize that ideas about *how* to protest play an important role in contention.[70] Others stress the enduring influence of *ideologies*, a subject to which we turn in Chapter 15.[71] One relatively recent theory of revolutions in the developing world, along somewhat similar lines, stresses the importance of "political cultures of opposition."[72]

As you approach the close of this chapter, you now know that scholars have a range of ways in which they conceptualize and explain contention and that they do not all agree. In general, though, theories might lead us to expect that several conditions would increase the likelihood of successful contention:

1. Some pre-existing grievances felt by one or more groups.
2. A weakening in the institutions that repress collective dissent, yet without sufficient political opening such that disputes can be resolved via formal political institutions.
3. The emergence of new methods or means of organizing and communication, whether they be technological (newspapers, social networking sites, enhanced transportation) or of some other form (semi-spontaneous organizing like the Montgomery Bus Boycott), or else new access to such means and methods.

4. Sufficient organizing success such that actors perceive some reasonable chance of further success.
5. The emergence of ways of talking and writing about underlying social problems that points toward contention rather than quiescence as the solution.
6. Organizational leadership that maintains the unity of contentious organizing rather than fracturing contention.

As you know, different theories place greater and lesser emphasis on each of these factors, and common sense tells us that they all matter. Drawing on the methods discussed throughout this book so far, think about how we might advance research from this point, determining with greater precision the relative weight of each of these factors and the precise ways in which they interact to produce successful organizing or revolt.

THINKING COMPARATIVELY

The "Arab Spring" of 2011

KEY METHODOLOGICAL TOOL

Deviant or Negative Cases

A "deviant case" is a case that has a notably different outcome from what one or another theory might predict. Such observations, also called "negative cases," are useful not because they necessarily invalidate a given theory but because they allow us to gain more leverage as we attempt to test hypotheses. Often, they do so by producing anomalous results that require a rethinking of the original theories. In this section, be attentive to the way in which the "negative case" of Saudi Arabia could cause a scholar to reconsider existing theory.

Beginning in spring 2011, many authoritarian governments in North Africa and the Middle East witnessed tremendous waves of contention. The protests began in Tunisia and spread quickly to many countries, with the most immediate consequence in Egypt, where hundreds of thousands of people crowded into Tahrir Square to demand change.

This truly momentous development encouraged further protests in other parts of the Arab world. Major protest action began in, among other places, Yemen, Libya, and then Syria. In the Libyan case, the dictator Muammar al-Qadhafi was quite willing to use massive force to repress protesters. Chillingly, authoritarian dictators seem to have learned the lesson that repression is the way to preserve power. NATO intervened militarily in Libya, ostensibly to protect civilians but ultimately to provide material assistance to rebels who eventually dislodged the Qadhafi regime. The outcomes in other cases have been mixed. The memory of the Arab Spring still inspires hope in many, but it did not democratize the region. So far, outcomes run the gamut from Tunisia's seemingly successful initial transition to democracy to pronounced state weakness in Libya, considerable repression in Egypt, and major gains for terrorist groups in Syria, not to mention great loss of life and massive displacement of people from their homes.

What should a theory of contention be able to explain about these events? We would want to include the following: (1) Why did this wave of contention emerge? (2) Why were the proponents of regime change successful in Tunisia and Egypt but not in Syria and only with NATO support in Libya? and, finally, (3) Why has no significant contention been seen in Saudi Arabia, where a number of similar conditions can be found? In other words, any theory of what caused the revolts in Tunisia, Egypt, and elsewhere should be able to account for Saudi Arabia as a "negative case" in which at least some of the key factors in the other cases are present but in which the outcome is sharply different. These are not the only interesting questions one can ask about the Arab Spring revolts and their aftermath, but here we focus on them, largely restricting our discussion to the events of 2011.

To work toward establishing hypotheses, let us first think about what our theories would predict, and then we will briefly consider some of the common and varying conditions present in our cases. See Table 12.2.

As you can see from this table, not all of the hypotheses generated from these theories are mutually exclusive. Indeed, you can probably see ways in which they could be combined. This does not mean that the underlying theories are fully compatible: certain general theoretical issues cannot be glossed over. For example, some versions of rational choice theory state that demand for revolution is constant, while relative deprivation theory says it varies. Nonetheless, we can draw on different theories as we attempt to explain the complexities of a series of cases.

A number of factors may have contributed to the emergence of the Arab Spring. Many commentators have noted that demographic pressures produced discontent. These are societies with a comparatively high number of young adults and few economic opportunities for them. Another clear factor is the sense of frustration that many in the Arab world feel with their countries' non-democratic status, particularly when judged against a world in which democracy has seemed ascendant for some decades. Others point to social media, arguing that Twitter and Facebook helped protesters to solve collective action problems, noting that some of the regimes have tried to restrict access to information technology.

What conditions were common in these societies before the wave began? Islam is the majority religion in all of them. Each began the sequence as an autocracy and, indeed, with a long history of authoritarianism. Each has relatively high poverty (though this varies in extent from case to case, as we shall see). Yet there are important variations along these dimensions. Note that the two cases where contentious action was most successful—Egypt and Tunisia—are not major oil exporters (Table 12.3).

This might suggest that *being* an oil exporter potentially thwarts this sort of contention, perhaps because oil export provides resources for the state to maintain legitimacy or even to repress opponents. Yet the lack of major government oil revenues is not a *sufficient* condition for successful contention, given that Syria also is not a major oil exporter and its regime has, despite serious opposition, held onto power. To some extent, though, this is a matter of scale. In relative terms, the Syrian government, at least in years prior to the conflict, derived considerable resources from oil exports.

Another point of variation concerns the relationship between religion and politics. While, as noted earlier, they are all majority-Muslim countries, there are important differences in this regard. Perhaps the sharpest contrast here can be found between Egypt and Saudi Arabia. Saudi Arabia is essentially a theocracy (though Islam in Saudi Arabia is Sunni Islam, meaning the clergy do not hold formal power, which is held by the royal family). The regime's legitimacy is maintained both by religious arguments and by the lavish

TABLE 12.2 | Contention: Theories, Hypotheses, and Evidence

Theory	Moving toward Hypothesis *What does the theory predict causes contention?*	Possible Instance *What would a case look like if it followed the theory?*
Relative Deprivation	Increased discontent due to declining status of key groups	Demographic and economic trends mean poor job prospects for young adults, who mobilize against regimes they see as barriers to advancement.
Political Opportunities/ Resource Mobilization	Political opening (from democratic reforms *or* fiscal weakening of the state) Pre-existing mobilization capacity among key groups	Low willingness/capacity to repress protests leads to more successful contention. More and larger pre-existing political groups leads to more contention.
Rational Choice Theory	Changes in the strategic situations faced by key actors	Lack of repression of early protests changes actors' views on risks of contention. Weak state responses make victory seem more likely, producing cascade of participation.
Cultural or "Framing" Theory	Changing ideas or cultural change before or during the process	Contention emerges and strengthens as the very idea spreads that radical change is needed (e.g., the "Arab Spring" idea).

TABLE 12.3 | Total Petroleum and Other Liquids Production, 2016 (in thousands per day)

Tunisia	52
Egypt	691
Libya	418
Syria	34
Saudi Arabia	12,387
Iran	4215

Source: US Energy Information Administration, http://www.eia.gov/countries/index.cfm

spending of oil revenues. Egypt has a long history of Islamic militancy, but for decades it was dominated by secular nationalists who attempted to marginalize political Islam. Framing theories of revolution might note that this could advantage the proponents of contentious action, since religious modes of dissent could likely be more readily used as a wedge in a society like Egypt than in Saudi Arabia. Of course, this can also produce problems for revolutionaries. The Arab Spring led the Muslim Brotherhood to power, but their overreach prompted resistance and their eventual fall, and some critics of the current regime suggest that Egypt has returned to "Mubarak-lite"-style governance.

Another issue is the degree of poverty faced by these countries. If the relative deprivation theory is right, we would expect to find one or another group experiencing economically generated discontent. While these issues are complicated, for the sake of simplicity here we will just look at per capita income (Table 12.4). Again for the sake of simplicity, we will take these data to indicate that Tunisia, Egypt, and Syria are likely to have a high degree of economically induced discontent, Libya a moderate degree, and Saudi Arabia a low degree.[73] Finally, if we examine the sequence of contention in these societies, we see an important difference in the *process* of contention. In four of the five cases (Egypt, Tunisia, Syria, and Libya), strong contentious action developed, but in two of them (Egypt and Tunisia) the military was unwilling to fully repress the regime's opponents in the early stages of collective action (Table 12.5). This suggests that the military and its linkage to the existing regime—which we can take to be a function of state capacity—are critical to outcomes. Focusing on general judgments of just these variables, we can summarize the cases as shown in Table 12.5.

If we take our negative case—Saudi Arabia—out of the comparison, a hypothesis suggests itself: Successful collective action appears to be a function of the state's failure to repress. Other features are held constant, with the exception of the fact that Libya is an oil exporter, which is perhaps relevant only insofar as it *facilitates* the state's repressive capacity. In other words, factors like economic discontent and the

TABLE 12.4 | 2016 Per Capita Income in Selected Countries (in US dollars)

Country	GDP Per Capita (USD)
Tunisia	3689
Egypt	3515
Libya	5602.55 (2011)
Syria	Not available
Saudi Arabia	20,029

Source: https://data.worldbank.org/indicator/NY.GDP.PCAP.CD?end=2016&start=2016&view=map

TABLE 12.5 | Contention in the "Arab Spring": Five Cases

	Major oil exporter?	Theocratic regime?	Economically generated discontent?	State/military willing to repress protest?
Tunisia	N	N	Y (high)	N
Egypt	N	N	Y (high)	N
Libya	Y	N	Y (moderate)	Y
Syria	N*	N	Y (high)	Y (so far, to the extent possible)
Saudi Arabia	Y	Y	N	Y (presumably)

* As stated in the text, the Syrian state has in recent years derived considerable revenues from oil export, even though the country's share in the total international oil market is small.

religious versus secular character of the regime appear to be constants and thus causally unimportant. This is broadly consistent with our "political opportunity theory" discussed previously. However, when we bring Saudi Arabia into the comparison, this no longer appears to be the case. Rather, Saudi Arabia, where no major contention has emerged, varies from the other cases in two respects: (1) it is a religious regime, and (2) it does not seem to have witnessed dramatic, economically generated discontent. In other words, the inclusion of this case makes these factors relevant, which is critical to the hypotheses suggested by framing and relative deprivation approaches. Note that it does not *demonstrate* their causal force, however.

The purpose of this exercise is to get you thinking about how to make comparisons and not to fully explain variation in the "Arab Spring" once and for all. Indeed, this task will likely take years, both because we need to see how these processes play out and because scholarship in political science often depends on many efforts by many scholars to generate and test hypotheses. What you can see here, however, is one way in which we may begin to proceed if we wish to make sense of emergent patterns in the "Arab Spring." Note how much case selection matters. What would we conclude if Saudi Arabia weren't included? Can you think of other cases that might change our conclusions if we included them? Or cases that point to causal factors that we have not considered here?

Chapter Summary

Concepts

- Comparative political analysts are interested in how and why conflict sometimes takes place outside of formal institutions.
- There are a number of forms that such conflict takes. We were especially attentive to the differences between revolutionary and non-revolutionary strategies to create change.

Types

- Social movements are probably the most common form of organized conflict in advanced industrial democracies. Social movements are commonly regarded as organized collective action in the pursuit of social reforms of one or another kind.
- Revolutions are perhaps less common in advanced industrial societies but quite common in modern societies more generally. Revolutions are usually thought of as producing dramatic change rather than mere reforms.
- *Social* revolutions change structures like the class system.
- Political revolutions change the state.
- Anti-colonial revolutions create newly independent states after removing colonial powers.
- Indigenous peoples in Western settler states may engage in contentious politics when their rights are continually repressed within a settler-dominated democratic system.

- Insurgencies shade into revolutions. We can distinguish them by the degree to which insurgencies take protracted military form, often in the absence of large-scale civilian mobilization.
- Terrorism can be studied as a tactic employed by participants in social movements, revolutions, and insurgencies or as a particular form for the organization of resistance. In the latter case, much attention is placed on "terror networks."
- "Everyday resistance" is the name scholars give to the ways that groups resist and express discontent in the absence of the resources needed for complex organization and coordination.

Causes and Effects

- There are at least four general types of theories of revolution, and these theories can, with some modification, be applied to other forms of contention.
- Theories of "relative deprivation" and "social disequilibrium" try to explain revolutions through focusing on an increase in the *demand* for revolutions. They look at the impact of modernization on existing political institutions and social hierarchies and suggest that when modernization affects these hierarchies, social equilibrium is broken and important groups seek to produce a new equilibrium through revolution.
- Theories of political opportunities and mobilization try to explain revolutions through focusing on *supply* of mobilization opportunities rather than demand for revolution. They suggest that new political opportunities, such as state collapse and the presence of useful ways of organizing dissent, matter most.
- Collective action theories argue that collective action problems are the main barrier to revolution. When revolutions do take place, the best way to explain them is to show how collective action problems were solved.
- Framing or cultural theory says that other theories must be supplemented by a focus on ideology or culture. Material conditions are not enough to produce revolutions. Rather, people need to have ideas that "frame" their grievances in a way that suggests that revolution is the legitimate solution.

Thinking Comparatively

- The "Arab Spring" of 2011 presents a set of interesting and useful cases for these theories.

Thinking It Through

1. This chapter ended with a brief discussion of the "Arab Spring." Based on the theories and concepts discussed here, why do you think some of the protests there were successful and others unsuccessful? What do these cases tell us about contention in general?
2. Did Idle No More have the basic ingredients for a social revolution? What forms of contention has the movement used, and how widespread is its support base?
3. In today's world, some groups claim to be making revolutions *through* democratic elections. In your view, is this possible? How would this change our definition of revolutions? Does it make sense to broaden our concept so as to include such cases? Why or why not?
4. All of the major forms of contention discussed in this chapter are hard to control and to lead. They often lead to unintended consequences and escape the grasp of those who began them. *Which* types of contention would be most difficult to lead, and why? Which ones might be a bit easier to lead, and why?
5. In this chapter, we considered numerous forms of contention, and then we focused on explanations of revolution. These explanations could potentially be applied to some of the other forms of contention as well. For which forms of contention do you think these explanations would be most successful? And for which do you think they would face the greatest difficulties? Why?

13 Nationalism and National Identity

In This Chapter

Syrian refugees near the Jordanian border, close to the town of Nasib, Syria, in 2017. (MOHAMAD ABAZEED/AFP/Getty Images)

The 20th century witnessed some of the greatest mass atrocities in human history, from the Nazi Holocaust to the deaths of millions through violence, starvation, and famine in China, Cambodia, the Soviet Union, India, Vietnam, and Bangladesh, among many other places. Earlier centuries, marked by slavery, colonialism, massacre, and other crimes were not much better, although there was little attention devoted to these horrors, partially because there were no mass media as we know them today. Canadians are also now aware that Indigenous peoples experienced cultural genocide through the Indian Residential Schools and the deliberate use of starvation tactics to "clear the plains" of Indigenous peoples in western Canada. Some have argued that government policies were genocide, not just cultural genocide. As historical scholarship advances, we are learning that no state has been free of originary violence—that is, the violence involved in creating modern territorial states on the homelands of other people.

After 1945, as a response to the horrific events in Nazi Germany in particular, the international community declared that it would never again allow **genocide**, the targeted and intentional destruction of people of a particular racial, ethnic, or national group. Although such destruction has continued around the world in subsequent decades, it was only in the late 1990s that much of the public realized that genocide had not been eradicated (though some observers were aware that it had never really disappeared). The genocides in both Rwanda (1994) and the former Yugoslavia (1995) were well documented, but the international responses to these crises diverged sharply. In the African case, the international community did very little, and peacekeepers stood by as the killing occurred because their mandate did not authorize genocide prevention. In the European case, NATO mounted a joint military effort, bombing Serbian forces, which brought an end to formal hostilities. In both cases, criminal tribunals were established to bring leaders to trial for genocide and crimes against humanity.

genocide Efforts to diminish or destroy a people and/or culture, prohibited by the United Nations Convention on the Prevention of Genocide (1948).

In the 21st century, genocide has continued, most notably in Sudan, and the international community has largely remained divided and confused about how to proceed. Other humanitarian disasters include the Rohingya Crisis in Myanmar and Bangladesh, the civil war in Yemen, and continued conflict in Syria, Afghanistan, and the Democratic Republic of Congo. To some extent, the lack of coherent international response may be due to a lack of sufficient will. But it may also be due to a failure to truly understand violence linked to political identities. If this is true, policy-makers may need to begin by understanding the nature and causes of national and ethno-national identities more generally. Comparative analysis of political identities and nationalism aims to help us better understand these issues. Why do some groups engage in violence against others? Is it mostly related to the identities themselves or to circumstances such as economic development or political institutions?

• • •

Concepts

We must begin by clarifying the meaning of the concepts of "identity," "the nation," and "nationalism."

Identity

What *is* **identity**? Probably the best way to begin thinking about it is at the level of the individual. At the most basic level, your identity is your sense of self. You have a sense of who you are and of what makes you special and unique. You also participate in attributing

identity The social label ascribed to an individual or group that locates the individual or group in political society more broadly.

identities to others, and you may be part of a community that helps you to understand your identity, group identity, and the identities of those outside of the community.

social identity theory An important theory in social psychology that sees personal identities as linked to and partially derived from group identities and roles.

As **social identity theory** argues, even our own personal identities are constructed on the basis of social sources, and the ongoing acts of having an identity and labelling others are social.[1] Every day, we construct symbolic representations of the social world in which we live and our place in it. Thus our personal identities—our senses of ourselves as individuals—are drawn from roles linked to role and group identities (e.g., student or professor, Indigenous or settler, Brazilian or Canadian, woman, man, or other, brother or sister) that our society makes available to us.

The identities that matter most in politics are group identities. Group identities can involve drawing boundaries between in-groups and out-groups, although the *ways* in which such boundaries are constructed may vary a great deal. For example, sometimes group identities are very sharply bounded, and individuals are not allowed to pass from one group to another.[2] In other situations, group boundaries are permeable, and one can choose whether or not to belong to the group in question. Likewise, certain sorts of identities are compatible, such as being simultaneously Spanish and Catholic, whereas others are likely to be perceived by some people as incompatible. This pertains for many racialized people in Western settler states being subjected to the question "but where are you *really* from?" It should be noted here that many Indigenous peoples have practised forms of more inclusive group identity in which kinship and interrelations between different groups are privileged.

Identities are *cultural*, *historical*, and *political*. This means that they are created by human societies and expressed symbolically, that they change over time, and that they influence and are influenced by the ways that *power* is distributed in society. We should

iStock.com/fstop123

PHOTO 13.2 Social identity theory argues that we construct symbolic representations every day of the social world in which we live and our place in that world. Our personal identities are drawn from roles linked to role and group identities that our society makes available to us.

therefore be attentive to *how* they are constructed by different individuals and groups, how their forms change over time, and how different individuals and groups, with varying access to resources, struggle to identify themselves and one another for their own purposes. In short, identities are the social labels ascribed to individuals or groups, locating the individual or group in political society more broadly.

Nationalism and the Nation

In this chapter, we focus on what might be the most important form of political identity in today's world, **national identity**. As suggested at the beginning of this chapter, for some the idea of **nationalism** conjures up images of stringent restrictions on immigration, of discriminatory behaviour, and even of genocide. And yet while nationalism and national identity can be and sometimes are linked to exclusion and violence, this is not the whole story.[3] They are also linked in some cases to inclusive citizenship and democracy. Indeed, modern democracy would not have emerged without nationalism and often exclusionary nationalism at that. In general, we could start by defining nationalism as the idea that nations exist and constitute the basic units of social and political life. **Nations**, in turn, are often defined as relatively large groups that think of themselves as *equal* and *sovereign*.[4] In other words, in modern politics, nations are thought of as the source of the state's legitimate authority. This is why all modern governments, even authoritarian ones, claim to speak on behalf of the "people" or "nation." To reiterate, nationalism is the view that we all have a national identity and that this identity is important. National identity says that we are members of nations and that these nations are sovereign and equal.

national identity An identity that locates one's social position in relation to national membership.

nationalism The view that the world is and should be divided into nations that are thought of by nationalists as sovereign and egalitarian.

nation A group thought of as sovereign and equal, typically comprised of a large, often geographically bounded population.

Types

The Academic Study of Nationalism[5]

The study of nations and nationalism is commonly divided among three schools: the primordialists, the modernists and perennialists, and the ethno-symbolists.

Primordialists see the nation as a natural phenomenon, a normal and understandable aspect of human relationships. In the 1950s and 1960s, the sociologists Clifford Geertz and Edward Shils emphasized the power of "primordial attachment" to the nation as a community with unique characteristics that must be preserved.[6]

By contrast, the *modernists* see the nation as an invented or constructed form of social organization. They argue that nations are often created by elites who seek to gain power within a state and use nationalism as a tool to control and manipulate the masses. According to this view, the idea of nationalism was a product of the Industrial Revolution when rural people began leaving their homes to seek work in the growing cities. Modernists such as Ernest Gellner argue that, having left their village identities, local dialects, and cultural traditions behind, these people had a deep need for a new identity that could be shared with people very different from themselves. Nationalism became a way of bringing disparate peoples together under the umbrella of an overarching "high culture" that had some similarities with traditional folk cultures but was also substantially different. The dislocation of urban spaces, the loss of former identity, and a sense of vulnerability all helped to make the national symbols and narratives promoted by the elites attractive.[7]

The precise content of national narratives is relatively unimportant. Gellner famously argued that "[t]he cultural shreds and patches used by nationalism are often arbitrary historical inventions. Any old shred and patch would have served as well."[8] Other well-known

PHOTO 13.3 Women making matches in London's East End in 1871. The Industrial Revolution caused the movement of rural people into cities to earn wages working in factories. Modernists see nationalism as a product of this movement because these people left their identities and traditions behind, which caused them to develop a new identity shared with others who were different from them.

modernists include Paul Brass, Benedict Anderson (who coined the term *imagined communities* to describe nations), and Tom Nairn, who developed an economic modernist model based on Marxism.[9]

A related group called the *perennialists* shares the modernists' opinion that nations are constructed but do not necessarily associate their origins with the Industrial Revolution. Liah Greenfeld asserts that nations in some cases were developed before industrialization. In England she traces the birth of the nation to the creation of the Church of England under King Henry VIII. Later nations developed in preindustrial rural Germany in the early 19th century and agrarian Russia in the 18th and 19th centuries. In these cases, other forms of association, such as religion and kingship, helped to bind individuals together as coherent "peoples."[10]

The third group of nationalism theorists is the *ethno-symbolists*, who argue that nations are constructed and invented but not necessarily by elites. According to Anthony D. Smith, many nations are based on pre-existing ethnic groups with their own sense of identity and their own history. Arguably, Smith's main contribution to the discipline of nationalism studies is his privileging of what he called *ethnies*: "named human populations with shared ancestry myths, histories and cultures, having an association with specific territory, and a sense of solidarity."[11] Not all ethnies become nations, but most nations are derived from ethnies, particularly "ethnic cores" that have the characteristics required to absorb and assimilate other ethnies and make them part of an emerging nation. Unlike the nation it may later become, a core ethnie needs to selectively borrow new elements from foreign groups through "controlled culture contact."[12] As the ethnic core expands and absorbs other ethnies, it incorporates their elements within its growing ethnic (and ultimately proto-national) culture.

In time, the ethnic core forms a coherent nation, with a national homeland, a unified economy, and unified myths and symbols.[13] For Smith, local history and identity are crucial elements in the construction of national myth. The communal past of a nation forms a "repository or quarry from which materials may be selected in the construction and invention of nations."[14]

Structuralism versus Constructivism

Modernists comprise a large share of scholars studying nationalism and national identity, and members of this large group disagree about many things. One major point of disagreement separates those who are more "structuralist" from those who are more "constructivist." The basic difference between these two approaches is not too difficult to understand, though there is a large debate in social science about what these terms mean. **Structuralists** see big, difficult-to-change parts of society—such as major features of the economy—as determining what really matters about national identity. **Constructivists** emphasize that nations are symbolic constructs and so place greater emphasis on the creative efforts of individuals and groups to define and redefine their identities.

structuralism An approach to nationalism studies that sees big, difficult-to-change parts of society as determining what really matters about national identity.

constructivism In nationalism studies, the view that nations are symbolic constructs and so places greater emphasis on the creative efforts of individuals and groups to define and redefine their identities.

An example of a structuralist theory is Gellner's linking of industrialization to national identity.[15] Gellner argued that national identity and nationalism are useful (or "functional") for industrializing societies because they promote social mobility, shared language, and common understandings. For Gellner, capitalism requires a homogeneous, interchangeable, socially and geographically mobile workforce as well as standardized language. Gellner posits that these needs lead to nationalism because nationalism encourages the social characteristics that capitalism requires. Nationalism takes a language of "the people" and gives it high status. The national state standardizes its usage through official documents, the education system, and so forth. Likewise, nationalism says that everybody in the nation is fundamentally equal, which breaks down hierarchical ties and gives rise to the interchangeability of modern workers.

An example of a constructivist theory is Greenfeld's argument that national identity is an imaginative response to contradictory public claims about a group's status.[16] She emphasizes social psychology, rather than economics, in analyzing the processes through which national identity emerges and thrives. To understand nationalism's emergence and growth, we must understand why the idea spread that humanity is divided into distinct "peoples" who are "sovereign" and "equal." For Greenfeld, the key preconditions for the development of national identity are problems in stratification systems through which societies hierarchically divide themselves, such as the class structure. Elite status-inconsistency—a condition present when the stratification system breaks down and elites are no longer sure of their status—leads some groups to seek to transform identity, and national identity often seems to such groups to serve their interests well.

These theories reveal just how different such structuralist and constructivist approaches can be but simultaneously reveal points of similarity. For example, the group status-inconsistency that Greenfeld emphasizes may often be due to "structural" changes in society such as shifting ways of organizing social and economic class or innovations in the ways that states recruit their staff. In other words, the fact that such a theory emphasizes social psychology and symbolic construction does not mean that it ignores structural characteristics of society.

Types of Nationalism

As we discussed in Chapter 1, political scientists can move up and down Sartori's ladder of abstraction in searching for more or less general conceptualizations of nationalism. At the level of greatest generality, scholars might look at the psychological preconditions of collective identity itself. A primordialist perspective might be useful in this case. At the same time, only modernist conceptualizations might offer sufficient specificity for asking questions about modern nationalism's *emergence*, since they are most able to draw clear qualitative distinctions between national identity and other identities out of which it might grow or that might otherwise resemble it in certain respects.

In order to ask and answer more specific comparative questions about national identity and other variables, however, one needs still more specific conceptualizations. These typically take the form of *typologies* of nationalism. Most commonly, typologies posit a choice between two main forms of national identity (see Table 13.1). We know these distinctions as **civic nationalism** and **ethnic nationalism**.[17] Civic nationalism is seen to be compatible with tolerance, liberal-democratic political institutions, and so forth because full citizenship and thus membership in the nation can theoretically be extended to anyone living within the state. Ethnic ones, however, like those of Germany or Russia, were based on the collective notion of the "volk," tended toward xenophobia, and were perhaps inhospitable to liberal-democratic institutions.[18]

civic nationalism A form of nationalism that says that you are a member of the nation if you are a citizen of its state.

ethnic nationalism A form of nationalism that says that you are a member of the nation because of your ancestry.

While different scholars parse these concepts in slightly different ways, the main issue here is a distinction between those societies that treat citizenship as technically open and as not based on ethnicity, and in turn take citizenship as the marker of national membership, and those that either have closed conceptions of citizenship (citizenship is and should be, according to such nationalisms, a biological inheritance) or that do not treat formal citizenship as a true marker of national belonging.

Sometimes this basic binary distinction takes on a slightly different form, such as in the distinction between "territorial" and "ethnic" nationalisms, though there is considerable overlap here with the civic–ethnic distinction.[19] **Territorial nationalism** is meant to refer to nationalism in which membership corresponds to residency in a territory and civic nationalism to citizenship in a state, but in the modern world these concepts are closely related.

territorial nationalism According to some scholars, a type of nationalism that closely resembles civic nationalism in that membership is fundamentally determined by where one is born or where one resides rather than by one's ancestry.

Greenfeld adds a further element to this civic and ethnic typological scheme, arguing that while ethnic nationalisms are always "collectivistic," civic ones can be either collectivistic or individualistic (for examples, see Table 13.2). This distinction can be rather difficult to understand.[20] The model of individualistic nationalism holds that nations are associations of individual persons. This suggests that, whatever the reality of the political community and the processes through which it is formed and maintained, it is conceived of by its members as voluntary or associative. Collectivistic nationalism, in contrast, sees the nation as

TABLE 13.1 | Traditional Typology of Nationalism

"Civic" or "Territorial" Nationalisms	"Ethnic" Nationalisms
France	Germany
United Kingdom	Russia
Canada	Central and Eastern Europe
Australia	

TABLE 13.2 | Greenfeld's Expanded Typology of Nationalism

CASE EXAMPLES

	Civic	**Ethnic**
Individualistic	United States United Kingdom	N/A
Collectivistic	France	Germany Japan Russia

having a kind of collective agency or will that transcends the agency or wills of individual members. According to Greenfeld, collectivistic nationalism increases the likelihood of authoritarianism.

Some critics allege that all such typologies are problematic because they appear to be linked to value judgments about different societies.[21] This concern deserves serious consideration. Typologies from political science exist to help us better analyze politics, but they may have other effects. If our categories too neatly sort the world in ways that make some actors appear to be more (or less) virtuous than others, we run the risk of creating damaging stereotypes.

Indeed, if the strongest claims made by proponents of typologies of nationalism and national identity are true—if there are differences between civic and ethnic nationalisms that have implications for both domestic and international conflict—it would be hard for many social scientists, *as citizens*, to avoid making value judgments about them. But this critique should be a helpful reminder to us that *as social scientists* we should remain careful to avoid the projection of our own values onto the cases we study. Typologies of nationalism remain important in the literature, but they are controversial, in part because all nations have an ethnic component, even and sometimes especially those that claim a civic identity.

Canada, Australia, the United States, Great Britain, and France are all seen in the literature as civic nations. Yet each of these states has practised forms of immigration restriction and segregation based on race, language, religion, and culture. Problems of structural racism persist in all of these civic nations, including such issues as discrimination in housing, employment, access to health care, and the judicial system. On a smaller scale, Quebec nationalism has long been associated with the descendants of the original French Catholic families who settled on Indigenous lands in the early 1600s. Quebec nationalism began very much based on ethnicity, religion, language, and common cultural elements. From the 1960s, it became more secular, and many in favour of separatism argue that the Quebec nation is defined by anyone who lives in Quebec, with a key characteristic of the nation being the ability to speak French. Yet the ethnic aspects of the nation appear when it comes to skin colour (particularly non-white) and religion (particularly Islam but historically Judaism as well). As discussed in the Canada Country Profile, the proposed Quebec Charter of Values was one such example of defining the nation in ethnic and religious terms. In 2018, the right-of-centre Coalition Avenir Québec won the provincial elections and formed the government. They introduced Bill 21, which would secularize the public service by prohibiting public employees (doctors, teachers, judges, etc.) from wearing symbols of their faith, including the Sikh turban, Muslim hijab, Jewish kippa, and the Christian crucifix.

In the current era of populist nationalism in Europe, North America, and around the world, civic states are demonstrating strongly ethnic characteristics, defining "us" and "them" on religious and ethnic terms. While anti-Semitism and racism against Asians, Africans, and others were common throughout much of the 19th and 20th centuries, civic nationalisms since at least the 9/11 terrorist attacks in 2001 have identified Muslims and immigrants and refugees from Muslim countries as being dangerous to the civic health of the nation. This too is a form of racism. With the rise of Donald Trump and the alt-right in the US, racism against African Americans and Latinos has also increased.

Causes and Effects: What Causes Ethno-National Conflict?

instrumentalism A type of explanation in social science that says that you can explain something by showing how its development or persistence is in the (usually material) interest of powerful individuals or groups.

Much of the recent interest in nationalism and related forms of political identity—as noted previously—concerns the widespread perception that national and ethnic conflict and violence have increased since the end of the Cold War. Recent research has shown, however, that the growth of such violence began decades earlier and that what appeared to be a spurt of such violence in the 1990s was a continuation of a long-run trend.[22] Moreover, most ethnically heterogeneous regions see very little intergroup violence.[23] Nevertheless, given the extent and seriousness of such violence—and the hope that policy based upon social-scientific knowledge can help us to reduce it—this is a particularly important area of research on political identities. There is relatively little theoretical consensus about how to explain ethno-national violence and indeed what *ethnic* violence is.[24] We need to clearly conceptualize both "ethnicity" and "violence" (and, of course, to remember that not all conflict is violent).[25]

To begin studying such ethno-national conflict, the comparative political analyst must answer several questions. First, what makes a conflict national or "ethno-national"? Related to this, does a conflict being "national" or "ethno-national" matter? In other words, can we understand a conflict better, or predict its likely course more effectively, if we know that it is linked to nationalism? Second, what type of conflict do we seek to explain? Third, what is the appropriate level of analysis to address the questions asked—for example, should our cases be distinct societies, localities, examples of group behaviour, specific events, and so forth?

As for the first question, scholars take a variety of views. Some have suggested that there are multiple types of ethno-national identity and that focusing on these different types might help us to account for variation in probabilities of violence.[26] A primordialist view of ethno-national identity, in contrast, might assume unchanging, irrational attachments to a given group. In addition, there are perspectives designated as constructivist (closely consistent with the "constructivist" view of nationalism discussed earlier) and as **instrumentalist**, meaning that the analyst assumes little significant affective attachment to the group but rather sees ethnicity as a product of political entrepreneurs seeking to manipulate populations in the pursuit of their own strategic ends. Finally, a number of scholars treat ethno-national identity as synonymous with "communal groups" more broadly for their research purposes.[27] For such analysts, it matters little whether a given group defines its boundaries in

JERRY LAMPEN/AFP/Getty Images

PHOTO 13.4 Late Yugoslav president Slobodan Milošević on trial for war crimes in Kosovo, at the UN War Crimes Tribunal in 2001. When the tribunal indicted Milošević in 1999, he was the first sitting head of state to be charged with war crimes by an international tribunal.

ethnic, racial, religious, or any other sorts of terms as long as the observable dynamics of conflict are the same.

Regarding the second question, about what type of conflict we seek to explain, some scholars have argued for a "disaggregation" of the concept of violence.[28] That is, there is more than one type of violence in need of explanation, and different kinds of violence might have different causes. The most fundamental distinction, perhaps, is between violence carried out by or via the state and violence that takes place between social actors independent of the state. Think of the difference between state-led efforts at genocide and, say, less centrally organized conflict between Hindus and Muslims in India. There are good reasons to suppose that the social and political conditions that underlie state-led genocide do not fully explain sectarian conflict outside the state, though they do have much in common. Much literature implicitly focuses on the former type, perhaps because state-led genocidal efforts have been so lethal and because they at least give the *appearance* of being preventable. However, genocide and other forms of intergroup violence, like periodic riots, can be analytically distinguished and likely require different explanatory approaches.[29]

Others note, importantly, that analysts must be attentive to *who* the parties to conflict are, since the "who" has great implications for the "why."[30] Lying behind such typologies are the analytical imperatives to (1) identify the major groups involved; (2) analyze their relative size and resources; (3) consider their relationship to the state and the society's stratification system; (4) take into account how they "frame" their own identities and those of other groups; and (5) understand the historical context of their relationships, given that these relationships influence both how their identities and the potential for conflict are culturally framed and the strategic calculations they are likely to make about the behaviour of contending groups.

Ultimately, as with all of comparative political analysis, our goal is to provide *explanations*. There are several existing explanatory strategies in this area of research. It is worth noting that many scholars combine bits and pieces of these different explanatory strategies.

Primordial Bonds

Primordialists tend to believe that national identity is essentially just another instance of a universal human tendency to form close (or "primordial") attachment to groups. The basic idea of primordialist explanations of ethnic conflict is that conflict takes place when pre-existing groups feel that their group and/or their identity is under threat. For instance, perhaps "globalization" is causing a group to feel that its identity is being diluted. Or perhaps members of another group are perceived to be out-competing them for jobs and other resources. Primordialist theories assume that these groups exist prior to the level of conflict and that it is people's "passions" and "loyalties" that cause the conflict.

Some scholars who are sympathetic to elements of primordialist theories would argue that primordialist explanations alone are not fully satisfactory because they need to be supplemented in order to explain conflict. Since primordialist views of ethnic groups and nations seem to assume the permanent character of these groups *and* that these types of identities exist in all or virtually all human societies, they may have trouble explaining why in only certain cases ethnic conflict takes place. For example, if Hutus and Tutsis, Bosnian Muslims and Serbs, or Indian Hindus and Muslims lived alongside each other for many years, why did conflict suddenly erupt between them at particular historical junctures? To answer such questions, primordialists often need to invoke some other explanatory element like economic crisis, political conflict, "modernization," or external pressure. To this extent, as we have seen in other chapters, scholars may need to draw on distinct theories, creating a "hybrid" model of conflict to fully explain many cases.

CASE IN CONTEXT

451

Why Are Natural Resources Sometimes a Curse? The Nigerian Case

Nigeria has some of the largest oil deposits in the world. So it must be a rich country, right? Actually, Nigeria remains one of the poorest countries in the world. While the Nigerian economy is one of the most important in Africa, historically it has performed poorly. Perhaps surprisingly, this may be *because* of the oil. A number of scholars have argued that countries like Nigeria suffer from what is sometimes called the resource curse because oil or other high-value commodities can potentially produce corruption, distort the formation and functioning of key institutions, crowd out investment in other areas, and affect a country's currency in negative ways.

For more on Nigerian economic development and the resource curse, see the case study in Part VI, p. 451. As you read it, keep in mind the following questions:

1. How has oil helped, and how has it hurt, Nigerian development?
2. What policies might the Nigerian case suggest to the leaders of a country that has just discovered large oil deposits?
3. If oil is so bad, why is Norway not poor like Nigeria? (Or does this indicate that other factors are involved?)

Associated Press/Saurabh Das

PHOTO 13.5 Natural gas burns as oil is welled in the Niger Delta region in Nigeria. Nigeria is a major oil producer, and yet its population remains among the world's poorest.

Cultural Boundaries

Culturalist/constructivist explanations argue that conflict is the result of the distinct ways in which groups and their boundaries are constructed. In other words, some ways of drawing boundaries increase the chances that one group will attack another. At first glance, this theory might seem very similar to the primordialist theory noted previously. However, it differs in seeing high variability in the ways that different groups think about and represent themselves (and others) and sees this variability as key to explaining conflict. Often, such theories are rooted in accounts of "types" of nationalism like those discussed in the previous section.

Thus, some argue that ethnic nationalisms exhibit a higher probability of engaging in violence. Others similarly suggest that the likelihood of conflict is increased by "barricaded" identities, which construct sharp distinctions between in-group and out-group members and depict out-group members as threatening. This idea can be contrasted with "bounded" identities, which facilitate having multiple different associations.[31] As with primordialist explanations, however, other factors likely need to be invoked to explain why conflict actually takes place when it does and why most "ethnic" or "barricaded" identities are not engaged in violence most of the time. Nations thought to construct boundaries in ethnic terms are not constantly at war, and even if it turns out that groups with "barricaded identities" are more likely to engage in violence, they are not constantly doing so, so some other variable must explain why violence emerges when it does.[32] Thus, we might see a society constructing exclusive, impermeable boundaries as a condition that increases the probability of violence but not a sufficient condition in and of itself.

Material Interests

Instrumentalist explanations make the assumption that people pursue "material" interests and that concerns like national pride or the dignity or "purity" of the ethnic group do not really matter much to them. The theory is called "instrumentalist" because it says that ethno-national identities are just used as "instruments" for the pursuit of other purposes. Instrumentalists' explanatory strategy, therefore, involves hypothesizing that certain conditions in given cases make it politically expedient for some actors to deliberately foment ethnic boundaries and conflict. For example, if one group engages in violence toward another, perhaps the underlying reason is that the first group wants access to resources controlled by their victims. As with other theories noted so far, simple versions of such explanations taken alone are incomplete, raising questions about how ethnic boundaries could be useful manipulative tools to begin with if strategic action is paramount. In other words, if everyone is rational and self-interested, why are some people ethnic/national chauvinists to begin with? Why does it help politicians' chances, in some cases, to play to such sentiments?

Rational Calculation

Rational choice explanations—which have much in common with instrumentalist approaches—aim to model the strategic calculus of actors in situations of potential ethnic conflict. What distinguishes such approaches from ordinary instrumental explanations is (1) their typical use of mathematical models and (2) their focus on modelling the ability of members of a group to anticipate and thus make rational choices about how to respond pre-emptively to the behaviour of members of the other group (and their own). The variables that must be considered in such models are many, including the perceived likelihood of the other group perpetrating violence, perceived likelihood of victory if conflict breaks out, and perceived costs associated with *avoiding* violence. As noted earlier, rational choice models do not necessarily assume that material factors are central and thus can be combined with any of the other perspectives mentioned here. For example, one could in principle combine a rational choice approach with a constructivist one, using constructivism to explain the exclusivist *preferences* of nationalist or ethnic chauvinist actors and rationalism to explain the choices they make given those constructed preferences.

Let us try to imagine how such explanations work (see Table 13.3). It would not be rational, for example, for you to redefine yourself as the sole member of a group that nobody has ever heard of: There would be no actual group to offer benefits, and nobody else would

TABLE 13.3 | Factors Influencing Ethno-National Identity: A Rational-Choice Approach

	Adopt the Majority Ethno-National Identity	Reject the Majority Ethno-National Identity
Few seek assimilation	Potential rewards if successful but high risk is present because potential costs include both in-group and out-group sanctioning.	No majority-group membership gains but risks of in-group and out-group sanctioning minimized.
Many seek assimilation	Likelihood of group sanctioning goes down. Rewards are still present but with fewer potential costs.	No majority-group membership gains and still no risk of in-group and out-group sanctioning.

recognize that membership. Likewise, if you were a member of a minority group in a highly segregated society, trying to assimilate to the majority identity might not be rational, since you would likely face resistance from both majority and minority group members. However, as larger numbers of those around you take the assimilation path, it may become increasingly rational for you to do so (depending, of course, on your preferences). According to scholars like David Laitin (see "Insights" box), these are the sorts of factors that shape the likelihood that someone will adopt a given ethno-national identity.

Somewhere along the line, there is a "tipping point" beyond which it becomes more rational to assimilate than to persist in one's minority-group affiliation.[33] Of course, identification with an ethno-national group in most cases has no connection to violence. But a similar logic to the preceding applies to participation in secessionist movements. Scholars use this logic to try to predict whether participation in such movements will "cascade," or spread through a group.[34]

INSIGHTS

Nations, States, and Violence

by David D. Laitin

Laitin uses a "rational choice" perspective to explain why some ethnic and national groups attempt to assimilate, why others try to secede, and so forth. He notes that most ethnic and national groups get along with little violence, though they may have grievances with one another, and argues that the rational calculation of interest explains why grievances sometimes result in violence. The spread of new identities depends on strategic decisions made by individuals about group affiliation, which in turn are shaped by the decisions of people around them. Individuals make choices about keeping or changing their own group affiliations based on three factors: economic benefit, "in-group status," and "out-group status." Group affiliation can affect one's income (because one's ethnic status can determine one's career prospects); it can influence one's standing within one's own group; and it can influence one's standing in the other group. For example, majority groups in some countries may condemn efforts by others to assimilate to the majority group, while the majority may encourage such efforts in other countries. Assimilation, secession, and other options are rational or irrational, depending on such factors.

David D. Laitin, *Nations, States, and Violence* (New York: Oxford University Press, 2007).

Social Psychology

Social-psychological explanations come in a variety of forms.[35] On one hand, these approaches focus on common patterns of boundary construction and the ways in which social categorization structures our perceptions of those around us. Thus, they partially overlap with cultural constructivism. On the other hand, many stress the importance of status differences, and the feelings of discontent and envy that these differences produce, in engendering conflict. The overarching idea, though, is that collectively held or group feelings and resentments lie behind conflict.[36]

In general, then, social-psychological theories focus on two things. First is the interactive process of the formation of group boundaries, the perception that "we are us" and "they are them." This relates to both the primordialist and constructivist approaches described previously (approaches that differ from each other most fundamentally with respect to the question of how such boundaries are established and how much they vary). The second is the relative social status of "us" and "them" in this connection. Many theories agree that some status configurations are more dangerous than others and also that "status dynamics"—ways in which status systems change—can precipitate conflict. As such, social-psychological theories of group violence are "demand side" theories, loosely analogous to the social-psychological theories of collective action discussed in the previous chapter. In other words, they attempt to explain violence by assuming that it is a response to an increase in intergroup grievances. These theories view increased grievances (or the ways structural circumstances, such as a system of group rankings, can generate resentments) as key to explaining the likelihood of violence.

Of course, for most research questions, none of these ideal-typical explanations alone will suffice, but thinking through these general explanatory strategies is a good place to begin as we try to construct hypotheses to explain specific cases of ethnic conflict.

INSIGHTS

Ethnic Groups in Conflict
by Donald L. Horowitz

Horowitz's account of ethnic conflict emphasizes (among other factors) the social psychology of group resentment. Horowitz notes that ethnically diverse societies can be ranked or unranked systems. In a ranked system, at least one ethnic group is subordinated to another (as in India's caste system). In unranked systems, ethnicity might correlate with social class, but one group is not structurally subordinated to another. In ranked systems, conflict typically takes the form of class warfare or social revolution, whereas in unranked systems conflict is often a drive to exclude, expel, or exterminate other groups. Among unranked systems, Horowitz further distinguishes between societies with many dispersed ethnic groups and those "ethnically centralized systems" with just a couple or several major groups. Major conflict centring on the state is more likely in ethnically centralized systems than in ethnically dispersed systems. While structural power relationships between groups matter, the driver of conflict is social-psychological: group resentment. Groups tend to compare themselves to other groups (a process exacerbated in many countries by colonialism) and often see themselves as entitled to higher status than other groups. Where differences in status persist, the potential ingredients for ethnic conflict are present.

Donald L. Horowitz, *Ethnic Groups in Conflict* (Berkeley: University of California Press, 1985; 2nd edn, 2000).

THINKING COMPARATIVELY

Ending Ethnic and National Violence

KEY METHODOLOGICAL TOOL

Large-N Studies

Most of the comparative analysis discussed in this book involves trying to discern causal sequences in a relatively small number of cases. This approach has great utility. Sometimes, however, we need to compare lots of cases to make sure that our conclusions are not artifacts of case selection or bias.

This is exactly what James Fearon and David Laitin did.[37] They noted that much research on ethno-national bias selects cases based on observed incidence of violence. That research then finds links to patterns of ethno-national identity. But Fearon and Laitin chose a different method, looking at a large sample including many cases of ethnonationally diverse or heterogeneous societies. They found that ethno-national diversity was a poor predictor of intergroup conflict. This does not mean that ethnicity and nationalism have nothing to do with rates of conflict. Indeed, more recent work by Lars-Erik Cederman, Andreas Wimmer, and Brian Min has argued that ethnic conflict can be predicted more successfully when we take into account the role of the state. This work suggests that the key to explaining such conflict is to examine the ways in which access to state power intersects with ethnic and ethno-national distinctions.[38]

Large-N studies of this sort—which deal with a large number of observations—can often help us to distinguish between findings that only hold for a small number of cases and those that capture general tendencies or relationships.

In this chapter's "Thinking Comparatively" section, we consider how comparative research can influence policy. As we noted at the beginning of this chapter, much of the practical "payoff" of research in this area is that we may be able to reduce the probability of intergroup conflict.[39] Policy prescriptions should be strongly influenced by what empirical evidence about conflict shows us about theoretical explanations. If it seems that constructivist explanations of violence are correct, we may hope to use policy to influence the formation of ethnic and national boundaries. If rational-choice theories are correct, we can use them to alter the calculus of interests of leaders in potentially violent situations, perhaps by making clear that they will face consequences for their actions if they pursue violence. In general, there are at least four main proposed strategies for managing conflict suggested by social scientists, and comparative political analysis is being used to assess their reliability. These are open questions. Which of these views do *you* find most persuasive? What sorts of evidence could help us to decide between them? Can you think of additional or supplementary approaches?

1. Institutional Approaches

By far the most influential proposal in political science has been that we may be able to reduce conflict by structuring institutions differently. There are several reasons for the popularity of this approach: among others, that (1) political science in general in recent years has relied heavily on institutional analysis and (2) institutions—unlike, say, culture more generally—seem to be relatively amenable to engineering, at least in theory.[40] Typically, scholars propose one or another version of federalism or "**consociationalism**" as the solution to ethnic conflict.[41] Those who favour federalist solutions can be divided into two groups. Some wish to see decentralized political institutions cut *across* ethnic ties, the goal being to reduce the likelihood that leaders of such groups could harness political institutions in support of the interest and aims of their group. Others wish to see federation cut *along* ethnic lines. For example, some policy-makers proposed a federated structure for Iraq that would have allowed considerable autonomy for Shia, Sunni, and Kurds. In situations where formal ethnic federalism is not feasible (for example, if the geographical settlement of different groups will not allow it), consociationalism calls for other methods for the systematic representation of ethnic groups as groups in the state.

consociationalism An institutional approach to managing potential conflict in polities with multiple groups, one that involves ensuring that each group has political representation.

2. Cultural and Civil Society Approaches

We have already noted that some suggest "peace-building" initiatives, or efforts to foster "positive intergroup contact," as key.[42] In an important study, Ashutosh Varshney argues against excessive reliance upon institutional solutions to intergroup conflict.[43] His analysis of group conflict in India reveals its local character and its roots in the structure of social networks. Conflict tends to take place mostly in urban areas and, indeed, in specific urban areas. Varshney's analysis led to the conclusion that the major variable that can explain the geographical distribution of conflict in India is the vibrancy of civic life: More specifically, in urban areas the presence of civic associations that cut across ethnic lines protects against violence, which in India took place disproportionately in areas with low levels of associational activity. The major policy payoff here would be to find ways to strengthen non-ethnic associationalism. While in some ways this approach is presented as an alternative to institutional strategies, it is better regarded as a complement to such strategies. In other words, we are still talking about efforts to shape organizations rather than directly addressing networks, identities, or behaviour.

3. Procedural and Judicial Approaches

Some scholars advocate using national and international judicial institutions to address problems of intergroup violence.[44] Rational choice and related forms of analysis draw important attention to the fact that the strategic considerations of both perpetrators and victims of violence shape outcomes over time. On one hand, it is important that potential perpetrators of violence have the reasonable expectation that there will be consequences if they harm others. On the other hand, once a cycle of violence has begun, it is important that at least some who have ties to such perpetrators do not so fear reprisal as to reach the judgment that ending violence would be too risky. Thus, some argue both for the importance of "individualizing responsibility" for the worst atrocities in ethnic conflict *and* for implementing forgiveness programs of one kind or another.[45] The de-escalation of South African conflict serves as a model for many proponents of this view.

4. International-System Approaches

More generally, international pressure can also reduce the violence carried out by states.[46] States and international actors can bring a variety of consequences to bear on transgressors of international human rights norms, and these consequences may have an important deterrent effect. Such approaches are most likely to be successful, many scholars believe, when (1) the claim that other states or the international community are likely to act seems plausible and (2) the potential perpetrator of violence is not already isolated internationally and thus has something to lose.

As you can see, these approaches are linked to the theories of conflict discussed previously. But how could we further test whether policies derived from theories will work? One approach would be to experiment with them, but for both practical and ethical reasons, this is not a real option. Therefore, we are largely dependent on comparing historical evidence from the real world, especially when it exhibits "natural experiments" that mimic experimental comparison. We can test existing theories of conflict through small groups of comparable case studies or through "large-N" studies. In either of these types of analysis, we would look for statistical correlations between variables suggested both by theory and by the observation of intergroup violence.[47]

As with many of the areas discussed in this book, this is an ongoing research agenda with lots of questions left to debate and resolve. The hope is that we can come to more fully understand the ultimate sources of intergroup violence and, by doing so, the most efficacious ways to reduce or prevent it.

Chapter Summary

Concepts

- Comparative political analysts are interested in classifying and explaining major political identities.
- National identity is an important modern political identity emphasizing popular sovereignty and equality.

Types

- National identities are conceptualized in three major ways by comparative political analysts; their positions are known to scholars as "primordialism," "modernism" and "perennialism," and "ethno-symbolism."

- Primordialists group national identity with collective identities more generally. For a primordialist, national identity is similar to tribal, clan, ethnic, or racial identity.
- Modernists believe that nationalism is different from the sorts of political identities that preceded it. Most believe that nations arose after the development of print media and the onset of industrialization and urbanization. In other words, nationalism and the Industrial Revolution are closely linked.
- Perennialists think that nationalism has been around for many centuries, but they do not see all collective identities as basically the same. Rather, they focus on one or another criterion that makes national identity different from more ancient identities (e.g., a common vernacular, control of a state).
- Ethno-symbolists focus on the historical roots of many nations through analysis of ethnic cores—the key myths, events, heroes, and symbols that make up ancient ethnic groups and modern nations.
- Some scholars argue that nationalism comes in different types. The most common distinction is between a "civic" or "liberal" type and an exclusive or "ethnic" type.

Causes and Effects

- Scholars have produced a range of theories to explain ethnic and national violence. We considered five of them in schematic form.
- One theory holds that "primordial attachments" are responsible for collective violence. From this point of view, in other words, explanations of collective violence must account for the emotional motivation of perpetrators. Such theories often suggest that such emotional motivations are encoded in our biology or in any case in our social nature, and threats to national identity (e.g., perceived imminent violence perpetrated by another group or fears about cultural dilution in the face of globalization) prompt the behaviour.
- Another theory holds that the nature of the cultural boundaries between groups strongly influences the probability of conflict. Groups that define cultural boundaries as impermeable and essential are, according to this point of view, more likely to engage in violence.
- A third theory holds that material interests are the main determinant of collective violence. In other words, according to this theory, when groups claim to be engaging in violence because of group affiliation, they are actually interested in increasing their access to material resources like money, water, food supplies, or technology.
- A fourth theory holds that collective violence is best explained through modelling the rational decision-making processes of group leaders and/or members.
- A fifth theory holds that collective violence is the product of social-psychological processes that go beyond the ways that cultural boundaries are constructed.

Thinking Comparatively

- We thought about major policy proposals for reducing or eliminating intergroup conflict, and we linked these proposals back to our earlier, causal theories of ethno-national violence.

Thinking It Through

1. In the "Causes and Effects" section of this chapter, we considered five major theories of intergroup/ethno-national conflict. These theories are not necessarily mutually exclusive. Sketch a hybrid theory that includes key elements of at least two of the theories discussed. Make clear (1) what is potentially gained through the linkage and (2) what, if anything, is lost about each of the theories included in the hybrid.
2. This chapter ends with a discussion of policy recommendations that have been made by political scientists who study ethno-national violence. We noted that they related to theories of ethno-national violence. However, some do not address "root causes," instead focusing on institutional solutions (like consociationalism) to problems that many theories would say are based on primordial, cultural, or material differences. Is this a contradiction? Why might someone who believes ethno-national conflict to have such geneses still prefer institutional solutions?
3. Why has Quebec nationalism (with one brief exception) not become violent? What institutional mechanisms and political arrangements have allowed Quebec nationalists to coexist peacefully with their counterparts in other provinces and in the federal government?
4. Pick a country you know well. Which of the three major perspectives on the historical origins of nationalism and national identity discussed in this chapter—primordialism, modernism/perennialism, and ethno-symbolism—do you think would be most useful for the analysis of nationalism in this case? Explain the reasons for your selection.

14 Race, Ethnicity, and Gender

In This Chapter

Former Canadian prime minister Kim Campbell speaking at the Daughters of the Vote event in the House of Commons on Parliament Hill, Ottawa, in 2017. (Sean Kilpatrick/THE CANADIAN PRESS)

In recent years, a number of countries have elected members of historically disadvantaged groups to the highest office. This trend has been especially notable in the Americas. Latin America, for example, has in the past decade seen the election of several important women as president: Michelle Bachelet in Chile, Cristina Fernández in Argentina, and Dilma Rousseff in Brazil. Unfortunately, by March 2018 all of these female leaders had left office, leaving the same historical gender gap as before. The Americas have also recently witnessed the election of presidents from other disadvantaged groups, such as Evo Morales in Bolivia, Luiz Inácio Lula da Silva in Brazil (before Rousseff), and Barack Obama in the United States. While Canada has not had a female prime minister for more than two decades and has never had an Indigenous person or a person of colour in this top spot, our provinces have had many female premiers, including, recently, Rachel Notley, Alison Redford, Christy Clark, Pauline Marois, and Kathleen Wynne. While constituencies have greeted these elections as a sign of political empowerment, it emphatically does *not* mean that race, ethnicity, and gender are no longer sources of political, social, and economic inequality. These elections are after all the exception rather than the norm. In the December 2018 issue of *Maclean's* magazine, for example, the cover displayed five white male conservative leaders, dubbed "the resistance." This was supposed to be about premiers and party leaders opposing the Liberal government's carbon tax, but it provoked a lot of debate and satirical commentary about the dominance of white men in blue suits over Canada's political system.

Photo by William F. Campbell/Timepix/The LIFE Images Collection/Getty Images

PHOTO 14.2 Whip-toting riot police in South Africa's *Apartheid* state in 1985. In 1948, the white-led National Party in South Africa institutionalized existing racial segregation policies by enacting them as a system of *Apartheid* laws. *Apartheid* (meaning "separateness") required non-white people (who were the majority of the population) to live in separate areas from white people, use separate public facilities, and have limited contact with white people and each other.

Gender continues to strongly shape political representation, economic position, and social status, thus remaining a key and often under-examined feature of comparative politics. Race and ethnicity matter, too, especially in our global culture in which international migration is so common and also in settler states that have always been multiracial.[1] Globalization is leading to important changes in the composition and identity of many countries. Perhaps more than ever before, our societies are racially and ethnically diverse (to varying degrees, of course) and increasingly transnational in character, yet diverse demography has not translated into equitable political representation.[2] In this chapter, we consider identities linked to gender, race, and ethnicity in relation to efforts to achieve empowerment and political representation.

Despite the importance of gender, race, and ethnicity, these subjects have often been minimized in the study of comparative politics. This tendency has started to change, in part because of **feminist** and **critical race** scholarship, yet the field still has a very long way to go. In this chapter, we first focus on gaining some clarity about the concepts of race, ethnicity, and gender. We then move on to related concepts such as gender discrimination and gender empowerment. Then we turn our attention to how some women and members of minority groups have worked to enhance their participation and representation in formal institutions. As we shall see, while efforts to more fully incorporate women and minority groups into formal political processes have a lot in common, they vary in important ways as well.

feminism A social and intellectual movement that aims to ensure equal rights for women and men.

critical race theory A movement in social, political, and legal theory that aims to discern and offer ways to combat the effects of racism and related forms of prejudice.

• • •

Concepts

Social scientists interested in these questions need to first define what we mean by race, ethnicity, gender, and sexual orientation. Though some of these concepts are related, they differ in important ways as well.

Race and Ethnicity

As we saw in Chapter 13, all human societies construct collective identities, which vary considerably depending on their context. Among other things, these identities often involve **boundaries** between an "in-group" ("us") and an "out-group" ("them").[3] One strategy for trying to understand various types and instances of collective identity is to focus on the nature of these boundaries. Different types of identities depend on contrasting ways of drawing lines between groups of people. Identities based on **race**, **ethnicity**, and **gender** draw these lines in overlapping and yet distinct ways.

We will unpack the related concepts of race and ethnicity later in the chapter; for now, we will just point to shared features of these categories of identity. Both suggest that people are divided into such groups, with the bases between groups allegedly established either by biological differences or by culture and tradition. Both treat group membership as important, and both can be sources of out-group discrimination and in-group pride. Different cases posit different sorts of boundaries between ethnic and racial groups, some more permeable than others. Unequal relationships between ethnic and racial groups can be caused and reinforced by formal and legal differences. For example, think of the denial of the federal vote for Indigenous peoples with status in Canada until 1960 or provincially in Quebec until 1969. Other well-known examples are the legislated racial segregation called *Apartheid* in South Africa from 1948 to the early 1990s and the explicit segregation under "Jim Crow" laws in the southern United States before the civil rights movement peaked in

boundaries Lines drawn symbolically between groups of people.

race The idea that human beings are divided into different groups, often thought of (erroneously) as biological categories.

ethnicity The quality that one has by identifying with or being ascribed membership in an ethnic group.

gender Culturally constructed roles or identities one has by virtue of being ascribed the status of male or female, to be distinguished from biological sex.

the 1960s. Alternatively, inequalities can be buttressed by more subtle forms of discrimination. Finally, as we discuss further in the "Types" section below, some people think of race and ethnicity as biological categories, though most social scientists reject this idea.[4]

As discussed in the previous chapter, there is a range of social-scientific views on the nature of national, ethnic, and racial identities. Some accounts emphasize constructivism, others instrumentalism, and still others primordialism (see Chapter 13 if you need to review these concepts and theories).

Gender

The first distinction that needs to be drawn here is between gender and sex.[5] From the point of view of social scientists, *sex* refers to biological differences between people as linked to reproductive potential. In other words, one's sex is the more or less objective quality that one has by virtue of being born biologically male or female. *Gender*, in contrast, is often seen as *cultural*.[6] This means that it is essentially symbolic. One way to formulate this is to say that gender is the way in which human beings "make sense" out of sex. For example, think of ideas like "masculinity" and "femininity." We may link these ideas to ways of acting and even different sorts of bodies. For example, in some cultures, maybe being very muscular is masculine, in others not; in some cultures, femininity and athletic prowess may go hand in hand, while in others femininity may be linked to perceived physical passivity. But given all of these differences, we know that ideas about gender (like masculinity and femininity) cannot be reduced to underlying sex differences. Indeed, some individuals' experienced gender does not "match" their biological sex in the traditional sense, and some individuals have **transgendered** identities.

transgender An identity in which one's gender does not conform to conventional matching with biological sex.

There are many debates among social scientists about the precise relationship between sex and gender. A dominant view is **social constructionism** (or social constructivism), which holds that biological sex does not determine gender. From this point of view, biology is not destiny. **Biological determinism**, the other end of the spectrum, asserts that gender is just a reflection of sex. As far as we are aware, no serious social scientists are true biological determinists in this sense. The debate is really between "strong" and "weak" versions of social constructionism. The "weak" version holds that gender is culturally constructed but that there may be some biological differences between women and men that limit or constrain this construction. For example, perhaps evolution has indeed encouraged some different tendencies in how one thinks about hierarchy or relationships or sexuality itself.[7] The "strong" version holds that any such tendencies are insignificant or do not exist at all.

social construction The process through which socially shared meanings and definitions are established and maintained.

biological determinism The view that a feature of social life, such as gender or ethnicity, is caused by underlying biology.

In other words, social scientists agree that gender is not *determined* by biological sex. This premise has some important implications. Perhaps most important, if gender is socially constructed, it can change over time. Gender might have meant something different in 1950s Canada or Great Britain from what it does today, for example. In other words, being a woman or a man decades ago was likely experientially different in many respects from what it is today (think of CBC's "Murdoch Mysteries," set at the turn of the 20th century, or the Netflix series "The Crown" about the British royal family). Note that if biological determinism is true, this change would be impossible. If gender can change over time, this means that (1) activists can try to shape it, at least to some extent, and (2) social scientists can try to map and explain the ways in which it has changed. Activities, identities, roles, jobs, even objects in the world can be seen as "gendered," and regardless of one's sex, everyone can participate in such gendered activities, perform such gendered roles, and exemplify different gendered styles, in varying ways and to different degrees.[8]

Sexual Orientation

When social scientists speak of sexual orientation in the most narrow sense, they refer to the fact that different people seek different sorts of sexual partners. Historically, in many societies a heterosexual, or "straight," sexual orientation has been held up as the standard. People with other orientations, such as gays and lesbians, were labelled as deviant and, as a result, often faced serious discrimination. Some scholars refer to this view, which takes heterosexuality as "normal" and preferred, as "heteronormativity" or "normative heterosexuality."[9]

Even today, same-sex relationships are subject to discrimination and are illegal in some countries and territories, but social movements have led to decriminalization and widespread acceptance in numerous locations. They have also expanded civil rights in other ways for persons of diverse sexual orientations, including, in some places, the extension of basic institutions like marriage, and they have elevated the status of people of diverse sexual orientations. In 2005, Canada legalized same-sex marriage, the fourth country in the world to do so and the first country outside western Europe. From 2013 to 2018, Kathleen Wynne, who has been in a same-sex marriage since 2005, served as premier of Ontario. The process of extending rights and ending discrimination is far from over, and even in countries where the rights of gay, lesbian, and transgendered persons have been increased the most, discrimination remains a serious issue.[10] In the Ontario case, the Wynne government initiated a major updating of the sexual education curriculum, which was then reversed when the Ford government took power in 2018.

Nathan Denette/THE CANADIAN PRESS

PHOTO 14.3 Students at a Toronto high school walk out of class in September 2018 to protest the Ford government's decision to scrap a modernized version of Ontario's sex-education curriculum. The modernized version, brought in by the previous Wynne government, had included discussion of online bullying, same-sex relationships, and gender identity.

Types

Different types of disadvantage and discrimination emerge in relation to categories such as race, ethnicity, and gender. At the same time, these categories may have different implications for potential empowerment.

Disentangling Race and Ethnicity

As with gender, some people imagine race to be a biological category. Scientifically, however, this way of thinking is inaccurate. As scholars have emphasized, there is far greater genetic variation within than between so-called racial groups.[11] The socially constructed (and thus non-biological) nature of race becomes even clearer when we look at the history of racial concepts. Categories such as "white" or "black" or "Asian" have changed over time. Indeed, to take just one example, in the 19th-century United States, Irish immigrants were sometimes defined as "non-white," and some groups from the Mediterranean such as Greeks and Italians were not considered "white" in the same way that Anglo-Saxons were in the 19th and early 20th centuries. Even today in much of Latin America and other parts of the world, racial categories are far more fluid and permeable than they are in the United States.[12]

racialization The historical process through which social relations become interpreted in terms of racial categories.

racial formation A concept developed by Omi and Winant (1994) that describes the process through which ideas of race are constructed and develop over time.

Scholars who study racial identity increasingly speak of certain stages or periods of **racialization** and **racial formation**, meaning times in which social distinctions pertaining to the idea of "race" became more pronounced.[13] Typically, these processes have to do with one or another group having an interest in closing off competition for status or resources—a sort of rational-choice model of how racism develops.[14] Much of this developed as European countries sought to colonize other parts of the world and justify their violent conquests and exploitation in the process.

When individuals and groups compete for social status, they often seek to formally exclude others from competition, making it easier for themselves.[15] Race has often been used for this purpose.[16] For example, Europeans drew distinctions between themselves and "black" individuals from sub-Saharan Africa for centuries, but when European colonizers of the Americas sought to enslave those individuals on a mass scale and to exploit Indigenous nations, they drew a clearer, "racialized" line between themselves, Indigenous populations, and Africans, trying to justify their different forms of exploitation.[17] White people came to benefit from these internalized views of race over time and unconsciously and consciously adopted racial hierarchies. It can be very difficult to see racism if it has developed in such an environment. Recent research suggests that those who are subjected to lifelong racism may internalize feelings of inferiority, which can have implications for health, employment, and almost every aspect of life.[18]

In summary, most scholars believe that race is not a real, biological fact but is instead a social construction. An identity is a "racial" identity when people in a society think that one or another group is significantly biologically different from other groups and view these imagined differences through the race concept. For this reason, race is only a useful category for comparative analysis when we are studying societies that think about themselves and others in terms of race. The term "racialized people" is becoming more common in Canada. In researching race and racialization, we aim to understand (1) how political actors think about race, (2) how ideas of race are constructed by different groups, and (3) whose interests are served by these different constructions. Some important comparative analysis aims to explain differences between societies' constructions and uses of race.[19]

ethnic group A group that identifies itself as having strong cultural commonality and a shared sense of long-running history, sometimes thinking of itself as a kind of kinship group.

The terms "ethnicity" and **ethnic group** are sometimes used as synonyms of race, but they are often applied more broadly. An influential conception of ethnic groups is as follows: "named units of population with common ancestry myths and historical memories, elements of shared culture, some link with a historic territory, and some measure of solidarity, at least among their elites."[20] Note that, defined in this way, ethnicity is conceptually broader than race: "Common ancestry myths" does not necessarily imply that those myths are thought to be biological, even if they often are understood to be so. If one chooses this sort of approach, the concept of "ethnic group" is a broader category of collective identity than the more narrowly defined "national identity" discussed in the previous chapter.[21]

Yet much work on questions of ethnicity and ethnic identity focuses not on the long-term past but on the nature of these identities and the roles they play in the contemporary world. Typically, it conceptualizes ethnicity as an identity that is not necessarily bound to a state (though states often influence ethnicity in a variety of ways). For example, Irish Canadians, Japanese Canadians, and Afro-Caribbean Canadians might be characterized as "ethnic groups" because while some members of these groups feel a sense of cultural belonging, they do not desire to form their own state as a result. Ethnicity, as such, can be consistent with membership in a broader civic or multicultural community in which individuals possess other collective identities besides their ethnicity.[22] Most often, social scientists think of ethnicity as based on cultural commonalities, ranging from shared rituals and practices to common language.

Ideas such as ethnicity are constructed in very different ways in different societies.[23] Thus, identities deriving from tribal forms of organization in some parts the world, those deriving from distinct units in hierarchical stratification systems in some African societies or in India, and those of "hyphenated Canadians" cannot for all research purposes be treated as instances of the same general phenomenon, yet social scientists may treat all such identities as "ethnic." In modern societies, the following components are likely to be building blocks for how ethnicity is identified: type of national identity, how the state deals with questions of citizenship and residency, formal and informal rules of national belonging and participation in public life, and the broader stratification system (which in most modern societies means the class structure).

More generally, the state plays a role in the ongoing construction of ethnicity, such as by making "official" decisions about how to use ethnic categories in the census or in laws and judicial decisions involving ethnicity.[24] It has made such decisions in cases involving questions of affirmative action in employment and in efforts by college and university admissions offices to ensure a diverse student body.

Discrimination Based on Race and Ethnicity

Both ethnicity and race often serve as the basis for discrimination, which can be both explicit and implicit. In a country like Canada or the United States, racial and ethnic identities have a pronounced impact on one's prospects for income, assets, education, marriage, and incarceration, among other outcomes.[25] While in the United States surveys show that explicit racism is much less prevalent than it once was,[26] members of minority groups continue to experience high rates of discrimination.[27] Much of the inequality based on race and ethnicity is not obvious to most observers.[28] Social scientists who study race and ethnicity almost universally agree that even as explicit racism has declined in societies like Canada and the United States, racial and ethnic disparities remain a serious problem.

Discrimination and its historical legacies take very different forms in different societies. Since race and ethnicity are socially constructed and because they intersect with other potential bases of cleavage in a variety of ways, there is no one set pattern of racial and ethnic discrimination.

Demographics cause variation in how race and ethnicity are constructed, and they link to discrimination as well. Societies with a long tradition as destinations for large-scale immigration can be expected to exhibit different dynamics from those of societies that have received little immigration. This observation might help to explain why some countries in western Europe, such as France, have faced challenges incorporating immigrant groups in recent years. Polities that presided over long histories of slavery may exhibit dynamics different from those of societies without such histories. Cultural traditions and beliefs likely matter as well. Finally, the principal actors involved vary from case to case. Actors that can be agents of discrimination include not just the state but other societal institutions, as well as groups and individuals within the society.

Gender Discrimination

The meaning of gender discrimination may seem fairly obvious. Many people are explicitly discriminated against on the basis of their gender. For example, a woman might be denied a job because she is a woman, or her work might be unpaid or paid less than the work of an equally qualified man.[29] In a number of countries, as with racial and ethnic discrimination, political action over decades has resulted in laws offering some protection against discrimination based on gender and sexual orientation. Yet again, the protection offered does not fully resolve the problem, and in a number of societies explicit job discrimination remains rampant. Beyond this, other forms of discrimination, perhaps less obvious, happen in virtually all societies.[30] While both men and women experience sexual harassment, women are far more likely to encounter it.[31] Yet social-scientific data suggest that—in addition to persistent discrimination of this kind—women are systematically disadvantaged in subtler ways as well.

Women are often paid less than men.[32] In a number of places, this inequality is explicit, and it still happens with frequency in advanced industrial and post-industrial societies like Canada, despite efforts to curb the problem. But think about ways in which women are subject to pay differentials *beyond* such explicit forms of discrimination:

- First, cultural pressures still sometimes emphasize that women bear special responsibility for raising children. As a result, "work–life balance" issues tend to be especially acute for women, and in just about any field, taking time off from the workplace means lower pay and slower ascent of the career ladder.[33] Women take time off not only to give birth but because in some cases they feel more pressure than male counterparts to stay home with children on an ongoing basis.[34]
- Second, employers often engage in anticipatory discrimination for these reasons. Women might be less likely to receive promotions—or even opportunities to demonstrate they deserve promotions or raises—because of expectations that their time may be divided between work and family.
- Third, discriminatory attitudes about women's abilities and competencies persist. For example, some people still believe, erroneously, that men are better at math and science and related technical subjects.
- Fourth, on a related note, the labour market itself is gendered.[35] Some jobs are considered by many to be stereotypically or characteristically male or female. Traditionally, jobs gendered as female have paid lower wages than those gendered as male. Thus, women could, within these categories, receive "equal pay for equal work" and *still*, when we think about the broader society, be paid unfairly in the aggregate.

These are just some examples of mechanisms through which gender discrimination in the labour market operates. Of course, they play out very differently in the wide range of contemporary societies.

In addition to pay inequality, women are often systematically disadvantaged because in many societies, parents invest more in the human capital of their sons than in that of their daughters.[36] In these instances, women are not competing on a level playing field because they have fewer resources. This tendency has been greatly reduced, however, in many advanced industrial and post-industrial societies. Indeed, in a number of countries, women consistently outperform men in the educational system.[37] Institutions of higher education increasingly have a hard time achieving gender balance between male and female students because women tend to have higher grades and better test scores. In fact, many colleges and universities may now be practising so-called "affirmative action" for men.

Beyond serious, ongoing, explicit, and subtle discrimination in economic life, women continue to face discrimination in the political sphere in virtually all societies, though societies vary substantially in the *extent* to which this is true.[38] It is only over the past century that women have acquired the right to vote in most countries (1918 in Canada among white women over the age of 21), in some far more recently, and in a few not at all. And even in countries with long-established traditions of women's suffrage, women politicians rarely occupy top posts at parity with men. As we shall see later in this chapter, there is much debate about why this is the case and what its main consequences might be. Women are less likely than men to hold office at all levels of government. Systematic disadvantage of women in politics most likely reinforces other forms of disadvantage, since research indicates that women in political office are more likely than men to aim to eradicate discrimination and related problems.[39] Beyond these issues, globally, women are considerably more likely than men to experience poverty and sexual violence.

Associated Press/Eric Risberg

PHOTO 14.4 Barbados Prime Minister Mia Mottley speaks during the opening plenary of the Global Action Climate Summit in San Francisco in September 2018. In May of that year, she became the first woman to hold this leadership position in her country.

Empowerment of Women and Minority Groups

empowerment An increase in the social, political, or economic capabilities of an individual or group.

Empowerment is the expansion of the socially defined capability of a given group.[40] The simplest way to think of empowerment is as the opposite of discrimination. That is, you might think about women or minority groups becoming empowered to the extent that they overcome such discrimination. This idea is helpful but only partially defines empowerment, which could, in principle, extend beyond the establishment of parity. We think of empowerment as expanding women's and minority group members' capabilities in all spheres of life that bear on politics.

Empowerment can be economic.[41] For example, prohibiting or undoing economic discrimination (such as in the labour market) based on gender, race, or ethnicity is a form of empowerment. Many agencies encourage economic development—another form of empowerment—by offering small loans specifically to women.[42] Similarly, many developing world societies, such as Brazil and Mexico, target women with "conditional cash transfers"; that is, they disburse funds to those who comply with certain conditions, such as enrolling children in school.[43] In part, this practice rests on evidence that women are more likely than men to invest such funds in the human capital of their families (i.e., health and education) rather than in personal consumption. Further, one can think of women's cooperatives—in which women not only pool resources but also create political structures that allow them to exert leadership—as potentially empowering. Government programs that provide services such as childcare and medical care to women can also be empowering.

Empowerment can also be cultural or symbolic. One example of symbolic empowerment is a low-status group engaging in collective action to elevate its status. Of course, status often goes along with economic class and political power, but we should not assume that it always does so or that it is not independently important.[44] The lesbian, gay, bisexual, and transgender (LGBTQIA+) movement stands out as one that has aimed to shape the status position of the populations it represents and supports. One aspect of the movement is working to expand the political representation of LGBTQIA+ people. It also seeks to promote positive depictions of LGBTQIA+ people, both in the media and in everyday life. This effort has involved lobbying media as well as more grassroots action such as gay pride parades and related events. Such actions aim to extend social benefits to in-group members in addition to demanding broader social acceptance and elevated status. Symbolic empowerment may be an important component in achieving political and economic empowerment, since politics and economics are ultimately cultural. Note that the movement was formerly seen as being LGBT but has now expanded to include recognition of a much larger range of sexual and gender identities. The plus sign is "Not just a mathematical symbol anymore, but a denotation of everything on the gender and sexuality spectrum that letters and words can't yet describe."[45]

Finally, empowerment can be political.[46] Political parties that aim to advance the goals of specific ethnic groups are also potentially empowering (for interesting reasons, as we shall see, political parties that represent women as a group are relatively rare[47]). Laws and interventions to ensure political opportunities for women and members of minority groups may be empowering as well. Perhaps most important, we can see empowerment in initiatives that increase women's and minority group members' representation in political offices.

On a related note, some scholars interested in women's empowerment have focused on "state feminism," which one political scientist defines as "the advocacy of women's movement demands inside the state."[48] This perspective reminds us that beyond social movement organizing and political competition for elected office, both elected and appointed officeholders inside the state bureaucracy can contribute to the empowerment of women and other groups in myriad ways.[49]

Feminism and Intersectionality[50]

Growing in popularity is intersectional feminism, which builds on work related to race and class. Intersectionality means that different forms of subordination often accompany each other—gender is only one of many variables. Feminists focusing on intersectionality may observe how sexism, racism, classism, ageism, ableism, and homophobia can all be part of the same burden women face. This theoretically means that while women may share some sort of solidarity as women, more affluent women may benefit from structures that oppress poorer women, while white women may benefit from hierarchies that marginalize Indigenous women and racialized women. Understanding feminism in this way helps to better make sense of the divisions between different groups of feminist scholars and activists and can also help to explain why alliances form within ethnic and class-based groups that seem to operate against what some forms of feminist thought would suggest.

Kimberlé Crenshaw (1989) is credited with promoting this form of analysis with her critique of how "African-American" and "female" were examined as mutually exclusive categories. She argued against a single-axis form of analysis, promoting instead a form of study that would take multiple points of identity into account at the same time (p. 139). In examining legal cases in which being black and being a woman were judged separately, she argued that "a single-axis framework erases Black women in the conceptualization, identification and remediation of race and sex discrimination by limiting inquiry to the experiences of otherwise-privileged members of the group." She focused on what she called the "multiply-burdened" (p. 140). Crenshaw's solution was to bring these different forms of discrimination together, since they all intersect and cause serious problems of health, safety, and well-being for women of colour. Carbin and Edenheim (2013) observe that "in the last 10 years the use of the concept intersectionality has practically exploded in European and North American gender research" (p. 233).

INSIGHTS

The Equity Myth: Racialization and Indigeneity at Canadian Universities

by Frances Henry, Enakshi Dua, Carl E. James, Audrey Kobayashi, Peter Li, Howard Ramos, and Malinda S. Smith

Using an intersectional lens, this team of noted critical race and gender theorists explores the status of women, Indigenous, and racialized peoples in Canadian post-secondary institutions. The authors interrogate the claim that universities have become more equal and respectful of diversity to the point where racism no longer exists on campus. Problematizing such claims, *The Equity Myth* explores the barriers to equality, many of which are complex, subtle, and wide-ranging, despite how some norms of equity and diversity have been institutionalized. Problems of unconscious gender and racial bias continue, while racialized and Indigenous faculty have some of the most precarious academic positions and some of the lowest wages. The book offers a comparative study that focuses on Canada but also draws on comparative analysis from the United States, Australia, and the United Kingdom. Survey data and interviews play a central role, demonstrating the continued need for change so that women, Indigenous peoples, and racialized people can secure the same access to a quality education and secure employment as the white male mainstream, which has traditionally dominated the Canadian university system (and still does). The book features detailed qualitative and quantitative appendices to support the findings of the authors.

Frances Henry, Enakshi Dua, Carl E. James, Audrey Kobayashi, Peter Li, Howard Ramos, and Malinda S. Smith, *The Equity Myth: Racialization and Indigeneity at Canadian Universities* (Vancouver: UBC Press, 2017).

CASE IN CONTEXT 361

Gender and Political Representation in Brazil: From Where Has Progress Come?

Historically, Latin America has been viewed, rightly or wrongly, as a region in which women face widespread discrimination. Yet in recent years, the women's movement has made notable advances in this region, such as in Brazil.

For more on the state of women's political empowerment in Brazil, see the case study in Part VI, p. 361. As you read it, keep in mind the following questions:

1. What have been the major successes of feminist activism in Brazil in recent years?
2. Why, according to political scientists, have gender-linked parties not been prominent in Brazil?
3. Why, nevertheless, has the Workers' Party tended to be more favourable to women's empowerment?

In the "Causes and Effects" section that follows, we focus on political empowerment because it is fundamental. Once a group is politically empowered, it has an expanded capacity to shape agendas. As a result, it can then push for other forms of empowerment.

Causes and Effects: What Factors Influence the Political Representation of Women and Minority Groups?

In this section, we consider factors affecting political representation of women and minority groups. As noted previously, we are narrowing our focus a bit, since we will pay less attention here to questions of economic and symbolic empowerment, though they are not unrelated. We focus on social movement mobilization, the creation of political parties based on gender or ethnicity, and institutional design tools such as quotas. Reflecting the literature on intersectionality, these potential causes of empowerment are not mutually exclusive but rather may go together.

Social Movement Mobilization

A key process through which women and minority groups have been empowered is social movement mobilization.[51] Indeed, this process often underlies the two other main processes we consider in this section: political parties and policy responses.[52] As noted in Chapter 12, social movements typically need to develop organizations to maintain their momentum and direction over an extended period: Political parties are one such type of organization. The development of a political party out of a social movement is a step in the institutionalization of that movement's concerns.[53]

Social movement mobilization can also be effective in other ways. It can act in the form of symbolic empowerment to expand the interests of a group. Thus, social movement activity can aim to transform political culture or popular attitudes about a group, such as LGBTQIA+ people (as we mentioned earlier). The civil rights movement in the United States is another clear example here. The movement's goals were many and included both the political and economic empowerment of African Americans, but one of its key aims was breaking down the symbolic barriers that facilitated many white Americans' support of or tolerance for discriminatory Jim Crow laws. Another example is Indigenous activism in Canada, which arose in 2012 against the federal government's plan to remove protections on lakes, rivers, streams, and other waterways. This and other legislation that was damaging for the environment and for Indigenous peoples led to the formation of Idle No More by a group of concerned educators and activists in Saskatoon. We looked at major theories of contentious action, including social movements, in Chapter 12.

Whether or not social movement activity focusing on questions of identity is novel, there is no disputing that it can be an effective strategy for empowering a group. As noted previously, one way it can work is through helping to establish and support political parties that represent the interests of a group.

Political Parties Based on Gender or Ethnicity

So how do political parties help to represent a group's interests? First, most modern electoral systems depend on political parties to organize and structure political competition. As a result of this process, parties bind political representatives together under common platforms, which can strongly influence votes and thus political decision-making. This influence varies from case to case, of course, and not all parties are equally capable of shaping the voting behaviour of party members. Another reason that parties can matter is that in some political systems, parties exist as either an official (e.g., contemporary China) or de facto (e.g., Mexico under the PRI) layer in institutional decision-making processes. As Chapters 9 through 11 demonstrate, the nature of the electoral system

INSIGHT

Global Indigenous Politics: A Subtle Revolution
by Sheryl Lightfoot

Sheryl Lightfoot is an Anishinaabe scholar of Indigenous politics and international relations and a Canada Research Chair at the University of British Columbia. She is also the advisor to the president of UBC on Indigenous issues. Her book is a fascinating exploration of how global networks of Indigenous peoples were able to create and secure passage of the United Nations Declaration on the Rights of Indigenous Peoples. The Declaration was passed in 2007 by 144 states, with only four countries voting against it: Australia, Canada, Aotearoa New Zealand and the United States. *Global Indigenous Politics* explores the decades-long rise of Indigenous organization at the international level, through domestic and pan-national organizations like the International Indian Treaty Council, founded in 1974, to more international organizations like the UN Expert Mechanism on the Rights of Indigenous Peoples and the United Nations Permanent Forum on Indigenous Issues. Lightfoot suggests that Indigenous peoples are not marginal actors but potentially crucial players, helping to develop new approaches and new norms in the conduct of international relations. As she observes, "global Indigenous politics is potentially forging major changes in the international system, as the implementation of Indigenous peoples' rights requires a complete re-thinking and re-ordering of sovereignty, territoriality, liberalism, and human rights."

The book also features detailed case studies of Canada and Aotearoa New Zealand and the arduous struggles in these countries to encourage settler governments to approve the Declaration. Indigenous peoples have collective rights to self-determination. The evolution of Indigenous rights domestically and internationally will be of crucial importance for students of comparative politics.

Sheryl Lightfoot, *Global Indigenous Politics: A Subtle Revolution* (New York: Routledge, 2016).

Sipa via AP Images

PHOTO 14.5 Grand Chief Wilton Littlechild of the Confederacy of Treaty Six First Nations (left) and Bolivian President Evo Morales (right) participate in an event at the UN headquarters in New York in 2017 to mark the 10th anniversary of the UN Declaration on the Rights of Indigenous Peoples.

and how the legislature and executive are structured affects the ways in which parties organized around an ethnic group might exert influence.

However party organization intersects with the formal organizational features of the state, parties are useful tools for pursuing group interests. When and why ethnic parties are formed is a somewhat complicated question. Several variables probably matter, but in interaction with one another.[54] In other words, none of them alone is likely sufficient to produce an ethnic party.

CASE IN CONTEXT

471

Why Has Saudi Arabia Made Such Little Progress on Women's Rights?

Saudi Arabia has an international reputation for being one of the worst abusers of women's rights, in part because of an extremely social conservative ruling ideology. Despite some very basic reforms in recent years, women continue to be subjected to widespread discrimination and repression.

For more on the status of women in Saudi Arabia, see the case study in Part VI, p. 471. As you read it, keep in mind the following questions:

1. To what extent is the low status of women's rights a reflection of Wahhabi religious beliefs?
2. What are the prospects for positive change in Saudi Arabia? Have government reforms been window dressing, or do they represent something more fundamental?
3. If Saudi Arabia became a constitutional monarchy, would women's rights improve?

The first such variable is demographic.[55] How racially and ethnically heterogeneous is the society in question? This is not to suggest that there is an ideal level of ethnic heterogeneity for the formation of ethnic political parties but that some level of heterogeneity is key. The relative shares of the population divided into each group, as well as the number of groups and the geographical dispersion of groups, can influence the probability of the formation of ethnic parties. This demographic variable interacts with several other variables, the most important of which are likely (1) the society's culture of ethnic affiliation more broadly (e.g., how does the culture in general handle ethnic attachment?) and, equally important, what other bases for political mobilization are available that might crowd out ethnic party organizing; (2) the nature of political competition in the society in question; and (3) the historical and structural relationships between ethnic groups.[56]

The way a society handles questions of ethnic affiliation more broadly might also be relevant to ethnic party formation. For example, does the society define national identity in ethnic terms, or does it view national identity as attached to citizenship?[57] Imagine a society that historically treats national identity in ethnic terms and where a large ethnic majority comprises this ethno-national group. We would expect this situation to affect the likelihood that either the majority group or any minority groups would seek political representation through parties.

Perhaps equally or even more important, other bases for social cleavage can crowd out ethnic attachment as a basis for forming political parties.[58] This is sometimes true of social class, for example. Sometimes a strong tradition of class-based organizing—think of a society in which people are mobilized as workers or as peasants—might reduce the likelihood of organizing around ethnicity.

The nature of political competition in a society seems to matter a lot as well. Ethnic parties seem to be more likely in parliamentary systems in which there is proportional representation. This is because it is more likely that an ethnic party could win some seats and play a role in a coalition government in such cases. Imagine a country in which 10 per cent of the population falls into an ethnic group that has faced some discrimination and members of this group seek to influence the political process in order to reduce this discrimination. A party could help in a system based on proportional representation because if a high percentage of group members voted for the party, it could win parliamentary seats and bargain to join a governing coalition.[59] However, if the society has a first-past-the-post system (i.e., the winning candidate simply needs the most votes), there is little likelihood that group members would rationally pursue party organization. The reason is that if the party was perceived to be linked to the needs of a minority ethnic group, it would have trouble reaching the vote threshold needed to win seats. Of course, depending on how such an electoral system is structured, a minority ethnic party could achieve reasonable representation under some conditions. For example, if an ethnic minority is geographically concentrated, constituting a majority in some areas, it might be in the minority at the national level but still capable of winning a number of seats in the legislature.

Finally, the nature of the historical and structural relationships between groups, including their relative power, could matter greatly in influencing the likelihood of ethnic party development. For example, historical discrimination against a group may motivate them to form a party.

So far in this subsection, we have been discussing political parties based on ethnic group membership. But what about gender? Interestingly, political parties based on gender are much rarer than parties based on ethnicity. Why might this be the case? Some scholars suggest that women-only political parties may not be popular because women are institutionally linked to men: Their interests as individuals and as members in other groups are tied in important ways to the interests of individual men and other members of those other groups.[60]

Institutions for Promoting Women's and Minority Group Representation

Many social movements and political parties seek to influence institutional design in ways that will expand a certain group's political representation. While social movement organizing and political party formation can acquire a degree of permanence, institutional design can potentially shape outcomes independent of the ongoing efforts of activists. In other words, this approach seeks to turn empowerment into an automatic feature of the political institutions of a given country.

The fundamental institutional design feature that has been used is a quota system, which reserves a certain number of candidacies or seats for members of a group.[61] This system has been implemented in a number of different ways. The biggest division is between "reserved-seat" systems and "candidate-quota" systems.[62] Reserved-seat systems are what they sound like: systems that reserve a certain number of seats for members of a particular group. For example, constitutions in some Latin American countries guarantee a specified number of seats for members of one or another Indigenous community. In Aotearoa New Zealand, Indigenous Māori voters have had special Māori seats in the national Parliament since 1867.

Reserved-seat systems are the oldest form of quota system, and they tend to have only a limited impact on the representation of women's groups.[63] This limited impact may be due, in part, to the politics of implementing them: agreeing to set aside a high percentage of all seats for members of a particular group may meet with political opposition in many circumstances.

The other major types of systems are "candidate-quota" systems.[64] Here the idea is to guarantee that a certain number of female candidates—or members of other groups as the case may be—are running in elections. One major way this takes places is within political parties. Although gender-based political parties are relatively rare, political parties may still address issues related to gender, or they may position themselves to capture the votes of those who favour gender equality. Thus, some parties will aim to formally or informally increase the number of female candidates within the party. When this is done formally, it is a party-level quota system. For example, a Social Democratic Party in country X might apply to itself the rule that 30 per cent of its candidates for legislative office will be women. Imagine that they face a Christian Democratic Party as their main opponent. That party will now have to make a strategic choice: One possible option among others would be to apply a quota that matches or exceeds that self-imposed quota on the Social Democrats in order to demonstrate that, despite other ideological and policy differences, the Christian Democratic Party is progressive on issues of gender equality.

Party leadership may succeed in self-imposing quotas in systems where proportional representation is the norm, given that party leadership tends to have more power to select its candidates in such systems. If voters vote for parties rather than individual candidates, it is easier for the party to impose formal rules on itself as it selects candidates. How do you think such an approach would work in the United States, where many candidates are not selected by party leaders but in primaries where voters choose the party's nominee? What would happen if the Democratic Party leadership decided that it wanted to adopt a 40 per cent quota for female candidates? Would the Republican Party follow suit?

Another way quota systems can be adopted is through a law or constitution stating that *all* parties must meet certain quota thresholds.[65] But the adoption of such a system can be difficult to achieve as well and would require major changes in how elections are organized. More generally, the likelihood of a country developing a quota system that applies to all parties would depend on each party's calculation of its own electoral prospects if such reforms are carried out, as well as each party's relative power. If a given party stands to benefit from new arrangements, it can be expected to support them, but if a party is either strongly ideologically opposed to the idea or stands to have trouble meeting quota requirements, it is likely to resist their universal imposition. Scholars debate which quota system is most effective.[66]

You can see the complexity of analyzing how, when, and why institutional design affects the representation of women or members of other groups. Two things, however, are clear. First, global efforts to expand political representation of women are clearly increasing, and different quota systems have led to important gains. Second, social-scientific interest in these issues is increasing as well—something to keep in mind for your next research project.

More generally, remember that the causes we have considered in this section are not mutually exclusive explanations of how empowerment takes place. Rather, they are potential tools for those who seek to empower minority groups, women, and other groups. In many cases of successful empowerment, these elements work together. For example, it is possible for social movement organizing to help produce both political parties and new institutional designs. However, parties and institutional design also influence the environment in which social movement organizing takes place. There seems to be no standard way in which these pieces fit together.

INSIGHTS

Quotas for Women in Politics: Gender and Candidate Selection Reform Worldwide

by Mona Lena Krook

Krook has developed an innovative approach to the study of empowering women through institutional design. She compares a number of cases of more and less successful adoption of reserved-seat and candidate-quota systems, and she draws the following general conclusions, among others:

1. The causal impact of a given variable is not universal but rather depends on interaction effects with other variables. Thus, there is no "one size fits all" approach to institutional design in this area.
2. Institutional design can affect three major arenas, those of "systemic," "practical," and "normative" institutions. Different sorts of institutional design efforts affect these arenas in different ways. Not only do formal institutional changes matter, but moral arguments about issues such as justice and equity do too.
3. Processes of change differ in quality. The more successful ones are "harmonizing sequences" in which changes build on one another and actors adjust for unintended consequences of previous stages, while "disjointed sequences" are less successful.
4. Many actors with a variety of goals are involved in these processes. These actors include, at the very least, state-level actors like politicians, actors in "civil society" like activists, and "transnational" actors like certain NGOs. It is exceedingly difficult to predict how such actors will interact.

Mona Lena Krook, *Quotas for Women in Politics: Gender and Candidate Selection Reform Worldwide* (New York: Oxford University Press, 2009).

THINKING COMPARATIVELY

Indicators of Gender Empowerment

KEY METHODOLOGICAL TOOL

Selecting or Creating Indicators

An indicator is a measure that indicates the presence, amount, or degree of a variable you are researching. Good indicators have to work effectively in at least two ways. First, they have to be true to the underlying concept you are researching. Second, they need to be actually measurable, meaning, among other things, that any observer using the indicator will see it in more or less the same way. Another way to say this is that indicators must comprise measures that are both "valid" and "reliable."

A useful recent indicator we have for studying women's empowerment is the GDI, or Gender Development Index, which is prominently featured in UN Development Reports. The GDI seeks to measure the extent to which women have political and economic control of their lives and environments in different societies. It is a composite indicator based on underlying measures of women's and men's shares of (1) political positions, (2) prominent economic roles, and (3) overall income.[67]

Imagine that we wanted to evaluate how well the United Kingdom and some of its former colonies are empowering women relative to Spain and its former colonies. Why would we do this? We might, for example, have looked at the Gender Development Index (formerly the Gender Empowerment Measure, or GEM) and got the impression that in the United Kingdom and formerly British Western settler states, women were better represented politically than in Spain and Latin America. The GDI on the surface is supposed to provide a measure of the political empowerment of women. Bringing together several indicators, this measure and its predecessor have been used in a number of United Nations reports in the late 2000s and for many purposes, despite criticism, was considered by many the best single measure of gender empowerment at that time.

If we look at Gender Development Index (GDI) ranks for 2016 for the former British colonies in which we are interested (see Table 14.1), we see that Australia ranks second, Canada and the United States share 10th place, New Zealand 13th, and the United Kingdom 16th. Ranks for former Spanish colonies are not this high, with only Spain at 27th place. Does this mean that former British colonies for whatever reason are sites of higher levels of political empowerment for women? This could be misleading. Since GDI is a composite measure, it captures economic empowerment as well. It may be that the strong showing of former British settler colonies (relative to former Spanish colonies) in terms of GDI is a consequence of higher levels of economic development in these societies.

Let's try a narrower indicator that can help us to better understand the *political* empowerment of women. What if we look at the percentage of women holding legislative office? This could give us a clearer indication of *political* empowerment, given that it won't include information about the relative *economic* standing of women, which we may consider to be a different question (see Table 14.2).

TABLE 14.1 | Gender Development Index (GDI) Global Ranks, Selected Countries

2	Australia
10	Canada
10	United States
13	New Zealand
16	United Kingdom
27	Spain
37	Chile
45	Argentina
54	Uruguay
68	Cuba
118	Bolivia

Source: UN, *Human Development Report, 2016,* http://hdr.undp.org/sites/default/files/2016_human_development_report.pdf.

TABLE 14.2 | Ranking of Percentage of Women in National Legislature, Selected Countries

Rank	Country	% Seats in Lower/Single House	% Seats in Upper House
2	Bolivia	53.1	47.2
4	Cuba	48.9	N/A
9	Ecuador	41.6	N/A
12	Spain	41.1	33.8
15	Nicaragua	39.1	N/A
17 (tied)	Mexico	38	33.6
22	Argentina	36.2	38.9
29	New Zealand	31.4	NA
44	Australia	26.7	38.2
49	Canada	25.2	38.6
57	United Kingdom	22.8	24.1
73 (tied)	United States	19.3	20.0

Source: Interparliamentary Union, 2015, *Women in National Parliaments*, http://www.ipu.org/wmn-e/classif.htm

Here, we see a very different pattern. In our set of comparative cases, Bolivia is on top, and the United States is on the bottom. New Zealand is the only former British settler colony in the top 30, and Bolivia, Cuba, Ecuador, Spain, Nicaragua, Mexico, and Argentina all outperform *all* the other former British settler colonies in our group (as do Costa Rica and El Salvador, though they do not rank as highly as the other Latin American countries listed in Table 14.2).[68]

Does this demonstrate that selected former Spanish colonies have higher levels of the political empowerment of women than former British colonies? Not necessarily. Can you think of some of the limitations of this indicator? One would be that legislative representation is not the only form of representation. Another might be that empowerment of a group, even political empowerment, likely extends well beyond having members of that group hold office. Both of these are concerns about the potential *validity* of this indicator as a measure of the underlying concept we are researching: political empowerment of women. What we see here is that a number of former Spanish colonies have achieved very high levels of legislative representation of women, outpacing former British settler colonies by this measure, which is interesting and deserving of comparative exploration. Using an intersectional lens, we could also ask whether these women were white or were Indigenous and/or racialized peoples as well, and we could also problematize their economic status. Perhaps white women from upper-class backgrounds have done very well in Latin American legislatures, while Indigenous women from poorer backgrounds have not.

The bottom line is that there is almost never a *perfect* indicator. (Indeed, the United Nations recently replaced the former GEM with the GDI in response to scholarly critiques.) All choices of indicators involve trade-offs. You should be mindful of these trade-offs and remember that indicators are only stand-ins for the underlying concepts you are researching. Indicators and measurements are crucial in understanding the extent to which women and ethnic and racial groups are empowered and active in politics. Conducting careful comparative research can give us greater insight into questions that matter to us on issues as profound as our very identities as people.

Chapter Summary

Concepts

- The meaning of concepts like race and ethnicity varies in relation to context. While some people think of race and sometimes ethnicity as biological, most social scientists view them as culturally constructed. As such, the term "racialized" is more often used.
- Gender is distinguished from biological sex, and most social scientists think of gender as cultural rather than biological.
- In recent years, a number of societies have grown more pluralistic and tolerant with respect to sexual orientation, although intolerance and violence remain high in many countries.

Types

- Race historically has almost always been linked to social actors' beliefs about biology, whereas ethnicity has emphasized cultural traditions. The concept of race in particular has been linked to exploitation.
- Discrimination based on both race and ethnicity is a common feature of many polities, historically and today. Discrimination has in some societies become more subtle over time but nevertheless continues. An intersectional analysis can demonstrate ways in which different forms of discrimination can converge.
- Discrimination based on gender is also a pervasive feature of polities, and gender discrimination remains a problem.
- Empowerment can be economic, symbolic, or political.

Causes and Effects

- One potential source of empowerment is social movement mobilization.
- Another is political parties, and parties tend to be more viable for ethnic groups seeking empowerment than for gender groups.
- Institutional design strategies like reserved seats and quotas can also be used in support of empowerment.

Thinking Comparatively

- A thought experiment about relative gender empowerment in the former colonies of Spain and the United Kingdom demonstrates the pros and cons of two major indicators of political empowerment.

Thinking It Through

1. The theme of empowerment is much discussed in this chapter, including dimensions of empowerment and ways in which development is conceptualized and measured by social scientists. But what *is* empowerment? Develop your own conceptualization, and link it back to the discussion in the chapter. What, if anything, is missing?
2. We discussed political, economic, and cultural or symbolic empowerment. How are these dimensions related? Is one more fundamental than the others, and, if so, why? If a group wants to improve its position, would it be best advised to begin by focusing on one or another form of empowerment?
3. Imagine now that you have been asked to consult with social movement activists who represent poor rural women of a particular ethnic group. They tell you that their ethnic, gender, and class status compound each other and that their interests really are distinct from those of other groups. They would like your technical assistance as they aim to build a social movement. In particular, they would like your advice about how to "frame" that movement. What questions do you ask them, and how do you advise them? How is this case different from organizing around "women's issues" or the interests of a particular ethnic group?
4. Imagine that you are an "empowerment consultant." You have been contacted by the representatives of a political party that represents the interests of an ethnic group that has historically faced severe discrimination, one that is largely found in a particular area of the country and that constitutes about 10 per cent of the country's population. They tell you that their country is going to write a new constitution and that they have a number of delegates in the constitutional assembly. They want your advice about what sorts of institutional designs they should push for as they aim to protect the interests of their people. What do you need to know in order to give them advice? How would your answer depend on their answers?

15 Ideology and Religion in Modern Politics

In This Chapter

From left to right, Venezuelan president Hugo Chavez, Cuban president Fidel Castro, and Bolivian president Evo Morales wave to the crowd during a meeting among the three countries in Havana, Cuba in 2006. (Jose GOITIA/Gamma-Rapho via Getty Images)

If you were to walk last year through downtown Caracas, Venezuela, you might have seen huge banners with pictures of Argentinian Marxist revolutionary Che Guevara and slogans declaring the arrival of "21st-century socialism." Supporters of Venezuela's late president, Hugo Chávez, and his "Bolivarian Revolution" (named for Venezuelan revolutionary Simón Bolívar) extolled the virtues of the regime, which continued under Nicolás Maduro. The *Chavista* government was not alone in its socialist position, as governments in countries like Bolivia, Ecuador, and Nicaragua have taken a similar line.

Halfway across the globe, if you stroll through Tehran, Iran, you will encounter very different public symbolism. The Iranian government, which also calls itself "revolutionary," attempts to garner public support through justifying itself in religious terms—through the regime's close adherence to the Shi'a branch of Islam. Scholars who study relationships between religion and the state find that in much of the world, religion remains very influential.[1] Moreover, survey research shows that much of the world's population has religious beliefs.[2]

If you had told comparative political analysts in the 1960s that regimes like these would proliferate in the early 21st century, most would have disagreed sharply because they expected their particular understanding of modernization to render ideology and religion obsolete.[3] A large proportion of such theorists agreed that religion would fade from public life in coming decades.[4] Yet both ideology and religion continue to exert a strong influence on modern politics. In 2015, even in fairly secular Canada, some 30 per cent of people embraced religion, higher than the 26 per cent who rejected it. Almost half of respondents—44 per cent—declared themselves "somewhere in between."[5]

Their persistence has led analysts to ask a series of questions: How has the role of religion in modern societies changed as societies have modernized? Why haven't ideologies such as communism disappeared? Finally, the persistence of ideology and religion draws attention to important, perennial questions of social and political theory concerning the role of ideas in politics. To what extent do religions and ideologies affect political processes? As we outlined in Chapter 5, some analysts argue that certain religious ideas increase the likelihood of economic development. Related theories, mentioned in Chapter 6, suggest that certain religious ideas promote democratization.[6] These are unsettled questions, and there is a lot of interesting work to be done in this area of comparative politics.[7]

• • •

Concepts

political culture The symbolically encoded beliefs, values, norms, and practices that shape the formal distribution of power in any given society.

modernity A contested term that refers to a type of society, typically one experiencing economic growth and with a relatively strong state, among other characteristics.

modernization The process through which a society becomes "more modern," which is typically understood to mean having an advanced economy and, sometimes, a democratic polity.

Both ideology and religion, when considered from the perspective of political science, are examples of what scholars call **political culture**. This means, essentially, that they are different types of *representations* that people hold about politics and related matters. People have all sorts of beliefs, but ideological and religious beliefs tend to be deeply held and therefore may be highly impactful. This does not mean that religion and ideology are the same thing, of course, as we discuss in this chapter. Ideologies are explicitly political in their orientation, whereas religions might have political implications but are broader belief systems that extend well beyond politics.

Given that our interest is in understanding ideology and religion in *modern politics*, and since much analysis concerns the relationship between these phenomena and **modernity**, we start by discussing the concepts of modernity and **modernization**. Note that you have already seen these concepts come up from time to time in earlier chapters.

Modernity and Modernization

"Modernity" is one of the most important labels in contemporary political life and is a cultural construction, tracing its origins to a particular time and place.[8] In other words, people (primarily European and North American thinkers) created the concept of modernity, and like all ideas that bear on competition for status and power, it served certain interests and did not serve others. Most fundamentally, the idea of "the modern" helped to both motivate and justify European and American colonial projects in Africa, the Middle East, Latin America, the Pacific, and Asia.[9] Indeed, this concept was perhaps one of the most formidable tools of those colonial projects' "soft power."[10] The European powers and some members of the Westernized classes in the subjugated, colonized populations agreed that such societies needed modernization. The watchwords of this vision were *technical efficiency*, *education*, *literacy*, *civilization*, and ***secularism*** (favouring secular—non-religious—culture). It is not surprising, therefore, that anti-colonial resistance was, in its first generation, typically carried out using this same conceptual language:[11] Rather than being seen as agents of modernization, colonizers were reinterpreted as being barriers to it. Bound up with the notion, sometimes explicitly and sometimes implicitly, were the corollaries that modernization was both a necessary and an inevitable process.

secularism The ideological complex that favours secular (non-religious) culture.

Transforming ideas like "modernity" and "modernization" into social-scientific concepts is a difficult task, since we do not want to reproduce the biases found in the original concepts.[12] Indeed, some scholars have called for the abandonment of these concepts altogether and advance some persuasive arguments in support of their ideas. In this book, we argue that the concepts are still worth using, partly because most of the world continues to talk about modernity and modernization. Political scientists and scholars in related fields generally mean several things by modernity and modernization, or they focus on several distinctive features of modern or modernizing societies.[13] First, they often characterize modernity by growth-oriented, or capitalist, economies rather than "traditionalistic" economic systems in which there is little accumulation of wealth over time. Second, they often characterize modernity by its open system of stratification, meaning that social position in modern societies is not fixed at birth. In "modern" societies, according to this view, social, political, and economic forms of mobility are both possible and legitimate. Third, they often characterize the chief political form of modernity as the modern, bureaucratic state; they see centralization and bureaucratization of power as hallmarks of modernity. Finally, as noted in Chapter 13, some scholars see national identity as a distinguishing marker of modernity. As we discuss later, scholars increasingly note that modernization can take a variety of forms.[14]

Ideology

Most comparative political analysts think of **ideologies** as highly organized and rationalized systems of ideas that directly bear on politics.[15] According to this way of thinking, your ideas about your tastes in music, fashion, food, and so forth may not be ideological.[16] But whether you know it or not, your thinking about politics is probably shaped by an ideology. This ideology most likely contains ideas about what rights people should have and where these rights come from, ideas about whether individuals matter more than groups or vice versa, ideas about how the economy ought to be organized, and ideas about how collective decisions should be reached. Some people can be considered very ideological, meaning that they think a lot and very clearly about these things or even that they are rigidly devoted to their views about them, but all of us are influenced by ideologies to some degree.[17]

ideology A systematically coordinated and cognitively salient set of beliefs focused on politics.

Major political ideologies include liberalism, fascism, and socialism, each of which we discuss further later in the chapter. It is worth noting that these major political ideologies are largely secular and either oppose or sideline religion as a basis for organizing politics. Some scholars have gone as far as arguing that ideologies are like "secular religions."[18]

Religion

functional definition Definition that aims to define a given phenomenon by what it *does*.

substantive definition Definition that aims to define a given phenomenon by what it *is* rather than by what it does.

Mainstream analysts tend to think about religion in two basic, contrasting ways: by using **functional definitions** and by using **substantive definitions**.[19] Functional definitions specify what religion *does*. They define religion by its ability to foster social integration, to give people a sense of order through creating and telling myths about history and the cosmos or by its ability to motivate collective action. If we use a functional definition, we see lots of things—including modern ideologies—as religion. For certain research purposes, this view may be helpful.

More often, as we have seen throughout this book, when doing comparative analysis we want to make clear distinctions so that we can locate and explain variation. Substantive definitions of religion help to make this possible. A substantive definition focuses on the content of religious belief or organization, its "substance" rather than just what it does. For example, a substantive definition might say, "Religions are systems of belief that grant a prominent place to a single overarching deity." For many purposes, though, this particular definition would not be helpful, since a number of religions (e.g., Buddhism) do not have gods and many others (e.g., animism and Hinduism) have many gods or god-like entities. More commonly, though, substantive definitions of religion argue that what separates religion from other aspects of culture is that it gives prominence to some transcendent force (i.e., one beyond the normal or merely physical human experience).[20] This might be a deity, a goal such as Nirvana, or even the Platonic ideal of "the good."

Along these lines, some analysts define religion substantively as a cultural system or network of beliefs and organizations that are oriented toward the transcendent.[21] Note that this definition, unlike most functional ones, allows us to then pose empirical questions about religion's growth, decline, or changing features because we can track change about beliefs in the transcendent over time.

Secularization, Religion, and Modern Politics

secularization The process through which (according to some theories) societies become less religious as they become more modern.

As we noted previously, for a number of years comparative analysts thought that religion would decline in the modern world. They called this idea "**secularization**" or "secularization theory," and they came up with a number of reasons for their prediction.[22] Some noticed that as societies modernized, new religious groups emerged, giving people greater religious choice. For example, in modern Canadian society—unlike in, say, medieval France—one can choose from a wide variety of world religions and in particular from a large array of Christian denominations. Some scholars thought that this pluralism would undermine religious belief because religious people would be less likely to have their beliefs constantly reinforced by like-minded people around them.[23] Others thought that modernization would cause religion's decline because of the importance of science and technology in the modern world. According to this point of view, "rational" explanations would replace "irrational" religious ones, leaving some people "disenchanted."[24]

Scholars have noticed, however, that this theory seems to describe only one small part of the world: western Europe.[25] Much of the world is very religious, and some claim that

Blackfox Images/Alamy Stock Photo

PHOTO 15.2 Baitun Nur Mosque in Calgary, Alberta, is the largest mosque of the Ahmadiyya Muslim Community in western Canada. Citizens and residents of Canada today can choose from a variety of world religions and are free to establish their own places of worship throughout the country.

over the longer term, societies like the United States have actually become *more* religious.[26] Moreover, since societies with the highest birth rates tend to be more religious than societies with low birth rates, we may see continuing increases in global religiosity in coming decades.[27] Canada, by contrast, is becoming less religious over time.

Comparative analysts continue to note some important changes in religion's role as societies modernize, however, and the old theories of secularization are not all wrong. Scholars today do not agree on whether we should call these changes "secularization," but they widely agree that we should distinguish between any change in religious belief itself and changes in religious *institutions* or *organizations*.[28] It seems that when societies modernize, religious institutions or organizations tend to become increasingly **differentiated** (independent) from the state, although, as we shall see, the extent of this varies.[29] Along similar lines, in some, but not all, modern societies, religious institutions and organizations become **privatized**.[30] This means that they become increasingly independent not just of the state but of the **public sphere**: They lose their status in support of public claims. For example, in societies with a strong tradition of privatizing religion, such as France, efforts by the church to influence major political decisions are viewed negatively. Much of the comparative analysis of religion and politics today involves mapping institutional or organizational changes and then trying to explain the different patterns that emerge. For example (as we discuss in more detail in the "Types" and "Causes and Effects" sections), some societies separate church and state and then organize religions as denominations.[31] Some almost fully privatize religious institutions and organizations, while others allow the state to control them. Comparative analysis seeks to explain these variations.

differentiation The process through which institutions become increasingly autonomous from one another, including the reduction or other change in the linkages between religion and other institutions.

privatization In the context of the social-scientific study of religion, this refers to the process of religious practice being confined to the private sphere.

public sphere The space in which public life and deliberation take place (as opposed to the "private sphere").

Religious Conflict

Religious conflict is not surprising in a world with major ideological and religious differences, especially as religion's relationship to politics is in flux.[32] Many analysts assert that religion has served and will continue to serve as a motivator for international conflict, and we certainly have seen dramatic examples of religiously inspired violence across national boundaries in recent years. Others draw our attention to cases where pluralism within a polity causes great tension that leads to violence. Analysis of such cases is often complicated by the fact that religious difference tends to go along with other types of difference, such as regional and ethnic identity. As such, many of the theories discussed in Chapters 12 and 13 are used to explain religious conflict as well.

Types

In this section, we begin by describing and exemplifying the major forms of ideology visible in modern politics. We then move on to do the same for the major patterns of religious involvement in politics.

Modern Ideologies

As noted previously, the main families of modern political ideologies are liberalism, fascism, and socialism. This list is not exhaustive of the ideological universe, of course, but these are the most important major ideologies that political scientists have analyzed.

Liberalism

liberalism An ideology that emphasizes individual freedoms, representative democracy, and the market economy.

Liberalism is probably the most widespread and influential of modern ideologies. Indeed, it is so widespread that sometimes analysts do not even notice that it is an ideology. Thus, scholars who declared that ideologies would disappear in modern society often did not include liberalism in this prediction.[33]

Like all complex ideologies, liberalism takes many forms, and not all of them are fully consistent. In general, though, the ideology of liberalism holds that (1) individuals are and should be more important than groups; (2) individuals' relationships with the state should be organized through democratic citizenship; (3) a democratic political system should be representative, and it should have constitutional limits that protect the rights of individuals; and (4) free-market capitalism is the best, and for many the most "natural," way of organizing the economy.

social democracy An ideological movement that favours both representative democracy with respect for basic individual rights and state action to promote relative economic and social equality.

libertarianism A form of liberalism focused on individual rights and especially concerned with minimizing the role of government.

Our fourth point is that different variants of liberalism take different stances on the state's role in the economy. Many analysts consider **social democracy** to be a variant of liberalism, though it owes a great deal to socialism as well: It promotes state management of the economy as a means of preserving representative democracy. Broadly, liberalism is a continuum, from **libertarianism**—the view that the state's involvement in the economy and social life should be minimal—to social democracy.

We should briefly mention "conservatism" in this context. In early 19th-century Europe, conservatism was a distinct ideology, one that aimed to restrain modernization processes, defend monarchy, and preserve religious organizations in their traditional positions. We can still today speak of conservatism as a strong cultural tendency in many societies. Indeed, in some societies it could still be treated as a distinct ideology. Yet in many societies conservatism has come to constitute a form of liberalism. In contemporary Canada, the United States, and western Europe, few conservatives would go as far as questioning liberalism's emphasis on representative democratic institutions and markets.

Fascism

The ideology (or family of ideologies) known as **fascism** was very prominent in the 20th century, which saw fascist governments in Spain, Portugal, and Italy, among other places.[34] Some analysts also classify national socialism (the ideology of the German Nazi Party) as fascist, while others see it as a distinct form given its totalitarian aspirations and more virulent, race-based form of government.

fascism An ideology associated with regimes like the Nazis and that of Italy's Benito Mussolini, favouring authoritarianism, militarism, and right-wing nationalism.

Fascism can be distinguished from liberalism in several ways. First, fascism does not share liberalism's respect for the individual. Rather, fascist ideology holds that the state, as the embodiment of the nation, is most important. In the paradigmatic case of Italian fascism under Mussolini, fascism was grounded in a nationalism that sought to recover the "glorious" history of Ancient Rome. Second, in line with fascism's lack of concern for the individual, the political programs associated with it typically do not make much effort to protect the individual's rights. Third, fascism is anti-democratic in that it views an authoritarian protector for the nation (e.g., Francisco Franco in 20th-century Spain) as preferable to liberal democracy, which it argues can be co-opted by ideologies and actors hostile to the nation's interests. Finally, while fascists often embrace capitalist economics, they typically promote state capitalism, in which the state has control of production and the use of capital.

Liberals criticize fascism not only for its lack of respect for individual rights but for the horrific human rights abuses that have been carried out in its name. Socialists critique it for these reasons as well and often add the critique that, in their view, fascism is fundamentally about preserving the capitalist economy. Indeed, some socialists believe that capitalism will inevitably fall back on fascism as its ultimate defender.

Socialism

Perhaps the most widely discussed ideology (or family of ideologies) is **socialism**. Though there are many forms of socialism, by far the most influential socialist was Karl Marx, although the ideology predated him, with a range of European socialists such as French theorists Charles Fourier and Pierre-Joseph Proudhon and British theorists John and Robert Owen. Marx constructed his socialism as a critique of liberalism.

socialism An ideology (or family of ideologies) that emphasizes economic equality as a key goal, to be pursued in large measure through state action.

According to Marx, the freedoms promised by liberalism were illusory.[35] For example, Marx said, you might believe you can liberate people by giving them freedom of speech or religion, but this belief is based on a misunderstanding of freedom and the ways in which we are unfree. The main problem in modern society, from this point of view, is not that authoritarian regimes limit people's ability to make their own choices but that our economic system alienates us. In our ideal state, Marx says, we would experience fulfillment through labour. But capitalism, which divides our

Matteo Bazzi/ANSA via AP

PHOTO 15.3 People take part in a Liberation Day march in front of Milan's Duomo Cathedral in Italy in April 2019. Liberation Day celebrates the end of fascist dictatorship in Italy during World War II.

labour via manufacturing and the bureaucratic organization of office work, makes it impossible for us to find fulfillment in this way. Marx further argued that capitalism impoverishes the majority as it enriches a parasitic minority. To solve these problems, socialists like Marx argued that revolution is necessary. The working class must take control of the state and use it to promote the collective ownership of factories and other elements of the productive process, which are controlled by "capitalists." Once this happens, Marx hoped, socialism will eventually give way to *communism* in which there will be no forced division of labour and, thus, no alienation. These ideas inspired much of the world in the 20th century, leading to the establishment of socialist or communist regimes in China, Vietnam, Russia, Cuba, and many other places. Many socialists, however, became disillusioned with these regimes. Some saw them as brutal and dehumanizing, with little likelihood of ever producing the promised world, free of alienation. Some of these disillusioned individuals turned to the ideology of liberalism. Within it, a subset attempted to construct a modified version—social democracy, which (as mentioned earlier) aims to preserve representative democracy and the respect for individual rights through active state management of the economy. Social democrats have been some of the most ardent supporters of the welfare state discussed in Chapter 4. Moreover, they are hard to locate within the typology of ideologies we have developed here. Some would see social democrats as liberals because of their emphasis on democratic institutions and freedoms. Others would see them as socialists, since many social democrats emerged from the socialist tradition and since they tend to favour more state spending than do liberals. Finally, despite the emergence of social democracy in the 20th century, there are still numerous proponents of more traditional socialism in the world, and some have played an important role in protest against globalization and related phenomena.

Modern Forms of Religion in Politics

In much of the world, religious and political institutions are intertwined.[36] Even in Canada, which remains a fairly secular country, Queen Elizabeth II (the head of our executive branch through the governor general) is both the Queen of Canada and the "Supreme Governor" of the Church of England.[37] Most governments at the organizational level are involved with religious organizations. Governments often regulate religions, stipulating what they can and cannot do. Governments also affect religious organizations financially. Many governments offer religious organizations direct financial support. Others give them tax advantages. Finally, numerous societies have **established religions**, meaning there is an official religion of the state, such as in the United Kingdom.[38] Yet even in such cases, we see some level of differentiation between religious and political institutions.

established religions Religions that are granted official status and support by the state.

Lay and Religious States

Most societies see increasing differentiation of religious and political institutions as they modernize. This does not happen in the same way everywhere, though there are several common patterns. A prominent one is the "laïcist" pattern in which the state seeks to completely dominate and privatize religion.[39] The core idea is that public life must be "**lay**" rather than religious: The state is seen as sharply antagonistic to religious organizations as if competition between them were zero-sum. One of the most important examples of this pattern is France. In a society exhibiting this pattern, it is not just that the there is a separation between church and state but that, culturally, religion tends to be considered a matter of private conscience and nothing more. What this means will become clearer later when we discuss denominationalism.

lay state State that establishes a formal separation of religion and public life.

We should note that laïcism sometimes goes along with socialism in ideology. There are liberals who favour a laïcist approach—and, indeed, the earliest architects of laïcism in both France and Latin America considered themselves liberals. However, most modern socialist regimes have been laïcist in their approach to religion, including the Soviet Union, Maoist China, and Cuba since soon after Castro came to power in 1959.

In societies with laïcist systems, there are often minority groups and religious organizations that favour the inverse set of arrangements: a theocratic state or at least one in which a single religion is given support. Moreover, sometimes these individuals triumph and overturn lay states.

We can speak of societies such as Iran as "**religious states**." Like lay states, their proponents often view competition between religion and a secular state as zero-sum. The difference is that they favour the religious side. Religious states vary a lot, and some are more tolerant of minority religions and of secular people than others. Saudi Arabia, for example, has no tolerance for other religions within its borders and promotes a restrictive view of Sunni Islam known as Wahhabism. Costa Rica, which takes Roman Catholicism as the state's official religion is, by contrast, fairly tolerant of religious difference. One way of gauging a state's religious tolerance is to see how large the non-mainstream religious communities within the state are and whether their activities are restricted either by government laws or by various informal restrictions.

religious state State in which religion is a key part of official politics, often involving religious establishment, religious legitimation of the state, and restrictions on religious minorities.

CASE IN CONTEXT

472

Yemen's Civil War: What Is the Saudi Role?

Since 2015, Saudi Arabia has been intimately implicated in a civil war in neighbouring Yemen. During the Arab Spring in 2011, Yemen's long-serving authoritarian leader, Ali Abdullah Saleh, handed over the presidency to his deputy, Abdrabbuh Mansour Hadi, who was unable to maintain control of the country. Hadi's government broke down in 2015 because of the rise of the Houthi, a predominantly Shi'a movement. (Shi'a Muslims are about 15 per cent of the population versus Sunni Muslims, who are around 80 per cent.) The Houthi wanted more transparent and representative government and an end to Hadi's Sunni-dominated regime, which they argued was too close to Saudi Arabia. When the Hadi government collapsed, a coalition of eight Sunni Arab countries (led by Saudi Arabia) began air raids on Yemen with the goal of returning Hadi to power. Iran, a Shi'a-dominated country, provided arms and aid to the Houthi. While the major players in the conflict all practise the Islamic faith, there are major splits between Sunni and Shi'a populations that have led to countries taking one side or another in this civil war.

Sami Abdulrhman/picture-alliance/dpa/AP Images

PHOTO 15.4 Yemeni women wave flags during a rally in March 2019 organized by the Iran-backed Houthi rebels to commemorate the fourth anniversary of the Saudi-led military campaign on Yemen.

See the case study on Yemen's civil war and the Saudi role in Part VI, p. 472. As you read it, keep in mind the following questions:

1. Has Saudi Arabia committed human rights abuses in Yemen? Why has the United States supported the Saudi position?
2. Why has the United Nations categorized this war as "the world's worst man-made humanitarian disaster"?
3. If the Houthi had not targeted Riyadh with ballistic missiles in 2017, would Saudi Arabia have become so heavily involved?

denominationalism A system or set of beliefs that privileges denominational forms of religious organization.

religious pluralism The situation in which there are multiple religious organizations within a given society (the opposite of **religious monopoly**).

denomination A type of religious organization, prevalent in the United States, among other places, that is voluntary and accepts the principle of religious pluralism

Denominationalism

Scholars take full **denominationalism** to be somewhat exceptional. The main example of a fully denominational system is the United States. One could argue, though, that societies with growing **religious pluralism**, such as Brazil, might be moving toward a denominational model. In addition, *some* societies where established religions coexist with religious pluralism and high tolerance for religious difference share certain characteristics of the denominational model.

To fully understand denominationalism, we must first understand the concept of the denomination. If you live in Canada, you are probably used to hearing religious groups referred to as "**denominations**," which are different from "churches" in the traditional sense and "sects."[40] A "church," as social scientists usually use the term, typically tries to make itself mandatory in a given territory and to link itself to the state (social scientists who study religion use this word in a more restrictive sense than you probably do). A sect, in contrast, often tries to turn *away* from the state and from public life and is typically defined as a group that removes itself from some other religious organization. Denominations are in a middle ground between churches and sects, engaging in public life but respecting pluralism (at least in principle) and considering membership to be voluntary.[41]

Examples of denominations include the Anglican Church and the United Church of Canada, with branches throughout the country, while sects have fewer numbers and are often concentrated in some geographic regions. Examples include the Hutterites and the Doukhobors, which are sects from central and eastern Europe that eventually set up communities throughout western Canada.

A society in which religious difference is organized denominationally tends to see many different religious groups and organizations. Unlike in a laïcist society, however, denominations do not consider politics to be off limits. In a denominational society such as Canada, religious leaders of all persuasions routinely make pronouncements about public life. Majorities in many denominational societies consider religious motivations appropriate in politics, as long as one or another religious group is not ultimately favoured by the state, though sometimes this leads to controversy.

Some scholars have viewed denominationalism very positively as offering a good way to manage religious difference. As a result, there is some discussion about whether and to what extent it can be exported.[42] Views on this matter depend largely on explanations of denominationalism's origins. If its origins lie in institutional design, perhaps it is exportable. If they lie in difficult-to-change features of a society, such as levels of religious pluralism and diversity, it would be harder to export to countries without similar conditions.[43] If this is the case, however, perhaps denominationalism can develop spontaneously in different societies. We should note that denominationalism often coincides with the ideology of liberalism. At the same time, many proponents of liberal ideology are laïcist and worry that denominationalism can lead to states treating majority religious groups preferentially. Further, they worry that it may lead to failure to fully protect the rights of minority religious groups, depending on demographic factors and disproportionate political influence.

INSIGHTS

Religion and Canadian Party Politics

by David Rayside, Jerald Sabin, and Paul E.J. Thomas

Rayside, Sabin, and Thomas examine the relationship between the state and religion in distinct geographical regions of Canada, with chapters on Catholicism in Newfoundland and Labrador, the special case of Quebec, the decline of conservative religion in Alberta, and the rise of evangelical religion in the North. The authors explore three main areas of contention. The first concerns the traditional denominational conflict between Catholics and Protestants, which began as France and Great Britain competed for control of Indigenous lands, goods, trading routes, and peoples. The second key issue concerns the overall climate of secularism since the 1960s whereby new political divisions have developed between political reformers and religious conservatives. The third area of contention since the 1990s has been on the recognition of non-Christian rights, with a focus primarily on Islam but also on Judaism, Hinduism, and other religions. While this book focuses primarily on Canada, the authors also draw explicit comparisons with religious belief and policies in other Western industrialized countries, including the United States.

David Rayside, Jerald Sabin, and Paul E.J. Thomas, *Religion and Canadian Party Politics* (Vancouver: UBC Press, 2018).

Causes and Effects: Why Do Religion and Ideology Remain Prevalent in Modern Politics?

Since religion clearly remains an important part of politics in most of the world, we examine causal arguments about the changing role of religion and ideology in modern politics. We begin with religion and then turn to ideology.

Why (and How) Does Modernization Alter Religion's Role in Politics?

Virtually all mainstream scholars agree that "modernization" changes religion's role in politics. They may disagree about the details, but generally they hold that (1) as societies modernize, religious organizations tend to be increasingly differentiated from other organizations, especially the state; (2) as economic development increases, religious belief tends to decline somewhat—*maybe* not as much in more religiously diverse societies, though this is subject to much debate.

Modernization Theory and Secularization

As we noted earlier in the chapter, traditional secularization theories hypothesized that "modernization" would lead to religion's decline. Most often such theories did not distinguish between (1) decline in rates of religious belief and practice (measured through surveys of beliefs or of attendance at religious services) and (2) changes in religion's public role. In addition, these theories often focused on particular features of modernization, such as increasing social mobility, increasing pluralism, and the growth of Western science.

Over the past couple of decades, secularization theories have been heavily criticized.[44] Yet some scholars have continued to promote them, often assembling powerful evidence

INSIGHTS

Sacred and Secular: Religion and Politics Worldwide
by Pippa Norris and Ronald Inglehart

Norris and Inglehart test secularization theory against data drawn from the World Values Survey from 1981 to 2007. They hypothesize and argue that societies with high levels of human development have more "existential security" and less need for religion. Their argument is based on several assumptions. First, they assume that religion's main function is to help people deal with what they call "existential insecurity." In other words, religion comforts people in the face of suffering and death. They then assume that, as development increases, suffering is decreased and death delayed. Life expectancies rise, debilitating illnesses are reduced, and infant and child mortality decline. They suggest that this should lead to a decline in religiosity, and they test their hypothesis by analyzing the relationship between increasing human development and levels of religious belief. They find much support for it, since increasing human development leads to some decline in religiosity in general. However, they encounter some anomalies, most notably the case of the United States, which has both high levels of human development and high religiosity. They explain this anomaly by noting the high levels of income inequality in the United States relative to other countries with similar levels of human development.

Pippa Norris and Ronald Inglehart, *Sacred and Secular: Religion and Politics Worldwide*, 2nd edn (New York: Cambridge University Press, 2011).

(see the "Insights" box on *Sacred and Secular: Religion and Politics Worldwide*). The evidence assembled by scholars such as Norris and Inglehart is hard to ignore. That being said, critics of this theory make two arguments worth consideration. First, it could be that some confounding variable helps to explain religion's relative decline in some societies. Second, not all scholars are convinced by Norris and Inglehart's explanation of why the United States has high religiosity despite its high level of development. In any case, the controversy over secularization theory rages on.

The "Religious Economies Approach"

Over the past two decades, many scholars have proclaimed a new paradigm in the social-scientific analysis of religion.[45] It is distinguished from other work in the field by its heavy reliance on methods derived from economics and rational choice theory. Indeed, it is sometimes referred to as the "supply side approach" to religion.[46] Whereas previous theories treated questions of religiosity as being ultimately about variations in levels of religious *demand*, the "religious economies approach" posits that a generic level of religious demand is a constant and that what explains variation in religiosity is the nature of the *religious market* in any given society. As with all markets, the theory further assumes, monopoly is bad, since competition spurs innovation and the tailoring of specific (here religious) products to market preferences. Thus, the United States, which has high levels of religious pluralism and no established (monopoly) religion, has high levels of religious belief. European societies, which generally have low levels of religious pluralism and, often, established religions, exhibit low religiosity. Canada falls somewhere in between. This approach has been hugely influential, aided by the increasingly visible role of religion in public affairs. Sociologist Rodney Stark has argued that the world is growing *more* religious because of increasing religious specialization. He claimed that medieval Europe (so often the historical benchmark for religiosity) was not really that religious because it had high levels of "**religious monopoly**."[47]

religious monopoly The situation in which one major religion dominates the religious landscape within a given society (the opposite of **religious pluralism**).

While the "religious economies approach" has been influential, empirical evidence on the impact of levels of pluralism is mixed. Some studies have found that pluralism is linked to increased religiosity, while others have found the opposite and still others have found no discernible effect.[48] Some scholars also criticize the approach's rather narrow focus on questions of attendance at religious services or on self-reported measures of religious belief rather than on institutional shifts.

Institutional Theories

Much work in the comparative analysis of religion and politics takes a different tack, focusing on institutions and organizations. These theories aim to explain how and why religious organizations become differentiated from others, particularly from the state, and why religion becomes privatized.[49]

The classical sociological approach to these questions viewed societies as complexes of interdependent institutions that function together *systemically*, meaning they are connected by ordered networks.[50] Traditional forms of this approach held that societies are *functionally integrated*, or that linkages between social institutions depend on their related and overlapping functions. An institution such as the state may have as its core functions the preservation of order and the coordination of collective projects, whereas a religious institution might have as its core function the creation of societal legitimacy, providing a narrative that supports the existing social order. Note that in many societies these functions overlap: A religious organization such as a church, mosque, or synagogue might help to legitimize the state, which in turn might protect and support the religious organization.

According to differentiation theories, as societies modernize, they generate an increasing number of interdependent institutions. For example, in a relatively simple society, socialization could take place via the large, intergenerational family. But when the process of socialization becomes more complex—for example, when it begins to require specialized knowledge that family members do not have—new institutions must form to serve these new requirements. Thus, once societies reach a certain level of complexity, there is a need for a separate educational system. When the complexity increases even more, differentiation increases *within* that educational system (e.g., separation of primary, secondary, and post-secondary education; longer and more complex post-graduate training; greater field-specific technical training, and so on). This differentiation of non-religious institutions would gradually reduce the scope and autonomy of religious institutions, turning them into one institution among others rather than society's core integrating institution.

Such an account raises the question of why some societies might incline toward greater complexity to begin with. Many, perhaps most, scholars have assumed that increasing complexity (and therefore differentiation) is rooted in economic processes. Adam Smith, Emile Durkheim, and Karl Marx—representatives of very different traditions—all saw the increasing division of labour as the motor in this process. From this general point of view, the source of ongoing differentiation in modern societies is capitalism. Note that this account of why capitalism and economic development might lead to secularization is very different from Norris and Inglehart's view, discussed in an "Insights" box earlier in the chapter. Norris and Inglehart assume that the psychology of the individual actor is the mechanism connecting development and secularization. Differentiation theories, on the other hand, typically assume that the mechanism exists at the level of institutions rather than individual psychology.

Not all theories of differentiation look like this, however. Some are more actor-centred and suggest that differentiation takes place if and when powerful individuals and groups *want* it to take place. For example, some scholars have argued that the differentiation of religious and educational institutions in the 19th-century United States and Canada did not happen simply because of the society's increasing complexity. Rather, they argue, it happened because some key, socially mobile groups benefitted from drawing a sharp distinction between science and religion and from bounding clear institutional turfs for each.[51]

Why Didn't Ideology (and History) End?

Scholarly attention to religion has, to some extent, displaced attention to secular ideologies in recent years. This trend is probably best explained by current events and contemporary history: Religion has *seemed* to matter more in recent political conflict. In recent years in particular, there has been resurgence of both the left and the right around the globe.[52] Conservative evangelical Christianity and some conservative forms of Islam have been influential in a diverse range of societies (for example, conservative evangelicalism has been influential in the United States while conservative Islam has been influential in Afghanistan, among other countries). In many societies, right-wing actors, both religious and secular, have attempted to scale back or dismantle the welfare state—we see this very clearly in the United States. On the left, we have seen some actors turn to social democracy, which is consistent with the arguments of those who forecast an "end to ideology." Social democrats and liberals in general believe that some version of capitalism should be allowed and that liberal-democratic government is preferable to authoritarianism. Others on the left, however, seek an ideology that will stridently oppose liberalism, such as "**21st-century socialism**."

"21st-century socialism" Ideology of government supporters in some contemporary societies (e.g., Venezuela, Bolivia) that aims to emphasize the allegedly more participatory and democratic features of these governments.

INSIGHTS

The End of History and the Last Man

by Francis Fukuyama

In this famous, controversial, and sometimes misunderstood book, conservative theorist Fukuyama argues that political conflict has been seen as ideological struggle since the beginning of modernity. Many different visions of the good life have contended with one another, from socialist to religious conservative. Liberalism was only one contender among many until the fall of the Soviet Union delegitimized socialism. Then, claims Fukuyama, no alternative to liberalism was left standing, and a consensus emerged about market relations in economics, liberal democracy in politics, and open stratification in society.

Many read Fukuyama's thesis as if he were simply arguing that the "good guys" won the Cold War, though his argument is more ambivalent, suggesting that the end of great ideological struggles would make it harder to find meaning and achieve great things. This argument has been the subject of major debates, most notably between its supporters and those of Samuel Huntington's "Clash of Civilizations" argument. Critics of Fukuyama say he failed to see other sources of division and conflict, that the fall of the Soviet Union does not invalidate all leftist regimes and ideologies, and that his account is teleological, meaning it assumes that history has a particular destination, or "end," toward which it is directed.

Francis Fukuyama, *The End of History and the Last Man* (New York: The Free Press, 1992).

Efforts to articulate "21st-century socialism" have been particularly important. The idea here is to incorporate and respond to criticisms made of 20th-century socialism—for example, that it was anti-democratic and allowed for the establishment of *new* oppressive bureaucratic hierarchies and that it was often murderous on a mass scale—without throwing out socialism's core aspirations. Proponents of 21st-century socialism, therefore, tend to accept the Marxist critique of capitalism as essentially exploitative and alienating and hope for a utopian future. They suggest that this can be achieved via a form of political decentralization that they call "participatory democracy."[53]

In various parts of the developing world—especially in several Latin American countries in recent years, particularly Venezuela, Bolivia, and Ecuador, among others—these ideas have captured the imaginations of self-described revolutionary governments. Nicolás Maduro (and his predecessor, Hugo Chávez) in Venezuela and Evo Morales in Bolivia, and the many intellectuals and politicians associated with them, claim that ideological conflict remains. They claim that their governments constitute an alternative to liberalism, although it's not always precisely clear what that alternative is. In November 2019, Morales resigned amid controversy over the outcome of the recent Bolivian presidential election. He argued that a coup had taken place, and stepped down after nearly 14 years in power.

Religious opposition to liberal/secular modernity and alternative ideologies such as "21st-century socialism" share some things in common and are in other ways very different. Contemporary Venezuela and Iran have sometimes made common cause, probably not only because they share some common interests but because their ideological positions are sufficiently compatible, at least in the short run. What is shared? First and foremost, perhaps, is a clearly articulated opposition to the United States. But beyond this, they share a criticism of liberal modernity as falsely universalizing a particular kind of experience *and* as hiding deeper alienation and exploitation. It is for this reason, in part, that Chávez and others like him could compellingly use religious discourse even as he and the Catholic Church remained in sharp conflict.[54]

INSIGHTS

The Clash of Civilizations and the Remaking of World Order

by Samuel Huntington

Within political science, conservative theorist Samuel Huntington was one of the earliest voices claiming that religion would play an important, indeed resurgent, role in contemporary geopolitics. In *The Clash of Civilizations*, he famously argued that the world was divided into a set number of distinct "civilizations" and that these civilizations were built around different cultural traditions and often incompatible values. What would replace old ideological conflicts between the Soviet Union and United States would be a clash between the world's civilizations, particularly between Islam and "the West." While many critics rightly derided this analysis as simplistic, reductionistic, even racist, it gained wide currency, particularly after the terrorist attacks of 11 September 2001. For many public commentators and media figures, Huntington's model of opposed cultural traditions was an explanation that vindicated the history of US foreign policy while more or less demonizing Muslim majority states. Huntington's thesis, built on earlier work by the controversial historian Bernard Lewis, laid part of the ideological basis for US President George W. Bush's "war on terror," which was primarily focused on regime change in the Middle East.

Samuel Huntington, *The Clash of Civilizations and the Remaking of World Order* (New York: Simon and Schuster, 1996).

INSIGHTS

Multiple Modernities

by Shmuel N. Eisenstadt

Many scholars have argued that contemporary ideological and religious conflict is less about "tradition" versus "modernity" and more about different "modernities," or different understandings of what modernity means. Seemingly conservative systems such as the contemporary Iranian regime incorporate elements of the "modern package." They revise the meaning of key terms, however, in relation to their cultural traditions and to the goals of those shaping the system: Iran's "democracy" may not be Europe's democracy.

According Eisenstadt, we can make sense of such cases by recognizing that there are multiple modernities. This label recognizes that the modernization processes witnessed in Canada, the United States, and western Europe are not the only available models but rather that modernity might take different forms in other cultural contexts. The concept of modernity may have roots in the West, but it was carried globally via processes of diffusion (especially, though not exclusively, via colonialism), and it has been reframed and reinterpreted wherever it has gone.[55] Many scholars have understood the pairing of capitalism in economics and liberal democracy in politics as the core features of modernity. These are only forms, however, of the more general phenomenon of growth-oriented economics and political systems. Thus, early critical modernities arose in the competing alternative ideologies of the 20th century: communism and fascism. From this point of view, the alleged "religious resurgence" of recent years should be considered another example of this process of emergent alternative modernities. While Eisenstadt's approach shares some ideas with Huntington's assessment, it differs notably in pointing to common underlying features of modern societies.

Shmuel N. Eisenstadt, "Multiple Modernities," *Daedalus* 129(1, Winter 2000): 1–29.

These issues have practical, policy-relevant importance. We can only hope to come to terms with contemporary international religious and ideological conflict if we can first understand its sources, and the foremost task here is to examine the nature and aspirations of regimes that define themselves as in conflict.

THINKING COMPARATIVELY

Is 21st-Century Populism an Ideology?

KEY METHODOLOGICAL TOOL

Knowing When to Use a Typology

We could always construct types and subtypes of any complex feature of politics. A key methodological question is when and why to do so. Typologies draw distinctions that highlight some similarities and draw out some differences, but when we compare cases, there are many potential similarities and differences on which we could focus. The choice to use a typology, as well as which one to use, should depend on the research question at hand. If you are tempted to use (or create!) a typology, ask yourself which similarities and differences would be emphasized by that typology as well as which similarities and differences might be obscured.

The early 21st century has been marked by the rise of a variety of movements and political candidates that have been labelled "populist." Is this an ideology? "Populism" is a word that can mean different things to different people, but generally it signifies that these movements and candidates tend to identify themselves with "the people" and to claim that some set of institutions or groups have been damaging the interests of the people and need to be removed from power.[56] Often, those institutions and groups are perceived to be "foreign." For example, many populists in Europe are nationalists who are critical of the European Union and its policies. In Greece, the populist Syriza movement blames the EU for austerity programs that have been imposed. Populists in a number of other European polities blame the EU for policies that allow refugees and other migrants to enter their countries. In Latin America, many populists blame the United States for its history of intervention in the region. But some—like contemporary Venezuela—also blame international institutions like Human Rights Watch for criticizing their regimes' human rights abuses, claiming that these organizations are lackeys of the United States or of European countries. Populists in the United States might simultaneously blame immigrants, globalizing trade deals, and the cultural attitudes of educated elites for their country's problems.

Jan-Werner Müller argues that populism can be identified by two characteristics. First, populists present themselves as opposed to "elites."[57] We can add that these elites may be foreign or domestic, but either way they are presented as being apart from the people and operating against their interests. Second, populism is "anti-pluralist," meaning that populist leaders claim to represent the people in its entirety. According to Müller, this makes populism always potentially anti-democratic, since pluralism—the idea that there are multiple versions of the good and a variety of groups deserving to be recognized—is a key feature of most democratic societies.[58] Another key scholar of populism, Cas Mudde, defines the phenomenon in a closely overlapping way, again emphasizing the opposition of populism to pluralism but adding that it is also opposed to elitism. Mudde emphasizes that populism is a "thin" ideology and as such can be mixed with other ideologies.[59]

To some extent, populism seems to upend traditional distinctions between "left" and "right." There are populists most would locate on the right, such as Donald Trump in the United States, Geert Wilders in the Netherlands, and perhaps Maxime Bernier in Canada with his People's Party. There are those that appear to be located much further on the left, such as Venezuela's Chavistas or, arguably and to a lesser extent, politicians like Bernie Sanders in the United States.[60] Indeed, there have been both right- and left-leaning varieties of Peronista populism in Argentina. Two scholars have recently argued that we should see left versus right and populist versus anti-populist as distinct ideological "dimensions."[61]

This raises the question of whether there are "types" of populism. Another way to put this is to ask whether, since populists vary so much, they fall into categories that we can use to better understand and predict their behaviour.

Some scholars suggest that there is a big difference between "inclusive" populism, which they say is common in Latin America, and "exclusive" populism, which they say is

CTK via AP Images

PHOTO 15.5 Geert Wilders, a populist politician in the Netherlands best known for his outspoken racism against immigrants and Muslims.

common in Europe.[62] According to such arguments, the first type is distinguished by the fact that it aims to open up access to the state and its benefits to people—typically, people with lower socio-economic status—who previously had not been included. Thus, for example, the populism of former Bolivian president Evo Morales could be thought of as "inclusive" because it represented "the people" as Indigenous persons and nations, rural populations, and others who have historically been marginalized. Those who promote this typology offer France's National Rally (formerly the National Front) as an example of "exclusive" populism. This is because they tend to define the white French population as "the people" and to treat historically marginalized groups like migrant populations as targets.

This distinction does seem to be meaningful. After all, the power and status of out-groups probably affect their vulnerability to populist regimes. So "exclusive populism" may be more damaging to already marginalized groups than "inclusive populism." And it may be possible, as some scholars have argued, that populism can be used to expand access to power and resources among disadvantaged persons in polities where many people have been largely ignored by the state.[63] Skeptics, though, would remind us that if populism undermines democratic institutions, any such gains might be temporary at best. Evidence from cases like Venezuela suggests that even "inclusive" populism can lead to authoritarian regimes that ultimately make most people worse off.

At the same time, we should avoid letting the distinctions in our typologies blind us to commonalities. For example, the similarities among populist regimes and movements may for many purposes be more important than the differences. First of all, many of the white French supporters of the National Rally may themselves feel disenfranchised and excluded from power. In a number of cases, working-class populist supporters seem to be drawn from populations who once supported socialist parties or parties of "labourers." The decline of these parties in some countries and their transformation into "third way" parties in others may have left a number of these individuals feeling unrepresented by the institutions of traditional politics. There may still be a difference between a disenfranchised person in the developing world supporting a populist candidate who claims she or he will redistribute resources and a middle-class person in a rich country who is anxious about the economy and increased migration who supports a xenophobic populist. But both may feel relatively disadvantaged in some way, and this may play a role in their shared receptiveness to populist ideas. If this is true, separating cases by this typology may make it harder to see common causal patterns.

The key point here is that whether a typology such as this will be useful depends very much on the reason one is making a comparison and the question one is asking. Any time that we distinguish or categorize, we highlight one or another characteristic in a set or subset of cases. We need to select the typology for our research purpose and be careful not to "reify" it, or treat it as more than a useful theoretical abstraction.

So, then, is populism an ideology? Most scholars could probably agree that populism influences things in ways similar to the way that ideologies have in the past and that it has important implications for how our polities and economies may be organized in the future. It includes a series of ideas we can identity, as the definitions from Müller and Mudde cited previously show (emphasis on "the people," suspicion of "elites" and "foreigners"). Whatever one might think of these ideas, they seem to shape the behaviour of many political actors in our world.

Chapter Summary

Concepts

- Religion and ideology are two major forms that ideas take as they shape politics.
- Ideology gets defined in lots of ways, but many scholars see it as systematically organized beliefs about how politics and society should be constructed.
- Religion, too, gets defined in many ways, but a large number of scholars see it as a system of beliefs and accompanying organizations that posit a transcendental source of meaning.
- Some scholars used to think that religion and ideology would both decline as societies modernize, but it now appears to most students of comparative politics that they continue to shape politics in meaningful ways.

Types

- The main modern ideologies are liberalism, fascism, and socialism. Much of 20th-century international conflict was interpreted in the light of these ideologies.
- There is consensus that while religion does not necessarily decline when societies modernize, religion does tend to undergo a process of differentiation. Scholars have tried to explain this in several ways.
- There are three main ideal-typical patterns of modern relationships between religion and politics: lay states, religious states, and denominationalism.

Causes and Effects

- Modernization theory argues that as economic development takes place, religious belief and practice will decline. We have mustered some very strong evidence in support of this theory, though there are also some anomalies.
- The "religious economies school" is most interested in the relationship between religious pluralism and religious belief. According to this theory, the more diverse the offerings in any given religious marketplace, the more religious belief and practice you will find. As with modernization theory, this approach has strong evidence behind it but also serious anomalies.
- Many theorists focus on changing relationships between religious organizations and the state rather than just looking at whether individual-level belief and practice go up or down over time. These scholars have produced a variety of theories to explain why some societies produce lay states, others religious states, and still others denominational systems.
- Strong evidence indicates that religion and ideology have not gone away but are, rather, at least as important factors in shaping comparative politics today as they were decades ago.

Thinking Comparatively

- The ideological landscape of contemporary Latin America points to the potential utility of different typologies in comparative analysis.

Thinking It Through

1. Canada and the United States have marked contrasts in their levels of religious belief and in the denominational ways in which each state organizes religious difference. How can some of the theories outlined in this chapter help us to analyze these differences? How can they account for why these differences exist?
2. As noted previously, some prominent actors in Latin America claim to be making a "revolution" in favour of "21st-century socialism." Some of their critics argue that this is no different from earlier forms of socialist ideology. What would the "21st-century socialists" say in response to this charge? Who do you think makes a stronger case, and why?
3. Proponents of the "multiple modernities" approach argue that modernization takes notably distinct paths in different cultural contexts. In contrast, traditional

modernization theory says that modernization is always the same basic underlying process, though cultural context shapes how it happens. How could we design a comparative analysis to judge between these two theories? Which cases would you select, and why? What questions would you ask about them?

4. We have seen that liberalism and socialism have been enduring political ideologies. The other major modern political ideology, fascism, has fewer proponents today. Has fascism likely disappeared? Why or why not? Under what circumstances might we expect to witness a resurgence of fascism?

PART V

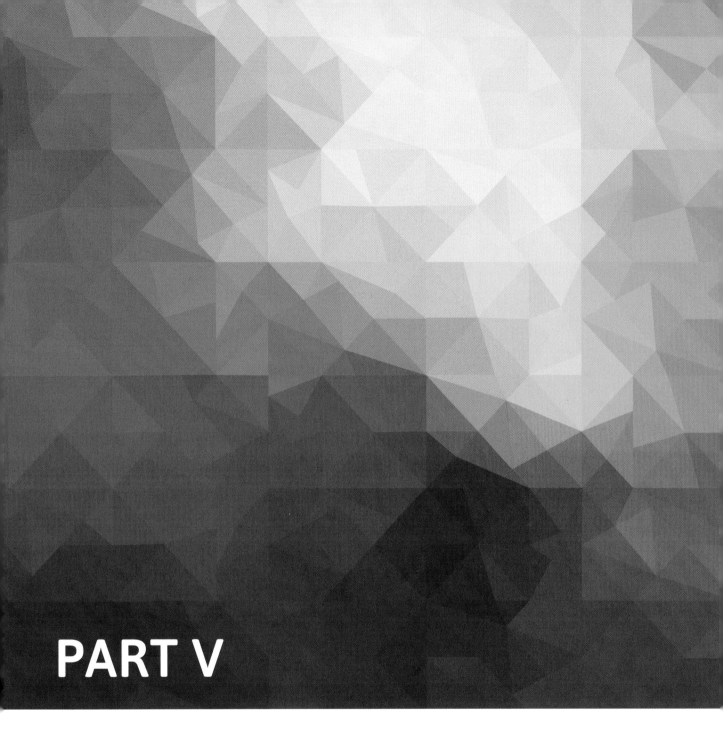

The Comparative–International Nexus

16 Comparative Politics and International Relations

In This Chapter

Students carry an inflated globe with the European Union flag during a "Fridays for Future" protest for urgent climate action in Muenster, Germany in 2019. (GUIDO KIRCHNER/AFP/Getty Images)

The years between 2009 and 2019 saw major economic upheaval across Europe as 19 of the continent's economies struggled desperately to save their common currency, the euro. The crisis came after several years in which eurozone countries (European Union countries whose currency is the euro) in southern Europe faced high levels of debt. Greece ultimately required a bailout from European funds—and then a second one in 2012—sparking fear of contagion, since Portugal, Ireland, Spain, and Italy also risked defaulting on their debts. As Europe's largest economy and the centre of the eurozone, Germany sought to hold the euro together without a massive bailout of the slower-growing economies. It pushed for strict controls on spending in the southern European countries, including requirements for austere budgets that would cut back on generous social programs and old-age pensions.

The complications were numerous: Although Germany called for austerity in southern European countries, it had benefitted from exports to those indebted countries, and banks in Germany, France, and abroad risked collapse if the euro fell apart. By 2012, the euro seemed to be hanging on by a precarious political and economic arrangement, one that involved a mix of cooperation and diplomatic fights among Europe's major allies. While the EU economies began to bounce back by 2016 and growth rates have risen in 2017 and 2018, there are still concerns that many of the larger structural problems have not been resolved. For example, in 2018, with a new right-wing government in power, Italy objected to the tight controls on spending and borrowing. The government, composed primarily of the populist Five Star Movement and an anti-immigrant League (formerly Northern League), wanted to spend more money and cut taxes. However, after Greece, Italy had the highest debt load in the EU, which meant that a lack of financial prudence could cause further problems for the euro.[1]

From a Canadian perspective, the EU represents the second-largest market for our goods and services, with trade in goods valued at €64.3 billion in 2016 and trade in services at €30.1 billion in 2015. What happens to EU economies has a marked impact on ours, and the federal government has sought to expand Canada's trade relationship through the EU–Canada Comprehensive Economic and Trade Agreement (CETA), which provisionally came into force in September 2017.[2] If a post-Brexit arrangement comes to pass, Canada will need to negotiate new and separate trade agreements with the United Kingdom.

In many respects and despite recent controversies, the EU has been a remarkable success story. After the devastation of World War II, Germany and France (along with Italy, Belgium, the Netherlands, and Luxembourg) led a process designed to bring Europe together economically and politically. It was clear that Europe wanted to avoid another cataclysmic war, and the continent's leaders felt that integration was the solution. The process began with a common market in coal and steel, which was symbolically rich in indicating shared sovereignty over the very materials needed for war. Integration later expanded into a broader common market between these countries, and the European Community took on new members: the United Kingdom, Denmark, Spain and Portugal (after the two countries became democracies), and Greece. Integration then widened and deepened further, moving beyond **free trade** to free movement of people across many European borders, increasing the role of the renamed **European Union (EU).** Alongside this process, the Berlin Wall fell in 1989, East and West Germany reunified in 1990, and the Cold War ended by 1991. The EU ultimately invited in most of the countries of central and eastern Europe, as well as countries in Scandinavia and even Mediterranean island nations. It also created the euro in 1999 for the majority of its countries, deepening its integration further even as it expanded to include 28 countries (see Map 16.1).

Yet throughout all of this integration, the countries of the EU have jealously guarded their sovereignty, and major decisions and treaties must be approved unanimously. The

free trade A policy or approach in which a government allows foreign goods and services to compete freely with domestic production, as contrasted with protectionism, which favours domestic production.

European Union (EU) The political and economic union of many European states, numbering 28 as of 2019.

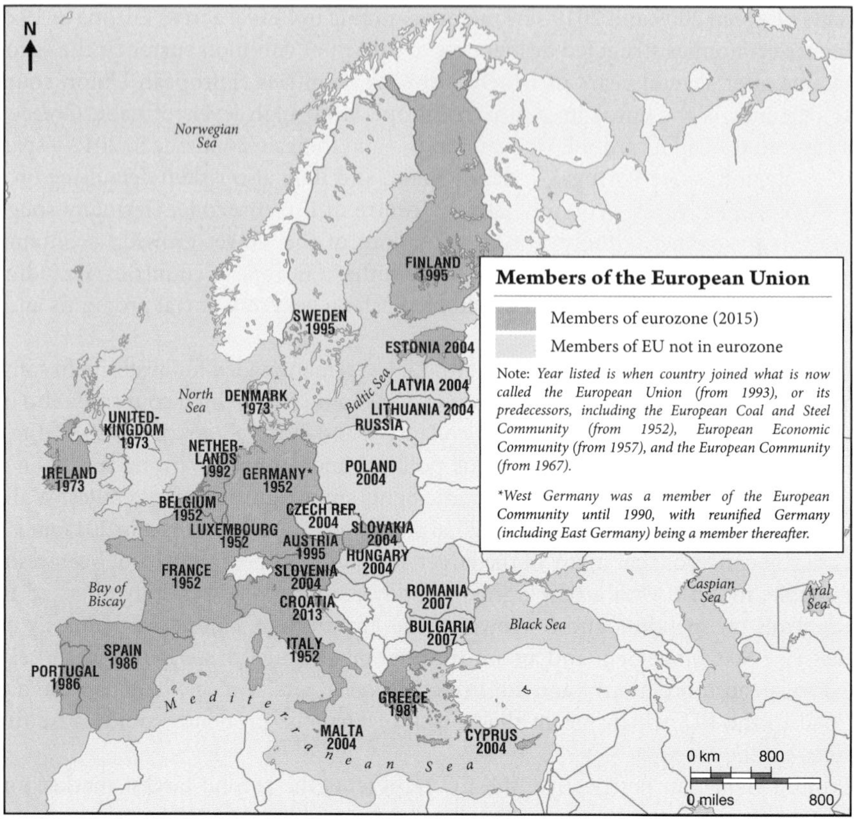

MAP 16.1 Members of the European Union.

Note: At time of publication, the United Kingdom had not confirmed an exit date from the European Union.

UK remains the only country to have actually voted successfully to withdraw from the EU. Some countries, such as Norway and Switzerland, opted to stay out of the EU altogether.

European integration since World War II thus offers one of the world's greatest contemporary examples of international cooperation, while it also demonstrates the challenges of this cooperation and the reality that most states engage in international relations with a view toward their own national interests. Whether the ambitious and remarkable European project of postwar unification is in the process of foundering or flourishing, it is important to note how the comparative politics of different countries interfaces with international relations.

• • •

Concepts

international relations The study of relations between countries and between actors in the international system.

foreign policy The set of policies toward foreign nations made by a national government.

Throughout this text, we have examined issues of comparative politics, which tends to focus on politics *within* different countries. In some instances, we have made reference to factors that cross borders, such as revolutions or processes of democratization that come in waves. Yet we have not focused directly on the many areas of **international relations** *between* countries, including war and peace and economic relationships. In discussing the actions of governments in international relations, we are often referring to decisions made in **foreign policy**.

We consider two main areas under the topic of international relations: international security and international political economy. **International security** in a traditional sense refers to issues of war and peace between nations and to issues of global security and conflict more broadly. As we discuss here and have noted previously, these issues include terrorism and terrorist acts committed by nonstate actors. In addition, civil wars and conflicts may take place within a state and yet involve the relations between states. For example, a rebel group that is trying to take over the government in one country may seek refuge in a neighbouring country. All of these issues of security and conflict fit in the domain of international relations, but they intersect with the comparative politics we have discussed throughout this book.

international security The study of issues of war and peace between nations and global security and conflict more broadly.

These are the standard "guns and bombs" descriptions of security studies, but the field has certainly expanded in recent decades to include what one might call non-traditional security issues. Canadian political scientist Peter Stoett, for example, dubs this traditional focus a minimalist interpretation and instead calls for a maximalist one, which includes global warming, refugee crises, environmental disasters, and many other issues that create insecurity not just for humans but for the planet itself.[3]

Beyond security studies, the other principal area of study in international relations is **international political economy**, which examines how the economic relations between countries affect politics and how political relations affect economies. In the modern world, countries trade in goods and services, and money flows across borders, often reaching trillions of dollars a day. Comparative politics and international relations intersect on political economy issues when it comes to questions of globalization, international trade, international finance, and efforts at integration or cooperation on economic issues.

international political economy The study of how the economic relations between countries affect politics and how political relations affect economies.

International relations issues do not always fit neatly in one or the other of the two main categories we've set out here. Consider, for instance, efforts to stop flows of illegal drugs across borders. Is this a question of international security or of international political economy? A plausible answer is "both." Similar arguments could be made for questions of refugees fleeing violence in one country or of immigration more generally. Many issues in the 21st century are **transnational** in that they cross borders. The range of issues linking comparative politics and international relations is vast, and we explore them in this chapter.

transnational Issues or institutions that cross international borders.

We will briefly examine some of the leading issues in which comparative politics and international relations overlap and affect one another. We look at how domestic politics affects international relations and how transnational issues affect the politics of different countries. Many of the issues we discuss are some of the great challenges and opportunities facing nation-states in the 21st century.

Issues

In this chapter, rather than address the "Types" we find in different social and political categories (such as types of revolutions, or types of development, or types of party systems), we focus on some of the leading issues in international relations that relate to comparative politics. These issues include economic globalization, immigration, transnational networks, and the global environment and sustainability.

Globalization and Trade

Globalization is one of the major trends in the world, a force shaping not only the economy but many aspects of everyday life. It refers to increasing interaction, both economic and cultural, between peoples and societies across national borders. Perhaps more than any other phenomenon, globalization epitomizes how international phenomena affect

globalization The increasing interaction, both economic and cultural, among peoples and societies across national borders.

comparative politics. We begin with a discussion of the economic relations that come with flows of goods, capital, and people across borders.

What crosses borders? First, traded goods do, in the form of imports and exports. These goods can include cars or food, minerals or natural resources such as cedar shakes and shingles, barrels of oil, milk products, or toys. Second, services are increasingly transnational. Examples include customer service call centres located in India or medical tourism that leads some residents of wealthy countries to seek out lower-priced surgeries in countries such as Thailand or Costa Rica. Third, money (or **capital**) crosses borders for a number of reasons. Many people and corporations have investments or own properties in other countries. Many immigrants living abroad send money home to their families or communities as well. And anything imported must be paid for, so money flows constantly. Finally, people cross borders, whether in search of opportunities for work or political freedoms, or to flee violence or strife in their home countries, or for recreation or business. With these transnational flows come challenges relating to the movements of goods, services, money, and people.

capital A factor of economic production consisting of accumulated wealth or financial resources available for investment.

international trade The economic exchange of goods, services, and capital across international borders.

Turning first to **international trade** of goods and services, economic interactions between countries have increased significantly in recent years. Many people in advanced, industrialized countries are aware that an increasing number of goods come from overseas, but the extent is still impressive: The clothes on your back may have been tailored in Bangladesh or Pakistan, the cellphone in your hand may have been assembled in Brazil or China, with parts from Malaysia, and the apple you had at lunch may have come from Chile. Increasingly, this is true of services as well, especially as technology makes it easier and cheaper to communicate around the world.

outsourcing In international trade and business, the practice of an economic actor contracting out to other actors, often overseas. (*See also* **offshoring**.)

offshoring In international trade and business, the practice of an economic actor basing some of its services or processes abroad rather than in its domestic market. (*See also* **outsourcing**.)

This increase in international trade has given rise to many concerns in wealthier countries about job **outsourcing** (contracting abroad) and **offshoring** (basing some services or processes abroad). This has been the basis of populist challenges (such as Donald Trump's "America First" trade ideas) to established economic and trading systems in many

Associated Photo/Paul Sancya

PHOTO 16.2 Trucks cross the Ambassador Bridge between Windsor, Ontario, and Detroit, Michigan, bringing goods back and forth across the Canada–US border. The bridge is part of the Windsor–Detroit Gateway, which is the busiest land border crossing between Canada and the United States.

countries. In some lower-income countries, it has also created enthusiasm about the prospects for growth. As wealthy countries rely on goods produced in emerging economies, and as emerging economies rely on markets in wealthy countries, the world economy becomes more **interdependent** (in that individual economies are dependent on one another) and interconnected.[4] The trend of increasing trade has thus given rise to many clichés about globalization, some of which may indeed have a grain of truth to them: The world is "flat" or "shrinking," we are living in a "global village," and we have never been closer.[5] This is not to say globalization is brand new: By some measures, the end of the 19th century, when Great Britain was the leading imperial power, was as globalized as any other time in history up to the past two decades. However, such globalization was highly skewed toward benefitting the colonial metropole at the expense of the colonies.[6] Today, countries have increasingly reduced their barriers to trade with one another over recent decades.

interdependence A relationship in which two or more actors (such as countries) are mutually dependent upon one another.

Trade between two or more countries—at least when it is voluntary—is based on the idea that the countries involved gain some advantage from trading. One of the leading principles in international trade and political economy is **comparative advantage**. This principle holds that countries can benefit from trade by specializing in the goods they can produce with the greatest relative efficiency and by trading for goods they produce relatively less efficiently.

comparative advantage In international trade, the idea that different countries or territories will have different relative advantages in the production of different goods and services, which forms the basis for gains from trade.

The following is a simple illustration to show the benefits of trade under the principle of comparative advantage. Imagine two countries, Pacifica and Atlantica, both of which have working populations that can produce shirts and phones. Pacifica is more populous, with 2000 people to Atlantica's 500. On the other hand, it takes somewhat fewer people in Atlantica to produce a shirt or a phone than it does in Pacifica (see Table 16.1). It takes five Atlanticans to make a shirt as contrasted with 10 Pacificans and 10 Atlanticans to make a phone as contrasted with 50 Pacificans. This is not necessarily because the skills of the workers differ by country but could perhaps be because there are more labour-saving machines in Atlantica, for example, which allow workers there to produce more rapidly. If Atlantican labour has advantages that allow it to produce more efficiently, how could these two countries gain from trading with each other?

For simplicity's sake, say Pacificans are interested only in buying more phones right now and Atlanticans are interested only in buying more shirts. The strategy for each country without trade would lead to 40 phones produced and purchased in Pacifica and 100 shirts in Atlantica:

Pacifica: *Have 2000 people produce 40 phones.*

Atlantica: *Have 500 people produce 100 shirts.*

But if the two countries can trade, the strategy for each country could be different. If the international price were four shirts to one phone, for example, the following is possible:

Pacifica: *Have 2000 people produce 200 shirts, then trade to Atlantica for 50 phones.*

Atlantica: *Have 500 people produce 50 phones, then trade to Pacifica for 200 shirts.*

TABLE 16.1 | Benefits of Trade under Comparative Advantage

Country	Population	Labour per Shirt	Labour per Phone	Possibilities without Trade	Possibilities with Trade (Price: 4 Shirts = 1 Phone)
Pacifica	2000	10 people	50 people	Make 200 shirts or 40 phones	Make 200 shirts, trade for 50 phones
Atlantica	500	5 people	10 people	Make 50 phones or 100 shirts	Make 50 phones, trade for 200 shirts

By specializing in the good they make relatively more efficiently and then trading, both countries are better off. Pacifica ends up with 50 phones instead of 40, while Atlantica ends up with 200 shirts instead of 100. The example would still work even if one country or the other wanted to trade only some of its product rather than all of it. And this example has two other noteworthy features. First, shirts require less labour to make than phones in each of the countries. Comparative advantage does not depend on countries differing on which product is easier to make than the other. Second, recall that a worker in Atlantica is more productive than a worker in Pacifica in making *both* shirts *and* phones, perhaps because of the machines they work with. Atlantica has an "absolute advantage" in both shirts and phones because both require less labour in Atlantica than in Pacifica. Yet comparative advantage still allows trade to benefit both countries, despite Atlantica's absolute advantage in both industries. This is the key lesson of comparative advantage, even though it is counter-intuitive for many people.

As for the politics of trade, some groups will clearly benefit from trade while others will suffer, at least in the short run. Critiques of economic globalization often focus on those who are disadvantaged by trade and who may be politically important actors. The economic gains from comparative advantage are in aggregate, and while they may appear good for consumers and some producers, the benefits are not equal for all producers.

In the preceding example, opening up to trade might actually put workers out of a job in the Atlantican shirt industry as Atlantica imports shirts from Pacifica and in the Pacifican phone industry as Pacifica imports phones from Atlantica. With exposure to trade, economic actors representing the relatively efficient sectors will benefit, and economic actors representing less efficient sectors may lose out. Free market economics may claim that these workers can simply move to the new industry (e.g., Atlanticans would move from making shirts to assembling phones), but this process is not simple: It can mean periods of unemployment and require retraining, for example. This change of industry can create economic, social, and political disruptions and uncertainty. Moreover, the more efficient phone-making gets, the more dependent upon technology (rather than human labour) its production might become, and it may be that those former shirt-makers in Atlantica end up working in lower-level service jobs, such as warehouse processing or retail. Finally, we should note that the process of offshoring production, if not adequately regulated or monitored, can result in environmental damage to the locations where production takes place. It can worsen environmental degradation around the world if production becomes "dirtier" overall by moving to countries with lower environmental standards.

For example, say that building phones requires a lot of capital investment to construct high-tech factories, while the shirt industry mainly requires labour and limited investment in some sewing machines. If Atlantica is relatively abundant in capital investment in the phone industry and Pacifica is relatively abundant in labour for making shirts, then Atlantican capital-owners will benefit from trade and Pacifican labourers will benefit.[7] Conversely, Atlantican labourers may not benefit as they find themselves competing with labourers in Pacifica, and Pacifican capital-owners may not benefit as they find themselves competing with Atlantican capital-owners. In an even simpler sense, ask yourself this: If you were the leader of Pacifica, would you want to have your economy based on producing shirts, or would you prefer to have your country produce higher-value and higher-tech goods like mobile phones? The answer to these economic questions often comes in the form of **protectionism**, or efforts by governments to protect domestic industries from foreign competition. The politics and demands of these different groups will influence the decisions made by governments. International trade is clearly an area where international politics affects the domestic and vice versa.

protectionism In international trade, the practice of a country protecting or giving favour to its own domestic producers.

International Institutions and Integration

Since World War II, countries have increasingly collaborated on economic and policy matters. This too links comparative politics to international relations because individual nation-states have made conscious decisions about international relations that are often based on domestic politics. Collaboration began between the advanced, industrialized countries and accelerated after the end of the Cold War. At the **multilateral** level between many countries (i.e., when three or more countries participated), cooperation took the form of freer and more open trade in goods, greater movement of capital and finance, and greater cooperation in international law to bring some criminals to justice.

Several **intergovernmental organizations (IGOs)** push for cooperation between countries and work toward conflict prevention. The **United Nations** is the most comprehensive of global institutions. It was designed after World War II to provide a global forum for diplomacy and conflict prevention, and it encompasses a number of agencies with missions to enhance security and development; these include the development organization UNICEF, the World Health Organization (WHO), and the United Nations High Commission for Refugees (UNHCR).

multilateral In international relations, the actions of three or more countries working together.

intergovernmental organizations (IGOS) The set of international organizations that push for cooperation between countries and work for the prevention or mitigation of international conflicts.

United Nations The most comprehensive global institution, which aims to prevent and manage conflict and to establish multilateral cooperation on matters of international law, economics, and human development.

Associated Press/B.K. Bangash

PHOTO 16.3 Refugees from Afghanistan in traditional dress at a reception organized by the United Nations High Commission for Refugees (UNHCR) on World Refugee Day in Islamabad, Pakistan, in 2018. Since 2001, World Refugee Day has been observed every June 20th to honour the strength, courage, and perseverance of refugees around the world.

international financial institutions (IFIs) Multilateral institutions, particularly the International Monetary Fund (IMF) and the World Bank, that have considerable leverage in the international economy.

integration In international relations, a process by which countries agree to collaborate economically or politically, to make some decisions collectively, and to shape common strategies.

Some multilateral institutions have had significant influence in the global economy and have been the source of much debate. This is especially true of the major **international financial institutions (IFIs)**, namely the International Monetary Fund (IMF) and the World Bank. These two organizations have had leverage in international politics, especially in the 1980s and 1990s. During that period, these institutions pressured developing countries to follow a free market model rather than a model that featured protectionism, investments by the government in state-owned enterprises, and greater state intervention in the economy (as noted in Chapter 5). This came to be known as the "Washington Consensus" because it reflected the policy recommendations of the World Bank and IMF, both of which are based in Washington, DC, along with the views of the United States government. Critics have argued that these draconian reforms hurt people and economies in developing countries and precipitated financial crises. Certainly these policies led to increased unemployment and a rollback of the welfare state in many countries.[8]

Apart from these global, multilateral institutions are a range of regional organizations. At this level, there is sometimes economic and political **integration** whereby countries agree to open up their economies to one another and shape common strategies toward other countries outside the regional bloc. There are many examples, including the Canada-U.S.-Mexico Agreement (CUSMA) and associations for free trade in South America, Pacific Asia, and regions of Africa, but the standout example is the EU, noted at the beginning of the chapter.

How the EU has achieved greater economic and political integration in a world of sovereign nation-states is one of the great questions of modern political economy. Over the decades from the 1950s to the present, much of Europe transitioned from a region of long-standing suspicions and historical animosities (such as between France and Germany) to a more closely integrated set of countries. They share a supranational set of political institutions and interdependent economies. As noted at the beginning of the chapter, European integration began as little more than a trade zone involving six countries and a common market in coal and steel. Over time, members reiterated a push for "ever closer union" between member countries. Subsequent treaties established the European Union, and its many member countries agreed to pool their sovereignty on some major issues. Besides the establishment of the euro, a notable example was the creation of the Schengen area, which eliminated internal border controls between the countries of the zone. The area encompasses the various EU countries on the continent (though not the United Kingdom or Ireland). The European Union now makes many of its decisions based on qualified majorities rather than on a "one country, one vote" principle.

We return to the example of the EU in the "Thinking Comparatively" section at the end of the chapter, but we note here that integration does not mean that nation-states have ceased to be important. In fact, even in the EU major decisions about issues such as foreign policy or taxation require unanimous consent of the member governments, meaning that each nation-state effectively has a veto. As one of the world's most integrated supranational bodies, the EU shows that most integration is still deeply dependent on the nation-state. At the same time, globalization and integration have occurred alongside the emergence of many identities below the level of nation-state, such as ethnic groups and regional groups, in countries from Russia to Ethiopia to Mexico. Thus, even as China has integrated with the world economy, the Uighur ethnic group in the west of the country has tried to secure greater autonomy, and even as Spain has integrated with the EU, the Catalonian and Basque regions have sought guarantees of greater autonomy from the Spanish central government, with Catalans holding a referendum on independence in 2017. The referendum was held by the regional legislature of Catalonia, and the legislature declared independence in October of that year. The Spanish parliament refused to recognize the legitimacy of the referendum and used emergency powers to dissolve the Catalan legislature, while the Spanish constitutional court found the referendum to be illegal and ordered the arrest of six separatist leaders.

This combination of integration from above the nation-state level and demands from ethnic or regional groups below has put the nation-state under pressure, but it continues to be the central actor in international relations and comparative politics.

Immigration

Another key area where domestic and international politics intersect is **immigration**, defined as the movement of people to foreign countries. Immigration is clearly an issue of international relations because it involves a country from which a person leaves (or emigrates), potentially one or more transit countries through which people pass, and a country to which the person immigrates. It is also a matter of comparative politics because it regularly becomes a major domestic issue in the countries involved.

immigration The movement of people to foreign countries.

The details of immigration debates vary from one country to another, but immigration patterns can be compared. In many prominent examples, the pattern is for immigrants to move from lower-income countries with limited economic opportunities to wealthier countries. Immigration often induces conflicts or tensions between citizens of the receiving country and the newcomers, and sometimes populist leaders stir up fears of immigration to gain votes at election time. For example, Donald Trump famously condemned Mexican immigrants as "rapists" when running for president and pledged to build a wall between the US and Mexico. As president, he has continued to promote the same xenophobic rhetoric.[9] Immigration is a major issue across Europe as well, though patterns of immigrants' countries

Press Association via AP Images

PHOTO 16.4 A referendum held in the UK in June 2016 asked voters whether the UK should leave or remain in the European Union. Nearly 52 per cent of voters chose the "leave" side. A key focus of the "leave" campaign had been the EU immigration policies.

of origin differ from one European country to another. In France, many of the tensions are with respect to North African immigrants and their descendants, who have been singled out for attack by political parties such as the Rassemblement National (the former Front National) and its leader Marine Le Pen. In Germany and northern Europe, there are large numbers of immigrants from Turkey and the Middle East who have been subjected to racism by right-wing parties and movements. A key focus of the "leave" campaign in the Brexit referendum was challenging EU immigration policies as too permissive. The image of Britain being inundated with immigrants was used to court British voters. One famous poster entitled "Breaking Point, the EU has failed us all" urged voters to "take back control of our borders" by voting the leave the EU.[10]

assimilation The practice of being integrated into another culture, especially with respect to immigration.

The issues surrounding immigration are numerous, contentious, and often blurred. One major issue is **assimilation** (being culturally absorbed by or integrated into another culture). Some immigrant groups may prefer to merge with the "mainstream" of society, while others prefer to retain their cultural autonomy. The more xenophobic members of these host countries may see immigrants as a threat to their economic livelihoods and national identity. Immigrants with a different skin colour, language, or religion may find integration impossible in a climate of intolerance.[11] Advocates of assimilation often argue that immigrants must adapt to the cultural practices and conceptions of liberal values in the countries to which they migrate. Immigrants, however, may rightly wish to retain their own cultural traditions. They may argue that respect for different traditions is a basic tenet of modern liberal societies and that assimilation to a dominant culture is not required. Further, some scholars have claimed that positions in favour of assimilation are often based on misconceptions and simplistic notions about people of other backgrounds.[12]

Middle-ground views tend to favour multicultural notions of citizenship protected by a liberal state. Debates over multiculturalism are common in advanced, industrialized countries like Canada that have substantial numbers of immigrants from developing countries, and immigration has become a major issue in domestic and comparative politics. Indeed, Canada's population contains a very high proportion of foreign-born immigrants—almost 22 per cent, according to the 2016 census. More than 250 different ethnicities are represented in the Canadian population.[13]

Many countries—especially, but not exclusively, those with civic forms of nationalism, as outlined in Chapter 13—have welcomed immigrants over time but face new challenges with each generation. Many Americans refer to the United States as a "nation of immigrants" while also calling for stricter limits on immigration and efforts to stop the flow of immigrants and deport those present. Of course, this ignores the fact that Europeans colonized the US in a long and violent history that included the massacre and forced displacement of Indigenous peoples, who were the original owners and occupants of what is now North America. Unfortunately, pride in a history of immigration can thus coexist with **nativism**, which seeks to protect the privileges of established groups of residents against the interests of immigrants. It can be manifested as overt racism, especially as we see now with the appeal of the alt-right among some people in the US and Canada. This position attempts to portray more recent immigrants as somehow inferior or threatening compared with previous waves. Sometimes even scholars make such claims, singling out groups like Hispanic or Islamic immigrants as less open to assimilation, less democratic, or less capable of economic integration.[14] Impartial reviews of the evidence, though, thoroughly refute such claims.[15]

nativism A political attitude that seeks to protect the interests of established groups of residents in a given country against the interests of more recent immigrants.

Immigration thus brings together issues in the social, economic, and political domains. The social side involves cultural assimilation and competing conceptions of what it means to be part of a nation. Some of the hottest debates on immigration are as much about money as they are about identity. On the economic side, immigration raises issues of competition

CASE IN CONTEXT

393

Globalization and Culture in France

As we have noted in previous chapters, France gives us many examples of how cultural and economic challenges interact when questions of immigration arise. France experiences ongoing debate about its demographic, economic, and political future in light of growing numbers of immigrants and the appeal of populist xenophobic parties promoting anti-Islamic sentiments. Immigration is a debate in most European countries today.

For more on these issues in France, see the case study in Part VI, p. 393. As you read it, keep in mind the following questions:

1. In what ways has France been ambivalent about the progress of globalization?
2. What might explain why the French were once quite favourable to globalization but have more recently become uncertain about it?
3. In what ways has France tried to mitigate the perceived downsides of globalization?

with domestic-born workers for jobs and for some public benefits. The political domain includes aspects of the social and economic sides but focuses on immigration as a policy issue, which is complicated because immigration is both a transnational and a domestic issue.

We should also note that just as immigration poses challenges, emigration—leaving a country to live in another—has some important economic implications for the countries left behind. One issue is the **brain drain**, or the fact that in many cases the most skilled and highly educated members of a population leave. In some of these circumstances, relatively poor countries have invested heavily in preparing some of their top young people to build their country, only to see them leave for better opportunities elsewhere. On the flip side, emigrants are often huge contributors to their home countries through **remittances** of cash or resources sent back home to families and friends. Further, some emigrants who have left their home countries have gone into exile for political or economic reasons because they are fleeing repression or lack of opportunity.

brain drain The departure or emigration of skilled and educated members of a population, especially with reference to developing countries in the international system.

remittances Cash or resources sent to a home country, often to family and friends, by emigrants.

Environment and Sustainability

Contemporary debates in comparative politics and international relations are not just about maximizing economic growth but also about the consequences of that growth around the world. A major worry is that the current consumption of resources and rates of environmental pollution are not **sustainable**, or capable of being sustained for future generations. At the local level, this has become a major issue in rapidly industrializing countries such as China, where environmental degradation has worsened dramatically through the pollution of air, water, and land. The result has been contamination and disease affecting many millions of people.

Environmental consequences from industrialization are horrific in many locations, yet the leading issue with respect to the environment at the global level is **climate change**. Climatologists and natural scientists agree that climate change is attributable in part to human-made causes.[16] Humankind's effect on the climate has come mainly through **greenhouse gas** (GHG) emissions. Pollutants such as carbon dioxide and methane are emitted

sustainability The notion, especially used with regard to the environment, that a resource is capable of being sustained for use or enjoyment by future generations.

climate change A set of changes to the earth's climate.

greenhouse gases (GHGs) Emissions of gases such as carbon dioxide and methane from industrial activity and consumption of fossil fuels that contribute to climate change.

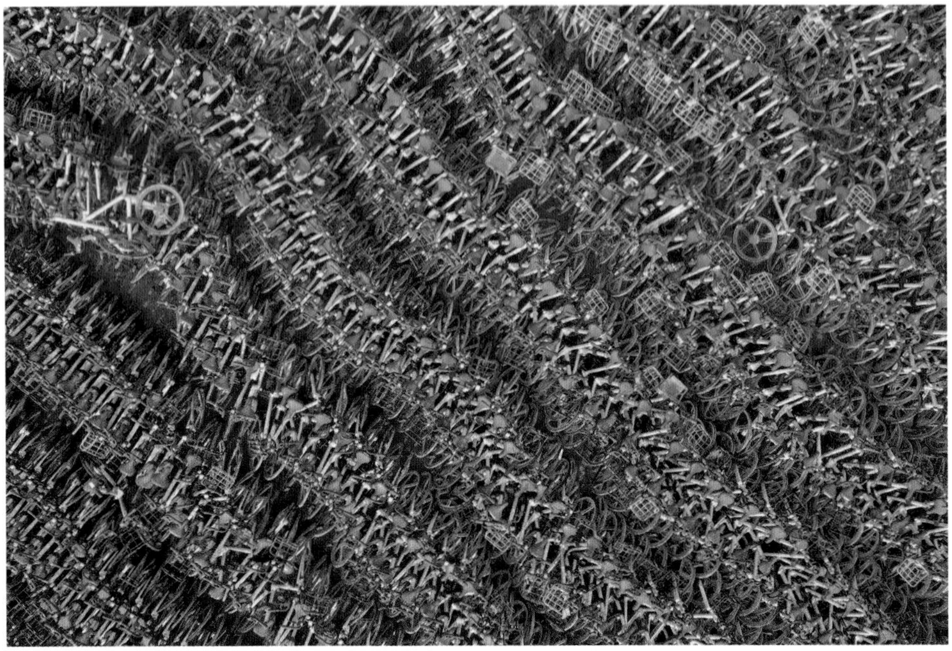
Press Association via AP Images

PHOTO 16.5 An aerial view of tens of thousands of abandoned bicycles from a bike-sharing service at a large empty space in Nanjing, China, in 2019. China has had to tackle the issue of abandoned bikes after bike-hiring services suddenly became popular across the country but quickly became oversupplied.

into the atmosphere and trap solar energy, warming the planet below, as in a greenhouse. Many of these pollutants come from fossil fuels used to produce energy, such as petroleum, coal, and natural gas. There is a need for more **alternative energy** sources, such as solar or wind power.

alternative energy Energy sources, such as solar or wind power, that are not derived from fossil fuels.

While China is often singled out as a major contributor to climate change, there are also major problems in Western countries, especially when political leaders refuse to acknowledge that climate change is a reality. The Chinese leadership does recognize the reality of climate change, whereas the Trump administration does not. As well, we may have political leaders who acknowledge the reality of climate change yet continue to promote environmentally destructive practices like the development of oil sands and the construction of pipelines.

Climate change estimates predict that global temperature averages will peak at two or more degrees Celsius above historical averages. This change is predicted to bring about other consequences, including melting of glaciers and ice sheets, rises in sea levels, flooding of coastal lowlands, increased numbers and severity of extreme weather events such as hurricanes and avalanches, desertification of marginal agricultural lands, and extinction of large numbers of animal and plant species. To the extent these events materialize, they will signify major, costly disruptions to peoples and societies across the planet. Droughts may lead to major conflict over food and water. Flooding may erase some cities.

Climate change and environmental sustainability present some of the most fundamental dilemmas in politics. One basic feature of pollution is that it is an **externality** from economic activity, meaning that the gains and costs from an activity do not accrue to the same actor. In the case of polluting, individual companies may gain profits from their production

externality An economic phenomenon in which the gains and costs from a given activity do not accrue to the same actor.

(or countries may grow economically from it), with the act of polluting as a by-product, but the costs of that pollution are passed on to others. Because polluters do not pay the costs to society associated with pollution, they do not have as much of an incentive to stop it. This condition represents a collective action problem and is a good example of the "free rider" problem we discussed in previous chapters. One of the leading discussions about pollution is on the difficulties of managing resources that are shared among many people (or countries) when all actors have an incentive to free ride—to maximize their own benefit while passing the costs of their action onto others.

Climate change is more than a scientific challenge: It is also a political challenge both within and across national borders. Most efforts to halt climate change involve securing commitments by sovereign states to reduce their greenhouse gas emissions over time. These agreements are not easily secured because they require cooperation and agreement among large numbers of actors and because there is little agreement on which countries should pay the costs of halting greenhouse gas emissions. In general, large developing countries such as China and India hold that the developed countries are responsible for most of the emissions to date and are thus primarily responsible for stopping climate change while lower-income countries catch up in development. Some developed countries, like the United States, respond that climate change was unknown when many of the rich world's emissions occurred and that much of the future damage will come from the developing countries.[17] Addressing climate change thus raises many of the central dilemmas in international politics. There have been successes in communities around the world in managing common resources, but scaling these efforts up to international levels through cooperation among nation-states is difficult.[18]

Transnational Networks

Many of the challenges facing nation-states in contemporary politics come from nonstate actors and especially from **transnational networks** of different actors working across borders. Some transnational networks are particularly worrying because they are criminal or violent, and comparative politics matters here because these networks thrive where states

transnational network A network of nonstate actors working across state borders.

INSIGHTS

The Tragedy of the Commons

by Garrett Hardin

Garrett Hardin's article is foundational in the study of common resources, and it has implications for many environmental challenges in the world today. The article focuses on the challenges of overexploitation of common resources by large and growing populations. Hardin's illustrative example of the tragedy is a pasture open to all herdsmen and their herds of animals. As each herdsman allows his herds to graze, the pasture is degraded a bit, and its resources (grass) are used up, yet each herdsman has an individual incentive to encourage his livestock to continue grazing. This situation ultimately leads to a depleted common resource because benefits from using the commons are individual but costs are shared by all. Hardin notes that this principle also operates with pollution in the atmosphere, except that users are not "taking out" natural resources but rather "putting in" contaminants and thus "using up" a resource shared by all. Possible ways to address the tragedy of the commons include assigning private property rights and requiring those who exploit natural resources to pay the costs associated with their use or through cooperative institutions and practices.[19]

Garrett Hardin, "The Tragedy of the Commons" *Science* 162(3859, 1968): 1243–8.

are weak, failing, or collapsed. Since 11 September 2001, the most famous of these has been al Qaeda, the Islamic fundamentalist terror group. One of the distinguishing characteristics of al Qaeda and other groups like it, as discussed in Chapter 12, is its decentralized structure and the fact that its ideology spreads to other like-minded organizations.[20] Stopping or defeating the al Qaeda network is thus not as clear-cut as defeating a nation-state in a traditional war.

Of course, not all transnational networks are criminal or violent; rather, globalization has generated a large number of transnational networks designed to leverage citizens' political voice. The emergence of transnational advocacy networks may be a key to facilitating greater governmental response to issues such as environmental protection and preventing violence against women.[21] In some circumstances, governments may not make needed changes unless pressured to do so by networks of advocates and activists that cross borders. The success of these networks may be due in part to their flexibility, which allows them to use strategies that are not available to governments.[22] Taking both terror groups and advocacy networks into account, it is both for better and for worse that transnational networks affect the politics and societies of countries around the world.

Nuclear Threats and Terrorism

The classic issues of international relations are those of war, peace, and conflict among nations. This may seem to be exclusively the domain of international relations and thus unrelated to comparative politics, but, as we will see in the section on "Causes and Effects," there is major debate about the role of domestic politics and domestic institutions in shaping international relations.

During the Cold War, the central issue in international relations was the conflict between the major powers: the United States and the Soviet Union. Weapons that created the possibility for mass casualties in civilian populations heightened the sense of urgency over war and peace. Some of these weapons are chemical, such as gases and biological weapons that can spread infectious bacteria, viruses, and other deadly agents through a population. But the class of weapons that received and continues to receive the most attention is nuclear weapons, capable of killing millions of people. The only military use of nuclear weapons (then called atomic weapons) was by the United States in the 1945 bombing of Japan at the end of World War II. However, there have been more than 2000 nuclear tests by eight countries since 1945, some of which have resulted in casualties.[23]

Nuclear weapons are known to be possessed by only a small number of countries: the United States, Russia, the United Kingdom, France, China, India, Pakistan, Israel, and North Korea. Iran has been working toward nuclear status. In many cases, countries have argued that developing nuclear weapons is a deterrent against attacks by other countries; this probably applies in many cases, such as the USSR seeking a deterrent to the United States or India seeking a deterrent to China and Pakistan in turn seeking a deterrent to India (see the "Case in Context: India in the 21st Century"). Many current nuclear powers are hoping to prevent further **nuclear proliferation**—the spread of nuclear technology—to other states.

nuclear proliferation The expansion of the number of countries and other actors possessing nuclear technology.

Terrorism is a significant issue in international security today. The definition of terrorism is greatly contested, as discussed in Chapter 12, but in the context of international relations for this chapter we may define it roughly as the use of violence to achieve political ends through psychological impacts on a civilian population. It is usually distinguished from acts of war in which militaries attack one another, but terrorism by this definition could occur during war when militaries target civilians. Often, terrorism is associated with **nonstate actors**, but countries such as the United States also declare other countries to be

nonstate actors In international relations, actors in international politics that are not nation-states; includes multinational corporations, transnational advocacy groups, and international criminal networks.

CASE IN CONTEXT

422

Iran and the Politics of Nuclear Proliferation

Iran has been developing the capacity to enrich and refine nuclear materials but halted such activities in 2015 by signing on to a nuclear agreement with the permanent five members of the UN Security Council (US, UK, France, China, and Russia) and Germany. The agreement called for Iran to stop enriching uranium and to allow international inspectors in return for an end to crippling economic sanctions against Iran. In May 2018, President Trump, however, unilaterally pulled the US out of the nuclear deal, generating a climate of considerable uncertainty.

For more on nuclear power in Iran, see the case study in Part VI, p. 422. As you read it, keep in mind the following questions:

1. Do you agree with President Trump's decision to pull out of the Iran nuclear deal? Why might regional actors like Israel support this move? Could it enhance Israel's security?
2. What should the other parties to the Iran deal do now? Does the US have to be part of any such agreement for it to be effective?
3. If you were a European decision-maker, how would you respond to Trump pulling out of this deal? How could this create a potential advantage for your country when seeking to increase its global profile?

"state sponsors of terrorism."[24] Some have also called the US itself a terrorist state for its military attacks against civilians in many countries, sometimes through targeted assassination and sometimes through drone strikes. The US has a long record of launching military strikes on countries with whom it is not at war.

It has often been said that the world changed on 11 September 2001 when the Islamic fundamentalist group al Qaeda launched a terrorist attack on the United States. The attack killed nearly 3000 Americans in New York's World Trade Center, the Pentagon in Washington, DC, and on an airliner in Pennsylvania. This led to a United States response

CASE IN CONTEXT

413

India in the 21st Century: Domestic Politics, Identity, and Security

It is often said that India and Pakistan have the world's "most dangerous border." The reasons for this assertion straddle the boundaries of comparative politics and international relations. Both countries are nuclear powers, both claim Jammu and Kashmir, and an additional range of domestic differences have resulted in long-standing tensions and conflict.

For more on these issues, see the case study in Part VI, p. 413. As you read it, keep in mind the following questions:

1. How do domestic politics and international security interact in India and Pakistan?
2. How do national and religious identity and political institutions affect relations between the countries?
3. Are the issues raised here best seen as issues of international relations, comparative politics, or both? Why?

that began to shape the foreign affairs of the post-9/11 period. Yet terrorism began long before 2001, and movements around the world have been classified as terrorist organizations. Examples include the Irish Republican Army (IRA) in the United Kingdom and Ireland, whose stated aim was the end of British presence in Ireland, and separatist organizations such as the Basque group ETA in Spain and the Tamil Tigers in Sri Lanka. Canada even had a short-lived terrorist organization—the Front de libération du Québec, which sought to bring about the separation of Quebec by force.

States often define terrorist groups as those seeking to overthrow or replace an existing state structure. Showing the ambiguities of such definitions, the white *Apartheid* regime in South Africa deemed the African National Congress a terrorist organization, but it was seen as a freedom movement by the majority of South Africans and ultimately by international public opinion. There have also been terror attacks committed in the United States by American citizens, such as the bombing of the Oklahoma City federal building in 1995 by Timothy McVeigh, which killed 168 people.

Causes and Effects: What Are the Main Causes in International Relations?

Several major theories of international security offer different explanations for conflict and cooperation between states. To illustrate these explanations, we will focus mainly how these theories work in the area of security, conflict, and peace rather than international political economy. We have addressed political economy in several other chapters (especially 4 and 5) and will return to it in the "Thinking Comparatively" section later in the chapter. The major theories we examine in this section are realism, liberalism, constructivism, and socialism. We note how comparative politics fits into (or does not fit into) each of these theories. In each case, we look at the theory and how it explains in general the prevalence of conflict or peace in international relations (IR).

Realism

realism In international relations, a theory that treats states in the international system largely as acting on the basis of national self-interest, defined often in terms of power, survival, and security.

unitary rational actor In international relations theory and especially realism, the idea that states act as if they were single individuals capable of making decisions on the basis of rational calculations about the costs and benefits of different actions.

Realism is one of the dominant theoretical approach to American international relations today and one embraced by a large proportion of American IR theorists, although it is less popular in other countries. From the perspective of comparative politics, realism is noteworthy for the ways it does *not* examine the internal politics of nation-states and finds relatively little room for domestic and comparative politics in international relations. The realist literature treats states in the international system largely as **unitary rational actors**—those capable of making reasoned decisions on the basis of national self-interest. This model holds that the main determinant of international action is self-interest, defined often in terms of survival and security.

Realists like to claim that their reasoning dates back to much earlier thinkers, most notably Thucydides in ancient Greece, Machiavelli in Renaissance Italy, and Thomas Hobbes, author of *Leviathan*, in 17th-century England.[25] These philosophers emphasized how human nature gave rise to conflict and necessitated seeking power in order to achieve security. The leading modern example of realist thinking in international relations can be found in the work of Kenneth Waltz.[26] Waltz's work is the foundation for much of contemporary realism and is known as "neorealism" to distinguish it from the classical realism of earlier 20th-century thinkers such as Hans Morgenthau and Reinhold Niebuhr. These theorists had a certain pessimism about human nature and saw international politics as being realistic about the prospects for war. However, their work was not as systematized as that of Waltz.

The conditions of anarchy and the balance of power are central to realism, but realism is a theory that contains many different perspectives. For example, Waltz's **defensive realism** holds that a lack of conflict and even cooperation can emerge under specific circumstances, namely when it is easier to defend than to attack and when states can see clearly what other states' intentions are.[27] On the other hand, John Mearsheimer's **offensive realism** holds that states are never satisfied with the status quo (the way things are) and will seek to maximize their power whenever they can, striving toward a hegemonic position where possible.[28]

defensive realism A realist theory that holds that peace or cooperation can emerge under specific circumstances, namely when it is easier to defend than to attack and when states can see clearly what other states' intentions are.

offensive realism A realist theory that holds that states will seek to maximize their power whenever they can.

Some of the work in realism features rational choice theory. Rational choice typically involves a formal model of strategic interactions between actors, often by conceiving of these interactions as "games" in which the "players" respond rationally to incentives and to the expected actions of other players, given their incentives. These games gave rise to the name **game theory**; they are designed to simplify a problem to its essence in order to analyze the actions of the players.

game theory A set of approaches to the study of strategic interaction between actors, often relying on mathematical modelling and assumptions of the rationality of different actors.

The most famous illustration is the **prisoner's dilemma**. In this game, one imagines two prisoners being interrogated separately by a jailer. Each prisoner can choose whether to "rat out" his fellow prisoner or not, and what each says affects the sentence of both prisoners (see Table 16.2). Each prisoner's cell in the table has two possibilities—to not tell or to rat out the other prisoner—giving four possible outcomes in the table. These outcomes are known as the **payoff matrix** because they reflect the payoffs the players get depending on their choices. The prisoners would be better off if both refused than if both were to rat out the other, so we might expect them to cooperate and not tell. Yet the result will be that both defect and rat each other out. Why?

prisoner's dilemma (game) A model of a game in which two actors would benefit from cooperation but each has individual incentives to defect from cooperation.

payoff matrix In game-theoretic models, the distribution of payoffs to players depending on the choices made.

Consider the situation from the perspective of prisoner 1 (called P1) by looking only at P1's payoffs. If P2 cooperates, P1 is better off defecting because he will go free. If P2 defects, P1 is still better off defecting as well because he gets five years instead of 10. No matter which strategy P2 chooses, P1 is better off defecting; put another way, no matter which row of the payoff matrix P1 finds himself in, he is better off in the "Defect" column. In the terms of game theory, P1 has a dominant strategy to rat out P2. By the same token, no matter what P1 decides, P2 is better off defecting and ratting out P1. So they both go to jail for five years even though they both would have been better off had they cooperated.

INSIGHTS

Theory of International Politics

by Kenneth Waltz

Waltz's theory of realism advances the idea that the actions of states can be explained primarily by the structure of the international system and the distribution of power within it. The central fact that shapes the behaviour of states is the *anarchy* of the international system in which there is no sovereign power. Given the anarchic system, the distribution of power within that system shapes how states act. States behave differently depending on whether the system has a single great power, two great powers, or multiple great powers. A *bipolar* world is one with two great powers, such as in the Cold War between the United States and the USSR. Waltz argued that this was the most stable arrangement. A *multipolar* system has many powers, such as in Europe in the 19th century and up to World War I. In a *unipolar* system, there is a single power, known as a *hegemon*. Waltz argued that the bipolar system would be especially stable because it enables countries to join with one power or the other to balance the efforts of the other to reach hegemony. This idea of the *balance of power* came to be one of the leading premises of realism.

Kenneth Waltz, *Theory of International Politics* (Reading, MA: Addison-Wesley, 1979).

TABLE 16.2 | The Prisoner's Dilemma

		Prisoner 1	
		Cooperate ("Don't Tell")	**Defect ("Rat out")**
Prisoner 2	**Cooperate ("Don't Tell")**	P1 gets 1 year, P2 gets 1 year	P1 goes free, P2 gets 10 years
	Defect ("Rat Out")	P1 gets 10 years, P2 goes free	P1 gets 5 years, P2 gets 5 years

In rational choice, cooperation between actors is possible under certain circumstances if the payoffs to each actor are best for them individually. This can often occur through repeated interactions.[29] For example, if the prisoner's dilemma happens with repeated interactions between the "players," then many more dynamic possibilities are opened up as players are able to signal their intentions to one another and to reward or punish one another over time. In addition, some scholars note that international institutions can be used to create circumstances for cooperation, as we discuss next, under "Liberalism." Realism is the predominant approach, or paradigm, in international relations, but liberalism places greater emphasis on how domestic institutions and politics shape the behaviour of states.

Liberalism

liberalism In international relations, a theory that holds states can have different preferences and internal structures that lead them to behave in different ways, especially with regard to the conduct of states that hold liberal values of democracy and free-market commerce.

Another prominent school of thought in American international relations has been **liberalism**, which holds that states can have different preferences and internal structures that lead them to behave in different ways. Liberalism pays greater attention to the role of domestic institutions in international relations, and it makes efforts to explain cooperation and peace between some states while also accounting for conflict in other circumstances. The liberal critique of realism holds that realism is best suited to explaining conflict and a lack of cooperation but that it fails to account for more optimistic outcomes. As a leading scholar of liberalism puts it, "[t]he Realist model of international relations, which provides a plausible explanation of the general insecurity of states, offers little guidance in explaining the pacification of the liberal world."[30] Liberal scholars argue that domestic institutions and comparative politics matter more. For example, free-market democracies that value individual liberties highly may be expected to act differently from totalitarian dictatorships. Cooperation and lack of conflict can emerge when like-minded states interact, when states have incentives to trade and exchange with one another, or when states comply with different institutional norms.

There are several strains of liberal thought.[31] One, known as "commercial liberalism," is based on the idea that countries engaged in economic interactions with one another have more incentive to be peaceful.[32] This line of logic dates back to the 18th-century economist Adam Smith. Another strain of liberalism is "liberal institutionalism," which argues that international institutions—such as free trade blocs, international forums, and international financial institutions—can mitigate the effects of anarchy and make more cooperation possible than realists expect.[33] One of liberalism's strongest claims is the existence of a **democratic peace**. This theory seeks to explain why democracies (almost) never go to war with one another and have not done so since the first democracies emerged in the 1700s.[34] The reasons for the democratic peace may be numerous (see the "Insights" box on "Kant, Liberal Legacies, and Foreign Affairs"), including common values and the ability of democratic regimes to observe the domestic debates going on inside other democratic regimes.

democratic peace A phenomenon associated with liberalism that holds that democratic countries will rarely if ever go to war with one another.

INSIGHTS

Kant, Liberal Legacies, and Foreign Affairs
by Michael Doyle

Doyle is a leading proponent of the democratic peace theory, and this book offers his synthesis of liberal theory along with treatments of other theoretical approaches. The treatment of liberalism traces the democratic peace to the philosopher Immanuel Kant, who argued that a "perpetual peace" would emerge between liberal republics. Doyle notes that democracies regularly go to war but almost never against other democracies. Thus, democratic peace holds *between* democracies but not between a democracy and an authoritarian regime. The reasons for this are numerous. First and foremost, in liberal regimes the voting public must consent to the costs of war, and decisions to go to war will not be undertaken lightly. Not being led simply by dictatorial rulers, liberal regimes deliberate carefully about war and do not enter it rashly. Second, democracies have an ability to observe one another's political processes and intentions rather transparently and extend to one another respect and a presumption of accommodation. And third, the logic of liberal regimes typically extends over into commercial or economic interests, which adds material reasons to the moral commitments that prevent conflict between liberal states.

Michael Doyle, "Kant, Liberal Legacies, and Foreign Affairs," *Philosophy and Public Affairs* 12(3, 1983): 205–35; and "Kant, Liberal Legacies, and Foreign Affairs, Part 2," *Philosophy and Public Affairs* 12(4, 1983): 323–53.

Several arguments in international relations focus on the importance of domestic politics. Some of them show how foreign policy decision-making does not come only from a calculation of a state's interest but also depends on the actors and interests involved in making the decision. When one looks inside the government to see how a decision is actually made, the "unitary rational actor" looks less clear. In addition to the presence of liberal institutions, the organizational processes for making decisions and the interactions between decision-makers and their advisers may be especially important in the final decisions made by governments.[35]

Constructivism

The third leading school of thought in international relations today is **constructivism**. Constructivism is an approach arguing that decisions made by states need to be understood in their broader, constructed context of social and political interactions. In particular, states will not simply view one another as having purely aggressive intentions. The contexts in which states interact may range from competitive to cooperative, and states may respond in many different ways.[36] One might not necessarily interpret all military exercises by other countries as overtly hostile, for instance, even if they do heighten the sense of alert. Here, too, comparative politics has some role in shaping international relations: Countries that have reason to trust one another may do so on the basis of histories or cultures that are partly shaped by domestic politics. One prominent formulation from constructivism holds that anarchy does not simply lead to conflict but rather depends on "what states make of it"[37] (see the "Insights" box on *Social Theory of International Politics*).

constructivism In international relations, a theory that holds that decisions made by states need to be understood in the context of social and political interactions and that behaviour is shaped by norms and values as well as narrowly defined interests.

Constructivists note the obvious in international relations—some states are part of large and complex alliance structures like NATO, and other states cooperate and cede aspects of their national sovereignty to supranational bodies like the EU. Some states with common values and shared traditions rarely go to war against one another and indeed have often enjoyed "special relations," such as the traditionally strong relations between Canada and the US or the US and Great Britain. This suggests that ideas matter a great deal in determining the character of the international system. Constructivists are also interested

INSIGHTS

Social Theory of International Politics
by Alexander Wendt

For Wendt, the anarchy of the international system does not necessarily give rise to states conflicting with one another. At the most fundamental level, states may view other states as enemies, as rivals, or as friends. When states expect one another to behave as enemies, war and conflict will be commonplace. Yet Wendt notes that recent centuries have often seen states treat one another as rivals rather than enemies. In these circumstances, states may compete and will not be at permanent war; they may develop a culture in which they often respect one another's sovereignty and do not represent existential threats to one another, though reversions to war are possible. Beyond this, states sometimes treat one another as "friends" and see themselves on the same team. Conflict is highly unlikely in these circumstances. Examples may be Canada and the United States or even contemporary France and Germany, which clearly view one another as partners today despite the horrific wars in their pasts. Wendt argues that states can internalize to different degrees these world views and that they will give rise to different types of politics between them.

Alexander Wendt, *Social Theory of International Politics* (Cambridge: Cambridge University Press, 1999).

in how attitudes and personalities play a key role in international outcomes. For example, the level of military power did not change significantly before President Ronald Reagan of the US and Premier Mikhail Gorbachev of the USSR sat down to negotiate the rollback of their country's respective nuclear arsenals in a series of summit meetings beginning in late 1985. However, fear of nuclear war and a high degree of trust between the two leaders helped to create the conditions for change. In short, the end of the Cold War was not the outcome of a system exerting pressure on decision-makers (as realists might suggest) but on decision-makers choosing to change the nature of the system.

Socialism

socialism In international relations, a theory that emphasizes the role of social classes in shaping politics and highlights the role of capitalist accumulation as a prime driver in international affairs.

Socialism wielded considerable influence for many decades as an explanation for the behaviour of actors in the international system. The peak of its appeal came during the Cold War, although since that time new variations on socialist theory have been proposed. While the end of the Cold War largely removed the prospect of Soviet-style communism as a viable way to address imperialism worldwide, socialist theory continues to have utility in diagnosing how the global political economy functions and especially who gains and who loses in this system. In general, socialist theory emphasizes the role of social classes in shaping politics and highlights the role of capitalist accumulation as a prime driver in international affairs. Many of the manifestations of socialism as it relates to international relations theory are in the area of international political economy, and we treated some of them—such as dependency and world systems theory—in Chapter 5 on development. Nonetheless, there are ways that socialist analysis relates to questions of violence and conflict. Most notably, Vladimir Lenin, the founding leader of the Soviet Union, theorized that brutal imperialism and domination and exploitation of poor countries was the logical consequence of capitalism's international efforts at accumulation.[38] This formulation thus took a theory of society, economy, and comparative politics and scaled it up to the level of international relations.

THINKING COMPARATIVELY

The EU and Levels of Analysis

KEY METHODOLOGICAL TOOL

Levels of Analysis

In our discussion linking comparative politics and international relations, we are considering different levels of analysis. In one prominent formulation, international politics can be seen through the lenses of three different levels: individual actors, domestic political institutions and groups within a country, and the international system.[39] Throughout much of this book, we have discussed the first two of these levels of analysis: how individuals and domestic political institutions (including groups and cultural norms) affect each other. We have looked comparatively to develop causal arguments about a range of topics: how domestic political groups shape democratic institutions, how and why individual people organize into groups, or how institutions give individuals incentives to behave in certain ways. International relations adds the international system as a third level of analysis. This level of analysis again affects the others and vice versa. One of the premises of this discussion is that domestic politics can affect international relations, and it has been shown that diplomacy and foreign policy are indeed conditioned on domestic politics.[40] Conversely, the international system affects domestic politics as well.[41] It is important to remain aware of the level of analysis at which your argument is operating, though there are often good reasons to consider multiple levels of analysis as part of your investigation.

This chapter has touched on some of the leading issues in international relations that relate to comparative politics. The discussion of "Causes and Effects" highlighted how different explanatory models in international relations reflect different perspectives on the importance of domestic politics and institutions to international relations. The range of topics in international relations is so vast that it is its own field, and this discussion in a text on comparative politics can only briefly mention a subset of the relevant issues.

Yet examining certain topics will reveal many of the key themes that link comparative and international politics. The EU is the world's quintessential example of efforts at supranational governance in which countries have given away a degree of real sovereignty. As such, it poses many of the central analytical questions addressed herein. For example, the crisis over the euro that started around 2009 brings up a host of dilemmas in international cooperation. How can countries ensure that others do not free ride? Can states trust one another to cooperate, or will each behave in its own self-interest? At the same time, there are even more fundamental questions, such as "What is Europe?" Is it a political unit that has overcome the challenge of anarchy by creating institutions? Is it a certain set of peoples, or is it changing definitively because of immigration, transnational movement of ideas, and the spread of globalization? There are more questions than answers when it comes to complex issues in international relations, as Europe illustrates. As we note in concluding, this uncertainty is important from the perspective of research in comparative politics: It means that the central questions are not resolved and that research areas and agendas remain open to the curious and motivated analyst.

The EU also shows that the debates between theoretical perspectives are unresolved, as has been the case in our other chapters. The fact of European cooperation over more than 60 years may support the ideas of liberalism and constructivism: Shared values and norms and a common political adherence to democratic institutions may have facilitated peace and cooperation. On the other hand, each of the countries in the EU has valued its own self-interest over integration on many occasions. The British government's decision to leave the EU as a result of the pro-Brexit vote in 2016 can certainly be seen as an example of realist thinking. While cooperation may support one or more of these theoretical perspectives, so too can the seeming breakdowns in cooperation give ammunition to realism, liberalism, constructivism, socialism, or other theoretical frameworks. Here, too, the example of the EU generates major debates that are not easily resolved except through further contestation of ideas.

Interestingly, to complicate things further, we can look to the Scottish independence movement. The Scottish Parliament held a referendum on independence in September 2014, which was ultimately defeated. However, the Brexit vote in 2016 changed the dynamic for Scotland, and in 2017 the Scottish Parliament gave the Scottish government the authority to request from the British Parliament a second referendum on independence. All of this is interesting because at one level it might seem as though Scotland is seeking to form an independent state and is thus acting in a realist way. However, a primary goal of the Scottish National Party (SNP) driving the referendum is actually for its country to rejoin the EU. SNP merchandise features a "Yes" alongside the stars and colours of the EU flag. These ideas suggest a more liberal and/or constructivist approach to how Scotland approaches the prospect of independence—more of a reconnection than a separation.[42]

The fundamental difference between comparative politics and international relations is that the former looks primarily at politics within countries while the latter looks primarily at politics between countries. We have noted in this chapter (and in previous chapters) that politics within countries affects politics between countries and vice versa: International forces sometimes shape phenomena such as democratization, development, nationalism, and revolutions. The EU shows how these **levels of analysis** interact (see the "Key Methodological Tool" discussion in the margin). In the EU, decisions made by the European Central Bank regarding the fate of the euro will have significant effects on politics in Germany, Greece, and Italy at the same time that politics in these countries will have major effects on the euro and on the decisions of the European Central Bank. Paying attention to the different levels of analysis in such situations is useful for developing a clear sense of how comparative politics and international relations each contribute to the study of politics globally.

levels of analysis In international relations, the different levels that can be the context of a study, including the individual level, the nation-state level, and the level of the international system.

We cannot resolve the fundamental issues of comparative politics and international relations here, of course. Even a start at doing so requires the combined efforts of thousands of social scientists and academics, diplomats and statespersons, members of advocacy and activist groups, not to mention millions (or even billions) of citizens. It requires a collective enterprise in seeking knowledge that is based both on collaboration and on disagreement and debate. We reiterate that the domestic politics of countries affects international politics and that international politics affects domestic politics as well, and we encourage you to further explore the major themes of these fields. We hope you will use the tools from this chapter and the text as a whole to participate in this exploration, making your own contributions to the knowledge that scholars of comparative politics continue to seek.

Chapter Summary

Concepts

- Comparative politics focuses largely on politics within individual countries, while international relations focuses on relations between countries.

Issues

- There are a large number of issues that link comparative politics and international relations, including globalization and trade, international immigration, transnational networks, nuclear and terrorist threats, global warming, and environmental sustainability.

Causes and Effects

- There are several main schools of thought in international relations, including realism, liberalism, constructivism, and socialism.

- Contemporary realism focuses on the supposed anarchy of the international system and the efforts of each nation-state to make itself secure in this system, which leads to frequent conflict.
- Liberalism emphasizes the effects of political institutions and domestic politics more than realism does and finds more factors that mitigate the likelihood of conflict.
- Constructivism emphasizes the social context in which international interactions happen and argues that anarchy does not necessarily lead to conflict.

Thinking Comparatively

- International relations often operates at a different level of analysis from comparative politics by looking at the international system, but the levels of analysis can interact.

Thinking It Through

1. We discussed the problem of global climate change in this chapter as a major issue facing the international community. Imagine that you are the prime minister of Canada and are thus responsible for coming up with a plan to address the problem. You need to consider three proposals prepared by your advisors, one based on realist assumptions about international relations, one based on liberal assumptions, and one based on constructivist assumptions. How would these proposals differ?
2. Substitute the problem of nuclear proliferation for climate change in the previous question. How would your three proposals differ? Now compare your answers to these questions. Does theoretical perspective affect these problems of international politics in the same way across different issues or in different ways?
3. Take a main phenomenon discussed in any of the institutional chapters in this book (Chapters 8–11), such as presidentialism vs parliamentarism, proportional representation vs district systems, federalism vs unitarism, or multiparty systems vs two-party systems. How might these variations in institutional design influence the likely behaviour of different states in the international system?
4. The foreign policy doctrine of US President George W. Bush from 2001 to 2009 was based on the ideas that the United States was an indispensable leader as the world's hegemon and that it should act unilaterally and pre-emptively as necessary to prevent threats from arising. It also held that US action should promote regime change in favour of democracy in order to enhance American security. Does this sound like a realist doctrine, a liberal doctrine, or a constructivist doctrine? Why?
5. Following from the question above, how might one use international relations theory to interpret Donald Trump's foreign policy? In what important ways does it differ from that of George W. Bush? What are some similarities?
6. The European Union has achieved significant economic integration in recent decades, but it still makes many of its major decisions by unanimous consent. One of the dilemmas of the EU has been the trade-off between "broadening" the union to more members and "deepening" the integration among existing members. Why might these two goals be seen as potentially contradictory? If you were a government leader in France or Germany, which of these two directions would you want to see the EU favour, and why?

PART VI

Country Profiles and Cases

Brazil

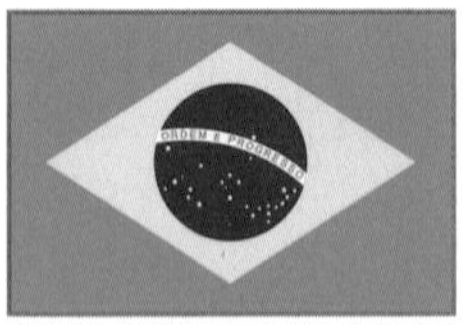

PROFILE

Key Features of Contemporary Brazil

Population:	207,353,391 (July 2017 est.)
Area:	8,514,877 square kilometres
Head of State:	Jair Bolsonaro (president, 2019–present)
Head of Government:	Jair Bolsonaro (president, 2019–present)
Capital:	Brasília
Year of Independence:	1822
Year of Current Constitution:	1988
Languages:	Portuguese (official), Spanish, German, many Indigenous languages
GDP per Capita:	$9,821.40 (World Bank estimate 2017)
Human Development Index Ranking (2015):	79th (high human development)
Trading Relationship with Canada (2016):	• Imports $2,915,290,687 • Exports $1,544,129,003 https://globaledge.msu.edu/countries/canada/tradestats

Sources: *CIA World Factbook*; World Bank World Development Indicators; United Nations *Human Development Report 2016*

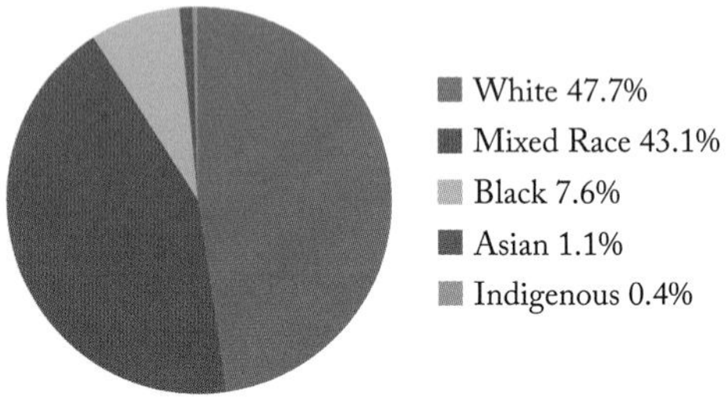

Ethnic Groups in Brazil
Source: *CIA World Factbook*

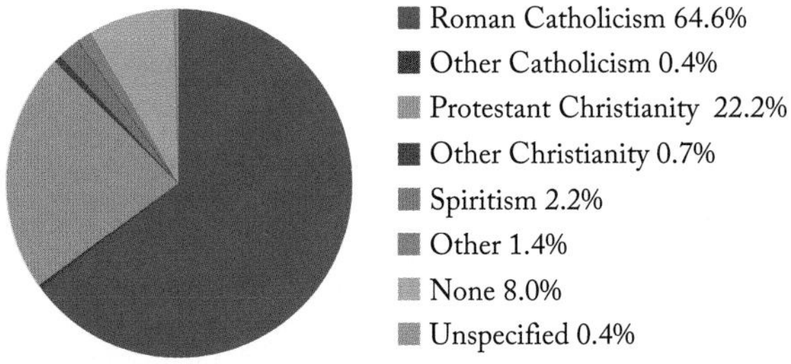

Religious Affiliation in Brazil
Source: *CIA World Factbook*

Introduction

Brazil has always been of interest to comparative political analysts. The country has in recent years achieved considerable economic growth and consolidated its democracy after years of alteration between democratic and authoritarian rule. It has also exercised more global influence than ever before. Brazil stands out in Latin America for several important reasons. First, it is the only Portuguese-speaking country in the region, though its population comprises a large proportion of the total Latin American population. Second, it emerged from European colonialism as a geographically intact unit despite its strong regional tensions, whereas Spanish America split up into many smaller countries. Third, and related to this, Brazil gained its independence without a war but, in essence, with the help of the Portuguese royal family. This and subsequent events have led some to describe Brazil as a non-revolutionary society in which gradual change is predominant. Slavery lasted longer in Brazil than in most societies, and it entered the 20th century with an agrarian economy and a highly unequal social order (Roett 2011; Skidmore 2010). Indigenous peoples have also been subject to mass killings and government policies designed to deprive them of their traditional lands. Overall, Brazil's development has had a range of positive and negative features as successive governments have woven a coherent society together.

Brazil is characterized by pronounced regional differences. The country is geographically enormous, and settlement

VENEZUELA
GUYANA
SURINAME
French Guiana (FRANCE)
COLOMBIA
Boa Vista
NORTH ATLANTIC OCEAN
Equator
Belém
Amazon
Manaus
Amazon
São Luís
Fortaleza
Teresina
Natal
Recife
Rio Branco
Palmas
Maceió
B R A Z I L
PERU
Salvador
Brasília
BOLIVIA
Campo Grande
Rio Grande
Belo Horizonte
Vitória
PARAGUAY
São Paulo
Santos
Rio de Janeiro
CHILE
Curitiba
SOUTH PACIFIC OCEAN
ARGENTINA
Porto Alegre
SOUTH ATLANTIC OCEAN
URUGUAY
0 200 400 Kilometers
0 200 400 Miles

patterns and economic bases in different regions vary considerably. The large cities of the southeast, such as São Paulo and Rio de Janeiro, include huge populations and are more closely linked to the global economy, especially São Paulo. While this area can be viewed as a "region," historically there were tensions *between* these cities, with Paulistas and residents of Rio sometimes vying for national influence. More striking contrasts, however, are found between this and other regions, including the relatively poor Amazonian region, which contains large Indigenous populations, and the northeast, where some of the earliest settlement was established on the basis of sugar cultivation. This area, too, remains relatively poor when compared to the southeast.

In religious terms, Brazil remains a society of high vitality. The Catholic Church is still important to a large share of the population, and Brazil has contributed importantly to theological developments in past decades like liberation theology and the establishment of ecclesiastical base communities. At the same time, Brazil also has one of the highest rates of Protestant adherence in Latin America, and Pentecostal forms of Protestantism have been particularly important, especially among poorer populations.

Historical Development

Brazil began as a quintessentially agricultural society, with early inroads by both Dutch and Portuguese colonialists (on the colonial period, see Fausto 1999 and Skidmore 2010). In the end, it became the principal colonial possession of the Portuguese crown. Prior to its colonization, Brazil was home to numerous Indigenous peoples. In 2010, the United Nations estimated that there were still around 897,000 Indigenous peoples alive, divided into 305 communities and speaking some 274 languages. The region of Vale do Javari contains the greatest proportion of Indigenous peoples in Brazil (UNESCO). Over time, the Indigenous populations fell from an estimated 3–5 million before colonization to their present numbers. Genocidal massacres and other forms of state-sponsored violence have characterized Brazilian history, and killings continue even now (Barbara 2017). The Bolsonaro regime has introduced legislation to transfer responsibility for Indigenous lands from the ministry of justice to the ministry of agriculture. The plan is to convert at least some Indigenous lands to farms.

The colonizers developed an economic model based on plantation agriculture, with the initial focus in the northeast, where sugar cane was the main product for export. Later in the colonial period, this was supplemented by mining. The 18th-century expansion of mining activities, especially in Minas Gerais, had important implications for the political structure of the Portuguese colonies and for Brazil's future. Perhaps the most important effect was the shift in regional elite power and in colonial administration as the northeast city of Salvador ceased to be the main colonial port, with Rio de Janeiro taking over that role. Rio was also the capital until it was moved to the new planned city of Brasília in 1960.

Historical Development Timeline

What is now Brazil originally contained Indigenous nations, with a population estimated at between 3 and 5 million people.

1500 Portuguese mariner Pedro Alvares Cabral is the first European to explore Brazil.

1500s Portuguese crown attempts to colonize Brazil by granting captaincies (*Capitanias*) to nobles, but few successful outposts are established. Diseases, enslavement, and massacre are responsible for the deaths of hundreds of thousands of Indigenous peoples.

1600s French and Dutch excursions establish inroads along Brazil's coast but depart by mid-1600s.

1808 The Portuguese monarchy flees Portugal and establishes residence in Brazil.

1821 Portuguese monarchy returns to Portugal.

1822 Dom Pedro, a prince and son of Portugal's king, declares Brazilian independence from Portugal and remains in Brazil as emperor.

1888 Princess Isabel abolishes slavery by decree while Emperor Dom Pedro II is away in Europe.

1889 The military deposes Emperor Dom Pedro II and establishes a republic, now known as the Old Republic (*República Velha*); constitutional democracy is largely limited to land-owning males.

1880s–1920s	Economic boom based on agricultural exports (coffee, sugar, etc.) to Europe.
1930	General Getúlio Vargas takes presidency.
1930s	Great Depression interrupts world trade, cuts off imports, and harms the economy; this gives impetus to Brazil's fledgling industrialization in the medium term.
1937	President Vargas proclaims "New State" (*Estado Novo*) along fascist lines.
1946	Brazil returns to democratic rule.
1954	Vargas commits suicide while president (1951–4), having been elected some years after his previous removal.
1960	President Juscelino Kubitschek moves capital to new city of Brasília.
1964	Military overthrows President João Goulart in coup d'état.
1964–82	Military rules Brazil in "bureaucratic-authoritarian" style; industrialization deepens.
1982	Massive street protests for direct elections (*Diretas Já!*), with trade union leader Luiz Inácio Lula da Silva a prominent figure; democratic elections are held for governors.
1985	Presidential election is held; Tancredo Neves is elected but dies before taking office; José Sarney becomes president.
1988	Constitution is passed by Brazil's Constituent Assembly.
1988–94	Growing inflation problems and economic crisis.
1992	President Fernando Collor (1990–2) resigns amid corruption scandal.
1995–2003	Presidency of Fernando Henrique Cardoso (a sociologist) ends economic crisis, begins to see economic growth, better social services, and declining inequality.
2003–11	Presidency of Luiz Inácio Lula da Silva, a former Marxist trade union leader and head of the Workers' Party (PT); continued economic growth and declines in inequality, as well as an expanding international role for Brazil.
2011	Dilma Rousseff of the PT becomes Brazil's first female president.
2015	Rousseff begins her second term.
2016	Rousseff is impeached because of a financial scandal. Her vice-president Michel Temer takes over with Senate approval.
2019	Far-right populist leader Jair Bolsonaro is sworn in as president. Massive fires consume parts of the Amazon rainforest.

The transition to independence in Brazil was relatively peaceful. There had in the late colonial years been a couple of minor rebellions (Fausto 1999), including the well-known Inconfidência Mineira, but nothing that remotely threatened the regime. Napoleon was invading Portugal, and the royal family, under Dom João, moved the court to Rio de Janeiro and continued to govern from there. Dom João remained there until 1821, when a revolt back home forced him to return to Lisbon. Approximately a year after his return, his son Pedro, who had been sent as regent, declared independence. He was soon named emperor. Between the rule of Pedro I, the long rule of Pedro II, and a regency in between, the Brazilian empire would last until the 1880s. Brazil's empire was quite conservative, uniting the government, the Catholic Church, and agricultural elites (Roett 2011, 26–7).

Over the course of the 19th century, the nature of Brazilian exports changed, but its key economic activity remained the export of primary products. Coffee was a key export, and this created problems because coffee prices had a tendency to fluctuate widely, meaning that business was hard to predict, and sometimes ruined farmers. This also contributed to the relative weakness of the Brazilian state. Just the same, Brazilian politics remained surprisingly stable in this period. Brazil *was* involved, though, in the most infamous international war of Latin American history, the "War of the Triple Alliance," which pitted Brazil, Argentina, and Uruguay against Paraguay and resulted in the devastation of the latter country. Brazil suffered heavy losses and experienced fiscal difficulties as a result of its involvement.

While European industrial modernization theory became popular during the 19th-century development, Brazil's economy remained dependent on a plantation agriculture economy. The situation changed after the abolition of slavery in 1888 and after Pedro II was deposed a year later. An elite-led republic was created soon after, and Brazil started to resemble the more typical Latin American pattern, with political instability and weak institutions serving as obstacles to development.

The next major development in the political history of Brazil was the coup d'état that brought Getúlio Vargas to power in 1930. Vargas was a populist, and he largely worked to undercut the influence of the regional oligarchies, though he did retain ties to some elite groups (Roett 2011; Skidmore 2010). Vargas encouraged industrial magnates and labour alike, and the latter became an increasingly important force in Brazilian politics in this period. Vargas was also a state-builder and a centralizer. The Brazilian state he helped to develop was also one with militaristic features, and Vargas eventually became a dictator. While Brazilian troops fought with the allies in World War II, Vargas was deposed following the end of the war.

In the coming years, political instability continued—Vargas was even brought back in 1951, though he killed himself in office rather than be deposed again in 1954. Amid the disorder, Brazil continued with a program of economic nationalism and import-substituting industrialization. The country's record in this connection was mixed. Growth was irregular and often slow, and inequality remained notoriously high, but the country had a more diversified industrial base than did many of its neighbours. Under Juscelino Kubitschek (1956–60), the modernist capital of Brasília was established. In 1964, following a military coup, the country succumbed to the wave of "bureaucratic-authoritarianism" that was to dominate the region for some years (O'Donnell 1973; Stepan 1971).

This military regime sought to take an active role in shaping the development process and deepening industrialization (O'Donnell 1973). It saw Brazil's strong unions and demands for worker advantages as factors that prevented the accumulation of capital needed for Brazil to become an advanced, industrial society. Accordingly, it centralized power and repressed dissidence. The military promoted industrial investment from foreign and domestic sources in an attempt to convert Brazil's industry from making the likes of textiles and sugar to making more sophisticated products like steel and automobiles for consumption in Brazil itself. The military partially succeeded, presiding over some deepening of industrialization that represented a substantial portion of the "Brazilian Miracle" of the postwar era (Evans 1979; Cardoso and Faletto 1979). Ultimately, however, making the necessary investments required more and more state spending and debt. In the long run, the borrowing culminated in the 1980s debt crisis. Growing pressures for political liberalization signalled the exhaustion of military rule.

The military controlled the process of liberalization in the initial stages but found itself pushed to make greater moves toward full democracy (Haggard and Kaufman 1995). Political pressure for democratization came from many political actors. By the mid-1980s, millions took to the streets to demand elections, with many led by trade union leader and political hopeful Luiz Inácio Lula da Silva. The protests led to massive rallies in the 1980s calling for "Direct Elections Now" (*Diretas Já!*), which the business community increasingly supported. As the military regime recognized its loss of power, it agreed to elections for state governors in 1982, followed by national elections in 1985.

In 1990, Fernando Collor became the first directly elected president of Brazil after the military regime. His presidency was marked by scandals and a failed economic policy that led to impeachment in 1992; Vice-President Itamar Franco governed until the next elections in 1994. The two following presidents governed Brazil for two terms each, for a total of sixteen years, and these years saw relative improvements in addressing Brazil's economic and social challenges (Roett 2011). Fernando Henrique Cardoso's government (1995–2003) consolidated a new economic policy—The *Plano Real*—together with a new currency (the *real*) that brought a relatively stable economy and the beginnings of a decline in inequality. This was followed by the two terms of Luiz Inácio Lula da Silva (2003–11), known simply as Lula. He was a founding member of the Workers' Party (*Partido dos Trabalhadores*, PT) and a union leader who was once a Marxist but governed in a centrist fashion. Dilma Rousseff of the PT was elected in 2010 as Lula's successor, but was impeached by the Senate in 2016 because of a scandal involving bribery and kickbacks at the government-run oil company Petrobras. Rousseff was replaced by her deputy, Michel Temer. Lula da Silva was also put on trial for his suspected role in the scandal. Hundreds of thousands of Petrobas employees and others dependent on contracts from this state-owned giant lost their jobs (Watts 2016).

In 2019, Jair Bolsonaro, a former military officer and leader of the right-wing Social Liberal Party, took office as president. He is a nationalist, anti-communist, and populist leader who promotes social conservative policies. Much of his appeal lay in his promises to reverse economic stagnation and clean up corruption.

Regime and Political Institutions

The executive in Brazil's federal system is directly elected, with the vote tally for the presidency based on the national popular vote. If no candidate receives a majority in the first round, a second-round runoff election is held between the two leading candidates. The term of office is four years, and the president is limited to two terms. According to the constitution, the president has considerable powers, including the ability to decree certain laws for a limited time (30 days), with the so-called "provisional measure" (*medida provisória*). While formal powers are useful, most presidential prerogatives of significance can be consolidated only by extensive negotiating and bargaining with other parties, individual legislators, and the state governors and city mayors who support these legislators.

Judicial power in Brazil resides in the Federal Supreme Court (*Supremo Tribunal Federal*—STF), which has the authority to pronounce on the constitutionality of law. The constitution reserves substantial responsibilities, functions, and resources for the state governments as well.

Regime and Political Institutions

Regime	Federal republic, representative democratic elections
Administrative Divisions	27 federal units: 26 states (*estados*) + Federal District of Brasília
Executive Branch	President
Selection of Executive	Direct election by national popular vote; voting is compulsory; runoff between top two candidates if none receives 50 per cent in the first round
Legislative Branch	Bicameral Congress (*Congresso Nacional*) Lower chamber: Chamber of Deputies (*Câmara dos Deputados*) Upper chamber: Senate (*Senado Federal*)
Judicial Branch	Federal High Court (*Supremo Tribunal Federal*) has some power of judicial review
Political Party System	Multiparty system, with four to five leading parties: PSL (far right), PT (left/centre-left), PSDB (centrist, technocratic), MDB (centrist, traditional), DEM (centre-right, traditional)

Political Culture

In many ways, Brazilian society is renowned for bringing together elements of distinct traditions. Brazil has large numbers of Indigenous peoples, people of African descent, and descendants of migrants of European and Asian origin. However, the myth of racial harmony is largely a myth, masking a society still dominated by problems of anti-black racism and intolerance for Indigenous peoples. For example, white Brazilians on average earn 57 per cent more than their black counterparts and comprise 71 per cent of legislative representatives. Black Brazilians comprise 64 per cent of the prison population, and 71 per cent of those murdered in 2017 were black (dos Santos Carvalho Carinhanha 2018).

Brazil is, like many countries, in the processes of rapid modernization. Its complex culture can be seen, for example, in the combination of highly advanced centres of efficiency in certain aspects of the state, combined with old-fashioned patronage-based bureaucracies (Evans 1989). Some diplomats in Brazil's Foreign Ministry and economists at its Central Bank are among the world's best, while many legislators, ministers, and judges (and some presidents) have been notoriously corrupt. Brazil is home to some of the world's most advanced industries—in petroleum exploration, aircraft manufacture, and mobile phone assembly, among other areas—but is also home to poverty that rivals the poorest countries on earth. A cultural element that works its way into politics is the notion of *jeitinho*, or "finding a little way." This has a connotation of skilfulness and cleverness, but can also lead to corruption and getting ahead at another's expense, as the Petrobas scandal has ably demonstrated.

Political Economy

Brazil has emerged to become one of the most dynamic economies in the developing world, but it is also characterized by shocking inequalities, extreme poverty, rampant corruption, high costs of doing business, and among the world's highest tax rates. It is one of the renowned BRIC countries that are projected by many to be economic giants of the future: Brazil, Russia, India, and China. While it still faces huge difficulties in integrating its diverse population into the modern economy, Brazil has developed dramatically from its export-oriented agricultural base in the 19th century, when the country was dominated by oligarchic plantation owners who exported coffee, sugar, and other products to Europe.

The country's economic history accounts for much of where Brazil is today. Brazil began to industrialize in earnest in the late 19th century, and this process accelerated through the 1920s, especially in the south and southeast of the country. The Great Depression and its collapse of world trade was initially a catastrophe for South America's agricultural-dominated economies, which lost their markets around the world. But the decline in trade led Brazil to produce more of its own industrial goods (such as textiles, cement, and processed foods) rather than relying on imports. This led to more advanced industrialization and the "Brazilian Miracle" after World War II. Under both democratic rule (1946–64) and military rule (1964–80s), Brazil moved from production of simple industrial goods to a much more intensive economy that produced appliances, automobiles, electronics, petrochemicals, and even airplanes. The industrialization extended wealth to a broader cross-section of society, creating an urban middle class of workers, managers, and professionals. From 1968 to 1973, Brazil's GDP had an average growth of more than 10 per cent a year, but economic collapse in the 1980s led to shuttered factories and sent millions out of work and into the less secure, informal economy of street vending and odd jobs. Soon thereafter, excessive government spending led to hyperinflation and further decline. Finally, in the 1990s, the country stabilized under President Fernando Henrique Cardoso (1995–2003) and grew impressively once again in the years under President Luiz Inácio Lula da Silva (2003–11).

Poverty and inequality remain Brazil's greatest economic challenges. For years, Brazil was reputed to be the most economically unequal society on earth, with only a fraction of very wealthy people and huge numbers of people living in poverty in rural areas or in urban shantytowns known as *favelas*. As Brazil has grown methodically over the past decade or more, inequality has fallen but still remains at very high levels. The improvements have been helped along by policy changes, especially new and improved social programs. The governments of Cardoso, Lula, Rousseff, and Temer created and expanded social programs that provided modest cash benefits to low-income families that have their children vaccinated and stay in school. Poverty reduction has been a long-term goal of many governments, but this will not be an easy task in such a large and diverse country.

CASE STUDIES

CASE STUDY

Chapter 3, Page 55

Democratic Consolidation in Brazil

Brazil has moved back and forth between authoritarianism and democracy for much of its existence as an independent country. The country was an empire for the period from 1822 to 1889, followed by a republic from 1889 to 1930. Both of these had some formal democratic institutions, including elected legislatures and relatively liberal laws that enfranchised large numbers of people by 19th-century standards, but both were in practice dominated by landowning elites (Graham 1990). The 20th century saw a coup leading to military rule from 1930 to 1945, followed by a democratic republic from 1945 to 1964, which in turn fell to another military coup. Brazil's military regime fell under the category known as bureaucratic-authoritarian (see Chapter 6) from 1964 to the 1980s. A gradual transition to the current democratic republic began in 1982, resulted in a presidential election in 1985, and was codified in the Brazilian constitution of 1988.

Brazil's numerous experiences with regime change feature prominently in studies of democratization and democratic breakdown, partly because it is a large and important country in Latin America and partly because the historical evidence can provide support for several different theories of regime change (O'Donnell, Schmitter, and Whitehead [1986] 1993; Stepan 1971; O'Donnell 1973; Evans 1979).

The study of democracy in Brazil goes beyond the question of transition from one regime type to another. Perhaps the most important issues today for those studying Brazilian politics are about democratic consolidation. Since 1988, Brazil's democracy has achieved some consolidation, with repeated elections that have seen incumbents voted out of office and the election of Lula da Silva, whose candidacy was at one point unacceptable to the military. The country has protections for civil liberties as well, and a return to outright authoritarian rule seems unlikely in the near future. Yet that does not mean Brazil has created effective representation or equal opportunity for all citizens. The rule of law does not extend equally to everyone everywhere in Brazil: Some areas (both remote rural areas and parts of major cities) are almost lawless and ruled by criminals, while corruption is considerable in the police and in many political institutions. Racism remains a serious problem for black and Indigenous Brazilians.

One of the most interesting transitions in recent years has been a set of economic and policy changes that have improved the well-being of the lowest-income people in Brazil. The most famous is the *Bolsa Familia*, or Family Allowance. This program, known as a "conditional cash transfer," provides direct income from the government to poor families on the condition that they keep their children in school and keep their vaccinations up to date. The program predates the Lula presidency, but it was dramatically expanded on a nationwide basis under Lula (Zucco 2008). This set of changes brings poorer Brazilians into greater contact with state institutions, such as the education and health systems. This raises the prospect of strengthening relations between the state and society at large, which is one measure of what democratic consolidation is about.

CASE STUDY

Chapter 14, Page 298

Gender and Political Representation in Brazil: Where Has Progress Come From?

Like most modern societies, Brazil has struggled to provide gender equity. Also like most modern societies, it still has a long way to go on this issue. That said, the country has made considerable progress in recent years, especially since the 1990s, perhaps symbolized by the fact that the country recently had a two-term female president, Dilma Rousseff. Comparative political analysts ask how and why this progress has been made, in part because understanding the sources of both progress and failures may help future organizers and party leaders to make further progress, both in Brazil and elsewhere.

Some of the political successes of the Brazilian women's movement include the following:

1. Women's suffrage in 1932, though this proved moot in the Estado Novo (1937–45, when women were equally *unable* to vote) and in later authoritarian governments.
2. The decriminalization of divorce in 1977, with reforms in the late 2000s making divorce easier to obtain. This is important because typically, women without the right to divorce are more likely to be stuck in dangerous situations like ongoing domestic violence and it is widely held in today's world that people should be free to enter into and exit relationships consensually.
3. Creation of the *Conselho Nacional dos Direitos da Mulher* (CNDM, the National Council on Women's Rights) in 1985 and the *Secretaria Especial de Políticas para as Mulheres* (SEPM) in 2003. This was a consequence of important women's movement activism in civil society, and it essentially coincided with the re-emergence of Brazilian democracy. The CNDM has been involved in numerous important feminist initiatives (Macaulay 2006, 48).
4. In 1996, the passage of a law proposed by the PT (Workers' Party) establishing minimal candidate quotas of 30 per cent for both men and women. This means that parties are required to run slates of candidates at least 30 per cent of whom are women.
5. Dilma Rousseff's two terms, beginning in 2010. Her general unpopularity in 2016, which led to her impeachment, does, however, indicate continued gender bias.

Fiona Macaulay (2006, 39) notes that an interesting feature of recent Brazilian experience is that advances on gender issues at the national level have not often come from the state but rather from the Partido dos Trabalhadores (the party of both Rousseff and Lula da Silva), though some proposals have come from actors from a variety of parties and even though gender has not historically been an axis of "party system cleavage" in Brazil. This latter point is not especially surprising, particularly given that gender-based parties, unlike ethnicity-based parties, are rare for reasons discussed in Chapter 14 (see Htun 2004; Htun and Power 2006). More interesting is the fact that PT has, in comparative terms, nominated many more female candidates than other parties and has more consistently focused on gender issues. Macaulay's analysis suggests that this is partly due to the role that female activists and party operatives have played within the PT.

Macaulay further points to the fact that Brazil has a fairly decentralized federal political system and that local and state-level reforms have also been beneficial to women in some areas (Macaulay 2006, 35). The downside of this, of course, is that women's rights and their enforcement vary from area to area as well. Despite progress on issues of gender and politics in Brazil, serious problems remain, including limited representation of women's issues, a higher rate of poverty for women than for men, and a notably high rate of domestic violence. Many would also point to Brazil's strong restrictions on abortion in this connection.

Research Prompts

1. We have noted that Brazil is sometimes considered a "non-revolutionary" society in which transitions are gradual. Be that as it may, it is demonstrable that Brazil stands out in the Latin American context for the degree to which its transition to independence was peaceful. Why might this be? What would major theories of revolution say about this, and how might this case (in comparative Latin American perspective) help us to consider the relative merits of those theories?
2. After decades of mixed performance, Brazil has recently achieved solid economic growth. What would the major theories of development considered in Chapter 5 say about this case? What can Brazil's experience tell us about those theories?
3. Jair Bolsonaro has been criticized for his stance on Indigenous rights and for his right-of-centre populist message. What can we predict may be some of the consequences of his administration for Indigenous peoples?
4. Brazil has alternated between democracy and authoritarianism for some time, with a strong authoritarian tradition. It has had notable democratic success but the current government has been criticized for being illiberal. Is democracy likely to last? Why or why not? Be sure to draw both on facts about Brazil and on theories of democratic consolidation in your response.

Online Case Studies

Go to **www.oup.com/he/DickovickCe** to find more case studies online, including:

- Brazil's Landless Movement
- Does the Global Economy Help or Hurt Developing Nations Like Brazil?
- Electoral Rules and Party (In)Discipline in Brazil's Legislature

Canada

PROFILE

Key Features of Contemporary Canada

Population:	35.6 million (July 2017 est.)
Area:	9,984,670 square kilometres
Head of State:	Queen Elizabeth II (1952–present). Represented by Governor General Julie Payette
Head of Government:	Justin Trudeau (prime minister, 2015–present)
Capital:	Ottawa
Year of Independence:	1867 Confederation as a settler dominion; 1931 Statute of Westminster; Indigenous peoples remain subject to settler government and the Indian Act
Year of Current Constitution:	1982
Languages:	English and French (official), with many Indigenous languages including Cree, Oji-Cree, Anishinaabe, Innu, Inuktitut, Mi'kmaq, Dene, Athabaskan languages, etc.
GDP per Capita:	$45,032.10 (World Bank estimate 2017)
Human Development Index Ranking (2015):	10th (very high human development)

Sources: *CIA World Factbook*; World Bank World Development Indicators; United Nations *Human Development Report 2016*; 2016 Census Canada, https://www12.statcan.gc.ca/census-recensement/2016/as-sa/98-200-x/2016022/98-200-x2016022-eng.cfm

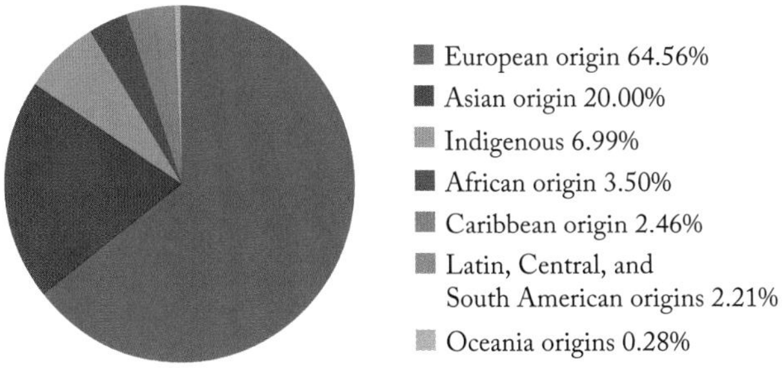

Ethnic Groups in Canada

In ethnic terms, the 2016 census lists a predominantly European population with growing ethnic diversity.

Source: Statistics Canada, 2016 Census

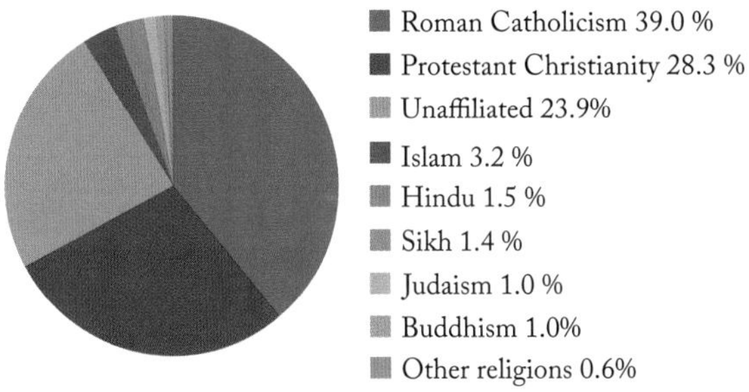

Affiliation in Canada

The majority of the population is nominally Christian. As in other Western countries, many Christians do not attend church regularly.

Statistics Canada, National Household Survey, 2011, Table 4. https://www150.statcan.gc.ca/n1/daily-quotidien/130508/dq130508b-eng.htm

Introduction

Canada is a Western settler state, an English-French bilingual country with a growing Indigenous population and an attractive destination for many immigrants from around the world. Canada is the world's second largest country in terms of size, with six time zones, but ranks 38th in terms of population. Canada is highly urbanized, with 81.4 per cent of the population living in urban areas. Ninety per cent of people live within 160 km of the US border. Ontario, Quebec, and British Columbia are the three most populous provinces. With 2–3 million lakes, Canada has more fresh water than all

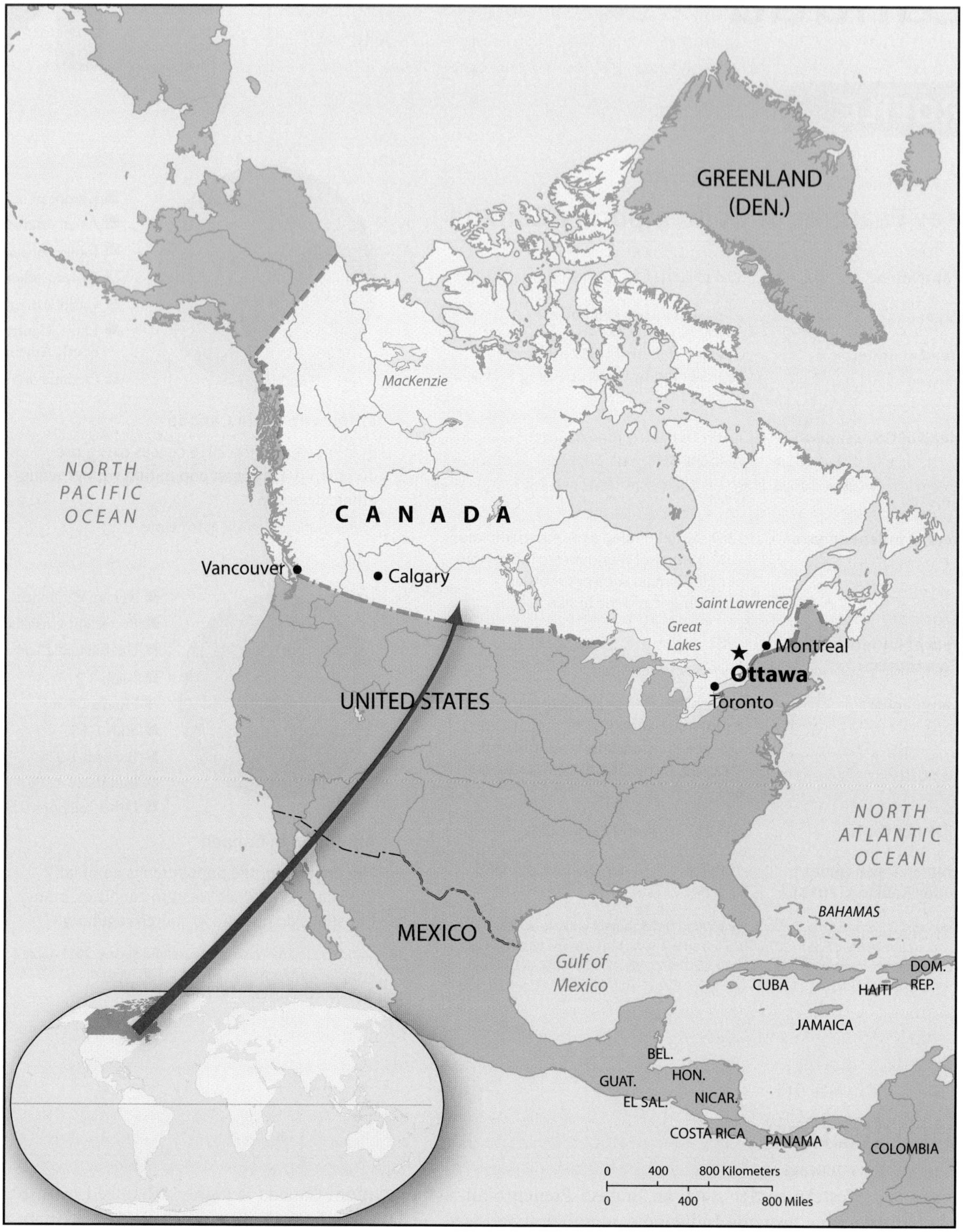
GREENLAND
(DEN.)
MacKenzie
NORTH
PACIFIC
OCEAN
CANADA
Vancouver
Calgary
Saint Lawrence
Great
Lakes
Montreal
Ottawa
Toronto
UNITED STATES
NORTH
ATLANTIC
OCEAN
BAHAMAS
MEXICO
Gulf of
Mexico
CUBA
HAITI
DOM.
REP.
JAMAICA
BEL.
GUAT.
HON.
EL SAL.
NICAR.
COSTA RICA
PANAMA
COLOMBIA
0 400 800 Kilometers
0 400 800 Miles

the other countries of the world combined. It is also abundant in other natural resources, including timber, precious metals, coal, oil and natural gas, gold, and other commodities (*CIA World Factbook* 2018). Since World War II, it has moved from agriculture to a highly diversified economy in manufacturing, services, and technology.

Historical Development

The original lands of Turtle Island were and still are the traditional territories of Indigenous peoples, whose creation stories trace their presence in what is now Canada to time immemorial. Linguistically, Indigenous peoples have been divided into at least 50 separate languages and 12 distinct language groups, seven of which are in British Columbia. There are also six cultural areas throughout the country: "Northwest Coast, Plateau, Plains, Subarctic, Arctic, and Northeast" (Jones, Smith, and Francis 2000, 17–18).

Early European exploration began with Leif Erikson's visit to what is now Newfoundland in the 11th century, following which was the Italian explorer Giovanni Caboto, who was working for the English Crown. French explorer Jacques Cartier mapped parts of the land and claimed much of Canada for France. In the 1600s, the English and French formed companies to trade in furs and other goods with Indigenous peoples. Various commercial and other alliances were developed, as well as rivalries. Both empires began developing coherent networks of colonies and brought in settlers from Europe as traders and farmers.

By 1763, the British had militarily defeated the French, and the former French colonies came under British rule. In part to avoid further bloodshed, the British agreed in 1774 to recognize the French language and the Catholic faith. This allowed French language and culture a level of autonomy that helped to make the future country bilingual. The British also signed a range of treaties and agreements with Indigenous nations.

That Indigenous nations were self-determining political actors was affirmed through the 1764 Treaty of Niagara. Some 2000 Indigenous representatives from 24 nations met with William Johnson (speaking for the Crown) and established a system of relationships for selectively sharing lands with the Crown. The treaty established clear lines of authority and gave the Crown responsibility for keeping local colonial administrations in line so that they would not bother Indigenous peoples in the practice of their governments and in their use of their resources and lands. The treaty's oral implications recognized Indigenous self-government and "an alliance between sovereign nations" (Jai 2017, 121–2).

After the American Revolution, which began in 1776, large numbers of Empire Loyalists fled from the 13 newly independent American states (they had yet to form a union) to the Canadian colonies, creating a society that was loyal to the British and anti-revolutionary. Settler numbers greatly increased in the 1800s, with tens of thousands of immigrants coming from the British Isles.

During the 1850s and 1860s, the Americans began expanding their state, going to war against Mexico and annexing large tracts of land. During the 1860s, the US government encouraged Irish Fenian mercenaries to invade and hold Canada for ransom to secure the independence of Ireland from British rule. The growing threat posed by an expansionary US prompted Canadian colonial officials to discuss creating a coherent country. Four colonies agreed to join together in 1867 (Quebec, Ontario, Nova Scotia, and New Brunswick), forming the Dominion of Canada. Further colonies joined Confederation: British Columbia, Manitoba, and Prince Edward Island in the 1870s, Alberta and Saskatchewan in 1905, and finally Newfoundland in 1949. Indigenous nations were not consulted about this process, and the treaties were largely set aside.

In the 1880s, the federal government, alongside the four main Christian denominations in the country, began a network of Indian Residential Schools. Under the Indian Act, Indigenous children were obliged to attend settler-run schools. This became compulsory in 1920. Overall, some 150,000 Indigenous children attended these schools, which were designed to destroy Indigenous languages, spiritual practices, and identities. In 2015, the schools and the government's policies of forced assimilation were described as cultural genocide.

Universal suffrage took some time to come about. Women over the age of 21 gained the right to vote federally in 1918, but it took considerably longer for women to be able to vote in provincial elections, with Quebec not allowing women to vote until 1940. While women could stand for election to the House of Commons (the first female MP was Agnes Macphail in 1921), women were barred from serving in the Senate and indeed, according to the Supreme Court of Canada in 1928, were not "persons" under the British North America Act of 1867. This decision was reversed by the British Privy Council in 1929 (Marshall and Cruickshank 2015).

Canada gained independence from the British Crown in 1931 with the Statute of Westminster and gained full legislative and legal autonomy with the passage of the Canadian Constitution in 1982.

Canada participated in both world wars, fighting alongside the British and other Western allies. Canada also became a central player after the Second World War in the creation of the United Nations in 1945, was a founding member of NATO in 1949, and sent troops to the Korean War from 1950 to 1953. Canada, through Prime Minister Lester Pearson, also created UN peacekeeping to help diffuse the Suez Crisis of 1956, for which Pearson received the Nobel Peace Prize. Since that time, more than 150,000 Canadian troops have served as peacekeepers around the world (Granatstein 2016).

Canada enacted forms of socialized health care and other welfare programs during the 20th century. A piecemeal welfare state developed during the early 1940s in response to the Great Depression, which lasted during the war years but was largely scaled back afterwards. The Conservative government of John Diefenbaker laid much of the basis for the welfare state today. Socialized medicine dates provincially back to Saskatchewan in the 1940s when the Co-operative Commonwealth Federation (CCF) government of Tommy Douglas set up a province-wide health scheme in 1947. By 1966, the Liberal government of Lester Pearson had introduced a national scheme with funding shared between the federal and provincial governments. He also introduced a permanent unemployment insurance scheme and a national pension plan (Moscovitch 2016).

Canada was founded on the national myths of an English–French partnership, and ideals of bilingualism and biculturalism remain important. The 1867 British North America Act set out both languages as legislative and judicial in Quebec and at the federal level. It also recognized the right to denominational schools—Protestant and Catholic. In 1969, the Royal Commission on Bilingualism and Biculturalism concluded that Canada should be made officially bilingual in all federal institutions and laid the basis for the 1969 Official Languages Act, which legislated the "equality of status" of both languages in the federal Parliament and in federal public services. Provincially, New Brunswick is officially bilingual, while Quebec in 1974 chose French as its only official language ("Bilingualism," 2015). Prime Minister Pierre Trudeau was seeking to diffuse desires on the part of some Québécois for a separate state. In 1967, the Mouvement Souveraineté-Association had been formed by René Lévesque. In 1976, the Parti Québécois under his leadership came to power on the promise of holding a referendum on independence, both of which they duly held in 1980. This was the first of two referenda, which failed to secure the independence of Quebec.

Demographically, Canada at first maintained strict racial immigration policies, and Asians, East Indians, Africans, and other non-European groups were restricted from immigrating. The rules were loosened by the end of the 1960s and in 1971. Under the Liberal government of Pierre Trudeau, policies of official multiculturalism were introduced, opening immigration to a range of non-European countries such as those in the Caribbean, Asia, and Africa. A ministry of multiculturalism was formed in 1973, and in 1988 a Multiculturalism Act was introduced (Moscovitch 2016).

Both bilingualism/biculturalism and multiculturalism help to frame the political culture of Canada and have also sometimes acted to undermine the Indigenous identities of the country. Canada was based on treaties and other agreements between Indigenous nations and the British Crown. Most articulations of national identity do not fully acknowledge this. Indeed, at the same time that biculturalism and multiculturalism were being introduced, Trudeau's Liberal government sought through its 1969 White Paper on "Indian Policy" to do away with the legal status of First Nations, end the treaties, and assimilate Indigenous peoples with settler Canadians—making them "equal." At the same time, the Liberals sought to provide French Canadians with special status and to introduce a new multicultural framework. Organized opposition to the White Paper led to its rejection in 1970. By 1973, the Canadian Supreme Court ruled in *Calder v. British Columbia* that Indigenous land title pre-dated the European occupation of North America, and by 1982 Indigenous treaty rights were recognized and affirmed under section 35 of the Constitution (Lagace and Sinclair 2015).

As in the UK and the US, the 1980s was a time when welfare state benefits were reduced, in Canada under the Progressive Conservative administration of Brian Mulroney. Mulroney privatized many national industries and developed the basis of the free trade agreement with the US in 1988. In 1993, a Liberal government under Jean Chrétien took power, which improved some aspects of the welfare state and also negotiated the North American Free Trade Agreement between Canada, the US, and Mexico, which entered into force in 1994. During his time in power, Quebec separatism became a serious issue again, and it was rejected in the 1995 referendum by a margin of less than 1 per cent. When Chrétien retired in 2003, former finance minister Paul Martin became prime minister. His time in office was mired in a financial scandal in which various supporters of the Liberal Party in Quebec were secretly provided with government funding to sponsor events as a means of boosting federalism in the province. Martin's government was defeated two years later by a vote of non-confidence. One notable outcome of this period was the Settlement Agreement over the Indian Residential Schools. The agreement was the outcome of the largest class action suit in

Canadian history and was negotiated between the federal government, the four main Christian churches that ran the schools, and representatives of the survivors. In addition to financial compensation, a Truth and Reconciliation Commission was created to investigate and document the truths of what had occurred during this lengthy period.

The Conservative Party of Stephen Harper was elected as a minority government in 2006 and remained in power until 2015. The government shifted Canada to the right in economic terms, lowering corporate and business taxes and courting closer military ties with the United States. Harper took a strong stand on supporting Israel and was very critical of both Iran and Russia as well as the UN. The Harper government established a range of policies that were seen as pro-military, pro–oil and gas, and harmful for Indigenous peoples. The Indigenous-led movement Idle No More began in 2012 in opposition to many Harper-era policies.

In 2015, Justin Trudeau's Liberal government was elected on a promise of increased transparency in government and what he called "sunny ways." Trudeau's record has been mixed in policy terms. He sought to expand the welfare state and greatly increased the number of Syrian refugees welcomed into Canada. He created a gender-balanced cabinet and launched a national inquiry into missing and murdered Indigenous women and girls. While professing to be pro-Indigenous, the Liberal record on Indigenous issues has been inconsistent. Trudeau's government supports the incorporation of the UN Declaration on the Rights of Indigenous Peoples into federal legislation. He has also pledged to create a viable nation-to-nation relationship with Indigenous peoples. While some of his policies have moved in this direction, Trudeau has also promoted the oil sands industry and the expansion of oil and gas pipelines across Indigenous lands. The government bought the Trans Mountain pipeline project in mid-2018, only to have the Federal Court of Appeal quash its approval of the pipeline expansion on the grounds that Indigenous nations had not been properly consulted.

In 2019, two female cabinet ministers resigned: former Minister of Justice and Attorney General of Canada Jody Wilson-Raybould and former President of the Treasury Board Jane Philpott. Wilson-Raybould was the first Indigenous person to occupy these prestigious positions. Both cabinet ministers resigned over the SNC-Lavalin affair. In this political scandal, the Quebec multinational was charged with fraud and corruption over bribery of Libyan government officials in order to obtain construction contracts. Wilson-Raybould asserted that the Prime Minister's Office had engaged in political interference and obstruction of justice by pressuring her to back off on a criminal prosecution of SNC-Lavalin in order to save jobs in Quebec. The scandal was a blow to Trudeau's prestige and eroded public trust in the Liberal government.

Historical Development Timeline[1]

Undated	Indigenous peoples establish communities throughout Turtle Island, developing sophisticated societies with their own languages, cultures, governance structures, and relationships with lands, waters, plants, and animals.
11th Century	Viking explorers establish a temporary settlement in what is now Newfoundland.
1497	Italian explorer Giovanni Caboto maps the coastlines of Cape Breton and Newfoundland for the Kingdom of England.
1534	French explorer Jacques Cartier travels up the St Lawrence River and claims waters and lands for the Kingdom of France.
1583	England declares Newfoundland an overseas colony.
1600s	Indigenous peoples form alliances with European fur traders, primarily the Dutch, French, and English.
1627	France creates the Company of New France to oversee the fur trade and also to administer its colonies in "New France."
1670	London businesspeople create the Hudson's Bay Company to trade in furs and other commodities with Indigenous peoples.
1756–63	The Seven Years' War between the French and British leads to the defeat of the French empire in North America and the British acquisition of New France.
1774	The British government recognizes Roman Catholicism and the French language in British North America.
1791	Lower Canada (Quebec) and Upper Canada (Ontario) are created as separate colonies.
1812–14	During the War of 1812, the US attempts to invade and take over Canada, only to be repelled and lose the war.
1841	The "United Province of Canada" is created when "Canada East" (Quebec) and "Canada West" (Ontario) are joined together.
1867	Confederation with the passage of the British North America Act unites four colonies to create the Dominion of Canada. Sir John A. Macdonald serves as Canada's first prime minister.

continued

1870-3 Manitoba, British Columbia, Prince Edward Island, and the Northwest Territories join Confederation.

1885 Completion of the Canadian Pacific Railway, which was a key condition for BC's entry into Confederation.

1893 The first three Indian Residential Schools are established by the federal government and the mainline Christian churches.

1898 The Yukon is created from a portion of the Northwest Territories.

1905 Alberta and Saskatchewan join Confederation as provinces.

1914 Canada enters World War I, provoking domestic divisions between English and French Canadians over whether Canada should fight in a British war.

1918 Women gain the right to vote in federal elections.

1920 Attendance in state-run schools for Indigenous children is made compulsory. A large proportion of children are forced to attend residential schools.

1935 William Lyon Mackenzie King begins his time as Canada's longest-serving prime minister. With occasional breaks, he will stay in office until 1948.

1939 Canada enters World War II in support of Britain and its allies.

1949 Canada helps to found the North Atlantic Treaty Organization (NATO). Newfoundland joins Confederation.

1957 Canada and the US form the North American Air Defense Command (NORAD) for coordinated air defence of North America, primarily against the threat of Soviet invasion or nuclear attack.

1960 Indigenous peoples with status under the Indian Act are legally allowed to vote in federal elections. Provincially, they cannot vote until 1963 in New Brunswick and Prince Edward Island, in Alberta until 1965, and in Quebec until 1969.

1965 Canada's red and white maple leaf flag is adopted.

1968 Pierre Trudeau's Liberal Party wins federal elections. In Quebec, the Parti Québécois (PQ) is created on a platform of Quebec independence as a separate country.

1970 The Front de libération du Québec, a terrorist organization, kidnaps a British diplomat and murders a provincial cabinet minister, seeking independence for Quebec.

1976 The PQ wins the provincial elections under René Lévesque.

1980 The PQ holds a referendum on independence, which is rejected by almost 60 per cent of Quebec voters.

1982 The Constitution Act, including a Charter of Rights and Freedoms, ends the UK's legal control over Canada.

1984 Brian Mulroney's Progressive Conservatives take power, moving Canada in a more right-of-centre direction.

1993 Mulroney resigns, and Kim Campbell becomes the first female prime minister. Her tenure does not last long, and after the federal election, Jean Chrétien's Liberal Party takes power. A lasting legacy of this era is the North American Free Trade Agreement, signed between Canada, the US, and Mexico.

1995 In a second PQ-led referendum, Quebec voters narrowly reject independence.

1999 Nunavut is created as Canada's third territory, the first territory with a majority Indigenous population.

2003–5 After Chrétien's retirement from public life, Paul Martin becomes prime minister. Martin and the Liberals face a major scandal over the misuse of federal money. Following a commission of inquiry into the scandal, Martin's minority government is defeated in a vote of non-confidence.

2006 Stephen Harper and the Conservative Party form a minority government.

2007 Lawyers for the federal government, Canada's main Christian churches, and survivors of the Indian Residential Schools (IRS) sign a settlement agreement to compensate survivors and create a Truth and Reconciliation Commission (TRC). Harper provides an official apology to the survivors of the IRS system in 2008.

2010 The TRC begins regional and national hearings into the IRS system.

2011 Harper and the Conservatives form a majority government. They act to formally withdraw Canada from the Kyoto Protocol, an international accord on controlling climate change.

2012 Indigenous groups found the Idle No More movement in reaction to the Harper government's policies toward Indigenous peoples, the environment, and other issues.

2015 The TRC releases its final report with 94 Calls to Action for government, the churches, and society. The report concludes that the Canadian state committed cultural genocide against Indigenous peoples. Justin Trudeau and the Liberal Party form the government.

2017 Trudeau backtracks on his promise to reform the electoral system.

2018 The North American Free Trade Agreement (NAFTA) is opened to renegotiation after US President Trump expresses dissatisfaction with the agreement.

2019 SNC-Lavalin affair leads to resignation of two prominent female cabinet ministers. Canada holds its federal election and Justin Trudeau and the Liberal Party are re-elected in a minority government. A "Wexit" movement for western separatism forms, and the Bloc Québécois gains a large number of seats in the Parliament. The British Columbia legislature passes legislation incorporating the UN Declaration on the Rights of Indigenous Peoples into provincial law.

Sources: *CIA World Factbook*; BBC News, "Country Profile Canada"

Regime and Political Institutions

Canada is a federal system. Its bicameral Parliament in Ottawa features a 338-seat House of Commons and a 105-seat Senate. The House of Commons is elected using a first-past-the-post electoral system. While a fixed election term is now a part of the Canada Elections Act, in practice the prime minister can choose to hold an election earlier by notifying the governor general. The Senate is based on appointments by the prime minister and is not subject to elections; the model is based on the British House of Lords, although Senate seats are not hereditary. Canada uses a Westminster parliamentary system, which means that the largest party typically forms the government. The leader of the largest party becomes prime minister and appoints a cabinet. The prime minister also appoints justices to the Supreme Court, who serve until the age of 75.

The provinces and territories all have unicameral legislatures subject to regular elections. Provincial legislatures also adhere to the Westminster model. In both federal and provincial politics, three parties have traditionally been dominant: the Liberals and Conservatives tend to alternate between government and opposition federally, but at the provincial level, the New Democratic Party (NDP) has also served as the government in many provinces. Coalition governments are rare, although the current provincial government in British Columbia is a coalition of the NDP and the Green Party.

While Queen Elizabeth II is the official head of state, the monarch's domestic representative plays the key ceremonial and legal roles. Federally, the Queen's representative is the governor general, appointed by the prime minister for a seven-year term. Provincially, the prime minister appoints lieutenant governors for five-year terms. While there has been some discussion of Canada becoming a republic, this would require major constitutional change. Theoretically, the Canadian system provides fewer checks and balances than the American system and gives the prime minister tremendous political power at the federal level over the judiciary, both houses of Parliament, the cabinet, and all federal departments and agencies.

Indigenous governance remains a major challenge to the legitimacy of the Canadian state. From the 18th century, the British Crown negotiated a series of treaties with Indigenous nations. Some parts of the country are on unceded land (including most of BC), which means they are not covered by treaties, so while there is a Crown assertion of sovereignty, there is no legal basis for the assertion. The 1982 Constitution recognizes three classifications of "Aboriginal" peoples: First Nations, Inuit, and Métis. Within these categories, the state has divided Indigenous peoples into those with "status" and those without. Having status means in most cases being subject to the Indian Act (1876). Those with status are recognized as being members of a particular First Nation, and they may vote for their nation's chief and council and have access to a range of services funded by the federal government. Numbers of Indigenous peoples are growing because of higher birth rates and an increase

Regime and Political Institutions

Regime	Constitutional monarchy, with parliamentary democracy
Powers in Constitution	Formal Constitution from 1982, including a Charter of Rights and Freedoms, outlining powers of the federal, provincial, and territorial governments along with the power of the judiciary. Section 35 also recognizes pre-existing Indigenous rights.
Administrative Divisions	Federal government, 10 provinces, and three territories.
Executive Branch	Prime minister (and cabinet)
Selection of Executive	Elected by House of Commons
Legislative Branch	Bicameral Parliament Lower chamber: House of Commons (338 seats) Upper chamber: Senate (105 seats)
Judicial Branch	Interprets statutes, has right of judicial review
Political Party System	Three-party system; Conservatives (Tories) and Liberals are two main parties; New Democratic Party is third party.

in self-identification. The 2016 census indicates that there are 1,673,785 Indigenous peoples, comprising 4.9 per cent of the country's population (Galloway and Bascaramurty 2017). Unfortunately, Indigenous education, housing, governance, and health care have been chronically and severely underfunded for decades by every federal government.

The 1996 Royal Commission on Aboriginal Peoples (RCAP) recommended the establishment of a House of First Peoples, and other suggestions for Indigenous representation have included guaranteed seats for Indigenous peoples in the House of Commons and/or at the provincial and territorial levels. This is a model used in Aotearoa New Zealand. The RCAP also identified between 60 and 80 Indigenous nations that might viably exercise political rights to self-determination, which would imply regrouping more than 600 bands into larger governance structures (Palmater 2011). Provincially and territorially, Indigenous peoples are represented by regional organizations such as the Federation of Sovereign Indigenous Nations (Saskatchewan) and the Chiefs of Ontario (Ontario), while federally, the Assembly of First Nations represents the chiefs of the individual First Nations throughout the country. While these organizations enjoy some Indigenous support, there is also criticism that they are not traditional Indigenous forms of governance and that they owe their creation and continuation to the Indian Act and other colonial policies.

Political Culture

Canada was ostensibly founded on the partnership of two colonizing peoples—the descendants of French and British explorers and settlers. Indigenous peoples have largely been frozen out of the political cultures of the country, although this is slowly changing as the government and Canadians have begun to grapple with the many harms of the colonial process. (See "Case Study: What Is the Future of Reconciliation between Indigenous peoples and the Canadian Settler State?")

Bilingualism and biculturalism have traditionally been important aspects of Canada, providing a mark of differentiation from the United States. Official biculturalism builds on the national mythology that two founding peoples (English and French) formed Canada in 1867. While English is spoken by almost 87 per cent of Canadians, 58 per cent as their first language, 22 per cent speak French as their first language. Quebec retains a French civil law system derived from the Napoleonic Code, while the rest of the country uses a British common law system.

Since the 1970s, multiculturalism has also become an important aspect of national identity. While the Harper government reduced immigration levels, they rose under the Trudeau government. A key promise of the government was increasing the refugee quota for Syrians from 40,000 in 2016 to 43,000 in 2018 with plans to increase this number to more than 48,000 by 2020 (Perreaux 2017; Immigration, Refugees and Citizenship Canada).

An extensive welfare state has been an enduring source of pride for Canadians, who often try to distinguish themselves from Americans and seek to be more "European" in terms of social policy-making. Indeed, a sense of rivalry with the United States has been an enduring feature of Canadian political culture. Kim Nossal has described what he calls a "contingent anti-Americanism," contingent on political events in the US and "stimulated by the dislike of particular policies or personalities in any given U.S. administration" (Nossal 2005, 7–8). As such, Canadians were very much anti-Bush but pro-Obama and are now anti-Trump.

UN peacekeeping has traditionally been an important part of Canadian identity. While Canada is a member of NORAD and NATO, military power has not been a significant ingredient in national identity, and Canada's defence budget often hovers below 1 per cent of GDP (2016). The Harper government sought to promote military history as a key aspect of identity, and before he became Conservative Party leader in 2004, he was publicly supportive of US military forays into Afghanistan and Iraq, a view he maintained as leader of the opposition and as prime minister. The Trudeau government has kept military spending relatively low, and Canada's defence expenditures are 114th in the world (*CIA World Factbook 2017*).

Political Economy

Canada is a market-oriented economy with a very high standard of living. The economy is focused on services and manufacturing, which it has moved to since World War II from being a primarily agricultural economy. Canada is a member of the G7 and is one of the world's most productive economies.

Canada has a growing oil and gas sector, rooted primarily in Alberta and Saskatchewan. Its proven oil reserves are the third largest in the world after Saudi Arabia and Venezuela. Canada is becoming increasingly dependent on trade in oil and gas, and partly for this reason, the Harper government withdrew from the Kyoto Protocol in 2011.

Despite a downturn after the 2008 financial crisis, Canada has bounced back because of a more strongly regulated banking and financial sector. The economic structure is similar to that of other Western countries, with services accounting for more than 70 per cent of the economy, industry at 28 per cent, and agriculture well below 2 per cent. In 2017, Canada's GDP per capita was $48,100. The unemployment rate was 6.5 per cent (*CIA World Factbook 2017*).

A considerable percentage of its two-way trade is with the United States. Canada also has free trade agreements with the European Union. Canada maintains 12 consulates general throughout the US in addition to an embassy and three additional trade offices. In 1989, a Canada-US Free Trade Agreement was signed, followed in 1994 by the North American Free Trade Agreement (NAFTA), renegotiated in 2018 following the election of Donald Trump. In 2017, the US bought 76.4 per cent of Canada's exports and supplied 51.5 per cent of its imports (valued at more than $680 billion), with China behind at 4.3 and 12.6 per cent for exports and imports and Mexico at 6.3 per cent imports. The US is the largest market for Canadian oil, natural gas, electricity, and uranium. Some commentators have worried that Canada is too dependent economically on the US, which is perhaps part of the reason that Canada has sought to diversify its markets, signing on to free trade with the European Union in 2016 and pursuing free trade agreements with Asia-Pacific countries.

As of 2018, Canada was a party to 14 free trade agreements and was also a founding member of the World Trade Organization (WTO). Canada is continuing to negotiate an agreement with members of the Trans-Pacific Partnership, which, if successful, would provide Canada with free trade with more than 60 per cent of the world's economy (Export Development Canada).

Sources for economic data in this discussion: CIA World Factbook 2018; World Bank World Development Indicators 2017.

CASE STUDIES

CASE STUDY

Chapter 4, Page 78

How Does Canada Compare in Terms of Gender Equality?

In the 2015 federal election, 88 women were elected to the House of Commons, representing 26 per cent of the total in a country where women make up 50 per cent of the population. This put Canada in 50th place globally in terms of female representation, well below Rwanda, Cuba, Bolivia, and Sweden (CBC News). Historically, there has been only one female prime minister—Kim Campbell in 1993, who was in office very briefly. Female representation has been slightly better at the provincial level. Recently there have been several female premiers, including Rachel Notley (Alberta 2015–19), Kathy Dunderdale (Newfoundland and Labrador 2010–14), Eva Aariak (Nunavut 2008–13), Alison Redford (Alberta 2011–14), Christy Clark (BC 2011–17), Pauline Marois (Quebec 2012–14), and Kathleen Wynne (Ontario 2013–18). Currently there are no female premiers in Canada.

Political scientists have often asked: *why are there not more women in politics?* The reasons for low female representation are often divided into supply and demand factors. As Joanna Everitt explains, the "supply side" explanations often involve a lack of financial resources for women, gendered social roles, a low number of female political role models, and women self-selecting themselves to not run for office. On the "demand side," political cultures at the municipal, provincial, and federal levels may be unwelcoming to women, and party gate-keepers (usually men) can block women from running or can simply avoid recruiting them (Everitt 2015, 178; on gatekeeping and party structure, see O'Neill 2015).

How can the situation be improved? Everitt suggests the key is having more female role models—the more women in power, the more other women will be empowered to enter the political system. This will, in turn, have an influence on the political culture. The flip side is that if women politicians are treated badly and become mired

continued

in sexism, this may act as a deterrent to other prospective candidates (Everitt 2015, 178). In their 2014 book *Stalled: The Representation of Women in Canadian Governments*, Trimble, Arscott, and Tremblay ask why representation has not improved significantly since the 1980s and 90s. They note a range of factors, which include a negative political climate for women, even threats and harassment.

Money and access to financial resources is another key issue highlighted. By 2017, women made only 74 cents for every dollar made by a man, and for women with disabilities, as well as Indigenous and racialized women, the figure was worse—67 cents. In 2015, a study of TSX-listed companies demonstrated that almost 50 per cent of companies had no female directors while only 29 per cent had one. The very high costs for childcare are seen as one reason why women are being held back, alongside problems of continued discrimination and the fact that women do far more unpaid work than men, primarily related to child and elder care (Global News 2017).

Everitt points out that proportional electoral systems are generally much better for female representation (Everitt 2015, 180). This has been clearly noted in New Zealand where after a mixed member proportional system (MMP) was introduced in 1993, female representation greatly increased to the point where there have been three female prime ministers since that time, together with a larger representation of women in cabinet and Parliament as a whole. Nagel has noted of the NZ system that MMP has "helped elect higher percentages of women, Pasifika and Asian MPs. For many supporters of MMP, representational fairness is the primary goal and virtue of the system" (Nagel 2012). Electoral change could play an important role in bringing about gender equity in politics in Canada. It is long overdue.

CASE STUDY

Chapter 6, Page 118

What Is the Future of Reconciliation between Indigenous Peoples and the Canadian Settler State?

Historically, Indigenous peoples have been marginalized in the European colonization of what is now Canada. They were not a party to Confederation, had their traditional governments dismantled, could not vote federally until 1960, had their spiritual practices outlawed, and were forbidden from leaving the reserves without a pass. As James Daschuk has noted of the 19th century, policies of starvation, decimation of food supplies, and denial of rations were used in western Canada to reduce the political challenges posed by Indigenous nations to European settlement and to get them to move to isolated reserves (Daschuk 2013, 183). A network of Indian Residential Schools run by the federal government and the four main Christian churches forcibly assimilated a large proportion of Indigenous children into settler society (Miller 2010, 138). From the 1950s, tens of thousands of Indigenous children were taken from their families and communities and put into foster and adoptive care—in what has become known as the "Sixties Scoop" (Vowel 2016, 181).

As noted in the history section, in 2007 a Settlement Agreement with residential school survivors provided compensation and established the basis of a Truth and Reconciliation Commission. In its five-volume report in 2015, the TRC officially concluded that Canada had committed cultural genocide against Indigenous peoples, and individual commissioners also argued that genocide as defined under international law had also been committed in the schools. The report outlined 94 Calls to Action—a broad range of recommendations. Currently, a reconciliation process is underway, and the federal and some provincial and territorial governments are making efforts to increase knowledge of Indigenous histories and cultures. However, cultural inclusion will not be enough.

Canada is not a wealthy country by accident, and it has, like all other settler states, profited from its control of Indigenous lands. Currently, Indigenous reserves comprise around 0.2 per cent of the Canadian land mass, with the federal and provincial Crowns owning almost 90 per cent of the land. The state has generally profited from the arrangement. For example, as Lee Maracle recently highlighted, the Attawapiskat First Nation is one of the poorest in Canada, yet the De Beers diamond mine generates some $6 billion annually, with the federal government claiming a significant share for having leased Cree lands to this South African company. The reserve itself gets only about $1 million, along with some manual labour jobs for the Attawapiskat Cree. In many parts of the country, the provincial and federal governments control the subsoil or mineral rights to reserve lands (which are still legally "held in trust" by the government and not owned by individual First Nations), denying Indigenous peoples the ability to profit from the royalties generated by their own lands (Maracle 2017, 965, 968; Indigenous Foundation Arts).

CASE STUDY

(Chapter 8, Page 170)

Is Quebec Independence Now off the Agenda?

Canada is one of the most interesting cases for the study of how federalism relates to secession. Quebec is the only province that is predominantly French-speaking and was one of the key founding provinces of the country in 1867. Much of the rest of the country is English-speaking. Many Québécois see themselves as constituting a separate nation, with their national attributes consisting of the French language, their historical ties to territory, and the culture they have developed during more than four centuries of settlement. Quebec has sought to be recognized as a "société distincte," or a distinct society, within Canadian history and politics. During the 1960s, a movement for Quebec independence developed as the province became more urbanized and industrialized.

In 1980 and 1995, the Parti Québécois, which has been devoted to the independence of Quebec, held two referenda on independence. The first failed by a wide margin, the second by barely 1 per cent of the vote. For the PQ, a key point of contention was the exclusion of Quebec's voice from the 1982 Constitution. The government of Quebec refused to sign onto the Constitution because they would lose their veto over future constitutional changes and were also concerned that French language rights would not be protected. The federal government tried twice to bring Quebec into the Constitution, with the Meech Lake Accord of 1987 and the Charlottetown Accord of 1992. Both attempts failed, and there seems to be little political will for a third attempt.

In 2013, the PQ government tried to implement a Charter of Values (*Charte des valeurs québécoises*) that seemed to be focused on promoting secularism in Quebec society. It would have prohibited the wearing of "conspicuous" religious symbols for most provincial employees. This seems to have been directed primarily at Muslim women wearing the hijab, niqab, or burqa. It was publicly perceived as dog-whistle politics against Muslims and played a role in the defeat of the PQ by the Liberals in the 2014 provincial election.

While independence seems to be less popular than it was historically (certainly among younger voters), the anti-Muslim and intolerant views in general against immigrants seem to remain salient in electoral politics. In 2018, the Coalition Avenir Québec (CAQ), a political party founded in 2011, gained considerable support for a renewed call for a ban on facial coverings and tests for immigrants in Quebec values and the French language (with the threat of deportation for those who fail). The CAQ gained 74 seats in the 2018 elections, forming the government, with the Liberals (who lost half of their seats) as the official opposition. The PQ dropped from 30 to 9 seats, losing their party status for the first time in five decades. CAQ promotes a right-of-centre social policy agenda, and Premier François Legault has also pledged not to hold a referendum on independence. He has, true to his election promise, introduced Bill 21, which will ban provincial employees from wearing conspicuous religious symbols such as the turban, hijab, or kippah.

Research Prompts

1. Canada remains the only Western country with an exclusively first-past-the-post electoral system. Assess the prospects for electoral reform federally and provincially. How likely is such reform? Would such reform increase the representation of women, Indigenous peoples, and racialized communities?
2. As Quebec becomes more multicultural, will this reduce the prospects for Quebec sovereignty, or will newcomers to Quebec also seek to create an independent state?
3. Canada is highly dependent on the US for trade in goods and services. How is the current Trump administration affecting the Canadian trading regime? Are we likely to see differences in trade patterns as the US becomes more protectionist and more willing to use tariffs to protect domestic industry?
4. Many political commentators contrast the relatively strong welfare state in Canada and the country's generally centrist political system with the lack of a similar social safety net in the United States. What do you think accounts for those differences?
5. Compare the level of gender representation in Canada and other Western countries. What could Canadians learn from examples where female representation is higher?

Online Case Studies

Go to **www.oup.com/he/DickovickCe** to find more case studies online, including:

- Should the Senate Be Reformed to Be More Accountable and Democratic?
- Why Does It Take So Long to Choose a Leader?

Note

1 Adapted from BBC News 2018.

China

PROFILE

Key Features of Contemporary China

Population:	1,379,302,771 (July 2017 est.)
Area:	9,596,961 square kilometres
Head of State:	Xi Jinping (president, 2013–present)
Head of Government:	Li Keqiang (premier, 2013–present)
Capital:	Beijing
Year of Independence:	Never formally colonized, with the exception of Hong Kong, despite European imperial involvement in the 19th century. People's Republic of China established in 1949.
Year of Current Constitution:	1982
Languages:	Mandarin is the majority language. There are numerous dialects and minority languages.
GDP per Capita:	$8,827.00 (World Bank estimate 2017)
Human Development Index Ranking (2015):	90th (high human development)
Trading Relationship with Canada (2016):	Trading Relationship with Canada (2016): • Imports $48,641,696,239 • Exports $15,832,275,983 https://globaledge.msu.edu/countries/canada/tradestats

Sources: *CIA World Factbook*; World Bank World Development Indicators; United Nations *Human Development Report 2016*

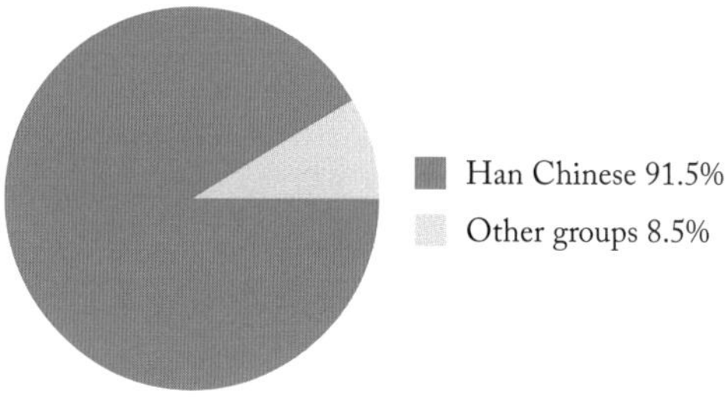

Ethnic Groups in China

Source: *CIA World Factbook*

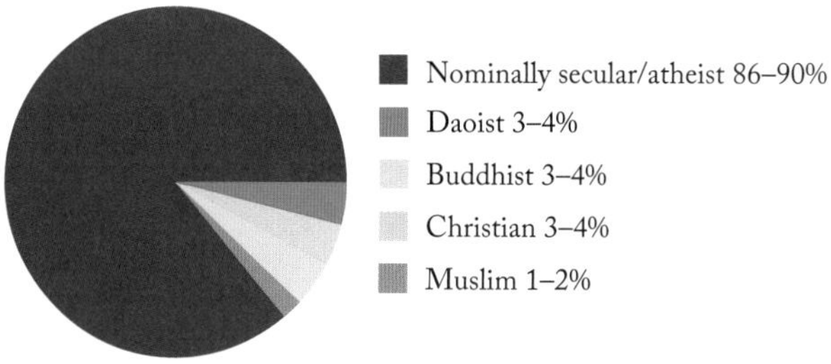

Religious Affiliation in China

Source: *CIA World Factbook*

Introduction

For a comparative politics scholar, China is one of the most fascinating countries. It raises numerous questions and issues about economic development, democracy, the relationship between political parties and the state, and the causes and consequences of social revolutions, among many others. For Canadians, China is our second-largest trading partner after the United States, and our relationship with this country will continue to grow.

Of course, a leading issue in the politics of China is the question of how it has rapidly become the world's second-largest economy and a major global power just a few short decades after being characterized by extreme poverty.

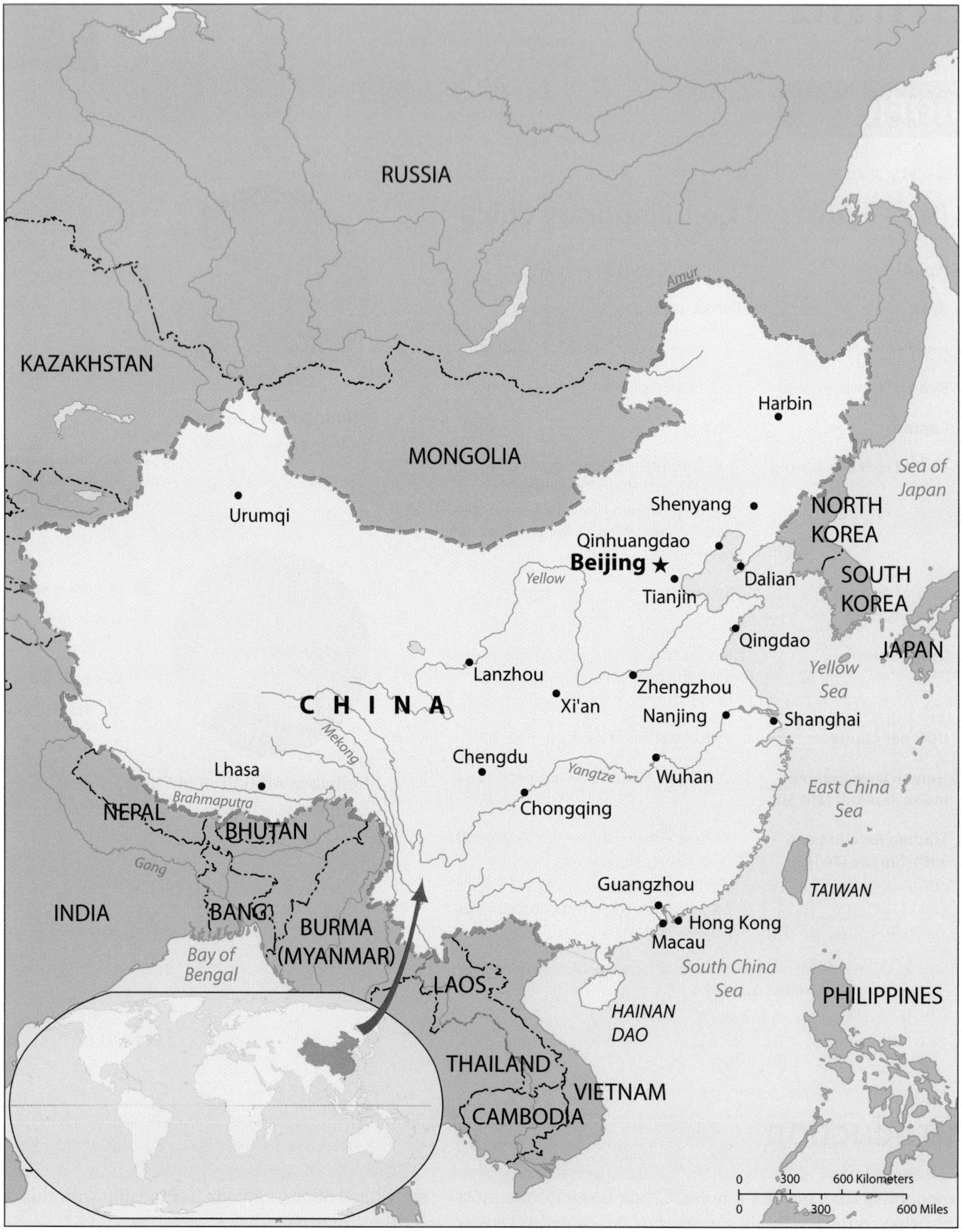
RUSSIA
Amur
KAZAKHSTAN
MONGOLIA
Harbin
Sea of Japan
Urumqi
Shenyang
NORTH KOREA
Qinhuangdao
Beijing
Yellow
Dalian
Tianjin
SOUTH KOREA
Qingdao
JAPAN
Lanzhou
Yellow Sea
Zhengzhou
C H I N A
Xi'an
Nanjing
Shanghai
Mekong
Chengdu
Lhasa
Yangtze
Wuhan
East China Sea
Brahmaputra
Chongqing
NEPAL
BHUTAN
Gang
Guangzhou
TAIWAN
INDIA
BANG.
BURMA (MYANMAR)
Hong Kong
Macau
Bay of Bengal
South China Sea
LAOS
PHILIPPINES
HAINAN DAO
THAILAND
VIETNAM
CAMBODIA
0 300 600 Kilometers
0 300 600 Miles

It has done so in a non-democratic, one-party state that restricts many basic freedoms. The implications of China's rise for the future are massive, both within China and around the world. We examine these issues of political economy and the regime in this profile.

Another striking thing about China from the point of view of political science is the degree of political, economic, and cultural unity that it has managed to achieve despite its enormous size (in terms of both geography and population) and diversity. China is among the most geographically diverse countries in the world. Its land mass encompasses more than 9.5 million square kilometres.

China's population currently stands at around 1.4 billion, making it the largest country in the world in population terms. Demographers expect Chinese population growth to slow in the coming decades, and some suggest that India's population will overtake China's, though the accuracy of this forecast remains to be seen. More than 90 per cent of the population falls into the Han ethnic category. Yet the remaining 8.5 per cent of the population falls into numerous groups (small in percentage terms because of China's large population but still numerous in absolute terms). These categories include the Manchu (the ethnic group that was dominant during the Qing Dynasty), Tibetans, Mongols, Zhuang, and Uighur, among others.

In terms of religion, China's state is officially atheist in character, owing, in part, to the legacy of Marxism. The above chart shows the percentage of the population that professes allegiance to several major religions. Students should keep in mind that some scholars estimate higher levels of religious belief and practice than these data suggest (see Pew Forum 2008). China is a large, complex, heterogeneous society in which one major ethnic group (Han Chinese) predominates. The state is officially secular, but underneath this surface a number of citizens are religious, and both Christianity and Islam continue to grow (Weiming 1999). It has a varied geography and some striking demographic patterns. These basic features form the context through which we try to understand China's political development.

Historical Development

China stands out among most modern countries for how long it has existed as a large-scale and more or less unified civilization. Indeed, China has been a distinct geopolitical entity for *millennia*. As we shall see, however, this does not mean that it does not change or that it is not changing now. The beginning of the history of Imperial China is conventionally dated at 221 BCE, and historians have traced the sequence of imperial regimes that followed. The history of *modern* China, however, begins in the later years of the Qing Dynasty (1644–1912). The Qing Dynasty entered into difficulties in the 19th century as a result of several key factors: foreign intervention, fiscal difficulties, internal instability, and a changing geopolitical environment (for an overview of this period, see Spence 1990; Fairbank and Goldman 2006).

China in the 19th century faced increasing foreign intervention. Western nations imposed their own "rights" to trade with China, using force when necessary. This even included British merchants smuggling opium into the Chinese market. When China tried to resist, they were twice militarily coerced (in the 1840s and 1850s), and among other things Hong Kong became a Crown colony of the British Empire. Beyond direct interference, European powers also interfered in China's traditional sphere of influence, particularly in so-called "French IndoChina." It is important to understand that China considered itself to be one of the world's great civilizations, and their relative weakness in the face of European powers was experienced as humiliating. At the same time, the Qing Dynasty found itself in serious fiscal difficulties. It was unable to consistently raise the revenues that were required to protect itself and to maintain internal order (Fairbank and Goldman 2006, 187; Spence 1990). Partially as a result, the country witnessed serious internal disturbances. Among them were the Taiping Rebellion of the 1850s and 1860s, which killed many millions of people before the Qing eventually put it down. This was only the most important of a series of 19th-century rebellions against the Qing. During this same period, China's neighbour Japan underwent dramatic changes, and by the end of the century emerged as a major regional power, defeating China itself in the Sino-Japanese War of 1894–5 and then defeating Russia in the Russo-Japanese War of 1904–5.

Not surprisingly, many in China decided that greater openness to both Japan and the West would be needed, in terms of both technology and political ideas. By the first decade of the 20th century, the Qing regime was embracing reforms and even toying with constitutionalism. However, this was not enough to stop the growing discontent, and a political revolution (the "Chinese Revolution of 1911") toppled the Qing in 1912. The most important leader in this movement was Sun Yat-sen.

Historical Development Timeline

1644–1912	Qing Dynasty
1839–42	First Opium War (with Britain)
1842	Treaty of Nanking. Britain takes Hong Kong and imposes trading rights for itself.
1850–73	Taiping (1850–64), Nien (1853–68), and Panthay (1855–73) Rebellions
1856–60	Second Opium (or "Arrow") War with Britain and France
1860	Convention of Peking imposes humiliating conditions on China
1894–5	Sino-Japanese War (China defeated)
1898	Hundred Days' Reform, ended by coup d'état
1899–1901	Boxer Rebellion, ended by foreign intervention (eight foreign powers)
1911–12	Revolution of 1911
1912	Fall of the Qing Dynasty,foundation of Guomindang (GMD or Nationalist Party), establishment of the Republic of China, which then falls into disorder and civil conflict
1920–1	Chinese Communist Party founded
1925	Death of Sun Yat-sen, founder of the Guomindang
1926	Chiang Kai-Shek leads "Northern Expedition," achieving partial political unification
1931	Japanese invasion of Manchuria
1934–5	The "Long March" of the Communists, who face repression at the hands of the Nationalists. The march facilitates Mao's rise within the group and the move toward the countryside.
1936	Beginning of the "Anti-Japanese War," which can be thought of as the beginning of the Second World War in China
1937	Japanese invasion of Manchuria (northeast China) in lead-up to World War II
1946–9	After end of World War II, civil war between Nationalists and Communists continues.
1949	Communists victorious, Nationalists exiled to Taiwan
1949	People's Republic of China is proclaimed.
1950–2	Major land reform is carried out.
1950–3	Korean War in which China backed North Korea against US-backed South Korea
1955–6	Major agricultural collectivization is carried out.
1957	The "Hundred Flowers Campaign" in which dissent is encouraged but then punished
1957, 1959	The "Anti-Rightist" Campaigns in which alleged enemies of the revolution are repressed
1958–60	The "Great Leap Forward"—an effort to force industrialization and meet often unrealistic production goals. Among other things, this produces a famine that leads to millions of deaths, some say as many as 20 million or more.
1966–9	The "Cultural Revolution" and massive political repression, especially in the late 1960s, though some think this period lasts until Mao's death. The government encourages students to root out alleged enemies of the revolution. Among others, Deng Xiaoping loses his position, only to be rehabilitated in 1974.
1976	Arrest of the "Gang of Four," prominent Communist leaders of the Cultural Revolution
1976	Mao Zedong's death
1978–9	Deng Xiaoping consolidates his dominance in the post-Mao transition. Deng Xiaoping reforms begin, which open China to greater private enterprise and foreign trade and begin to dismantle the collectivization of agriculture, leading to greater agricultural productivity.
1989	Tiananmen Square assault by military on protesters, centrepiece of repression of movement for political reform
1993	Jiang Zemin assumes presidency.
1997	China officially takes over Hong Kong from United Kingdom.
2001	China becomes member of World Trade Organization (WTO).
2003	Hu Jintao assumes presidency.
2008	Beijing Olympics are taken by many as a sign of China's ascendancy.
2007–10	China becomes world's second-largest economy, largest exporter, largest holder of foreign currency reserves, and largest polluter.
2013	Xi Jinping becomes president, and Li Keqiang becomes premier.
2016	Xi is recognized as "core leader," providing him with a wide range of informal powers. Mao Zedong, Deng Xiaoping, and Jiang Zemin have all previously been recognized as core leaders.
2018	Trade war develops between the United States and China over issues such as subsidies, tariffs, technology transfer, and intellectual property.

Unfortunately, this revolution did not bring about stable, constitutional government (on this period, see Fairbank and Goldman 2006; Spence 1990). Rather, China descended into the period of "Warlordism" (Schoppa 2010, 47–8). In short, the existing state broke down, and local power brokers were responsible for much of the order that remained. It was in this context that some of the political forces that still shape China were created. In the 1920s, Chiang Kai-shek, leader of the Nationalist Party (the Guomindang, or GMD), successfully established central political order in much of China. Yet this victory was never absolute. The Communist Party had been established in the early 1920s, with the earlier groundwork set by the "May Fourth Movement," and the Nationalists and Communists existed in tension. At times, the Communists followed Comintern orders to cooperate with the Nationalists and at other times not. Likewise, Chiang Kai-shek and the Nationalists alternated between cooperation with and coercion of the Communists. After 1945, the Communists, under the leadership of Mao Zedong, gradually defeated the Nationalists, who retreated along with Chiang Kai-shek to Taiwan. In accomplishing this, the Communists were greatly aided by the work they had done in organizing peasant communities.

In 1949, Mao declared the People's Republic of China (PRC). At first, the new regime was very much in line with Soviet-style communism, but over time they took a different course (Teiwes 2010). A key emphasis on the PRC was to encourage the collectivization of agriculture and forced industrialization. In 1958, Mao declared the "Great Leap Forward." This is often thought about by scholars as one of the clearest examples of the "voluntarism" of Maoist thought. Whereas traditional Marxism had emphasized that underlying structural conditions would determine the sequencing of revolutionary processes, Maoism held that through a great act of the collective will, China could *force* modernization. Unfortunately, the "Great Leap Forward" produced famine rather than modernization. The main reason was that agricultural collectives felt obligated to exaggerate their productivity and the state in turn demanded so-called excess grain production (Fairbank and Goldman 2006, 368–74). Millions died.

Politically, China under Mao was a party dictatorship, one in which the party was clearly personally controlled by Mao himself. Mao thought that revolution needed to be "permanent" and that the bourgeois "class enemies" of the workers could be anywhere. For this reason, he encouraged self-criticism. Indeed, in the late 1950s he initiated the "Hundred Flowers Campaign" (Spence 1990, 569–73). The idea was that intellectuals and others would criticize and thus improve the revolution. However, Mao was less than satisfied when his own policies became the object of criticism. He and others soon denounced these critics as "rightists." This phenomenon was even clearer in the "Cultural Revolution" of the late 1960s (Spence 1990, 602–17; Fairbank and Goldman 2006, 383–405). Mao tried to organize a movement to target "rightists" and alleged enemies of the revolution, but soon the student "Red Guard" groups escaped his control. Many were attacked and killed, and still others lost their jobs and were imprisoned or sent to work with the peasants in the countryside. Purges touched all levels of the society, including future leader Deng Xiaoping.

Mao died in 1976, and after a brief period a new, reformist generation came into leadership (Gilley 2010). Deng himself was the central figure here. Greater intellectual freedom was allowed, and the regime began to make economic reforms. At first, many of these reforms were concerned with agricultural policy, and then China slowly and strategically privatized some state firms, moving toward a model of "market socialism." It also skilfully increased its integration with the global economy. China's growth in recent decades has been truly astonishing, with hundreds of millions lifted out of poverty.

Politically, the reforms have been less noteworthy. The central goal seems to have been the preservation of the power of the Communist Party, which has been ideologically flexible. Just the same, the party continues to describe itself as Maoist, and, at least ostensibly, capitalist reforms in the economic sphere are presented as preparing the way for fuller socialism in the future. The regime has expanded the role that citizens can play in local politics, and internal party politics are no longer just the product of the deliberation of a single individual—this became especially clear under the leadership of Jiang Zemin—but for the most part important decision-making remains securely walled off from "the people."

Regime and Political Institutions

The central feature of the Chinese regime is the single-party system, and decision-making effectively rests with a small group of Communist Party of China (CPC) elites in the top state organ known as the Politburo. The legislature (NPC) is elected by intricate systems that ensure both Communist Party dominance and top-down control. It is indirectly elected by lower-level assemblies that stretch down to the local level: village-level assemblies choose representatives

Regime and Political Institutions

Regime	Authoritarian
Powers in Constitution	Unitary system; written constitution; officially socialist
Administrative Divisions	22 provinces (and China claims Taiwan as the 23rd) Five autonomous regions (including Tibet) Four municipalities (Beijing, Shanghai, Tianjin, and Chongqing) Two special administrative regions (Hong Kong, Macau)
Executive Branch	Three top positions with executive functions: President of People's Republic of China; secretary-general of Communist Party; and chairman of Central Military Council Politburo is executive committee of the Communist Party and includes top leaders of the party Head of government is the premier, recommended by president and approved by legislature; leads the State Council that oversees administration
Legislative Branch	National People's Congress (NPC); elected in indirect elections from village level up to NPC
Selection of Executive	Indirect; president selected by NPC
Judicial Branch	Supreme Court elected/appointed by NPC and its committees
Political Party System	Single dominant party: Communist Party of China (CPC)

in *towns*, who select representatives in turn to larger *counties*, and the indirect elections continue upward to the levels of *prefectures*, *provinces*, and finally up to the NPC at the top. At each level, the CPC dominates and ensures that only its party members are selected for the higher levels of the legislature.

The executive branch has several prominent positions. The president is the formal head of state, while the secretary-general leads the CPC. In practice, a single person often holds both positions, along with the role of commander in chief of the military, and is known as the "paramount leader." The premier, who is responsible for the ongoing operations of the government and for implementing laws, is nominated by the president and approved by the NPC. This system ensures that policies set by the Politburo and the executive pass into law.

Political Culture

Political cultures are complex and multifaceted. As such, mapping political culture is a complex task, above all in a large society like China. A typical strategy is to focus on important features or currents of a given country's political culture. Here we briefly focus on two of the most important currents in Chinese political culture: Confucianism and Maoism.

Confucianism is traced back to Confucius, a philosopher who lived from around 551 to 479 BCE. Confucianism emphasized formal education, the importance of public ritual, a strict code of ethical responsibility, respect for hierarchy, and piety toward one's family and ancestors (Harrison 2001). While many find these ideas intrinsically appealing and interesting, we can argue that they became influential in part because the Chinese imperial state employed them for many centuries in its efforts to maintain its legitimacy and staff itself. Imperial examinations based on Confucianism determined who would be able to hold which official jobs. This enhanced and maintained Confucianism's prestige in pre-modern China, since it was associated with both the state and high social status.

Maoism attempted to replace Confucianism in the sphere of political culture, viewing this as necessary to modernization. For this reason, some analysts are critical of claims about the contemporary consequences of traditional Confucianism, since they argue that there is little continuity between pre-modern Confucianism and contemporary Chinese political culture. Maoism—in China often called

"Mao Zedong Thought" (Joseph 2010, 135–50)—is a variant of Marxism. It emphasizes the importance of class struggle, sees history as the story of class exploitation, and calls for a future in which the division of labour and associated exploitation will be reversed. However, Mao made major revisions to previous versions of Marxism. The two most important are (1) the centrality of the peasantry in Maoist thought and (2) Maoism's voluntarism. Mao emphasized the revolutionary potential of peasants and concentrated his organizing among them. He regarded them as virtuous, often punishing wayward elites by sending them to work with peasants for "re-education."

In the years following Mao's death, Maoism has become more open and flexible. It remains, at least formally, the core ideology of the state. Nevertheless, some China observers wonder if Maoist "market socialism" is really socialism—or Maoism—at all. Confucianism, which was officially to have been replaced, has been gradually endorsed by China's elites. Some students of culture would argue that the Confucian legacy, despite Mao's opposition to it, had never really disappeared. Thus, both of these key strands of Chinese political culture remain important in today's China, as intellectuals work to revise aspects of each that are viewed as inconsistent with the modern world (e.g., traditional Confucianism's critical stance toward commerce).

At the same time, China has many of the features of industrialized societies, and a growing question is how middle-class consumers (especially in cosmopolitan urban areas) will coexist with Confucian or Maoist views in an increasingly entrepreneurial society. In recent years, much of China's elite and masses alike have embraced a vision that "to become rich is glorious." The country has embraced many aspects of capitalism, even as the government tightly limits political rights and intervenes heavily in the economy. China's political culture thus draws upon multiple strains of long-standing philosophy "made in China," even while taking on some of the cultural features of other contemporary societies in an age of global communications and exchange.

Political Economy

Despite a long and rich history and culture, China spent centuries in a state of economic stagnation that continued up to the 1980s. China's economic model changed dramatically, however, after the rise of Deng Xiaoping in 1978. Deng instituted reforms that opened China up to greater capitalism, with the most prominent changes being opening agriculture and industry to private ownership.

China's recent embrace of greater openness to market forces has had dramatic effects. Industry flourished, especially along the coast, as China pushed economic growth based on cheap exports and became the "workshop of the world." Wages were (and remain) low by Western standards but often represented significantly increased income from that which was available in rural areas. It may be that since the reforms were passed, more than 800 million people have come out of poverty, to cite a recent World Bank study (Press Trust of India 2017). China has become the world's leading exporter and second-largest economy, based in part on export-led growth in manufacturing and related investment. It has gone from being one of the world's poorest countries to middle-income status in just three decades.

Despite the apparent success of market-friendly reform, China is far from purely capitalist. The state continues to play a major role in the economy, including in ways that some global competitors say gives China "unfair advantage." For instance, China has required that major foreign investors wishing to invest in China must partner with Chinese companies in "joint ventures." This ensures that Chinese companies benefit from investment and the transfer of skills, knowledge, and technology. These and other state interventions are in addition to controlling the currency to promote exports.

China's political economy still has several major challenges. One of the most pressing is the continued poverty of rural areas and the related problem of high and growing inequality. Second, China's environment is degraded because of pollution that has come with industry. Many cities have heavily polluted water supplies and awful air quality from factory emissions and the shift from bicycles to ever more cars for transportation. Third, China faces a demographic challenge that many wealthy countries face but even more so: Its "One Child" policy from 1979 limited the birth rate for many years (and was only ended in 2016), but it also means a rapidly aging population that may struggle in the future to care for its growing number of elderly citizens. A final major challenge is the rule of law for intellectual property as China has been a haven for digital piracy and "ripping off" patents and copyrights of major international companies. In short, while China is in many respects an economic success story, it will continue to face major challenges to continued growth.

CASE STUDIES

CASE STUDY

Chapter 11, Page 233

The Chinese Party System

China has the most influential and important dominant-party system in the world today. The country functions essentially as a single-party system, though some other parties are nominally allowed. China's Communist Party has held onto power for almost seven decades through a combination of factors. The various mechanisms for ensuring the dominance of the Communist Party are useful to understand, especially since the meaning of "Communist" in Communist Party has shifted so dramatically with the many changes in China over the past several decades.

The first and most obvious factor is the tight linkage between the Communist Party, the Chinese state bureaucracy, and the military. The party controls the state apparatus and can call on the military as needed to protect the regime. Through years of Communist dominance, the state and military have contributed to single-party rule. This has sometimes taken place with violent repression by the military, as in Tiananmen Square in 1989 and in purges by leader Mao Zedong in previous decades. It has also happened on an ongoing basis through the use of state organs to harass certain opposition forces that might pose a threat, imprison prominent dissidents, and control the media (including new media such as Google's China-based search engine and social media). Many of these efforts to minimize opposition have been passed by the National People's Congress (NPC), but they rely upon the state for enforcement.

A second factor is the electoral system, which provides built-in advantages for the Communist Party. The most important feature is the indirect election process by which local councils elect members of governing councils at higher levels and so on up to the NPC. For instance, national-level legislators are selected by provincial legislators, who are in turn selected by council members at lower levels. The result of this indirect election process is absolute dominance for the Communists at the national level in Beijing. While it is possible for independents and even some members of other small parties to elect a single delegate or two at the local level, it is exceedingly difficult for enough independents to be elected to get an independent or member of another party at the next level up. The well-established, well-resourced Communists are present in every local election throughout the country and dominate the indirect elections to higher levels; this means a virtual single-party state at the national level, with the only exceptions being other parties that are closely "allied" to the Communists and basically under Communist control.

A third set of factors has to do with the Communist Party's legitimacy, including its actual performance in government. China's economic growth under Communist Party rule has been remarkable. While it is difficult to get an independent view of Chinese public opinion, even international news reports suggest that many Chinese are relatively satisfied with government performance and are thus not pressing for immediate moves toward a multiparty system. This idea that a government's legitimacy can be based on economic performance has often been tested in a democracy, and it also seems to have held in some authoritarian and exclusionary systems (Epstein 1984).

CASE STUDY

Chapter 12, Page 262

The Chinese Revolution

The case of China allows us to consider two issues of concern to us in the study of contention and revolutions. First, it highlights the question considered in Chapter 12 about how to define revolutions and even subtypes like "political revolutions" and "social revolutions." Second, it focuses attention on the importance of mobilization in successful revolution, a factor highlighted by resource mobilization and political opportunity theories. Interestingly, the case of China considered alone gives at least some support to *all* of the theories considered in Chapter 12.

The reason that China highlights the definitional issue is that the country went through a long process of social change, and it is therefore difficult to precisely date when revolution began. As discussed in the preceding historical narrative, China saw major changes over the course of the 19th century, including foreign intervention, domestic revolts (some of which, like the Taiping Rebellion, were revolutionary in intention), and fiscal problems. This led many to seek the modernization of both state and society. At the same time, the state came to be perceived as weak because of those very same fiscal difficulties, the trouble it had in maintaining domestic order, and in particular its loss in the Sino-Japanese War. State weakness—sometimes called "state breakdown"—is seen by many scholars as an essential precursor to revolution. The late Qing state responded by implementing an ineffectual reform program, a factor sometimes stressed by relative deprivation theories of revolution.

In 1911 and 1912, contention reached a level most scholars would consider revolutionary, and yet what took place at that time was not a "social revolution" in the sense defined in Chapter 12. The fundamental emphasis was on the transformation of political structures: the end of the Qing Dynasty and the creation of a republic. Of course, as our brief historical narrative shows us, the republic was weaker than expected, and China descended into the period of "Warlordism." Now, this certainly had consequences for social structures (just as the successful creation of a strong republic would have), but these consequences were indirect.

It was within this context that the rival parties involved in the next stage of the revolutionary process developed, the Nationalists (heirs to the early republicanism) and the Communists (Averill 1998). As the reader knows from the previous historical narrative, the Communists were ultimately triumphant. The most important factor that scholars have used to explain this difference is their advantage in mobilization capacity (Skocpol 1979, 252–62). While the Nationalists were in power, they were often ineffective, and some of their members acquired a reputation for corruption (Schoppa 2010, 59), although some recent scholars argue that the Nationalists were more capable state-builders than traditional accounts suggest (see a brief discussion of these and related issues in Edmonds 1997). In the rural areas controlled by the Communists during the conflict, they were focused on the establishment of peasant organizations, indeed, as early as the late 1920s. This strategy—which is linked to Maoism's emphasis on peasants as revolutionary actors, which Marx would have rejected—paid enormous dividends in the 1940s when peasants helped the Communists defeat the Nationalists once and for all. Of course, proponents of other theories of revolution could point to other factors that might help to explain the Communists' success. Cultural or framing theories could point to the salience of Maoist ideology. Relative deprivation and political opportunity theories could point to the ongoing weakness of the state.

Finally, it is important to note that the Chinese Revolution did not end in 1949. Mao was a proponent of "permanent revolution." Indeed, at least ostensibly, it is still going on today. More realistically, perhaps, we could say that it was carried out in stages during Mao's rule. Collectivization of agriculture, the "Great Leap Forward," and the "Cultural Revolution" (Perry 1998) were all key episodes in the Maoist effort to remake the underlying structures of Chinese society.

Research Prompts

1. Consider economic development and democracy in China, and review the discussion of these same themes in the country case materials on India. Both societies have been "modernizing" rapidly, but they have done so in very different terms. India first embraced democracy and only more recently has achieved rapid economic growth. China has achieved dramatic growth, but so far has seen very little democratization. What accounts for these different trajectories? Which theories can you draw on from the thematic chapters of this textbook to explain the variation between these two cases? How might we empirically test the hypothesis that you generate?
2. If Mao were alive today, what elements of his thought would he see in how modern China is governed? Does much remain of his ideological legacies, either positive or negative?

3. Compare the Chinese Revolution to the Russian Revolution. Both were intended to be Marxist revolutions, but they exhibited notable differences. How were these revolutions different, and how might a social scientist *explain* their differences?
4. Compare the overview of Chinese political history with our overview of Mexican political history in the Mexico country case materials. Both societies have had long-standing, highly complex civilizations stretching back centuries. However, Mexico experienced direct colonialism, whereas China's struggle with European imperialism was often indirect. What are the major implications or consequences of this difference for Chinese and Mexican political development? How could one use major theories of comparative politics to begin generating ideas in response to this question?
5. China is governed through a complex set of political institutions. Compare and contrast this with Iran. Can you hypothesize about why authoritarian regimes might have such intricate sets of governing institutions? Do these compare or contrast with any other countries that have witnessed authoritarian rule in the 20th century—such as Brazil, Germany, Mexico, Nigeria, Japan, or Russia? What selection of cases might best enable you to test your preliminary hypothesis?

Online Case Studies

Go to **www.oup.com/he/DickovickCe** to find more case studies online, including:

- How Did China Become a Global Economic Power?
- Is China Destined for Democracy?
- Who Governs China?

France

PROFILE

Key Features of Contemporary France

Population:	67,106,161 (July 2017 est.)
Area:	643,801 square kilometres
Head of State:	Emmanuel Macron (president, 2017–present)
Head of Government:	Edouard Philippe (prime minister, 2017–present)
Capital:	Paris
Year of Independence:	France was never formally colonized. Many date the consolidation of the French state to the era of Louis XIV (1643–1715) and the birth of modern France to the French Revolution of 1789.
Year of Current Constitution:	1958
Languages:	French
GDP per Capita:	$38,476.7 (World Bank estimate 2017)
Human Development Index Ranking (2015):	21st (very high human development)
Trading Relationship with Canada (2016):	• Imports $4,515,505,282 • Exports $2,569,717,143 https://globaledge.msu.edu/countries/canada/tradestats

Sources: *CIA World Factbook*; World Bank World Development Indicators; United Nations *Human Development Report 2016*

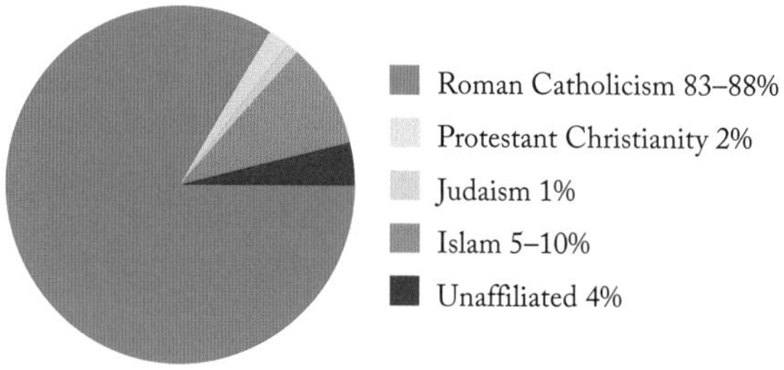

Religious Affiliation in France

Source: *CIA World Factbook*

Introduction

France has historically been situated at the centre of western Europe. This is true not only geographically but in terms of France's identity and culture. At least since Charlemagne united significant portions of western Europe in the eighth and ninth centuries, presenting his kingdom as the successor to the Roman Empire, many have considered France the central carrier of European civilization. France also maintained an enormous empire from the 18th to the 20th centuries, colonizing portions of North America, the Caribbean, the Pacific, Asia, and Africa.

Geographically, France extends from the English Channel in the north to the Mediterranean in the south. The Pyrenees divide it from Spain (and the tiny mountain country of Andorra) in the southwest, and it shares its eastern border

IRELAND
UNITED KINGDOM
NETHERLANDS
Dunkirk
English Channel
Lille
BELGIUM
Rhine
GERMANY
Cherbourg
Le Havre
Rouen
Brest
LUX.
Paris
Nancy
Strasbourg
Orléans
Nantes
Tours
Seine
Dijon
Bay of
Biscay
F R A N C E
AUS.
SWITZERLAND
Lyon
Saint-Etienne
Bordeaux
Grenoble
ITALY
Rhône
Toulouse
Montpellier
Nice
MONACO
SPAIN
Marseille
AND.
Toulon
Mediterranean
Sea
CORSICA
(FR.)
0 70 140 Kilometers
0 70 140 Miles

with Belgium, Luxembourg, Germany, Switzerland, and Italy. In addition to its mountainous areas (both the Pyrenees and the Alps as well as the smaller Jura and Massif Central), it has good farmland, being most famous for the production of grapes and cereals. French agriculture has historically excelled in the production of wine, cheese, and other items considered by international consumers to be luxury products.

Today's France is interesting to scholars of comparative politics for numerous reasons. First, while some people tend to think of European societies as consistently stable and evidencing consistent, progressive development over time, France's passage to political modernity was extraordinarily rocky. It also played out in striking fashion the contrast between democratic-republican and authoritarian centralist forms of politics, settling on a "mixed presidentialist" system in the Fifth Republic (which still goes on today) that continues to stimulate much debate. France also showed us what conflict between civic republicanism and a monopolistic church could look like, pioneering a certain kind of secularism, often called *laïcité*.

It is difficult to estimate the relative share of the population comprised by different ethnic groups in France. This is because France places restrictions on national statistical surveys that document the ethnic and racial identities of respondents, in part because of a strong cultural tradition proscribing such questions. The *CIA World Factbook*, the main source we have used here for data on the ethnic composition of the other countries considered in this book, does not list estimated percentages of ethnic groups in France. It notes simply that French ethnic groups include "Celtic and Latin with Teutonic" as well as "Slavic, North African, Indochinese, and Basque minorities." Of these groups, the North African minority—many from France's former colony of Algeria—and sub-Saharan Africans may be the most politically important.

Many in this group may list Islam as their religion, though the majority are probably non-practising. Adherents of Islam probably constitute somewhat less than 10 per cent of the French population. The majority of the French population is at least nominally Catholic, but, as in much of Europe, most are not regular church attendees. Some sources (e.g., Kuru 2009, 244) estimate that just over half of the French population (55 per cent) adhere formally to a religion.

Historical Development

As noted, France has travelled a challenging road to political modernity. In 1789, France gave us what many consider the first modern revolution (Arendt 1963; Furet [1988] 1995), deposing the Bourbon monarchy, establishing a republic, abolishing the nobility (*noblesse*), and opposing the power of the Roman Catholic Church and ultimately repressing it. The revolution even temporarily created a new calendar, with the beginning of the revolution the starting point from which future years would be counted.

After a decade of radicalization and increasing confusion, Napoleon Bonaparte took power (see the discussion in Parry and Girard 2002, 7–24). Napoleon was an early example of what modern authoritarianism might look like, with lots of references to "the people" and even plebiscites and other elements of democracy. He further spread modern politics through conquest, centralizing political authority and imposing Napoleonic law in numerous countries—it still serves as the basis for law in much of the world today—and also raising nationalism in the resistance he engendered. In Quebec, for example, the current Civil Code of Quebec (1994) is in part based on the Napoleonic Code of 1804.

Ever since the time of Napoleon's domination, people have debated whether his regime consolidated or reversed the revolution. The best answer is probably to say that it did both. On one hand, he re-established order, proclaiming himself emperor, establishing a concordat with the Church, and creating a new "nobility" that was distinct from the hereditary *noblesse* of the prior regime. On the other hand, he spread many of the revolution's achievements to the rest of Europe and beyond.

Napoleon was once deposed after military defeat and sent to an island exile, but he escaped and briefly resumed his efforts before being defeated again at Waterloo. Following Napoleon's demise, France saw the restoration of the old Bourbon monarchy that had lost power in the great revolution of 1789. Louis XVIII and Charles X governed as constitutional monarchs (Furet [1988] 1995, 270–2), however, even if they and some of their supporters might have preferred absolutism. In other words, there was no full return to the system from before the revolution.

In 1830, Charles X was replaced by Louis-Philippe in the "July Revolution" (see Parry and Girard 2002, 55–9). Called the "Citizen King" because of his stronger and more consistent support for the "constitutional" in "constitutional monarchy,"

Louis-Philippe would hold the throne until 1848, when a revolutionary wave shook Europe. In France, this brought about the "Second Republic." By the end of the year, Louis-Napoleon Bonaparte was elected president. The nephew of the former emperor, he declared *himself* Emperor Napoleon III in 1851, ushering in the Second Empire. Napoleon III was known for encouraging industrialization and economic modernization, and Paris was redesigned, producing much of the infrastructure and plan for the city as it is known today (Parry and Girard 2002, 63–9; Schwartz 2011, 60–1). This was also a time of increasing French geopolitical ambitions as Napoleon III waged military campaigns, increased French colonial activity, and invaded Mexico, installing a member of the Hapsburg family as Emperor Maximilian there in the 1860s. Eventually, though, military activity was Napoleon III's downfall. He was defeated by Bismarck's Prussia in the Franco-Prussian War of 1870 and almost immediately lost power in France. This transition marked the beginning of France's Third Republic.

The Third Republic—which would last until World War II—is considered by some to have been a French "golden age" (Parry and Girard 2002, 74). It was a period of great flowering in the arts and literature, but it also saw a great deal of political and social activity and controversy and has been seen by many in France as a period of instability.

France was badly shaken by World War I. Like the rest of the participants in other countries, neither the army, nor the politicians, nor the citizens fully anticipated the nature of trench warfare, with its enormous loss of life, terrible conditions, and seemingly infinite stalemates. France was eventually among the victors, but the conflict played an important role in producing the next European crisis. France insisted that Germany pay huge indemnities, and its preparatory strategy for the next possible war with Germany was based on its experiences in World War I, involving a single, supposedly impregnable line of defence called the Maginot line.

The indemnity imposed on Germany contributed to the economic and social problems that conditioned Hitler's rise to power. While Hitler rose in Germany, France saw a different pattern, most notably with the left-wing "Popular Front" government headed by Leon Blum, which was formed in 1936 (Parry and Girard 2002, 163–9). The short-lived government was accompanied by strikes and labour mobilization, but France was highly polarized in this period, and the Popular Front government was over by 1938. When war came, Germany bypassed the Maginot Line with relative ease. The French state collapsed, and the Vichy Government was established under Marshal Philippe Pétain. This government was long seen as a puppet of the German occupiers, though more recent historical evidence suggests that the Vichy government played an active role in decision-making and collaborated with the Nazis, participating in the deportation of Jews. At the same time, many thousands of French men and women participated actively in the resistance, as well as in the Free French, led by Charles de Gaulle.

After the allied victory, de Gaulle would become president of the "Fourth Republic." During this period, France focused on reconstruction and economic development. France went through several decades of strong economic performance and *relative* political stability. In this same period, France lost most of its former empire, especially with decolonization in Africa in the 1960s.

France's empire was once second only to the British Empire, although it is not as well studied in English-speaking countries. The French language and forms of culture were spread throughout the colonies alongside French models of education, but French rule was often spectacularly exploitative and brutal, especially in Asia and Africa. The spread of the so-called *mission civilizatrice* (civilizing mission) was often accomplished by force. While some countries gained their independence relatively quickly, the French also fought lengthy wars to prevent independence movements from succeeding. The bloody conflicts in Vietnam (1946–54) and Algeria (1954–62) are but two examples, with almost 1.5 million casualties in Algeria alone (Kalman 2010; Ramdani 2012). France has still to fully come to terms with this period of its recent history.

A prominent feature of France's postwar politics was the process of European integration, which has often been led by France in tandem with democratic Germany. Beginning in 1950, France and Germany—along with Italy, Belgium, the Netherlands, and Luxembourg—agreed to free and open trade in coal and steel. This was seen as economically significant but even more important symbolically and politically because it meant the two countries would be openly trading the raw materials needed for war. Further integration came in 1957, when the Treaty of Rome extended the economic cooperation to create a European Economic Community. Further extensions of the European project came with expansion to many other countries (now 27) and the deepening of integration through free trade, free flows of labour and capital, and the creation of today's common currency, the euro. The former European Coal and Steel Community of 1950 has now become the broader and deeper European Union (EU).

Today, France is considered to be, with Germany, one of the two most powerful state-level actors in the EU. Yet it faces a number of significant questions. First, has its system of immigration and assimilation broken down? Second, what will happen to the French welfare state? Is it in need of reforms and if so, which reforms, and will it be politically possible to produce them? Finally, what will be France's role in the Europe of the future, given the enormous questions that the EU now faces as it struggles to coordinate region-wide monetary policy with state-level fiscal policy? One of the intriguing facts about contemporary France is the degree to which many of these decisions will be taken at a European level. It should be noted, though, that France (like other countries in the EU) has a national veto on most important matters.

Historical Development Timeline

800	Charlemagne consolidates rule in much of western Europe.
1000s–1700s	Rivalry between France and Britain through Middle Ages includes numerous wars.
1334–1453	Hundred Years' War between France and Britain.
1643	Louis XIV becomes King of France, rules for more than 70 years.
1789	French Revolution begins with the storming of Bastille prison; self-proclaimed National Assembly issues Declaration of the Rights of Man and Citizen.
1793	The most violent part of the French Revolution begins, known as the Reign of Terror; King Louis XVI executed by guillotine.
1799	Napoleon's seizure of power.
1804	Napoleon's coronation as emperor.
1812	Invasion of Russia.
1814	Napoleon's defeat and imprisonment.
1815	Napoleon returns but is soon defeated by British at Battle of Waterloo.
1814–30	Bourbon Restoration of Louis XVIII (1814–24) and Charles X (1824–30).
1830	July Revolution.
1830–48	July Monarchy of Louis-Philippe ("Citizen King").
1848–52	Revolution of 1848 and the Second Republic.
1848	Louis-Napoleon Bonaparte elected president of the republic.
1852	Louis-Napoleon Bonaparte named Emperor Napoleon III, beginning the "Second Empire" (1852–70).
1870–1	Franco-Prussian War, in which France is soundly defeated.
1870	The Second Empire ends shortly after Napoleon III's forces are defeated by Prussia (under Bismarck) at the Battle of Sedan in September 1870.
1870–1940	Third Republic.
1871	Paris Commune.
1894	Conviction of Alfred Dreyfus.
1906	Dreyfus officially exonerated by a military commission
1914–18	First World War.
1936–8	Short-lived "Popular Front" government.
1939–45	Second World War.
1940–4	Vichy Government, which collaborates with the Nazis.
1944–6	After the fall of the Vichy government, a provisional government is in place.
1946–58	Fourth Republic.
1946-56	War in Vietnam, eventually taken over by the United States.
1954–62	War in Algeria, culminating in Algerian independence in 1962.
1958–present	Fifth Republic.
1958	Constitution establishes "mixed presidentialist" system.
1966	France leaves NATO.
1968	Major student protests in Paris (and numerous other countries).
1981	François Mitterrand is elected president (the only Socialist elected to this post during the Fifth Republic) and governs until 1995.
1995–2007	Presidency of Jacques Chirac.
1999	France adopts the euro.
2007–12	Presidency of Nicolas Sarkozy.
2009	France returns to NATO.
2012–17	Presidency of François Hollande.
2017–present	Presidency of Emmanuel Macron.
2018	France wins the FIFA World Cup; le *Mouvement des gilets jaunes* (yellow vest movement) begins, focused on redress for economic inequalities.
2019	Treaty on Franco-German Cooperation and Integration (Treaty of Aachen) is signed, promoting closer economic, cultural, and security cooperation. Notre-Dame de Paris catches fire in April.

Regime and Political Institutions

France has a *semi-presidential* system of government, also called a *presidential-parliamentary* system. This hybrid has both a directly elected president and a prime minister, with the former the head of state and the latter the head of government. Presidential elections are followed by elections to the legislature, after which the president nominates a prime minister to run the government. However, prime ministers serve at the discretion of the legislature, and the lower house (the *Assemblée Nationale*, or National Assembly) may force resignation of the government at any time by a simple majority voting for censure. In practice, this has meant that the president appoints a prime minister only after consulting the leader of the largest party in the legislature to determine the latter's wishes.

The upper legislative chamber, the Senate, has nearly co-equal powers with the National Assembly, but the National Assembly takes the lead on most legislative debates and legislation. A sophisticated system of checks and balances includes the president's ability to dissolve the legislature and call new elections but no more than once in any given year. By convention, the prime minister has greater power over domestic politics and the president more power over foreign affairs, but these lines can be blurred, especially when the president and the legislative majority are from different parties, a situation known as *cohabitation*.

Finally, a judicial body known as the Constitutional Council has the power to review major laws before their passage and can rule them unconstitutional and thus invalid; this council may also hear appeals to laws and similarly rule on constitutionality. The council is composed of nine members, three each appointed by the president and the leaders of the two legislative houses, as well as all former French presidents not actively involved in politics.

Political Culture

Probably the most distinctive feature of French political culture is the historical relationship between a left-wing, secularist, republicanism and a more conservative and less egalitarian alternative, often associated with Roman Catholicism. Both right- and left-wing thought in France had origins among the 18th-century *philosophes*, and the very designations "left" and right" emerged in the French Revolution. From the beginning, the French left radically opposed hierarchy and royalty, promoting democracy and republicanism as alternatives. Viewing the Roman Catholic Church as linked to royal politics and the nobility (and indeed being the "First Estate" prior to the revolution) and

Regime and Political Institutions

Regime	Republic, democratic
Administrative Divisions	27 regions (of which 22 are in "metropolitan France" and five are overseas); smaller divisions are departments, arrondissements, cantons, and communes
Executive Branch	Semi-presidential; president and prime minister
Selection of Executive	Direct election of president, in two rounds, with second-round runoff between top two candidates; appointed prime minister
Legislative Branch	Bicameral Lower chamber: National Assembly (*Assemblée Nationale*) Upper chamber: Senate (*Sénat*)
Judicial Branch	Several top authorities: Court of Cassation (*Cour de cassation*) as court of final appeal for individuals; appointed Constitutional Council (*Conseil constitutionnel*) has authority to rule laws unconstitutional and invalid
Political Party System	Multiparty system with several parties in Parliament, generally with one large party on the centre-right (currently the Union for a Popular Movement, UMP) and the Socialist Party on the centre-left; also the National Rally (formerly National Front) (far right), Communist Party (far left), and other moderate and fringe parties

noting its substantial control over land, schooling, and much lawmaking, a radical left aimed to eliminate these "regressive" social actors. This tradition was largely critical of Napoleon as well as the Second Empire of Napoleon III (1852–70). Over the course of the 19th century, many of its proponents turned to socialism and communism. While by the middle of the 20th century it was clear that communism on the Soviet model was not a viable option for France, the communists were important in the resistance against Hitler. Many communists were seen as national heroes of the Resistance, and aspects of communist ideology remained popular with intellectuals and the working classes. After the war, the larger French left favoured social democracy and helped to construct the French welfare state.

The right-wing tradition is also quite heterogeneous and has also changed over time. Some of the supporters of the restoration monarchies of Louis XVIII and Charles X were out-and-out royalists, but even they were relatively few. In the 19th century, the French right favoured maintaining and even expanding the privileges of the Catholic Church. Supporters included not only the remnants of the old nobility but also wealthy industrialists. More than anything, they favoured the maintenance of social order.

As part of France's imperial expansion, an "ethnic" conception of the French nation developed, suspicious of "cosmopolitanism," anti-black, anti-Asian, anti-Semitic, and often Islamophobic. This tradition may have witnessed its most extreme expression in the collaborating Vichy regime during World War II. It lives on in the National Rally (formerly the National Front) party of Marine Le Pen, a xenophobic party that is above all preoccupied with immigration, especially immigration by Muslims, while also having a history of anti-Semitism. This group was for many years politically marginal, but the party achieved notable success in the 2002 presidential elections under its former leader Jean Marie Le Pen. The National Front did very well in the 2014 EU Parliament elections, shocking many observers both in France and internationally. Its current leader, Marine le Pen, did well in the first round of the 2012 elections and again in 2017. Le Pen changed the name of the party to the National Rally (NR) in 2017 in an effort to soften its racist image. The NR has encouraged more mainstream parties to move to the right on immigration issues.

Political Economy

France has one of the world's most advanced economies and has had for some time. Measured in terms of the Human Development Index, its citizens live in one of the 20 best-off economies in the world. The French economy is among the 10 largest in the world (in the top five when measured simply by income and top 10 when measured in terms of what that income can buy), and it has one of the highest GDPs per capita. Moreover, citizens benefit from relatively generous welfare-state benefits (discussed further a bit later in this section). They also pay higher taxes than citizens in countries with less generous welfare states: Indeed, government revenues amount to nearly 50 per cent of GDP.

The French economy has historically privileged an important role for the state through regulation, government ownership of firms, and redistributive efforts. In recent years, as societies with welfare states entered into a period of "retrenchment" following the economic crises of the 1970s, there were some efforts to scale back this state involvement, particularly under conservative presidents Jacques Chirac and Nicolas Sarkozy. The state has partially divested itself from some of its holdings, though it has had a bit more trouble freeing itself from welfare obligations and deregulating the labour market because it has faced public resistance when it has attempted to do so.

The French economy in some ways is a typical "post-industrial" economy. Note that this does not mean that there is no industry but rather that services are dominant. Indeed, industry accounts for 20.1 per cent of GDP. Agriculture only accounts for 2 per cent, with services accounting for 77.9 per cent of GDP (2017 estimate, per *CIA World Factbook*).

France has relatively low income inequality, near the average for eurozone countries. Its Gini coefficient is 0.29 (World Bank 2017 estimate), where 0 would mean perfect equality and 1 would mean perfect inequality. Canada's is 0.32. France also has relatively low poverty. Historically, it has suffered from relatively high levels of unemployment, which some analysts have attributed to the rigidity of its highly regulated labour market. Some would argue that this is a function of the French state's ongoing involvement in the economy. However, other advanced economies have, sadly, "caught up" with France in unemployment. Some, notably its neighbour to the south, Spain, have far more serious unemployment problems.

The French welfare state has been resilient in the face of efforts to roll it back (Prasad 2006). It has, as noted previously, seen considerable privatization, and there have been pushes toward deregulation, but the state continues to play an enormous role in the French economy, and the welfare state remains generous.

CASE STUDIES

CASE STUDY

Chapter 10, Page 207

Electing the French President: What Do Runoffs Do?

In France in 2002, most voters were surprised as the results came in for the first round of presidential voting. In this first round of French elections, the nationwide popular vote is tallied for the many candidates, and a candidate is elected only if he or she secures an outright majority, which is uncommon. In the absence of a majority, the top two candidates have a runoff to determine the winner. This system allows citizens to vote for their most preferred candidate in the first round, then vote for an "electable" candidate in the second round. Typically, the runoff had amounted to a showdown between the leading candidate of the centre-right (often called the "Gaullist" candidate after French war hero and later president Charles de Gaulle) and the candidate of the centre-left Socialist Party. But in 2002, with the first-round vote split between many candidates on the left, the Socialist candidate Lionel Jospin performed poorly and came in third with 16 per cent behind centre-right candidate Jacques Chirac (just under 20 per cent) and the far-right candidate Jean-Marie Le Pen, leader of the National Front, who took just under 17 per cent of the vote. The runoff came down to the right versus the far right.

For some, Le Pen's first-round success served as a condemnation of the French practice of having elections with a "runoff" between the top two candidates: It gave a huge platform and political spotlight to a candidate on the fringe (though the National Front has done surprisingly well in subsequent elections). What happened next had the opposite effect, though it was predictable: Jacques Chirac won 82 per cent of the vote in the runoff, and Le Pen won less than 18 per cent.

This raises the issue of whether runoffs are good or bad for representation and democracy. While anomalies such as the Le Pen result can emerge in the first round, proponents of the system can argue that it performed exactly as intended: It allowed French voters to express their initial preference, then weeded out the more extreme candidate. It also signalled the frustration of voters with the Socialist Party, which allowed that party to reshape its platform for the future rather than simply resting on its laurels as the presumptive leader of the left. Just as important, the runoff ensures that the individual elected president ultimately receives more than 50 per cent of the votes in a presidential election. That is, the president ends up with a clear mandate of over half of French voters electing him or her.

The runoff features frequently in elections in Latin America and Africa where presidentialism is common. In these countries, there are particular historical and social reasons that can make the runoff appealing. In Chile in 1970, the Marxist Salvador Allende was confirmed president by Congress after receiving less than 37 per cent of the vote; three years later, a military coup to overthrow the elected president resulted in nearly two decades of brutal dictatorship. And in Africa, presidential elections can result in voting along ethnic lines in the first round but broader coalition-building across ethnic lines to win in the second round. It is worth considering how history might have been different—and whether violence and democracy would be affected—if a French-style runoff system had existed in Chile in 1970 or did not exist in some African countries today.

CASE STUDY

Chapter 12, Page 256

The French Revolution

The French Revolution took place amid major structural problems in 18th-century French society (Furet [1988] 1995; Doyle 2003). In this period, France, like much of early modern Europe, remained an "estate society" divided into three groups: a nobility with special privileges, the clergy, and commoners. The social status of the nobility, however, was weakened by the ongoing efforts of the centralizing, absolutist Crown. As the monarchy and its state grew stronger, the nobility felt increasingly marginalized. At the same time, the French absolutist state, largely through its involvement in foreign wars (especially the American Revolution), faced major fiscal difficulties (Doyle 2003). Indeed, by the late 18th century it was nearly bankrupt. Meanwhile, periodic problems in food distribution and rural poverty ensured that much of France's rural population felt discontent. Finally, the spread of the Enlightenment and of nationalism provided the bases for an intellectual critique of the old regime (Greenfeld 1992; Bell 2001).

The revolution began as a series of efforts to reform the French state. The Crown called an "Assembly of Notables," but the assembly declared that the Estates General, which had not met since the early 17th century, needed to be called. When the Estates General convened, it was divided in the customary manner into the three estates mentioned previously. However, before long politics and propaganda forced representatives of the first two estates to join the latter one, the core idea being that the French nation shouldn't be divided by estates, since all of its members should be equal. The third estate *was* the nation, as Sieyes declared (Furet [1988] 1995, 45–51). In other words, the Estates General was reinterpreted as being something like a modern, national legislature (though the leaders of the Estates General remained bourgeois and nobles, along with some clergy, and not "popular" actors).

Reform quickly devolved into a novel form of collective behaviour that was surprising even to its most central participants and those who attempted to lead and control it. Street actions began, and mobs attacked the Bastille prison on 14 July 1789, wishing to destroy a reviled symbol of the arbitrary authority of the monarch to imprison opponents at will. By 1792, the monarchy had fallen amidst increasing violence—much perpetrated by mobs known as the "*sans culottes*"—opening a period known as the "Terror" in which perceived enemies of the revolution were murdered in large numbers. Robespierre was a key figure in this period, perpetrating the paranoid violence that ultimately consumed him. This was followed by a period of relaxation known as the "Thermidorian reaction" and, finally, by the rise of Napoleon. On one hand, Napoleon appears a conservative figure, since, for example, he declared himself emperor. But on the other hand, he can be viewed as a revolutionary whose mission was to spread the French Revolution to the rest of Europe through an imperial war.

What struck so many contemporaries was the revolution's *destructive* nature. It seemed intent upon an eradication of the old society and the replacement of all of its forms by new, "revolutionary" ones. This included the creation of a new, revolutionary calendar, the efforts to destroy the Church and its teachings, the war on the nobility, the destruction of many architectural sites, and so forth. The French Revolution subsequently became the model for many later revolutionaries and its ideals inspirational for nationalists and republicans everywhere. At the same time, it surprised nearly everyone involved, and those who attempted to control it quickly learned that they had helped to unleash social forces beyond their ability to lead (Arendt 1963).

CASE STUDY

Chapter 16, Page 339

Globalization and Culture in France

France's relationship with globalization has been complex. In the late 19th century, France was a lead "globalizer" and colonizer. If you travel in the developing world today, you may learn that the architecture built in the 19th century had a marked French influence. French ideas were extraordinarily influential around the globe in this period, at least in more cosmopolitan social sectors in many societies. Colonialism helped to spread French culture, language, law, and society, and generations of colonization led to the development of francophone and francophile societies throughout the world.

In the 20th century, though, France grew more ambivalent about globalization, and its role was overtaken by the United States. Cultural forces from Hollywood to hip hop have reshaped French film, literature, music, and the arts. Within the French economy itself, there has often been an emphasis on craftsmanship and small-scale production. At the same time, France in the 20th century did establish

continued

major corporations but often did so with state support; examples of major French companies that were state-owned or nationalized at one time include the car company Renault, the oil giant Total, and several major banks and utilities.

A common refrain in France has been the need to develop in a "French way," resisting Americanization and globalization. Economically, this is linked to common tropes in French culture: Societies fully immersed in global capitalism "live to work," whereas some French citizens would argue that the French "work to live." France has thus been somewhat skeptical of multinational businesses and of the consequences of international trade agreements, and it has even tried to limit the spread and use of English words in French business.

While ambivalent about some aspects of globalization, France has also been a key mover of deeper integration in continental Europe since World War II. It has sought to develop strong economic ties to Germany and other economies while developing in a way that relies heavily on elements of free markets yet continues to guarantee an active role for the state in the economy. It has been a strong supporter of the European Union, and in 2011 France, along with Germany, exercised a considerable influence over how the EU responded to the fiscal crises in Greece and Italy and worries over Portugal and Spain as well. France also retains major global linkages to former colonies, particularly in North Africa and sub-Saharan Africa. People of North African origin—especially from Algeria and Morocco—constitute an important group in French society. Indeed, France largely won the FIFA World Cup because of its very talented players of African origin, among them Kylian Mbappé, Ousmane Dembélé, Adil Rami, Nabil Fekir, and Samuel Umtiti.

Research Prompts

1. France has runoff elections, and the United States does not. What are the major consequences of this difference? Would you expect the consequences of this difference to play out in the same way in a wider range of comparative cases? Why or why not?
2. France is a society that has had many revolutions and one in which revolution has become a key idea in the culture. Brazil is a society that, despite promoting social change in important, novel, and influential ways, has largely been free of revolutions as such. Can you explain this difference?
3. There are similarities and differences between French culture in France and in Canada, in part because Quebec was settled before the French Revolution. What are some key differences in terms of language and culture between France and Quebec?
4. The French welfare state has survived "retrenchment" more successfully than a number of others, despite some changes, including the privatization of a number of formerly state-owned enterprises. How do you explain its staying power? Will it likely remain strong in the future?
5. The United Kingdom has a fairly small extreme, xenophobic right wing (represented by the British National Party), whereas in France this group has been larger (though the National Rally still represents a minority of French citizens). Is this difference a function of different ideas of nationhood, different historical experiences, different patterns of decline of traditional left-wing parties, different political institutions, or something else?

Online Case Studies

Go to **www.oup.com/he/DickovickCe** to find more case studies online, including:

- Authoritarian Persistence in 19th-Century France
- Religion and Secularism in France
- The State in France

Germany

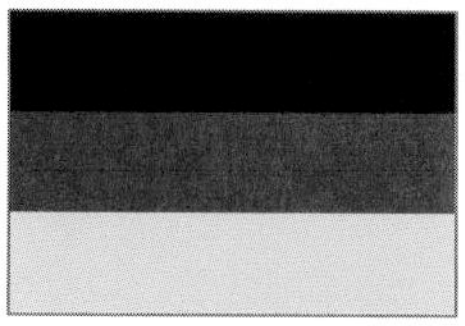

PROFILE

Key Features of Contemporary Germany

Population:	80,594,017 (July 2017 est.)
Area:	357,022 square kilometres
Head of State:	Frank-Walter Steinmeier (president, 2017–present)
Head of Government:	Angela Merkel (chancellor, 2005–present)
Capital:	Berlin
Year of Independence:	Unification achieved in 1871; reunification in 1990
Year of Current Constitution:	1949
Languages:	German
GDP per Capita:	$44,469.90 (World Bank estimate 2017)
Human Development Index Ranking (2015):	4th (very high human development)
Trading Relationship with Canada (2016):	• Imports $13,045,172,576 • Exports $2,960,590,236 https://globaledge.msu.edu/countries/canada/tradestats

Sources: *CIA World Factbook*; World Bank World Development Indicators; United Nations *Human Development Report 2016*

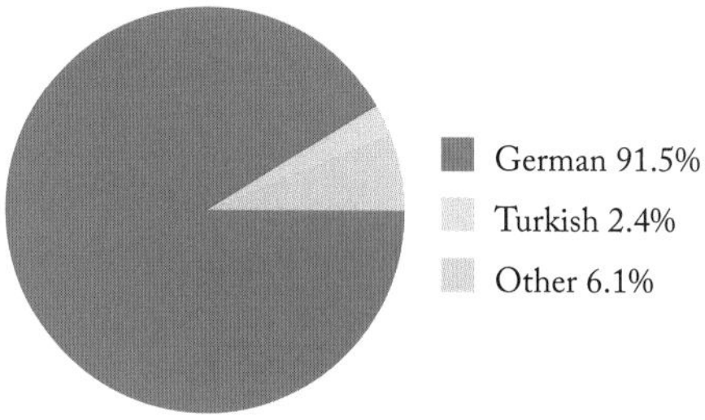

Ethnic Groups in Germany

Note that most of those in the "other" category are from or descend from citizens of other European societies, including Russia.

Source: *CIA World Factbook*

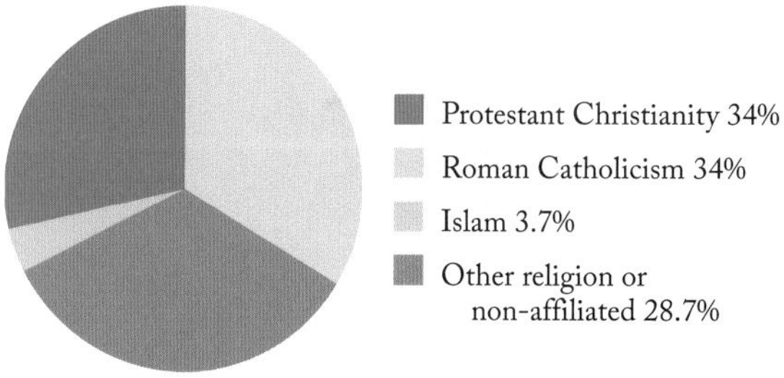

Religious Affiliation in Germany

Source: *CIA World Factbook*

Introduction

Germany is a country of enduring interest to political scientists for a number of reasons. Its historical state-building process draws attention, both because of the early success of Prussian state-builders and because of the relatively late development of the unified German state (1871) after years of decentralization and nationalist aspiration. Germany is also of interest because of its development trajectory because it achieved relatively rapid industrialization and economic growth in the mid- to late 19th century and came to be the pre-eminent European economic power after its political unification. The country, as we will see, is frequently cited as a prototypical case of ethnic nationalism, meaning that boundaries between Germans and others are typically understood in ethnic terms rather than as a function of citizenship. As such, Germany is frequently contrasted with France, and a robust social-scientific literature seeks to explain this difference. Moreover, there are major debates about whether German culture is changing or has changed in this connection.

DENMARK
SWEDEN
North Sea
Baltic Sea
Kiel
Rostock
Lubeck
Wilhelmshaven
Bremerhaven
Hamburg
NETHERLANDS
Bremen
Berlin
Hannover
POLAND
Magdeburg
Duisburg
Essen
GERMANY
Düsseldorf
Leipzig
Kassel
Cologne
Dresden
Bonn
BELGIUM
Frankfurt
Wiesbaden
CZECH REPUBLIC
LUX.
Saarbrucken
Mannheim
Nuremberg
Karlsruhe
Stuttgart
Danube
Rhine
FRANCE
Munich
AUSTRIA
0 30 60 Kilometers
0 30 60 Miles
ITALY
SLOVENIA

Germany is also of interest as a society that has witnessed rapid and consequential political transitions. It has seen authoritarianism (with some democratic features) under Bismarck and Kaiser Wilhelm II and then democratization in the wake of World War I. Democratic consolidation, however, failed in that period, and the Weimar Republic had collapsed by 1933. The country then witnessed the rise of a totalitarian regime. Finally, after Germany's defeat in World War II, it has seen the successful consolidation of a representative democracy, initially in the West but continuing in all of Germany with reunification after the collapse of Soviet power. Indeed, many see potential lessons in the success of this democratic consolidation. Today, Germany is a European and global leader, with robustly democratic politics, a strong economy (a highly advanced one that has managed to maintain strength in the export of manufactured goods), and a return to international influence. This is doubly so as the United States seems to be reducing its global persuasiveness under the Trump administration.

Germany's geography has historically been shaped by political division, most notably in the forced division between East and West Germany after World War II. Previously, much of its long-run history of political disunity caused the region to be dominated by Prussia in the east and Austria (today not a part of Germany) in the south, with smaller states in the west. Religious variation exacerbated subregional differences, with southern parts of the German region having large Catholic populations (in Austria and Bavaria, for example) and with the north tending toward Protestantism. As is the case in much of western Europe, German society has seen noteworthy secularization. The majority of the population is still nominally Christian, and there is a small Muslim population, many of Turkish descent. The question of how immigrants will be incorporated into German society remains an important issue of interest to scholars and has been the source of considerable public debate (see discussion in Fetzer and Soper 2005).

Historical Development

Germany's modern history is extraordinarily complex, owing in part to the many political units that composed the state. Indeed, until 1871 there was no "Germany" in the sense of a single nation-state but rather a complex configuration of smaller states and principalities as well as free towns (Kitchen 2006, 9; Berger 2004). At the same time, a vague sense of German identity had developed over the course of the 18th century. At first, this identity was very "cosmopolitan" and focused on the idea of Germany as a cultural community (Greenfeld 1992; Berger 2004). However, the Napoleonic invasions transformed German identity, leading to efforts to define Germanness *against* what French civilization was taken to represent (Kitchen 2006; Greenfeld 1992).

In the post-Napoleonic years, aspirants to a German nation-state would have to make do with a loose confederation of existing units, established at the Congress of Vienna, with both Austria and Prussia exerting leadership. The German state unified in the wake of Prussia's defeat of France in the Franco-Prussian War in 1871 (see Kitchen 2006). The united Germany—which excluded Austria—was organized as an empire, referred to as the "Second Reich." Otto von Bismarck, a Prussian "junker" (aristocrat) who is considered the architect of unified Germany and who had led Prussia and the North German Federation in the years prior, was named chancellor, a post that he would hold until 1890.

Bismarck is important not just because of Germany's unification and the way in which Germany's unification influenced European power politics—following the Franco-Prussian War, Germany emerged as Europe's central power—but also because of the way he managed domestic politics. Bismarck governed largely as a conservative but made use of some ideas from the moderate left. Perhaps most important was the establishment of welfare state functions—disability, unemployment, and health insurance, as well as pensions—in the 1880s (Esping-Andersen 1990, 24), to be expanded in the 20th century (Mares 2001, 60–3; Hentschel 2008, 793–801). These programs were not as generous as later welfare state programs would be, nor as generous as the social democrats wanted. The German imperial state also extended suffrage to all males.

In economic terms, late 19th-century Germany saw continued industrialization and growth. The country came to rival Britain in many respects (Kitchen 2006). Its economy was particularly strong in some areas, like chemical

Historical Development Timeline

1648	Treaty of Westphalia signals rise of modern nation-state system; present-day Germany governed by many principalities.
1815	End of Napoleonic Wars; Congress of Vienna gives rise to loose Germanic Confederation led by Prussia (present-day northern Germany) and Austria.
1834	Establishment of the Zollverein (Customs Union) in the Confederation.
1848	Revolutionary upheaval in Europe, including in German states.
1864	German-Danish War over Schleswig-Holstein.
1866	Led by Chancellor Otto von Bismarck, Prussia defeats powerful Austria in Austro-Prussian War.
1870	Prussia defeats France in Franco-Prussian War.
1871	Unification of Germany under Prussian leadership.
1904	In what has been called the first genocide of the 20th century, German forces decimate the Herero and Nama populations of what is now Namibia, part of their colonial empire. Both groups were poisoned, massacred, rounded up into concentration camps, and worked to death. A tiny fraction of their pre-genocide population remained.[1]
1914–18	World War I. Germany joins Austria-Hungary and Ottoman Empire as Central Powers vs Great Britain, France, and Russia as Allies; United States enters war on side of Allies in 1916.
1918	Armistice ends World War I, with Great Britain and France demanding reparations from Germany and demilitarization of Rheinland.
1919–33	Weimar Republic presides over hyperinflation and Great Depression.
1933	Hitler elected chancellor as head of National Socialist (Nazi) Party, establishes "Third Reich."
1939	Germany invades Poland; Great Britain and France declare war on Germany.
1939–45	World War II. The Holocaust, led by Adolf Hitler and the Nazi Party, results in the extermination of 6 million Jews as well as members of many other groups. Germany invades and occupies much of western Europe, bombs Britain extensively, and invades Russia, but ultimately retreats. Retreat from Russia in 1943 and D-Day in 1944 (Allied invasion of occupied France) signal beginning of the end of Third Reich.
1945	Allies (including Soviet Union, Great Britain, United States, France) take Berlin. Third Reich falls; Hitler commits suicide. Soviets occupy East Germany; Americans, British, and French occupy West Germany.
1945–89	Germany divided into communist East Germany and democratic/capitalist West Germany; major repression in East Germany.
1948	Berlin Airlift
1950	Treaty of Rome begins integration in western Europe of European Community, with West Germany and France leading.
1961	Berlin Wall raised overnight by Soviets and East German regime.
1989	Fall of the Berlin Wall signals end of communism.
1990	Reunification of East and West Germany as Federal Republic of Germany (Helmut Kohl, chancellor).
1980s–90s	European integration accelerates (Single European Act, 1987; Maastricht Treaty, 1992 through 1999).
2002	Euro begins circulating as new currency, with Deutschmark phased out.
2005	Angela Merkel, leader of the Christian Democratic Union Party, becomes Germany's first female chancellor.
2011–15	Countries in the eurozone face the need for financial bailouts, which are resisted in Germany.
2017	Federal elections see rising support for the anti-immigrant Alternative for Germany party.
2018	Merkel puts together a "Grand Coalition" between her party and the Social Democrats.
2019	Treaty on Franco-German Cooperation and Integration (Treaty of Aachen) is signed, promoting closer economic, cultural, and security cooperation.

engineering. Its research universities were important as well and were emulated elsewhere, including in the United States.

In terms of foreign policy, the state rushed to compete with more established colonial powers in the "scramble for Africa," though Germany never successfully established as large a colonial system (Kitchen 2006, 168–9). Unlike France and the United Kingdom, Germany entered the imperial game late and only maintained a small empire. Nevertheless, the German empire was equally brutal, and signs of the brutalities to come in World War II were visited on Germany's colonies in Africa.

Bismarck built his foreign policy around manipulating alliances such that France would be unable to make common cause with Russia, Austria, and/or the United Kingdom against the new German state.

Leadership was less capable following Bismarck's departure from office in 1890 (Kitchen 2006). After a Serbian nationalist linked to some figures in the Serbian government killed Archduke Franz Ferdinand of Austria, war began, and Germany joined Austria (Davies 1996, 875–95). Russia backed Serbia, and France and the United Kingdom allied with Russia. The United States would soon join the allies as well. World War I was a brutal conflict in which trench warfare was predominant. While some foresaw the implications of new military technology and strategy, many of the combatants and citizens on both sides were shocked by the tragedy of webs of alliances and concerns over national honour leading to millions of deaths in a war that was basically at a stalemate for much of its duration (Weber 1972, 363–70).

Germany's defeat meant the end of the empire. A new, republican government was formed. The new German state, known as the Weimar Republic because its constitution was established in the city of Weimar, was hampered from the start by a series of difficulties (Fulbrook 1990, 155). Despite great hopes, it would only survive for a bit more than a decade, collapsing as the Nazis ascended to power.

Some of the major problems were consequences of the Treaty of Versailles, which ended World War I. Despite the objections of some of its allies, France insisted on disabling indemnities for Germany to pay indefinitely. This condition generated discontent and provoked resentment among the German population that would later feed into critiques of the Weimar Republic's liberal order, and it also weakened the state's economic position (Fulbrook 1990, 163–4).

The situation was exacerbated when the global depression spread to Germany (James 2009). Society polarized politically, and institutional alterations to the Weimar Republic could not help. The National Socialist German Workers' Party (Nazis) did well in the 1930 and 1932 legislative elections, and its leader Adolf Hitler came in second, with approximately 37 per cent in the presidential elections of 1932 (Kitchen 2006, 249, 251). In 1933, Hitler was appointed chancellor, the position from which he would dismantle the Weimar order and, with it, German democracy.

Under Hitler, the Nazis quickly moved to undermine the rule of law and the existing constitutional order. They did so both through formal institutional means (e.g., the "Enabling Law" of 1933) and informally, such as during the "night of the long knives" in which the Nazis purged political elites (Fulbrook 1990, 178–87). Germany became a totalitarian police state.

The anti-Semitism that had been present in Germany for years (Kitchen 2006, 133–8), and had been a prominent part of Hitler's rhetoric, came fully out into the light of day (Fulbrook 1990, 196–203). Jewish identity was legally defined, and a series of discriminatory laws were passed. Violence against Jews became increasingly common, notably the mass violence of the Kristallnacht of 1938. Even more chillingly, the regime aimed to sequester Jews in concentration camps with ultimately genocidal purposes. Historians estimate that around 6 million Jews were murdered by the Nazis. Jews suffered more than most, but other groups, such as Poles, Soviet citizens, gypsies, homosexuals, and even some Christian religious actors, as well as political activists opposed to the Nazis, were also oppressed and murdered in great numbers.

Hitler's foreign policy was expansionary (Fulbrook 1990, 187–95), and Germany's territorial ambitions led to the Second World War. Germany took Czechoslovakia in 1938, and in 1939 Germany invaded Poland. At first, the Soviet Union was not part of the hostilities, Stalin and Hitler having signed a non-aggression pact, but the Nazis had no intention of long-term coexistence with a major socialist power (Kitchen 2006, 297–8, 301–4). While France quickly fell to Germany, with the collaborating Vichy regime put in place, Britain and later the Soviet Union fought persistently. Canada joined early as a part of the war effort, alongside other British dominions like Australia and New Zealand. They were joined by the United States after Japan's attack on Pearl Harbor in December of 1941. It took until 1945, but the Allies were eventually triumphant, and Germany was partially destroyed in the process.

The effort to reconstruct Germany—economically, politically, and socially—was daunting. The Soviet Union had occupied the eastern portion of the country while the United Kingdom, France, and the United States occupied the west. These would become two distinct states, the Federal Republic of Germany (West Germany) and the German Democratic Republic (East Germany). West Germany embraced liberal democracy and a mixed economy, with strong support for social democracy and a relatively robust welfare state. East Germany became a satellite state of the Soviet Union. Economic reconstruction of West Germany was greatly aided by funds from the United States in the form of the Marshall Plan (Davies 1996, 1080).

Against the skeptics, West Germany had success in building a largely tolerant, functional, democratic society, one that has largely been economically successful. A stable party system developed (Davies 1996, 1074), with the Christian Democratic Union Party and the Social Democratic Party being the most important (and they remain so today in unified Germany). Key leaders of both parties, like Konrad Adenauer (a Christian Democrat) and Willy Brandt (a Social Democrat), played key roles in the ongoing democratic consolidation of West Germany. The East German state, perhaps owing to its status as a satellite, was judged by most to be less successful, with poor economic performance over many years.

As part of the wave of revolutions that swept central and eastern Europe and brought the Soviet Union to an end, the Berlin Wall fell in 1989, and East and West Germany were unified in 1990. East Germany, owing to decades spent as a command economy and with political subordination to the Soviet Union, had a lower level of socio-economic development. The reunification of Germany resulted in major transfers of resources from west to east. Despite the fact that this has partially redressed the imbalances in economic development, differences are still visible.

Throughout recent decades, Germany has been a leader in the creation and expansion of the European Union. It was an initiator of the project of European integration, beginning in the 1950s with free trade in coal and steel and then moving to a common market, common trade policies, and ultimately to a common currency and open borders within parts of the continent. While the process of European integration has been remarkable, the region has fallen on more difficult times even as Germany has boomed economically. This has put the euro under pressure, with Germans facing a dilemma: The country is hesitant to bail out countries facing financial difficulties in the eurozone, but it also is the key player that must do so if the eurozone is to hold together.

Regime and Political Institutions

The head of government in the Federal Republic of Germany's parliamentary system is the chancellor, a position comparable to a prime minister. The chancellor is selected by the lower house of the legislature, the Bundestag (see the Chapter 9 case study on page 191) after legislative elections. Since no single party is usually able to attain a majority of seats in the Bundestag, Germany's chancellor regularly governs at the head of a coalition of two or more parties. The chancellor is almost always either from the Christian Democratic Union Party (CDU, an example being current chancellor Angela Merkel or, in earlier years, Helmut Kohl and Konrad Adenauer) or the Social Democratic Party (SPD, with examples like Gerhard Schroder and Willy Brandt). The chancellor's power is limited by Germany's federalism, which empowers representatives of the states (Länder) in the upper house (Bundesrat) to vote on all legislation affecting the states.

Regime and Political Institutions

Regime	Democratically elected federal republic
Administrative Divisions	16 Länder (states)
Executive Branch	Chancellor (head of government) President (head of state, ceremonial)
Selection of Executive	Selected by Bundestag
Legislative Branch	Bicameral Lower chamber: Bundestag; members elected by mixed system of districts, proportional representation Upper chamber: Bundesrat; members selected by Länder (state) governments
Judicial Branch	Constitutional Court with powers of judicial review
Political Party System	Multiparty, with frequent coalitions Main parties: CDU (centre-right), SPD (centre-left), Greens (left), Liberals (right), Left. Of these, the CDU and the SPD have historically been predominant.

Political Culture

Much attention has been focused on nationalism as a key feature of German political culture, with considerable preoccupation, understandably, with the Nazi regime of the 1930s and 1940s. A whole industry of scholarship attempts to unpack the relationship between that regime and the long-running German political-cultural tradition (see, for example, discussion in Greenfeld 1992; Goldhagen 1996; Browning 1992; as well as in Berger 2004). Precisely because this important conversation has received so much attention, we focus less centrally on it here.

Rather, we will note that a key aspect of German political culture—both East and West before reunification—has centred on how German identity can be reconstituted following that shameful episode in the nation's history. Indeed, this has perhaps been *the* central question of political culture since the Second World War, and Germany's experiences with political instability in the Weimar years and with totalitarianism in the 1930s and 1940s seem to have led the country to be healthily wary of radical polarization.

Germany has sometimes been at the forefront of efforts to experiment with direct democracy and related ideas. For example, a number of its states, particularly Bavaria, stand out for their frequent use of referenda. Perhaps more quixotically, a number of German localities have issued local currencies, at least some of them hoping to resist excess "commodification" and to retain local control of economic processes by doing so. The Green party has done well in Germany (indeed, Germany has had a strong environmental movement more generally). In recent years, because of public concern about immigration, the right-wing populist Alternative for Germany party has performed well in federal elections. In 2017, they came in third after cutting into the electoral popularity of both the Christian Democrats and the Social Democrats.

Political Economy

Germany is by most accounts the world's fifth-largest economy, coming behind only the United States, China, Japan, and India (on the basis of purchasing power). The industrial powerhouse was the world's largest exporter for some years before ceding that honour to China more recently. By virtue of its size and prominence, Germany is the engine of the European Union, the world's largest economic free trade area, which has a combined economy somewhat larger than that of the United States. The country's economic model contains many free market elements but also features an active state role in investment, in building human capital, and in providing support for the vulnerable. Economic decision-making since World War II has prioritized consensus between major economic actors, including corporations, labour unions, and the state.

From 1945 to 1990, the country was split into the capitalist West and the communist East, with the latter falling far behind West Germany economically. West Germany was quite successful after the war, as was Japan, which led to the theory that the loss in the war had eliminated the many "special interests" in politics that complicate reform; this would explain success relative to victors such as the United Kingdom and the United States (Olson 1984). After the fall of the Berlin Wall signified the end of the Cold War in 1989, Germany reunified in 1990 and resumed its place as one of the world's leading economies.

Per estimates for 2017, 30.7 per cent of Germany's GDP comes from industrial production, 68.6 per cent comes from the service sector, and only 0.7 per cent comes from the agricultural sector. Germany's unemployment rate was estimated at 3.8 per cent (*CIA World Factbook 2019*), which is quite low by European standards, especially since the economic crisis that began in 2008.

A big question for Germany's economy has been whether the eurozone will hold together. The question has arisen as several southern European economies (most notably Greece but also Spain, Portugal, and Italy) have lagged behind Germany and northern Europe in terms of productivity. This situation has raised the prospect that some countries might need to drop the euro as a currency to regain their competitiveness. From the perspective of many Germans, their southern neighbours have lived beyond their means for years (drawing support from economies such as Germany's) and now must make the painful adjustments necessary to compete. However, Germany too has depended on economically viable southern neighbours, both as markets for its exports and as destinations for a good deal of the capital in its banking sector. Perspectives critical of Germany have held that it is forcing other European countries to cut public services and reduce wages (perhaps because Germans are concerned about inflation), even though Germany has relied on the rest of Europe as well. This situation shows the interdependence of international economies in the present day and especially in Europe. Debates about the eurozone's future continue, and the situation has certainly been exacerbated as Germany and other EU member states negotiate the terms of Britain's withdrawal from the EU.

CASE STUDIES

CASE STUDY

Chapter 7, Page 141

Democracy and Authoritarianism in Germany

Many people know of German Nazism (1933–45) as the epitome of 20th-century totalitarianism, with its denial of basic human rights and its culmination in the atrocities of the Holocaust. But it is important to consider German history in the 20th century as a set of shifts between democratic and authoritarian rule. In other words, Nazism is not the whole story in Germany. This is a country that has seen oscillations between democracy and democratic breakdown, culminating in democratic consolidation over the past 70 years such that virtually no observers worry about the ongoing democratic status of contemporary Germany.

In the German Empire after unification, there were democratic elements, most notably that suffrage was extended to all males for voting in legislative elections. Yet few would describe this system as "democratic," since the chancellor (Bismarck until 1890) and the kaiser (Wilhelm I and II) held disproportionate power. After the collapse of this system as a result of the First World War, the country embarked upon an experiment with a democratic republic. Great effort was expended on the constitution of this Weimar Republic, but it would be for naught (for more on this fascinating period, see the essays in McElligott 2009). Serious economic problems, resulting from both the Treaty of Versailles and, later, the Great Depression, compounded the existent political polarization of German society. Political parties proliferated, and despite institutional changes meant to quell disorder, Hitler and the Nazis would eventually take power. It is unclear how long and in what form the Nazi regime would have lasted if it were not for the Second World War, but in any case military defeat brought the Nazi era to a close. This led to an externally imposed transition in East and West Germany.

Here, Germany's political history bifurcates until 1990. During the Cold War, Germany was divided into a democratic West Germany and a communist East Germany. Thus, the eastern part of today's Germany experienced both of the 20th century's most infamous forms of totalitarian rule: Nazism and Soviet communism.

The case of West German democratization is fairly singular. In other words, the degree to which it can serve as a model for other regimes seeking to make a democratic transition is limited. First of all, the authoritarian regime fell because it was defeated and then the country occupied by foreign powers. Second, those powers helped to shape the transition, both in political and especially in economic terms. Third, the nature of the authoritarian regime demanded such thoroughgoing repudiation that democracy's legitimacy was high (indeed, in general, the defeat of the axis powers was linked to a global wave of democratic prestige).

The case of unification is a bit more useful for comparative analysis, if for no other reason than not all of the aforementioned conditions apply to the case. So far at least, the unified Germany has defied fears that it would come to dominate Europe or revert to the authoritarian impulses that surfaced at various points in the country's history. Indeed, to most observers, the unified Germany appears to be a highly stable and successful democracy.

CASE STUDY

Chapter 9, Page 191

Institutional Design: Germany's Bundestag and Bundesrat

There are many ways to structure legislatures, and the German model is an intriguing one for other countries. Germany is a federal country in which the 16 states (Länder) have considerable authority, and it has a bicameral legislature with a chamber known as the Bundesrat to represent the states. The country also has a blend of different electoral systems for its lower house, known as the Bundestag. The mixed system is a case of careful institutional engineering that incorporates many different features.

In the Bundestag, the electoral system features elements of both district-based representation and proportional representation (PR). At each election, every German has two votes: one for a preferred candidate from the district and one for a preferred party; this is similar to the New Zealand example, discussed in Chapter 9. The district-based vote for a candidate means that each geographic constituency in Germany has its own representative, just like in district systems elsewhere in the world. But the party vote is tallied to ensure that the overall distribution of seats in the Bundestag reflects the partisan preferences of the country as a whole. After all the district representatives are calculated, the party vote is used to add "at-large" seats as necessary to the Bundestag. For example, a party that gets 24 per cent of the overall party vote but only earns 18 per cent of the district seats would be "compensated" with additional at-large seats to make its overall representation in the parliament proportional to its support. This gives the proportionality in the legislature associated with PR, even while giving each constituency its own representative as in district systems. All members of the Bundestag vote to elect a chancellor as the head of government.

The legislature also has another innovation: a modified version of the vote of no confidence. As with other parliamentary systems, Germany's chancellor and government can be dismissed by a vote of no confidence, but the form is known as a "constructive vote of no confidence." The twist in Germany is that those proposing to bring down the government must simultaneously present and support a new governmental majority coalition that will go into effect. This prevents opposition parties from reducing the government to permanent gridlock by bringing down governments without being able to propose a viable governing alternative.

Germany also has features that protect the 16 states in the federal system, mainly through the Bundesrat. The members of the Bundesrat are appointed by the respective state governments to represent the interests of that state. Each state's delegation to this upper chamber must vote as a bloc, otherwise its votes are not counted. With regard to powers, the Bundesrat has the right to vote on any matter that materially affects the 16 Länder, including matters of budgets and administration. While the powers thus have some constitutional limits, the amount of legislation deemed to affect the states is considerable, which gives the Bundesrat substantial authority. On issues that do not have special bearing on the states, the Bundesrat can still review legislation and offer objections, which can be overturned by the Bundestag.

In addition to these legislative arrangements, Germany has a ceremonial president who has relatively few powers. Germany's presidential selection is undertaken by a body that brings together the elected legislators of the Bundestag along with representatives of Germany's 16 Länder. The president is deemed to be impartial, and nominees are typically selected for their reputation for being non-partisan.

In combination, the various aspects of the German political system are intended to balance and distribute power in several ways. The party vote has the effect of ensuring that the most successful parties have a mandate to govern, while the constituency vote allows each geographic area to be represented by its preferred candidate. The constructive vote of no confidence allows for an unpopular government to be overturned while also placing a premium on governability. Finally, the delicate balance of powers between the Bundestag and Bundesrat is designed to ensure that federalism is protected, but so are the prerogatives of the parliamentary majority. This set of institutional designs shows that there is a nearly endless variety of possible models for structuring political systems.

Research Prompts

1. What would major theories of democratization and democratic consolidation say about the pattern of authoritarianism and democracy that Germany witnessed in the late 19th and 20th centuries? What are the implications of the German case for those theories?
2. As discussed in several of the case studies, Germany has often been considered a prototypical case of ethnic nationalism, and its nationalism has often been causally linked to its 20th-century totalitarian regime. Design a comparative analysis—drawing on several cases—that would allow us to examine this claim. Is yours an MSS or MDS design? Why?
3. Some argue that Germany is a case of state-led development. Others argue that market forces have played a central role in Germany's historical economic performance. How can these claims be reconciled? To what extent is either or both of these claims true?

4. What are the pros and cons of the institutional structure of Germany's government? Canada has toyed with various forms of electoral reform, with both the Liberals and NDP promising electoral reform in the 2015 election campaign. How might the German model work either at the provincial level or at the federal level? What changes would need to be made to better adapt it for Canada?

5. Germany was in certain respects a "late modernizer" within the European context. In particular, it is noteworthy that the country only achieved political unification in 1871. Situating Germany in its comparative European context, analyze the main consequences of this modernization pattern.

Online Case Studies

Go to **www.oup.com/he/DickovickCe** to find more case studies online, including:

- Consensus-Based Politics in Germany
- Ethnic Boundaries of the German Nation?
- The German State: Unification and Welfare

Note

1 Burke and Oltermann 2016.

India

PROFILE

Key Features of Contemporary India

Population:	1,281,935,911 (July 2017 est.)
Area:	3,287,263 square kilometres
Head of State:	Ram Nath Kovind (president, 2017–present)
Head of Government:	Narendra Modi (prime minister, 2014–present)
Capital:	New Delhi
Year of Independence:	1947
Year of Current Constitution:	1950
Languages:	English, Hindi; other major languages include Bengali, Tamil, Urdu
GDP per Capita:	$1,939.60 (World Bank estimate 2017)
Human Development Index Ranking (2015):	131st (medium human development)
Trading Relationship with Canada (2016):	• Imports $3,051,114,580 • Exports $3,006,946,340 https://globaledge.msu.edu/countries/canada/tradestats

Sources: *CIA World Factbook*; World Bank World Development Indicators; United Nations *Human Development Report 2016*

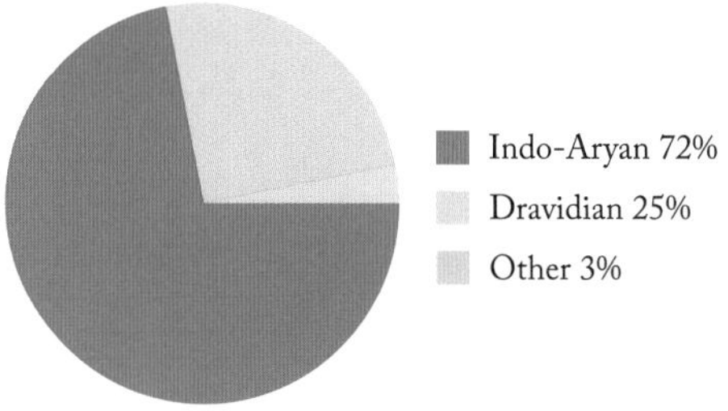

Ethnic Groups in India

Note that while the *CIA World Factbook* includes only three main groups, which are really language families that overlap with ethnicity, these categories include many smaller groups. Note, too, that caste distinctions in India are sometimes treated as similar to ethnic distinctions.

Source: *CIA World Factbook*

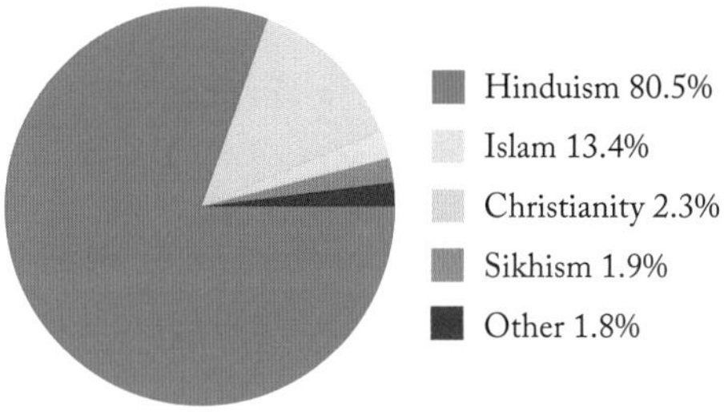

Religious Affiliation in India

Note that Hinduism is used as an umbrella term to cover a wide range of religious groups with different traditions, practices, and beliefs. Many of these groups would reject the characterization of being Hindu. In constitutional terms, even well-established groups such as Jains and Buddhists are nominally considered Hindu.

Source: *CIA World Factbook*

Introduction

India is the world's largest democracy and a surprising one given its size and history. India is a diverse society of more than 1 billion people, divided into different major religions, languages, and social groups (see the charts that follow). This diversity was perhaps even more striking under British colonial rule prior to 1947, since British India also contained both present-day Pakistan and Bangladesh, two Muslim-majority countries that together combine for more than 325 million people today. Prior to colonialism, India was largely decentralized, with the territory being ruled by many regional or local princes. It is a source of inspiration to many that India has retained its democracy for almost all of its some three-quarters of a century of independence, despite the ravages of poverty and hunger, social inequality, and a multitude of cultures and beliefs densely packed into the South Asian subcontinent.

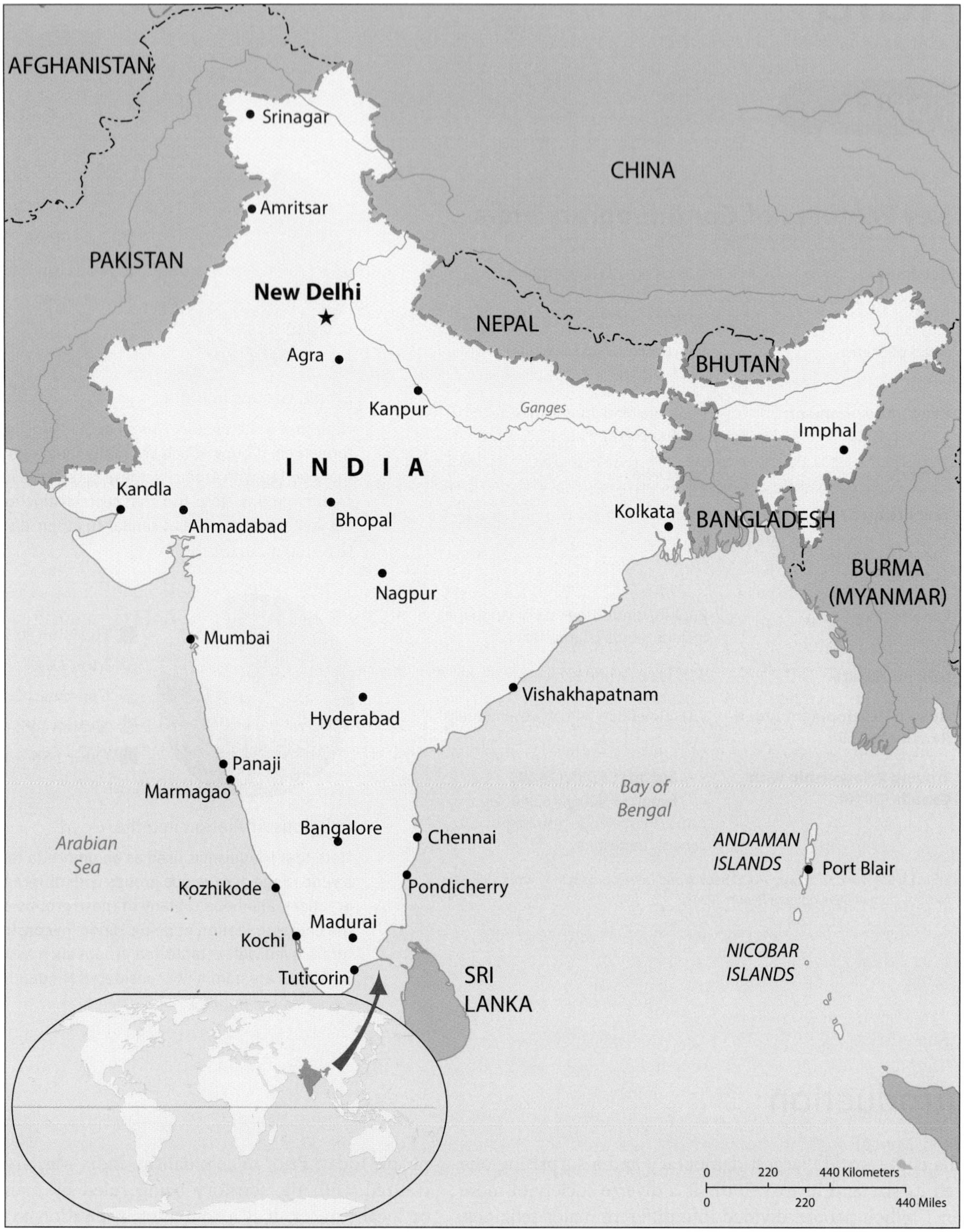
AFGHANISTAN
Srinagar
CHINA
Amritsar
PAKISTAN
New Delhi
NEPAL
Agra
BHUTAN
Kanpur
Ganges
Imphal
I N D I A
Kandla
Ahmadabad
Bhopal
Kolkata
BANGLADESH
Nagpur
BURMA
(MYANMAR)
Mumbai
Vishakhapatnam
Hyderabad
Panaji
Marmagao
Bay of
Bengal
Bangalore
Chennai
Arabian
Sea
ANDAMAN
ISLANDS
Port Blair
Kozhikode
Pondicherry
Madurai
Kochi
NICOBAR
ISLANDS
Tuticorin
SRI
LANKA
0
220
440 Kilometers
0
220
440 Miles

Even with its many social problems, India today is likely to be seen as a thriving hub of the future, renowned for technological innovation, engineering prowess, and entrepreneurial spirit. It has grown rapidly in recent years and has become a global leader in technology, science and engineering, and the service industry. It is likely to become the world's most populous nation in the next decades, and if much of that population can come out of poverty and into the middle class, it will, along with China, become one of the leading global powers as the 21st century progresses.

Historical Development

India is home to some of the world's most historic civilizations and is the source of several of the world's great religions, most notably Hinduism, which remains its majority religion, and Buddhism, which continues to have a tremendous influence in numerous East and Southeast Asian countries. The country's recorded history dates back millennia and consisted for centuries of a range of empires, small states, and principalities. It was for many centuries a crossroads of peoples, where cultures came together and new ones were created and where trade networks linked together. India's past involves some of recorded history's most compelling characters, including the emperor Ashoka, who in the four decades before his death in 232 BCE nominally united much of the region known as the Indian "subcontinent" and ordained a legal code that emphasized sectarian and ethnic tolerance. The subcontinent witnessed Greek invaders from the west under Alexander the Great and Turkic raiders from the north. Turks established states in north India by the early 1200s. The region was settled by Muslims, as well as Hindus and Buddhists, and was criss-crossed by merchants as it became a linchpin of the spice trade that connected east and west. Much of India was then united under the Mughal Empire up to the 1700s.

Despite its exceedingly rich prior history, the formation of modern India is often seen as beginning with the advent of European colonial rule, which began in the 17th century and lasted up to 1947. India was gradually colonized by many European powers over several centuries, though over time British colonialism came to dominate. British colonial rule did not begin with outright conquest but rather with the establishment of trading posts under the British East India Company (on the East India Company and the growth of colonialism, see Metcalf and Metcalf 2006). The company had a charter from the British monarch to establish a monopoly trade in India for products that included cotton and silk, tea, and opium. Given the richness of trade, British India came to be seen as the crown jewel of all European colonial possessions. It eventually encompassed present-day India, Pakistan, and Bangladesh and became central to the aims and aspirations of the British Empire.

After 18th-century conflict between England and France, the British East India Company gained colonial control over much of today's India, Pakistan, and Bangladesh. British colonialism gradually became more direct and intense over time. It met with resistance at various points but succeeded in part through playing various Indian actors against each other. The most serious 19th-century resistance against the British was the revolt of 1857–9 (sometimes called the "Sepoy Rebellion") after which the British state took over control from the East India Company and ruled India directly, effectively humiliating and "deindustrializing" the subcontinent (e.g., Allen 2011).

In the early 20th century, Indian resistance to British rule grew, with the Indian Congress Party leading the anti-colonial movement. Its key leader was Mohandas Gandhi (often known as Mahatma, or "great soul"), who led peaceful demonstrations, marches, and protests demanding home rule. Gandhi's methods pioneered non-violent resistance—later used by Martin Luther King in the United States—and were known in India as *satyagraha*. Gandhi's charismatic appeal to many millions of Indians was enhanced by his decisions to eat and dress simply rather than following the expectations of British culture (and, in part, for religious reasons). The other main political leader of Congress was Jawaharlal Nehru; also making common cause with them in the eventual demands for independence was Muhammad Ali Jinnah of the Muslim League.

Gandhi, Nehru, and Jinnah pressed for Indian independence from Britain, and the move to decolonization accelerated after World War II, but as independence approached Jinnah and the Muslim League insisted on a partition of India with an independent state for Muslims. (British colonialism, of course, played a critical historical role in exacerbating such divisions.) On 15 August 1947, India became independent but had split into a majority-Hindu India and majority-Muslim Pakistan. Pakistan included West Pakistan (present-day Pakistan) and East Pakistan (present-day Bangladesh), which were on opposite sides of India. The 1947 partition led to thousands of deaths and millions of refugees as Hindus left Pakistan for India and Muslims left India for Pakistan (both groups

Historical Development Timeline

321 BCE	Chandragupta Maurya founds the Mauryan Empire, which encompasses much of contemporary northern India, Afghanistan, Pakistan, and Bangladesh.
273–32 BCE	Ashoka expands the size of the empire to some 5 million square kilometres at its height.
68 CE	Kushan Empire is formed, which encompasses portions of northern India and Afghanistan.
200s	Gupta Empire controls much of the subcontinent until around 590. A number of other empires rise and fall over the next millennium.
1400s	Territory today encompassed by India was, by the 15th century, home to large numbers of empires, states, and religious traditions, including Hinduism, Buddhism, and Sikhism.
1498	Portuguese explorer Vasco da Gama reaches India, and the Portuguese establish a small state by 1505.
1600s	British East India Company begins trading in India and eventually consolidates control over most of the subcontinent, prevailing over French and Dutch competition.
1857	Major rebellion against rule of the British East India Company.
1858	Britain asserts direct Crown control over most of India and rules parts of India indirectly through "Princely States" of local nobles.
1876–9	British create famines in India as a result of droughts, and the British hoarding of food leads to between 6.1 and 10.3 million preventable deaths.
1896–1902	A second series of British-made famines results in between 6.1 and 19 million deaths according to contemporary records, including the medical journal *The Lancet* (which provides the figure of 19 million).[1]
1915–1930s	Mohandas Gandhi becomes leader of the Indian National Congress and leads protests against British rule, demanding home rule and eventually independence.
1919	Massacre of several hundreds of unarmed Indians at Amritsar by British troops under General Reginald Dyer.
1930s–40s	Anti-colonial movement accelerates with mass strikes and mobilizations, led by Gandhi and Jawaharlal Nehru of the Congress Party and Muhammad Ali Jinnah of the Muslim League.
1943	Bengal famine kills an estimated 2–3 million Indians in the Bengal province.
1947	Independence and partition of British India into India and Pakistan (with Pakistan including East Pakistan, or present-day Bangladesh); tensions and conflict emerge between Hindus and Muslims over partition, culminating in war and massive refugee flows of Indian Muslims to Pakistan and Pakistani Hindus to India.
1948	Mohandas Gandhi is assassinated by a Hindu fundamentalist who rejected Gandhi's calls for peace between Hindus and Muslims. Founder of Pakistan Muhammad Ali Jinnah dies of tuberculosis.
1950	India ends its symbolic links to Great Britain with adoption of new constitution that establishes a republic; India's "princely states" are incorporated into the nation's states and territories.
1962	War with China centred on a border dispute.
1964	Death of Jawaharlal Nehru.
1966	Indira Gandhi (daughter of Nehru and no relation to Mahatma Gandhi) becomes prime minister and continues most policies set by Nehru.
1971	India and Pakistan go to war over East Pakistan; former East Pakistan separates from West Pakistan and becomes Bangladesh.
1974	India explodes a nuclear device.
1975–7	"The Emergency": martial law under Indira Gandhi, who rules by decree and imprisons opposition leaders.
1977	Congress Party loses power for the first time.
1979	Indira Gandhi returns as prime minister.
1984	Indira Gandhi is assassinated by her Sikh bodyguards; riots ensue in which several thousand members of the Sikh minority are killed; Rajiv Gandhi (Indira's son) becomes prime minister.
1989	Protests increase in Kashmir, a Muslim majority area administered by India on the border between India and Pakistan.
1991	Rajiv Gandhi is assassinated by militants seeking a separate homeland for Sri Lankan Tamils and angry at India's intervention in the conflict.
1991	Pro-market economic reforms begin under finance minister Manmohan Singh (later prime minister), under pressure from the International Monetary Fund and the World Bank.

1992	Hindu nationalists destroy a mosque in Ayodhya that is of historical importance to some Muslims but also is in a location sacred to some Hindus.	**2008**	Islamist militants from Pakistan stage simultaneous terror attacks in Mumbai.
1996	Atal Bihari Vajpayee becomes prime minister as head of the Hindu nationalist Bharatiya Janata Party (BJP); governs only briefly but returns from 1998 to 2004.	**2014**	Narendra Modi of the BJP elected prime minister. The new state of Telangana is created in the south from a portion of the state of Andhra Pradesh.
2000s	India's economy booms, with growth rates occasionally reaching near 8 per cent.	**2018**	The government launches a goods and services tax, a major tax reform.
2004	Congress Party voted back into power with Manmohan Singh as prime minister.	**2019**	Seven-phase election (11 April to 19 May 2019) for the Lok Sabha (lower house of parliament), with Modi returning as prime minister and the BJP increasing its majority.

often walking on foot), with conflicts and massacres between the groups occurring in the process. Tensions continued after the assassination of Gandhi in 1948 by a Hindu fundamentalist who objected to Gandhi's efforts to reconcile and promote tolerance between Hindus and Muslims.

Indian politics in the first decades after independence was dominated by the Indian Congress Party. As India's first prime minister, Nehru led the country from 1947 to his death in 1964. His governments developed many lasting features of the Indian state and economy, most notably creating a very active and interventionist state. While some economic production remained in private hands, the state owned many large enterprises and regulated the economy heavily. In this mixed economy, India achieved some modest growth and developed strong educational programs in science and engineering while also working to improve agriculture.

Indira Gandhi ascended to the role of prime minister in 1966 and governed for more than a decade. She largely followed the policies set in place by her father, Jawaharlal Nehru, and built upon them with efforts to increase agricultural production in rural areas. On the international front, her government supported residents of East Pakistan who militated for independence from Pakistan in 1971; this led to a war with Pakistan that resulted in the independence of East Pakistan as the new nation of Bangladesh. Indira and her followers were accused of electoral fraud in the 1971 election by an increasingly restive opposition, and in response the government declared martial law in 1975. Known as "The Emergency," this period lasted nearly two years until 1977 and can be seen as the only period in which democracy suffered a setback in independent India. The Emergency ultimately ended in 1977 and cost the Congress Party control of the government for the first time. Indira Gandhi and the Congress returned to power in 1980, and the prime minister herself was assassinated by her bodyguards—of the Sikh minority—in 1984. This resulted in deadly anti-Sikh riots. In the meantime, the post of prime minister passed to Rajiv Gandhi, Indira's son and the next generation of the "Nehru-Gandhi dynasty" in the Congress Party. Rajiv was assassinated by a Sri Lankan Tamil separatist in 1991.

Through the 1990s and 2000s, India has witnessed several sources of violence and instability. The most important international conflict has been with Pakistan, especially as the two nuclear-armed powers contest the disputed region along their shared border. The Indian-administered province of Jammu and Kashmir has a Muslim majority, much of which wishes to come under Pakistani sovereignty, with another contingent advocating independence. Conflict erupts sporadically and was most tense when the two countries tested nuclear devices in a standoff in 1998. Sectarian conflict has a domestic component as well, with conflicts ongoing between Indian Hindus and the significant minority of Indian Muslims. A most dramatic conflict came when Hindu nationalists demolished a holy Muslim mosque by hand in Ayodhya in 1992 on the grounds that it had been built on the site of a temple marking the birthplace of the Hindu divinity Rama. Tensions mounted further when the Bharatiya Janata Party (BJP) governed in the period from 1998 to 2004 because the party promoted Hindu nationalist ideals while attempting to court some Muslim and Christian voters. The party maintained that Hindu should be India's leading cultural identity and should be fostered by state institutions.

Violence and conflict continue in contemporary India. In 2008, the international and domestic aspects of India's sectarian divide came together tragically when coordinated bombings and suicide attacks on prominent sites in the metropolis Mumbai resulted in several hundred deaths. Violence also takes on various daily forms that amount to more deaths but appear less in the news: India has high levels of social violence against women, with deadly abuse remaining common. An increasing phenomenon is sex-selective abortion, which has resulted in many "missing girls."

India has been led by reformist governments and prime ministers in recent years and amid many uncertainties has emerged economically in the last two decades. Prime Minister Manmohan Singh (a Sikh and the first non-Hindu to hold the post) governed from 2004 to 2014 and was formerly the finance minister who initiated important economic reforms in 1991. In 2014, Narendra Modi of the BJP was elected and subsequently re-elected in 2019. Some economic analysts responded to his election with enthusiasm, given the economic successes in the state of Gujarat under his administration.

Regime and Political Institutions

India is a federal parliamentary system with two chambers of parliament, the lower house called the Lok Sabha (with about 550 members, though the number varies) and the upper house known as the Rajya Sabha (with no more than 250 members), which represents the states. The Lok Sabha has the greater powers of the two: It elects the prime minister and can vote out the government with a vote of no confidence; the government is thus accountable to the Lok Sabha. The Lok Sabha also is the final authority on "money bills" regarding taxation and spending appropriations. In some cases, a government minister introduces legislation in the Lok Sabha, while in other cases individual members of the Lok Sabha introduce bills. Except for money bills, the Rajya Sabha has a role after bills pass the lower chamber. If the Rajya Sabha votes against a bill, a joint committee of the two houses is formed, with a majority prevailing. Since the Lok Sabha is more numerous, it has the advantage in such votes.

Other branches and powers of government also have roles. India has a formal, written constitution and a Supreme Court responsible for deciding on the constitutionality of law. As a federal system, important parts of Indian law are made at the state level. States have their own High Courts (with some states grouping together to share a High Court) and their own legislatures and executives. The state assemblies select most of the members of the national Rajya Sabha. The president is largely ceremonial but must assent to parliamentary bills for them to become law. Occasionally, the president may offer an objection to a bill and send it back to the legislature, but if it passes a second time, the president is constitutionally required to assent. On very rare occasions, the president may exercise a "pocket veto" by neither assenting to a bill nor returning it to the parliament.

Regime and Political Institutions

Regime	Federal representative democracy; parliamentary system
Administrative Divisions	29 states and seven union territories
Executive Branch	Prime minister as head of government (in parliament) President with largely ceremonial powers
Selection of Executive	Prime minister selected by parliament President elected by electoral college of parliament and state legislators
Legislative Branch	Bicameral parliament Lower chamber: Lok Sabha (House of the People) Upper chamber: Rajya Sabha (Council of States)
Judicial Branch	Supreme Court of India
Political Party System	Multiparty system, with two major parties leading coalitions at national level: Indian Congress Party (United Progressive Alliance) and Bharatiya Janata Party (National Democratic Alliance)

Political Culture

There are a number of noteworthy features of India's political culture. Perhaps the most singular feature of Indian political culture is its diversity. India is a strikingly heterogeneous and culturally complex society. It is the point of origin for two of the most important world religions: Hinduism and Buddhism, and India has an enormous Muslim population and notable Sikh and Christian populations, as well as other religions like Jainism.

India is also a society that has exhibited a high degree of inequality and stratification. This can be measured in terms of income, for example, because India has relatively high income inequality, but cultural sources of inequality are also notable. The most controversial has been that of caste. Caste is a source of controversy because it used to be asserted that caste was a long-standing tradition of Indian culture (Dumont [1966] 1981). While most historians argue that caste had featured in Indian life before the advent of British colonial rule, some historians (e.g., Dirks 2001) have argued that caste as we know it was at least partially a function of colonialists having used such distinctions to aid in subjugating and ruling India. Whatever the historical sources, caste distinctions have been important features of contemporary Indian politics, with political parties sometimes coinciding with castes and with some groups being favoured over others.

Another notable feature of modern Indian political culture—which exists in tension with the previously noted characteristic—is India's democracy. India is notable for being the world's largest democracy, and it achieved this well before its recent gains in economic development. Indians treat political and civil liberties as rights and entitlements, and this has given rise to social movements and protests, alternations in government, and a wide range of political parties, including important communist parties being elected to run some states.

India is known for its remarkable contradictions when it comes to how the political culture interacts with the economy. The country has a famously strong administration and civil service in the sense that top-ranking officials are accomplished, well-educated, and admired. On the other hand, the Indian state has been characterized by high levels of corruption, with bribes being expected from the lowest official up the chain to higher-ranking superiors. The result has been a state that has technical competence at the top but historically has failed to deliver needed services to the beneficiaries in the population. This contradictory nature of the political culture plays a role the persistence of extreme poverty.

Political Economy

India's political economy is seemingly a study in contrasts. The country's economic history has witnessed a combination of stagnation, modest growth, and more recent success. Under state planning and state-led development for much of its post-independence period from the 1940s through the 1980s, India had a middling level of economic success (Kohli 2004). Yet it was clear that the challenges remained as of the 1990s. One of the key features of the Indian political economy was noted earlier: the use of extensive government planning, intervention, and regulation. A leading manifestation of this was what came to be known as the "licence raj," or the complex system of regulations—often in the form of required licences and permits—that businesses needed to follow. This system was nominally supposed to ensure coordination, planning, and protections for workers, but it came to represent bureaucratic inefficiency that stifled innovation.

By the 1990s, the Indian state was seen as increasingly meddlesome, dysfunctional, corrupt, and in need of reform. A major response came in 1991 with a set of reforms that opened up India's economy somewhat. While India did not undertake any massive transition to free-market principles, the changes were significant by Indian standards. The change coincided with the end of the Cold War when the Soviet Union collapsed, having once been the command economy model that India (while remaining democratic) had sought to follow.

India's growth soon accelerated, though this is not attributable to the reforms alone. The country has grown rapidly in the years after 2002, averaging in the range of 8 per cent per year. This is even more impressive given that population growth has slowed in the country to closer to 1 per cent, meaning the growth per capita has accelerated. From an economy that was rather inefficient, modern enterprise has emerged in various forms, ranging from some of the most successful multinationals in the world (such as the Tata conglomerate) to remarkably innovative small-scale enterprises popping up as survival strategies in dirt-floor homes in the Mumbai slum of Dharavi. Much of India's growth has come in the diverse service sector, not only in manufacturing. Despite this, agriculture still employs about half of all Indians, often in the form of small-scale or subsistence agriculture on family plots.

The boom in the GDP growth rate does not imply that India's economic problems are solved. A leading feature to note in India is high levels of extreme poverty, prevalent in rural and urban areas alike. Despite the decades since the end of princely titles and the abolition of caste discrimination, there are powerful landed elites that control much of the wealth, while incomes for the poor are tiny and fragile. Equally striking juxtapositions are found in the massive and growing inequalities in India's major cities. Mumbai has become a classic example of this, being a centre both of the aforementioned corporate boom—with high-end real estate and a wealthy financial district—and the overcrowded slums (Mehta 2004). Regardless of innovation and entrepreneurship, work among the urban poor remains largely in the informal sector, with no benefits, much uncertainty, and hazardous working and living conditions.

CASE STUDIES

CASE STUDY

Chapter 5, Page 87

What Explains India's Recent Growth?

For many years after its independence from Britain in 1947, India achieved relatively slow growth on the order of about 4 per cent per year. Growth was hindered by extensive regulations and the "licence raj" that required many licences and approvals to conduct business. Under this system, state policy often favoured the well-connected rather than making decisions based on economic rationality and efficiency. Economic improvements have been more dramatic in recent years, and this change has followed the implementation of pro-market economic reforms in 1991 at the direction of Manmohan Singh. But what is India's development path, and does openness to the market alone explain its recent success?

There are a number of distinctive features of India's development. One is that India established a robust democracy *before* achieving a modern economy, whereas many theories lead us to expect the opposite sequence. This makes India a very interesting case for scholars who want to study how politics shapes economic performance. India's state action has long been shaped by the government's need to respond to the expectations of important economic actors and the populace at large, which makes it different from development initiatives attempted by authoritarian regimes that could have more closed patterns of decision-making (Kohli 2004).

India's recent growth has also been very interesting as a contrast to that of other developing countries, especially China. While China has achieved much of its rapid growth on the basis of investment in manufacturing, India has seen extensive growth in services as well and has boomed in part because of the growing consumption of its middle class as opposed to investment for exports to foreign countries. While India and China have highly skilled professional sectors, a difference is in the caricature of each development model: China is the "world's workshop," making plastic toys and simple electronics on the factory floor, while India is the world's "back office," home to many "call centres" that provide customer service and other support, as well as engineering, computing, and other services (see Friedman 2005 for a popular version of this argument). The reality is much more nuanced, but the distinction illustrates some features of the respective paths.

An additional striking feature of Indian development is that high levels of extreme poverty have still accompanied its growth over the past two decades. While poverty has been reduced, hundreds of millions are still extremely poor in India, living on less than a dollar a day. Scholars debate why extreme poverty persists in the country, with many stressing more growth as the remedy and others saying that only growth coupled with better governance, improved agricultural performance, and more effective investment in human capital will work (Sen 1999; Balakrishnan 2010).

As for the causes of the boom, a common argument is that the liberalization of the economy after 1991 was the key factor. This can certainly be supported by the timing of the boom, which began after the reforms had taken root, though critics could argue that the boom did not happen immediately following the reforms. Policy reform is not the only factor, however. Careful attention should be paid to the deeper historical origins of the contemporary Indian economy. In particular, the long emphasis on education under Nehru in such areas as science and technology has likely paid important dividends in subsequent decades as the beneficiaries of investments in education have entered the labour force (see Kohli 2004). The favourable international context has also mattered, including technological advances in telecommunications and information sharing that facilitated offshoring of service jobs to India's booming technology sector (Friedman 2005). In other words, while market reforms may have been a component of India's changing economic fortunes, the correlation between the two is not the same as proof of causation.

CASE STUDY

Chapter 16, Page 343

India in the 21st Century: Domestic Politics, Identity, and Security

In India, domestic and international politics are deeply intertwined. This is true on questions of security as well as in the economy. Especially important is the country's relationship with neighbouring Pakistan and how this reflects relations between Indians domestically. The challenge of India–Pakistan relations affects questions of nationhood, identity, violence, and government in India; in short, international relations affect almost everything addressed in the chapters of this book. On the flip side, India's domestic politics also affects its international relations. Comparative politics and international relations may be two subfields of political science, but they are not totally separable.

India's long and contested border with Pakistan is often called the "world's most dangerous border." It has been a source of conflict for more than 70 years. One of the most contentious points has long been the disputed region of Kashmir, which is claimed by Pakistan but is currently administered by India. The border between Pakistan and India is notoriously tense and is clouded by the prospect of nuclear standoff or even possible use of nuclear weapons. In 1998, Pakistan's testing of an atomic device resulted in India testing its own devices just days later; both tests were widely seen as provocative signals to the opposite country. Indeed, the development of nuclear weapons in Pakistan was fuelled in large measure by historical animosity toward India, which was a nuclear power as of the 1970s. Relations between the countries affect the domestic politics of each in many ways. For example, the very question of Indian nationhood and identity, the political party system, and the resulting policy-making in the Indian parliament have been affected by the question of Islam and the resulting rise of Hindu nationalist sentiment. This was at the origin of some of the popularity of the Hindu nationalist BJP, which governed from 1998 to 2004 and has since 2014, though the party addresses issues other than Hindu nationalism. India has an estimated 160 million Muslims, which is a minority of the country's population but still represents more than 10 per cent of the world's Muslims and the third-largest Muslim population in the world, after Indonesia and Pakistan (Pew Forum 2009).

Research Prompts

1. As a low-income democracy, India is seen as a "deviant case" for modernization theory when it comes to democratization. What comparative analyses could you set up to test hypotheses about the reasons behind India's democratic success? Would you prefer another low-income democracy elsewhere, such as Ghana in Africa? Or a low-income country neighbouring India that shares a region and some history but is not democratic, such as Pakistan? What would be the merits of your research design?

2. Do a brief search of the literature to find two or more states of India to compare on the question of economic development. What do you find are some of the main factors that emerge to account for why certain states have done better or worse than others?
3. India has developed economically at a much faster rate since making economic reforms beginning in 1991. What is the best argument you can make that India's economic boom of the past two decades has been based on something *other than* this set of reforms? What is the evidence you have to make this other claim?
4. If relations between India and Pakistan are deeply rooted in identity issues and history, what are the implications for policy-making that might contribute to peace going forward? Are there any factors that can be changed (unlike the demographics and history of the countries) that can contribute to a more optimistic outcome?

Online Case Studies

Go to **www.oup.com/he/DickovickCe** to find more case studies online, including:

- Democracy's Success in India
- Ethnicity and Political Parties in India
- Federalism and Differences in Development in India

Note

1 Davis 2000, 7.

Iran

PROFILE

Key Features of Contemporary Iran

Population:	82,021,564 (July 2017 est.)
Area:	1,648,195 square kilometres
Head of State:	Ali Hosseini Khamenei (Supreme Leader, 1989–present)
Head of Government:	Hassan Rouhani (president, 2013–present)
Capital:	Tehran
Year of Independence:	The Islamic Republic was founded in 1979, but Iran was never fully colonized and had been a distinct geopolitical entity in a variety of forms for centuries.
Year of Current Constitution:	1979
Languages:	Persian is the majority language. Other important languages include Turkic, Azeri, Kurdish, and Luri, among others.
GDP per Capita:	$5,415.20 (World Bank estimate 2017)
Human Development Index Ranking (2015):	69th (high human development)
Trading Relationship with Canada (2016):	• Imports $11,936,210,216 • Exports $35,163,818 https://globaledge.msu.edu/countries/canada/tradestats

Sources: *CIA World Factbook*; World Bank World Development Indicators; United Nations *Human Development Report 2016*

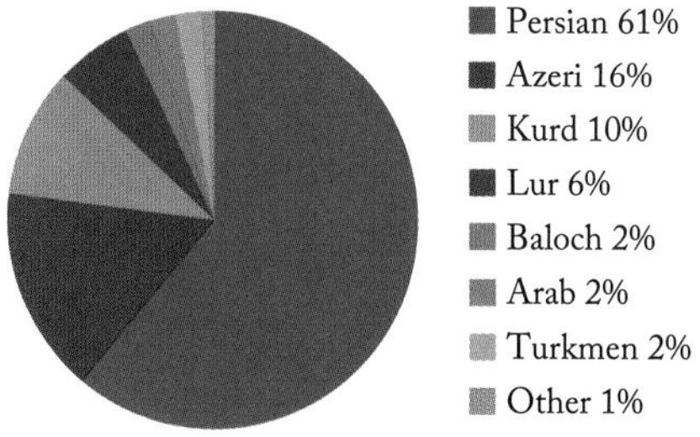

Ethnic Groups in Iran

Source: *CIA World Factbook*

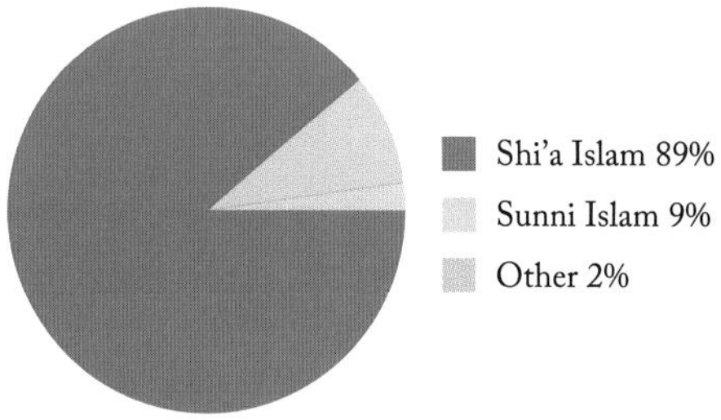

Religious Affiliation in Iran

Source: *CIA World Factbook*

Introduction

Iran is of interest to many political analysts because of its revolutionary regime and because of its foreign policy. In 1979, Iran witnessed a revolution against an authoritarian regime backed by the United States, yielding a strongly religious, anti-American regime. The United States has backed authoritarian governments in other Islamic societies in an effort to prevent governments like that in Iran from taking power there. Much attention has been focused on explaining contemporary Iranian politics. Iran has also been in the headlines for its nuclear ambitions and its conflict with the United States. In 2015, the "Iran Nuclear Deal" was reached between the Iranian government and the five permanent members of the UN Security Council plus Germany. Iran would stop its nuclear enrichment program in return for

KAZAKHSTAN
UZBEKISTAN
GEORGIA
AZERBAIJAN
ARMENIA
Caspian Sea
TURKMENISTAN
Tabriz
Now Shahr
Tehran
Mashhad
Kermanshah
Qom
IRAN
AFGHANISTAN
IRAQ
Esfahan
Birjand
Dezful
Yazd
Ahvaz
Abadan
Shiraz
Kerman
KUWAIT
Zahedan
Bushehr
SAUDI ARABIA
Asaluyeh
Bandar Abbas
PAKISTAN
Persian Gulf
Chabahar
QATAR
Gulf of Oman
U.A.E.
OMAN
0 110 220 Kilometers
0 110 220 Miles

an end to nuclear-based economic sanctions. However, US President Donald Trump decided in mid-2018 to unilaterally halt the agreement against the advice of European allies and most American policy-makers. This has meant that the Iranian situation is now more complex and more volatile than before.

The "revolutionary" character of the regime is itself a source of considerable interest. While in some respects the Iranian revolution resembled other major revolutions, it differed from many in that it did not clearly lean toward the political left, though some elements in the revolutionary coalition did (Parsa 2000; Kurzman 2004; Salehi-Isfahani 2009, 32–3). Indeed, it is hard to place the Iranian revolution in ideological terms. In certain respects, it is very conservative, and it often is described as such. Yet secular Marxists were part of the revolutionary coalition that helped to bring down the Shah, and even today there are features of the Iranian government that are left-leaning. As well, aspects of the government structure were modelled on the French republican system.

Historical Development

Iran has a long and fascinating history, dating back to the great Persian Empire (and earlier). Here we are interested in its contemporary history, which means that we need to begin with the 20th century. Our goal is to understand how Iran developed such that the Islamic Revolution could take place in 1979.

It is critical to understand that while Iran had not been formally colonized, it had been at the mercy of two imperial powers, Great Britain and Russia (and later the Soviet Union), for some years (Hambly [1991] 2008a; [1991] 2008b). This weakened the Qajar Dynasty, which had held power since 1795 in a monarchical system. Iran was largely a traditional religious society in which Shari'a law was practised and the clergy exercised some state-like functions (Keddie [1991] 2008, 179), but Western-derived ideas of nationalism and modernization had begun to seep into the country by the late 19th century (Moaddel 2005). In 1905–6, contentious action forced the Qajar to adopt a constitutional monarchy (Keddie [1991] 2008, 202–3). This is not to say that the Qajar regime was happy about such a development (Keddie [1991] 2008, 205–7), and the Shah in 1908 attempted to circumvent constitutionality but was forced from office. He would make a failed attempt to re-establish his authority two years later. The turn to constitutional monarchy did not, however, make the British and Russians any less likely to intervene in Iran, and in 1907 at the Anglo-Russian Convention they had essentially agreed to divide the country into zones where one or the other power would exert predominant influence (Keddie [1991] 2008, 205).

In 1921, Reza Khan helped to organize a coup d'état, with Sayyid Ziya al-Din Tabatabai emerging as prime minister and Reza Khan as minister of war (Keddie [1991] 2008, 210–12; Hambly [1991] 2008b, 219–21). Reza Khan would become prime minister himself in 1923 and then, in 1925, become the country's monarch (Hambly 2008b, 224–5), as Reza Shah Pahlavi, inaugurating the Pahlavi Dynasty, which would last until 1979. Reza Shah, like his son and successor, Mohammad Reza Shah (often referred to simply as "the Shah"), was secular, Westernizing, and modernizing in orientation. Notable projects included the establishment of a Western-style legal system, the expansion of the state bureaucracy, and the creation of the Trans-Iranian Railway. Reza Shah also tried to force his subjects to wear Western clothing, among other symbolic mandates (Hambly [1991] 2008b, 225–6, 230–2).

The Shah established close ties with Germany in the 1930s (Hambly [1991] 2008b, 241–3). During the Second World War, he attempted to maintain formal neutrality, but the Allies would not accept this, in part because they wanted to use the Trans-Iranian Railway to send supplies to Russia. As a result, Soviet and British troops occupied the country, and in 1941 the Shah resigned. This placed his son, Mohammad Reza Shah, on the throne. After some years, the Shah would be known as a strongly authoritarian ruler who used systematic violence to quell opposition.

A crisis would develop in the early 1950s after Mohammad Mosaddeq became prime minister (Hambly [1991] 2008a, 251–63). Mosaddeq, among other things, sought to nationalize Iran's oil industry (as had been done, for example, by Mexico with its own some years earlier). A coup d'état was launched, with support from both the United Kingdom and the United States, which wanted to ensure continued Western control over Iranian natural resources (Keddie [1991] 2008). There is no telling what would have happened had foreign intervention not brought down this government (Hambly [1991] 2008a, 254), but it is conceivable that Mosaddeq could have built on successful nationalization to expand Iranian democratization. In any case, this was not to be, and the Shah's authoritarian government negotiated generous terms for multinationals involved in the extraction of Iranian oil such that nationalization would not dramatically impinge on the interests of the oil companies (Hambly [1991] 2008a, 265).

Historical Development Timeline

1795–1925	Qajar Dynasty.
1906	Constitutional monarchy established after the "Constitutional Revolution."
1907	Anglo-Russian Convention, used to justify English and Russian spheres of influence within Iran and periodic intervention.
1908	Mohammad Ali Shah tries to undo the constitutional order but is forced from power.
1919	Anglo-Iranian Agreement, never implemented, but upon becoming public generates considerable discontent.
1921	Reza Khan becomes minister of war after helping to bring a coup that places Sayyid Ziya al-Din Tabatabai as prime minister (still under the Qajar Dynasty).
1923	Reza Khan (later to be Reza Shah) becomes prime minister.
1923	Ahmad Shah leaves the country, showing Qajar Dynasty's weakness.
1923	Major political reforms.
1925	Reza Shah Pahlavi becomes monarch (beginning of Pahlavi Dynasty).
1925–6	Establishment of European-style legal system.
1938	Completion of Trans-Iranian Railway.
1941	Reza Shah resigns following the country's occupation by the United Kingdom and the Soviet Union (part of World War II), leaving Mohammed Reza Shah in power.
1942	Formal alliance is formed between Iran, the United Kingdom, and the Soviet Union in the struggle against the Nazis.
1944	Death of Reza Shah.
1951–3	Tumultuous period in which the elected government of Mohammad Mosaddeq holds power, including efforts to nationalize the Iranian oil industry.
1953	Coup d'état, with backing from Britain and the United States, brings down the Mosaddeq government.
1954	Settlement of the oil industry question, with favourable terms for multinational corporations
1963	The "White Revolution" is announced and includes a number of reforms such as agrarian reform and women's suffrage.
1963	Exile of Ayatollah Khomeini
1973	Spike in global oil prices benefits Iran in the short term.
1978–9	Increasing social conflict, Iranian Revolution, and the return of Ayatollah Khomeini; the Shah departs Iran.
1979	Foundation of Islamic Republic; by the end of the year religious leaders come to dominate, and a new constitution is passed.
1979	Beginning of Iranian hostage crisis.
1980	Abolhassan Bani Sadr is elected as president but is impeached the following year.
1980–9	Iran–Iraq War.
1981	Release of American hostages shortly after Ronald Reagan takes office.
1981	Bani Sadr forced from power by Khomeini, further cementing the position of religious leaders in the revolutionary regime.
1981	Mohammad-Ali Rajai elected president but is killed within a month; Ali Khamenei, future Supreme Leader, assumes the presidency.
1988	Iran Air flight 655 is shot down accidentally by the United States, killing 290 passengers and crew members.
1989	Death of Ayatollah Khomeini; rise of Ayatollah Khamenei; election of Akbar Hashemi Rafsanjani to the presidency.
1997	Election of Mohammad Khatami to the presidency (perceived as more liberal, raising hopes of reform in both Iran and the West).
2005	Election of Mahmoud Ahmadinejad to the presidency (perceived as a hardliner, dampening hopes for reform).
2009	Ahmadinejad's re-election, apparently fraudulent, provokes major protests.
2013	Hassan Rouhani is elected president.
2015	Iran signs a Joint Comprehensive Plan of Action with the United States, China, Russia, France, Great Britain, and Germany to halt its nuclear enrichment program in return for an end to nuclear-related sanctions.
2017	Rouhani wins re-election with 57 per cent of the popular vote.
2018	The Trump administration unilaterally pulls out of the plan and threatens to punish European and other countries that do business in Iran.
2019	US-imposed sanctions cripple the Iranian economy, causing it to contract by 6 per cent.

The Shah's regime was an authoritarian developmentalist state (Foran 2005, 75–81). Mohammad Reza Shah, in a series of economic plans, aimed to continue the process of industrialization and modernization that had been started under his father, using oil revenues as a principal source of funding. In this he was fairly successful: Iran modernized somewhat rapidly, built a notable middle class with a cosmopolitan orientation, and established a notable higher education infrastructure. In political terms, the Shah was regressive, though he was willing to make reforms when he thought this would enhance his position. Thus the "White Revolution" of 1963 distributed land, extended suffrage (most notably to women), and made a number of other reforms (Hambly [1991] 2008a, 279–83). This should not be understood as purely benevolent largesse, however: The Shah faced civil discontent and protests, and his "White Revolution" was accompanied by efforts to repress his critics. For example, the Ayatollah Khomeini, a prominent cleric, was forced to leave the country in 1963. More generally, the Shah's state was highly repressive, and the security forces (the SAVAK) were notorious for torturing and murdering dissidents (Foran 2005, 77; Hambly [1991] 2008a, 290–1). It is worth further emphasizing that this regime was supported by Western powers like the United Kingdom and the United States, largely because of Cold War concerns.

The revolution took many by surprise. In 1978 and 1979, actors demanding change spanned the political spectrum and the religious–secular divide: It was by no means obvious that a conservative religious regime would emerge victorious from the Iranian Revolution, at least initially, though it is also clear that the religious component of the revolution was absolutely central to its success, since Khomeini was the one actor who seemed capable of unifying diverse revolutionary elements (Arjomand 2009). Secular Marxists were important in the opposition to the Shah's regime, and over time the middle class got on board as well. As often happens in revolutions, various groups likely felt that they would be able to control the process, and the secular allies of the clergy undoubtedly did not envision the regime that emerged. The clergy's consolidation of their power only took place over the first couple of years of the regime. Even in the constitutional order that was established, which places ultimate authority with the clergy, some democratic forms are present, with regular elections held for the presidency and the parliament.

During the post-revolutionary era, we could divide Iranian presidential politics into five main periods. The first is the instability of the early years. The second is the period of Khamenei's presidency, during which clerical authority was consolidated and the war with Iraq took place. The third is the period of Rafsanjani's presidency, after 1989, during which, as Arjomand notes (2009, 7), the system of "dual leadership" between the Supreme Leader and the president fully developed. Rafsanjani's presidency is also notable for efforts to rebuild the Iranian economy, which included some capitalist reforms. The fourth period encompasses Mohammad Khatami's reformist presidency beginning in 1997, which raised hopes for many that the regime would liberalize. Finally, the 2005 election of Mahmoud Ahmadinejad opened a period of conservative retrenchment.

Some expected that revolutionary Iran would not last, particularly given the international pressures that it faced, including the Iran–Iraq War (1980–9), but also the country's relative diplomatic isolation. Yet the regime consolidated its control, and it has remained in power since. The transition after Khomeini's death in 1989 was particularly important. Arjomand (2009) describes what followed, in the language of Max Weber, as the "routinization" or "institutionalization" of the "charismatic authority" of Khomeini, meaning that the revolution had to face the classic problem of going on without its mystical leader and turning the revolution into something that did not depend on that leader. Major constitutional reforms removed the office of prime minister, making the system more presidentialist, and in many ways the reforms also solidified the clergy's power and authority. Sayyed Ali Khamenei took over as the new Supreme Leader, a post he still holds. With the election of the relatively liberal Mohammad Khatami in 1997, some observers both in Iran and abroad felt that the regime might be opening to greater democratization, but these hopes were dashed after the election of Ahmadinejad in 2005. Ahmadinejad was both a hardliner *and* a populist whose demagoguery appealed to many of Iran's worse-off. Just the same, he faced opposition, and his re-election in 2009 was denounced by many as fraudulent. This led to major protests against the regime in the so-called "Green Revolution," supported by many prominent former leaders. Again, it seemed for a time that the regime might need to make major concessions, but the use of force brought the protests to a halt. Some have seen the 2017 re-election of Hassan Rouhani as signalling a loosening of some restrictions within the state. Rouhani is seen as a reformist within the Iranian context, especially in terms of economic openness to Western countries (Takeyh 2017).

Regime and Political Institutions

Iran's policy-making process is very complex, since both elected and non-elected officials play major roles in setting policy. The regime has a dual nature, with the elected features of a republic mixing with the institutions of theocratic rule by Muslim clerics. On one hand, Iran is a presidential system with a popularly elected president who governs with the cabinet. The parliament, known as the Majlis, is elected, and it exerts some checks on presidential power. However, another important policy-making body is the Guardian Council, a group of 12 clerics who have a range of important powers. They can approve or reject candidates for the presidency, for parliament, and for ministerial positions. They can also veto legislation made by the Majlis if they deem it does not fit with Islamic law or the Iranian constitution. Finally, the Supreme Leader is perhaps the central figure in Iranian politics. He too is a cleric (a high-ranking *ayatollah*), and he appoints half of the members of the Guardian Council as well as the head of the judiciary; the Supreme Leader also indirectly controls who is eligible for the other six posts in the Guardian Council, since the head of the judiciary nominates them for consideration by the Majlis. The Supreme Leader, not the president, has authority over the military. Moreover, the Supreme Leader must officially affirm the election of the president. Many commentators thus conclude that power lies ultimately with the clergy and not with the more "democratic" bodies in Iran, though these elected bodies are not mere puppets. Finally, there are additional consultative bodies in Iran: an Expediency Council advises the Supreme Leader, and an Assembly of Experts is empowered to elect the Supreme Leader after his predecessor dies, resigns, or is incapacitated; the Assembly of Experts is nominally empowered to review the Supreme Leader but has not done so in practice, perhaps in part because its composition is indirectly controlled by the Supreme Leader. These arrangements are discussed in more detail in one of the case studies that follow.

Political Economy

One of the most striking features of the Iranian Revolution and its aftermath is the damage that was done to the economy. Economic growth dropped dramatically in the years after 1979, with GDP per capita dropping by 50 per cent over the revolutionary regime's first decade before gradually recovering to around pre-revolutionary levels (Salehi-Isfahani 2009, 6–7). Part of this has to do with the fact that Iran is a major oil producer and the international oil market hit all oil exporters hard in the 1980s, with lower commodity prices in general contributing to the debt woes of much of the developing world in that period. As Salehi-Isfahani notes (2009, 7), bad policy and the long-standing war with Iraq also played major roles in the country's poor economic performance in this period. Not surprisingly, when Hashemi-Rafsanjani was elected in 1989, he embarked on economic reforms (Arjomand 2009, 56–8), including

Regime and Political Institutions

Regime	Theocratic state but with some features of presidential and parliamentary democracy
Administrative Divisions	Unitary state; 30 provinces + capital province of Tehran
Executive Branch	President and cabinet, but with a number of executive functions held by the Supreme Leader (non-elected) and the Guardian Council
Selection of Executive	Election from within a set of candidates approved by the Guardian Council
Legislative Branch	Elected parliament, called the Majlis. The Guardian Council can veto legislation.
Judicial Branch	Politicized judiciary controlled by religious conservatives, with Islamic law the basis of the system. Supreme Court and Judicial High Council are top bodies.
Political Party System	Multiparty system but with restrictions

privatization of some enterprises—though these moves were minimal, and public sector employment remained high—and changes made to financial markets. Economic performance in the 1990s was mixed, but with the oil boom of the 2000s Iran achieved notable growth and accompanying improvements in well-being (Salehi-Isfahani 2009, 8).

The most important problem that Iran faces, like that of other oil producers, is managing to achieve sustainable growth while easing its own dependence on oil. Iran was the world's third-largest oil exporter until recently, producing more than 4 million barrels per day and exporting more than 2.5 million (*CIA World Factbook*). However, this changed dramatically after 2011 when the United States and European countries placed sanctions on Iran for the country's continued efforts to develop a nuclear program. This move disrupted and slowed Iranian production, and the country's exports fell by one-half. Iran's dependence on oil is such that petroleum accounts for 60 per cent of exports (*CIA World Factbook*).

For the oil that stays in the country, the government has provided massive subsidies for energy consumption that were declared to be in the range of $100 billion per year up to 2010. These subsidies amounted to more than $1000 per person, which is estimated by the International Monetary Fund to be greater than the average income in many households. The country's oil dependence is visible if we look at various economic sectors' share of GDP: As of 2017, agriculture stands at 9.8 per cent, with services at 54 per cent and industry at about 36 per cent, of which a notable share is oil-related (*CIA World Factbook*). In addition to the problem of oil dependence and questions of the "resource curse" discussed in the Nigeria case, Iran's broader economy was damaged by sanctions. The economy began to grow again under the nuclear agreement but is facing a serious threat after President Trump's actions, which some even thought could bring about the end of the regime. Some Trump administration advisors even predicted that Iran's daily oil exports could be reduced by as much as 1 million barrels per day (Lowry 2018).

CASE STUDIES

CASE STUDY

Chapter 5, Page 99

Gender in Post-revolutionary Iranian Politics

Iranian society is notorious for gender inequality. It was hardly an egalitarian society before the 1979 revolution, and for most of the post-revolutionary period, religious elites have favoured policies and views that many would consider discriminatory. The consequence and legacies of this show up clearly in the quantitative data. In terms of women's political representation in the legislature, Iran is near the bottom, with only six seats in the Majlis (5.9 per cent) held by women (World Bank). Women in 2018 constituted only 16 per cent of the workforce, and their unemployment rate was twice that of men. Women are required to have a male guardian's permission to marry and their husband's permission to obtain a passport (World Bank).

The World Economic Forum's Gender Gap Index in 2017 ranked Iran 140th (out of 144). The country scores particularly badly in terms of "economic participation and opportunity" and "political empowerment." Iran's performance in terms of gender equality/inequality in the areas of "educational attainment" and "health and survival"—the other main components of the index—are also very poor, most of them close to the bottom of the world rankings (World Economic Forum).

At the same time, some scholars have argued that the picture is more complicated than these data suggest. Ziba Mir-Hosseini (1999) has argued that in some areas, women's participation in public life has improved, notably in the educational system and particularly in universities. Mir-Hosseini (1999, 7) points out that this may even be a function of religious traditionalism in a certain sense, since "the enforcement of hejab became a catalyst . . . by making public space morally correct in the eyes of traditionalist families, it legitimated women's public presence." In recent years, females are near parity with males in terms of primary and secondary educational enrolment, and women's enrolment in tertiary education *exceeds* that of men (Hausmann et al. 2010, 165).

Few would argue that the post-revolutionary regime in Iran is a feminist one. However, scholars remind us that beneath repressive surfaces, women and others work to expand women's rights in even the most difficult of circumstances.

CASE STUDY

Chapter 7, Page 134

Democratic Features of Authoritarian Systems? The Case of Iran

We saw in Chapter 6 that democracy and democratization are "moving targets" in the sense that standards and critical thresholds for democratic practice change over time. While few commentators would regard the current Iranian regime as *democratic*, it has some clear democratic *features*, and it is possible to argue that it is as democratic as the dictatorship of the Shah that preceded it. Iran does have an elected president and an elected legislature, the Majlis. Religious leadership can restrict individuals from running for these positions (and from serving in the cabinet as well), and it does so with regularity. However, Iranian voters are nevertheless often faced with real choices in these elections. The reform movement associated with Mohammad Khatami, elected in 1997, gives clear indication of this, as does the shift that came with Mahmoud Ahmadinejad's election in 2005. However, subsequent events make clear that not only do existing institutions work to limit and even exclude change but that institutional norms can be violated if necessary to preserve the status quo. Widespread perceptions of fraud in the 2009 re-election of Ahmadinejad led to protests that the regime quelled with violence.

Voters also have the ability to indirectly shape clerical rule. This is done through two institutional mechanisms. First, the elected Majlis can exert some influence over who is appointed to the Guardian Council. Second, the Assembly of Experts is actually an elected body. However, there is a catch. Only clergy can run in elections for this assembly. Just the same, the electorate can indirectly exert *some* influence through this mechanism. Of course, complex systems of indirect influence produce collective action problems for individuals seeking to make far-reaching changes.

Traditional religious regimes have historically insisted that sovereignty was divine and thus could only be discerned or exercised by religiously legitimated authorities. Most modern democratic states—even constitutional monarchies—tend to view sovereignty as vested in the people (this change owed greatly to the global spread of national identity). The institutional structure of the Iranian state, though, seems to imply a sort of dual sovereignty of the people and a deity, with the latter (whose will, again, can only be discerned by religious elites) exerting ultimate authority. This set of arrangements is itself a function of the conflictual nature of the process that produced the current regime. Some clerical actors were and are proponents of theocracy. Some other actors are proponents of popular sovereignty. The result is a sort of hybrid.

Many other states had historical periods in which sovereignty was blurred in this way. Prominent examples might be England in the 17th century and Japan after the Meiji Restoration, among many others. This could be taken to give optimism to those who hope for a more democratic Iran. However, we should not assume without further evidence that mixed sovereignty is a stage on a progressive, linear development. The fact that popular sovereignty and fully constitutional governance came to triumph in much of the world does not mean this will necessarily take place in Iran. In the meantime, we can only conclude, with Arjomand (2009, 6), that "theocratic government, participatory democracy, and populist social justice" exist in tension in Iran's post-revolutionary regime.

CASE STUDY

Chapter 16, Page 343

Iran and the Politics of Nuclear Proliferation

Iran has been in heated diplomatic conflict for years with many Western countries over its "nuclear ambitions" and its apparent desire to develop a nuclear weapon. One leading American concern is that Iran will target its regional neighbour Israel, which already has nuclear weapons.

For those hoping to prevent nuclear proliferation, one of the central challenges is preventing new countries from attaining nuclear weapons when they may have real incentives to develop them. Why would a country wish to have nuclear weapons? One simple answer of long standing in international relations theory is that the country thinks it will be more secure with nuclear weapons than it is without them. Applied to the case of Iran, it may believe it can deter an American or Israeli attack if it has a nuclear weapon it can use in retaliation. There may also be domestic reasons for building nuclear weapons, such as if the public, the military, and the energy industry push for it, for example (Sagan 1996). In normative terms, those seeking nuclear technology also note a double standard among those who have nuclear weapons yet seek to deny others the right to develop them.

The 2015 agreement seemed to be working well for Iran as well as the other six countries involved in the process. This was until President Trump decided to back out of the agreement. He argued that the deal was empowering Iran and endangering Israel, and he also disliked it because it was a centrepiece of Barack Obama's foreign policy legacy. The resolution of the Iranian nuclear issue is now increasingly uncertain, but the Iranian government as well as the Europeans and the Chinese leadership appear interested in continuing to work together. The United States remains the primary obstacle to any resolution of the problem, and as long as the administration remains convinced they can topple the Iranian regime, the problem will be hard to resolve.

Research Prompts

1. Do some background reading on the Iranian Revolution and on Egypt, and compare Iranian society in politics on the eve of the revolution to the society and politics of Egypt in the same period. Can you come up with a theory of why a revolution took place in Iran but not in Egypt at that time? How might you go about testing your theory? Now bring Turkey into the mix.
2. Compare the "Green Revolution" in Iran to the Arab Spring movements discussed in the "Thinking Comparatively" section at the end of Chapter 12. How does this case fit into the comparative framework discussed there?
3. Chapter 6 on democracy and regimes discusses the conceptualization of democracy and democratization at great length. As discussed here, Iran is a complex case in this connection. To what extent do you judge contemporary Iran to be a democratic society? What does Iran suggest about the general relationship between authoritarianism and democracy in modern societies?
4. The Trump administration has discussed the possibility of regime collapse in Iran. Would an end to the theocratic regime lead to a more pro-American type of government, or is the reverse more likely to be true? Based on your reading of events, how likely is regime collapse?

Online Case Studies

Go to **www.oup.com/he/DickovickCe** to find more case studies online, including:

- Constitutional Design: Theocracy in Iran
- Iran's Islamic Revolution and "Green Revolution"?
- Religion and Politics in Iran

Japan

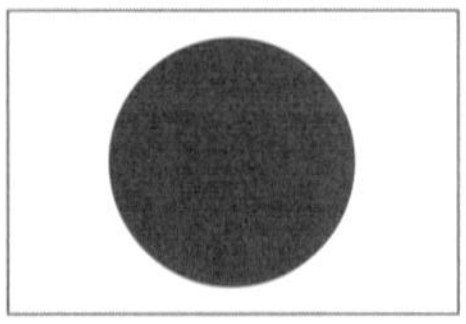

PROFILE

Key Features of Contemporary Japan

Population:	126,451,398 (July 2017 est.)
Area:	377,915 square kilometres
Head of State:	Emperor Kōtaishi Naruhito Shinnō (2019–present)
Head of Government:	Shinzo Abe (prime minister, 2012–present)
Capital:	Tokyo
Year of Independence:	Never formally colonized, though occupied by the Allies from 1945 to 1952
Year of Current Constitution:	1947
Languages:	Japanese
GDP per Capita:	$38,428.10 (World Bank estimate 2017)
Human Development Index Ranking (2015):	17th (very high human development)
Trading Relationship with Canada (2016):	• Imports $11,936,210,216 • Exports $8,089,163,101 https://globaledge.msu.edu/countries/canada/tradestats

Sources: *CIA World Factbook*; World Bank World Development Indicators; United Nations *Human Development Report 2016*

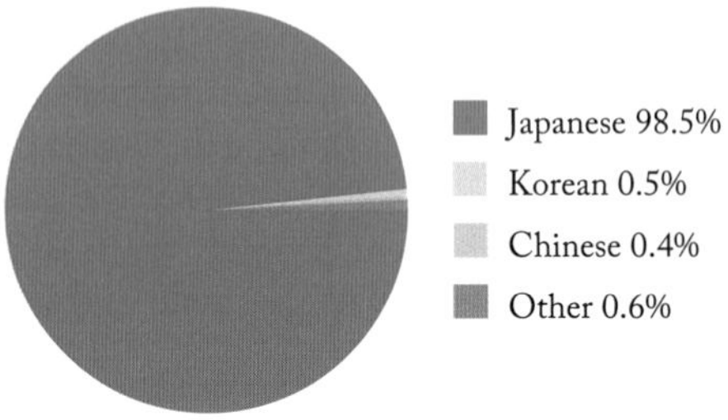

Ethnic Groups in Japan

Source: *CIA World Factbook*

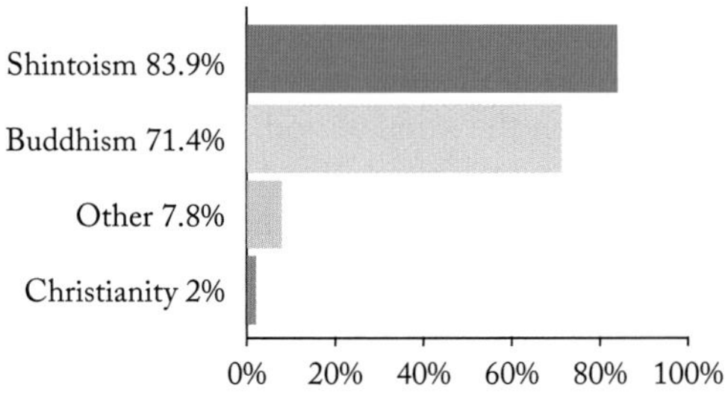

Religious Affiliation in Japan

Note that according to these data, the majority of the Japanese population adheres to both Shintoism and Buddhism, exceeding 100 per cent.

Source: *CIA World Factbook*

Introduction

Japan has long been a country of interest to comparative political analysts working on modernization processes. This is because Japan was, in many ways, the first non-Western society to "modernize" in the sense of developing a growth-oriented, industrial economy, a modern state, a modern national identity, and a system of social stratification based predominantly on economic class rather than ascriptive status-group membership. Japan's culture had been largely insular—as a matter of official policy—for several centuries until the middle of the 19th century. However, in the closing decades of the 19th century and throughout the first part of the 20th century, it achieved dramatic social transformation, becoming a modern state and then an empire almost overnight. Scholars have long been intrigued by this pattern. On one hand, it is intrinsically interesting from an intellectual point of view. On the other hand, many have hoped that Japan would hold the key to development that other nations could follow. Indeed, many of the "Asian Tigers" that achieved economic modernization took several pages from Japan's playbook.

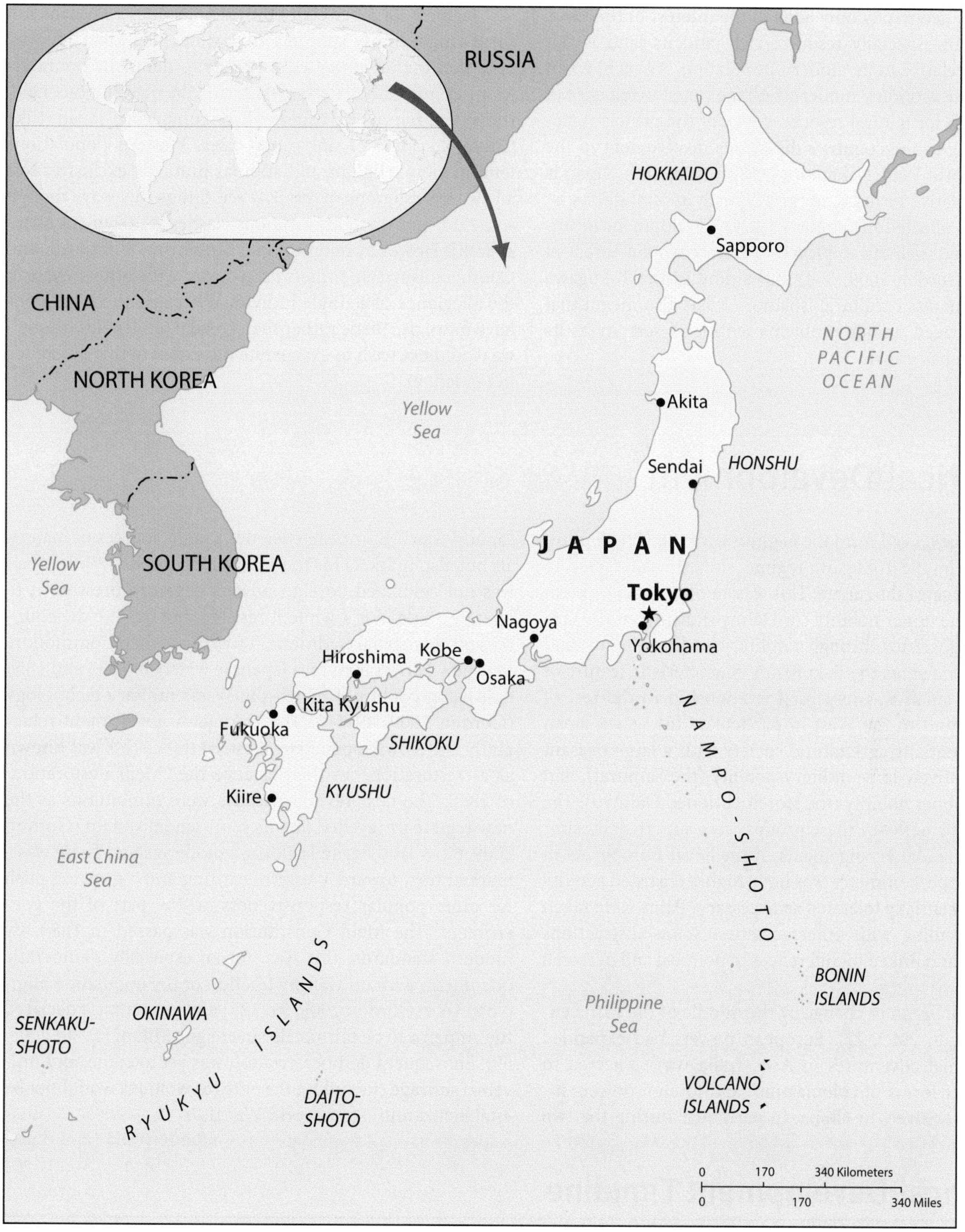
RUSSIA
CHINA
NORTH KOREA
SOUTH KOREA
Yellow Sea
Yellow Sea
HOKKAIDO
Sapporo
NORTH PACIFIC OCEAN
Akita
Sendai
HONSHU
JAPAN
Tokyo
Yokohama
Nagoya
Kobe
Osaka
Hiroshima
Kita Kyushu
Fukuoka
SHIKOKU
KYUSHU
Kiire
NAMPO-SHOTO
East China Sea
RYUKYU ISLANDS
OKINAWA
SENKAKU-SHOTO
DAITO-SHOTO
Philippine Sea
BONIN ISLANDS
VOLCANO ISLANDS
0 170 340 Kilometers
0 170 340 Miles

Japan's geography only adds to the interest of this case. Japan is not especially resource-rich, and its land is not abundant relative to its modern population. As such, when the Japanese economy modernized, the state looked abroad in its search for natural resources, one of the principal factors leading to the country's disastrous involvement in the Second World War (Nakamura [1988] 2008, 485). Japan is small in relative terms, a series of mostly mountainous islands. This affected the country's early development in important ways, helping to protect it from constant threat of invasion (Gordon 2009, 3–4) and aiding in the Tokugawa efforts to maintain cultural isolation. It has also meant that Japan has faced unique problems with land scarcity as its population has grown.

Japan is 98.5 per cent ethnically Japanese. Perhaps not surprisingly, most students of Japanese national identity note that the Japanese nation tends to define its boundaries in ethnic rather than civic terms. In the religious field, some caution is in order when comparing Japan (like China) to some of our other cases. Western populations tend to view religious affiliation as mutually exclusive. Not all eastern religions *necessarily* see things this way (though some do, and there are religious clashes in Asian countries as well). However, religions like Buddhism, Shintoism, and Confucianism can sometimes coexist with others even in the allegiance of a single individual because these religions have more ritualistic rather than creedal tendencies (though we would not wish to exaggerate the extent of this difference in tendency).

Historical Development

Japan was governed from the beginning of the 17th century until 1868 by the Tokugawa regime, sometimes referred to as the Tokugawa shogunate. This was an oligarchical system in which the upper nobility (or Daimyo) displaced the emperor and governed through a military leader (shogun) and his state (known as the Bakufu). A characteristic feature of Tokugawa Japan was its closed relationship to the rest of the world and to the West in particular. Tokugawa Japan was an essentially agricultural society with a large peasant class, a relatively large military nobility (the Samurai), and a smaller upper nobility (the aforementioned Daimyo). The relationships between these groups were superficially similar to the feudal arrangements in medieval Europe. As in feudal Europe, commerce was not a highly regarded activity and was essentially tolerated as necessary: Pains were taken to avoid trading with other societies. Status distinctions were rigid and linked to differences in political and personal rights.

This all began to change by the middle of the 19th century (Gordon 2009, 22). European powers had expanded their colonial adventures in Asia. India was subjected to more direct forms of colonization, and foreign powers intervened decisively in China, in particular during the two "opium wars." European societies sought sources of materials but also markets for the sale of their goods. While Japan was not colonized, foreign powers began to pressure it to open to trade. For a while it resisted, but despite the country's proud martial traditions, it was clear when Commodore Matthew Perry sailed into Japanese waters in 1853 and 1854 that Japan could not match the West's military technology (Gordon 2009, 49–50). The Tokugawa government reluctantly and slowly opened to Western trade. This was known as a "restoration," in this instance the "Meiji Restoration" of 1868. The next several decades were tumultuous as the new regime unravelled Japan's semi-feudal system (Gordon 2009, 62–4) and began building a modern state. There was a marked turn toward Western learning and a growing push for more popular responsiveness on the part of the government. The Meiji Constitution was passed in 1889. By modern standards, this was not an especially democratic document, with only a tiny fraction of the population eligible to vote (Gordon 2009, 91, 125) and given that it declared the emperor to be ultimately sovereign (Mitani [1988] 2008, 59). Subsequent democratization was yet to come, and universal suffrage (including the vote for women) would not be established until after World War II.

Historical Development Timeline

1600–1868	Tokugawa regime.
1853	Commodore Perry (United States) arrives, demanding that Japan open itself to trade with the West.
1867–8	Meiji Restoration, which is ostensibly conservative but which will produce a program of modernization and Westernization.
1870–3	Major reforms.

1877	Satsuma revolt.
1889	Meiji Constitution, which establishes constitutional monarchy and limited parliamentary system.
1890	Elections held under the Meiji Constitution.
1894–5	Sino-Japanese War; Japan occupies Taiwan by 1895.
1904–5	Russo-Japanese War.
1910	Japan colonizes Korea, signifying expansionist phase of Japanese Empire.
1914–8	Japan is a combatant in the First World War, allied with Britain, France, the United States, and Russia.
1923	Japan suffers the deadliest earthquake in its history.
1931	Japan invades Manchuria on Chinese mainland, establishes Manchukuo government.
1937–41	Second Sino-Japanese War.
1941	Japanese bombing of Pearl Harbor begins Japan's involvement in the Second World War on the side of Axis powers Germany and Italy.
1941–5	War in the Pacific, with Japan fighting US and other Allies on islands and atolls and in regions from the Philippines to near Japanese coastline.
1945	The United States drops atomic bombs on Hiroshima and Nagasaki; Japan surrenders.
1947	Constitution of 1947 is proclaimed, re-establishing democracy and including women's suffrage.
1953–70s	"Japanese Miracle," a period of dramatic economic expansion.
1991–2001	Economic crisis and the "Lost Decade."
1993–4	LDP briefly loses power but remains the largest party in Diet; coalition government initiates electoral reforms.
1995	Aum Shinrikyo cult/terror organization releases deadly sarin gas in Tokyo subway; 13 people are killed, and many more are injured or incapacitated.
2009	LDP loses control of government as DPJ wins general election.
2011	Massive earthquake and resulting tsunami results in more than 15,000 deaths and reactor meltdowns at the Fukushima nuclear power plant.
2012	Shinzo Abe elected prime minister as LDP regains control of government.
2013	The International Olympic Committee chooses Tokyo to host the 2020 Olympics.
2014	Abe and the LDP win snap elections. The government earlier changed its security policies to allow Japanese defence forces to fight overseas.
2016	Two major earthquakes rock the island of Kyushu; 44 people die and at least 100,000 people are displaced.
2017	Abe and the LDP again win snap elections. Parliament passes legislation allowing Emperor Akihito to abdicate if he so chooses.
2018	Akihito sets the date of his abdication for 30 April 2019.
2019	Crown Prince Naruhito succeeds his father as emperor, becoming the 126th person to hold the position. The Reiwa (or "beautiful harmony") era begins.

Japan went through many striking changes in the period from the 1880s to the Second World War, modernizing its economy, society, and state. The country transformed its social structure by doing away with samurai status differences and built a modern state (Gordon 2009, 64–6). It also began to achieve rapid economic development (Crawcour 2008, 386–7) during and after the First World War. In the same period, from 1890 to 1910, Japan began to flex its military muscle outward in Asia. It first won a major war against China (1894–5) and claimed present-day Taiwan as a colony. It then won a war with Russia (1904–5) and later claimed Korea as colony (1910), among many other islands and territories. In a matter of decades, the country moved from being a predominantly agricultural society to being one of the world's major economic and military powers.

A distinguishing feature of this process was the strong role that the state played in allocating capital for productive use as it industrialized. The state owned or controlled many firms, and the state linked itself to private firms that received state assistance in accessing capital and in other ways (Crawcour 2008, 414). In some areas, like heavy industry, the state maintained its involvement for strategic reasons even though it took decades to achieve profitability (Crawcour 2008, 422, 435). The state also played an important role in the development of railways, Japanese shipping, and other infrastructural developments (Crawcour 2008, 393–9) as well as through creating a system of commercial law (Gordon 2009, 95), a factor that institutional economists would emphasize (e.g., North 1990). The Japanese economy took off during World War I because Japanese producers for export could take advantage of the disruption of existing supply chains to access markets. Economic historians consider Japanese economic performance to have been strong in relative terms throughout not just the 1920s but also the 1930s, though the country did experience frequent financial crises, and the effects of the Great Depression were notable (Nakamura [1988] 2008).

Japanese economic and military expansion took place under an increasingly aggressive, militaristic, and nationalistic regime. Japan invaded Manchuria on the Chinese mainland in 1931 and attempted to establish control of much of the Pacific in subsequent years. When World War II came about, Japan allied with Nazi Germany and fascist Italy. In 1941, Japan's attack on Pearl Harbor, Hawaii, brought the United States into the war. After more than three years of total war fought across the Pacific Ocean, American forces closed in on Japan and prepared for invasion. In 1945, however, American forces established air supremacy over Japan and firebombed Tokyo and other Japanese cities, leaving hundreds of thousands dead. President Harry Truman then authorized the dropping of two atomic bombs on the Japanese cities of Hiroshima and Nagasaki on 6 and 9 August 1945. Japan surrendered six days later.

After the tragedies of World War II, Japan began economic and political reconstruction under American-led Allied military occupation until 1952. A lasting impact of postwar reconstruction was the beginning of Japan's remarkable economic performance; it is estimated that the Japanese economy grew at the tremendous rate of almost 10 per cent per year between 1945 and 1973 (Kosai 2008, 494). Again, the state played a large role in the economy: The government strategically supported the redevelopment of the coal and steel industries, utilizing the so-called "priority production method" (Kosai 2008, 500–1). The state, in cooperation with private enterprise, later implemented "rationalization plans" for key industries (Kosai 2008, 516–18). Beginning in the early 1960s, the government relaxed regulations on foreign trade, which helped Japanese exports in their subsequent boom (Kosai 2008, 522–7).

Democratization progressed along with economic growth in the years during and after the Allied occupation, with a series of new constitutional guarantees in the constitution of 1947 (Fukui [1998] 2008, 156). This owed both to the occupation authorities insisting on democratization *and* to Japanese efforts. Japan's democratization over this period also may be due to the Japanese economic success of the postwar years: strong economic growth and the emergence and development of a middle class, which clearly took place in postwar Japan (Fukui [1998] 2008, 204), are associated with democratic consolidation. One lasting aspect of the peace was a constitutional commitment not to deploy its military overseas.

Postwar Japan became a democracy, albeit one with a notable limitation: It was dominated by a single party, the Liberal Democratic Party of Japan (LDP) for most of the postwar period. The LDP's hegemony is a bit more complex than it appears at first glance, and this was not simply a single-party system. During the early years after Allied occupation, a multiparty system developed, but by the 1960s the LDP had come to win majority governments consistently. Japan was still technically a pluralistic and competitive political environment, but the LDP managed to defeat its (socialist and other) opponents and to regularly win legislative majorities, thus not needing to form coalitions. Many commentators and citizens felt that this reduced responsiveness to citizen concerns. A system developed in which representatives established local ties and worked to enhance the interests of local constituencies, organized partially through exclusive sets of social networks called *koenkai* (Kabashima and Steel 2010, 3–4, 15–17). In Japan's system, voters voted for one individual within a district, but often multiple LDP candidates were running within the district. To differentiate themselves from other LDP candidates, politicians sometimes turned to personal networks and even corruption (Kabashima and Steel 2010, 15–17). This led to complex factionalism and divisions within the LDP. While the LDP exerted near hegemony for decades, they occasionally had to form coalition governments as well, and the Democratic Party of Japan (DJP) remained an electoral adversary.

Beginning in the late 1980s, it became clear that the LDP's grip on power was weakening, and it had to form coalitions to govern in the 1990s as many voters became disenchanted with parties more generally (LeBlanc 1999, 5). The party fell out of power briefly in 1993–4, though it remained the largest party in the Diet. During the 1990s, difficulties and frustrations mounted as the country experienced financial crisis and a prolonged period of stagnation. Some have suggested that this ended the implicit bargain in Japan's postwar democracy in which the LDP governments were continually returned to power in exchange for sustained economic growth.

Another factor in the LDP's long dominance was the fragmentation of the opposition, but this was finally overcome when the DJP took over the government after a resounding win in elections in 2009. From the point of view of some democratic theorists, alternation in power constitutes an advance because it suggests the possibility of increased pluralism and competition. In 2012, the LDP returned to power and again won elections in 2014 and 2017.

Regime and Political Institutions

Japan has a parliamentary system with a ceremonial emperor. The bicameral parliament has a lower chamber in which 300 of 480 seats are elected by district constituencies and the remaining seats are elected by proportional representation in different "blocks" or regions of the country. The upper chamber has most of its members elected in their respective prefectures, with a remainder voted in by proportional representation as well. The House of Representatives is the more powerful body, being able to overrule the House of Councillors on budget and finance matters and override the House of Councillors with a two-thirds majority on other matters. In the late 20th century, perhaps the most distinguishing feature of the policy-making process in Japan was the dominance of the LDP. Because of the extent of this dominance (Kabashima and Steel 2010, 15–17), the LDP did not need to be fully responsive to the wishes of the electorate. Rather, the state was a place in which political elites worked with the business community to manage Japanese economic performance. Following the rise of coalition governments, though, and accelerating through the DJP's recent successes, we *may* be seeing an increase in responsiveness to citizens (Kabashima and Steel 2010). On one hand, commentators note a decline in public trust of political parties. On the other hand, a number of population segments are involved in civil society. All else being equal, political activity among the citizenry and pluralist competition between parties could be expected to increase accountability.

Political Culture

Scholars interested in Japanese political (and economic) culture have emphasized a number of themes, but perhaps the most distinctive one is the allegedly collectivistic and egalitarian character of Japanese beliefs and practices (Kunio 2006), particularly with regard to their manifestation in Japanese *economic culture*. Japan has relatively low levels of income inequality (Kosai 2008, 512). Some assert that this might be partially due to the cultural foundations of business management in Japan. Yoshihara Kunio goes as far as to add alleged cultural orientations toward materialism, savings, high valuation of educational attainment, and a strong work ethic as key components of Japanese economic culture (2006, 83), even as he stresses the institutional dimensions of Japan's economic performance as well. It should be noted, however, that these low levels of inequality and high savings are most noteworthy in the postwar era and not as true for earlier periods.

Regime and Political Institutions

Regime	Constitutional monarchy (parliamentary democracy with ceremonial emperor)
Administrative Divisions	Centralized, unitary government; 47 prefectures
Executive Branch	Prime minister and cabinet
Selection of Executive	Selected by parliament, ceremonially appointed by emperor
Legislative Branch	Bicameral parliament (Diet) Lower chamber: House of Representatives Upper chamber: House of Councillors
Judicial Branch	The Japanese Supreme Court (which has 14 justices and one chief justice) is the ultimate judicial authority in the country.
Political Party System	Multiparty system. Dominated by the LDP for decades, though the DJP governed 2009–12; political environment is one of pluralistic competition, with the LDP and the DJP as the two strongest contenders.

Much has been made of Japanese corporate governance as a lens into Japanese culture. Japanese firms seem to differ from Western firms in key respects. Major Japanese industrial firms have relationships with their (especially male) employees that many define as paternalistic, providing extensive benefits and nearly guaranteeing lifetime employment for good conduct. The notion that all are part of a "team" or even a "family" is relatively strong. Within Japanese firms, one tends to see a strong sense of solidarity, while status differences are mitigated by cultural norms that discourage massive income inequality within the firm. In a typical corporation in the United States, the salaries of executives dwarf those of entry-level employees, but in Japan the ratio of executive to entry-level employee salaries tends to be notably lower.

Of course, this is not a perfect system. Relations between workers and management may be less conflictual than in many other countries, but labour has a relatively weak position vis-à-vis corporations: Workers have difficulty establishing industry-wide organizations and demanding change rather than pursuing institutionally structured negotiation. This was at least partially a product of the LDP's policy of reducing union strength (Manow 2001, 44). In addition, strong cultural norms of employment security and relative equity might affect the competitiveness of Japanese firms over the long haul. Moreover, the alleged collectivism and "team orientation" of Japanese firms may be a factor in the notably high rates of discrimination against women (including lack of equal participation in the benefits of employment and sexual harassment) that exists in Japanese workplaces. Finally, the culture of Japanese firms has sometimes been seen as a hindrance, requiring reform. The firms that developed in the early years of Japanese industrialization—the *zaibatsu*—were highly concentrated and monopolistic (Gordon 2009, 96–7). They would later be partially broken up in the postwar years, but large conglomerates known as *keiretsu* persisted, with an example being Mitsubishi. Centred around huge banks, they were an integral part of postwar industrialization, but they later came to symbolize the possibility of crony capitalism, with cozy relationships between economic and political elites.

Political Economy

Japan, as we have noted, was the first non-Western society to develop sustained economic growth, in many ways establishing a path that has been followed, with variations, by the so called Asian Tigers (e.g., South Korea, Singapore) and, more recently, even China. This it did, in part, through state coordination, by the state strategically favouring certain sectors and helping to coordinate the deployment of capital for productive purposes. The Japanese state had a history of working well with the large, industry-spanning corporations that were so important to Japanese growth in the 20th century (see Evans 1989).

Japan was one of the world's great economic success stories of the 20th century. While economic development picked up during the interwar period, it was especially following reconstruction and American occupation after World War II that Japan built major global enterprises and became an export powerhouse, with examples of leading firms including Toyota and Honda in the automobile industry and Sony and Toshiba in electronics. The tradition of strong growth slowed by the 1980s and went into crisis in the early 1990s. The causes of the crisis were complex, but they included an overheated real estate market that collapsed and serious problems spreading throughout the financial system (much like in the United States in 2008). The government responded very slowly and only "bailed out" the banking system toward the end of the decade. Japan's economy has never completely recovered.

In recent years, there has been considerable debate over the country's economic policy under Prime Minister Shinzo Abe. After nearly two decades of low growth, Abe promised a set of dramatic policies (commonly referred to as "Abenomics") to jumpstart the economy. These policies included increased government spending and loose monetary policy that lowers interest rates; it was hoped that this would encourage consumers to spend after many years of stagnation (and that this would helpfully raise prices after many years of price declines that had discouraged spending). Abe also promised structural reforms that would encourage easier hiring and firing, thereby making the labour market more flexible. Indicators have been mixed: The Japanese stock market more than doubled from the time Abe took office, but growth has been sluggish when compared to the growth of global GDP and the country's debt has continued to increase.

Despite some concerns about Japanese economic performance in recent years, the country's basic economic indicators are still sound. According to the *CIA World Factbook*, the country's unemployment rate stood at an enviable 2.9

per cent in 2017. (It should be noted that the unemployment rate is calculated on the basis of the number of people in the labour force as the denominator, so Japan's large elderly population that is out of the labour force may affect this number.) GDP per capita in PPP stood at $42,700, and in terms of human development indicators, Japan is among the global leaders. The Japanese economy accomplishes this while maintaining a level of income inequality substantially better than that found in the United States and comparable to that of the western European welfare states (though these states slightly outperform Japan in terms of this indicator). Its Gini level stood at 32.1 in 2013, making it comparable to many western European countries and giving it a markedly lower level of inequality than the United States.

Japan was famous for its manufacturing for export, which stood at the heart of the "Japanese Miracle" that ran from the 1950s to the 1970s, but today services are predominant, accounting for 69.3 per cent of GDP in 2017, with industry accounting for 29.7 per cent and agriculture at 1 per cent.

The economic indicators in this section are drawn from the CIA World Factbook.

CASE STUDIES

CASE STUDY

Chapter 5, Page 88

Gender Empowerment in Japan?

Historically, women's participation in Japanese politics has received little emphasis, both in popular discussion and in the academic literature, in part because of discrimination and in part because of the (male) elite-centredness of much work in political science (LeBlanc 1999). What scholars have uncovered has largely not been good. Japan stands out, when compared to its peers in terms of socio-economic development, for the relatively low political empowerment of women. For example, its Gender Inequality Index (GII) put Japan in 19th place globally according to 2017 data (United Nations Development Programme (UNDP) 2018). In terms of women's legislative representation, 9.3 per cent of elected representatives were women, a drop from a high of 11.3 per cent in 2010 (World Bank).

In 2017, the numbers were not encouraging, and the Inter-Parliamentary Union ranked Japan 158th among 193 countries for female representation in national parliaments in 2017. The nation had moved up slightly from its position in the previous survey, 163rd place. Compared with other developed economies, Japan was last. Gender studies professor Shin Ki-Young notes that Japanese women have had a hard time with the balance between their work and personal lives, part of a legacy of male dominance. If "fulfilling a leadership role means giving up on a 'private' life and adapting to a male way of working," Shin argues, women may not wish to pursue a career. She posits: "what we need is a working environment that is accommodating" (Murakami 2018). Beyond questions of political representation, it is worth noting that Japan stands out as a country where gender discrimination in employment and everyday life is quite high. In 2017, women comprised only 13 per cent of management positions (Larmer 2018).

Overall, while better jobs for more women will be crucial for the health of the Japanese economy, there are major structural problems to overcome, such as a need for much more state-funded childcare for working mothers, as well as a major change in attitudes toward women. A 2018 study of the problems of gender in the Japanese workforce concludes that despite some changes, "the traditional expectations, which primarily reduced female roles to family life, have remained" (Eszter 2018).

CASE STUDY

Chapter 9, Page 190

The Hybrid Electoral System of the Japanese Diet

Japan's parliament, called the Diet, is bicameral, having been established in its current form by the constitution of 1947, which was crafted under the American occupation that followed Japan's surrender in World War II. Yet electoral procedures for the Diet have changed, most substantially in the electoral reform of 1994 that dramatically altered Japanese politics. The Diet is now elected by a hybrid system that includes features of both district-based and proportional representation. In 2017, the numbers of representatives in both houses were slightly reduced under new electoral laws.

The lower (and more powerful) chamber in Japan is called the House of Representatives and was modelled in part on the American chamber of the same name and in part on the British House of Commons. Currently, this lower house is comprised of 465 representatives elected by a system that mixes single-member districts with proportional representation. Of the 465 representatives, 289 win seats in specific district elections, and an additional 176 are chosen based on party lists in 11 different regional blocks around the country. All representation thus has a territorial component, though the 176 seats was an attempt to introduce proportionality into the system. The House of Councillors is the upper chamber, with 146 members selected from Japan's 47 prefectures, while an additional 96 members are directly elected at a national level (in a single nationwide district). The legislative chambers are not symmetric in their powers because the House of Representatives has the authority to overrule the House of Councillors and also selects the prime minister. Most laws gain approval from both chambers to pass, but a two-thirds majority in the House of Representatives can pass legislation even over the negative vote of the House of Councillors.

The system is notable not only for its hybrid structure but also for how it reformed a previous system. From 1947 to 1994, the electoral system consisted of districts that would elect three to five representatives according to whichever candidates received the most individual votes. The old electoral system for the House of Representatives, called the "single nontransferable vote" (SNTV) system, has been argued to be more proportional than majoritarian systems with single-member districts, but in Japan it seemed to favour the long-dominant Liberal Democratic Party (LDP).

The reformed system finally came about in 1994. At that time, the LDP had at last lost governing power, though it remained the largest party in parliament. The reform of 1994 was intended to change a party system that had for a long time been characterized by individual politicians cultivating support from local networks; this system was to be replaced with one in which parties would take more programmatic stances (Horiuchi and Saito 2003, 672). Another consequence of the 1994 reform was to reduce the power of rural areas, which had been overrepresented for decades, and give more equal representation to urban areas.

Research Prompts

1. Compare the modernization paths of China and Japan. In what ways are they similar, and in what ways are they different (in terms of both politics and economics)? Using theories from Chapters 3–7 (and, possibly, Chapters 12 and 13 as well), develop hypotheses to explain the variation that you noted in response to the first part of this prompt.
2. Compare the period of LDP hegemony in Japan to the experience of Mexico under the PRI. How did each party cement its control? To what extent did the nature

of single-party dominance vary? What similar and different causes lay behind single-party dominance? Then bring China into the comparison. What might this comparison suggest about what seem to be the main factors that influence types of single-party dominance in more and less democratic societies?

3. Compare long-running economic development in the United Kingdom, Germany, and Japan. Be especially attentive to the role of the state in these cases. How do the cases contrast? What are the implications of your comparison for the theory that state involvement is bad for economic development?
4. In Chapter 15, we introduced the concept of "multiple modernities" that scholars like S. M. Eisenstadt have developed. Japan is often regarded as a Western-style modernizer. Is Japanese modernity "Western," or does it have its own distinct characteristics?

Online Case Studies

Go to **www.oup.com/he/DickovickCe** to find more case studies online, including:

- How Did Japan's Dominant Party Win for So Long?
- Importing National Identity in Japan?
- Resource Management in Japan
- State-Led Development in Japan

Mexico

PROFILE

Key Features of Contemporary Mexico

Population:	124,574,795 (July 2017 est.)
Area:	1,964,375 square kilometres
Head of State:	Andres Manuel Lopez Obrador (president, 2018–present)
Head of Government:	Andres Manuel Lopez Obrador (president, 2018–present)
Capital:	Mexico City
Year of Independence:	Often cited as 1810 when the movement for independence began, but actual independence was established in 1821.
Year of Current Constitution:	1917
Languages:	Spanish; Nahuatl; Mayan; other Indigenous languages.
GDP per Capita:	$8,902.80 (World Bank estimate, 2017)
Human Development Index Ranking (2015):	77th (high human development)
Trading Relationship with Canada (2016):	• Imports $25,075,246,229 • Exports $5,761,602,546 https://globaledge.msu.edu/countries/canada/tradestats

Sources: *CIA World Factbook*; World Bank World Development Indicators; United Nations *Human Development Report 2016*

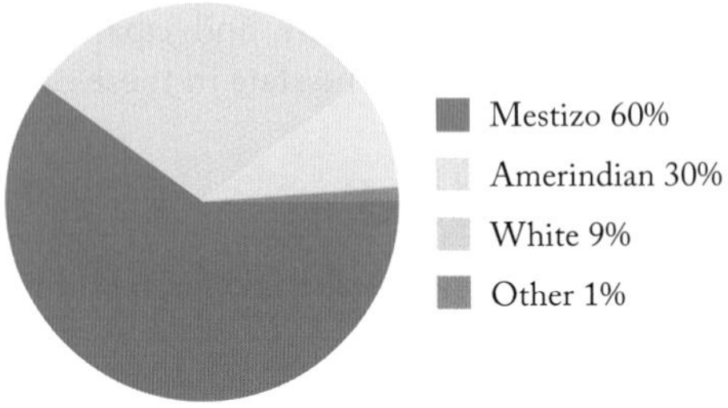

Ethnic Groups in Mexico

Source: *CIA World Factbook*

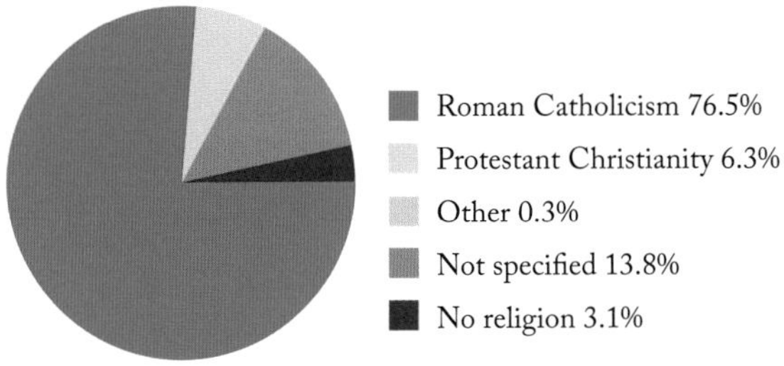

Religious Affiliation in Mexico

Note that we have included Jehovah's Witnesses (1.1%) in the "Protestant Christianity" category.

Source: *CIA World Factbook*

Introduction

Mexico receives a great deal of attention from political scientists for numerous reasons. One of the most important is that it is a large country bordering on a culturally very different one with a contrasting political and economic history (Camp 2007, 1–9), thus facilitating comparisons. Another is that its economic and political histories are fascinating and set up many other potential comparisons that allow us to gain some leverage over a number of theories of comparative politics. In economic terms, it has alternated between periods of growth and stagnation, and the state's economic policy has shifted on numerous occasions over the decades. Since 1994, it has been economically integrated with the rest of North America via first the North American Free Trade Agreement and now the Canada-United States-Mexico Agreement (CUSMA). It has more generally increased its global economic integration in recent years. Along with Brazil, it has had moderate success

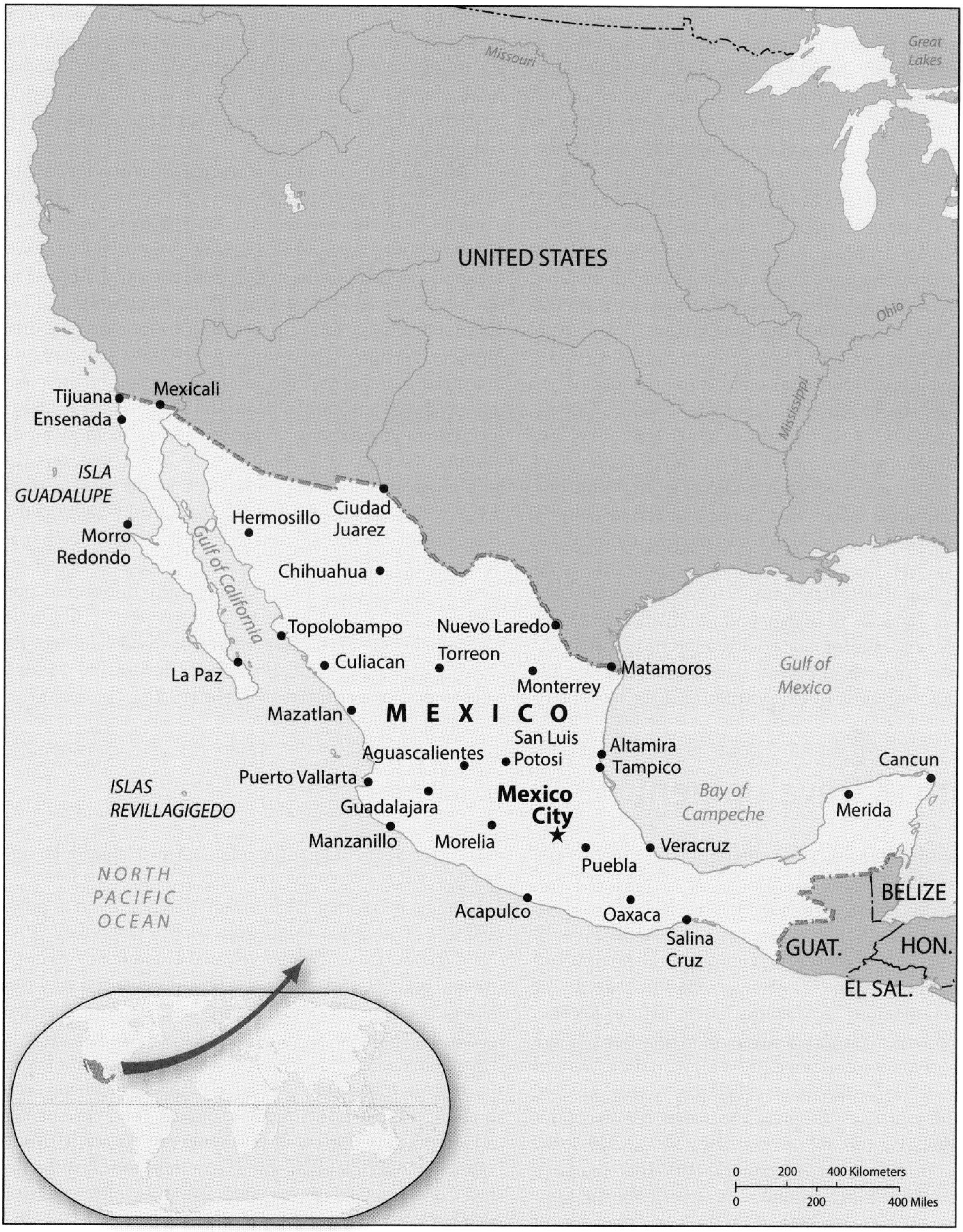

Great Lakes
Missouri
UNITED STATES
Ohio
Mississippi
Tijuana
Mexicali
Ensenada
ISLA GUADALUPE
Hermosillo
Ciudad Juarez
Morro Redondo
Gulf of California
Chihuahua
Topolobampo
Nuevo Laredo
Culiacan
Torreon
La Paz
Matamoros
Monterrey
Gulf of Mexico
Mazatlan
MEXICO
San Luis Potosi
Altamira
Tampico
Aguascalientes
Cancun
Puerto Vallarta
ISLAS REVILLAGIGEDO
Mexico City
Bay of Campeche
Merida
Guadalajara
Manzanillo
Morelia
Veracruz
Puebla
NORTH PACIFIC OCEAN
BELIZE
Acapulco
Oaxaca
Salina Cruz
GUAT.
HON.
EL SAL.
0 200 400 Kilometers
0 200 400 Miles

in recent decades in establishing a diversified industrial base. Yet severe poverty is a persistent problem, and economic difficulties are linked to serious political challenges, including severe problems of violent crime linked to the state cracking down on the production and trafficking of illegal drugs. Tens of thousands of people have died in the drug wars since 2006.

Historically, Mexico has occasionally been thought of as having a strong state, since the state has often been interventionist in Mexico's history. In terms relative to the rest of Latin America at the time, the decades of late 19th-century dominance by Porfirio Díaz saw fairly strong development (Mörner 1993, 6) in which the state encouraged foreign capital to build railways and to transform the countryside, promoting a more commercial agricultural model and beginning to establish industrial activity in the cities (Meyer and Sherman 1987, 431–79; Krauze 1997, 218). Likewise, the state that emerged from the Mexican Revolution (which began in 1910), after serious instability and around one million deaths, was a state that came to intervene actively in the economy, for example in Mexico's early nationalization of oil (1938). The post-revolutionary regime also acted strongly against the Roman Catholic Church, dramatically reducing its capacity to act in politics (Blancarte 1992). However, Mexico was for many decades prone to instability and irregular transfers of power; even in the years of relative stability promoted by the Institutional Revolutionary Party's (Partido Revolucionario Institucional, or PRI) dominance for much of the 20th century, authoritarianism was the norm (a variation on the "party dictatorship" model). In recent years, the country has struggled with serious problems of organized crime and drug trafficking (O'Neil 2009).

Mexico has many interesting characteristics for detailed study. It (1) is geographically diverse; (2) has a highly unequal society with considerable heterogeneity and cultural diversity; and (3) emerged from an unequal post-colonial society in which multiple exogenous shocks disrupted the traditional social structure. In terms of geographical and cultural diversity, the sharpest contrast is between the drier, northern portion of the country, which is the centre of most industrial activity, and the southern portion of the country, which has a tropical climate and is poorer, with a larger Indigenous population. Exogenous shocks to Mexican development included numerous foreign interventions that both changed domestic politics and, in the most extreme instance of war with the United States in the 1840s, led to massive loss of territory. To this list we could add the impact of foreign capital during the Porfiriato and the social dislocation experienced by the rural, largely Indigenous populations, and it is not hard to understand why important groups of rural poor were willing to follow leaders like Pancho Villa and Emiliano Zapata during the Mexican Revolution (Womack 1968; Knight 1990a).

Historical Development

Mexico was arguably the most important of Spain's colonies in the "New World" (Thomas 1993). This was mainly due to its economic value, which had two main sources. First, it had mining wealth, and Spain was a mercantilist power, meaning that it viewed the maximization of holdings of gold and silver ("bullion") as fundamental to state power and the key measure of economic performance. Second, Mexico had large, complex Indigenous civilizations before European conquest (most notably the Maya in the south and the empire of the Mexica, often called the "Aztecs," centred in today's Mexico City). This meant that state-like structures could be built "on top of" the existing political and social institutions in the society (Mahoney 2010). This was similarly the case in the area around today's Peru, for the same reasons (in this case, the Inca civilization was the relevant one). Thus, both Mexico and Peru famously became "cores" of the Spanish colonial system, while areas like the Southern Cone (today's Argentina and Chile), Venezuela, and parts of Central America remained "peripheral" to that system until the closing years of Spanish colonialism (Halperín Donghi 1993).

Being a colonial core meant that the central power paid lots of attention to Mexican society (Mahoney 2010). Colonial Mexico had more colonial bureaucracy than peripheral regions, and it had a more complex social structure, in large measure because of the amount of wealth generated by mining. Perhaps not surprisingly, its efforts to achieve independence followed a path that differed in certain key respects from the pattern witnessed in more peripheral areas. In places like Buenos Aires and Caracas, local elites tended to be strong supporters of independence (Lynch 1973). In places like Mexico, such elites were less sure, and the first stages of the revolt against Spain came out of the Mexican periphery. Indeed, Mexico only became independent when a *liberal* revolt in Spain caused some Mexican conservatives, most notably Augustin de Iturbide, to change sides, favouring a conservative government at home versus a liberal government from Europe (Meyer and Sherman 1987, 294–308;

Anna 1998). In all of Latin America, politics in the 19th century was divided between conservatives and liberals, but the conservatives were both stronger and more conservative in Mexico than in many other places (see Krauze 1997). Perhaps most important, Mexican conservatives helped the Roman Catholic Church to maintain strength and privileges that were almost without parallel in the region, two of the most important being the Church's enormous landholding and the fact that it was allowed to operate a parallel legal system through which its clergy could be tried (Lynch 1986; Gill 2008). This ongoing polarization was an important factor in the War of the Reform in the 1850s and the revolution beginning after 1910, as well as the subsequent Cristero Rebellion in the 1920s.

Historical Development Timeline

2000 BCE–900 CE	A range of Indigenous civilizations began and flourished during this period, including the Maya, the Olmec, the Zapotec, and the Teotihuacan civilizations.
900–1521	Numerous city states rose and fell during this time. The early period was marked by the rise and the fall of the Toltec, while the Aztec empire grew to prominence during the 1400s. A revitalized Mayan civilization also developed.
1521	Beginnings of European colonization and the destruction of many Indigenous civilizations. The conquest of Indigenous nations was often brutal and accompanied by mass murder and enslavement. Mexico was incorporated administratively into the Viceroyalty of New Spain.[1]
1810	"The battle cry 'Grito de Dolores' marks beginning of independence movement".
1821	Plan of Iguala and its "Three Guarantees" and the establishment of Mexican independence.
1833–4	Valentín Gómez Farías attempts anti-clerical and other reforms. Santa Anna displaces Gómez Farías, prompting a period of conservative rule.
1836	Independence of Texas.
1838–9	The "Pastry War" (French invasion)
1846–8	US war with Mexico in which a considerable portion of Mexican national territory was annexed, including much of present-day Arizona, California, Colorado, Nevada, New Mexico, and Utah.
1853	Gadsen Purchase transfers more Mexican land to the United States.
1855	Ley Juárez introduces anti-clerical reforms.
1856	Ley Lerdo forces alienation of Church lands.
1857	Liberal constitution of 1857.
1858–61	War of the Reform.
1862	European intervention, led by France.
1864–7	Rule by Emperor Maximilian, imposed by French forces.
1867	Return to liberal government, under Juárez.
1876–1911	The Porfiriato, during which Porfirio Díaz dominates Mexican politics.
1910	Díaz "defeats" Madero in a fraudulent election that is the opening scene of the Mexican Revolution.
1911–13	Presidency of Francisco Madero.
1913–14	Presidency of Victorino Huerta, which begins with a coup d'état and the murder of Madero.
1914–20	Presidency of Venustiano Carranza, proponent of "constitutionalism."
1920–4	Presidency of Alvaro Obregón.
1924–8	Presidency of Plutarco Elías Calles, who creates the party that later becomes the PRI.
1926–9	Cristero Rebellion.
1928–34	Period in which Calles dominates but does not hold the presidency.
1929	Founding of PRI (at the time called the PNR).
1934–40	Presidency of Lazaro Cárdenas, which includes nationalization of oil in 1938 as well as major agrarian reforms.
1968	Major student protests quelled with violence.
1988–94	Presidency of Carlos Salinas de Gortari, known for its liberal economic reforms.
1994	North American Free Trade Agreement (NAFTA) enters into effect.
1994	Beginning of Zapatista National Liberation Army (EZLN) activities under Subcomandante Marcos.
1994–2000	Presidency of Ernesto Zedillo.
1994	Peso crisis, resolved with major aid from the United States under Bill Clinton.
2000	Election of Vicente Fox of PAN signals the end of PRI hegemony in Mexico.
2006–12	Presidency of Felipe Calderón.
2006	A new anti-drugs police force is created, but drug violence increases and by 2008, an estimated 4000 people have been killed during the Calderón era alone. In 2009, an estimated 6500 people are killed in the drug war.

continued

2012-18	Presidency of Enrique Peña Nieto.
2016	President Nieto declares that Mexico will not pay for any prospective border wall with the United States. Mexico announces plans to legalize same-sex marriage.
2018	Presidency of Andres Manuel Lopez Obrador begins. NAFTA is replaced with the Canada-United States-Mexico Agreement (CUSMA).

In the early years of the republic, Mexico descended into what scholars call "caudillismo," which essentially means rule by authoritarian leaders. The Mexican state was at least partially a vehicle for the pursuit of the private interest of a "predatory" elite rather than an organization in which rule of law, equal access, and institutional legitimacy were established. While the institutional trappings of a liberal republic were in place, the holder of the presidency ultimately answered to a military elite, and in Mexico this meant Antonio López de Santa Anna. His authority rested on his reputation as a great warrior and his ability to establish a private army to outcompete potential domestic rivals. Santa Anna lost power after the unsuccessful effort to stop the declaration of the independent Republic of Texas. He would temporarily gain it back after heroic service against the French in the "Pastry War" and then lose power again in subsequent years, gaining it again during the US invasion of Mexico, and losing power for good in 1855, when the Revolution of Ayutla (1854–5) brought the liberals to power (Hamnett 1994).

After so many years of political instability and protection of conservative interests, the liberals were eager to dramatically remake Mexican politics (Krauze 1997, 157–9). This they attempted to do in the constitution of 1857 and in two major reforms, which expanded civilian power over the clergy and forced the Church to sell its massive properties. However, the Church's conservative allies were unwilling to accept the new order, and a major civil war, known as the War of the Reform (1858–61), broke out (Hamnett 1994). Eventually, the republic was able to defend itself against conservative insurgents.

In 1871, Porfirio Díaz ran on a campaign of "no re-election." Having lost, he began a revolt, which culminated in his taking power in 1876. In certain respects, this signalled a return to caudillismo, since he would govern, though not always formally holding office, until 1910. Díaz courted foreign investment and presided over some growth in manufacturing, the construction of a notable system of railways, and the transformation of agriculture (Meyer and Sherman 1987, 431–79; Krauze 1997). These developments produced some dislocation and upset traditional ways of doing things. Perhaps agricultural changes were the most important because they broke up traditional local landownership patterns and helped to concentrate land in the hands of a small elite (Camp 2007, 38) and introduced wage labour as the basis of the rural economy in at least some areas. As many scholars have pointed out, this, and social inequality more generally, would play a major role in the discontent that fuelled the Mexican revolution beginning in 1910 (Camp 2007, 42; Knight 1990a). In particular, Emiliano Zapata's insurgency was focused, above all, on landownership (Womack 1968).

The revolution had as its proximate cause the revolt of Francisco Madero, who had run against Díaz and lost in a fraudulent election (for a definitive account of the revolution, see Knight 1990a; 1990b). Madero was essentially a northern elite and a liberal. He was soon joined in his efforts by distinct social groups, the most important of which were led by Francisco ("Pancho") Villa in the north and Zapata. These groups sought to redress problems of economic inequality and not just political issues. Scholars disagree about when, precisely, the revolution ended, and we cannot trace here all of its twists and turns. Note, though, that Madero governed until he was assassinated by Victoriano Huerta in 1913. Huerta was in turn displaced by Venustiano Carranza in 1914. It was under Carranza that the revolutionary constitution of 1917 was passed. Carranza was forced out in a revolt in 1920 led by Álvaro Obregón, and Obregón would himself assume the presidency. Several years later, Obregón would be followed by Plutarco Elías Calles, who would found the party that would become the PRI and who would dominate Mexican politics—both directly and indirectly (Krauze 1997, 404–37)—until Lázaro Cárdenas was elected in 1934. Elías Calles is best known for consolidating the system of PRI party dominance that would endure until 2000 and for presiding over the period of the Cristero Rebellion, a major civil war in which insurgents aimed, unsuccessfully, to defend the Roman Catholic Church from the state's alleged depredations (Blancarte 1992). Cárdenas is best remembered for his populist politics, for his role in further solidifying Mexican corporatism, for the nationalization of Mexican oil, and for his efforts at agrarian reform (Krauze 1997, 438–80).

In Mexico, for a time at least, many judged this approach to be successful, yielding the so-called "Mexican miracle" (Basañez 2006, 297) of medium-term sustained economic growth. Economically, though, the country entered into crisis—like most of Latin America—in the 1980s. In the early 1990s, President Salinas de Gortari introduced important liberal economic reforms. Scholars debate the relationship between these reforms and the subsequent economic turbulence, including the peso crisis of 1994. Also in the early 1990s, Mexico witnessed the beginning of an insurgency in the southern state of Chiapas, protesting liberal reforms and "globalization" more generally. In later years, Mexico's citizens became more and more interested in breaking the PRI's stranglehold on power. The National Action Party (Partido Acción Nacional, or PAN) successfully won the presidency with Vicente Fox in 2000. PAN is a centre-right party that tends to be less anti-clerical than the PRI (indeed, the Catholic Church played a role in Mexican democratization, as it did elsewhere during "third wave" democratization). It also continued with economic liberalization. Fox was succeeded by President Felipe Calderón. Calderón had some success but faced difficulties generated by his efforts to control drug gang activity, especially in border states. PRI candidate Enrique Peña Nieto won the 2012 presidential elections. In 2018, leftist candidate Andres Manuel Lopez Obrador won the presidency in the midst of drug-related violence as well as renegotiations of NAFTA with the US and Canada. He came to power through the support of a coalition of left and right parties known as the Juntos Haremos Historia (Together We Will Make History). He has pledged to combat crime through better education and job opportunities, while also promising to crack down on corruption. He is also seen as an economic protectionist (CNN Library 2018).

Regime and Political Institutions

Mexico's political system is strongly presidentialist, though it has become less so in recent years as multiparty competition has become a reality (Camp 2007, 181–3). In the years of PRI dominance, this was highlighted by the extraordinary power that the president had both within the institutional framework of the state *and* within the party. The executive branch plays a critical role not just in the administration of the state but also in conceiving and proposing legislation. Indeed, historically, the extent to which legislation is proposed by the executive in Mexico has been significant (Camp 2007, 181–2). Camp notes two additional sources of the legislature's relative weakness (2007, 187–8). First, representatives cannot be re-elected immediately after serving a term. Second, the research staff of the legislature is small and poorly funded, whereas the executive's staff is robust.

The judicial system has also suffered historically from relative weakness and lack of independence, though this has changed somewhat in the wake of reforms passed in the 1990s (Camp 2007, 189–92). Since the defeat of the PRI in 2000, there has been greater competitiveness in the electoral system.

Regime and Political Institutions

Regime	Federal republic, democratic (more fully so in recent years, especially since PAN victory in 2000 presidential election)
Administrative Divisions	31 states as well as the Federal District of Mexico City
Executive Branch	President
Selection of Executive	President is elected by popular vote. Note that presidential selection has changed notably in recent years.
Legislative Branch	Bicameral Congress Lower chamber: Chamber of Deputies (*Cámara de Diputados*) Upper chamber: Senate (*Senado*)
Judicial Branch	Supreme Court of Justice, composed of 11 justices (one the "president" of the Supreme Court). Justices are nominated by the executive and approved by the legislature.
Political Party System	Multiparty system, though for much of the 20th century Mexican politics was completely dominated by the PRI. The PAN broke this monopoly in 2000, and the presidency is held by the leader of MORENA.

Political Economy

Mexico is an important emerging economy, increasingly integrated with the broader global economy. Its economic history has been mixed, alternating between periods of growth and crisis. As discussed previously, it was, in economic as well as political terms, one of Spain's most important colonial possessions. In the 19th century, political instability caused economic problems, since a predictable political and economic environment is necessary for investors and other economic actors to act optimally. In the later 19th century, modern economic infrastructure was built during the Porfiriato, but the social dislocations caused in part by this process yielded later instability. The Mexican Revolution ushered in another period of instability, which likely held economic performance back, though it is arguable that the fruits of development in subsequent years were somewhat more equitable as a result of this process. Finally, as in much of Latin America, Mexico turned to import substitution as its development strategy in the middle of the 20th century. This set of policies coincided with fairly consistent and strong economic growth for several decades, though even at the end of this process Mexico was left with high inequality and notable poverty.

Today's Mexican economy is dominated by services (64 per cent of GDP) and industry (31.5 per cent), with agriculture accounting for less than 4 per cent of GDP (2017 estimates, *CIA World Factbook*). Unemployment is at least formally quite low at present, estimated at 3.6 per cent (2017 estimate, *CIA World Factbook*). As the *CIA World Factbook* notes, Mexico has a high rate of *underemployment*, however. What this means is that many Mexicans do not have satisfactorily remunerative jobs and a large percentage (around a quarter of the labour force) works in the informal economy. This is very common in the developing world, and it is worth keeping in mind because it affects the extent to which unemployment rates in developed and developing societies are comparable measures. Mexico does continue to suffer from high income inequality. Its Gini coefficient stands at 43.4 (World Bank 2017 estimate).

The Mexican state has historically played an important role in economic management. As noted previously, during the Porfiriato the state endeavoured to attract and protect capital. Its role in the economy grew after the revolution and under the PRI (Camp 2007, 45), particularly beginning in the 1930s and 1940s. Mexico practised state-led development, nationalizing enterprises like oil (creating the giant Pemex firm) as well as railways, engaging in land reform (which generally tended toward the distribution of relatively small landholdings), and adopting a strategy of import-substituting industrialization, protecting domestic industries. It invested heavily in infrastructure as well. This was the period of the "Mexican miracle" (Basañez 2006, 297), which produced steady growth, relatively low inflation, and rapid industrialization. Unfortunately, Mexico suffered, along with the rest of Latin America, from the debt crisis of the 1980s, related here to the dramatic decline in oil revenues, which exacerbated the state's difficulties in paying its debts. Consequently, the country faced serious economic difficulties—including an increase in poverty and the expansion of the informal economy—and Mexico slowly turned toward reform. Mexico followed prescriptions to privatize a number of industries, including banks that had undergone emergency nationalization in 1982, though the state continues to own Pemex, CFE (a major power company), and other enterprises. The Mexican economy has also seen the growth of agribusiness in recent years. Mexico has come to be more integrated with the global economy, particularly through NAFTA (which came into effect in 1994), aiming to bolster growth through industrial exports. This strategy has produced gains, though it has also left the country vulnerable to global economic forces, including the peso crisis of 1994 and the country's serious exposure to the global economic crisis beginning in 2008.

CASE STUDIES

CASE STUDY

Chapter 3, Page 45

Why Aren't There Major Ethnic Parties in Mexico?

Mexico had complex Indigenous civilizations prior to European contact, which were decimated by the violence of the colonization process. In subsequent years, people of European descent have on average fared better in Mexico than Indigenous peoples, even though the majority of the Mexican population is of mestizo background and the next largest group is of predominantly Indigenous ancestry. Given the country's history of inequality and ethnic discrimination, why have Indigenous groups not organized via ethnic political parties in Mexico?

This sort of question cannot be answered definitively because it is asking, in essence, about a counter-factual. In other words, logically, the question is indistinguishable from the question "What would have caused ethnic political parties to have formed in Mexico?" The best way to provisionally answer such a question is to generate potential causes that plausibly would have increased the probability of the formation of such parties, but there is clearly no formula such that "if characteristic X had been present in Mexican society, ethnic parties *would* have developed."

What sorts of features might have encouraged the formation of ethnicity-based parties in Mexico? Among others, we might expect (1) salient and impermeable boundaries between ethnic groups; (2) the lack of other frameworks for mobilization of the subaltern population; and (3) the opening of political space within which such parties could form and have some prospect of electoral success (since, from certain points of view, party organization is irrational if it cannot lead to increasing a group's power).

Historically, in Mexico these conditions tended not to apply. While inequality has been a pervasive feature of Mexican society and while ethnicity has been a major dimension of inequality, the boundaries between ethnic groups have historically been fluid (Camp 2007, 26). The majority of the population, as noted before, is of mestizo background (Krauze 1997; Camp 2007, 81), which could facilitate some freedom in self-identification. In addition to the fact that the cultural boundary between the categories "Indigenous" and "mestizo" is permeable (as is, to a more limited extent, the boundary between "mestizo" and "white"), the very predominance of mestizos in the society undercuts the likelihood of a party linked to mestizo or Indigenous identity. Moreover, other frameworks—frameworks that preclude mobilization around specific ethnic identities—have been salient in Mexican political history. Mexican national identity, at least since the early 20th century, has been marked by the idea of ethnic mixing. Mexican immigrants in the United States will sometimes use the word "raza" to refer to their identity as Mexican or Chicano/a. In addition to this sort of national frame, Mexico's revolutionary tradition tended to frame dissent in relation to class. Thus, Zapata's insurgency during the revolution, which included many mestizo and Indigenous actors, largely privileged a peasant or rural labourer identity rather than an Indigenous identity as such. Further, the corporatist mode of interest mediation developed under the PRI (particularly under Cárdenas) likely cut against ethnic affiliation because it again organized people in relation to their economic activity rather than their ethnic status. Finally, Mexican parties were established at certain critical junctures in which conditions likely did not favour ethnic mobilization as the basis for party affiliation.

Does this all mean that ethnicity is unimportant in Mexican politics? Not at all. Indigenous communities have mobilized in numerous ways (Hernández Navarro and Carlsen 2004), and it is always possible that more influential ethnic parties will emerge in the future. Factors that might contribute to this possibility could include the much-documented role of international NGOs in helping to organize ethnicity-based political mobilization, the modelling effects of such organization in other parts of Latin America in recent years, and the ongoing effects of political opening and democratic consolidation in Mexico. One might expect this sort of outcome to be more likely in areas like Chiapas, where a larger portion of the population is Indigenous, where historical discrimination, inequality, and poverty have been especially high, and where the EZLN ("Zapatista") insurgency has been based.

CASE STUDY

Chapter 7, Page 139

The Mexican State and Rule of Law

One of the distinguishing features of modern states (in addition to their relative autonomy, bureaucratic mode of organization, and so forth) is that they have established the *rule of law*. This means that, at least ideal-typically, a fully functioning modern state (1) has a legal-rational framework for resolving conflict; (2) enforces that framework transparently; and (3) enforces it equally rather than privileging one or another set of actors based on network ties or some other sort of affiliation.

The Mexican state has done this at various times in its history with varying degrees of success. As Mörner (1993, 6) notes, the state was relatively weak after independence and then grew in strength during the Porfiriato, entering a period of weakness during the revolution and its immediate aftermath before gaining capacity again in the middle of the 20th century. In very recent years, there has been a great deal of concern about increasing levels of violence, drug trafficking, ongoing corruption, and the seeming inability or unwillingness of components of the Mexican state (army, police, and the judicial system) to curb criminal activity. Some areas of Mexico, it is alleged, largely lie outside of the state's real jurisdiction. In some towns in parts of the country, drug gangs essentially exercise state-like functions, resolving disputes and maintaining order of a certain sort.

How could we explain the presence and influence of powerful criminal organizations that make a mockery of the state's "monopoly on the legitimate use of force"? Several basic factors are likely decisive. First, there must be gains to be made above those made in licit activity for an important segment of the population. Otherwise, there would be little incentive to *engage* in illicit activity. This would suggest that continued economic development would help to reduce organized, nonstate violence (of course, organized nonstate violence makes economic development more difficult to achieve). Second, the risks must not be so high as to discourage a large number of criminals from participating in illicit activity. In contemporary Mexico, as in many parts of the developing world, the risks that state enforcement poses to criminals is relatively low because of high rates of *impunity*. The state cannot or will not enforce the law in certain areas, dramatically reducing the cost (in terms of risk) for illicit activity. Finally, illicit groups must have the resources necessary to seek their chosen ends, and these resources can be both material and organizational. Material resources include both guns, which in the case of Mexico are often trafficked from the United States where there is little gun control, and money, again from the United States. Organizational resources include the ongoing existence of criminal gangs, as well as their established ties, via corruption, to state actors.

Interestingly, a number of commentators have tied the escalation in Mexican drug violence to reform. Some of this has to do with the fact that the PRI historically sometimes worked *with* criminal networks rather than aiming to squash them (O'Neil 2009, 65). Moreover, at lower levels of the organizational structure of the state, police corruption was common under the PRI (Davis 2006) and remains so. Where and when the PAN came to hold office, linkages between the PRI and drug traffickers were broken, producing non-institutional (and thus often violent) responses (O'Neil 2009, 65). Exogenous factors were important as well, including US efforts to restrict the flow of trafficking in the Caribbean region. If the costs of one path get too high, traffickers will look for another path, and trafficking through Mexico rose dramatically in response to changing patterns of US enforcement (O'Neil 2009, 66; Davis 2006, 62). Of course, this necessarily bolstered the position of Mexican illicit organizations. Thus, at the same time, Mexican criminal organizations had greater profits, more autonomy, and a reason to become more independent. Then the Mexican government attempted to stamp them out. At this point, the organizations had little choice but to fight back.

It is worth noting that some commentators have seen linkages between Mexican democratization (O'Neil 2009; Davis 2006) and rising crime in Mexico. Indeed, the rise in crime witnessed in Latin America from the 1980s on does roughly mirror the pattern of regional democratization. Could it be, as some authors have asked, that democratization and rule of law don't always go hand in hand? Others (Magaloni and Zepeda 2004) have looked at economic data, though, and argued that while democratization *seems* the culprit, its near simultaneity with rising crime is largely coincidental and that the most important variables associated with rising crime are income inequality and economic difficulties. This is an ongoing debate in the field.

Research Prompts

1. The "Mexican Miracle" was achieved, in part, through policies of import substitution. In more recent years, the country has taken a more market-friendly approach. What would our theories of development from Chapters 4 and 5 say about this sequence?
2. Think about the years of the PRI's dominance in Mexico. The regime was clearly authoritarian, but it had some democratic elements. How would you classify it in terms of the ideas of democracy and authoritarianism discussed in Chapters 6 and 7? As you conduct research, what do you find other scholars saying about this issue?
3. Do a little outside research to compare the development of national identity in Mexico to other cases (good choices for comparison might be Argentina, Chile, Colombia, and Venezuela). What, if anything, is distinctive about the Mexican case?
4. In the preceding case study on "Why Aren't There Major Ethnic Parties in Mexico?" we noted that Mexico's political parties have not been organized predominantly along the lines of ethnicity. Conduct some research, and find a Latin American case where ethnicity *has* been a key basis of political organizing. What accounts for the difference?
5. Have Mexican views of the United States changed since Donald Trump became president? Do you think the Trump administration has influenced voting behaviour and voter preferences in Mexico?

Online Case Studies

Go to **www.oup.com/he/DickovickCe** to find more case studies online, including:

- Industrialization, Modernity, and National Identity in Mexico
- Mexico's "Perfect Dictatorship" and Its End
- The PRI and Corporatism in Mexico

Note

1 BBC News 2018.

Nigeria

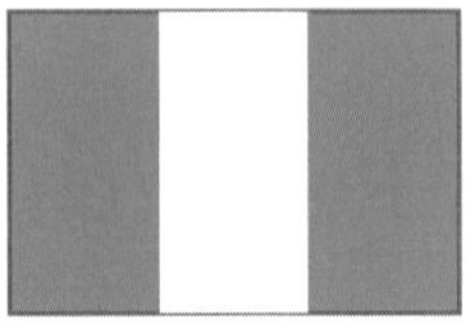

PROFILE

Key Features of Contemporary Nigeria

Population:	190,632,261 (July 2017 est.)
Area:	923,768 square kilometres
Head of State:	Muhammadu Buhari (president, 2015–present)
Head of Government:	Muhammadu Buhari (president, 2015–present)
Capital:	Abuja
Year of Independence:	1960
Year of Current Constitution:	1999
Languages:	English (official), Hausa-Fulani, Yoruba, Igbo, many others
GDP per Capita:	$1,968.60 (World Bank estimate, 2017)
Human Development Index Ranking (2015):	152nd (low human development)
Trading Relationship with Canada (2016):	• Imports $1,189,743,411 • Exports $236,673,248 https://globaledge.msu.edu/countries/canada/tradestats

Sources: *CIA World Factbook*; World Bank World Development Indicators; United Nations *Human Development Report 2016*

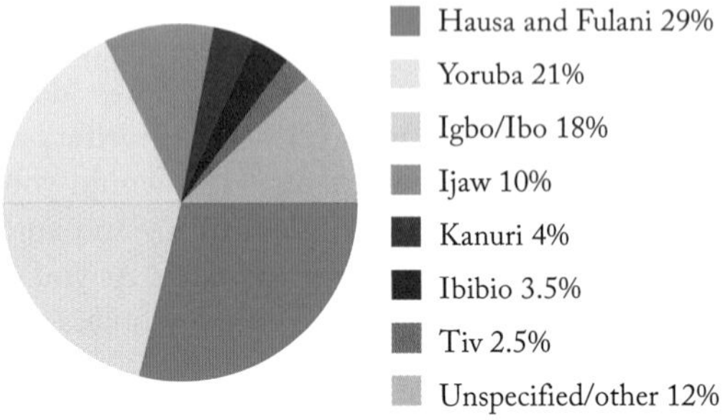

Ethnic Groups in Nigeria

Note that the Nigerian population includes hundreds of ethnic groups, but these are the most numerous.

Source: *CIA World Factbook*

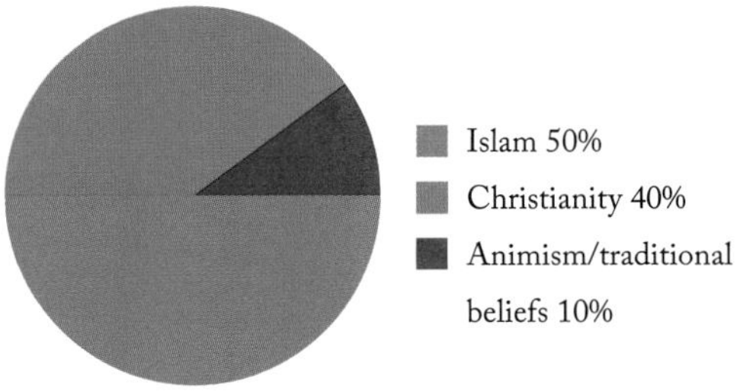

Religious Affiliation in Nigeria (estimates)

Source: *CIA World Factbook*

Introduction

Nigeria is the largest country in Africa and has been subject to enduring interest among political scientists for several reasons. Of these, the two most important are that (1) it is a prominent example of the perils of oil dependence (Karl 1997) and (2) it has been the site of considerable inter-ethnic conflict. Indeed, these issues, discussed herein, are not unrelated. Also related are the relative weakness of Nigerian institutions, development problems, and the lessons that Nigeria might offer about how political modernization can take place in a post-colonial society.

Yet Nigeria is a country of great cultural diversity and has provided the world with Nobel laureates and other artists, writers, and musicians. It has a lively media scene with hundreds of television and radio stations as well as 86 million Nigerians online (as of 2016) and more than 7 million daily Facebook users in 2015 (BBC News: Africa 2017). Nigeria is the largest society in Africa, and many believe that if it can overcome its history of underdevelopment and ethnic conflict, it would have great potential. Indeed, though there are many concerns, the country has been democratic for almost two decades, a source of considerable optimism.

Nigeria's diversity encompasses both religious and ethnic difference. In terms of ethnicity, there are many groups,

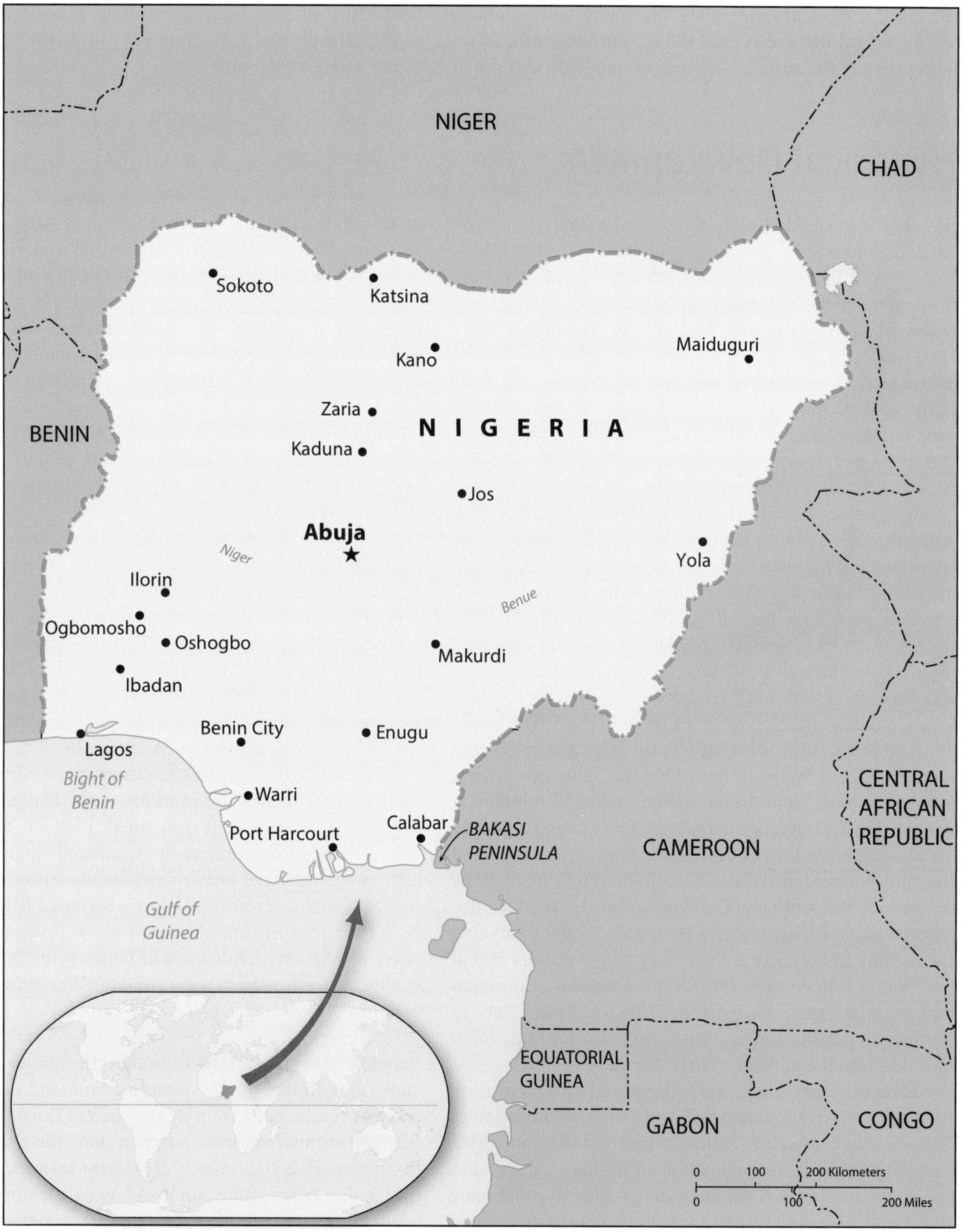
NIGER
CHAD
BENIN
NIGERIA
Sokoto
Katsina
Kano
Maiduguri
Zaria
Kaduna
Jos
Abuja
Niger
Yola
Benue
Ilorin
Ogbomosho
Oshogbo
Makurdi
Ibadan
Benin City
Enugu
Lagos
Bight of Benin
Warri
Port Harcourt
Calabar
BAKASI PENINSULA
CAMEROON
CENTRAL AFRICAN REPUBLIC
Gulf of Guinea
EQUATORIAL GUINEA
GABON
CONGO
0 100 200 Kilometers
0 100 200 Miles

though the most prominent are the Hausa and Fulani in the north and the Yoruba and the Igbo in the south. In religious terms, the society is diverse as well, with about half the population practising Islam, about 40 per cent adhering to Christianity, and the remainder mostly practising traditional African religions.

Historical Development

Before British colonial rule, Nigeria had a variety of different Indigenous state structures (Falola and Heaton 2008). In northern Nigeria, where Islam had made its way from the Arabian peninsula centuries earlier, there were relatively well-established states. Among the large population of the Hausa-Fulani ethnic groups—which today are the largest ethnic group in Nigeria—there were rather large and militarily capable units. In the south, where the Yoruba and Igbo peoples predominate in the southwest and southeast, respectively, people generally lived in smaller political groups such as villages or clusters of villages.

Interaction with Europe and the global economy took shape through early explorations by Europeans and the establishment of the slave trade along the coast of West Africa, including Nigeria. The Portuguese were the first to establish a trading post in the late 1400s, and several other countries were later involved along the Nigerian coast. After establishing authority through a combination of military intimidation and bargaining with local groups, European powers established a trade in which slaves were taken to the Americas.

The British ultimately became the principal colonizing force in Nigeria when in the 1800s the European powers undertook what came to be known as the "Scramble for Africa." The scramble was largely a land grab and a geopolitical contest between Great Britain, France, Portugal, and Belgium, which staked their claims to dominate most of the territory on the continent; Germany claimed several territories as well, and Spain played a lesser role, with Italy staking claims only in the early 20th century. These powers met at the Berlin Conference in 1884–5 and divided the continent into colonial states. Many of the British colonies were in southern and eastern Africa, but Nigeria was the largest and most important colony in western Africa.

Over the course of the late 19th and early 20th centuries, Britain increased the extent and depth of its colonization of Nigeria, slowly asserting authority over the vast land. This happened through a combination of military subjugation and negotiation with Nigerian leaders willing to collaborate with the British. The system came to be known as indirect rule (Falola and Heaton 2008, 110–16; Lange 2009; Dorward 1986, 402–4) because the British did not send large numbers of forces to occupy Nigeria but rather sought to exert authority by using Indigenous leaders as intermediaries with local populations; in a perversion of African forms of rule, this often involved the appointment of village chiefs and other customary leaders by the British administrative authorities. The system served the interests of the colonizers, but it set the tone for a long run of unaccountable government across much of Africa (cf. Mamdani 1996). By the time of the First World War, Commissioner Frederick Lugard had established a form of indirect rule over nearly all of present-day Nigeria. He unified the northern and southern colonies into a single political unit, which formed the basis for today's nation-state, with its large size and its conflicts between regions.

As World War II came to an end, the European powers had increasing difficulty maintaining colonial control. Nationalists gained in prominence in most of the colonies (see discussion in Williams 1984 and Falola and Heaton 2008, 136–57), empowered in part by the increasing recognition of the contributions Africans had made in the war. One of Nigeria's leading nationalists was Nnamdi Azikiwe, whose writings first became known in the 1930s. By the 1950s, it was clear that colonialism in Africa was on its last legs.

Nigeria achieved independence from Great Britain in 1960. It remained a dominion of the United Kingdom until 1963, meaning it remained part of the British Commonwealth and nominally considered the British monarch as a ceremonial head of state while retaining political independence and self-rule. Nigeria became a federal republic in 1963, the principle of federalism was instituted, and the governing system divided power between the three regions of Nigeria: the Northern region and the Western and Eastern regions in the southern half of the country.

Ethnic and regional tensions emerged early on as the populous north came to dominate the parliament, with votes split almost purely along regional and ethnic lines, and this resulted in a coup by elements of the military from the Igbo ethnicity in the Eastern region. The coup came to be known as the "Igbo coup." This characterization has been disputed, but the name stuck and signalled the increasing alienation of the Igbo from the northern Hausa-Fulani as well as the western Yoruba. Though the eventual military leader chosen as president, Yakubu Gowon, was from central Nigeria and was seen as a compromise selection, the tensions between Igbos and other groups worsened.

Historical Development Timeline

1000s–onward	A range of kingdoms, empires, and city states are formed, including the Oyo, Benin, and Hausa kingdoms and the Borno dynasty.[1]
1500s–1800s	Period of slave trade along the coast of West Africa, including Nigeria; slaves are taken to the Americas.
1800s	Period of initial establishment of British colonies in present-day Nigeria; Sokoto Caliphate governs many of the Hausa-Fulani groups in the north; smaller groups govern among Yoruba, Igbo, other groups in the south.
1850s–1900	Increasing colonization of Nigeria by Great Britain.
1900–19	Era of Lord Frederick Lugard, British administrator who establishes indirect rule using traditional authorities as intermediaries and unifies colonies of Nigeria.
1960	Independence from Great Britain.
1966	Military coup overthrows civilian government.
1966–75	Presidency of military leader Yakubu Gowon.
1967–70	Biafra War.
1976	Assassination of military leader Murtala Mohammed (president, 1975–6).
1979	Military leader Olusegun Obasanjo (1976–9) turns power over to civilian Shehu Shagari.
1983	Military takes control again under General Muhammadu Buhari.
1985–93	Presidency of military leader Ibrahim Babangida; human rights abuses worsen.
1993	Military holds elections but annuls them after apparent victory of businessman Moshood Abiola.
1993–8	Presidency of General Sani Abacha; corruption and human rights abuses reach their worst levels, with regular torture and execution of dissidents.
1995	Abacha regime executes political activist and author Ken Saro-Wiwa.
1998	Abacha dies suddenly in office, followed soon after by the sudden and suspicious death of civilian rival Moshood Abiola.
1999	Nigeria returns to civilian rule under former general Olusegun Obasanjo.
2003	Obasanjo is re-elected for a second term.
2007	Umaru Yar'Adua is elected president but is in grave health for most of his presidency.
2008–11	Tensions worsen between northern Muslims and southern Christians.
2010	As many as 1000 people are killed in clashes between Christians and Muslims in the city of Jos and elsewhere in central Nigeria.
2010	Yar'Adua dies of natural causes; Vice President Goodluck Jonathan becomes president.
2011	Goodluck Jonathan is elected to full presidential term.
2011-15	Increased terrorist activity by Islamist extremist group Boko Haram, including deadly bombing of a UN compound in Abuja, kidnapping of schoolgirls, and massacres in several towns across northern Nigeria.
2015	Muhammadu Buhari, a former military dictator, is elected president, defeating incumbent Goodluck Jonathan.
2017	Activists launch a large-scale stay-at-home protest advocating independence for the southeast.
2019	Federal elections see Buhari elected to a second term with more than 55 per cent of the vote. Buhari's party, the All Progressives Congress, wins majorities in both the House of Representatives and Senate.

In 1967, the Nigerian Civil War (also known as the Biafra War) broke out, pitting the Eastern region and its Igbo majority against the federal government (Falola and Heaton 2008, 175–80). The conflict was over autonomy, with the Igbo seeking to establish the independent state of Biafra and gain control of the rich oil holdings found in their region. After three years of bloody conflict in which more than 1 million people died—mostly on the Igbo side—the federal government won the war, and Nigeria remained a single country.

The 1970s saw another succession of military rulers, with power passing to presidents Murtala Mohammed (a northerner), who was assassinated, and then Olusegun Obasanjo (a southwestern Yoruba). Obasanjo ultimately proposed free elections and the establishment of a new republic and turned power over to civilian leader Shehu Shagari, a northern Muslim. Shagari and the republic did not see out their term, however, as the military seized control again under General Muhammadu Buhari, citing extensive corruption and fraud under Shagari. Military rule continued under President Ibrahim Babangida, who ruled from 1985 to 1993, but governing conditions did not improve. In particular, corruption continued unabated despite the imprisonment of several high-ranking officials and the execution of violent criminals. While Babangida was initially popular, he came under pressure to redemocratize as a wave of democracy swept across Africa in the early 1990s.

The military held elections in 1993, but when prominent businessman Chief Moshood Abiola looked to be the victor, the military annulled the results. This paved the way for the presidency of military General Sani Abacha (see Falola and Heaton 2008, 229–34), who earned the dubious distinction of being the worst dictator in Nigeria's less-than-proud history of corrupt and authoritarian presidents. The regime stood accused of engaging in torture on a regular basis. During his reign, Abacha and his family were rumoured to have accumulated several billion dollars in assets. In 1998, Abacha's rule came to a sudden end when he died in office. Rumours soon emerged that he was poisoned; the rumours gained in popularity when his death was soon followed by the sudden and suspicious death of Chief Moshood Abiola, the presumptive winner of the 1993 elections.

After Abacha, a transitional military government under General Abdulsalami Abubakar moved to draft a new constitution, establish a new republic, and return Nigeria to civilian rule by 1999. In elections that year, former general and one-time military president Olusegun Obasanjo won the presidency handily. This Christian southerner selected a Muslim northerner as vice president and governed at the head of the People's Democratic Party (PDP), which crafted a cross-ethnic coalition. Obasanjo remained relatively popular in Nigeria's challenging political environment and was re-elected for a second term in 2003. He then ceded power in 2007 to another PDP president, the Muslim northerner Umaru Yar'Adua. Yar'Adua was ill for most of his presidency, and authority was largely exercised by Vice President Goodluck Jonathan after 2009. In 2010, Yar'Adua died, and Jonathan became president; he later won a full term of office running as an incumbent in 2011. Anger at Jonathan's corruption and mismanagement led in 2015 to the election of Muhammadu Buhari, who ran as an anti-corruption candidate, calling himself "Mr Honest" and proclaiming a "broom revolution" to clean up the greed of the federal government. However, when he ran for re-election in 2019, the problems of corruption had not changed much, according to Transparency International (Maclean and Egbejule 2019).

Ethnic and regional tensions came to the fore again in recent years in Nigeria with a string of clashes between Christians and Muslims and with the emergence of Islamist fundamentalist groups. Much of the violence has occurred along the central belt of Nigeria, along the fault line between the Muslim-dominated north and the Christian-dominated south. Over these same years, the Islamist extremist group Boko Haram has emerged as a significant threat to stability, having coordinated and led deadly bombings and attacks of markets, police stations, polling stations, and international agencies in cities such as Bauchi and the capital Abuja, over recent years killing thousands of people and becoming internationally notorious for its mass abduction of schoolgirls in 2014 and again in 2018. The group calls for stricter enforcement of Islamic Shari'a law in Nigeria, where it is applied to some extent in the northern states, and for the outright rejection of modern education, and has claimed an affiliation with ISIS.

Regime and Political Institutions

According to its constitution, Nigeria now follows the policy-making processes that exist in many other presidential systems. The legislature passes bills through both houses—the National Assembly and the Senate—and the president signs the bill into law or vetoes it. In the case of a veto, the National Assembly can override the president by a vote of two-thirds in both chambers. Laws are subject to constitutional review by the independent Supreme Court. And as a federation, Nigeria has states that exercise considerable authority as well in a way that is semi-autonomous from the central government.

Political Culture

Nigeria routinely appears among the worst on lists by Transparency International when it ranks the most corrupt countries on earth. Politics has been plagued by corruption for decades, under military and civilian regimes alike. The issue of corruption is linked to the distribution of spoils to different groups. Groups of people in Nigeria often view

Regime and Political Institutions

Regime	Federal republic, democratically elected since 1999
Administrative Divisions	36 states + Federal Capital Territory (Abuja)
Executive Branch	President
Selection of Executive	Direct election by national popular vote; runoff among top two candidates if none secures 50 per cent in first round; to win in first round, candidate must also secure at least 25 per cent of the vote in at least two-thirds of the states.
Legislative Branch	Bicameral Lower chamber: House of Representatives Upper chamber: Senate
Judicial Branch	Supreme Court, appointed by president, confirmed by Senate
Political Party System	Multiparty but with leading/dominant parties: All Progressives Congress (APC) and the People's Democratic Party (PDP)

elected representatives from their group as being responsible for providing for an "extended family," and a whole ethnic group can sometimes be seen as just such an extended family.

While corruption has been an enduring problem, Nigeria features a great deal of mobilization, and the citizenry has often taken on the central government in various ways. The country witnessed significant movements for autonomy in the 1990s, not to mention a major civil war in the 1960s over regional autonomy. Many movements have emerged in the Niger Delta, the locus of much of Nigeria's oil that is also one of the poorest and most polluted regions of the country. Resistance there has ranged from non-violent citizens' protests to the emergence of armed separatist groups, as well as criminal gangs seeking profit from kidnappings or banditry.

Political Economy

Nigeria has a low average income compared to many of the countries profiled in this book. Yet the country is an economic giant by African standards due to its large population and a petroleum industry that is the source of much of the nation's revenue. New estimates suggest it is the largest economy in Africa south of the Sahara, surpassing South Africa.

The most important single sector in Nigeria's economy is petroleum extraction. Oil revenues account for more than 90 per cent of export earnings and more than three-quarters of the government's revenues. The country brings in large amounts of money and relies on natural resources rather than broad-based taxes to support government spending. Oil shapes the country's patterns of economic growth and inequality. In terms of economic growth, the country's performance depends in part on the international price for oil, though Nigeria's dysfunctional political economy has repeatedly resulted in the squandering of revenues when the price for Nigeria's main export is high.

The running theme in Nigerian politics has been corruption and the misuse of state resources, and as we noted before, Buhari's appeal has been his promise to crack down on corruption. In Nigeria, the particular style of political economy has given rise to terms such as "neopatrimonialism" (Bratton and Van de Walle 1997). The main implication of these terms is that those in state office view the resources of the state as available for their own personal use rather than for public services. State officials at all levels make use of government funds to favour themselves and their own families, ethnic groups, or other favoured constituents. The system views the officeholder as a "patron" and these recipients of resources as "clients," from which come the terms *patron–client relations* and *clientelism*.

Apart from the extraction of petroleum (and now natural gas) and the rents it generates, Nigeria is a large and relatively advanced economy by African standards. The country does have a developed industrial sector, and it is the leading manufacturer in West Africa, though it is not a world leader in industrial technology: Many products are simple consumer goods such as processed foods and beverages, textiles, and basic household products. Agriculture, meanwhile, still employs an estimated 70 per cent of Nigerians and accounts for almost 22 per cent of GDP (*CIA World Factbook 2017*). In urban areas, large numbers of Nigerians work in the informal sector, the largely unregulated part of the economy in which workers try to eke out a modest living without formal contracts or guaranteed wages. Among the many millions working in Nigeria's vast and dynamic informal sector are street vendors, hawkers, small merchants, and providers of a range of services, from messengers and couriers to mechanic shops. Finally, Nigeria is an African leader in communications, with major industries ranging from mobile phone networks to "Nollywood," the Nigerian film industry that distributes movies across Africa at a rate faster than Hollywood itself.

CASE STUDIES

CASE STUDY

Chapter 10, Page 217

Federalism and the States in Nigeria: Holding Together or Tearing Apart?

Nigeria is a crucial case in examining whether constitutional engineering and design, particularly with regard to federalism, can contribute to stability and democracy. Federalism has been essential to efforts to address one of Nigeria's leading political challenges: ethnic and regional divisions. The subject of federalism and autonomy came to the fore most dramatically with the Nigerian civil war from 1967 to 1970.

A principal tactic of the central government to hold the country together has been to increase the number of states, which have gone from an original three regions at independence to 36 today. This happened in a series of steps. Independent Nigeria began with three regions—Northern, Western, and Eastern—each of which was associated with a particular dominant ethnic group: the Hausa-Fulani, Yoruba, and Igbo, respectively. The Mid-West Region was added in 1963. In the lead-up to the Nigerian civil war, the central government moved to reorganize the four regions into 12 states. The civil war then pitted the Eastern region against the rest of Nigeria, and after the rebels surrendered, the military government responded by creating seven more states in 1976 and two additional states in 1987. In 1991, President Babangida announced that the number of states would increase to 30, and six more states were added in 1996 (Suberu 2001, xxiv–vi). The numbers thus went from three to four regions, then to 12 states and on to 19, to 21, to 30, and finally to 36 states.

Why would subdividing the states and increasing their number matter for stability? The approach has been largely about ethnic arithmetic (see Suberu 2001). In Nigeria, the central government has used the creation of new states in an attempt to multiply the number of administrative divisions in Nigeria. The theory was that this would eliminate the big divisions between the largest ethnic groups as an important factor in Nigerian politics and would substitute for this new administrative boundaries that citizens would focus on. At the same time, those living in the newly created states often favoured the proposals for two reasons. First, the smaller ethnic groups in Nigeria sought their own states to avoid domination by the Hausa-Fulani, Yoruba, and Igbo. Second, the creation of states in a particular area meant they would share in the distribution of the country's revenues. This gave incentives for many groups to favour new states, though at different times Nigeria's dominant ethnicities have opposed plans they believed would weaken them in the delicate balance of power.

Most new states were created by the military governments rather than through public consultation, and the justifications have ultimately been about national stability (see Suberu 2001, 80). The creation of states in the 1960s was based on the idea of balance: No region should be able to dominate the federation. As the civil war approached and the Igbo-dominated Eastern region threatened to secede, the military in power gained some support from non-Igbos in that region by offering to grant them new states (Suberu 2001, 87–9). Similarly, a panel in the 1970s argued that Nigeria would not remain stable without further subdivision; this resulted in the 19 states as of 1976 (Suberu 2001, 90–1). The logic played out in slightly different ways in subsequent divisions but always with an eye toward governability. Beyond creating states, the federal government has taken a number of other steps that supports them, most notably guaranteeing substantial revenues to the state and local governments. At the same time, while creating these states the central government has also attempted to centralize many powers.

Giving different ethnic and regional groups their own authority and resources could either improve stability and increase the likelihood of democracy or harm those prospects. It could help by allowing each group some say in its own affairs and some role in government, preventing winner-takes-all politics in national elections. Or it could draw such stark dividing lines between groups that it might give rise to secessionism or civil war. The Nigerian approach has been to give more small groups additional say and to blur (or redraw) the lines between the large groups.

Has it succeeded? The evidence can be interpreted in different ways. On one hand, Nigeria has remained intact after the civil war of the late 1960s, which is a non-trivial achievement in a society that is so fractured along ethnic, religious, and regional fault lines. On the other hand, the creation of new states has not ended ethnic or sectarian tensions. Politics in Nigeria is still centred around the division between the north, the southwest, and the southeast that troubled the country at independence. The 2015 presidential election, for instance, had an electorate divided geographically, with Buhari winning the north and the southwest, while the defeated incumbent Goodluck Jonathan won in his native southeastern region. In 2019, Buhari again won the north, while his main challenger, Atiku Abubakar, was from the northeast region of Adamawa state.

The creation of states has created new divisions in Nigerian politics but has not overcome the old divisions (Suberu 2001, 110). Nigeria still witnesses a spiral of intergroup conflict. Demands for more states or greater federalism are unlikely to mitigate conflict at this point and may only serve to appease different groups clamouring for the resources that come with getting a state. Federalism might have changed the nature of conflict, but it has not necessarily stopped it.

CASE STUDY

Chapter 13, Page 280

Are Natural Resources Sometimes a Curse? The Nigerian Case

Nigeria has the largest population and the second-largest economy in sub-Saharan Africa, but it is not an economic success story. Instead, Nigeria—a major oil producer—is often held up as an exemplary case of the "resource curse." You would expect that discovering oil would be very good for an economy, and in some cases it can be, especially if the economy is already robust and diversified when oil is discovered. But often oil and similar high-value commodities produce unanticipated problems. The first is called the "Dutch Disease." Exporting oil brings in lots of foreign currency. The ready supply of, say, dollars means dollars are not seen as valuable relative to the national currency; the domestic currency rises in value, and this hurts other exports because these goods are expensive for foreigners in dollar terms. Along the same lines, the potential profitability of oil makes it a magnet for big capital investment, thus crowding out investment in other industries. Oil-producing countries thus often see other areas of their economies decline.

Equally important, the global price for oil is cyclical. Economies like Nigeria tend to see boom and bust cycles that prevent them from achieving development. High prices at one point in time can leave a country vulnerable to downturns in the price of its main export commodity.

Oil dependence also affects politics and often for the worse (Karl 1997; Herbst 2000, 130–3). The easy access to oil money has a rather subtle effect: It stunts the growth of important relationships between the state and the society at large. Politicians can have incentives to make bad policy in oil-rich countries. "Easy money" from oil can make states such as Nigeria more likely to simply offer handouts to their "clients" and to the populace during boom times. States with substantial cash flows from oil often do not develop a capacity to tax the population. This may sound like a low-tax paradise, but without taxation the populace is less likely to see the government as a set of institutions to be held accountable for its governing performance.

continued

Rather, citizens become accustomed to government simply distributing benefits. This can result in a destructive relationship between state and society, especially in oil-producing countries. Such a counterproductive relationship is not universal but may be most likely in places such as Nigeria with high prior levels of inequality (cf. Dunning 2008). In addition to domestic challenges, the politics of oil and natural resources also involves international actors such as oil companies. This is because developing countries themselves often lack technical capacity in areas that require advanced technology and may also lack the capital needed for investment, at least at early stages. Such countries thus commonly rely on licences to foreign companies, or the use of foreign advisors, or joint ventures between major multinational companies and relatively weak states (Kohli 2004). This leaves another form of dependence. The impacts of interactions with foreign actors are hotly debated, but in Nigeria low state capacity, partially dating back to weak state development under British colonialism, seems not to mix well with oil. In short, despite the enormous wealth that Nigerian oil has created for some, it has left the country with high levels of poverty and inequality and with institutional problems that will make overcoming these challenges difficult.

Research Prompts

1. British colonialism in Nigeria ended more than 50 years ago. To what extent does the legacy of colonialism still affect the politics and economy of Nigeria today? How can we determine what contemporary outcomes are the result of historically distant factors like colonialism as opposed to more recent factors such as the events of the late 1990s?
2. Nigeria is used by scholars of development as a quintessential example of economic failure and underperformance. Viewing the history of Nigeria's political economy, does Nigeria's weak economic performance over the decades give more credence to proponents of market-led development or proponents of state-led development? What would be the recommendations from both market-led and state-led development advocates for Nigeria?
3. Compare and contrast Nigeria's development experience with one of the other developing countries mentioned in Chapter 5: Iran, China, or India. What do you learn from the comparison, and are there any comparative lessons that you can draw for why development does or does not happen?
4. One unavoidable element of Nigeria's political life seems to be corruption. Can we say this corruption is caused by oil and other natural resources? By political culture? Economic realities? Or political institutions? Which of these do you find to be the leading the cause, and how can you know?
5. Conflict in Nigeria is often said to have at least three components: ethnic, religious (or sectarian), and regional. Which of these divisions in Nigerian society is the primary cause of the conflict? Can you trace the historical evolution of conflicts in Nigeria to determine which of them is the leading causal factor?
6. Nigeria has implemented numerous institutional reforms to limit violence and conflict. These include the creation of more states in the federation and provisions requiring presidents to win a substantial proportion of the vote across many states. Is it possible to determine what the effects of these reforms have been on conflict and ethnic tension? How might you approach this question and research it to be able to offer an answer? How might comparative study help?

Online Case Studies

Go to **www.oup.com/he/DickovickCe** to find more case studies online, including:

- The Presidency in Nigeria: Powers and Limitations
- The Nigerian Civil War, or Biafran War: Nationalism and Ethno-national Conflict in a Post-colonial Society
- What Is a Weak State, and Can It Be Changed? The Case of Nigeria

Note

1 BBC News: Africa 2019.

Russia

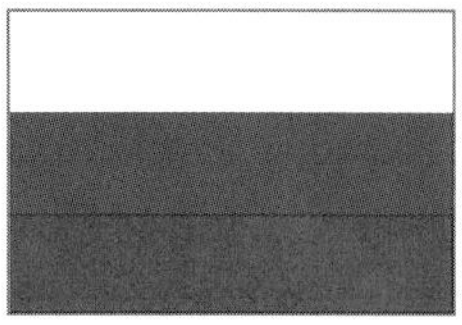

PROFILE

Key Features of Contemporary Russia

Population:	142,257,519 (July 2017 est.)
Area:	17,098,242 square kilometres
Head of State:	Vladimir Putin (president, 2012–present)
Head of Government:	Dmitry Medvedev (premier, May 2012–present)
Capital:	Moscow
Year of Independence:	The Russian Empire dates back to 1721, and independent states comprising much of Russia predate that founding. The current state became independent of the Soviet Union in 1991.
Year of Current Constitution:	1993
Languages:	Russian is spoken by most citizens; there are more than 100 other languages in the Russian Federation: Tatar and Ukrainian are among the most important.
GDP per Capita:	$10,743.10 (World Bank estimate, 2017)
Human Development Index Ranking (2015):	49th (very high human development)
Trading Relationship with Canada (2016):	• Imports $704,086,289 • Exports $458,234,353 https://globaledge.msu.edu/countries/canada/tradestats

Sources: *CIA World Factbook*; World Bank World Development Indicators; United Nations *Human Development Report 2016*

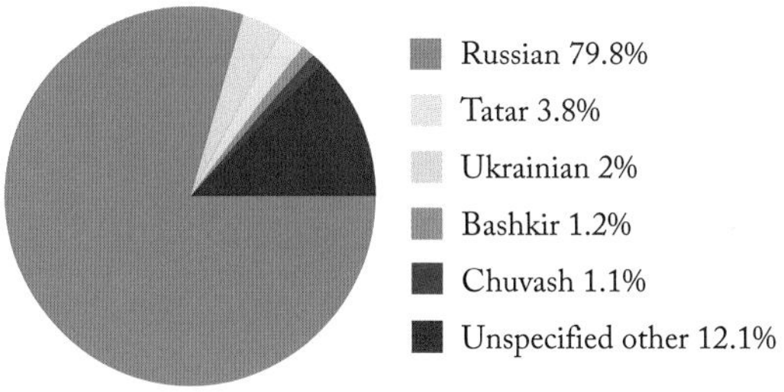

Ethnic Groups in Russia

Note that there are numerous smaller groups as well, including Chechens, captured in the "unspecified/other" category here.

Source: *CIA World Factbook*

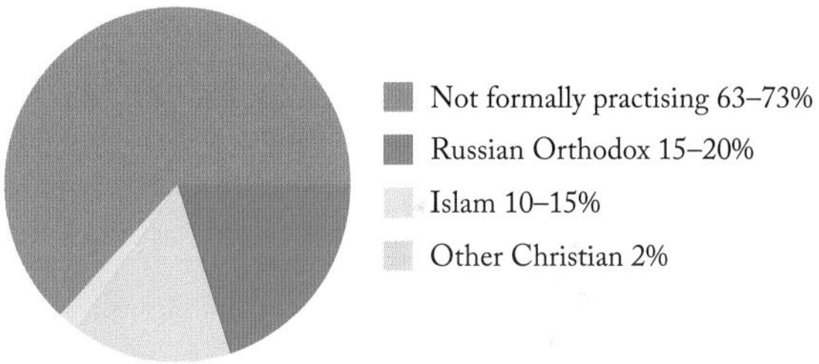

Religious Affiliation in Russia, 2006 Estimates of *Practising* Religious Populations

Note that some of those counted as "Russian Orthodox" may be only nominally so.

Source: *CIA World Factbook*

Introduction

The Russian Federation is, in geographic terms, the largest country in the world, with Canada in second place. Its land is highly varied, stretching from temperate areas to the Arctic and from western Europe to the Sea of Japan. Its people and their culture are varied as well. Both its people and its expanse of land have captured the imagination of writers for generations, and many have felt that there is something ineffable about Russia. However, what is of still greater interest about Russia to comparative political analysts is the country's tumultuous political and economic history. Russia, as we will see, has over the past century gone from being a reactionary Tsarist regime, to creating the Soviet Union, during which it

aimed to completely remake the society and to spread socialist revolution around the globe, to watching the Soviet Union collapse to be replaced by a relatively weak government, and finally, under Vladimir Putin, to the restoration of centralized authority. Contemporary Russia is Exhibit A in political scientists' efforts to describe so-called "hybrid" or "competitive authoritarian" (Levitsky and Way 2010) regimes discussed in Chapter 7 of this volume.

Russia's 1917 revolutions—both the one that removed the tsar from power and the subsequent one, which gave the Bolsheviks control of the state—inspired waves of imitators. The Soviet Union formed one of the two poles in the Cold War that structured global affairs for half a century: It would be difficult to exaggerate the extent of this long conflict's impact, especially on the populations of those countries where proxy wars between the poles were fought. At the same time, the Soviet Union's brutality, particularly under Joseph Stalin, pushed many global political actors away from socialism and toward liberalism and social democracy. Russia is also of interest to students of identity politics. Debates abound concerning the nature of Russian national identity and the timing and causes of its emergence and spread. These questions become particularly complicated in the Soviet years. As a Marxist regime, the Soviet Union was officially internationalist, but a number of observers see it as having been a vehicle for Russian national aims, and Stalin himself was a theorist of nationalism (Stalin 1994). Russian nationalism has typically been considered to fall into the ethnic type (Greenfeld 1992), and Russian history gives numerous examples of repression of ethnic minorities.

Russia's post-communist transition is of particular interest to comparative analysts, in part because of the pattern of authoritarian persistence that it reveals. Russia has never developed a sustainable, fully functioning democracy, and the lengthy Putin regime is a contemporary example of this situation.

Historical Development

Many accounts of modern Russia begin with Peter the Great, who in the late 17th century attempted to forcibly modernize the country. Some of these reforms changed the social structure in important ways. For example, he imposed a "Table of Ranks" that re-engineered the Russian social hierarchy, making noble status dependent on state service and creating the possibility to *achieve* nobility through partially meritocratic competition (Ascher 2009, 63; Greenfeld 1992). He personally studied Western techniques for shipbuilding and other technologies that he expected would increase Russia's power and prestige, and he brought foreign experts to Russia in large numbers (Ascher 2009, 58–65). Some of his reforms were more symbolic as well and invited a cultural turn to the West (Hughes 2008, 68–77; Bushkovitch 2012, 82–3, 94–8). Not all of these moves were popular, but there was little doubt that Russia under Peter was stronger than it had been in previous years. Russia played a central role in the Great Northern War that dramatically reduced Swedish power, much to Russia's benefit (Ascher 2009, 61–2).

Subsequent years saw some decline (Ascher 2009, 66–7), but Russia encountered another strong leader in Catherine the Great, who seized the throne in a coup d'état in 1762. Catherine was known as a patron of the European Enlightenment (on Russian culture under Catherine, see Hughes 2008, 81–8). She turned to Western models as she aimed to increase Russia's power and status and increased the administrative reach and centralization of the state to assert Russia's role as a geopolitical power. The first half of the 19th century saw the rule of Alexander I and Nicholas I. Alexander is best remembered for leading Russia as it defeated Napoleon in his famous invasion (in which the French occupied Moscow but were eventually defeated by Russian resistance and the harsh Russian winter). Both Nicolas I and Alexander I, though, presided over a period in which Russia failed to continue its path of modernization (Ascher 2009, 80–1). Much of this changed beginning in the 1860s under Alexander II, who implemented a number of reforms. The most important was the emancipation of the serfs (Bushkovitch 2012, 188–93) and state peasants, which commenced between 1861 and 1866. Material conditions of peasants, though, in many cases did not improve over the several decades that they paid for the land they received.

During the 19th century, Russian nationalism spread as Russian literature and cultural production grew. Moreover, that nationalism acquired a strongly populist component, epitomized in the Narodnik, or "To the People," Movement in the early 1870s (Service 2009, 17–18). Among other things, Russian intellectuals went to live with poor peasants in hopes of helping to lead a movement, which met with little success. However, discontent and agitation would continue. Most notably, Tsar Alexander II was assassinated in 1881. His successor, Alexander III, endeavoured to undo many of the reforms of the previous decades (Ascher 2009, 125–30).

Historical Development Timeline

1682–1725	Reign of Peter the Great, seen as Western-oriented modernizer of Russia.
1762–96	Reign of Catherine the Great, another Westernizer but nevertheless autocratic and a critic of the French Revolution.
1812	Invasion of Russia by Napoleon of France; French reach Moscow but then retreat, and Napoleon is defeated.
1815	Congress of Vienna.
1853–6	Crimean War pits Russia against France, Great Britain, and the Ottoman Empire.
1861–6	Beginning of the process of emancipation of the serfs and state peasants.
1881	Assassination of Tsar Alexander II.
1905	1905 Revolution (brings about constitutional monarchy).
1917	Russian Revolution(s) that topple the tsar and bring the communists to power.
1918–21	Russian Civil War.
1921	Vladimir Lenin's New Economic Policy (NEP).

continued

1924	Death of Lenin, which leads to Joseph Stalin's rise to prominence.
1928–33	First Five Year Plan and introduction of a command economy.
1929	Consolidation of Stalin's authority; Leon Trotsky is forced into exile.
1933–7	Second Five Year Plan.
1935–8	Period notable for Stalinist purges, including 1937–8 mass executions (the "Great Terror").
1938–41	Third Five Year Plan (ends prematurely because of the Second World War).
1939	Soviets sign non-aggression pact with Nazi Germany, including secret agreement to divide up Europe; World War II begins in Europe.
1941	Germany invades Soviet Union.
1941–5	Soviet involvement in World War II, in which more than 20 million Soviets die; Hitler invades the Soviet Union but ultimately retreats in a major turning point in the war in Europe.
1945	Soviets occupy Berlin with the fall of Hitler.
1946–89	Cold War, an ideological, military, and economic rivalry between the communist world led by the Soviet Union and the capitalist world led by the United States.
1949	Soviets test atomic bomb.
1953	Death of Stalin.
1956	USSR cracks down on dissent in Hungary with invasion.
1957	USSR launches Sputnik satellite.
1961	Berlin Wall erected; Soviet Union becomes first country to send man into space.
1968	USSR crushes "Prague Spring" movement in Czechoslovakia.
1972	SALT I treaty as policy of détente between the USSR and the United States commences.
1989	Fall of Berlin Wall and collapse of Soviet-led communism in eastern and central Europe (Poland, Czechoslovakia, East Germany, Hungary, Bulgaria, Romania); Soviet Union begins to unravel.
1991	Communist hardliner coup to replace Mikhail Gorbachev results in street mobilizations for further reform; USSR collapses and divides into 15 countries; Boris Yeltsin becomes president of independent Russia.
2000	Vladimir Putin is elected president.
2008	Dmitry Medvedev is elected president, with Vladimir Putin as prime minister.
2012	Vladimir Putin is re-elected president amid allegations of electoral irregularities and widespread public protests; Putin nominates Dmitry Medvedev as prime minister.
2014	Russia annexes the Crimean peninsula, a Russian-majority region in neighbouring Ukraine, and Russian-backed separatists in eastern Ukraine seek to join with Russia. Canada, among other countries, condemns the annexation.
2015	Russia intervenes militarily in Syria against the wishes of NATO allies to buttress President Bashar al-Assad's regime.
2016-17	Russia is accused of meddling in the US presidential election in favour of Donald Trump and against Hillary Clinton.
2018	Putin re-elected president in a weak field of opposing candidates. Russia hosts the FIFA World Cup, and Putin holds a summit meeting in Helsinki, Finland, with US President Donald Trump.
2019	The Muller Report documents aspects of Russian interference in the 2016 US election.

Demands for change came to a head in the first years of the 20th century. Note that Russia was relatively exceptional in this period (in the European context) for still being a non-constitutional monarchy. Russia's highly educated, literate, and partially Westernized nobility, along with non-noble intellectuals, were painfully aware of this sign of "backwardness." The country had begun state-led industrialization (Service 2009, 4–5), and while industrial workers were only a tiny fraction of the overall population, they were important agitators concentrated in the largest cities in what would be called the Revolution of 1905 (Carr [1979] 2004, 2; Fitzpatrick 1994, 33–4). Another critical factor was Russia's poor showing against Japan in the Russo-Japanese War of 1904–5, which seemed to signal state weakness and the need for reform. The revolution itself consisted largely of a series of strikes and other actions (Fitzpatrick 1994, 32–3). It also unleashed a series of pogroms. The goals of the "revolutionaries" varied considerably. Some were simply disaffected peasants and urban workers; others were committed ideologues. The revolution ended with Russia becoming a constitutional monarchy.

The years after the 1905 revolution saw agrarian reform that would increase private landholding as well as other changes. However, the decisive event that helped to trigger the Revolution of 1917 was the First World War. Russia suffered heavy losses, and its troops faced difficult conditions. The war lost public support, and the relative military weakness of the state was again exposed. The year 1917 was the key year, with two critical revolutionary stages. In March, street protests led to the fall of Tsar Nicholas II and his government. A provisional government was formed by the legislature (the Duma), but it was soon rivalled by "Soviets" (councils) of workers, peasants, and general military personnel in other parts of the country. In short, it was not entirely clear who was in charge of Russia. Before long, the Bolsheviks, a radical socialist group, took over the Soviets, and the provisional government fell, leaving the Soviets in charge. This would be followed by withdrawal from World War I early the next year and ongoing civil war between Bolsheviks (who renamed themselves the Communists) and Mensheviks. Contrary to Lenin's expectations, the rise of the Soviet Union did not trigger a wave of successful proletarian revolutions throughout Europe (Ascher 2009, 167–8). The new government soon began to increase the already notable role of the state in the Russian economy, and it began agrarian reforms, pitting poorer peasants against those who were better off. Some of this was relaxed with Lenin's more pragmatic "New Economic Policy," beginning in 1921 (Service 2009, 123–49; Bushkovitch 2012, 318–19). Lenin died in 1924, setting off a struggle within the party for supremacy. By 1929, Joseph Stalin consolidated his authority, purging numerous alleged opponents, often using "show trials" and forced confessions to maintain the appearance of legitimacy. This behaviour would continue after the war. Millions died or were imprisoned under Stalin.

The Stalinist regime set out to extend socialist revolution. The first Five Year Plan (1928–33) aimed to both force rapid industrialization and to collectivize agriculture (Fitzpatrick 1994, 129–41). It was somewhat successful with regard to the former goal, but the latter goal was largely a failure in economic and human terms, costing millions of lives (Service 2009, 181). The second (1933–37) and third (1938–41) Five Year Plans continued Stalin's efforts to achieve state-led full industrialization. The last of these efforts was disrupted by the invasion by Nazi Germany. For the first two years of that war, the Soviet Union remained uninvolved because of a non-aggression pact that Hitler and Stalin had signed in 1939 (Kitchen 2006, 297–8, 301–4). But in 1941 Hitler changed course and invaded the Soviet Union (Bushkovitch 2012, 378–82). The fighting on the eastern front was brutal and the loss of life enormous. While the allies emerged victorious, the process was very costly for the Soviet Union. At the same time, it ended up greatly expanding the territory controlled by the Soviet Regime, notably eastern Europe and much of central Europe, which in the years after the war became Soviet satellite states.

The settlement at the end of World War II set the stage for the Cold War. The Soviet Union and the United States jostled for global influence, and proxy wars were fought in a number of developing countries, causing considerable suffering and loss of life. For both sides, fears of the prospect of nuclear war were part of daily life. Stalin died in 1953 and was followed by long terms for Khrushchev and Brezhnev. Khrushchev aimed to "de-Stalinize" the country, repudiating the purges and other forms of oppression that had claimed so many and making a number of reforms. The fact that they criticized Stalin's atrocities should not lead us to conclude, however, that they were not willing to repress civilians themselves, as a number of citizens of Russia and of Soviet satellite states were to learn (Davies 1996, 1102–4; Service 2009, 435–500).

After Brezhnev's death in 1982, there was a series of short-lived leaders until Mikhail Gorbachev was selected in 1985. Gorbachev embarked on a series of reforms (Davies 1996, 1121; Bushkovitch 2012, 448–51). In the economic sphere, this involved trying to expand the role of markets so as to preserve socialism through enhancing productivity and efficiency. Part of this was inspired by China's economic reforms of 1978. It was clear to all in the Soviet world that change was necessary, and once it became clear that Gorbachev would not repress protest in central and eastern Europe with the force that previous Soviet leaders had used, those countries began to seek independence. Poland was the initial leader, and its Solidarity Movement struggled for years in its efforts to bring about a transition, with a successful and peaceful revolution taking place in 1989, followed shortly thereafter by a wave of similar ones throughout the region (Ash 2002). Communist elites in the Soviet Union were alarmed, not surprisingly. Eventually some of them launched a coup d'état against Gorbachev in an effort to restore centralized control. The plan backfired, and when the dust settled Boris Yeltsin was in charge of the Russian Federation (the Soviet Union was gone).

Gorbachev had hoped to save communism: Yeltsin moved to end it. He presented himself as a democrat, though his governing style was somewhat autocratic. He was able to inaugurate a new, more democratic constitution for the Russian Federation (Service 2009, 522–8). Yeltsin embraced radical free-market reform (McFaul 2008, 359–61), quickly privatizing key industries and helping to create what commentators now sometimes refer to as Russia's "crony capitalism." A relatively small group of wealthy individuals benefitted disproportionately from privatization schemes, and economic performance was consistently poor, yielding an increase in poverty (Ascher 2009; Service 2009, 518–19, 540–1). Rule of law declined precipitously as well (Service 2009, 519, 534; Bushkovitch 2012, 452–3). Economic problems were exacerbated by the disappearance of Soviet social entitlements, and euphoria gave way to frustration and, for some, to nostalgia (Service 2009, 529). Yeltsin's inconsistent leadership did not help matters, nor did the war in Chechnya. In 1999, Yeltsin elevated Vladimir Putin, first to the post of prime minister and then acting president, and Putin was then elected president in 2000.

Russia under Putin shifted back to a form of personalized authoritarianism and has not led in the direction of a functioning liberal, representative democracy. Putin's key goals seem to have been to (1) solidify his own power base; (2) centralize authority (Service 2009, 552); (3) strengthen the state; (4) curb the influence of the business leaders, or "oligarchs," who might oppose him and his allies; and (5) resume a more assertive foreign policy. Under Putin, Russia has reasserted control over its traditional spheres of influence. Notable examples are Russia's decisive victory over Georgia in 2008 and its military involvement in neighbouring Ukraine, including Russia's annexation of Crimea in 2014. Russia has also intervened in Syria to support its ally President Bashar al-Assad. A sustained increase in oil prices in the mid-2000s contributed to consistent Russian economic growth and aided Putin's efforts.

Putin has solidified personal control of Russian politics. While the government has formally independent branches, few doubt his authority. This is perhaps clearest in electoral politics in which Russia is a case of so-called "competitive authoritarianism" (Levitsky and Way 2010). Putin formally satisfied the rules regarding term limits, temporarily moving to the position of prime minister while a protégé, Dmitry Medvedev, ascended to the presidency. While some commentators thought Medvedev might adopt an independent line, it soon became clear that Putin would remain the central figure in Russian politics. Putin was re-elected to the presidency in 2012 and again in 2018, with numerous allegations of electoral irregularities and widespread public protests. The authoritarian character of the contemporary Russian regime is also revealed by the government's selective targeting of political opponents for prosecution (Service 2009, 550). In 2016, Russia was roundly condemned for meddling in the US presidential and congressional elections and has also been linked to funding a range of populist and right-of-centre parties throughout Europe.

Regime and Political Institutions

Russia is a semi-presidential system. The president and the prime minister both have considerable powers. However, in reality in recent years, institutions are not as strong and independent as a review of their formal features might lead us to suppose. Most observers believe that even in his years as prime minister, Vladimir Putin was the true decision-maker on key issues, not then-president Dmitri Medvedev. Presidential powers are strong on paper. The president can even veto no-confidence votes in the legislature, though they are subject to override in the Duma. In practice, Putin's personal authority seems more important than formal powers. Personalism is not restricted to the executive itself: Political parties have come to be associated with leading individuals in several cases. In short, contemporary Russian politics still has some minimal democratic features, but few observers now regard it as a functioning democracy.

Regime and Political Institutions

Regime	Federal republic
Administrative Divisions	83 or 85 units in the federation, of which 21 (or 22) are formally republics; since annexation in 2014, Russia has claimed Crimea as a constituent republic and the Crimean city of Sevastopol as a federal city, but many countries, including Canada, do not diplomatically recognize this change.
Executive Branch	Semi-presidential: president and prime minister
Selection of Executive	President is elected and appoints the prime minister.
Legislative Branch	Bicameral Lower chamber: State Duma Upper chamber: Federation Council
Judicial Branch	Supreme Court is the highest judicial authority. A Constitutional Court is responsible for judicial review. There is a separate Superior Court for economic issues, called the Supreme Arbitration Court of the Russian Federation.
Political Party System	Russia's is nominally a multiparty system, though the independence and efficacy of some of the parties is in serious doubt. Important parties include United Russia (the party of Putin), the Communist Party, the Liberal Democratic Party of Russia, and A Just Russia.

Political Culture

Russia has long struggled with its relationship with western Europe. One strong political cultural tendency has been toward Westernization and modernization. This has meant different things at different times and for different constituencies, including constitutional monarchy, democratization, economic development, literary and artistic achievement, and even the turn to socialism. Another tendency, though, has pulled in the opposite direction, emphasizing the idea of a distinctively Russian, Slavic, or Orthodox identity that is different from, and perhaps superior to, western European culture.

Linked to this has been Russia's historical ability to dominate the nations in its periphery, which has lent the country a sense of important geopolitical status. Thus, it is hardly surprising that Russian political culture after the fall of the Soviet Union showed signs of frustration and loss, bordering on what sociologists call "status-inconsistency," as central and eastern Europe withdrew and moved into the orbit of western Europe and the United States. Russia's concerns about some of these countries' entry into NATO can only be partially explained in terms of national security interest, since this interest is blended with concerns about national pride and the sense that Russia has a natural or historically established "right" to dominate these countries. Russia underwent a transition from being a society that saw itself as being on the "right side of history," with allegedly scientific certainty of eventual triumph, to one that saw much of the globe view the society's political and economic structures as backward. These tendencies have no doubt facilitated the authoritarian features of the Putin years, since he presents himself as the one person capable of restoring Russia's "rightful" place in the international status hierarchy (Service 2009, 549).

Another key feature of Russia's political culture has been widespread corruption. Many commentators, both in Russia and abroad, allege that Russian economic liberalization was mismanaged, leading to oligarchical politics in the 1990s. Supporters tried to justify Putin's more authoritarian turn as a necessary response to such developments, yet in certain respects it has led to weak rule of law and ongoing corruption in both economics and politics, even while order was restored (Brown 2006, 395).

Political Economy

Russia is a fascinating case for political economists because it has witnessed a shift from a largely agrarian economy, to state-led industrialization and central planning under the Soviet Union, to a bumpy transition to a market economy. The Soviet system was a command economy, with the state responsible for major decisions about investment, production targets, and the social organization of economic life. Some would allege that the Soviet system failed because it did not give sufficient incentive to entrepreneurial activity and encouraged a culture of dependency. On one hand, popular dissatisfaction with the market reforms of the 1990s *might* be taken to indicate a sense of citizen entitlement of this sort. On the other hand, the "shock therapy" strategy of Russian privatization and the political and economic corruption that followed might be to blame for this reaction. Perhaps more measured economic reforms—with less tumultuous economic and social consequences—would have mitigated the impact of changes.

The Russian economy saw relatively strong performance in the first part of this century. Russia saw high GDP growth in the 2000s, owing in part to high oil prices. The global recession hit Russia hard in 2009. Growth rates were −2.8 per cent in 2015, −0.2 per cent in 2016, and only rose to a positive number in 2017 (1.8 per cent) (*CIA World Factbook 2018*).

At present, with the recent fall in oil prices, potentially serious economic problems loom, and this could be exacerbated by international sanctions against Russian banks and companies following Russia's incursion into Ukraine in 2014. Russia remains a society with a relatively high level of industrialization. Of its GDP, 4.7 per cent is produced by the agricultural sector and 32.4 per cent by industry, with the service sector accounting for the remaining 62.3 per cent, according to 2017 statistics (*CIA World Factbook*). The oil and natural gas industries are particularly important components of the Russian economy, and the country depends upon the proceeds of its exports to Europe.

Russia faces a series of social problems linked in different ways to its economic fortunes, including high rates of alcoholism and drug addiction, a high crime rate, relatively low life expectancy, and a very low birth rate, particularly among ethnic Russians, producing challenging demographic issues. Life expectancy fell notably as economic problems mounted in the years after the transition, while poverty jumped dramatically alongside high rates of crime.

CASE STUDIES

CASE STUDY

Chapter 10, Page 211

Oligarchy, Democracy, and Authoritarianism in Russia

Russia's political development has been mixed since the fall of the Soviet Union in 1991. An optimistic burst of activity in the early 1990s pushed the country from Soviet rule toward a greater emphasis on individual rights, but the country is now widely considered to be under authoritarian rule, or at least to be moving decisively toward centralization. At best, Russia can be seen as a hybrid regime with many authoritarian features that blends in some elements of electoral democracy. Russia's trajectory since 1991 is one in which a democratizing moment has been followed by a return to more centralized power and decision-making by a closed set of economic and political elites.

In the early 1990s, as the former Soviet Union crumbled, Russia moved toward more open and democratic rule under the erratic president Boris Yeltsin. The country also moved to a more open economy as privatization turned state enterprises over to private hands. Despite the excitement of the reforms, the strongest lasting image of this period is probably the dysfunctional transfer of economic power in which Russia developed only weak state institutions and lacked a rule of law. This gave rise to a corrupt network of "oligarchs," newly wealthy tycoons who operated in a style reminiscent of the mafia, especially in the areas of oil and natural gas. Privatization was seen going in step with democratization by giving individuals more freedoms, but the practice led to the creation of mega-rich corporate bosses that came to dominate the economy because of privileged connections to the state at the time of privatization. The result was a massive concentration of wealth in the hands of a few elites who were well connected to the state. The oligarchs exercised considerable control in Russian politics under Yeltsin and contributed to the breakdown of the rule of law, even bankrolling Yeltsin's campaign in exchange for options to purchase state assets at favourable prices (Rose, Mishler, and Munro 2006, 64).

While the emergence of the oligarchs thus undermined the rule of law under Yeltsin in the 1990s, cracking down on them also compromised democracy and facilitated the rise of new authoritarianism under Vladimir Putin. During his presidency, Putin used state power to suppress powerful adversaries, most notably the oligarchs. A key period was 2003 to 2005. During that time, the Putin government jailed Russia's wealthiest oligarch, the outspoken Mikhail Khodorkovsky, and prosecuted him on charges of tax fraud. The Putin administration renationalized his oil firm, Yukos, transferring the resources to the Russian state, in what was widely seen as a deliberate attack on the power of oligarchs who might get out of line (for example, by funding political opponents of Putin and his allies). The move signalled that Putin would allow no dissent, though the government would work with oligarchs who supported Putin and his version of "managed democracy" (Colton and McFaul 2003; Goldman 2004, 36). Many of the wealthy beneficiaries of Russia's 1990s privatization have either learned to work closely with the state or have been harassed by the state. The oligarchy has thus increasingly come under state pressure or state control. Putin himself has profited immensely from his long tenure in power. Recent estimates put his financial worth at between $70 and $200 billion, although it is virtually impossible to confirm any amount (Kottasová 2018; Hanbury and Cain 2018).

One of the key features of Russia's authoritarian rule has thus been the removal of alternative sources of power. The moves to sideline those oligarchs who were critical of Putin's rule have been part and parcel of a broader centralization of power and control. One leading commentator notes that Russia is actually quite similar to other authoritarian regimes in middle-income countries: It is not a totalitarian dictatorship, but "Putin has reduced the role of parliament, increased state control over the media, and overseen the renationalization of two major oil companies" (Treisman 2011, 342). The assertion of power over political institutions has gone hand in hand with the state's establishment of control over the economy. We return to Putin and his style of rule in the case studies that follow.

CASE STUDY

Chapter 11, Page 237

Personalism and the Party System in Russia

Russia illustrates the challenge and importance of party system institutionalization. During the Soviet period from 1918 to 1991, the party system was focused on the single party, the Communist Party. After the collapse of the Soviet Union, Russia became a country where the political party system lost much of its structure. Russia saw some major parties emerge—and the Communists remained a minority party—but many of these parties came and went. In more recent years, Vladimir Putin has accumulated more power, but not through constructing a well-institutionalized party to contest democratic elections. On the contrary, Russia's poorly institutionalized party system has facilitated authoritarian tendencies even in the absence of single-party rule.

To continue building on the themes of the previous box, the Putin years have seen significant centralization of power. But the United Russia party that has backed Putin has taken a back seat to a more personal system of rule. Personalism is not limited exclusively to Putin and the United Russia party. Another leading party has also become associated with their particular leadership: the Liberal Democratic Party under the erratic and unpredictable xenophobe Vladimir Zhirinovsky. Perhaps more significant, Russians felt little affinity for parties even after the transition from Soviet rule to a multiparty system in the 1990s (Mainwaring 1998). President Boris Yeltsin was nominally an independent during his time in office. This meant that the political party system never institutionalized before the Putin years; instead, Russians generally expressed dissatisfaction with the emergence of party options, which may have contributed to a desire for a strong central hand in the long run (Sharafutdinova 2011). In other words, the weak institutionalization of parties—with their weak links to society and lack of consistent programmatic alternatives—facilitated the rise of powerful actors such as Putin who work around institutions.

This prevalence of personalism in Russian politics is a clear demonstration of how political development and political institutions interact. Russian authoritarianism consists of centralized decision-making that is tightly linked to the personalism of the president. Similarly, the legislature has been reshaped in a way that facilitates central control, while the structure of the executive seen in Chapter 10 clearly facilitates personalism. In short, the various features of Russian politics work together to create a top-down system. Personalism is thus a theme that shows how the various institutions of government link to other features of a society's political culture.

CASE STUDY

Chapter 12, Page 261

The Russian Revolution

Karl Marx expected that the great revolution against capitalism would come in highly developed capitalist societies like Britain. If he had lived long enough to see it, he might have been surprised that it was in *Russia* where the most iconic revolution in his name would be made (Fitzpatrick 1994, 26–7).

The setting for the Russian Revolution of 1917 was developed over many years. By the late 19th century, it was clear that the tsarist regime (Russian monarchs were called tsars) was falling behind the rest of Europe and needed reform. In 1905, this produced Russia's so-called "liberal revolution," which ended with a weak constitutional monarchy. However, this did not stop political agitation. Though Russia was a largely agrarian society, figures like Leon Trotsky (and Vladimir Lenin, though he was in exile for many years), as well as lesser-known figures, led or influenced socialist organizing in the face of ongoing repression. Lenin in particular is famous for insisting on party discipline (Fitzpatrick 1994, 30–1): Though

continued

his group was numerically smaller than some other groups demanding change, their organization and unanimity may have been key to their success. Russia's involvement in the First World War weakened the state's position in society, and the tsar fell in early 1917. In the fall, the provisional government collapsed, and the Soviets, largely controlled by the Bolsheviks, assumed increasing authority. Russia withdrew from the First World War in early 1918, and civil war broke out between groups of "red" and "white" Russians. This conflict lasted several years, but in the end the Bolshevik forces were victorious.

Through this process, the Soviet Union was born. Until its demise in 1991, the Soviet Union declared itself to be a Marxist revolutionary regime. Among other things, it aimed to ultimately collectivize all of the "means of production," doing away with the capitalist division of labour. That is, the state looked to take over economic activity, from industrial factories to agriculture to shops. According to Marxist theory, this would do away once and for all with exploitation and other classes beyond the working class. Eventually, there would be no more need for a coercive state. This is not what happened in practice. While the regime was indeed somewhat successful in redistributing wealth, it was very authoritarian. Indeed, the state became highly coercive and totalitarian, attempting to control not just the economy but even political thought. Especially under Joseph Stalin, the Soviet Union's human rights abuses were legion (Service 2009, 220–9). Millions were killed by the state. The regime also came to dominate much of central and eastern Europe following World War II.

The Russian Revolution was one of history's most dramatic social revolutions. It radically transformed not just the structure of politics in Russian society but the state's role in the economy and the nature of social stratification both within that society and in the world outside of it. In fact, by becoming the leading example of communism, it had a transformative effect on politics around the world.

Research Prompts

1. Russia has a notable tradition of authoritarian politics. How would you account for authoritarian persistence in Russia? What would the major theories from Chapter 7 say about this case?
2. Compare the reforms of Gorbachev to the reforms of Deng Xiaoping in China. What is similar about the circumstances they faced, and what are the major differences in this respect? What was different about their respective strategic approaches to reform? To what extent can the recent political and economic trajectories of these two societies be traced to different approaches to and processes of reform?
3. The Russian Revolution of 1917 produced a dramatic series of political, social, and economic changes. Compare that revolution to the French and Chinese revolutions. Can a common causal framework explain all three? What if we add the Iranian Revolution to the mix?
4. Russia is a useful case for proponents of the idea that the contemporary world is increasingly populated by "hybrid," "grey zone," and "competitive authoritarian" systems. What does Russia show us about the democratic status of such systems? Is a "hybrid" regime half-democratic? Or is democratization a threshold status of which hybrid regimes fall short?
5. Russian politics is characterized by personalism and a high degree of centralization and authoritarian decision-making, which is reflected in various institutions. Would reforming one of these institutions alter Russian political culture, or would changing institutional designs be ineffective without a deeper change in the culture? If institutional reform would be helpful, what institution would be the most useful one to change?

Online Case Studies

Go to **www.oup.com/he/DickovickCe** to find more case studies online, including:

- Communist Ideology in Practice: Russia and the Soviet Union
- Executives in Russia: Formal and Informal Powers

Saudi Arabia

PROFILE

Key Features of Contemporary Saudi Arabia

Population:	33,091,113 (July 2018 est.)
Area:	2,149,690 square kilometres
Head of State:	Salman bin Abdulaziz Al Saud (King and Custodian of the Two Holy Mosques since January 2015)
Head of Government:	Salman bin Abdulaziz Al Saud (prime minister since January 2015)
Capital:	Riyadh
Year of state formation:	1932
Year of Current Constitution:	1992
Languages:	Arabic
GDP per Capita:	$54,500 (World Bank estimate 2017)
Human Development Index Ranking (2018):	39th (very high human development)
Trading Relationship with Canada (2016):	• Imports $2,022,190,583 • Exports $1,119,892,872 https://globaledge.msu.edu/countries/canada/tradestats

Sources: *CIA World Factbook 2018*; World Bank World Development Indicators; United Nations *Human Development Report 2016*

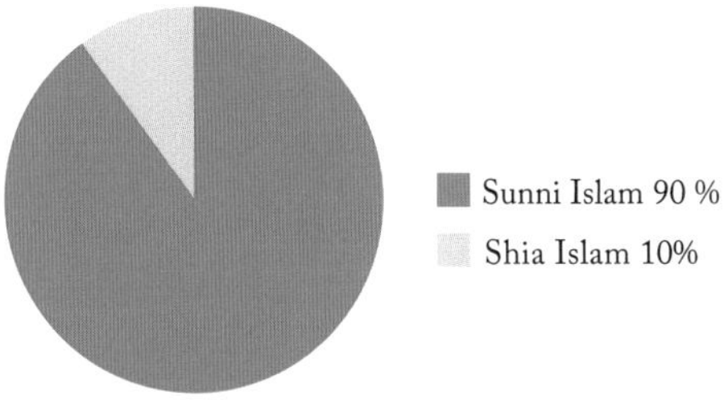

Religious Affiliation in Saudi Arabia

Ninety per cent of the population are Sunni Muslim, as is the ruling regime. Ten per cent are Shia and face some discrimination by the government. Other religious beliefs are not recognized, and there is no freedom of worship outside of officially sanctioned channels. A large and varied expatriate community comprising about 30 per cent of the population practise a range of other faiths, but only Muslims may hold Saudi citizenship.

Source: *CIA World Factbook 2018*

Introduction

Saudi Arabia is a unique country and society. First, it is an absolute monarchy, ruled by one of a succession of kings tracing their lineage to the founder of the state, Abdul Aziz bin Abdul Rahman Al Saud. The king also serves as prime minister and Custodian of the Two Holy Mosques (located in the cities of Mecca and Medina). Second, the regime is closely allied with clerics who follow the Wahhabi variant of Sunni Islam and have considerable power over civil society. Wahhabism is an extremely conservative branch of Islam that has led to repression of basic human rights. Third, Saudi Arabia is extremely rich, thanks to its enormous oil revenues, but the money has been unequally distributed and problems of corruption and mismanagement are high. Fourth, while the Arab Spring led to regime transformation throughout the Middle East region,

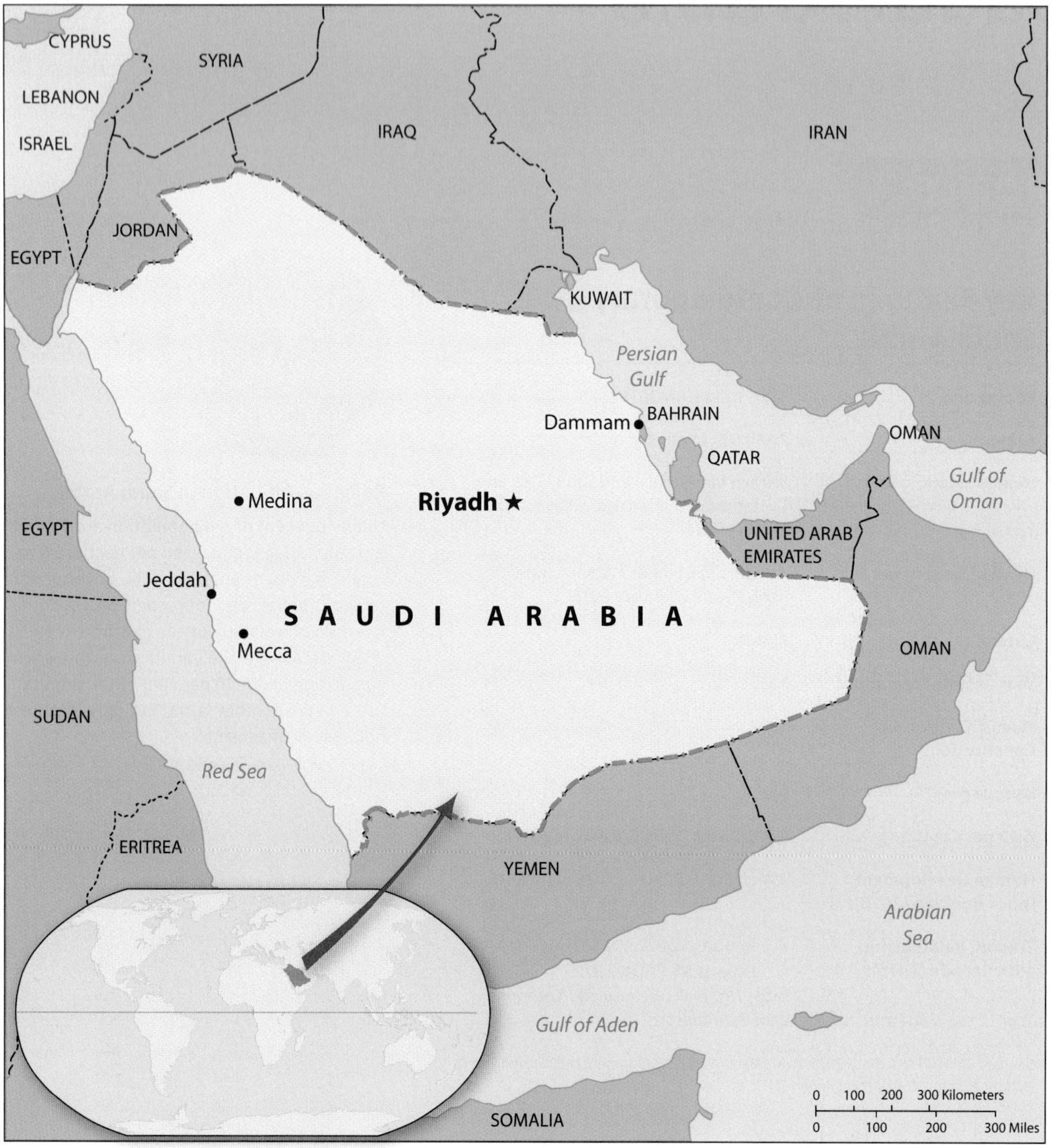

the kingdom is surprisingly stable. Since 2017, Crown Prince Mohammed bin Salman bin Abdulaziz Al Saud (known as MBS) has been trying to diversify and modernize some aspects of the economy, while at the same time centralizing political and economic power for himself. Most of the repressive aspects of the regime remain intact, especially as it relates to women's rights in general and more specifically the rights to assembly, free speech, and mobilization in support of change. With a large young population and considerable oil wealth, Saudi Arabia has the potential to transform itself. However, there are significant challenges ahead.

In regard to ethnic groups, the majority of Saudi citizens are ethnically Arab and speak Arabic. The country is divided into regions, which maintain strong regional and tribal identities. There is a large proportion of foreign workers in the country who are not citizens.

Historical Development

Saudi Arabia, which occupies 80 per cent of the Arabian peninsula, is home to Mecca and Medina, the two holiest cities in the Islamic world. The country is extremely dry, with only 2 per cent arable land and a permanent water crisis for its inhabitants. Initially, much of the population were nomadic Bedouin, but the population by the 20th century had become sedentary (Bowen 2008, 2–4).

There have been three Saudi states in recent history. The first was founded in 1744 when the Sunni Muslim scholar Muhammad bin Abdul Wahhab formed an alliance with Muhammad Ibn Saud, the emir of Diriyah. Together, Ibn Saud and Wahhab and their followers took control of the city of Najd and then the holy cities of Mecca and Medina. Egypt defeated the kingdom in 1818, but the partnership between the Saudis and the Wahhabis continued over the centuries, culminating in Wahhabism's adoption as the official state-sponsored version of Sunni Islam in Saudi Arabia (Blanchard 2008).

A second kingdom was built in 1824, which lasted until 1891. The genesis of the current kingdom dates to the end of the 19th century. In 1890, the family of Abdulaziz ibn Abdul Rahman ibn Faisal ibn Turki ibn Abdullah ibn Muhammad Al Saud (also called Ibn Saud) was driven into exile. By 1902, Ibn Saud had taken control of Riyadh, then Najd in 1906. Modern Saudi Arabia developed after World War I with the collapse of the Ottoman Empire. Ibn Saud took Mecca in 1924, Medina in 1925, and Asir in 1926. Finally, in 1932, the kingdom of Saudi Arabia was unified, with Ibn Saud assuming the throne. By May 1933, Standard Oil of California had negotiated an exclusive agreement to search and drill for oil in the country in exchange for annual royalties. In 1938, they made their first discovery. Standard Oil and Texaco formed a partnership, which in 1944 became the basis of Aramco (Arabian American Oil Company). This would eventually become the world's largest exporter of petroleum (Lawson 2017; al Dabaan; Alyas 2018).

After World War II, the regime drew closer to the US, and the US provided technical assistance and helped to establish key government ministries. However, there has been very little development along any form of Western democratic path. Rather, the royal family and religious elites have maintained control over the kingdom. Ibn Saud had 45 sons who all became princes, and the princes and their descendants divided into factions, sometimes allied, sometimes competing against one another. Conflict within the enormous ruling family has dominated most of the life of the kingdom, culminating in the formal deposing of King Saud in 1964, which was legitimated by religious elites. Another king (Faisal) was assassinated in 1975 and quietly replaced by King Khalid (Lawson 2017; Al Dabaan).

Regional and religious divisions have meant that the country does not have a strong sense of unity, and there has been friction between Sunni and Shia and between various types of conservatives and reformers. During the 1950s and 1960s, fears of leftist ideologies and forms of nationalism provoked the regime to respond to domestic unrest in the kingdom. In Egypt, Gamal Abdel Nasser was extremely popular, and leftist Ba'ath socialist parties gained power in Syria and Iraq. The solution to potential unrest in Saudi Arabia was a massive welfare state, funded by the oil revenues pouring in. King Faisal, who ruled from 1964 until 1975, is credited with greatly increasing the wealth and prominence of the kingdom.

There were, and continue to be, major grievances within the state from a wide range of groups. However, political challenges were often met with material rewards, diffusing many problems that other regimes had faced (Hertog 2016, 4, 8). While Saudi Arabia is clearly authoritarian, it has sought to buy compliance from its population. Well over half of all Saudi workers are employed by the government. A comprehensive welfare state includes subsidized transport, education, health, and other public goods (Hertog 2016, 2). The welfare state expanded after 1975 when King Khalid embarked on a USD $141-billion expansion of social services and infrastructure, as well as promoting further industrialization.

The year 1979 was particularly difficult for the government. In that year, the Iranian Revolution took place, while Wahhabi activists took over the Grand Mosque in Makkah. This period saw a hardening of religious control over the educational system in Saudi Arabia, and a more conservative variant of the faith was implemented (Montagu 2015, 5). There was activism and agitation in the mainly Shia areas of the Eastern Province, which were generally less wealthy. The Saudi government spent considerable money on infrastructure and public projects to pacify the population. (Lawson 2017).

US strategic policy for much of the early Cold War relied on alliance-building with Saudi Arabia and Iran (under the Shah's rule). After 1979, the US lost its Iranian ally and leaned more heavily on the Saudi alliance (Alyas 2018). The Saudi government took a strong stance against communism throughout the world, especially after the Soviet invasion and occupation of Afghanistan in 1979 (Bowen 2008, 7). Saudi nationals saw liberating Afghanistan from Soviet control as an important duty. The Taliban and later al Qaeda both emerged from this type of political and religious radicalization. Some Wahhabi clerics were supportive of these movements, although al Qaeda, led by Saudi national Osama bin Laden, was vigorously opposed to the Saudi regime (Blanchard 2008).

In 1982, King Khalid died and was replaced by King Fahd, who drew closer to the religious establishment as a means of strengthening his rule. Through the king, the ulama (religious leaders) promoted stricter laws in adherence with Wahhabi doctrine, and clerics were placed in key government positions. Three new Islamic universities were opened, and Fahd adopted the new title "Custodian of the Two Holy Places" instead of the previous title "King." Fahd's regime was difficult because the price of oil dropped during this time and debt soared (Lawson 2017).

The 1990 Iraqi invasion of Kuwait constituted a major crisis for the regime. The government was obliged to call for American assistance, and by 1991 more than a half a million US forces were in the region, a majority of them based in Saudi Arabia (Alyas 2018). On the conservative right, many were angry that the Americans were there. Reformers saw this as an opportunity to press for social and political reforms, including a constitutional monarchy (Lawson 2017).

After Fahd suffered a major stroke in 1995, Crown Prince Abdullah worked to introduce further reforms to pacify religious critics of the regime, including the release of some imprisoned Islamist activists. Violence continued, and this was the period when Osama bin Laden became influential and al Qaeda began detonating bombs in Saudi Arabia. After the 9/11 terrorist attacks in 2001, anti-regime protests continued, with accusations that the regime was too pro-American (Lawson 2017).

Abdullah took over as monarch in 2005 after Fahd's death, but reform efforts amounted to little. Sectarian and Islamic dissent continued, necessitating further funds being released into the economy to mollify the population. Around the time of the Arab Spring in 2011, two petitions were given to the king calling for a constitutional monarchy. Abdullah then released $70 billion to expand welfare programs, provide increased money for civil servants, and build more low income housing (Lawson 2017).

In January 2015, Abdullah died, and Salman bin Abdulaziz Al Saud became ruler. Under his regime, changes have taken place within the kingdom. Initially, King Salman confirmed Abdullah's choice as crown prince, Muqrin bin Abdulaziz Al Saud. However, he soon obliged Muqrin to step down in favour of his nephew Muhammad bin Nayef. In 2017, King Salman's son Mohammed bin Salman was appointed crown prince and Nayef was stripped of his positions (Lawson 2017).

Crown Prince bin Salman is very much seen as the power behind the throne, influencing an ageing king in failing health, who some argue is in an early stage of dementia. While King Salman is still in control, his son has taken over much of the day-to-day running of the kingdom (Saber and Riedel 2019). In 2017, bin Salman launched a reform program known as Vision 2030 and has been actively courting hundreds of billions of dollars in foreign investment in infrastructure and industrial development projects. He has travelled throughout the West, courting politicians like Donald Trump and Jared Kushner, and has promised major investments and trade opportunities with India, Pakistan, and other countries. The regime seeks to transform the kingdom into an "investment powerhouse" and "an epicenter of trade and the gateway to the world," to cite the foreword to the document (Vision 2030, Foreword).

While Saudi Arabia is not considered particularly unstable or fragile, it is important to note that other regimes that were toppled in the Arab Spring, such as those in Libya, Egypt, and Tunisia, were not seen as fragile either. However, regime change appears unlikely in Saudi Arabia. Iran does not pose a strong military threat, nor do Yemen or Bahrain. Domestically, there are no groups with sufficient military power to topple the government (Stares and Ighani 2017).

As bin Salman centralizes power, he is creating a more stable authoritarian system (see case study: "The Rise of Mohammed bin Salman (MBS): Reform or Repression?" on page 90) (Stares and Ighani 2017). Saudi society is very young, with the majority of the population under 30. Despite the repressive nature of the regime, the Internet is used by 93 per cent of Saudis, and 2.4 million are Twitter users, with Saudis accounting for almost 50 per cent of Twitter users in the Arab world (Stares and Ighani).

In 2018, bin Salman's international reputation was cast in jeopardy when journalist Jamal Khashoggi was murdered in the Saudi consulate in Istanbul, Turkey, by a group of Saudi nationals, who strangled him, then dismembered his body. Khashoggi was a columnist for the *Washington Post* and a member of one of the kingdom's more prominent families. He was an outspoken critic of the regime as well. International condemnation was immediate, and bin Salman was accused of having ordered the assassination. The Khashoggi affair, combined with the now more public abuses of women's rights and the atrocities in the Yemeni civil war, have all raised red flags about bin Salman's leadership.

Historical Development Timeline[1]

1744	Emirate of Diriyah is created by Muhammad ibn Saud, who founds the House of Saud (the dynasty in power today) and creates an alliance with the followers of Wahhab.
1818	Egyptian forces defeat the first Saudi state.
1824	Second Saudi state begins after the al Sauds occupy the city of Riyadh.
1891	Internal conflict leads to the collapse of the state.
1902	Abdul Aziz bin Abdul Rahman Al Saud captures Riyadh.
1912	The Wahhabi organization *Ikhwan* (or Brotherhood) is founded, which proves crucial to Ibn Saud's later military and political success.
1915	The Treaty of Darin is signed between Ibn Saud and Great Britain. Ibn Saud becomes a British ally in the war against the Ottoman Empire.
1932	The Kingdom of Saudi Arabia is born.
1938	After the discovery of oil, the US-owned Arabian American Oil Company (Aramco) begins production. Saudi Arabia is identified as one of the world's top sources of petroleum.
1953	Following the death of Abdulaziz, Crown Prince Saud becomes king.
1960	Saudi Arabia helps to found the Organization of Petroleum Exporting Countries (OPEC), with Iran, Iraq, Kuwait, and Venezuela.
1973	Arab members of OPEC launch an oil embargo against Western countries that supported the Israel military during the Yom Kippur War.
1975	Following the assassination of King Faisal, Khalid becomes king.
1981	Saudi Arabia helps to found the Gulf Cooperation Council.
1982	Crown Prince Fahd becomes king after the death of his brother King Khalid.
1990	Iraq invades neighbouring Kuwait; Saudi Arabia requests US intervention. The Kuwaiti government is sheltered in the kingdom.
1991	The US and its allies send troops to defend Saudi Arabia and liberate Kuwait.
1992	A "Basic System of Government" is announced, laying out the responsibilities of the monarch.
1999	A select group of Saudi women are permitted to attend the Consultative Council.
2001	After the 11 September terrorist attacks in New York and Washington, it is learned that 15 of the 19 hijackers were Saudi citizens.
2004	Al Qaeda steps up its terror attacks throughout the kingdom.
2005	The kingdom holds its first municipal elections. Abdullah is crowned king after the death of his brother Fahd. Saudi Arabia gains membership in the World Trade Organization.
2011	The Arab Spring and regional unrest prompt the king to increase welfare spending.
2011	Women gain the right to vote and to stand for election to municipal councils.
2014	General Dynamic Land Systems Canada signs a contract with the Saudis for approximately 1000 light-armoured military vehicles (LAVs).
2015	King Abdullah dies, and Salman bin Abdulaziz Al Saud is crowned king. King Salman appoints his son Muhammad bin Nayef as crown prince.
2016	King Salman introduces economic reforms aimed at diversifying away from oil.
2017	King Salman names Mohammed bin Salman as crown prince and successor, and Prince Nayef is stripped of his positions.
2018	*Washington Post* reporter Jamal Khashoggi is assassinated in Istanbul.
2019	The European Commission announces it will add Saudi Arabia to its list of "high-risk jurisdictions for money laundering and terrorist financing."

Regime and Political Institutions

Saudi Arabia has an absolutist monarchy whereby the monarch and his advisors control most aspects of the government. While the monarch has absolute power in the sense that he is not officially bound by a constitution, any elected body, or a national court system, he is constrained by the religious infrastructure of the state. The monarch's legitimacy rests on his following Sharia, or Islamic, law. He is also held in check by the large number of Ibn Saud's descendants, who have considerable power bases of their own.

Regime and Political Institutions

Regime	Absolute monarchy
Administrative Divisions	13 regions
Executive Branch	The king is both chief of state and head of government.
Selection of Executive	The monarchy is hereditary. The king is assisted in governing by a Council of Ministers, which he appoints every four years.
Legislative Branch	The Majlis al-Shura is a consultative council of 150 members appointed by the king to serve four-year terms of office.
Judicial Branch	All appointments are subject to royal decree. The High Court is comprised of a chief and is divided into circuits. A 10-member Supreme Judiciary Council makes recommendations to the monarch about appointments. Lower courts include a Court of Appeals, a Specialized Criminal Court, and a Labour Court.
Political Party System	No political parties are permitted

Under the Basic Law of 1992, the king must be a male direct descendant of Ibn Saud and is chosen with the approval of the religious leaders (the ulama). Since 1953, a Council of Ministers, comprising around 25 cabinet officials, prepare and implement policies on the king's instructions. The Council of Ministers represents the views of princes, business people, and other elites. Below them, a 150-member Consultative Council serves at the pleasure of the king. Below these institutions are 13 regional governorships, generally all held by princes. Four regions are of special significance: Mecca and Medina for religious reasons, Riyadh for political reasons, and the Eastern Province due to its rich endowments of oil. Political parties and electoral lists are forbidden in the country, but forms of regular consultation are traditional to Arab leadership (Bowen 2008, 13–16).

The ulama is also central to regime legitimacy. It is a group of between 7000 and 10,000 Islamic religious leaders comprising teachers, judges, clerics, and others. Of these, around 30 to 40 comprise an influential Council of Senior Ulama, which was created in 1971 as an official consultative body between the king and religious leaders. The monarchy recognizes the special religious status of the council, and in return ulama leaders support the regime and underwrite even the most controversial policies (Metz 1992). While the council must officially give its approval before a new king can ascend the throne and could theoretically stand against government policies, in practice this has rarely happened, and the council is used primarily to justify government policy. Council members and the institution itself rely on government funding and have no independent source of income.

Political Culture

The official state religion of Saudi Arabia is the Wahhabi variant of Sunni Islam. Wahhabism believes in a strict and narrow interpretation of Islam, and followers call themselves Salafis (which means "followers of the forefathers"). The movement began during a time when Islam was diagnosed as having fallen to magic, sorcery, and superstitious practices. Wahhab preached a return to the fundamentals and advocated a form of puritanical Islam. Beliefs include a ban on alcohol, tobacco, other stimulants, dancing, music, and immodest clothing. Codes of modesty are enforced by religious police known as the Mutaween (or "Authority for the Promotion of Virtue and Prevention of Vice"). Punishments for breaking the rules include public flogging, amputation, and execution (Krusch 2018; Lawson 2017). There were approximately 154 executions in 2016 and 146 in 2017.

The state has an extremely poor record of human rights and is classified by the Economist Intelligence Unit as authoritarian, with extremely low scores for civil society and human rights. Of 200 countries studied in 2018, Saudi Arabia came in 159th with a score of 0.00 for "electoral processes and pluralism" (Economist Intelligence Unit 2018). We should note that Wahhabism is not a form of Islam practised in most other Muslim-majority countries, where women can and do vote and take part in civic life. Muslim-majority countries have elected women as heads of state and heads of government, such as in Pakistan, Bangladesh, Indonesia, Senegal, Turkey, Kosovo, Kyrgyzstan, and Mali.

Saudi Arabia remains divided along several lines. The first is between reformers and conservatives. One recent study suggests that religious conservatives make up some 60–70 per cent of the population. They favour tradition and stability and "do not want the change or reforms that the government has been attempting" (Montagu 2015, 5). Those in favour of reform, or who find the regime too rigid, sometimes vote with their feet. For example, there are more than 100,000 Saudi professionals living in Bahrain and 12,000 in Dubai and a migration of young Saudis to other Gulf Arab states in search of economic opportunity and a better way of life (Montagu 2015, 12).

The country is also relatively youthful, and times are changing. As one recent study notes: "Saudi Arabia has a very considerable number of media-savvy, educated young people, many of whom are unemployed and frustrated, who wish to be part of government decision-making but are currently barred by the absence of formal channels" (Montagu 2015, 2).

Civil society organizations are relatively few in number and are weak; a large proportion are charities affiliated with the government. Civil society as a whole remains underdeveloped in a country subject to significant centralized control and restrictive laws. Strict counter-terrorism laws from 2014 have circumscribed rights to speech and assembly still further. Even peaceful dissent and critique of corruption can be harshly punished, as well as any form of demonstration seeking reforms or change. The Ministry of Interior has considerable powers to monitor activities, and police use flogging, travel bans, dismissal from employment, and imprisonment and have used live ammunition on demonstrators (ICNL 2019). While the government is supposedly engaged in reforms, such as allowing movies to be shown in cinemas and allowing women to drive, crackdown on dissent continues, and activists and intellectuals continue to be imprisoned (Al Jazeera News, 2019b).

Political Economy

During the late 1930s, Saudi Arabia was found to have the world's largest oil reserves, comprising about 25 per cent of global supply. As well, the oil was of very high quality ("light," meaning it is less viscous and easier to extract and transport) and was also located close to the surface. Overall, this created a massive, easily obtainable source of income, which has fuelled the development of the Saudi economy (Bowen 2008, 4). Currently, the regime controls about 16 per cent of global oil reserves, and almost half of its GDP comes from oil revenue.

The Saudis were instrumental in founding the Organization of Petroleum Exporting Countries (OPEC) in 1960, an oil cartel that strongly influences the production, supply, and hence the price of oil internationally. The regime has acquired tremendous economic power because of this cartel (Alyas 2018). While initially Aramco was American-owned, as the state's wealth increased the Saudi regime had bought out this company in its entirety by 1980 (Alyas 2018). In 2019, Saudi Aramco was valued at more than USD $2 trillion, and this giant corporation currently employs more than 65,000 people (Al Jazeera 2019c).

With the speed of Saudi wealth came unaccountable spending from the 1960s, with little institutional control. The political system was an arena for Ibn Saud's sons to jostle for position, competing for access to key government ministries and their share of the wealth. The result was the rise of what many have described as "parallel fiefdoms" controlled by rival princes seeking leverage over one another. As Hertog explains:

> The Al Saud-controlled Ministry of Defense, National Guard and Ministry of Interior developed into full-fledged states within a state, each with hundreds of thousands of employees . . . their own health and education systems, residential cities and large land banks. As oil income grew and senior princes competed for patronage and generosity, their institutions sprawled" (Hertog 2016, 8–9).

Control of various ministries allows princes to award contracts to their companies through opaque processes. Access to credit and land are given preferentially to the princes, and royals have until recently enjoyed the ability to engage in arbitrary land confiscation. This dominance over the economy makes it extremely uncompetitive, and small firms are largely shut out of the system (Adeel Malik 2018).

The size of the royal family was estimated at 15,000 in 2018, with about 2000 princes controlling most of the kingdom's wealth. Overall, the family is said to have a net worth of around USD $1.4 trillion (Umoh 2018). The skewed development of the economy has led to major distortions in the provision of jobs and services. Women are systematically excluded, while subsidies tend to favour richer households. Those with close ties to government enjoy privileges others do not. The cost of maintaining this system was estimated at almost 10 per cent of GDP in 2011, according to the IMF (Hertog, 2016, 9–10). Corruption, mismanagement, and an economy overly dependent on oil have taken their toll. The economy experienced recession and a budget deficit in 2017, amounting to more than 9 per cent of GDP. It also has an unemployment rate of about 13 per cent (Al Jazeera 2017).

In 2017, Crown Prince bin Salman launched Vision 2030, a comprehensive reform package designed to diversify the economy and expand Saudi investments in a wide range of new areas. Another plan is the creation of a 334-km² entertainment complex, which will be a theme park and will provide jobs and opportunities for the younger population. Also planned is the creation of a business city called NEOM (BBC News 2017a; BBC News 2017b). The reforms also include increased rights for women and the promotion of what bin Salman calls "moderate Islam." In early 2019, the government cracked down on corruption and claims to have recovered some USD $106 billion in stolen funds, primarily from princes, business leaders, and senior government officials. This initiative has been called "shock therapy" and is designed to reduce the problems of corruption (Al Jazeera News 2019b).

Overall, reforms, such as they are, proceed slowly because the entrenched positions of the political elites make change difficult. It is likely that these new policies are designed to rebrand rather than reform the system.

CASE STUDIES

CASE STUDY

Chapter 5, Page 90

The Rise of Mohammed bin Salman (MBS): Reform or Repression?

Until recently, the Saudi regime has been dominated by the octogenarian sons of the country's founder. King Ibn Saud died in 1953, yet every Saudi king has been his son. King Salman was the first to recognize the need for a generational shift. In 2015, he appointed his nephew Prince Muhammad bin Nayef as crown prince and his son Prince Muhammad bin Salman (known as MBS) as deputy crown prince and defence minister at the young age of 29. Both men are grandsons of Ibn Saud.

Bin Salman's rise was unprecedented and broke with tradition. Normally, seniority was crucial, as was power-sharing among the various princes. Bin Salman, as a virtual unknown, became deputy crown prince, then moved quickly to crown prince, deputy prime minister, minister of defence, and the heir presumptive to the throne after possibly engineering the removal of his cousin Nayef (Mazzetti and Hubbard 2016).

Bin Salman has been adept at changing the nature of the power around the country's various fiefdoms. Part of his strategy has been to wrest control of key ministries from other princes and to centre control for himself. In practice, some described "multiple kingdoms" centred around princes and engaged in extensive patron–client relationships (Jay 2014). Bin Salman has sought to break up much of the old factionalized system.

While King Salman is officially in charge and on paper is the one ordering changes, it seems probable that bin Salman is behind most of it. As defence minister, he has been able to crack down on any potential military threat against his rule. His control of the intelligence services has also allowed him to reduce the power and influence of his princely rivals. In mid-2017, King Salman authorized the consolidation of all intelligence and counter-terrorism agencies under a new body controlled by bin Salman: the Presidency of State Security (PSS). The king has also replaced the leaders of the armed forces, bringing in a new generation of leaders, including about 800 officer appointments. Bin Salman now chairs the powerful Council for Economic and Development Affairs and also controls the Public Investment Fund (PIF), which manages the kingdom's investments. Under the PIF is Saudi Arabia Military Industries (SAMI) and the General Authority Military Industries (GAMI), both of which also report to the prince (Sayigh 2018).

The older generations and more conservative Saudis dislike the changes taking place, and as Mazzetti and

Hubbard describe, bin Salman is seen as "a power-hungry upstart who is risking instability by changing too much, too fast." However, he is admired by many young people for being "an energetic representative of their generation who has addressed some of the country's problems with uncommon bluntness." Indeed: "The kingdom's news media have built his image as a hardworking, businesslike leader less concerned than his predecessors with the trappings of royalty" (Mazzetti and Hubbard 2016). The crown prince, however, has also sought the trappings of wealth, including buying a $300-million French chateau near Paris, a $450-million painting "Salvator Mundi" by Leonardo da Vinci, a $500-million yacht, and other luxury items (Umoh 2018).

Bin Salman's Vision 2030 seeks to diversify the economy so as to move away from volatile oil prices. The plan responds to cuts that corresponded to a drop in oil revenue. He has avoided dealing too closely with the older clerics at the Council of Senior Scholars, who are often seen by youth as being out of touch. He has instead aligned himself with younger clerics who have a large following on social media. Many of these younger clerics, however, are also deeply conservative, but they are more adept at promoting Wahhabi views in modern ways (Mazzetti and Hubbard 2016).

As one commentator noted in 2018, putting bin Salman's reforms and King Salman's legacy into context:

> Yes, Salman has allowed women to drive, to run their own businesses and to attend sports events. Cinemas have opened and rock concerts been staged. But the king remains the absolute ruler of a kingdom that practises torture, beheads dissidents and exports a barbarous foreign policy, including prosecuting one of the most brutal wars of modern times in Yemen (Kenan Malik 2018).

MBS will continue to be a controversial figure, especially as more details of the Khashoggi assassination come to light amid other information about the repressive nature of the Saudi regime.

CASE STUDY

Chapter 14, Page 300

Why Has Saudi Arabia Made Such Little Progress on Women's Rights?

Saudi Arabia has a justifiably negative reputation as one of the world's worst countries for women's rights. Wahhabi Islam informs the way the state controls the activities of women. Under the guardianship system, women must be under male guardianship from a father, husband, brother, or son. The guardians have control over decision-making for the women concerned, who are treated akin to legal minors. Widespread domestic violence and abuse has been documented, much of it unpunishable within the judicial system. Women cannot obtain a passport or go on foreign travel without guardian approval. Women must have the consent of a guardian to marry; there is no minimum marriage age, and child marriages continue in the present day. Men can marry up to four wives at one time. Employers may insist that women have permission from their guardian to work. Policies of gender segregation are strictly enforced in employment situations, and certain jobs are off limits to women.

A man may divorce his wife at any time without her consent and without even needing to inform her of his intention to obtain a divorce. Once divorced, a former wife has no right to custody of her children. On the death of a male relative, a woman may only inherit half of what a man can inherit.

In 2001, women gained the right to have and carry personal identity cards. This change was significant because before this time women had no legal means of proving their identity, which created problems for women in disputes over property or inheritance. In this year, ID cards were issued to guardians, and women needed their permission to obtain them. Starting in 2006, women have been able to obtain ID cards without guardian permission.

Saudi women achieved a number of firsts within the past decade, which demonstrates how restrictive the regime has been and still is. The first female government minister was appointed in 2009, and in 2012 the first female

continued

Olympic athletes were allowed to represent the country at the Olympics in London. A year later, women were permitted to ride bicycles and motorcycles in recreational areas as long as a male relative was present. In 2015, women were granted the right to vote and to stand for office in municipal elections.

It was only in 2018 that women were allowed to enter sports stadiums, previously a male-only venue. That year was also notable for the lifting of the ban on women driving. Women could now drive without guardian permission or guardian supervision in the car. However, many women activists were jailed and tortured for seeking this privilege. Women continue to be detained for activism, making it clear that what has been occurring is not reform but rather rebranding or strategic "women-washing" (Mahdawi 2018). According to Human Rights Watch (2019), Saudi Arabia's guardianship system is the most repressive in the region (Human Rights Watch 2019; Bleiker 2019).

CASE STUDY

Chapter 15, Page 316

Yemen's Civil War: What Is the Saudi Role?

Since 2015, Saudi Arabia has been intimately implicated in a civil war in neighbouring Yemen. The roots go back to the Arab Spring in 2011 when Yemen's long-serving authoritarian leader, Ali Abdullah Saleh, handed over the presidency to his deputy, Abdrabbuh Mansour Hadi. Hadi proved to be a weaker leader than Saleh and was unable to deal with the corruption and lack of adequate food and employment, as well as religious, ethnic, and geopolitical unrest in the country.

Hadi's government broke down in 2015, largely over his inability to deal with widespread political unrest. Much of this centred on the Houthi, a predominantly Shia movement (Shia are about 15 per cent of the population versus Sunni, who are around 80 per cent), which vocally criticized government corruption as well as the outsized influence of Saudi Arabia and the United States. The Houthi wanted more transparent and representative government and were joined by other Yemenis, including Sunnis and members of Saleh's former security forces. The deposed leader Saleh formed a strategic alliance with the Houthi, which lasted until 2017. In 2014 and 2015, the Houthis became a significant armed force and took control of the much of the northern province of Saada and the city of Sanaa, Yemen's capital. Hadi attempted to negotiate with the Houthi, offering to form a "unity government," but his overtures were rejected and he was forced to flee in early 2015.

Soon after, a coalition of eight Sunni Arab countries began air raids on Yemen with the goal of returning Hadi to power. This included Saudi Arabia. A civil war ensued, which continues today. In November 2017, the Houthi targeted Riyadh with ballistic missiles, which provoked a strong military backlash from the Saudis and a tighter blockade of the country. Food insecurity and famine are now major problems in Yemen, and the United Nations has dubbed this "the world's worst man-made humanitarian disaster." More than 22 million Yemeni people were categorized as food insecure in December 2018, with 10 million of them severely food insecure (BBC News 2019; Al Batati). Twenty-two million rely on humanitarian assistance to survive, and 3 million have been displaced from their homes.

The Saudi role in the war has been criticized for bringing about thousands of civilian deaths through indiscriminate aerial bombing, as well as precipitating famine-like conditions in much of the country (Amnesty International 2015). The Houthi human rights record is problematic as well. In 2018, Human Rights Watch noted the widespread use of child soldiers, as well as hostage-taking, summary executions, arbitrary detention, and torture. The Houthi have also been indiscriminately shelling civilians (Human Rights Watch 2018).

Religious sectarianism seems to play a key role, with the Sunni-led government in Saudi Arabia supporting Hadi's predominantly Sunni government against the predominantly Shia Houthi. Iran (a Shia-dominated theocratic regime) has been supporting the Houthi through arms and other means (Wintour 2018). Overall, the kingdom's reputation has soured since this conflict began.

Research Prompts

1. Despite its being an absolutist monarchy, there has been little significant internal dissent within the kingdom. What might account for Saudi Arabia continuing a strongly hierarchical system when the Arab Spring of 2011 changed the nature of many other regimes in the region?
2. Many critics of the Saudi regime in the kingdom have been calling for a constitutional monarchy for several decades. What might such a regime look like? Would it have some elements similar to constitutional monarchies in Europe?
3. Like Saudi Arabia, Qatar has a considerable number of Wahhabi followers. What accounts for their embrace of this variant of Sunni Islam? Why has it not spread to other parts of the Arab world?
4. Why does the United States continue such a close alliance with Saudi Arabia despite their human rights record and absolutist regime? Under what conditions might this alliance weaken or even end?

Online Case Studies

Go to **www.oup.com/he/DickovickCe** to find more case studies online, including:

- How Has Saudi Arabia's Welfare State Saved the Regime?

Note

1 BBC News: Middle East 2018; Bowen 2008, ix–xi; Al Jazeera News 2019a.

United Kingdom

PROFILE

Key Features of the Contemporary United Kingdom

Population:	65,105,246 (July 2018 est.)
Area:	243,610 square kilometres
Head of State:	Queen Elizabeth II (1952–present)
Head of Government:	Boris Johnson (prime minister, 2019–present)
Capital:	London
Year of Independence:	Never colonized. Political arrangements linking Northern Ireland, Scotland, Wales, and England have changed over time.
Year of Current Constitution:	Common law system; there is no formal constitution, though the Magna Carta dates back to 1215.
Languages:	English is the majority language. Other languages include Scots, Scottish Gaelic, Irish, and Welsh.
GDP per Capita:	$39,720.40 (World Bank estimate 2017)
Human Development Index Ranking (2015):	16th (very high human development)
Trading Relationship with Canada (2016):	• Imports $6,232,390,626 • Exports $12,907,490,266 https://globaledge.msu.edu/countries/canada/tradestats

Sources: *CIA World Factbook 2018*; World Bank World Development Indicators; United Nations *Human Development Report 2016*

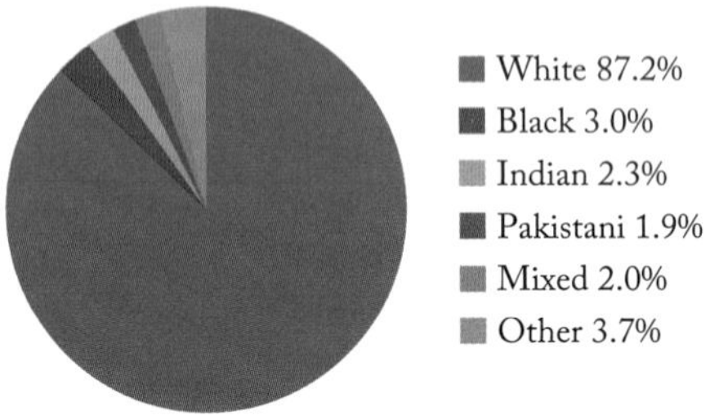

Ethnic Groups in the United Kingdom

Note that within the category "white," more than 80 per cent consider themselves English, with the bulk of the remainder being groups that consider themselves Scottish, Welsh, and Northern Irish.

Source: *CIA World Factbook*

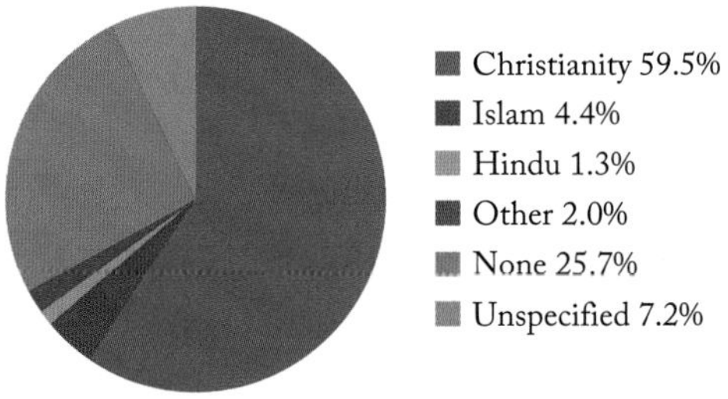

Religious Affiliation in the United Kingdom

Source: *CIA World Factbook*

Introduction

It is difficult to separate the history of the United Kingdom as an island society (comprising only about 244,000 square kilometres) from its former status as a global imperial power that once controlled one-quarter of the earth's surface. While it lacks a formal, written constitution, it was perhaps the society in which the idea of a "constitutional order" first emerged. Its Parliament survived the rise of absolutism, and constitutional monarchy was established early, with the "Glorious Revolution" of 1688–9. Moreover, many scholars consider it to have been among the first societies, and possibly the first, to establish modern national identity (Hastings 1997; Greenfeld 1992; Kohn 1944). Finally, Britain was a lead colonizer, spreading many of its political practices abroad and often using military force to enrich itself at the expense of its colonies. While on the positive side Britain has spread models of democracy, law, and society, alongside the English

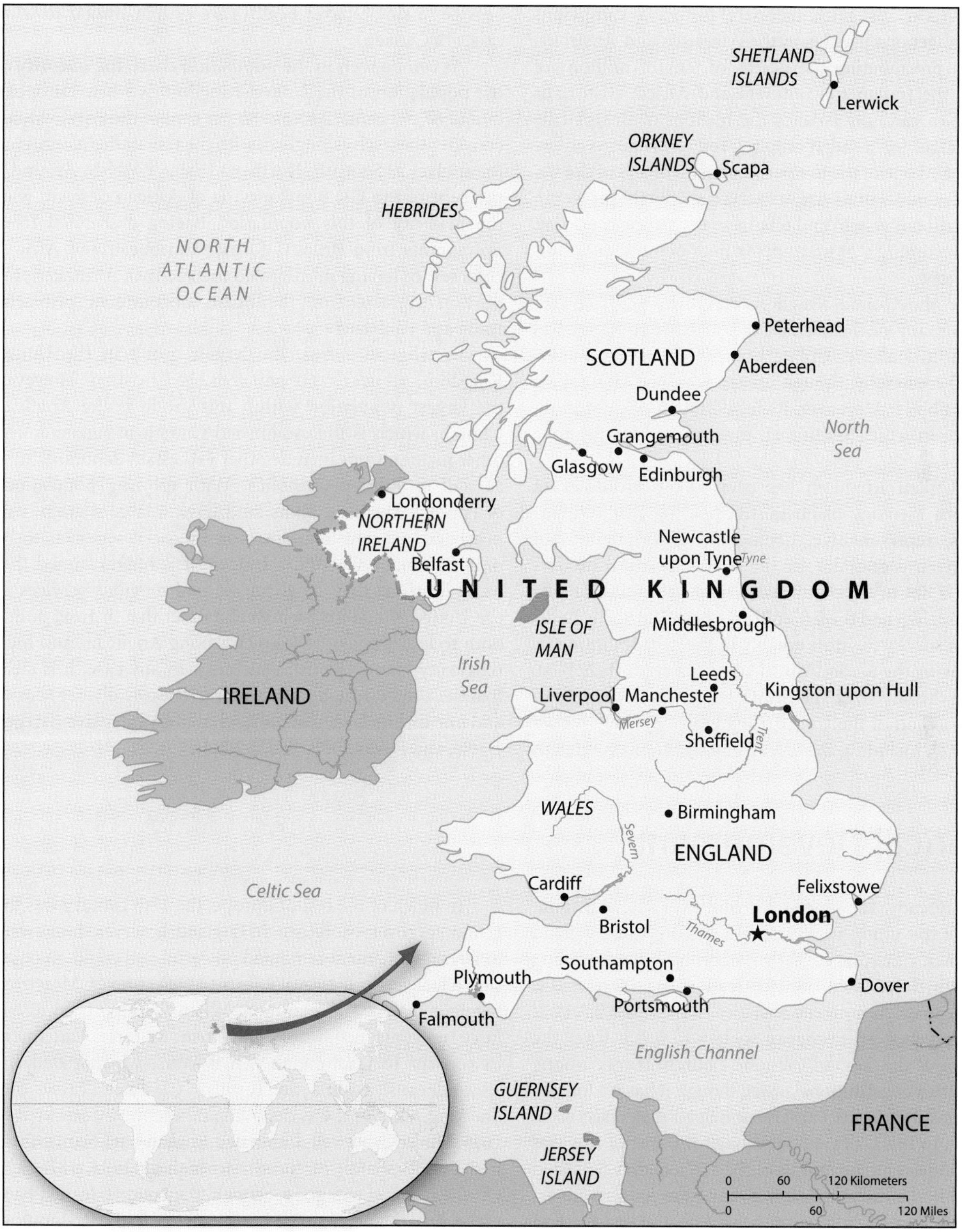
SHETLAND ISLANDS
Lerwick
ORKNEY ISLANDS
Scapa
HEBRIDES
NORTH ATLANTIC OCEAN
Peterhead
SCOTLAND
Aberdeen
Dundee
North Sea
Grangemouth
Glasgow
Edinburgh
Londonderry
NORTHERN IRELAND
Belfast
Newcastle upon Tyne
Tyne
UNITED KINGDOM
ISLE OF MAN
Middlesbrough
Irish Sea
Leeds
IRELAND
Liverpool
Manchester
Kingston upon Hull
Mersey
Sheffield
Trent
WALES
Birmingham
Severn
ENGLAND
Celtic Sea
Cardiff
Felixstowe
Bristol
London
Thames
Southampton
Plymouth
Dover
Portsmouth
Falmouth
English Channel
GUERNSEY ISLAND
JERSEY ISLAND
FRANCE
0 60 120 Kilometers
0 60 120 Miles

language, it also instigated successful genocidal campaigns against Indigenous peoples in the Americas and Australia, as well as precipitating the deaths of tens of millions of people in the Indian subcontinent and Africa. Historians are trying to carefully balance the realities of British rule with nostalgia for a faded empire. Today Britain is a key NATO ally and one of the five permanent members of the UN Security Council. For its size, it exerts considerable power in the international system and retains a very strong economy. It is also becoming a more complex multicultural and multifaith society.

While the United Kingdom was historically a lead society in many of these areas, it is now often viewed as highly traditionalistic. Unlike France, it still has a constitutional monarchy, though Queen Elizabeth II's role is largely symbolic. Moreover, its legal system is a common law system in which traditional practice is determinative of outcomes.

The United Kingdom has been a key promoter of the modern ideology of liberalism, holding that individual rights; representative, democratic government; and market-driven economics are the keys to political modernity. This is not to say that it has lacked a tradition of left-wing organizing, and the left in Britain has historically had a number of successes, most notably in the decades immediately following the Second World War (Clarke 2004, 221–4). Alongside this ideology, the British left played a key role in the construction of the United Kingdom's relatively robust welfare state, including the highly popular National Health Service (a single-payer health care system similar to what exists in Canada).

As can be seen in the population chart, the majority of the population of the United Kingdom is white European (about 87 per cent). Around 80 per cent of these individuals consider themselves English, with the remainder identifying themselves as Scottish, Northern Irish, or Welsh. Around 3 per cent of the UK population is of African descent, with the majority of this population having descended from immigrants from Britain's former Caribbean and African colonies (or having immigrated themselves). A smaller proportion originates from the Indian subcontinent (primarily India and Pakistan).

In religious terms, the largest group in the United Kingdom, at nearly 60 per cent, is Christian. However, the largest population within this group is the Anglican Church, which is the established Church of England. The other major groups include other Protestant denominations as well as Roman Catholics. With growing populations of Hindus, Muslims, Sikhs, and Jews, a large share of this nearly 60 per cent is understood by social scientists to be only nominally Christian. Indeed, it is often claimed that more Muslims than Anglicans attend religious services in the United Kingdom each week (a fact that, if true, points both to low levels of religiosity among Anglicans and high religiosity among British Muslims). In any case, it is clear that the United Kingdom is now a religiously diverse society and one in which secularization has been extensive (Berger, Davie, and Fokas 2008; Bruce 2004).

Historical Development

As noted already, the United Kingdom (or Great Britain, and before the union with Scotland and Ireland, England itself) is often viewed as an "early modernizer." It was among the first growth-oriented, modern economies and, relatedly, among the first "commercial societies" (Greenfeld 2001). It was the first western European society to break from the dominance of the Roman Catholic Church. It was among the first with a constitutional order, though it has no formal, written constitution. Its Parliament helped it to resist royal absolutism in the 17th century, though the cost of this was civil war. Indeed, in the middle of the 17th century it existed as a republic before the Restoration of the Stuart monarchy in 1660. Some scholars argue that England was the first society to establish a modern national identity (Hastings 1997; Kohn 1944; Greenfeld 1992). Finally, according to some scholars (e.g., Pincus 2009), its "Glorious Revolution" of 1688–9 was the first modern revolution.

In much of the rest of Europe, the 17th century was the century of royal absolutism. In England, however, things were different. Parliament remained powerful and could on occasion effectively resist royal efforts to collect taxes. Moreover, religious dissent was common. When the king tried to enforce religious orthodoxy and then to force Parliament to consent to taxation, the Civil Wars, which pitted the "Roundheads" against the royalist "Cavaliers," broke out. The king, Charles I, was deposed and eventually executed in 1649. Oliver Cromwell dominated English (and Scottish and Irish) politics until his death (Kishlansky 1996, 187–212). Once Cromwell was gone, though, the country turned back to the Stuarts, and Charles II was crowned in the Restoration. He was followed by James II, who was criticized because of his Catholic leanings. Perhaps more important, James II set about to dramatically strengthen the state, including building a larger navy and a standing army (Pincus 2009). With the

Historical Development Timeline

1215	Magna Carta.
1530–4	Break from Rome.
1580s–1700	First wave of English colonialism.
1600	Establishment of East India Company.
1642–51	Civil Wars.
1649–59	Cromwell and the Protectorate (1653–9).
1660	Restoration (Charles II).
1688–9	Glorious Revolution (William and Mary).
1694	Creation of the Bank of England.
1707	Act of Union (England and Scotland).
1714	Hanoverians inherit the throne (George I).
1756–63	Seven Years' War.
1776–83	American Revolution.
1801	Act of Union.
1807	Slave Trade Act.
1832	Reform Act of 1832.
1833	Slavery Abolition Act coincides with the beginnings of Indian indentured labour to various sugar colonies in the Caribbean and the Pacific.
1845-9	British-made famines in Ireland result in the deaths of approximately 1 million people from starvation and famine-related diseases.
1876-1900	British-made famines in India lead to the deaths of between 12 and 29 million Indians.
1899-1902	Boer War in South Africa, where the British imprisoned about one-fifth of the Boer population in concentration camps.
1911	National Insurance Act (early, very limited welfare state development).
1914–18	World War I.
1918	Limited women's suffrage.
1921	Emergence of Irish Free State.
1930	Women's suffrage.
1938	Munich Pact.
1939–45	World War II.
1942	Beveridge Report (very influential in subsequent welfare state development).
1940–5	Churchill government.
1943	Bengal famine in India as Churchill diverts food to British soldiers in Greece and elsewhere. Results in up to 4 million deaths.
1945–51	Labour government with Clement Atlee as prime minister. Creation of British welfare state, including National Health Service (1948).
1947–60s	Waves of decolonization in India, Africa, the Caribbean, and elsewhere, touched off by Indian and Pakistani independence in 1947.
1949	Independence of Ireland (except Northern Ireland).
1951–5	Second Churchill government (Conservative). Conservative governments will continue until 1964.
1956	Suez Crisis.
1951-60	Mau Mau uprising against British rule in Kenya leads to the British imprisoning 1.5 million Kenyans in concentration camps and the killing of up to 100,000 by imprisonment and starvation.[1]
1964–70	James Harold Wilson government (Labour). Labour governments will succeed each other until 1979, with the exception of the 1970–4 (Heath) Conservative government.
1973	United Kingdom joins the Common Market (EC).
1976–9	James Callaghan government (Labour).
1979–90	Margaret Thatcher government (Conservative). Some efforts to reduce the scope of the welfare state, including notable privatizations.
1982	Falkland Islands War.
1991	First Iraq War.
1997	Scottish and Welsh voters choose to create their own legislatures.
1997–2007	Tony Blair government (Labour).
2002	Eurozone begins, but the United Kingdom opts not to participate.
2003	Beginning of Second Iraq War.
2007–10	Gordon Brown government (Labour).
2010–16	David Cameron governments (Conservative/Liberal Democrats Coalition from 2010 to 2015, Conservative majority after 2015 election).
2014	Scotland referendum on independence fails, with 45 per cent voting for independence.
2015	Referendum on departure of Britain from the European Union leads to success for the Brexit side.
2016	Theresa May becomes prime minister after Cameron resigns over Brexit.
2017	Conservatives win the election, confirming May as prime minister.
2019	May tries in vain to negotiate a Brexit deal with the EU. There are several failed votes in Parliament to approve a Brexit deal. The UK and EU reach agreement for a Brexit extension until 31 October. In local council elections, the Conservatives lose more than 1300 local council seats. May announces her resignation on 24 May and is replaced by former foreign secretary Boris Johnson in June. A further extension on Brexit to 31 January 2020 was granted.

support of some well-placed Britons, the Dutch Stadtholder, William of Orange, invaded. He faced almost no resistance, and he and his wife, Mary (who was a Stuart), were crowned king and queen in the "Glorious Revolution." In general, this period witnessed heightened political activity, with coffee-house discussion and pamphlet writing, which some have argued led to the creation of the first modern "public sphere" (Habermas 1989). It also witnessed the development of the two parties, the Whigs (more liberal) and the Tories (more conservative), who would dominate British politics for many years (Kishlansky 1996, 313–35).

The 18th century largely witnessed the expansion of the empire, with notable military success, both in the War of the Spanish Succession (1701–14) and in the Seven Years' War (1756–63), though it failed in its effort to hold onto the colonies that became the United States. It did, however, lay the basis for the creation of the Canadian colonies, including the incorporation of Quebec into the empire. Commercial society grew, and in the second half of the century Britain saw the beginnings of the Industrial Revolution in which technologically adapted manufacturing, especially of textiles, dramatically expanded productivity (Harvie 2010, 475–81). This had numerous consequences as it slowly changed the nature of labour and led eventually to the urbanization of British society. In the religious field, new forms of Protestantism emerged and spread, especially Methodism, which would play a critical role in the abolition (of slavery and the slave trade) and reform movements (of British politics) that began to develop by the end of the century.

The 19th century, for much of which Queen Victoria held the throne, was a time of expanding liberalism and suffrage domestically, alongside the expansion of British colonialism (Harvie 2010; Matthew 2010). Beginning early in the late 18th century and accelerating in the 19th, some British leaders advocated expanding the electorate and updating parliamentary representation to make it more representative of the industrializing and urbanizing society that Britain had become. At the same time, popular actors came to make more demands on government (Tilly 1997). The Reform Act of 1832 expanded the vote, though one still needed to have property to vote. Further voting reform took place in 1867 when suffrage was extended, though only to (some) males and in a way that by today's standards would still be considered highly restricted.

The British Empire provided considerable economic advantages for many white British subjects and fuelled the economic growth of their country at the expense of the colonies. It relied on considerable force against people in the colonies, who often found themselves deprived of the same rights for which British citizens were fighting at home. For example, in India the British East India Company funded a private army of 260,000 and systematically eroded Indian manufacturing industries, whose share of world exports dropped from 27 per cent to 2 per cent in the 19th century. India became Britain's biggest source of revenue and generated colossal sums for its growing aristocratic and middle classes, while also subsidizing about a quarter of the imperial military budget (Tharoor 2017). A series of man-made famines in India during the British raj resulted in the deaths of tens of millions of people. The famines continued even during World War II, when Churchill famously said in 1943: "I hate Indians. They are a beastly people with a beastly religion. The famine was their own fault for breeding like rabbits" (Osborne 2016). These famines built on similar policies in British-controlled Ireland, arguably the first English colony.

In the decades after the end of the empire and an overly romantic view of British history, much of the truth of the brutality of British rule is now coming to light. Dealing with this history and its legacies is a painful topic for many British people, as it is for those in their former colonies.

In part this is because Britain's 20th-century experience was largely shaped by the two world wars and the Great Depression, so British memories of this period have been painful too (Morgan 2010b; Clarke 2004). World War I was enormously costly in terms of both lives and resources. Britain, like most of the world, suffered serious economic difficulties in the late 1920s and the 1930s. The country aimed to stay out of World War II, but it was eventually forced to participate in the war after Germany invaded Poland. Fighting was intense, and Britons had to face constant German air raids, which killed an estimated 60 thousand civilians (Morgan 2010b).

In the postwar years, the Labour Party worked to construct the British welfare state (Clarke 2004, 216–47). The welfare state has been somewhat reduced in subsequent years, especially during the administration of Margaret Thatcher (1979–90), but important components of it have been resilient (Prasad 2006). Another major 20th-century development was the shrinking and eventual disappearance of the British Empire (Clarke 2004). Once it had stretched across the globe, but in the mid- to late 20th century almost all of the United Kingdom's colonies achieved independence, though most retained some ties to Britain and to each other through the Commonwealth of Nations. The United Kingdom also slowly achieved partial, if controversial, integration with Europe, joining the European Communities in 1973, though it decided not to adopt the euro and even as powers were partially devolved to Scottish and Welsh legislatures in the late 1990s. In 2015, a majority of British voters chose to leave the EU in a referendum known as Brexit (short for "British Exit" from Europe). In March 2017, the Conservative government under David Cameron invoked Article 50 of the Treaty on

European Union (TEU) on withdrawal, beginning a two-year withdrawal process. By 2018, Theresa May's government was seeking to negotiate a trade agreement with the EU before Britain officially withdrew from the EU in March 2019. No agreement was reached, and a series of Brexit bills before Parliament were all voted down. The EU and UK agreed to a Brexit extension until 31 October 2019 in order to continue negotiating, and then further extended the negotiations into 2020. Both the Conservative and Labour parties contain pro- and anti-Brexit factions, and there is considerable voter anger and political uncertainty. In the local council elections held in May, the Conservatives lost 1333 local council seats, and Labour lost 82 as compared to the previous election. This was seen to clearly signal voter dissatisfaction with both parties. The Liberal Democrats and the Greens scooped up most of these lost seats.

Regime and Political Institutions

Government in the United Kingdom is based on the principle of parliamentary sovereignty, which holds that Parliament (and particularly the House of Commons) is the supreme lawmaking body and that whatever it votes into law is deemed constitutional. Acts of Parliament are not subject to judicial review and can be overturned only by subsequent acts of Parliament. While the legislature is supreme, the executive branch of government is powerful, being led by a prime minister who is selected by majority vote of the House of Commons.

The prime minister is routinely the leader of the party winning the most seats in the parliamentary elections, and they in turn select a cabinet that proposes and presents most bills for passage into law by the broader House. This government remains in office for a term of up to five years as long as it maintains the "confidence" of the House of Commons; elections must be held at least every five years, and the executive can be re-elected for multiple terms. Parliament has the power to "bring down" the prime minister's government by a majority vote of no confidence (or by defeat of a major bill, which is often interpreted as a vote of no confidence), while the prime minister has the power to dissolve Parliament and ask the monarch to call a new election. Dissolution may happen either when the executive believes Parliament is unable to govern or when the prime minister senses an electoral advantage in calling an election. In general, bills proposed by the prime minister's government are passed by the House of Commons because of strong discipline within political parties.

Despite the principle of parliamentary sovereignty, there are some practical limitations on Parliament. Nominally, the monarch calls elections and invites winning parties to form government, though the monarch's role is

Regime and Political Institutions

Regime	Constitutional monarchy with parliamentary democracy
Powers in Constitution	No formal written constitution but widely considered to include certain established laws and rights that are assumed to have constitutional status
Administrative Divisions	Great Britain (includes England, Scotland, and Wales) and Northern Ireland; three island dependencies (Isle of Man, Jersey, Guernsey); more than a dozen overseas territories (British Virgin Islands, Cayman Islands, Gibraltar, Falkland Islands, etc.)
Executive Branch	Prime minister (and cabinet)
Selection of Executive	Elected by House of Commons
Legislative Branch	Bicameral Parliament Lower chamber: House of Commons Upper chamber: House of Lords
Judicial Branch	Interprets statutes but has no right of judicial review
Political Party System	Two-party to three-party system; Conservatives (Tories) and Labour are two main parties; Liberal Democrats are third party.

almost exclusively ceremonial. Parliament itself is governed by traditions, customs, and constitutional interpretations. Although Parliament could theoretically pass any law it wants, it routinely stays within the bounds of common interpretations of the British constitution. A final restraint on Parliament in recent years has seen some devolution of power from the UK Parliament to assemblies in the regions or "countries" (the Scottish Parliament and the Welsh Assembly), as well as some recognition of the powers of the European Union to legislate on certain matters that are binding on British law. This will invariably change if the UK leaves the EU.

Political Culture

Political culture in the United Kingdom, as in other countries, is heterogeneous and dynamic. Several themes have been particularly important in the political culture of late 20th- and 21st-century Great Britain and are, therefore, worth special mention.

The first theme concerns the shifting nature of liberalism and the relationship between class affiliation and party loyalty. A highly stratified society, the United Kingdom in the early to mid-20th century saw a strong relationship between working-class membership and Labour Party support. By the 1970s, however, this had begun to change (Morgan 2010b). On one hand, this change might be attributed to the stagflation the British economy faced in that decade. On the other hand, the United Kingdom witnessed a familiar pattern in the political-cultural development of post-industrial societies. Rising incomes and a major shift in the composition of the labour market—a move away from manufacturing and toward services—have generally been found to change political culture, rendering it more individualistic and less tied to communities and classes (Inglehart and Welzel 2005). By the 1970s, Labour was in crisis, and it did not take power again until it had courted middle-class service sector workers (Morgan 2010b; Clarke 2004, 401–39). This "New Labour" contended with a resurgent liberalism, which preceded it in the form of the reforms of Margaret Thatcher's governments (1979–90) and, to a lesser extent, the government of her successor John Major (1990–97) but also, more recently, following the electoral success of David Cameron and later Theresa May of the Conservative Party.

Another major theme in the changing political culture of 20th-century Britain was the redefinition of British identity in the wake of the collapse of the British Empire. This is doubly the case since many people from the former colonies have made Britain their home and have played influential roles in British politics, such as Sadiq Khan, the current mayor of London, who comes from a working-class Pakistani family. A large number of British Indian, Pakistani, and black MPs serve in the House of Commons. In the 2017 elections, 52 MPs from ethnic backgrounds were elected to Parliament, alongside 45 longer-serving ethnic minority members of the House of Lords. Relatedly, the role of the monarchy in British political culture has gradually changed, but the monarchy remains an important symbol of the nation, especially with the next generations of royals: Prince William and Catherine and their three children and Prince Harry and Meghan and their son. Here too the royal family has become slightly more multicultural because Meghan Markle (Duchess of Sussex) is of mixed white and African-American ancestry. There is certainly a growing resurgence of regional-national identities and the growth of a multicultural understanding of citizenship (Modood 2007). The population of the United Kingdom has been noted for its relatively high level of "euro-skepticism," which has resulted in Brexit.

Political Economy

As mentioned in other sections of this country profile, the United Kingdom has had a central role in the history of global political economy. It was the site of origin for many ideas about free trade even as it used its military power to create a financially exploitative network of colonies. The UK was the launching point for the Industrial Revolution, and it played an important role in constructing the global economy through its formal colonialism and informal efforts to trade with other parts of the world.

Like many other countries that industrialized early, Britain has become a post-industrial economy, meaning, in essence, that services (which account for 80.4 per cent of GDP) dramatically outstrip manufacturing (19 per cent) in economic importance. Britain is also notable for the small share that agriculture plays in its GDP, constituting only 0.6 per cent (CIA 2017 estimate). The country is among the wealthiest countries in terms of GDP per capita in the world (World Bank 2017 estimate: $43,600), and its estimated unemployment rate as of 2017 stood at 4.4 per cent, relatively low given recent global economic difficulties.

There is a considerable discussion of the economic impact of Brexit and Britain's departure from the EU. If this is coupled with a second Scottish referendum on independence, Britain may be substantially reduced in size and economic power.

The welfare state in the United Kingdom has faced political opposition since the early 1980s. As such, it makes an interesting comparison with France, which saw no Margaret Thatcher arise in that decade (see further discussion in the French case). One major theory focuses on the politics of retrenchment, noting that in places like the United Kingdom (and the United States), the welfare state was created by parties on the left in response to the crises of the middle of the 20th century (the Great Depression and World War II). This creates the possibility of a strident opposition from across the spectrum (Prasad 2006; Huber and Stephens 2001).

Sources for economic data in this discussion: CIA World Factbook; World Bank World Development Indicators.

CASE STUDIES

CASE STUDY

Chapter 3, Page 54

No Constitution? No Supreme Court? Constitutionality in the United Kingdom

For two countries that are so historically and culturally intertwined, the United Kingdom and the United States have dramatically different democracies. The United Kingdom is a constitutional monarchy with no single constitutional document, no judicial review of the constitutionality of laws, a prime minister elected chief executive by the legislature, and a principle of legislative supremacy; this contrasts with the United States, centred around a Constitution, separately elected legislatures and executives, a Supreme Court, and a set of checks and balances and separations of powers between government actors.

Many countries follow certain aspects of the British model, but the aspect most unique to the United Kingdom is probably the lack of a single constitutional document. Rather than one core written charter that is amended periodically (as in most countries), the United Kingdom deems several documents to have constitutional significance. As the country developed its unified political system over the course of many centuries, several major acts shaped British political tradition. The constitutional documents include the Magna Carta of 1215 but also a range of other laws of great significance and stature. These include the Bill of Rights of 1689, which emphasized certain limitations on the power of the monarchy, and the Acts of Settlement of 1701, which established patterns of succession to the throne. In a sense, the United Kingdom has a "written" constitution but one that relies on a range of written documents rather than a single one. More generally, the "British Constitution" is partly shaped by tradition, custom, and a common cultural understanding of basic laws, powers, and functions of different political actors.

The British constitution is one of the most flexible in the world, at least according to the law. This is not solely because the United Kingdom has an "unwritten" constitution, though this certainly relates to the question of how the constitution can be changed. Rather, the flexibility comes from the fact that in the British system, Parliament is sovereign. What does this mean? When Parliament passes a law, it is by definition constitutional because the legislating body is the highest political and legal authority in the land. Contrast this with the United States in which the Constitution is the ultimate sovereign authority: Even Congress and presidents must act in accordance with its principles.

The same holds for Canada, where our Supreme Court also has the power of judicial review and the federal Parliament and the provincial and territorial legislatures are obliged to follow the 1982 Constitution and especially the Charter of Rights and Freedoms in passing legislation. Where Canada differs from the US is the fact that provincial leaders can invoke the "notwithstanding clause" whereby Article 33 of the Constitution allows provincial leaders to bypass or override the Charter for up to five years.

So why does the British Parliament not simply overturn long-standing parts of the constitution on a whim? Why has there not been massive "zigzagging" in terms of what the constitution means, from one election to the next, as

continued

new parties take power and lose power? In reality, custom and tradition prevent Parliament from overturning the founding laws of the polity. Much as American or Canadian political parties would probably not envision getting rid of core elements of their constitutions, so too does the British system exhibit constitutional stability from one elected government to the next.

The unwritten constitution and the fact of parliamentary sovereignty have one more implication for constitutionality in the United Kingdom: There is no role for the judiciary in ruling on whether a law is constitutional. In most countries, some judicial body has the power to rule on whether laws passed by the legislature are compatible with the written constitution. If that judicial body, such as the Supreme Court in Canada, finds a law unconstitutional, it may strike it down. But if Parliament is sovereign and there is no single constitution, there is no place for judicial review. Thus, the United Kingdom had no real "Supreme Court" until the 2000s, and even now its powers are limited to specific questions relating to issues of devolution of power to Scotland and Wales, along with very restricted responsibilities in the area of legal revision.

CASE STUDY

Chapter 9, Page 204

The United Kingdom and the Westminster Model

The United Kingdom is called the "Mother of Parliaments" because its Parliament dates back to at least the 13th century, when King John convened the nobility of England as an advisory council that controlled the economy. In 1215, the nobility sensed the king's weak position and need for the support of nobles to raise revenue for the Crown, so they insisted upon a "Great Charter"—the Magna Carta—and thereby secured various rights with respect to property and requirements for royal consultation of the nobles. Since that time, Parliament has steadily gained power relative to the monarch, most notably beginning in the 17th century with the English Civil Wars and their aftermath (1642–60) and with the Glorious Revolution of 1688. Initially comprised of nobles (lords) and later also of commoners, these Parliaments evolved from advisory councils to become powerful legislatures that eventually asserted their sovereignty over the monarch. These origins can still be seen today in the existence of the House of Commons and the House of Lords.

From these origins has come the system known worldwide as the Westminster system, named for the region of central London where the government resides. Parliament is considered the country's supreme and sovereign political power. While parliamentary sovereignty is the central fact of the United Kingdom's political system, a variety of institutional mechanisms gives the executive substantial power to push legislation through Parliament. The legislature votes, but the cabinet and the prime minister forward most legislation on the assumption that the "backbenchers" in the governing party will support the government's proposal. This model of parliamentary democracy has been used around the world, not least because of the influence of Britain's colonial empire on many of today's independent countries, from the giant India to tiny islands in the Caribbean.

In the British parliamentary model, the House of Commons is now the dominant chamber. It houses the executive branch of the prime minister and the cabinet and has almost sole responsibility for passing laws, approving budgets, and holding the executive accountable; it can cause the government to fall by a vote of no confidence. Members of the House of Commons are chosen in single-member districts in a "first-past-the-post" system in which the largest number of votes in a district suffices to elect a member of Parliament (MP), even if this is only a plurality and not a majority. This electoral system is widely viewed as favouring the largest parties and punishing smaller parties.

The House of Lords is marginal by contrast, as is the monarchy. Though they were the founding body of Parliament, Lords progressively lost power to the Commons over the centuries as the United Kingdom modernized and expanded the franchise. The House of Lords now possesses some limited ability to slow Commons' policy-making process by requesting further review. Major reforms in 1999 dramatically reduced the number of hereditary lords, and debate continues about eliminating hereditary peerages entirely. The queen or king, meanwhile, retains powers to invite parties to form a government or accept a resignation, but these are almost purely ceremonial.

This Westminster system is partially emulated in many other countries, though some countries established their own parliaments and assemblies independently of the United Kingdom in their early histories. There are few other places that precisely follow the House of Commons/House of Lords model; in most places with bicameral legislatures, the role of the upper chamber is more explicitly territorial, representing states, provinces, or regions. The lower chambers around the world, meanwhile, are elected in a variety of different electoral processes, as Chapter 9 shows.

Research Prompts

1. Compare and contrast state formation in the United Kingdom and France. What is similar and what is different about the timing and nature of state-building in each case?
2. Compare and contrast the United States, the United Kingdom, and Canada on the question of judicial review. In the cases, what are the relative consequences of having or not having judicial review? What conclusions can you draw about the costs and benefits of judicial review?
3. Analyze in comparative perspective the construction of the welfare state in the United Kingdom after the Second World War. What are the major implications of the fact that it was the Labour Party that constructed it? How does this compare to the American and French cases?
4. Some have argued that the yes side for Brexit was a result of Britain's unhappiness with the EU's relatively open immigration policies. Others claim that Brexit was primarily about EU regulation and bureaucracy. What accounts for the pro-Brexit vote? Does this referendum really represent the interests of most British voters?
5. Britain was an imperial power for many centuries and greatly enriched itself at the expense of its colonies. While this history was largely glossed over in the past, many of the more negative aspects of British colonialism are now coming to the fore. Assess the merits of this debate over British history and imperial legacies. Where does the balance lie?

Online Case Studies

Go to **www.oup.com/he/DickovickCe** to find more case studies online, including:

- National Identity in the United Kingdom
- Political Economy of Britain
- The State in the United Kingdom

Note

1 Parry 2016.

United States

PROFILE

Key Features of the Contemporary United States

Population:	329,256,465 (July 2018 est.)
Area:	9,826,675 square kilometres
Head of State:	Donald Trump (president, 2017–present)
Head of Government:	Donald Trump (president, 2017– present)
Capital:	Washington, DC
Year of Independence:	1776/1783
Year of Current Constitution:	1787 (ratified 1788)
Languages:	English; many others, including most prominently Spanish and Asian and European languages
GDP per Capita:	$59,531.70 (World Bank estimate, 2017)
Human Development Index Ranking (2015):	10th (very high human development)
Trading Relationship with Canada (2016):	• Imports $210,250,896,474 • Exports $296,607,266,017 https:/globaledge.msu.edu/countries/canada/tradestats

Sources: *CIA World Factbook 2018*; World Bank World Development Indicators; United Nations *Human Development Report 2016*

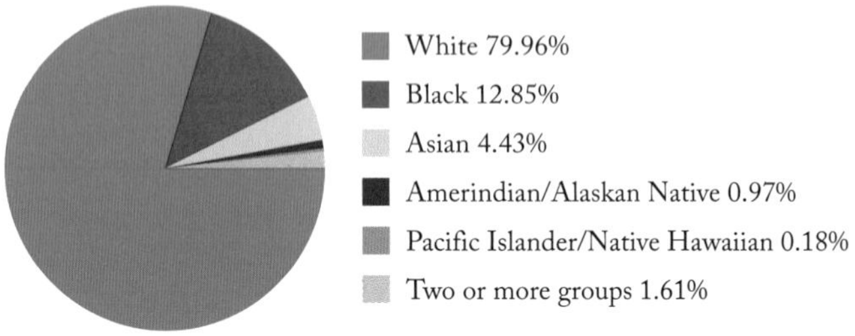

Ethnic Groups in the United States

Note that Hispanics, not captured here as a group because of the categories used when data is collected in the United States, are estimated to constitute about 15 per cent of the population. Most persons of Hispanic ancestry or ethnic identification show up here in either the "white" or "black" categories.

Source: *CIA World Factbook*

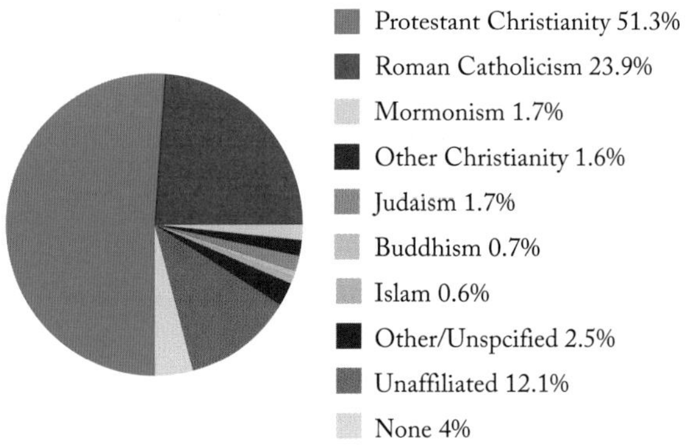

Religious Affiliation in the United States

Note that again these data are dependent on how categories are determined and measured. Some scholars would want to draw a distinction within the category of "Protestant Christianity" between evangelical Christian denominations and "mainline" Protestant denominations. In recent decades, the former have been growing or at least maintaining strength while the latter have seen some declines, and social scientists' predictions about future trends have varied (Wuthnow 2007).

Source: *CIA World Factbook*

Introduction

The United States has been the world's only comprehensive superpower for some three decades, with overwhelming dominance in terms of its unrivalled military power and reach in a worldwide network of bases, its global cultural power, and the world's largest economy. In terms of information technology, entrepreneurship, and innovation, the US has proven to be exceptional. It is also a lynchpin of and key influence over most of the financial and political institutions that comprise the global rules-based international order, such as the United Nations Security Council, the North Atlantic Treaty Organization, the International Monetary Fund, and the World Bank. The US is also one of the more unequal Western countries in the world, has the highest rates of gun violence, and is also the most religious Western country. With the world's oldest continuing constitution, the US possesses a centuries-old political system with some obvious strengths and weaknesses. The US is worthy of detailed study as both a model of some forms of development and as a cautionary warning. Canadians have a long history of being close observers of the United States in all of its positive and negative qualities.

Let us note several key features of the United States that make it especially interesting for the student of comparative politics. First, it was the earliest large-scale modern society to embrace democracy and republicanism. As such, it was viewed by its founders and by subsequent generations as a kind of experiment. It has been relatively stable, governed under a single constitution for centuries, and it rose from being a successful commercial and agricultural society to a major industrial power to a key "post-industrial" society. Scholars debate whether and to what extent the United States is "exceptional" in its liberal democracy, its "denominational" approach to organizing the place of religion in public life (Niebuhr 1929), and its lack of a comprehensive welfare state comparable to those of other Western countries (Kaufman 2002). The United States stands out among the major advanced industrial and post-industrial societies for the weakness of its welfare state and its dramatic problems of economic and social inequality.

Additionally, American-style democracy has deteriorated in recent years as populism and illiberal forms of rule have increased. In 2018, the Economist Intelligence Unit rated the US as a "flawed democracy," as compared to Canada's "full democracy" status. They note: "The US has fallen in the global rankings over the past decade, from 18th place in the 2008 Democracy Index, to 25th in 2018. This primarily reflects a deterioration in the functioning of government category, as political polarisation has become more pronounced and public confidence in institutions has weakened" (Economist Intelligence Unit, 11).

Finally, while those at the top of the American economic and political system remain predominantly white, American society as a whole is both ethnically and religiously heterogeneous. This periodically produces tension, and waves of large-scale immigration have often been met by waves of xenophobia and intolerance (Kennedy 1999, 14–15). Perhaps related to this heterogeneity is the degree of religious pluralism characteristic of the society, a feature that has been linked by some scholars to its comparatively high levels of religiosity (Iannaccone, Finke, and Stark 1997). Indeed, the United States is far more religious than one might expect it to be based on its level of economic development (Norris and Inglehart 2004).

Historical Development

Before the onset of European colonization, millions of Indigenous peoples divided into cultural and linguistic nations lived in and controlled the land mass that is now known as North America. Indigenous peoples were subjected to a high degree of violence during the lengthy process of European colonization, which today would be considered genocide. This included the deliberate spread of European diseases, forced marches, policies of starvation, bounties on scalps, massacres, and decades of "Indian wars." Indigenous peoples were also targeted with forced assimilation through residential schooling, white adoptions, and other means. Currently, Indigenous peoples are classified for the purposes of US law as "domestic dependent nations." They have some rights to their own forms of local government, police forces, schools, and courts but are seen to exercise their limited sovereignty within the American state (Vicaire 2013; Fredericks 1999). As the National Congress of American Indians lays out, there are currently 573 federally recognized Indian Nations, alongside a range of "state recognized tribes located throughout the United States recognized by their respective state governments" (National Congress of American Indians (NCAI) [2017] 2019).

Geographically, today's United States includes areas that were colonized by Spain, the Netherlands, France, and

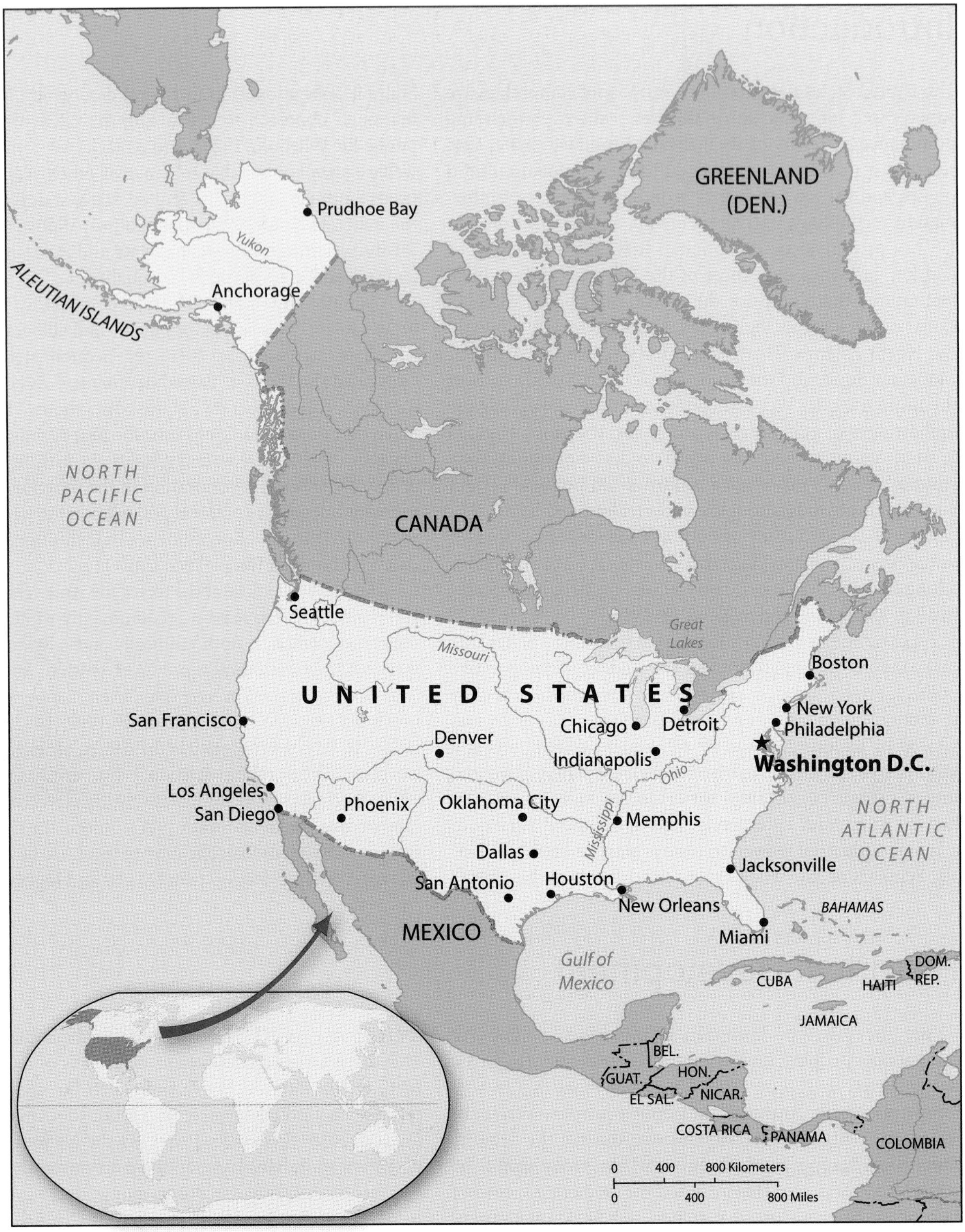
GREENLAND
(DEN.)
Prudhoe Bay
Yukon
Anchorage
ALEUTIAN ISLANDS
NORTH
PACIFIC
OCEAN
CANADA
Seattle
Great
Lakes
Missouri
Boston
UNITED STATES
New York
Philadelphia
San Francisco
Chicago
Detroit
Denver
Indianapolis
Washington D.C.
Ohio
Los Angeles
San Diego
Phoenix
Oklahoma City
Memphis
Mississippi
NORTH
ATLANTIC
OCEAN
Dallas
Jacksonville
San Antonio
Houston
New Orleans
BAHAMAS
MEXICO
Miami
Gulf of
Mexico
CUBA
HAITI
DOM.
REP.
JAMAICA
BEL.
GUAT.
HON.
EL SAL.
NICAR.
COSTA RICA
PANAMA
COLOMBIA
0
400
800 Kilometers
0
400
800 Miles

England and includes portions of what was once Mexico. For most of the British period, the 13 colonies in North America were not considered the most important of Britain's colonial possessions. Caribbean societies like Barbados and Jamaica were far more significant as sources of wealth (Dunn [1972] 2000), as India later would be. However, by the mid- to late 18th century, the Crown was becoming increasingly interested in its North American colonies as both markets for British manufactured goods and a potential source of revenue. While some slavery was practised in the North before independence, it became the basis of much of the southern plantation economy. When independence was established, the movement was predominantly led by white elites from these two regions.

Even after gaining independence, it was unclear if the new nation would survive as a polity. A number of views about what should replace British colonialism were in circulation, but the new country finally settled on the constitutional system that remains in place to this day (Wood [1969] 1998). The US Constitution established a division of powers across three branches of government and a separation of powers between the central government and the states. The Constitution outlines the basic system of governance and establishes the principles of the rule of law that "constitutes" the basic political compact. This compact did not include Indigenous peoples, enslaved or free Africans, or women and was based on particular conceptions about who constituted an autonomous rational subject. Comprised of just seven articles and a small number of sections, the entire document fits comfortably onto a handful of pages. Yet it has proved robust enough to withstand more than two centuries of change with only 27 amendments during that period, despite major economic and political developments and several wars that challenged the existence of the United States as a republic.

Some of the amendments to the Constitution have been substantial, and broader social change has altered the United States polity considerably over the years. Here we briefly highlight three main developments in that connection: the extension of suffrage and full participation in the life of the society to groups that were once excluded; the creation of the modern party system that has dominated American politics now for decades; and the growth of the state and, in particular, of the welfare state in the 20th century.

Let us begin with the gradual extension of full citizenship. Claims that "All men are created equal" glossed over the fact that a great deal of exclusion and inequality was at the root of the American republic, especially anti-black racism. Over the course of the 19th century, tension built over the persistence of slavery. Abolitionists campaigned against it, while slave owners and their supporters justified it. Presidents and other elected officials worked to balance power such that the status quo could persist—in which southern states could continue slavery and northern states could meekly oppose it—but eventually this became impossible. The country's defining event of the 19th century, the Civil War (1861–5), was fought over this issue (McPherson 1988). After four years of bitter fighting and 620,000 casualties, the Union side was victorious. In the initial postwar years, African Americans had social and electoral success in a number of southern regions. But much of this depended on the presence of northern troops during Reconstruction, which ended in the late 1870s. After this period, local majority-group actors in the South used force to re-establish exclusive control over political organizations and then wrote explicit racial discrimination into law, creating what was called the "Jim Crow South" with its sharp racial segregation.

At the same time, African Americans who moved to northern cities often discovered that discrimination was also present there (for an evocative account, see Wilkerson 2010). Jim Crow only fell in the face of social organizing, social movement activity, and extensive litigation. Indeed, when the federal government, under pressure, began to enforce equal access to voting, education, and other rights in the 1960s, it faced resistance from some southern populations and even from state-level leaders like George Wallace (Patterson 1996, 579–89). Social scientists point to ongoing evidence of job discrimination, substantially lower incomes and asset levels, substantially poorer public health indicators, and higher incarceration rates among African Americans as evidence that both historical legacies and ongoing discrimination remain issues (Brown et al. 2003).

The evolution of the modern party system is linked to these developments. On one hand, the fact that the United States has a two-party system is partially a function of its "winner take all" approach to elections, but this does not explain why the two parties have developed as they have and linked themselves to the interests and support of the groups that they have. In the initial years of the republic, the major conflict was between so-called "federalists" and "democratic republicans." The former favoured stronger central power (indeed, both groups were proponents of "federalism" as such) and a national bank, while the latter group felt more strongly about having a weak central government with stronger state and local governments. Over time, the federalists were essentially replaced by the Whigs. The Civil War,

Historical Development Timeline

Indigenous nations are sovereign in the territory of what is now North America from time immemorial. The Spanish, Portuguese, and British will later invoke a "Doctrine of Discovery" to legitimate the taking of Indigenous lands and their transformation into European colonies.

1600s	Establishment of early colonial settlements at Jamestown, Virginia (1607), Plymouth, Massachusetts (1620), and other sites along the Atlantic coast.
1754–63	French and Indian Wars, conflict between English and French settlers, along with Indigenous allies, in present-day United States and Canada.
1775	Beginning of American Revolution after years of tension between colonies and British Crown over taxation and representation.
1776	Signing of Declaration of Independence.
1781	Articles of Confederation take effect as first attempt at independent American government.
1783	Surrender of British forces at Yorktown, Virginia, signifies end of American Revolution.
1787	Constitution drafted, ratified by states in 1788.
1791	Bill of Rights, the first 10 amendments to the Constitution, takes effect.
1803	Louisiana Purchase.
1812	War with Great Britain, ends in 1815.
1820	Missouri Compromise works out a racial compromise between northern free states and southern slave states.
1840s	Annexation of Texas and Mexican-American War greatly expand US territory.
1850s	Rising tensions between North and South.
1861	Civil War begins.
1863	Emancipation Proclamation.
1865	End of Civil War; President Abraham Lincoln assassinated.
1870s	Reconstruction.
1880s	Peak of the Gilded Age.
1898	Spanish-American War.
1916–18	American involvement in World War I on the side of Allies.
1920	Women's suffrage movement results in vote for all adults.
1929	Great Depression begins, lasts through 1930s.
1933–45	Presidency of Franklin Delano Roosevelt, who champions the New Deal (including social security) and leads the US through most of World War II.
1941	US enters World War II after the Japanese bombing of Pearl Harbor, Hawaii.
1945	World War II ends with US dropping atomic bombs on Japanese cities Hiroshima and Nagasaki.
1950s–60s	Civil rights movement; *Brown v. Board of Education* (1954) Supreme Court decision; Civil Rights Act (1964); Voting Rights Act (1965).
1963	Assassination of President John F. Kennedy.
1963–69	Presidency of Lyndon Baines Johnson, who both increases US involvement in the Vietnam War and expands the welfare state via his "Great Society" programs.
1969–74	Presidency of Richard Nixon, which included continued war in Vietnam, partial rapprochement with China, and the decision to float the dollar on currency exchanges rather than pegging its value to gold; Nixon resigned in August 1974 as he faced impeachment for the Watergate Scandal.
1974–7	Presidency of Gerald Ford, which included the end of the Vietnam War.
1977–81	Presidency of Jimmy Carter, with a renewed emphasis on human rights in foreign policy but economic problems domestically.
1981–9	Presidency of Ronald Reagan, which includes partial retrenchment of the welfare state and a more aggressive foreign policy.
1989–93	Presidency of George H.W. Bush, which includes war in Iraq and end of the Cold War.
1993–2001	Presidency of Bill Clinton, which includes notable economic growth and the fiscal solvency of the state, the signing of the North American Free Trade Agreement, and welfare reform.
2001–9	Presidency of George W. Bush, which includes the 11 September attacks, wars in Afghanistan and Iraq, and the financial crisis of 2008, causing a major recession.
2009–17	Presidency of Barack Obama, which includes passage of the Affordable Care Act and the improvement of US foreign relations.
2016	Presidency of Donald J. Trump begins.
2017–ongoing	President Trump encounters challenges in reforming health care and in conducting foreign policy with allies. Scandals about Russian tampering in the US election, a showdown with North Korea's Kim Jong-Un, and other diplomatic issues signal a decline in US prestige internationally.
2019	Democratic candidates begin their primary process to select a presidential candidate. The House of Representatives begins impeachment proceedings against President Trump.

though, was a critical juncture. Abraham Lincoln, the candidate of the little-known Republican Party, was elected in 1860, and the party competition that emerged in subsequent years meant that the Democrats would be strong among predominantly white voters in the South and Republicans in the North. Moreover, African-American political actors tended to be strongly Republican. This changed in the 20th century (Kennedy 1999), particularly during the years of the Great Depression, when Franklin Delano Roosevelt's expansion of the welfare state appealed to many groups of minority voters, including African Americans, workers, and members of immigrant groups. For a time, there was considerable tension in the Democratic Party between more conservative, often southern, traditionalist party members and supporters of the more "liberal" (in the American sense) trajectory of the Democratic Party in the postwar years. More recently, following Richard Nixon's famous "Southern Strategy" (Patterson 1996, 702, 741–2), the Republicans established their strongest base in the South, and regions like the northeast have become staunchly Democratic.

The welfare state in the United States is underdeveloped if you compare it to those found in other advanced industrial societies such as Canada, France, Germany, or the Scandinavian countries. The American welfare state was really created in Franklin Delano Roosevelt's "New Deal" in the 1930s (Kennedy 1999). This is the period in which social security—the American form of social insurance that both provides retirement benefits and also support in the event of a wage earner's disability or death—was established, along with some forms of housing assistance, periodic relief programs meant to provide work and other forms of assistance during the Great Depression, and increased regulation of the labour market.

The second major period of construction of the American welfare state (Patterson 1996, 524–92) was during the presidency of Lyndon Baines Johnson (1963–9). Here, major health care programs like Medicare (which provides health care to retirees) and Medicaid (which provides care to some individuals who otherwise could not afford it) were established, as were numerous other social welfare programs such as Head Start and Food Stamps (technically called the Supplemental Nutrition Assistance Program), among others.

Ronald Reagan took office in 1980, strongly opposing the welfare state features established by the New Deal and the Great Society programs. Reagan, his Republican successor George H.W. Bush, and Democrat Bill Clinton rolled back many aspects of the welfare state. This continued under George W. Bush and to a lesser extent under Barack Obama, who reformed the publicly funded health care system. Donald Trump campaigned on eliminating "Obamacare," but he has not been able to do so. Both parties, despite major differences, continue to share the belief that Medicare and social security should be preserved.

Regime and Political Institutions

The predominant features of the American political system are the separation of powers among various levels and institutions of government. This includes not only the set of "checks and balances" between the legislature, the executive, and the judiciary but also the separation of power between the federal government and the 50 states. At the federal level, the United States Congress is a bicameral legislature comprised of a House of Representatives and the Senate; each representative in the House is selected in one of 435 districts around the country, with each district representing more than a half-million Americans. Every state has a minimum of one seat for a representative in the House, and the number of districts per state ranges from one in the least populous states (such as Wyoming) to 53 in California. This representation in the House, which is roughly proportional to a state's population, is counterbalanced by the two senators for each state. Either chamber can propose bills it wishes to see become law, but the bill must pass both houses of Congress, then be signed into law by the president. Alternatively, the president can choose to veto the bill, which can then be overturned only by a two-thirds majority vote in both houses of Congress. In addition, the federal judiciary can strike down laws it deems unconstitutional. This provides the judicial check on the other branches; the check on the judiciary in turn is that its judges are nominated by the president and approved by the Senate.

States and local governments have a great deal of responsibility in social services. States do much of the work in administering programs for the poor (such as Medicaid and income support), while localities have especially significant responsibilities in education. Local executives such as mayors also oversee services such as local roads, sanitation, and the police.

Regime and Political Institutions

Regime	Federal republic, democratically elected
Administrative Divisions	50 states, each of which has counties, cities, towns, etc. Also District of Columbia (federal capital) and several overseas territories and dependencies.
Executive Branch	President
Selection of Executive	Elected by "electoral college," with delegates awarded depending on popular vote in each state or electoral district
Legislative Branch	Bicameral Congress House of Representatives (lower chamber) elected in single-member districts Senate (upper chamber), two senators per state
Judicial Branch	Federal court system led by Supreme Court with powers of constitutional review
Political Party System	Two-party system: Democratic Party, Republican Party

Political Culture

American political culture, like political culture everywhere, has multiple streams and features. However, certain key themes stand out. For primarily white settlers, these themes have traditionally included skepticism of governmental authority, which extends back at least to the revolutionary era; so-called "rugged individualism"; the American "frontier mentality"; an isolationist tendency with respect to foreign policy but alongside an important militarist strain; and the idea of the "American dream" and the associated idea of meritocratic equality.

The tradition of skepticism may, to some extent, have its origins in the early stages of colonialism. When the country became independent of British rule, its founders clearly did have in mind "limited government," and government powers expanded in several key stages and in response to crises and changing conditions in subsequent years. Still, having founding documents and traditions that so clearly express skepticism of government means that the political culture, no matter how much it changes, always has these points of reference.

The notion of "rugged individualism" carries the image of single persons and small families struggling, without aid, against nature. Much of this developed as white settlers moved onto Indigenous territories and sought to take them over. In general, comparative researchers find a strong individualist tendency in American political culture.

Political Economy

The United States is the world's largest economy as of 2018, despite recent challenges and the rise of China. The 20th century was a time of dramatic expansion of American manufacturing, epitomized by the rise of the automobile industry (Kennedy 1999, 20–1). Economic setbacks came with the Great Depression of the 1930s, the oil crises of the 1970s, and the global financial crisis of 2007–9, but the American economy continues as a world leader. By the 21st century, the economy had shifted away from low-skilled, labour-intensive manufacturing as a result of automation and increasing imports of products built overseas (and, therefore, the outsourcing of much industrial work to developing countries). The economy has become more "service-oriented," including many professionals with university degrees and many working in retail sales. Inequality has increased notably as these trends have unfolded (Patterson 2005, 351–3).

The United States does not have the highest GDP per capita, as it lags behind several countries that are banking centres and several oil-exporting countries with small populations. Moreover, inequality in the United States is high compared to that in other wealthy countries, and more than 10 per cent of the population falls below the poverty line. This suggests that the issue of development is relevant even in this seemingly powerful economy. Health indicators and education lag behind those of many countries in both Europe and Asia. Some minority groups, such as African Americans, have faced centuries of systemic injustice and structural racism.

The American economy faces several significant challenges at present, especially after the deep recession of 2007 to 2009 and the slow recovery and high unemployment that persisted in its aftermath. In the short term (as of late 2018), the central challenge is one of continuing to restore demand while capitalizing on the momentum that has developed in the labour market. Many Americans worry about the size and sustainability of the national debt and are concerned that the imbalance may worsen as a result of continued low taxes and increased spending for an aging population in the coming years.

Despite these many challenges, the American economy is diversified and robust in many areas and is home to many of the largest and most successful corporations in the world as well as a leading centre of technological innovation and finance. The United States also features countless small businesses and is renowned for its culture of entrepreneurship. As a result, the United States continues to draw talent and capital investment from around the world, and it looks set to remain a global economic powerhouse into the future.

CASE STUDIES

CASE STUDY

Chapter 6, Page 125

Is American Democracy in Trouble?

Many of today's more robust democracies have had tumultuous histories. Think, for instance, of Germany or France, which over the past two centuries have seen both democratic and authoritarian regimes (with Nazi Germany as perhaps the most notorious totalitarian regime in modern history). Other countries, though, saw slow and steady democratization over time. Canada, the United Kingdom, and the United States stand out as Western examples of the latter pattern. Does this mean that polities like the United States are securely democratic?

Very few political scientists fear the imminent demise of American democracy, but scholars do vary considerably in terms of *how* safely institutionalized they consider that democracy to be. Some argue forcefully that democracy is being eroded. Think, for a moment, about what the different theories of democracy discussed in Chapter 6 might suggest about this case. What are the implications of each theory for the *survival* of democratic regimes? What risk factors might increase the probability of democratic decay?

One worry that some scholars have voiced concerns rising income inequality (e.g., Hacker and Pierson 2010). The gap between rich and poor Americans is much wider today than it was several decades ago. According to scholars like Hacker and Pierson, this change has dangerous implications, and we might expect it to be self-reinforcing, since the "beneficiaries" of expanding income inequality exert disproportionate influence in the political process and might block efforts to reduce inequality. Much of this inequality is racialized too: For example, African Americans are disproportionately affected by the growing gaps between rich and poor.

Another worry links to a different theory of democratization discussed in the chapter, the "cultural" theory. Some years ago, political scientist Robert Putnam (2000; for a similar set of concerns see Bellah et al. 1985) published a book called *Bowling Alone* in which he argued that the habits, tastes, and modes of participation that had been operative in the United States since its founding were in decline. According to Putnam, the voluntarist tendencies that were conducive to robust civic participation were giving way to individualism and isolation. The implication, again, is that the failure to practise democratic habits—or to maintain a democratic culture of civic participation—could undermine democratic institutions.

continued

Other commentators have more recently worried about the rise of populism, particularly the Trump phenomenon and the president's constant denunciation of mainstream media as "fake news." As we mention here and in Chapter 6, the Economist Intelligence Unit has downgraded the US from a full democracy to a flawed democracy ("Democracy Continues Its Disturbing Retreat," 2018). The Trump presidency has demonstrated that the constraints on the presidency many Americans have taken for granted are conventions, not laws, and can be set aside. At the same time, the 2018 mid-term elections had some of the highest voter turnouts in recent memory, and Republicans lost control of the House of Representatives. Now a Democratic Party majority is blocking many Trump actions, demonstrating that the system of checks and balances can work in practice. As Konrad Yakabuski wrote of the mid-terms in the *Globe and Mail*, "as discouraging as the spectacle in the White House may be, it is in moments such as this that the true genius of the U.S. Constitution and the resilience of the country's democracy are revealed." In short, he argues, "Democracy in America is down, but not out" (Yakabuski 2019).

We encourage *you*, though, to *think like a comparativist* in coming to judgments about whether the US democratic system is in trouble or not. Try to put the comparative approach to work in thinking about these critical issues.

CASE STUDY

Chapter 9, Page 195

The United States Congress: Dysfunctional or Functioning by Design?

Some of the leading debates about how representative democracy truly is in the United States focus on the functioning of Congress and especially the Senate. Consider one question: Would it seem democratic if elected officials representing about 12 per cent of the population could block legislation that the other 88 per cent wants? Probably not, assuming the law in question does not violate any basic civil rights. Yet this could happen in the United States, at least in theory. The Senate features significant malapportionment and provides major leverage to smaller and less populous (often rural) states.

The power of a minority in the Senate can be further enhanced by certain rules that have been applied with increasing frequency. For instance, even a minority of senators can block legislation, given the use of such tactics as the "filibuster" (or, more formally, a cloture vote), which requires a supermajority of 60 out of 100 senators to end a debate and move to a vote on a bill. In the most extreme scenario, legislation in the United States could be stopped by 41 senators representing only about 12 per cent of the country's population.

Representation in the House of Representatives is also subject to manoeuvres that can distort representation. The districts for elections depend on the results of the census, which takes place every 10 years. As states grow in population, they may be awarded additional seats among the 435 in the House, while these seats are taken away from states declining in population. This realignment gives rise to redistricting, or the drawing of new maps that define the boundaries of congressional districts. The shape of districts is a hotly contested issue, since it shapes the likelihood of who is elected to office. For instance, imagine a large urban area shaped like a large circle that is large enough to merit two congressional seats. Say the population of the whole area is comprised of 40 per cent Democrats, mostly located in the urban centre, and 60 per cent Republicans, mostly located in the suburbs that ring the city. Should the map-makers draw districts that cut the circle in half along its diameter with a straight line? Or should they create one congressional district for the urban centre and one for the suburbs? The "straight line" solution might well give two Republican seats (since Republicans would outnumber Democrats by a ratio of 3:2 on either side of the dividing line), while the "centre and ring" solution would probably give one seat in the House to each party (since the Democrats would dominate in the inner city and the Republicans in the district in the suburbs). The chosen solution may be determined by which party (if either) controls the redistricting process. In some instances, the map-making becomes an elaborate process known as "gerrymandering" in which incumbents who see an advantage in drawing a map a certain way create districts with bizarre shapes designed to help themselves and/or hurt their political opponents.

CASE STUDY

Chapter 16, Page 336

The United States and the World: A Love–Hate Relationship?

Internationally, the United States has traditionally been viewed as one of the key proponents of globalization and as one of the societies the culture and economy of which have most benefitted from increasing global integration.

There has been a long-standing tension in American politics between shutting the United States off from the world and engaging with it. George Washington famously urged the United States not to get involved in foreign wars, and for many years the United States had a very small standing army, owing to an "isolationist" tendency in American political culture. Where it did seek influence, such as in the Americas (Schoultz 1998), it used a combination of soft and hard power but in most cases without formally establishing colonies (see Puerto Rico, Hawaii, and the Philippines for key exceptions). A recent study by McPherson outlines that from 1800 to 2019, "US troops have intervened thousands of times in Latin America and have occupied its countries on dozens of occasions." Interventions took place during five eras in US relations with the region: "expansion of the continental republic from 1811 to 1897, the war in Cuba and the apex of occupations (1898–1933), the Good Neighbor years (1934–53), the Cold War (1954–90), and the post–Cold War period (1991–2018 and ongoing)" (Oxford Research Encyclopedias).

Both President Woodrow Wilson in World War I and President Roosevelt in World War II had to work very hard to convince the country to participate in those wars. However, through participating the United States gradually began to serve a global role from which it would be difficult to extricate itself, and US global involvement accelerated rapidly after World War II as it worked to help rebuild Japan and Europe, to counter the influence of the Soviet Union, and to restore international order in a manner consistent with its interests. Much of the responsibility for the enforcement of global order was assumed by the United States, which was instrumental in creating NATO, the United Nations, and international economic actors like the World Bank and the International Monetary Fund. The United States emerged as the most important state proponent of economic liberalism, and it has been instrumental in pushing for trade agreements like NAFTA and its successor and the General Agreement on Tariffs and Trade (GATT). Of course, the US has benefitted economically, politically, culturally, and militarily from maintaining this hegemonic control over global affairs.

In coming years, the United States will face new pressures and challenges related to globalization and the changing global order. China's influence in the Pacific will continue to rise, and both powers will need to be cautious as they gradually sort out how they will interact. Under the Trump administration, the US has seemed to pull away from traditional allies. Trump in 2018 engaged in a trade war with Canada over several commodities. He also insulted Canada's Prime Minister Justin Trudeau. During NATO meetings in 2018, Trump also seemed to go out of his way to disparage his closest European allies, chiding them for not spending enough on defence and even claiming that Germany was a "captive" of Russia for being too dependent on its oil and gas supplies. Trump also took the unprecedented step of engaging in a tariff war with China, with threats exchanged to impose tariffs on potentially hundreds of billions of dollars' worth of goods and services. While the fundamentals of the US economic and political systems are sound, there are major debates within the US about what sort of society is most desirable for its people. Internationally, governments throughout the world are increasingly questioning the future of US leadership.

Research Prompts

1. Consider the discussion of basic American political institutions in this country profile and its accompanying case studies, and then consider these materials alongside the discussion of the same institutions in the materials on France and the United Kingdom. What are the major differences in political institutions in the countries? What would any large-scale comparative analysis of political institutions in the three countries need to explain?
2. The "institutional chapters" in this volume have asked you to move beyond Canada, the United States, and the

United Kingdom in terms of your thinking about political institutions. In the other country profile materials, find three cases that differ from the United States in some important way in terms of political institutions. Why are these models so different? What are the advantages and disadvantages of each for politics in the respective countries?

3. Look in the country profiles at discussions of the welfare state in Canada, France, the United Kingdom, and the United States. You will see that different welfare states developed at different paces and with different consequences (for example, some spend more than others). How might you explain these variations?
4. Both the United States and the United Kingdom have, at different points in their history, been proponents of protectionism and then free trade. Based on your reading of these cases and their profiles, do you expect that we will see the same pattern in China? Why or why not?
5. Compare and contrast the key points of the politics of ethnicity in the United States and India. Both countries have pasts that include racial and ethnic discrimination, and empirical evidence suggests that discrimination continues to disadvantage some groups in each society. Does this take place in the same way? Why are there differences in how ethnic diversity is reflected in patterns of political representation in the two countries?
6. In recent years, the United States has largely promoted globalization while France has been ambivalent. This seems to have switched with the elections of Presidents Macron and Trump. What explains this shift?

Online Case Studies

Go to **www.oup.com/he/DickovickCe** to find more case studies online, including:

- Did Free Markets Help the United States Get Rich? Will They in the Future?
- Is Judicial Activism in the United States a Problem?
- "The Most Powerful Person in the World"? Checks on American Presidents

GLOSSARY

absolute deprivation A condition of being deprived of resources below some given threshold, as distinguished from *relative* deprivation.

administration The bureaucracy of state officials, usually considered part of the executive branch, that executes policy.

alternative energy Energy sources, such as solar or wind power, that are not derived from fossil fuels.

alternative vote Voting system in which voters rank candidates and the votes of low-ranking candidates are reallocated until a winner is determined.

anti-colonial revolutions Revolutions brought by subjugated populations against colonial powers, typically with the purpose of removing them so that the society in question can achieve independence.

apportionment The process by which legislative seats are distributed among geographic constituencies.

argument The placement of evidence in logical form in support of a position or claim.

assimilation The practice of being integrated into another culture, especially with respect to immigration.

authoritarianism A form of government or regime that is non-democratic.

authoritarian persistence The ongoing continuation of an authoritarian regime such that democratic transition does not take place.

authoritarian regime A non-democratic regime.

bellicist theory Theory associated with scholars such as Charles Tilly, who argue that interstate wars were decisive in the creation of the modern state.

bias A preference for one idea or perspective over another, especially a preference that may result in unbalanced use of evidence or in analytical error.

bicameral legislature Legislature with two chambers, which may have equal or unequal powers.

biological determinism The view that a feature of social life, such as gender or ethnicity, is caused by underlying biology.

boundaries Lines drawn symbolically between groups of people.

brain drain The departure or emigration of skilled and educated members of a population, especially with reference to developing countries in the international system.

bureaucracy The organization of unelected officials, often considered part of the executive branch, that implements, executes, and enforces laws and policies.

bureaucratic-authoritarian regime A type of authoritarian regime, common in Latin America and elsewhere in the mid- to late 20th century, that was associated with control of the state more by a group of elites (often military) than by a single individual leader.

cabinet The group of senior officials in the executive branch, including ministers, who advise the head of government or head of state.

capital A factor of economic production consisting of accumulated wealth or financial resources available for investment.

case In comparative analysis, a unit or example of a phenomenon to be studied.

catch-all parties Political parties that are flexible on their ideological positions and aim to attract support from a broad range of interest groups and voters.

causation The property that obtains when one thing can be shown to cause another.

chamber An assembly or body of a legislature, often referring to one of two such bodies in a bicameral legislature.

citizenship A form of relationship between the state and individuals subject to its control in which citizens have certain basic rights and are in some way represented in the state.

civic nationalism A form of nationalism that says that you are a member of the nation if you are a citizen of its state.

civil rights Rights of individuals to participate in civic life, including freedoms of assembly and speech, access to information, and equal access to institutions, among others.

civil society The set of organizations in civic life outside the state through which inhabitants (citizens but also residents) associate and articulate and advance their interests; includes civic associations, interest groups, and volunteer organizations.

civil wars Sustained military conflict between domestic actors.

class structure The ongoing and patterned relationships between "classes," typically understood as groups of individuals linked together by economic interest or activity.

clientelism The practice of exchanging political favours, often in the form of government employment or services, for political support.

climate change A set of changes to the earth's climate.

coalition A group of two or more political parties that governs by sharing executive power and responsibilities.

collective action Action undertaken by individuals and groups to pursue their ends in formally or informally coordinated ways, often in pursuit of some common or public good such as expanded civil rights or sustainable use of common resources.

collective action The pursuit of political or social goals by members of a group.

collective behaviour A paradigm for understanding various forms of contention, popular for part of the 20th century, which emphasized the irrational, social-psychological dynamics of protest.

committee In a legislature, a body composed of a group of legislators convened to perform a certain set of tasks.

comparative advantage In international trade, the idea that different countries or territories will have different relative advantages in the production of different goods and services, which forms the basis for gains from trade.

comparative checking The process of testing the conclusions from a set of comparisons against additional cases or evidence.

comparative politics The subfield of political science that aims to analyze multiple cases using the comparative method.

competitive authoritarianism A form of government or regime that allows somc political competition but not enough for it to qualify as fully democratic.

concentration (of party system) Contrasting with fragmentation, the extent to which political power and representation in a party system are characterized by relatively small numbers of relatively large parties.

concept An idea comparativists use to think about the processes we study.

conceptualization The deliberate process through which we create and select social-scientific concepts.

congress A form of legislature, typically associated with a presidential system in which there is a separation of powers.

consociational Systems that use formal mechanisms to coordinate different groups sharing access to power.

consociationalism An institutional approach to managing potential conflict in polities with multiple groups, one which involves ensuring that each group has political representation.

consolidation The process through which a new democratic order becomes institutionalized and therefore more likely to endure.

constituency A group of voters or a geographic district that legislators or other elected officials represent.

constituency system An electoral system in which voters select representatives from specific-geographic constituencies.

constitution Fundamental and supreme laws, usually written in a charter, that establish the basis of a political system and the basis for other laws.

constitutional design Features of constitutions that shape the basic features of the political system, such as separation of powers and responsibilities between levels of government and branches of government.

constitutionalism The limitation of government through a constitution.

constitutional monarchy A political system in which a monarch such as a king, queen, or emperor plays a role as a head of state but has powers limited by a constitution and/or a legislature.

constitutional republic A polity without a monarch in which the basic rules of politics are laid out in a constitution.

constructivism In nationalism studies, the view that nations are symbolic constructs and so places greater emphasis on the creative efforts of individuals and groups to define and redefine their identities.

constructivism In international relations, a theory that holds that decisions made by states need to be understood in the context of social and political interactions and that behaviour is shaped by norms and values as well as narrowly defined interests.

contention The name, most associated with scholars like Sidney Tarrow and Charles Tilly, referring to the pursuit of collective goods largely outside of formal political institutions.

corporatism A system of interest group representation in which certain major groups are officially designated as representatives of certain interests and have a more structured interaction with the government in power and with the state's administration.

correlation A relationship between two variables in which they tend to move in either the same direction (positive correlation) or in opposite directions (negative correlation).

coup d'état The use of force or threat of force, typically by the military or a coalition involving the military, to impose a non-electoral change of government.

critical race theory A movement in social, political, and legal theory that aims to discern and offer ways to combat the effects of racism and related forms of prejudice.

decree An executive-made order that has the force of law despite not being passed through a legislature.

deductive reasoning The process of moving from general claims or theories to specific observations or predictions about a phenomenon or set of cases.

defensive realism A realist theory that holds that peace or cooperation can emerge under specific circumstances, namely when it is easier to defend than to attack and when states can see clearly what other states' intentions are.

deflation Decline in the prices of goods and services, often associated with depressions or serious slowdowns in economic activity.

delegative democracy A hybrid form of regime that is democratic but involves the electorate "delegating" significant authority to a government.

democracy A form of regime associated with "rule by the people" that signifies rights and liberties for citizens, including political rights to participate in elections and civil liberties such as freedom of speech.

democratic breakdown The process through which a democratic regime partially or completely loses its democratic status.

democratic consolidation The process through which, after a transition from authoritarianism, a polity strengthens its democracy.

democratic peace A phenomenon associated with liberalism that holds that democratic countries will rarely if ever go to war with one another.

democratic transition The process through which a non-democratic regime becomes democratic.

democratization The process of a regime becoming more democratic, including both democratic transition and democratic consolidation.

denomination A type of religious organization, prevalent in the United States, among other places, that is voluntary and accepts the principle of religious pluralism.

denominationalism A system or set of beliefs that privileges denominational forms of religious organization.

dependency A theory that argues that developing countries cannot simply embrace free trade because this will lead to ever-increasing wealth disparities between them and the advanced economies.

dependent variable In hypothesis testing, the dependent variable is the effect or outcome that we expect to be acted on (or have its value altered) by the independent variable.

development A process by which a society changes or advances, often measured in terms of economic growth, but also sometimes measured in terms of quality of life, standard of living, access to freedoms and opportunities, or other indicators.

deviant case (outlier) A case that does not fit the pattern predicted by a given theory.

differentiation The process through which institutions become increasingly autonomous from one another, including the reduction or other change in the linkages between religion and other institutions.

diffusion The process through which a practice or idea spreads locally, nationally, and globally.

direct democracy A conception of democracy that places great emphasis on direct citizen involvement in politics, especially involving plebiscites and/or citizen assemblies.

direct election With regard to executives, an electoral system in which voters cast a vote directly for the head of government or head of state.

dissolving the legislature The practice of a chief executive disbanding the legislature, often accompanied in a democratic regime by the calling for new elections.

districting The process by which districts or other geographic constituencies are created for the purposes of elections.

dominant-party system Party system in which a country contains only one large political party that predominates politically, often controlling the legislative and executive branches of government.

economic management States' efforts to shape the economic performance of their societies, especially in fiscal and monetary policy.

effective number of parties A measure designed to capture the number of meaningful parties in a party system that weights the number of parties represented by their size.

electoral authoritarianism A name applied to situations in which authoritarian regimes nominally compete in elections.

elite parties Political parties in which membership and scope were largely restricted to a small number of political elites.

empirical Drawn from observations of the world.

empirical critique An effort to point to important evidence that does not support a conventional version of any given theory.

employment Ongoing, regular access to paid work.

empowerment An increase in the social, political, or economic capabilities of an individual or group.

endogeneity The name given to any circumstance in which two variables exhibit mutual or reciprocal effects.

environmental sustainability The quality that one or another practice has with being compatible with the long-term health of the environment.

established religions Religions that are granted official status and support by the state.

ethnic group A group that identifies itself as having strong cultural commonality and a shared sense of long-running history, sometimes thinking of itself as a kind of kinship group.

ethnicity The quality that one has by identifying with or being ascribed membership in an ethnic group.

ethnic nationalism A form of nationalism that says that you are a member of the nation because of your ancestry.

European Union (EU) The political and economic union of many European states, numbering 28 as of 2019.

everyday forms of resistance Efforts to resist or obstruct authority that are not clearly organized over time, such as work stoppages, slowdowns, and sabotage.

evidence A set of facts or observations used to support a proposition or hypothesis.

executive The branch of government, or the individual(s) at the top of that branch, that executes or administers policies and laws in a country.

executive–legislative relations The set of political relationships between the executive branch of government, which executes laws/policies, and the legislative branch, which often has the authority to pass those laws/policies.

executive order An order made by a chief executive or top official to the bureaucracy that determines how the bureaucracy should enact or interpret the law.

export-led growth A strategy for achieving economic growth dependent on sending natural resources or agricultural or industrial products for sale in foreign markets.

externality An economic phenomenon in which the gains and costs from a given activity do not accrue to the same actor.

extreme poverty A conception of poverty defined by the United Nations and the World Bank that involves setting a certain line below which people will be defined as poor, typically understood in terms of the inability to purchase a certain set of basic goods or services.

failed state A state that cannot or does not perform its expected functions.

falsifiability The testability of a theory or hypothesis. A good hypothesis could be logically demonstrated to be false by evidence.

fascism An ideology associated with regimes like the Nazis and that of Italy's Benito Mussolini, favouring authoritarianism, militarism, and right-wing nationalism.

federalism System of government with constitutional design of separation of powers between the central government and subnational governments.

feminism A social and intellectual movement that aims to ensure equal rights for women and men.

first-past-the-post Electoral system in which the candidate with the most number of votes is elected, regardless of whether a majority has been attained.

fiscal measures Measures of a government's revenues and/or expenditures.

fiscal policy Budget setting, which is dependent on generating revenue followed by government spending.

foreign policy The set of policies toward foreign nations made by a national government.

formal institutions Institutions that are governed by formal rules and typically linked to complex organizations like the state or corporations.

formal powers The powers possessed by a political actor, such as a chief executive, as a function of their constitutional or legal position.

fragmentation (of party system) Contrasting with concentration, the extent to which political power and representation in a party system are characterized by relatively large numbers of relatively small parties.

framing The way in which a given problem or situation is described and understood, with implications for how it might be addressed.

free rider Someone who benefits from a collective or public good without contributing to it.

free trade A policy or approach in which a government allows foreign goods and services to compete freely with domestic production, as contrasted with protectionism, which favours domestic production.

functional definition Definition that aims to define a given phenomenon by what it *does*.

game theory A set of approaches to the study of strategic interaction between actors, often relying on mathematical modelling and assumptions of the rationality of different actors.

gender Culturally constructed roles or identities one has by virtue of being ascribed the status of male or female, to be distinguished from biological sex.

generalizability The quality that a given theory, hypothesis, or finding has of being applicable to a wide number of cases.

genocide Efforts to diminish or destroy a people and/or culture, prohibited by the United Nations Convention on the Prevention of Genocide (1948).

gerrymandering Creation of districts of irregular shape or composition in order to achieve a desired political result.

Gini coefficient The most common measure of income inequality in any given population, usually expressed as a number between 0 and 1, with 0 being total equality and 1 being maximal inequality.

globalization The increasing interaction, both economic and cultural, among peoples and societies across national borders.

government In the context of executives, the set of top elected executive officials and high-level political appointees that shapes and orients policy; also refers to the broader administrative apparatus of the state.

grand coalition A governing coalition composed of two or more major parties that hold a supermajority of legislative seats and represent a supermajority of the electorate.

greenhouse gases (GHGs) Emissions of gases such as carbon dioxide and methane from industrial activity and consumption of fossil fuels that contribute to climate change.

gross domestic product (GDP) The total value of goods and services produced in a given country or territory; per capita GDP is divided by the population.

gross national income (GNI) A measure of the total income of all of a country's citizens, whether living in their home country or abroad.

guerrilla tactics Military techniques designed to produce ongoing stalemate, usually employed in situations of asymmetric military capability.

head of government The top executive official responsible for forming governments and formulating and implementing policies.

head of state A person with executive functions who is a country's symbolic representative, including elected presidents and unelected monarchs.

historical institutionalism An approach to theorizing that places emphasis on the power of institutions to shape the behaviour of individuals and how this operates over time.

Human Development Index (HDI) A composite measure developed by the United Nations to provide a broad view of annual development and well-being around the world, based on income, life expectancy, and literacy and school enrollments.

hybrid regime A class of regime that appears to be neither fully democratic nor fully authoritarian, such as electoral authoritarianism, delegative democracy, and illiberal democracy.

hyperinflation Exceedingly high inflation, which dramatically erodes the value of money over time.

hypothesis A specific prediction, derived from a theory, that can be tested against empirical evidence.

identity The social label ascribed to an individual or group that locates the individual or group in political society more broadly.

ideology A systematically coordinated and cognitively salient set of beliefs focused on politics.

illiberal democracy A polity with some democratic features but in which political and civil rights are not all guaranteed or protected.

immigration The movement of people to foreign countries.

impeachment A process by which a legislature initiates proceedings to determine whether an official, often a top-ranking executive official, should be removed from office.

impersonality A quality attributed by some scholars to modern states, which are presumed to be less likely to be identified with the personalities of their leaders.

independent variable In hypothesis testing, an independent variable is one that we expect to "act on" or change the value of the dependent variable.

indicator An element or feature that indicates the presence of an underlying factor.

indirect election Electoral system in which representatives are chosen by other elected officials rather than directly by the citizenry at large.

inductive reasoning The process of moving from specific observations to general claims.

inequality In the social sciences, the differential distribution of access to goods like power, status, and material resources.

infant mortality A major public health indicator, which typically measures the number of infants per 1000 born who do not survive until the age of one year.

inference The process through which we aim to test observable implications (often about cause and effect) of any given theory; also refers to conclusions reached through this process.

inflation Increase in the prices of goods and services.

informal powers Those powers possessed by an office holder that are not "official" but rather based on custom, convention, or other sources of influence.

institution A regularized or patterned activity that shapes the behaviour of individuals and groups, including formal organizations like the state or political parties as well as more informal institutions such as norms and values.

institutionalism An approach to theorizing in comparative politics and related fields that places emphasis on the power of institutions to shape the behaviour of individuals.

instrumentalism A type of explanation in social science that says that you can explain something by showing how its development or persistence is in the (usually material) interest of powerful individuals or groups.

insurgencies Contention with formalized military conflict.

integration In international relations, a process by which countries agree to collaborate economically or politically, to make some decisions collectively, and to shape common strategies.

interdependence A relationship in which two or more actors (such as countries) are mutually dependent upon one another.

interest aggregation The process by which individuals' preferences are brought together to make collective decisions, often through political parties and the party system.

interest articulation The process by which political actors express their demands, needs, or wants in a political system, often through interest groups.

interest groups Organizations that make demands in the political system on behalf of their constituents and members.

intergovernmental organizations (IGOs) The set of international organizations that push for cooperation between countries and work for the prevention or mitigation of international conflicts.

international financial institutions (IFIs) Multilateral institutions, particularly the International Monetary Fund (IMF) and the World Bank, that have considerable leverage in the international economy.

international political economy The study of how the economic relations between countries affect politics and how political relations affect economies.

international relations The study of relations between countries and between actors in the international system.

international security The study of issues of war and peace between nations and global security and conflict more broadly.

international trade The economic exchange of goods, services, and capital across international borders.

iron law of oligarchy The idea, developed by Robert Michels, that collective action always produces new elites.

isomorphism In institutional theory, the quality that two or more organizations have by virtue of being structurally very similar.

judiciary The branch of government responsible for the interpretation of laws in courts.

judicial activism Term used, often pejoratively, to characterize judicial actions that actively reinterpret legislation and thus imply exercising powers typically reserved for the legislative branch.

judicial review System of constitutional interpretation in which judges rule on the constitutionality of laws passed by legislature and executive.

lay state State that establishes a formal separation of religion and public life.

legislature Assembly or body of representatives with the authority to make laws.

level of analysis The level (e.g., individual, organizational, societal) at which observations are made or at which causal processes operate.

levels of analysis In international relations, the different levels that can be the context of a study, including the individual level, the nation-state level, and the level of the international system.

liberalism An ideology that emphasizes individual freedoms, representative democracy, the protection of private property, and the market economy.

liberalism In international relations, a theory that holds states can have different preferences and internal structures that lead them to behave in different ways, especially with regard to the conduct of states that hold liberal values of democracy and free market commerce.

libertarianism A form of liberalism focused on individual rights and especially concerned with minimizing the role of government.

life expectancy The average age until which members of a society (or some group within society) live.

literacy rate The percentage of a population who can read.

lower chamber In a bicameral legislature, the house that typically has a larger number of legislators than the upper chamber and often represents the national vote either more proportionally or through smaller geographic constituencies.

malapportionment Apportionment in which voters are unequally represented in a legislature, such as through relatively greater numbers of legislators per capita for low-population areas and lesser numbers of legislators per capita for high-population areas.

market-led development An approach to economic management in which the state aims to control private economic behaviour as little as possible.

mass parties Parties consisting of large numbers of citizens as members and that undertake massive political mobilization.

measurement bias A measure is biased if it will not produce comparable results for all observations.

measurement error Either an episodic error, such as improperly recording data, or a systematic error, meaning that a measurement does not fully reflect what it is designed to measure.

measurement validity Whether a given measure effectively captures or represents what we are researching.

median voter The voter who is theoretically exactly in the middle of the distribution of voters.

minimum connected winning coalition A minimum winning coalition in which all parties in the coalition are "connected" or adjacent to one another on the political spectrum.

minimum size coalition A governing coalition that is closest to the threshold needed to govern, typically 50 per cent of the legislative seats plus one seat.

minimum winning coalition A governing coalition that contains no surplus parties beyond those required to form a government.

mobilization The engagement of individuals and groups in sustained contention.

modernity A contested term that refers to a type of society, typically one experiencing economic growth and with a relatively strong state, among other characteristics.

modernization The process through which a society becomes "more modern," which is typically understood to mean having an advanced economy and, sometimes, a democratic polity.

modernization theory A theory that traces democracy to broad social changes, especially economic development and the changes that accompany it.

modern state A concept used to distinguish states in the modern world from earlier forms of political centralization; it includes features such as extensive bureaucracy, centralization of violence, and impersonality.

monarch A head of state in a monarchy, who usually inherits a position for life and may have either substantial political powers or very limited ceremonial powers.

monetary policy States' efforts to shape the value of a society's currency, often through the use of a central bank in the case of a modern state.

most-different-systems (MDS) A research design in which we compare cases that differ with respect to multiple factors but in which the outcome is the same.

most-similar-systems (MSS) A research design in which we compare cases that are similar with respect to a number of factors but with distinct outcomes.

multilateral In international relations, the actions of three or more countries working together.

multi-member constituencies (MMC) Electoral system in which constituencies have more than one representative.

multiparty democracy A democracy in which at least two parties compete for power.

multiparty system A political party system consisting of more than two significant parties that have opportunities to govern.

nation A group thought of as sovereign and equal, typically comprised of a large, often geographically bounded population.

national identity An identity that locates one's social position in relation to national membership.

nationalism The view that the world is and should be divided into nations that are thought of by nationalists as sovereign and egalitarian.

nativism A political attitude that seeks to protect the interests of established groups of residents in a given country against the interests of more recent immigrants.

neoliberalism An ideological tendency that favours liberal democracy and market-led development and a reduction of state influence over economic activity.

new institutionalism The name given to the turn to institutional theory in the past several decades in economics, political science, and sociology.

nonstate actors In international relations, actors in international politics that are not nation-states; includes multinational corporations, transnational advocacy groups, and international criminal networks.

normative Concerned with specifying which sort of practice or institution is morally or ethically justified.

nuclear proliferation The expansion of the number of countries and other actors possessing nuclear technology.

offensive realism A realist theory that holds that states will seek to maximize their power whenever they can.

offshoring In international trade and business, the practice of an economic actor basing some of its services or processes abroad rather than in its domestic market. (*See also* **outsourcing.**)

open-ended question A question that, in principle, is open to numerous possible answers.

open-list proportional representation Electoral system in which voters choose a candidate but votes are aggregated by political party to determine the allocation of seats across parties.

operationalization The process through which we make a concept measurable.

organization Institutionalized group such as a state, corporation, political party, social movement, or international body.

outcome Typically used as a synonym for "effect," something that is produced or changed in any social or political process.

outsourcing In international trade and business, the practice of an economic actor contracting out to other actors, often overseas. (*See also* **offshoring.**)

parliament A type of legislature, often associated with systems in which the legislators vote on the leadership of the executive branch and the formation of a government.

parliamentarism A system of government in which the head of government is elected by and accountable to a parliament or legislature.

parliamentary sovereignty System in which the constitutionality of laws passed by legislature and executive are not subject to constitutional interpretation by judiciary.

partisan powers The powers accruing to a government official, such as a chief executive, by virtue of the official's leverage or power over members of a political party.

party system Patterns of party politics characterized by the number of relevant parties in a country.

party system institutionalization The degree to which a party system is stable and remains so over time, as measured by such characteristics as the persistence of parties, the stability of their ideologies, and the degree to which they are distinct from the specific individuals that lead them.

path-dependent The name given to historical processes in which future developments are shaped or partially determined by events at previous stages in those processes.

patronage The use of government favours, typically in the form of employment, to garner political support.

payoff matrix In game-theoretic models, the distribution of payoffs to players depending on the choices made.

peak organization Top associations, such as labour federations and large business organizations, that bring together many like-minded organizations.

personalistic dictatorship A form of authoritarianism in which the personality of the dictator is highlighted.

pluralism A system of interest group representation in which groups compete openly to influence government decisions and public policy and in which specific groups do not have official preferential access to decision-making.

political culture The symbolically encoded beliefs, values, norms, and practices that shape the formal distribution of power in any given society.

political economy The interaction or interrelationship between politics and the economy in a given country or internationally, including how politics affects economies and how economies affect politics.

political opportunities The availability of political options to redress grievances.

political party A political organization that seeks to influence policy, typically by getting candidates and members elected or appointed to public office.

political revolutions Revolutions, the main effect of which is to alter political institutions rather than social and economic structures.

political rights Rights of individuals to participate in political life, including the right to political speech, the right to vote, and the right to join political associations.

populism A political approach in which leaders, often heads of government and top executive branch officials, make direct appeals to "the people" and seek to develop direct political ties with the masses.

portfolio The set of duties and tasks that correspond to a given ministerial office.

poverty The state of being poor, as measured by low income, deprivation, lack of access to resources, or limited economic opportunities.

poverty line A specified threshold below which individuals or groups are judged to be in poverty.

precarious work Where workers are denied the same rights given to permanent employees. This can mean lower wages, more dangerous working conditions, lack of union protection, a higher possibility of being fired, and reduced social benefits. Women, racialized peoples, and migrants comprise the majority of such workers.

president An executive leader who typically combines the functions of head of state and head of government and is not directly responsible to a legislature.

presidentialism A system of government in which a president serves as chief executive, being independent of the legislature and often combining the functions of head of state and head of government.

prime minister A chief executive in a parliamentary system of government.

prisoner's dilemma (game) A model of a game in which two actors would benefit from cooperation but each has individual incentives to defect from cooperation.

privatization In the context of the social-scientific study of religion, this refers to the process of religious practice being confined to the private sphere.

procedural definition of democracy A conception of democracy, contrasted with a substantive definition, that emphasizes the minimal standards, procedures, or rules that a country should have in place to govern political life.

proportional representation (PR) In its pure form, an electoral system in which voters choose a preferred party and seats are allocated to parties according to the percentage of the vote the party wins.

protectionism In international trade, the practice of a country protecting or giving favour to its own domestic producers.

public goods Goods or services, often provided by a government, for use by all members of a society and for which one person's use of the good does not compromise anyone else's use of the good. Examples include public health care, education, national defence, infrastructure, and a healthy environment.

public sphere The space in which public life and deliberation take place (as opposed to the "private sphere").

purchasing power parity (PPP) An adjustment made to income measures to account for differences in cost of living.

qualitative A form of analysis that aims to discern relationships between events or phenomena as described in narrative form, such as an account of a historical process.

quantitative Quantitative analysis aims for the mathematical discernment of relationships between variables, typically involving a large number of cases or observations.

race The idea that human beings are divided into different groups, often thought of (erroneously) as biological categories.

racial formation A concept developed by Omi and Winant (1994) that describes the process through which ideas of race are constructed and develop over time.

racialization The historical process through which social relations become interpreted in terms of racial categories.

rational institutionalism An approach to theorizing in comparative politics and related fields that places emphasis on the power of institutions to shape the behaviour of individuals, one that often focuses on implications of institutions for individuals' strategic choices.

realism In international relations, a theory that treats states in the international system largely as acting on the basis of national self-interest, defined often in terms of power, survival, and security.

referendum A popular vote on a specific issue.

regime change Any major change of regime type, including democratization, democratic breakdown, or certain types of authoritarian persistence in which one type of authoritarian regime gives way to another.

regime type The form of a political regime, such as democratic versus authoritarian, as well as subtypes, such as personalistic dictatorships or totalitarian regimes.

relative deprivation The state of having or feeling that one has less than other members of one's reference group (including one's own group over time).

religious monopoly The situation in which one major religion dominates the religious landscape within a given society (the opposite of **religious pluralism**).

religious pluralism The situation in which there are multiple religious organizations within a given society (the opposite of **religious monopoly**).

religious state State in which religion is a key part of official politics, often involving religious establishment, religious legitimation of the state, and restrictions on religious minorities.

remittances Cash or resources sent to a home country, often to family and friends, by emigrants.

representation In legislatures, the process by which elected legislators reflect the interests and preferences of voters in their constituencies.

representative democracy A conception of democracy in which politicians and institutions are understood to represent the electorate, who nevertheless can constrain their behaviour through periodic elections and other forms of participation.

revolution A form of collective action in which some large-scale, structural change is either attempted or accomplished.

rule of law A system that imposes regularized rules in a polity, with key criteria including equal rights, the regular enforcement of laws, and the relative independence of the judiciary.

runoff Electoral system in which the top candidates after a first round of voting compete in one or more additional rounds of voting until a candidate receives a majority.

Sartori's ladder of abstraction The idea that we can organize concepts on the basis of their specificity or generality.

scope conditions The conditions or range of cases for which an argument works.

secularism The ideological complex that favours secular (non-religious) culture.

secularization The process through which (according to some theories) societies become less religious as they become more modern.

semi-presidential system A mixed or hybrid system combining aspects of presidentialism and parliamentarism.

separation of powers The division of powers in a government system between branches of government or between levels of government.

single-member constituency (SMC) Electoral system in which voters choose a candidate and the winner is elected by earning the most votes or by winning a runoff vote.

single-party system An authoritarian system in which parties besides the single dominant party are banned or disallowed.

single transferable vote (STV) Electoral system in which voters rank candidates and the winners' surplus votes are reallocated to other, lower-ranking candidates until a slate of representatives is chosen.

social capital Advantage that individuals or groups hold by virtue of their social relationships.

social construction The process through which socially shared meanings and definitions are established and maintained.

social democracy An ideological movement that favours both representative democracy with respect for basic individual rights and state action to promote relative economic and social equality.

social identity theory An important theory in social psychology that sees personal identities as linked to and partially derived from group identities and roles.

socialism An ideology (or family of ideologies) that emphasizes economic equality as a key goal, to be pursued in large measure through state action.

socialism In international relations, a theory that emphasizes the role of social classes in shaping politics and highlights the role of capitalist accumulation as a prime driver in international affairs.

social movement organization An organization that has been created to help maintain and lead social movement activity over time.

social movements Ongoing, organized collective action oriented toward a goal of social change.

social networks Structures of social ties and connections among individuals.

social revolutions Revolutions that dramatically change social structures.

sovereignty The key way the authority of the modern state is conceptualized: states are understood to be the ultimate authority within their specifically demarcated territories.

state The most important form of political organization in modern politics, which, in its ideal form, is characterized by centralized control of the use of force, bureaucratic organization, and the provision of a number of public goods.

state breakdown Dramatic decline in state capacity.

state capacity The ability of the state to achieve its objectives, especially the abilities to control violence, effectively tax the population, and maintain well-functioning institutions and the rule of law.

state interventionism An approach to economic management in which the state plays a central role, not just through enforcing contracts and property rights but through active interventions such as coordinating investment, supplying credit, and, in many instances, the establishment and running of state-owned enterprises.

state-led development An approach to economic management in which the state plays a prominent role in coordinating the behaviour of economic actors and intervening in the economy.

state of emergency A condition allowed by some constitutions in which guarantees, rights, or provisions are temporarily limited, to be justified by emergencies or exceptional circumstances.

state system The condition that many of the most important actors in international relations are states, which can be understood as systemically linked to one another.

strain theory A theory suggesting that major social change causes social "strain" or conflict, which increases demand for revolution.

strategic voting The practice of voting in a way that does not reflect one's ideal preference in order to prevent electoral outcomes one thinks are worse, such as voting for a second-best candidate one thinks can reasonably win.

structuralism An approach to nationalism studies that sees big, difficult-to-change parts of society as determining what really matters about national identity.

subaltern Marginalized groups and individuals in a hierarchical system where other groups are dominant.

substantive definition Definition that aims to define a given phenomenon by what it *is* rather than by what it does.

substantive definition of democracy A conception of democracy, contrasted with a procedural definition, that views a polity's democratic status as dependent on the satisfaction of certain substantive ends, such as the extension of broad rights or the reduction of income inequality.

sustainability The notion, especially used with regard to the environment, that a resource is capable of being sustained for use or enjoyment by future generations.

term limit Restriction on the number of times or total amount of time a political official can serve in a given position.

territorial nationalism According to some scholars, a type of nationalism that closely resembles civic nationalism in that membership is fundamentally determined by where one is born or where one resides rather than by one's ancestry.

terrorism In the context of revolutions or insurgencies, a tactic used by some participants that involves violence directed at non-military targets.

theocracy An authoritarian state controlled by religious leaders or a state with very strict religious restrictions that uses religion as its main mode of legitimation.

theoretical critique An effort to show that a given theory has logical limitations.

theory A general set of explanatory claims about some specifiable empirical range.

thesis A statement for which one argues on the basis of evidence.

Third World Revolutions A concept developed by John Foran holding that revolutions in the developing world have special characteristics.

totalitarian regime A form of authoritarian regime that aims to control everything about the lives of its subject population, such as in the Soviet Union under Stalin and Germany under the Nazi Party.

transgender An identity in which one's gender does not conform to conventional matching with biological sex.

transition The movement from an authoritarian regime to a democratic one.

transnational Issues or institutions that cross international borders.

transnational network A network of nonstate actors working across state borders.

trust The extent to which an individual has confidence in the reliability or good conduct of others.

"21st-century socialism" Ideology of government supporters in some contemporary societies (e.g., Venezuela, Bolivia) that aims to emphasize the allegedly more participatory and democratic features of these governments.

two-party system A political party system consisting of two significant parties that have a duopoly on opportunities to govern.

underemployment When workers are employed less than they wish to be or below their skill level.

unemployment The lack of ongoing, regular access to paid work.

unicameral legislature Legislature with a single chamber.

unitarism System of government in which the central government is predominant and the powers of subnational governments are limited to those delegated by the centre.

unitary rational actor In international relations theory and especially realism, the idea that states act as if they were single individuals capable of making decisions on the basis of rational calculations about the costs and benefits of different actions.

United Nations The most comprehensive global institution, which aims to prevent and manage conflict and to establish multilateral cooperation on matters of international law, economics, and human development.

upper chamber The chamber in a bicameral legislature that is usually smaller in number of legislators, often representing larger geographic constituencies such as states or provinces.

utility The value that people derive from resources to which they have access.

variable An element or factor that is likely to change, or vary, from case to case.

variation Difference between cases in any given study of comparative politics.

veto An act of executive power in which an executive rejects a law passed by a legislature.

vote of no confidence A vote taken by a legislature that expresses a lack of support for the government or executive, which, if successful, often results in the dissolution of the government and the calling of new legislative elections.

welfare state A state that provides a basic safety net for its population, often accomplished through social insurance, public health care, public education, and poverty relief.

within-case comparison The comparative analysis of variation that takes place over time or in distinct parts of a single case.

world society theory A theory associated with scholars such as John Meyer, who argue that basic organizational features of the state system are cultural and have diffused globally.

NOTES

Chapter 1

1. *Stanford Encyclopedia of Philosophy* 2011.
2. Ross 2006, 127, 152.
3. We emphasize *why* questions here for heuristic purposes—to help you learn and discover for yourself. Well-posed *why* questions very often lead to social-scientific explanations. However, as Jon Elster (2007) reminds us, we should not equate good explanations with the answers to *why* questions. Furthermore, in actual social science, the place where a *why* question ends and a *how* question begins can sometimes be difficult to say.
4. If one is primarily interested in the causes of education policy in different countries, the safest way to formulate the question may be "What are the causes of education policy?" or "Why does education policy vary across countries?" If one is primarily interested in the consequences of systems of government, one might ask, "What are the consequences of systems of government for policy?"
5. Weber 2009, 4–5.
6. For a sophisticated and classic discussion of these issues, see Weber 1949.
7. Gerring 2001.
8. Collier and Levitsky 1997; Collier and Adcock 1999.
9. There is much debate about how standardized concepts should be in political science. Some argue that concepts should be standardized and agreed upon to mean the same thing from one work of scholarship to the next. Others argue that since no concept is perfect, scholars should be free to offer conceptual innovations depending on their specific projects as long as they are clear.
10. Conceptualization is also challenging for several additional reasons. It is bound up with our own values, making it challenging to define issues such as democratization, gender, or revolutions without bringing to mind lots of connotations. In addition, while ordinary language is precise enough for daily life, it is often riddled with internal contradiction and lack of conceptual clarity. Many concepts have multiple and distinct meanings across different contexts and from person to person, leading to confusion and miscommunication.
11. This is also sometimes referred to as Sartori's "ladder of generality." See Sartori 1970; Collier and Levitsky 1997.
12. Jago 2017, 719–22.
13. Gerring 2009.
14. Putnam 1993.
15. These terms date back to the work of the political theorist John Stuart Mill in the 19th century. See Mill 1846.
16. That is, some argue that social science issues in probabilistic rather than deterministic explanations. For an example, see Lieberson and Lynn 2002.
17. Dunning 2012.

Chapter 2

1. A clue that further explains what a hypothesis is can be found in the word itself, whose etymology includes the prefix *hypo*, meaning "less than." This suggests that a hypothesis is an idea that is "less than a thesis" until it receives some evidence to support it.
2. We thank one of our anonymous reviewers for this formulation.
3. If you are interested in understanding in more detail *why* this is the case, you might want to read a classic book by Karl Popper (1963) called *Conjectures and Refutations*. Popper argues that scientists should actually *try* to *disprove* their hypotheses or conjectures.
4. A long tradition of work in the history and philosophy of science since at least Kuhn (1963) gives us reason to be suspicious of such idealized portrayals as descriptions of how theories actually change, but most social scientists think that we should *aspire* to these ideals.
5. The quantitative approach requires some knowledge of key descriptive statistics and how to formulate and test hypotheses in a general sense, but it also depends upon knowledge of rules of probability and probability distributions. Statistical methodologies formalize the process of testing hypotheses and allow researchers to speak with numerical confidence about the precision of their findings.
6. The best-known work making this argument is King, Keohane, and Verba 1994 (or KKV, as it is often called).
7. Or, alternatively, "What does country A have more of than country B?" For example, it may be that variable levels of human capital and education influence development. Country B is not presumably totally lacking in education and human capital but has generally lower levels of these things.
8. This is partially adapted from Staffan Lindberg's work on democratization in Africa (2006, 118).
9. Even more troubling are cases in which we could use another mathematical identifier and say $X = Y$, that is, X is defined as being equal to Y. (To continue the logic using mathematical notation for a moment, even $X \approx Y$ can be a problem. This is because there is so little separating cause and effect that the argument becomes uninteresting.)
10. Inglehart and Welzel 2003.
11. Endogenous comes from *endo-*, meaning "within," and *-genous,* meaning "origin," suggesting that the origin of a phenomenon comes from within the phenomenon itself. So if X causes Y but Y also causes X, then X is causing itself.
12. Charity Intelligence Canada 2019.
13. See, for example, Babbie (2010, 95), who writes of a closely related example of a statistical association between ice cream sales and drowning rates.
14. See Lipset 1959.
15. For an overview, see Cassidy 2013.
16. One example that was hypothesized to exist for a long time was the supposed "Bradley effect" in which some American voters would profess to pollsters a preference to vote for an African-American candidate but would then vote for a white opponent when alone in the voting booth. The hypothesized reason was that some of those surveyed would not want to seem to the pollster that they had a racial bias, even if they really held one. The result would be an overestimation of the number of voters favouring the black candidate.

Chapter 3

1. Morgan 2007.
2. Anthropologists and historians have noted many kinds of states, going back thousands of years. Most comparative political analysis, however, is focused on the *modern* state, and thus we focus exclusively on this form here. Throughout the chapter, we use the term *state* to refer to the "modern state."
3. Weber 1946, 78.
4. Strayer ([1970] 2005), in a classic study, sees the state as originating in medieval Europe, particularly in England and France, but his argument is really that some of the key characteristics of modern states were established in this period. Few political scientists would see 12th- or 13th-century France or England as modern states.
5. Over time, a number of actors, especially elites, did increasingly seek the king's protection. See Strayer [1970] 2005. See also North, Wallis, and Weingast 2009.
6. Strayer stresses the importance of early efforts of the Crown in France and England to establish control over the law in establishing state structures. Strayer [1970] 2005, 26–33.
7. Tilly [1990] 1992, 69.
8. North, Wallis, and Weingast 2009.
9. For a discussion of some of these issues, see Giddens 1987.
10. Hayes 2018.
11. In referring to the goals of the state, we are using a kind of shorthand. The state, as such, does not have goals. Rather, the individuals and groups that compose it and make claims on it have goals. However, sometimes such goals become "institutionalized" over time, and states carry them on even when nobody is actively campaigning for them.
12. Tilly [1990] 1992; Levi 1988.
13. Levi 1988, 2.
14. On the concept of stateness, see Evans 1997 and Fukuyama 2004.
15. Fukuyama 2011.
16. Donkin 2011.
17. Pérez Díaz 2014.
18. Putnam 1993.
19. Ostrom 1990, 41.
20. See Migdal 1988; Putnam 1993.
21. Weber 1978, 956–1003. On bureaucracy and the state, see also Poggi 1990.
22. Poggi 1990, 74–5; Greenfeld 1996.
23. As Strayer [1970] 2005, 58, puts it, "Sovereignty requires independence from any outside power and final authority over men who live within certain boundaries."
24. Sahlins 1991.
25. Bell 2014, 420–1.
26. Belshaw 2016, 726–7.
27. Huntington 1957.
28. Weingast 1997.
29. Moreover, it does so unequally. See Pettit and Western 2004 and Western 2006.
30. Foucault 1977.
31. Note that this does not mean that strong states necessarily tax a *lot* but just that they tax successfully and regularly.
32. The quintessential example may be England's "Glorious Revolution." See Pincus 2009.
33. For example, see Karl 1997.
34. Scott 1999.
35. Loveman 2014.
36. Hardin 1997.
37. For an example of a theory that focuses on predatory elites, see Levi 1988.
38. On weak states as being failures to contain predation, see Bates 2008. See also North, Wallis, and Weingast 2009, discussed in the next section.
39. Tilly [1990] 1992; Centeno 2002.
40. Tilly [1990] 1992; W. McNeill 1982. See also Downing 1992.
41. Spruyt 2007.
42. McNeill and McNeill 2003; Chirot 1994.
43. Centeno 2002.
44. Herbst 2000.
45. Tilly 1975, 42.
46. Tilly [1990] 1992, 30.
47. Marx 1978, 187.
48. Evans, Reuschmeyer, and Skocpol 1985.
49. Gorski 2003; Greenfeld 1996.
50. Gorski 2003; Foucault 1977; see also Taylor 2007.
51. Among others, Greenfeld (1996) emphasizes nationalism as a critical prerequisite for the development of the modern state. As we shall see, other scholars see the state as the source of national identity. It is probably closer to the mark to see the development of the state and national identity as endogenous, as defined in Chapter 2.
52. Spruyt 1994; Wallerstein [1974] 2011; Meyer et al. 1997.
53. Lenin 1939.
54. Wallerstein [1974] 2011.
55. DiMaggio and Powell 1983.
56. Meyer and Rowan 1991.
57. For a partly critical perspective, see Wimmer and Feinstein 2010.
58. Strayer [1970] 2005.
59. North, Wallis, and Weingast 2009.
60. Colley 1992.
61. Pincus 2009.
62. Greenfeld 1992.

Chapter 4

1. There is another sense in which scholars also use the phrase "political economy" that is beyond the scope of our text. For some, it refers to using the methods of economics—especially formal algebraic models of decision-making and strategic interaction—and applying them to political problems. We occasionally make reference to these sorts of approaches throughout the text, especially when we draw on "rational choice" or "rationalist" theories, but for the sake of clarity, we do not use "political economy" in that context.
2. Abedi 2017.

3. Long 2016.
4. Tencer 2017; Statistics Canada, "Household Income in Canada: Key Results from the 2016 Census."
5. The Gini Index is a measure very similar to the Gini coefficient that varies from 0 to 100 instead of from 0 to 1.
6. Conference Board of Canada, "Income Inequality."
7. International Labor Rights Forum, "Precarious Work."
8. This argument, which can be found in most basic economics textbooks today, dates originally to Ricardo 1817.
9. Schlefer 2012.
10. Matthews 2014.
11. "Crash Course," 2013.
12. Levi-Faur 1997, 359–70, see 360–7.
13. Tse 2016.
14. Bell 2001.
15. Esping-Andersen 1990.
16. For a critical view, see Wilensky 1975.
17. Arendt 1963; Foucault 1977; Taylor 2007.
18. See discussion in Pierson 2006, 12–14.
19. Hayek [1944] 1994.
20. Esping-Andersen 1990; Huber and Stephens 2001.
21. Ibid.
22. Howard (2007) argues that the US welfare state is not so much small or weak as it is poorly designed.
23. Prasad 2006.
24. Mettler 2011.
25. Esping-Andersen 1990, 29.
26. "Asia's Next Revolution," 2012.
27. Goodman and Peng 1996.

Chapter 5

1. Sen 1999.
2. Poverty may also be understood as occurring when people are deprived of certain capabilities, as we discuss later (Sen 1999).
3. Pogge 2008, 103; Collier 2007.
4. See the World Bank website: http://www.worldbank.org.
5. Press 2017.
6. See Sen 1999 on how this process has happened in Kerala and in the country of Sri Lanka.
7. Gregson 2017.
8. This distinction was made persuasively by Sen 1999.
9. In many societies, women bear greater work burdens (both outside and inside the home) yet see fewer of the benefits of economic development. We discuss this in Chapter 14.
10. Sawchuk 2011. More detail specifically related to health outcomes can be found at Greenwood, De Leeuw, Lindsay, and Reading 2015.
11. Anaya 2014.
12. Abedi 2017.
13. See Escobar 1995.
14. Stiglitz, Sen, and Fitoussi 2010.
15. Nadasdy 2016, 2–3.
16. Rosenstein-Rodan 1943.
17. Carroll 2010.
18. See Mahoney 2010 and Pierson 2004, among many others.
19. Tocqueville 1998, 513.
20. Kennedy and Bailey 2009, 365.
21. Tocqueville 1998, 133.
22. Manuel 2017.
23. Imai 2017, 371, 396
24. On "bonding" and "bridging" capital, see Putnam 2000. On "structural holes," see Burt 1992.
25. We discuss religion in politics in Chapter 15 (and note the possible relationship between religion and regime type in Chapter 6), but the link between religion and development merits some comment here.
26. Rifkin 2004.
27. Guo 2003.
28. Zhang and Zhu 2012, 256, 269–70.
29. Almond 1991.
30. Lenin [1917] 1948.
31. Representative and influential works included André Gunder Frank's *Capitalism and Underdevelopment in Latin America: Historical Studies of Chile and Brazil* (1967) and Walter Rodney's *How Europe Underdeveloped Africa* (1981).
32. Prebisch 1950.
33. Wallerstein [1974] 2011.
34. Cardoso and Faletto 1979; Evans 1979.
35. See World Bank 1997. One of the authors behind the World Bank's 1997 *World Development Report* was Peter Evans, who was a leading figure in the revised version of dependency theory. Another leading dependency theorist, Fernando Henrique Cardoso, went on to become president of Brazil (1995–2003), where he undertook many pro-market reforms but also presided over efforts to build state capacity and strength.
36. Collier 2007.
37. For a sophisticated historical interpretation of this, see Acemoglu, Johnson, and Robinson 2001, as outlined in the "Insights" box.
38. The World Values Survey, available online: http://www.worldvalues survey.org.
39. Such questions were asked in slightly different forms in Evans 1995 and Kohli 2004.
40. Bajpai 2019.
41. Kohli 2004.
42. See Amsden 1992; Kohli 2004.
43. Amsden 1992.

Chapter 6

1. Indeed, important work on conceptualizing, defining, and measuring democracy and democratization is ongoing in today's political science. See, for example, Coppedge et al. 2011.
2. While this distinction between procedural and substantive definitions is conventionally drawn and important, we wish to emphasize that there is a grey area between them. Gerardo Munck, for example, following Robert Dahl, defines democracy as procedural but sees it as a substantive good. Munck 2009, 129.

3. See Dahl 1971 and Schmitter and Karl 1991 for a concise summary.
4. On competitive authoritarianism, see Levitsky and Way 2002; 2010 (discussed in Chapter 7). On the related concept of electoral authoritarianism, see Schedler 2006.
5. Schmitter and Karl 1991.
6. Elections Canada, "Voter Turnout by Age Group" for the 2015 federal general election.
7. Huntington 1991; Markoff 1996.
8. Linz and Stepan 1996.
9. Economist Intelligence Unit 2018.
10. See the discussion in the country materials at the back of this book.
11. On the concept of democratic consolidation, see Schedler 1998.
12. Linz and Stepan 1996, 5.
13. Lipset 1959; 1960; Inglehart and Welzel 2005; Rueschemeyer, Stephens, and Stephens 1992.
14. Almond and Verba 1963; Putnam 1993.
15. Huntington 1991; Markoff 1996; for an alternative sort of structural/systemic approach, see Bollen 1983.
16. Linz 1990a, 1990b; Stepan and Skach 1993.
17. An actor-centred theory can be found in the four-volume series edited by O'Donnell, Schmitter, and Whitehead (1986). See in particular volume 4, by O'Donnell and Schmitter, entitled *Transitions from Authoritarian Rule: Tentative Conclusions about Uncertain Democracies*.
18. For more on causal mechanisms in social science, see Elster 2007.
19. Lipset 1959, 1960.
20. Inglehart and Welzel 2005.
21. The best known comparative study of this sort is probably still Almond and Verba 1963.
22. For a scholarly discussion of some of these issues, see Fukuyama 1995.
23. Belli 2016.
24. Jackson 2017.
25. Huntington 1991.
26. Ibid., 100–6.
27. Meyer et al. 1997.
28. Stepan 1999.
29. Linz 1990a, 1990b.
30. The broader social theory question underlying this issue is often called the "structure–agency problem," the main idea of which is that it is often difficult to sort out how much of a social or political process is due to the intentional behaviour of individuals and how much of it is due to social structures or institutional constraints.
31. For one well-known view on variables and "proper names" in research, see Przeworski and Teune 1970.
32. O'Donnell, Schmitter, and Whitehead 1986.
33. See Putnam 2000.
34. Collier, Mahoney, and Seawright 2004.
35. George and Bennett 2005.
36. Jago 2017, 719–22.

Chapter 7

1. Mlambo 2014, 17.
2. Burke 2017; 2018.
3. Embassy of Canada to Zimbabwe website, 2018.
4. Adorno et al. 1950.
5. According to anthropologists and historians, there is astonishing variability in the political systems of the hunter-gatherer societies in which we spent most of our evolutionary history, but in general they were more egalitarian than the more complex societies that emerged after the development of settled agriculture and the creation of pre-modern states. See McNeill and McNeill 2003.
6. On the democratic wave, mentioned in Chapter 6, see Huntington 1991. On contemporary authoritarianism, see Levitsky and Way 2010.
7. For classic treatments of democratic breakdown, see Linz and Stepan 1978 and Valenzuela 1978.
8. For a thoughtful consideration of hybrid regimes, see Diamond 2002.
9. For a seminal treatment of totalitarian rule, see Arendt [1958] 2004.
10. See some discussion of these issues in the country profile materials at the back of this book.
11. See, for example, Žižek 2002.
12. On "sultanistic regimes," see Chehabi and Linz 1998.
13. Laub 2016.
14. On Africa's personalistic dictatorships, see Jackson and Rosberg 1982 and Decalo 1985.
15. Verbitsky 1996.
16. O'Donnell 1973.
17. Levitsky and Way (2010, 3) add to this the fall of the Soviet Union and its consequences.
18. Collier and Levitsky 1997.
19. Zakaria 2003.
20. O'Donnell 1994.
21. Schedler 2006.
22. Levitsky and Way 2002, 2010.
23. Levitsky and Way 2010.
24. For this reason, some scholars have emphasized the importance and potential difficulty of transitioning away from clientelism as societies democratize. See the discussion in Fox 1994.
25. See Brownlee 2007 and Levitsky and Way 2010 on this issue.
26. Myre 2014.
27. European Commission 2016.
28. Corrales and Penfold 2011; Smilde and Hellinger 2011; Levitsky and Way 2010.
29. See the many excellent essays in Mahoney and Thelen (2010) on historical institutionalism.
30. On coalitions and institutions, see Hall 2010.
31. Skocpol 1973.
32. This is an implication of a number of the findings of Inglehart and Welzel 2005.
33. The attentive reader will recognize this as key to Inglehart and Welzel's neo-modernization theory of democratization, discussed in the previous chapter. Inglehart and Welzel 2005.

34. North, Wallis, and Weingast 2009.
35. Paige 1997.
36. Roberts 1995.
37. See, for example, Migdal 1988, discussed briefly in Chapter 3.
38. Bates 2008.
39. See Jackson and Rosberg 1982.
40. Greenfeld 1997.
41. Véliz 1980.
42. Palmer 1980; Wiarda 2003.
43. Almond and Verba 1963; Inglehart and Welzel 2005.
44. For an overview, see Wintrobe 2007.
45. Olson 1965; Lichbach 1995. See also discussion of these issues in Chapters 11 and 12.
46. Economist Intelligence Unit 2018, 49.
47. Çalışkan 2018; Stelgias 2015; Human Rights Watch 2018.
48. Economist Intelligence Unit 2018, 2, 17–18.
49. Associated Press 2017.

Chapter 8

1. For an exploration of constitutional design issues relating to the legislative and executive branches, two of the leading works are Sartori 1994 and Lijphart 1999.
2. "British North America Act, 1867."
3. "Constitutions Acts, 1867 to 1982."
4. Russell 2017, 477–8.
5. "The Canadian Constitution."
6. Niskanen and Tupy 2005.
7. Government of Canada. "Oath of Citizenship."
8. Mills 1997.
9. "The Declaration of Independence."
10. Moses 2000, 94.
11. "Constitution Act, 1867."
12. Borrows and Coyle 2017, 3–4.
13. Borrows 2017, 17.
14. Jai 2017, 121–2.
15. Mills 2017, 238–9.
16. Call to Action #45.
17. Josefsen 2010.
18. This is sometimes referred to casually as the "fourth branch" of government, though most civil servants and administrators are technically part of the executive branch.
19. State-level rulings can be very significant not only for state residents (obviously) but also in broader national debates, as in recent years when the top courts in states such as Massachusetts, Iowa, and New Jersey ruled that the state must extend same-sex marriage rights or equivalent benefits to gay couples.
20. The high court may uphold lower court rulings by simply refusing to "hear the case" of a challenge or appeal.
21. Before 2009, the House of Lords was for a long time a quasi-judicial body that offered commentary on decisions by the House of Commons but could not overrule it.
22. Depending upon one's historical perspective, federalism may date back to the ancient world when rulers such as Alexander the Great used decentralized authorities to govern distant parts of their far-flung empires. These rulers used local magistrates, representatives, or agents to ensure governability. At other points in history, small territories sought the advantages of uniting certain powers under common rule, even while they retained authority and autonomy locally. In many cases, these arrangements could be best characterized as *confederal*, with examples including different "leagues" of city-states and united provinces and principalities in Europe as the modern nation-states came into being.
23. On this, see Riker 1964; Stepan 1999.
24. There are several ways to specify the concept of federalism without specific reference to constitutions. For some scholars, federal countries are determined by other features: whether subnational governments have some representation at the national level, usually through an upper chamber in the legislature (such as a senate) that is designed to defend the interests of the subnational units or independent legislatures at the subnational level, such as state assemblies, which ensure democratically elected subnational government. See Wibbels 2005.
25. Examples of small federal island nations are Comoros and Federated States of Micronesia.
26. "Provincial Districts."
27. As a character in *Monty Python and the Holy Grail* once suggested with respect to the divine right of kings as opposed to constitutional government, "supreme executive power derives from a mandate from the masses, not from some farcical aquatic ceremony."
28. The most famous early example was the signing of the Magna Carta in England in 1215 when English nobles defeated the forces of King John and demanded that he approve a "Great Charter" that conferred rights on the nobility and required the participation of Parliament in certain decisions. This was by no stretch a full-blown democracy (the rights were for the nobility and not for commoners), but it did establish an important principle that the ruler was at least partially constrained by the will of those governed.
29. Examples might be found in the Middle East, such as with the House of Saud in Saudi Arabia.
30. Of course, democratic regimes as well may fail to enforce certain constitutional rights, since these rights are regularly subject to interpretation and are not always perfectly implemented.
31. Hirschl 2010.
32. Riker 1964.
33. See Stepan 1999.
34. Russell 2017.
35. Minsky 2017; Schwartz 2013.
36. See Wibbels 2005; Rodden 2006; Rodden, Eskeland, and Litvack 2003.
37. See Dworkin 1977; 1986.

Chapter 9

1. "Parliament Prayer Changes" 2017.
2. The United States is an exception to the rule among democratic countries in that many presidents have not held

elective office at the national level prior to their election, instead coming often from the governorship of a state. It is for this reason of political socialization that some scholars prefer parliamentary government—in which the legislature chooses the executive—over a system in which the president is directly elected: It weeds out "outsiders" unfamiliar with how the system works and favours politicians who have come through the political system. Of course, a contrary argument can be found among those who find the political classes to be too insular and who want outsiders who are willing to "shake up" a political establishment that might be seen as lazy, or corrupt, or sclerotic.
3. Or, if retiring, they may work to ensure that their preferred candidate takes their place.
4. Mayhew 1974.
5. These qualifications may include getting a certain number of signatures on a petition to support the candidacy or perhaps making a cash deposit (which may be refundable, if the candidate polls enough votes in the election). The reason for placing such restrictions on the ballot is to ensure that the electoral authorities can control the number of candidates and that elections are contested only by "serious" candidates and parties.
6. "NDP Announces BC Referendum on Proportional Representation," 2017.
7. Many of the changes come down to how "remainders" are dealt with when it comes to assigning seats. The various methods include the D'Hondt method, the Sainte-Laguë method, and the largest remainder method.
8. "Trump Declares a National Emergency, and Provokes a Constitutional Crisis," 2019.
9. In that chapter, we discuss the work of Duverger 1954.
10. See Cox and McCubbins 1993; Mezey 1979; Shepsle and Weingast 1981.
11. See the various chapters in Morgenstern and Nacif 2002 for an examination of party discipline using several Latin American cases.
12. There are limitations on votes of no confidence in many countries. As noted in the Germany "Case in Context," a vote in that country must be a "constructive vote of no confidence," meaning that the members of the parliament proposing to bring down the government must simultaneously propose a new government to take its place. This is designed to discourage excessive "cycling" from one failed government to another.

Chapter 10

1. Furi 2008, 36. http://publications.gc.ca/collection_2008/psc-cfp/SC3-132-2008E.pdf.
2. Aberbach, Putnam, and Rockman 1981.
3. We emphasize *directly elected* presidents in this section, distinguishing them from prime ministers in the section on parliamentarism. But there are rare occasions, such as in South Africa, when a head of state is elected in an indirect fashion as a prime minister yet is called a "president."
4. As noted previously, some parliamentary executives are even called by the confusing moniker of "President."
5. On political business cycles, see Nordhaus 1975.
6. See Brownlee 2007 and Levitsky and Way 2010 on this issue.
7. This may seem self-evident, but there is a substantial literature documenting the importance of these institutional designs.
8. CBC Archives, "The Day Joe Clark's Short-Lived PC Government Came to an End."
9. Examples may be the need for an expression of national unity at a time of war or national tragedy or sacrifice. Under these circumstances, several parties may agree to put certain aspects of political competition aside for the good of the nation. Another example is the desire to create a supermajority, as in South Africa, where the African National Congress had a strong majority and needed only the support of one or two very small parties to have the supermajority needed to amend the constitution.
10. This may be an explicit rule or a commonly accepted norm. In many cases, the ceremonial head of state (such as the king or queen) will call upon the largest party to form the government.
11. Some of the most significant and influential ministries sought by coalition partners are the Ministry of Finance (or Economy) and the Ministry of Foreign Affairs, which correspond to the Secretary of the Treasury and the Secretary of State in the US government, respectively. Coalition partners may prioritize control over other ministries depending on their interests. For example, a Green Party may seek the Ministry of the Environment, an anti-immigration party may want the Ministry for Home Affairs (or Interior), and a rural party representing farmers may seek to control the Ministry of Agriculture.
12. This exercise is a modified version of that used in Lijphart 1999.
13. Neustadt 1960.
14. See Geddes 1994.
15. See Geddes 1990.

Chapter 11

1. Government of Nunavut website: Consensus Government.
2. See Kirchheimer 1966; Kitschelt 1994.
3. Kirchheimer 1966.
4. See Michels [1911] 1962, 367.
5. Some African countries, such as Ethiopia or Tanzania, did indeed have highly ideological single-party systems, while many former French and Belgian colonies in West and Central Africa had single-party regimes without strongly identifiable ideologies.
6. Zakaria 1994.
7. Lijphart 1999, 76–7.
8. See Lijphart 1999.
9. Laakso and Taagepera 1979.
10. Rae 1968.
11. See Mainwaring and Scully 1995.

12. Parties also differ in terms of how "disciplined" they are. That is, they differ on the extent to which party members follow the wishes of the party leadership. This was considered in the chapters on legislatures and executives.
13. Mainwaring and Scully 1995.
14. Collier and Collier [1991] 2002; Wiarda 1997, 73.
15. See Schmitter 1974.
16. Collier and Collier [1991] 2002; Katzenstein 1985.
17. We are thankful to an anonymous reviewer for suggestions on the discussion of authoritarian and democratic forms of corporatism.
18. There are hybrids and combinations of the two systems; see Chapter 7 for further detail.
19. Yarvin 2017.
20. See Sartori 1976, 336.
21. The literature here is extensive, and it relates to issues of incumbent advantage, redistricting, and other issues beyond the scope of this chapter. A partial and early review of the question of safe seats can be found in Mayhew 1974.
22. Marx and Engels [1848] 1998; Lenin 1902.
23. See Fukuyama 1992, among others.
24. See Dahl 1989, among others.
25. Associated Press 2017.
26. See Evans 1995.

Chapter 12

1. Canadian Press 2012.
2. Levitz 2013.
3. Katz 1999; Martin 2008.
4. The basic distinction between class, status, and power as dimensions of social stratification can be found in Weber 1946.
5. Tilly and Tarrow 2007, 4–11 and passim.
6. Ibid., 5–6.
7. Scott 1985.
8. Alvarez, Dagnino, and Escobar 1998, 16–18.
9. Pérez Díaz 2014; Shils 1997, 320–5.
10. At the same time, it is important to remember that civil society is not autonomous from power and status. See Alvarez, Dagnino, and Escobar 1998, 16–18.
11. Tilly and Tarrow 2007.
12. Tarrow 2005.
13. Lindholm and Zúquete 2010.
14. Michels [1911] 1962, 342–56.
15. Podur 2017
16. For a classic account of the US civil rights movement from the perspective of social movement theory, see McAdam 1982.
17. Burns 1997, 4–5, 10–11, 15.
18. Tilly and Tarrow 2007, 108.
19. Ibid., 29–36, 108.
20. Some scholars even refer to contemporary societies as "social movement societies." See Tarrow 2011, 5–6, 117–18, and especially the essays in Meyer and Tarrow 1998.
21. It should be acknowledged that if this distinction holds, it is only a matter of degree.
22. See discussion in Pincus 2007, 398–9.
23. Huntington 1968, 264–6.
24. Brinton 1952, 41.
25. Skocpol 1994, 5.
26. Skocpol 1979, 4–5.
27. Not all scholars agree that the distinction between coups and revolutions is easily made. For more on conceptualizing and explaining coups d'état, see Belkin and Schofer 2003; Johnson, Slater, and McGowan 1984; and Powell and Thyne 2011.
28. In his classic treatment, Huntington refers to these as the "eastern model" of revolution. Huntington 1968, 266–7.
29. Arendt 1963; Kumar 2005.
30. Foran 2005.
31. See Stathis Kalyvas's differentiation of civil wars from other forms of conflict on these grounds. Kalyvas 2007, 417.
32. Metelits 2009, 3.
33. Kalyvas suggests that revolutions are a type of civil war, but not everyone agrees. Kalyvas 2007, 417.
34. Centeno notes that they partially resembled civil wars. Centeno 2002, 47.
35. O'Leary and Silke 2007, 388–90.
36. Tilly 2004; Oberschall 2004, 26.
37. Sanderson 2010, 172.
38. Tilly 2004, 8–9.
39. See Chapter 13; Rummell 1997.
40. Senechal de la Roche 2004, 1–2.
41. Black 2004, 17.
42. Senechal de la Roche 2004, 2; Black 2004, 16.
43. Senechal de la Roche 2004, 2; Black 2004, 15, 23.
44. O'Leary and Tirman 2007, 6–7.
45. Gibbs 1989, 330; Bergesen and Lizardo 2004, 38.
46. Hobsbawm 1981.
47. Scott 1985.
48. Ibid., xvi.
49. Smelser 1962, 1–12.
50. Tilly and Tarrow 2007, 9–10.
51. Some are further apart than others. Most social movements, for example, have not even the remotest connection to terrorism.
52. See the insightful discussion in Buechler 2004.
53. Smelser 1962.
54. Toch 1965.
55. Brinton 1952, 33–6, 278.
56. Gurr 1970, 22–122 and passim.
57. Huntington 1968, 275.
58. Goldstone 1991.
59. See Goldstone 2001 for an overview of these and related theories.
60. Some of these and other issues are reviewed in Goldstone 2001, 145–7. See also Parsa 2000.
61. The most important works on revolution from a rational choice perspective are Lichbach 1995; 1998. See also Coleman 1990, 489–502; Tullock 1971; and Finkel, Muller, and Opp 1989.

62. Lichbach 1998.
63. Olson 1965; Lichbach 1995.
64. Of course, some political opportunity theorists *are* attentive to cultural factors. For example, see McAdam 1996, 25.
65. Hunt and Benford 2004, 437–8.
66. Melucci 1989; Castells, 2010.
67. On framing and "frame analysis," see Goffman 1974; Gamson 1992; and Benford and Snow 2000.
68. Greenfeld 1995.
69. Kumar 2005; Arendt 1963.
70. Tilly and Tarrow 2007.
71. Oliver and Johnston 2000.
72. Foran 2005.
73. A full analysis, of course, would question this assumption, looking at other indicators of development in order to be sure that high per capita GDP in the context of high inequality may not mask significant sources of economic discontent on the part of key populations.

Chapter 13

1. Tajfel 1981; Stets and Burke 2000, 225; Brewer and Gardner 1996; Greenfeld and Eastwood 2007.
2. On symbolic boundaries, see Lamont and Molnár 2002.
3. Calhoun 1997, 2–3.
4. The author who has most clearly and consistently defined them in this way is Greenfeld 1992; 2001. For a partially overlapping definition see Anderson [1983] 1991.
5. From "The Academic Study of Nationalism" in Garner, Ferdinand, Lawson, and MacDonald 2016.
6. Smith 2010, 55–8.
7. Gellner 1983, 57.
8. Ibid., 56.
9. Ozkirimli 2000.
10. Greenfeld 1992.
11. Smith 1998, 191.
12. Smith 1990, 35–9.
13. Ibid., 40, 64–5.
14. Smith 1996, 37.
15. Gellner 1983.
16. Greenfeld 1992.
17. For a partially critical perspective, see Brubaker 1999.
18. A good example of this view is Kohn 1944.
19. Brubaker 1992; Greenfeld 1992.
20. Smith 1986, 134.
21. Marx 2003; Hechter 2000, 6–7.
22. Harff and Gurr 2004; Fearon and Laitin 2003.
23. Laitin 2007.
24. Brubaker and Laitin 1998.
25. Ibid.; see also Varshney 2002.
26. Jowitt 2001.
27. Horowitz 1985; Varshney 2002.
28. Brubaker and Laitin 1998.
29. For one typology of such conflicts, see Chirot 2001, 7.
30. Harff and Gurr 2004.
31. Jowitt 2001. See also Greenfeld and Chirot 1994.
32. On "barricaded identities," see Jowitt 2001.
33. Laitin 2007.
34. Laitin 2007 uses the term "cascading" to describe spreading participation in secessionist movements.
35. See related theories discussed in Chapter 12. For the application of these theories to ethno-national conflict, see Horowitz 1985; 2001.
36. In addition to Horowitz, see Greenfeld 1992 and Petersen 2002 on these issues.
37. See Fearon and Laitin 1996; 2003; Laitin 2007.
38. Varshney 2002.
39. Cederman, Wimmer, and Min 2010.
40. For an accessible overview of research in this area, see Harff and Gurr 2004.
41. Some scholars of nationalism have urged caution about simple institutional policy recommendations such as democratization. For an interesting argument in this connection, see Snyder 2000.
42. For a classic discussion of consociationalism, see Lijphart 1977. For consideration of the relative performance of some consociational systems, see Lemarchand 2007.
43. Kaufman 2001; Pettigrew and Tropp 2011.
44. For a discussion of the complexities involved in doing so, see Sikkink 2011; Teitel 2011; and Drumbl 2007.
45. Chirot 2001, 20–4.
46. See especially Harff and Gurr 2004.
47. For an example, see Harff 2003.

Chapter 14

1. We discuss immigration further in Chapter 16.
2. On transnationalism, see Khagram and Levitt 2008; Ong 1999.
3. Barth 1969; see also the work by social identity theorists discussed in Chapter 13.
4. American Anthropological Association website: *Race: Are We So Different?* See also Duster 2005.
5. Kimmel 2000.
6. Lovenduski 2005, 6.
7. Costa, Terracciano, and McCrae 2001, though, find cross-cultural variation in gender role stereotypes, noting that this is a problematic finding for theories that argue for strong evolutionary shaping of gender roles. There is a vibrant debate about these issues in psychology.
8. England et al. 1994; Eccles 1987.
9. On the social construction of heterosexuality as the norm, see Katz 2007.
10. There is a growing comparative literature on LGBTQIA+ movements in different global regions. For example, on LGBTQIA+ movements in Latin America, see Corrales and Pecheny 2010 and de la Dehesa 2010.
11. American Anthropological Association, website: *Race: Are We So Different?* 12. On the Irish and the racial category of "whiteness" in the United States, see Roediger 1999, 133–63. On race in Latin America, see Winn 1992, 271–307.
13. See, for example, Omi and Winant 1994.

14. Gans 2005.
15. Sorenson 2001.
16. Fredrickson 2003; Gans 2005.
17. See the overview of this history in Fredrickson 2003 as well as in Pagden 2009, who stresses both the importance and the limits of racist and racist-like attitudes in colonial expansion, and Cañizares-Esguerra 2009, who suggests that the idea of race as justification for colonial domination was developed by overseas colonials rather than by European actors.
18. Garcia and Esparza 2006.
29. Marx 1998.
20. Smith 1995, 57. Note that he refers to such groups as "ethnie."
21. Smith famously argues that national identities *grow out of* but are not fully reducible to ethnic identities.
22. For this reason, some distinguish between ethnicity and race on the grounds that ethnicity may be more a matter of choice, with multiple affiliations possible, whereas race may be more a matter of external ascription and thus inescapable. This perspective is expressed in Fredrickson 2003, among many other works. For a fuller discussion of some of the differences between the concepts of race and ethnicity, see Cornell and Hartmann 1998, 25–35.
23. Posner 2005.
24. For one example, see Loveman 2009.
25. Brown et al. 2003; Pettit and Western 2004.
26. Herring 2002.
27. Pager and Shepherd 2008, 182.
28. Brown et al. 2003.
29. Henderson and Jeydel 2010, 238–42; Roth 2006.
30. Moreover, according to some analysts, gender inequality seems to negatively affect societal-level economic performance. See Dollar and Gatti 1999.
31. On sexual harassment, see Henderson and Jeydel 2010, 124–30.
32. Ibid., 116; Padavic and Reskin 2002, 121–47.
33. For a recent discussion of these and related issues, see Haveman and Beresford 2012.
34. For an interesting analysis of some of the cultural sources of such conflicts, see Blair-Loy 2003 as well as Haveman and Beresford 2012.
35. Padavic and Reskin 2002, 6–16. On consequences of this, see also Blau and Kahn 1992.
36. On health, education, and related arenas of inequality and disadvantage, see the extended discussion in Henderson and Jeydel 2010, 266–302.
37. Jaschik 2011.
38. On political underrepresentation, see Squires 2007, 22–4, 32, and Henderson and Jeydel 2010, 5–6.
39. Henderson and Jeydel 2010, 22–31.
40. Here we use the concept of "capability" as developed by Amartya Sen (see Chapter 5).
41. Indeed, some theories suggest that economic empowerment is fundamental. For example, see Blumberg 1984. For a partially contrasting view emphasizing culture and beliefs, see Ridgeway and Correll 2004.
42. For a critical perspective, see Izugbara 2004.
43. On the efficacy of conditional cash transfer programs, see Rawlings and Rubio 2005 and Handa and Davis 2006.
44. Weber 1946.
45. Gold 2018.
46. As noted before, political empowerment can take many forms, including women's representation in political institutions. On women's representation in legislatures, see Sawer, Tremblay, and Trimble 2006.
47. Htun 2004.
48. Lovenduski 2005, 4.
49. See the essays in Stetson and Mazur 1995, as well as Squires 2007, 32–8.
50. Adapted from Garner et al. 2017, 116-17.
51. Henderson and Jeydel 2010, 37–64. For a model analysis of ethnic groups' social movement mobilization, see Yashar 2005.
52. Van Cott 2005.
53. Of course, some would argue that Michels's "iron law of oligarchy" still applies in such cases.
54. Krook (2009) makes the same point with response to successful cases of quota system adoption. She draws on work by Charles Ragin and others that suggests that social and political outcomes are not just products of constant relationships between certain sets of variables but rather products of more complex interaction effects.
55. For one strong view on the relationship between the size of ethnic groups and group affiliation, see Posner 2005.
56. As noted in the "Insights" box, some of these factors are highlighted by Van Cott (2005).
57. For a review of these concepts, see Chapter 12.
58. Van Cott 2005.
59. Indeed, proportional representation seems to lead to women's holding elected office at a higher rate, at least in more economically developed countries. See Matland 1998.
60. On the impact of cross-cutting affiliations on group party formation, in addition to Htun 2004, see Dunning and Harrison 2010. The latter work suggests that under some conditions other forms of cross-cutting affiliation can weaken the potential for ethnic groups to form political parties.
61. On quotas and quota systems, see Franceschet, Krook, and Piscopo 2012; Krook 2009; and Squires 2007.
62. Krook 2009, 6–9.
63. Ibid. See also discussion of reserved-seat systems in general (not just for women) in Reynolds 2005. More generally, for an overlapping approach, known as consociationalism, see Lijphart 1977.
64. For a more detailed discussion of different types of quota systems, see Krook 2009. Some scholars have argued that quotas are not as effective at changing attitudes and behaviour as their advocates sometimes claim. See Zetterberg 2009.
65. Krook 2009, 7–9; Henderson and Jeydel 2010, 15.
66. On the effectiveness of quota systems more generally, see Krook 2009; Squires 2007, 53–60; and Franceschet, Krook, and Piscopo 2012.

67. The indicator referred to here is calculated annually in the United Nations Human Development Reports, available at http://hdr.undp.org/en/reports. For further information on the Gender-Related Development Index (GDI) and the Gender Empowerment Measure (GEM), see http://hdr.undp.org/en/statistics/indices/gdi_gem (accessed 13 August 2012).
68. South Africa, incidentally, is ranked 10th, but it is a special case.

Chapter 15

1. Fox 2008.
2. Norris and Inglehart 2004. Norris and Inglehart, as we will see later, *do* believe that religion declines when societies modernize.
3. Bell [1960] 2000; for a more recent version of this sort of argument, see Fukuyama 1992.
4. Berger 1967.
5. Hutchins 2015.
6. See discussion in Freston 2008 as well as in Woodberry 2011 and Woodberry and Shah 2004.
7. On the complex relationship between religion and democratic politics more generally, see Stepan 2000.
8. Appadurai 1996; Coronil 1997.
9. On this point, see the writings of Partha Chatterjee, among others; for example, see Chatterjee 1993; 1997.
10. On the concept of "soft power," see the work of Nye 1990.
11. See the very interesting discussion of Islamic encounters with Western modernity in Moaddel 2005.
12. Though, as scholars like the anthropologist Talal Asad (2003) have pointed out, we do not always succeed in our efforts to avoid doing so.
13. For a classic statement of "modernization theory," see Inkeles and Smith 1974 as well as Berger, Berger, and Kellner 1973. For a more recent version, see Inglehart and Welzel 2005 and Norris and Inglehart 2004.
14. Eisenstadt 2000.
15. This means that not all political beliefs should be thought of as "ideology." For classic statements, see Geertz 1973a and Converse 1964. For a highly sophisticated discussion of the many ways in which the term has been used by political scientists, see Gerring 1997.
16. Unless your wardrobe is specifically crafted to express your political views.
17. Karl Marx's followers go as far as suggesting that ideologies are simply reflections of underlying class interests.
18. See, for example, Boli 1981.
19. Berger 1974.
20. Greenfeld 1996.
21. On viewing religion as a "cultural system," see Geertz 1973b. On transcendence as a key, substantive feature of religion, see Greenfeld 1996 and James 1902.
22. For an overview and relatively recent example, see Bruce 2002.
23. Berger 1967.
24. Weber 1958.
25. Berger 1999; Berger, Davie, and Fokas 2008.
26. Stark 1999.
27. Kaufmann 2010.
28. Casanova 1994.
29. Ibid. See also Bell 1977.
30. The concept of "privatization" has been most clearly discussed by Casanova 1994.
31. Niebuhr 1929.
32. Juergensmeyer 1993; Kepel 1994.
33. Fukuyama 1992.
34. For a historical overview, see Payne 1995.
35. Marx 1978a and 1978b.
36. Fox 2008.
37. BBC 2011.
38. Fox 2008.
39. Blancarte 2008.
40. On churches and sects, see the classic work of Weber (1969) and Troeltsch (1969). On denominationalism as a distinct category, see Niebuhr 1929 as well as Casanova 1994; 2007.
41. It is important to remember that these are all "ideal types" and that in the real world we will find many exceptions and cases that do not neatly fit into one or another of these categories.
42. See José Casanova's (2007) thoughtful comparison of immigration and religious pluralism in western Europe and the United States in this connection.
43. This is closer to Niebuhr's classic (1929) view.
44. For a summary, see Gorski and Altinordu 2008.
45. See, for example, R. Stephen Warner 1993.
46. Finke and Iannaccone 1993.
47. Stark 1999.
48. Chaves and Gorski 2001; Voas, Crockett, and Olson 2002.
49. Casanova 1994; Chaves 1994; Martin 2005.
50. See discussion of traditional and more recent approaches to differentiation theory in Chaves 1994.
51. Smith 2003.
52. See Lindholm and Zúquete 2010. On the left, see Levitsky and Roberts 2011.
53. See discussion of these issues in the essays in Smilde and Hellinger 2011.
54. Smilde and Pagan 2011.
55. For a partially overlapping argument, see Meyer, Boli, Thomas, and Ramírez 1997.
56. For a deep dive into the conceptualization of populism, see Weyland 2001.
57. Müller 2016, 2.
58. Ibid. 3–6.
59. Mudde 2004, 543–4.
60. On populism in Venezuela, see especially Hawkins 2010.
61. Ostiguy and Roberts 2016.
62. Mudde and Rovira Kaltwasser 2013.
63. For example, see Laclau 2005.

Chapter 16

1. McHugh 2018.
2. European Commission, "Countries and Regions: Canada."
3. Stoett 1999.
4. On interdependence, see Keohane and Nye 1977.
5. See Friedman 2005.
6. See Wolf 2004.
7. Rogowski 1987.
8. For two leading perspectives on this debate, see Wolf 2004 for a perspective favouring the free market and Stiglitz 2002; 2007, on a critique of the international financial institutions.
9. Jacobs 2018.
10. Johnston 2017.
11. Some of these "debates" may be explicit and take the form of dialogue, while other "debates" may be more implicit, with their implications revealed more in terms of decisions and behaviours of the immigrant groups.
12. For one of the recent major statements arguing in favour of assimilation to protect a national identity, see Huntington 2004. For a classic statement about the tendency to essentialize foreign cultures, particularly those of the Middle East, see Said 1978.
13. Statistics Canada 2017.
14. Huntington 2004.
15. Portes and Rumbaut 2006.
16. For reports on this issue, see the Intergovernmental Panel on Climate Change (IPCC) at http://www.ipcc.ch.
17. See Singer 2004 for a discussion of the ethics of this debate.
18. On the characteristics that make for successful governance of the commons, see Ostrom 1990.
19. See Ostrom 1990.
20. Burke 2004.
21. Keck and Sikkink 1998.
22. Ibid.
23. Arms Control Association.
24. As of April 2019, the US list of state sponsors of terrorism consisted of North Korea, Iran, Sudan, and Syria (see US Department of State, "State Sponsors of Terrorism," https://www.state.gov/j/ct/list/c14151.htm).
25. Thucydides [n.d.] 1974; Machiavelli [1532] 1984; Hobbes [1651] 1996.
26. Waltz 1954; 1979.
27. Walt 1998, 31.
28. Mearsheimer 2001.
29. Axelrod and Hamilton 1981, 1392.
30. Doyle 1983a, 218.
31. See Walt 1998, 32.
32. Moravcsik 1997, 515.
33. Keohane 1984.
34. Doyle 1983a; 1983b; 1997.
35. Allison 1971.
36. Wendt 1992.
37. Wendt 1999.
38. Lenin [1917] 1996.
39. Waltz 1954.
40. Putnam 1988.
41. Gourevitch 1978.
42. Scottish National Party (SNP) 2016; SNP Store website.

REFERENCES AND FURTHER READING

Chapter 1

Collier, David, and Robert Adcock. 1999. "Democracy and Dichotomies: A Pragmatic Approach to Choices about Concepts." *Annual Review of Political Science* 2: 537–65.

Collier, David, and Steven Levitsky. 1997. "Democracy with Adjectives: Conceptual Innovation in Comparative Research." *World Politics* 49(3): 430–51.

Dunning, Thad. 2012. *Natural Experiments in the Social Sciences: A Design-Based Approach*. New York: Cambridge University Press.

Elster, Jon. 2007. *Explaining Social Behavior: More Nuts and Bolts for the Social Sciences*. New York: Cambridge University Press.

Gerring, John. 2001. *Social Science Methodology: A Criterial Framework*. Cambridge: Cambridge University Press.

——— 2009. "The Case Study: What It Is and What It Does." In Robert E. Goddin, ed., *Oxford Handbook of Political Science*, 1133–66. New York: Oxford University Press.

Jago, Robert. 2017. "Canada Problem." In Kiera L. Ladner and Myra J. Tait, eds, *Surviving Canada: Indigenous Peoples Celebrate 150 Years of Betrayal*. Winnipeg: Arbeiter Ring Publishing.

Lieberson, Stanley, and Freda Lynn. 2002. "Barking up the Wrong Branch: Scientific Alternatives to the Current Model of Sociological Science." *Annual Review of Sociology* 28: 1–19.

Mill, John Stuart. 1846. *A System of Logic, Ratiocinative and Inductive*. New York: Harper.

Putnam, Robert D. 1993. *Making Democracy Work: Civic Traditions in Modern Italy*. Princeton, NJ: Princeton University Press.

Ross, Rupert. 2006. *Returning to the Teachings: Exploring Aboriginal Justice*. Toronto: Penguin Random House.

Sartori, Giovanni. 1970. "Concept Misformation in Comparative Politics."*American Political Science Review* 64(4): 1033–53.

Stanford Encyclopedia of Philosophy. 2011. "Aristotle's Political Theory." Accessed 17 April 2019. http://plato.stanford.edu/entries/aristotle-politics.

Weber, Cynthia. 2009. *International Relations Theory: A Critical Introduction*. 3rd edn. London: Routledge.

Weber, Max. 1949. "Objectivity in Social Science and Social Policy." In Edward A. Shils and Henry A. Finch, eds. and trans., *The Methodology of the Social Sciences*, 49–112. New York: The Free Press.

Chapter 2

Babbie, Earl. 2010. *Methods of Social Research*. 12th edn. Belmont, CA: Wadsworth, Cengage Learning.

Cassidy, John. 2013. "The Reinhart and Rogoff Controversy: A Summing Up." *The New Yorker*, 26 April. https://www.newyorker.com/news/john-cassidy/the-reinhart-and-rogoff-controversy-a-summing-up.

Charity Intelligence Canada. 2019. "Breakfast for Learning." https://www.charityintelligence.ca/charity-details/595-breakfast-for-learning.

Inglehart, Ronald, and Christian Welzel. 2003. "Political Culture and Democracy: Analyzing Cross-Level Linkages." *Comparative Politics* 36(1): 61–79.

King, Gary, Robert Keohane, and Sidney Verba. 1994. *Designing Social Inquiry: Scientific Inference in Qualitative Research*. Princeton, NJ: Princeton University Press.

Kuhn, Thomas. 1962. *The Structure of Scientific Revolutions*. Chicago: University of Chicago Press.

Lindberg, Staffan. 2006. *Democracy and Elections in Africa*. Baltimore, MD: Johns Hopkins University Press.

Lipset, Seymour Martin. 1959. "Some Social Requisites of Democracy: Economic Development and Political Legitimacy." *American Political Science Review* 53(1): 69–105.

Popper, Karl. 1963. *Conjectures and Refutations: The Growth of Scientific Knowledge*. London: Routledge and Kegan Paul.

Chapter 3

Bates, Robert. 2008. *When Things Fell Apart: State Failure in Late-Century Africa*. New York: Cambridge University Press.

Bell, Duncan. 2014. "Beyond the Sovereign State: Isopolitan Citizenship, Race and Anglo-American Union." *Political Studies* 62: 418–34.

Belshaw, John Douglas. 2016. *Canadian History: Post-Confederation*. BCcampus.

Centeno, Miguel Angel. 2002. *Blood and Debt: War and the Nation State in Latin America*. University Park: Pennsylvania State University Press.

Chirot, Daniel. 1994. *How Societies Change*. Newbury Park, CA: Pine Forge Press.

Colley, Linda. 1992. *Britons: Forging the Nation*. New Haven, CT: Yale University Press.

DiMaggio, Paul J., and Walter W. Powell. 1983. "The Iron Cage Revisited: Institutional Isomorphism and Collective Rationality in Organizational Fields." *American Sociological Review* 48: 147–60.

Donkin, Karissa. 2013. "Social Media Helps Drive Idle No More Movement." *Toronto Star*, 11 January. https://www.thestar.com/news/canada/2013/01/11/social_media_helps_drive_idle_no_more_movement.html.

Downing, Brian. 1992. *The Military Revolution and Political Change*. Princeton, NJ: Princeton University Press.

Evans, Peter. 1997. "The Eclipse of the State? Reflections on Stateness in an Era of Globalization." *World Politics* 50(1): 62–87.

———, Dietrich Reuschemeyer, and Theda Skocpol. 1985. *Bringing the State Back In*. New York: Cambridge University Press.

Foucault, Michel. 1977. *Discipline and Punish: The Birth of the Prison*. Trans. Alan Sheridan. New York: Vintage Books.

Fukuyama, Francis. 2004. *State-Building, Governance, and World Order in the 21st Century*. Ithaca, NY: Cornell University Press.

——— 2011. *Origins of Political Order: From Prehuman Times to the French Revolution*. 1st paperback edn. New York: Farrar, Straus and Giroux.

Giddens, Anthony. 1987. *A Contemporary Critique of Historical Materialism.* Vol. 2: *The Nation-State and Violence.* Berkeley: University of California Press.

Gorski, Philip S. 2003. *The Disciplinary Revolution: Calvinism and the Rise of the State in Early Modern Europe.* Chicago: University of Chicago Press.

Greenfeld, Liah. 1992. *Nationalism: Five Roads to Modernity.* Cambridge, MA: Harvard University Press.

———. 1996. "Nationalism and Modernity." *Social Research* 63(1): 3–40.

Hardin, Russell. 1997. "Economic Theories of the State." In Dennis C. Mueller, ed., *Perspectives on Public Choice: A Handbook*, 21–34. New York: Cambridge University Press.

Hayes, Molly. 2018. "Black People More Likely to Be Injured or Killed by Toronto Police Officers, Report Finds." *Globe and Mail*, 10 December. https://www.theglobeandmail.com/canada/toronto/article-report-reveals-racial-disparities-in-toronto-polices-use-of-force.

Herbst, Jeffrey. 2000. *States and Power in Africa: Comparative Lessons in Authority and Control.* Princeton, NJ: Princeton University Press.

Huntington, Samuel. 1957. *The Soldier and the State: The Theory and Politics of Civil–Military Relations.* Cambridge, MA: Belknap Press of Harvard University Press.

Karl, Terry Lynn. 1997. *The Paradox of Plenty: Oil Booms and Petro-States.* Berkeley: University of California Press.

Lenin, Vladimir. 1939. *Imperialism, the Highest Stage of Capitalism: A Popular Outline.* New York: International Publishers.

Levi, Margaret. 1988. *Of Rule and Revenue.* Berkeley: University of California Press.

Loveman, Mara. 2014. *National Colors: Racial Classification and the State in Latin America.* New York: Oxford University Press.

McNeill, J.R., and William H. McNeill. 2003. *The Human Web: A Bird's-Eye View of World History.* New York: W.W. Norton.

McNeill, William H. 1982. *The Pursuit of Power: Technology, Armed Force, and Society Since A.D. 1000.* Chicago: University of Chicago Press.

Marx, Karl. 1978. "The German Ideology: Part I." In Robert C. Tucker, ed., *The Marx-Engels Reader*, 2nd edn. New York: W.W. Norton.

Meyer, John W., John Boli, George M. Thomas, and Francisco O. Ramírez. 1997. "World Society and the Nation-State." *American Journal of Sociology* 103(1): 144–81.

Meyer, John W., and Brian Rowan. 1991. "Institutionalized Organizations: Formal Structure as Myth and Ceremony." In Walter W. Powell and Paul J. DiMaggio, eds, *The New Institutionalism in Organizational Analysis*, 41–62. Chicago: University of Chicago Press.

Migdal, Joel S. 1988. *Strong Societies and Weak States: State-Society Relations and State Capabilities in the Third World.* Princeton, NJ: Princeton University Press.

Morgan, Glyn. 2007. *The Idea of a European Superstate: Public Justification and European Integration.* Princeton, NJ: Princeton University Press.

North, Douglass C., John Joseph Wallis, and Barry R. Weingast. 2009. *Violence and Social Orders: A Conceptual Framework for Interpreting Recorded Human History.* New York: Cambridge University Press.

Ostrom, Elinor. 1990. *Governing the Commons: The Evolution of Institutions for Collective Action.* New York: Cambridge University Press.

Pérez Díaz, Victor. 2014. "Civil Society: A Multi-Layered Concept." *Current Sociology* 62(6): 812–30.

Pettit, Becky, and Bruce Western. 2004. "Mass Imprisonment and the Life Course: Race and Class Inequality in U.S. Incarceration." *American Sociological Review* 69(2): 151–69.

Pincus, Steve. 2009. *1688: The First Modern Revolution.* New Haven, CT: Yale University Press.

Poggi, Gianfranco. 1990. *The State: Its Nature, Development, and Prospects.* Stanford, CA: Stanford University Press.

Putnam, Robert. 1993. *Making Democracy Work: Civic Traditions in Modern Italy.* Princeton, NJ: Princeton University Press.

Sahlins, Peter. 1991. *Boundaries: The Making of France and Spain in the Pyrenees.* Berkeley: University of California Press.

Scott, James. 1999. *Seeing Like a State: How Certain Schemes to Improve the Human Condition Have Failed.* New Haven, CT: Yale University Press.

Spruyt, Hendrik. 1994. *The Sovereign State and Its Competitors.* Princeton, NJ: Princeton University Press.

——— 2007. "War, Trade, and State Formation." In Carles Boix and Susan Stokes, eds, *Oxford Handbook of Comparative Politics*, 211–35. New York: Oxford University Press.

Strayer, Joseph R. [1970] 2005. *On the Medieval Origins of the Modern State.* Princeton Classic edn. Princeton, NJ: Princeton University Press.

Taylor, Charles. 2007. *A Secular Age.* Cambridge, MA: Belknap Press of Harvard University Press.

Tilly, Charles. 1975. "Reflections on the History of European State-Making." In Charles Tilly, ed., *The Formation of National States in Western Europe*, 3–83. Princeton, NJ: Princeton University Press.

——— [1990] 1992. *Coercion, Capital, and European States, AD 990–1992.* Oxford: Blackwell.

Wallerstein, Immanuel. [1974] 2011. *The Modern World-System*, vol. 1: *Capitalist Agriculture and the Origins of the European World-Economy in the Sixteenth Century.* Berkeley: University of California Press.

Weber, Max. "Politics as a Vocation." 1946. In H.H. Gerth and C. Wright Mills, eds, *From Max Weber: Essays in Sociology*, 77–128. New York: Oxford University Press.

———. 1978. *Economy and Society*, Vol. 2. Ed. Guenther Roth and Claus Wittich. Berkeley: University of California Press.

Weingast, Barry R. 1997. "The Political Foundation of Democracy and the Rule of Law." *American Political Science Review* 91(2): 245–63.

Western, Bruce. 2006. *Punishment and Inequality in America.* New York: Russell Sage Foundation.

Wimmer, Andreas, and Yuval Feinstein. 2010. "The Rise of the Nation State across the World, 1816–2001." *American Sociological Review* 75(5): 764–90.

Chapter 4

Abedi, Maham. 2017. "Rise of Income Inequality in Canada 'Almost Exclusive' to Major Cities: Study." *Global News*, 14 July. https://globalnews.ca/news/3599083/income-inequality-canada-cities.

Arendt, Hannah. 1963. *On Revolution*. New York: Viking Press.

"Asia's Next Revolution." 2012. *The Economist*, 8 September. https://www.economist.com/leaders/2012/09/08/asias-next-revolution.

Bell, David A. 2001. *The Cult of the Nation in France: Inventing Nationalism, 1680–1800*. Cambridge, MA: Harvard University Press.

Conference Board of Canada. "Income Inequality." Accessed 17 April 2019. http://www.conferenceboard.ca/hcp/provincial/society/income-inequality.aspx.

"Crash Course: The Effects of the Financial Crisis Are Still Being Felt Five Years On." 2013. *The Economist*, 7 September. https://www.economist.com/news/schoolsbrief/21584534-effects-financial-crisis-are-still-being-felt-five-years-article.

Esping-Andersen, Gøsta. 1990. *The Three Worlds of Welfare Capitalism*. Princeton, NJ: Princeton University Press.

Foucault, Michel. 1977. *Discipline and Punish: The Birth of the Prison*. Trans. Alan Sheridan. New York: Vintage Press.

Goodman, Roger, and Ito Peng. 1996. "The East Asian Welfare States: Peripatetic Learning, Adaptive Change, and Nation-Building." In Gøsta Esping-Andersen, *Welfare States in Transition: National Adaptations in Global Economies*, 192–225. Thousand Oaks, CA: Sage.

Hayek, Friedrich A. [1944] 1994. *The Road to Serfdom*. 50th anniversary edn. Chicago: University of Chicago Press.

Howard, Christopher. 2007. *The Welfare State Nobody Knows: Debunking Myths about U.S. Social Policy*. Princeton, NJ: Princeton University Press.

Huber, Evelyn, and John D. Stephens. 2001. *Development and Crisis of the Welfare State: Parties and Policies in Global Markets*. Chicago: University of Chicago Press.

International Labor Rights Forum. "Precarious Work." Accessed 17 April 2019. https://laborrights.org/issues/precarious-work.

Levi-Faur, David. 1997. "Economic Nationalism: From Friedrich List to Robert Reich." *Review of International Studies* 23: 359–70.

Long, Heather. 2016. "U.S. Inequality Keeps Getting Uglier." *CNN Business*, 22 December. http://money.cnn.com/2016/12/22/news/economy/us-inequality-worse/index.html.

Marx, Karl. [1867] 1996. *Das Kapital: A Critique of Political Economy*. Washington, DC: Regnery Publishing.

Matthews, Chris. 2014. "The 'Invisible Hand' Has an Iron Grip on America.' *Fortune*, 13 August. http://fortune.com/2014/08/13/invisible-hand-american-economy.

Mettler, Susan. 2011. *The Submerged State: How Invisible Government Policies Undermine American Democracy*. Chicago: University of Chicago Press.

Pierson, Christopher. 2006. *Beyond the Welfare State? The New Political Economy of Welfare*. Malden, MA: Polity Press.

Prasad, Monica. 2006. *The Politics of Free Markets: The Rise of Neoliberal Economic Policies in Britain, France, Germany, and the United States*. Chicago: University of Chicago Press.

Ricardo, David. 1817. *On the Principles of Political Economy and Taxation*. London: John Murray.

Schlefer, Jonathan. 2012. "There Is No Invisible Hand." *Harvard Business Review*, 10 April. https://hbr.org/2012/04/there-is-no-invisible-hand.

Smith, Adam. [1776] 2003. *The Wealth of Nations*. New York: Random House.

Statistics Canada. "Household Income in Canada: Key Results from the 2016 Census." Accessed 17 April 2019. https://www.statcan.gc.ca/daily-quotidien/170913/dq170913a-eng.htm.

Taylor, Charles. 2007. *A Secular Age*. Cambridge, MA: Belknap Press of Harvard University Press.

Tencer, Daniel. 2017. "Canada's Income Inequality 'Surged Under Harper': Analysis." *Huffington Post*, 29 May. http://www.huffingtonpost.ca/2017/05/29/income-inequality-canada_n_16869570.html.

Tse, Edward. 2016. "The Rise of Entrepreneurship in China." *Forbes*, 5 April. https://www.forbes.com/sites/tseedward/2016/04/05/the-rise-of-entrepreneurship-in-china/#2ff144403efc.

Wilensky, Harold L. 1975. *The Welfare State and Equality: Structural and Ideological Roots of Public Expenditure*. Berkeley: University of California Press.

Chapter 5

Abedi, Maham. 2017. "World Happiness Report 2017: Canada Slips to Its Lowest Ranking Yet." *Huffington Post*, 20 March. http://www.huffingtonpost.ca/2017/03/20/world-happiness-report-canada_n_15492574.html.

Acemoglu, Daron, Simon Johnson, and James A. Robinson. 2001. "The Colonial Origins of Comparative Development." *American Economic Review* 91: 1369–401.

Almond, Gabriel. 1991. "Capitalism and Democracy." *PS: Political Science and Politics* 24(3): 467–74.

Amsden, Alice. 1992. *Asia's Next Giant: South Korea and Late Industrialization*. New York: Oxford University Press.

Anaya, James. 2014. "The Situation of Indigenous Peoples in Canada." *United Nations Human Rights Council*. http://unsr.jamesanaya.org/docs/countries/2014-report-canada-a-hrc-27-52-add-2-en.pdf.

Bajpai, Prableen. 2019. "North Korean vs. South Korean Economies: What's the Difference." *Investopedia.com*, 8 March. https://www.investopedia.com/articles/forex/040515/north-korean-vs-south-korean-economies.asp.

Burt, Ronald. 1992. *Structural Holes: The Social Structure of Competition*. Cambridge, MA: Harvard University Press.

Cardoso, Fernando Henrique, and Enzo Faletto. 1979. *Dependency and Development in Latin America*. Berkeley: University of California Press.

Carroll, Toby. 2010. *Delusions of Development: The World Bank and the Post–Washington Consensus in Southeast Asia*. London: Palgrave Macmillan UK.

Collier, Paul. 2007. *The Bottom Billion: Why the Poorest Countries Are Failing and What Can Be Done about It*. New York: Oxford University Press.

Escobar, Arturo. 1995. *Encountering Development: The Making and Unmaking of the Third World*. Princeton, NJ: Princeton University Press.

Evans, Peter. 1979. *Dependent Development: The Alliance of Multinational, State, and Local Capital in Brazil*. Princeton, NJ: Princeton University Press.

——— 1995. *Embedded Autonomy: States and Industrial Transformation*. Princeton, NJ: Princeton University Press.

Frank, André Gunder. 1967. *Capitalism and Underdevelopment in Latin America: Historical Studies of Chile and Brazil*. New York: Monthly Review Press.

Greenwood, Margo, Sarah De Leeuw, Nicole Marie Lindsay, and Charlotte Reading, eds. 2015. *Determinants of Indigenous Peoples' Health in Canada*. Toronto: Canadian Scholars Press.

Gregson, Jonathan. 2017. "Poorest Countries in the World." *Global Finance*, 13 February. https://www.gfmag.com/global-data/economic-data/the-poorest-countries-in-the-world.

Guo, Xiaoqin. 2003. *State and Society in China's Democratic Transition: Confucianism, Leninism, and Economic Development*. 1st edn. New York: Routledge.

Imai, Shin. 2017. "Historic Treaties and the Indian Act." *All Papers* 316. https://digitalcommons.osgoode.yorku.ca/all_papers/316.

Kennedy, David M., and Thomas Bailey. 2009. *The American Spirit: United States History as Seen by Contemporaries, Volume 1*. 12th edn. Boston: Cengage Learning.

Kohli, Atul. 2004. *State-Directed Development: Political Power and Industrialization in the Global Periphery*. Cambridge: Cambridge University Press.

Lenin, Vladimir Il'ich. [1917] 1948. *Imperialism: The Highest Stage of Capitalism*. London: Lawrence and Wishart.

Mahoney, James. 2010. *Colonialism and Postcolonial Development*. New York: Cambridge University Press.

Manuel, Arthur. 2017. "Until Canada Gives Indigenous People Their Land Back, There Can Never Be Reconciliation." *Rabble* (blog), 18 January. http://rabble.ca/blogs/bloggers/views-expressed/2017/01/until-canada-gives-indigenous-people-their-land-back-there-ca#.WIAw9l1F2Ko.twitter.

Nadasdy, Paul. 2016. "First Nations, Citizenship and Animals, or Why Northern Indigenous People Might Not Want to Live in Zoopolis." *Canadian Journal of Political Science* 49(1): 2–3.

Pierson, Paul. 2004. *Politics in Time: History, Institutions, and Social Analysis*. Princeton, NJ: Princeton University Press.

Pogge, Thomas. 2008. *World Poverty and Human Rights*. 2nd edn. Cambridge: Polity Press.

Prebisch, Raul. 1950. *The Economic Development of Latin America and Its Principal Problems*. New York: United Nations.

Press, Jordan. 2017. "Census: Children Make up One Quarter of 4.8M Canadians Living in Poverty." *Canadian Press*, 13 September. https://www.ctvnews.ca/canada/census-children-make-up-one-quarter-of-4-8m-canadians-living-in-poverty-1.3587472.

Putnam, Robert D. 2000. *Bowling Alone: The Collapse and Revival of American Community*. New York: Simon and Schuster.

Rifkin, Jeremy. 2004. *The European Dream: How Europe's Vision of the Future Is Quietly Eclipsing the American Dream*. New York: TarcherPerigee.

Rodney, Walter. 1981. *How Europe Underdeveloped Africa*. Washington, DC: Howard University Press.

Rosenstein-Rodan, Paul. 1943. "Problems of Industrialization of Eastern and South-Eastern Europe." *The Economic Journal* 53(210/211): 202–11.

Sawchuk, Joe. 2011. "Social Conditions of Indigenous Peoples." *The Canadian Encyclopedia*, 31 October. http://www.thecanadianencyclopedia.ca/en/article/native-people-social-conditions.

Sen, Amartya. 1999. *Development as Freedom*. New York: Anchor Books.

Stiglitz, Joseph, Amartya Sen, and Jean-Paul Fitoussi. 2010. *Mismeasuring Our Lives: Why GDP Doesn't Add Up*. New York: The New Press.

Tocqueville, Alexis de. 1998. *Democracy in America*. Ware, UK: Wordsworth Editions.

Wallerstein, Immanuel. [1974] 2011. *The Modern World-System, vol. 1: Capitalist Agriculture and the Origins of the European World-Economy in the Sixteenth Century*. Berkeley: University of California Press.

Weber, Max. 1958. *The Protestant Ethic and the Spirit of Capitalism*. New York: Charles Scribner's Sons.

World Bank. 1997. *World Development Report: The State in a Changing World*. Washington, DC: World Bank.

World Values Survey. http://www.worldvaluessurvey.org/wvs.jsp.

Zhang, Cuiping, and Xiaoxing Zhu. 2012. "Chapter 17: Confucianism and Market Economy." In Gregory P. Prastacos, Fuming Wang, and Klas Eric Soderquist, eds, *Leadership through the Classics: Learning Management and Leadership from Ancient East and West Philosophy*. Berlin: Springer Verlag.

Chapter 6

Almond, Gabriel A., and Sidney Verba. 1963. *The Civic Culture: Political Attitudes and Democracy in Five Nations*. Princeton, NJ: Princeton University Press.

Belli, Gioconda. 2016. "Why Has 'Macho' Latin America Elected More Female Leaders Than the US?" *The Guardian*, 7 November. https://www.theguardian.com/global-development-professionals-network/2016/nov/07/macho-latin-america-elected-more-female-leaders-than-us.

Bollen, Kenneth. 2003. "World System Position, Dependency, and Democracy: The Cross-National Evidence." *American Sociological Review* 48(4): 468–79.

Collier, David, James Mahoney, and Jason Seawright. 2004. "Claiming Too Much: Warnings about Selection Bias." In Henry Brady and David Collier, eds, *Rethinking Social Inquiry: Diverse Tools, Shared Standards*, 85–102. Lanham, MD: Rowman and Littlefield.

Coppedge, Michael, and John Gerring, with David Altman, Michael Bernhard, Steven Fish, Allen Hicken, Matthew Kroenig, Staffan I. Lindberg, Kelly McMann, Pamela Paxton, Holli A. Semetko, Svend-Erik Skaaning, Jeffrey Staton, and Jan Teorell. 2011. "Conceptualizing and Measuring Democracy: A New Approach." *Perspectives on Politics* 9(2): 247–67.

Dahl, Robert A. 1971. *Polyarchy: Participation and Opposition.* New Haven, CT: Yale University Press.

Economist Intelligence Unit (EIU). *EIU Democracy Index 2018—World Democracy Report.* Accessed 17 April 2019. https://www.eiu.com/topic/democracy-index.

Elections Canada. "Voter Turnout by Age Group." Accessed 17 April 2019. http://www.elections.ca/content.aspx?section=res&dir=rec/eval/pes2015/vtsa&document=table1&lang=e.

Elster, Jon. 2007. *Explaining Social Behavior: More Nuts and Bolts for the Social Sciences.* New York: Cambridge University Press.

Fukuyama, Francis. 1995. "Confucianism and Democracy." *Journal of Democracy* 6(2): 20–33.

George, Alexander L., and Andrew Bennett. 2005. *Case Studies and Theory Development in the Social Sciences.* Cambridge, MA: MIT Press.

Huntington, Samuel. 1991. *The Third Wave: Democratization in the Late Twentieth Century.* Norman: University of Oklahoma Press.

Inglehart, Ronald, and Christian Welzel. 2005. *Modernization, Cultural Change, and Democracy: The Human Development Sequence.* Cambridge: Cambridge University Press.

Jackson, Moana. 2017. "How about a Politics That Imagines the Impossible?" *E-Tangata,* 23 September. https://e-tangata.co.nz/news/how-about-a-politics-that-imagines-the-impossible.

Jago, Robert. 2017. "Canada Problem." In Kiera L. Ladner and Myra J. Tait, eds, *Surviving Canada: Indigenous Peoples Celebrate 150 Years of Betrayal.* Winnipeg: Arbeiter Ring Publishing.

Levitsky, Steven, and Lucan Way. 2002. "The Rise of Competitive Authoritarianism." *Journal of Democracy* 13(2): 51–65.

——— 2010. *Competitive Authoritarianism: Hybrid Regimes after the Cold War.* New York: Cambridge University Press.

Linz, Juan. 1990a. "The Perils of Presidentialism." *Journal of Democracy* 1(1): 51–69.

——— 1990b. "The Virtues of Parliamentarism." *Journal of Democracy* 1(4): 84–91.

———, and Alfred Stepan. 1996. *Problems of Democratic Transition and Consolidation: Southern Europe, South America, and Post-Communist Europe.* Baltimore, MD: Johns Hopkins University Press.

Lipset, Seymour Martin. 1959. "Some Social Requisites of Democracy: Economic Development and Political Legitimacy." *American Political Science Review* 53(1): 69–105.

——— 1960. *Political Man: The Social Bases of Politics.* Garden City, NJ: Doubleday.

Markoff, John. 1996. *Waves of Democracy: Social Movements in Political Change.* Newbury Park, CA: Pine Forge Press.

Meyer, John W., John Boli, George M. Thomas, and Francisco O. Ramírez. 1997. "World Society and the Nation-State." *American Journal of Sociology* 103(1): 144–81.

Munck, Gerardo. 2009. *Measuring Democracy: A Bridge between Scholarship and Politics.* Baltimore, MD: Johns Hopkins University Press.

O'Donnell, Guillermo, Philippe Schmitter, and Laurence Whitehead, eds. 1986. *Transitions from Authoritarian Rule* (4 vols.). Baltimore, MD: Johns Hopkins University Press.

Przeworski, Adam, and Henry Teune. 1970. *The Logic of Comparative Social Inquiry.* New York: Wiley-Interscience.

Putnam, Robert D. 1993. *Making Democracy Work: Civic Traditions in Modern Italy.* Princeton, NJ: Princeton University Press.

——— 2000. *Bowling Alone: The Collapse and Revival of American Community.* New York: Simon and Schuster.

Rueschemeyer, Dietrich, Evelyne Huber Stephens, and John D. Stephens. 1992. *Capitalist Development and Democracy.* Chicago: University of Chicago Press.

Schedler, Andreas. 1998. "What Is Democratic Consolidation?" *Journal of Democracy* 9(2): 91–107.

———, ed. 2006. *Electoral Authoritarianism: The Dynamics of Unfree Competition.* Boulder, CO: Lynne Rienner Publishers.

Schmitter, Philippe O., and Terry Lynn Karl. 1991. "What Democracy Is . . . and Is Not." *Journal of Democracy* 2(3): 75–88.

Stepan, Alfred. 1999. "Federalism and Democracy: Beyond the U.S. Model." *Journal of Democracy* 10(4): 19–34.

———, and Cindy Skach. 1993. "Constitutional Frameworks and Democratic Consolidation: Parliamentarianism versus Presidentialism." *World Politics* 46(1): 1–22.

Chapter 7

Adorno, Theodor W., Else Frenkel-Brunswik, Daniel J. Levinson, and R. Nevitt Sanford. 1950. *The Authoritarian Personality.* New York: Harper Press.

Almond, Gabriel A., and Sidney Verba. 1963. *The Civic Culture: Political Attitudes and Democracy in Five Nations.* Princeton, NJ: Princeton University Press.

Arendt, Hannah. [1958] 2004. *The Origins of Totalitarianism.* New York: Schocken Books.

Associated Press. 2017. "Jimmy Carter Says US Has Become More an 'Oligarchy Than a Democracy' in Speech Critical of Trump." *The Telegraph,* 13 September. https://www.telegraph.co.uk/news/2017/09/13/jimmy-carter-says-us-has-become-oligarchy-democracy-speech-critical.

Bates, Robert. 2008. *When Things Fell Apart: State Failure in Late-Century Africa.* New York: Cambridge University Press.

Brownlee, Jason. 2007. *Authoritarianism in an Age of Democratization.* New York: Cambridge University Press.

Burke, Jason. 2017. "Zimbabwe Opposition Promises Push for Reform after New Cabinet Revealed." *The Guardian,* 1 December. https://www.theguardian.com/world/2017/dec/01/zimbabwe-military-officials-given-key-jobs-post-mugabe-cabinet-emmerson-mnangagwa.

——— 2018. "Zimbabwe President Promises 'Free and Fair' Election in Five Months." *The Guardian*, 18 January. https://www.theguardian.com/world/2018/jan/18/zimbabwe-president-pledges-free-and-fair-vote-in-four-to-five-months.

Çalışkan, Koray. 2018. "Towards a New Political Regime in Turkey: From Competitive toward Full Authoritarianism." *New Perspectives on Turkey* 58: 5–33.

Chehabi, H.E., and Juan J. Linz, eds. 1998. *Sultanistic Regimes*. Baltimore, MD: Johns Hopkins University Press.

Collier, David, and Steven Levitsky. 1997. "Democracy with Adjectives: Conceptual Innovation in Comparative Research." *World Politics* 49(3): 430–51.

Corrales, Javier, and Michael Penfold. 2011. *Dragon in the Tropics: Hugo Chávez and the Political Economy of Revolution in Venezuela*. Washington, DC: Brookings Institution Press.

Decalo, Samuel. 1985. "African Personal Dictatorships." *Journal of Modern African Studies* 23(2): 209–37.

Diamond, Larry. 2002. "Thinking about Hybrid Regimes." *Journal of Democracy* 13(2): 21–35.

The Economist Intelligence Unit. 2018. *Democracy Index 2018*. Accessed 18 April 2019. http://www.eiu.com/Handlers/WhitepaperHandler.ashx?fi=Democracy_Index_2018.pdf&mode=wp&campaignid=Democracy2018.

Embassy of Canada to Zimbabwe website. 2018. "Canada-Zimbabwe Relations." November. http://www.canadainternational.gc.ca/zimbabwe/bilateral_relations_bilaterales/canada_zimbabwe.aspx?lang=eng.

European Commission. 2016. "European Neighbourhood Policy and Enlargement Negotiations—Conditions for Membership." Accessed 18 April 2019. https://ec.europa.eu/neighbourhood-enlargement/policy/conditions-membership_en.

Fox, Jonathan. 1994. "The Difficult Transition from Clientelism to Citizenship: Lessons from Mexico." *World Politics* 46(2): 151–84.

Greenfeld, Liah. 1997. "The Political Significance of Culture." *The Brown Journal of World Affairs* 4(1): 187–95.

Hall, Peter A. 2010. "Historical Institutionalism in Rationalist and Sociological Perspective." In J. Mahoney and K. Thelen, eds, *Explaining Institutional Change: Ambiguity, Agency, and Power*, 204–24. New York: Cambridge University Press.

Human Rights Watch. 2018. "Turkey: Events of 2018." Accessed 18 April 2019. https://www.hrw.org/world-report/2019/country-chapters/turkey#.

Huntington, Samuel. 1991. *The Third Wave: Democratization in the Late Twentieth Century*. Norman: University of Oklahoma Press.

Inglehart, Ronald, and Christian Welzel. 2005. *Modernization, Cultural Change, and Democracy: The Human Development Sequence*. New York: Cambridge University Press.

Jackson, Robert H., and Carl G. Rosberg. 1982. *Personal Rule in Black Africa: Prince, Autocrat, Prophet, Tyrant*. Berkeley: University of California Press.

Laub, Zachary. 2016. "Why Iran's Elections Matter." Interview with Mohammed Ayatollahi Tabaar. *Council on Foreign Relations*, 24 February. https://www.cfr.org/interview/why-irans-elections-matter.

Levitsky, Steven, and Lucan Way. 2002. "The Rise of Competitive Authoritarianism." *Journal of Democracy* 13(2): 51–65.

———. 2010. *Competitive Authoritarianism: Hybrid Regimes after the Cold War*. New York: Cambridge University Press.

Lichbach, Mark Irving. 1995. *The Rebel's Dilemma*. Ann Arbor: University of Michigan Press.

Linz, Juan, and Alfred Stepan, eds. 1978. *The Breakdown of Democratic Regimes*. Baltimore, MD: Johns Hopkins University Press.

McNeill, J.R., and William H. McNeill. 2003. *The Human Web: A Bird's-Eye View of World History*. New York: W.W. Norton.

Mahoney, James, and Kathleen Thelen, eds. 2010. *Explaining Institutional Change: Ambiguity, Agency, and Power*. New York: Cambridge University Press.

Migdal, Joel S. 1988. *Strong Societies and Weak States: State–Society Relations and State Capabilities in the Third World*. Princeton, NJ: Princeton University Press.

Mlambo, Alois S. 2014. *A History of Zimbabwe*. Cambridge: Cambridge University Press.

Myre, Greg. 2014. "Why Can't the Former Soviet Republics Figure out Democracy?" *NPR.org*, 19 February. https://www.npr.org/sections/parallels/2014/02/19/279464408/why-can-t-the-former-soviet-republics-figure-out-democracy.

North, Douglass C., John Joseph Wallis, and Barry R. Weingast. 2009. *Violence and Social Orders: A Conceptual Framework for Interpreting Recorded Human History*. New York: Cambridge University Press.

O'Donnell, Guillermo A. 1973. *Modernization and Bureaucratic-Authoritarianism: Studies in South American Politics*. Berkeley: Institute of International Studies, University of California.

———. 1994. "Delegative Democracy." *Journal of Democracy* 5(1): 55–69.

Olson, Mancur, Jr. 1965. *The Logic of Collective Action: Public Goods and the Theory of Groups*. Cambridge, MA: Harvard University Press.

Paige, Jeffery M. 1997. *Coffee and Power: Revolution and the Rise of Democracy in Central America*. Cambridge, MA: Harvard University Press.

Palmer, David Scott. 1980. *Peru: The Authoritarian Tradition*. New York: Praeger.

Roberts, Kenneth M. 1995. "Neoliberalism and the Transformation of Populism in Latin America: The Peruvian Case." *World Politics* 48(1): 82–116.

Schedler, Andreas, ed. 2006. *Electoral Authoritarianism: The Dynamics of Unfree Competition*. Boulder, CO: Lynne Rienner Publishers.

Skocpol, Theda. 1973. "A Critical Review of Barrington Moore's Social Origins of Dictatorship and Democracy." *Politics and Society* 4: 1–34.

Smilde, David, and Daniel Hellinger, eds. 2011. *Venezuela's Bolivarian Democracy: Participation, Politics, and Culture under Chávez*. Durham, NC: Duke University Press.

Stelgias, Nikolaos. 2015. "Turkey's Hybrid Competitive Authoritarian Regime; A Genuine Product of Anatolia's Middle Class." *The Levantine Review* 4(2): 201–16.

Valenzuela, Arturo. 1978. *The Breakdown of Democratic Regimes: Chile*. Baltimore, MD: Johns Hopkins University Press.

Véliz, Claudio. 1980. *The Centralist Tradition in Latin America*. Princeton, NJ: Princeton University Press.

Verbitsky, Horacio. 1996. *The Flight: Confessions of an Argentine Dirty Warrior*. New York: The New Press.

Wiarda, Howard J. 2003. *The Soul of Latin America: The Cultural and Political Tradition*. New Haven, CT: Yale University Press.

Wintrobe, Ronald. 2007. "Dictatorship: Analytical Approaches." In Carles Boix and Susan C. Stokes, eds, *Oxford Handbook of Comparative Politics*, 363–94. New York: Oxford University Press.

Zakaria, Fareed. 2003. *The Future of Freedom: Illiberal Democracy at Home and Abroad*. New York: W.W. Norton.

Žižek, Slavov. 2002. *Did Somebody Say Totalitarianism? Five Interventions in the Misuse of a Notion*. New York: W.W. Norton.

Chapter 8

Borrows, John. 2017. "Canada's Colonial Constitution." In John Borrows and Michael Coyle, eds, *The Right Relationship: Reimagining the Implementation of Historical Treaties*, 17–38. Toronto: University of Toronto Press.

———, and Michael Coyle. 2017. "Introduction." In John Borrows and Michael Coyle, eds, *The Right Relationship: Reimagining the Implementation of Historical Treaties*, 3–16. Toronto: University of Toronto Press.

"British North America Act, 1867," 30-31 Vict., c. 3 (U.K.). *Department of Justice*. Accessed 18 April 2019. http://www.justice.gc.ca/eng/rp-pr/csj-sjc/constitution/lawreg-loireg/p1t11.html.

Call to Action #45.Truth and Reconciliation Commission of Canada (TRC). http://trctalk.ca/call-to-action-45.

"The Canadian Constitution." *Department of Justice*. Accessed 18 April 2019. http://www.justice.gc.ca/eng/csj-sjc/just/05.html.

"Constitution Act, 1867." *Justice Laws Website*. Accessed 18 April 2019. http://laws-lois.justice.gc.ca/eng/const/page-1.html.

"Constitution Acts, 1867 to 1982." *Justice Laws Website*. Accessed 18 April 2019. http://laws-lois.justice.gc.ca/eng/const.

"The Declaration of Independence." Accessed 18 April 2019. http://knarf.english.upenn.edu/Docs/decind.html.

Dworkin, Ronald. 1977. *Taking Rights Seriously*. Cambridge, MA: Harvard University Press.

———. 1986. *Law's Empire*. Cambridge, MA: Harvard University Press.

Government of Canada. "Oath of Citizenship." Accessed 18 April 2019. http://www.cic.gc.ca/english/resources/tools/cit/ceremony/oath.asp.

Hirschl, Ran. 2010. *Constitutional Theocracy*. Cambridge, MA: Harvard University Press.

Jai, Julie. 2017. "Bargains Made in Bad Times: How Principles from Modern Treaties Can Reinvigorate Historic Treaties." In John Borrows and Michael Coyle, eds, *The Right Relationship: Reimagining the Implementation of Historical Treaties*, 105–48. Toronto: University of Toronto Press.

Josefsen, Eva. 2010. *The Saami and the National Parliaments: Channels for Political Influence*. Geneva: Inter-Parliamentary Union.

Lijphart, Arend. 1999. *Patterns of Democracy: Government Forms and Performance in Thirty-Six Countries*. New Haven, CT: Yale University Press.

Mills, Aaron. 2017. "What Is a Treaty? On Contract and Mutual Aid." In John Borrows and Michael Coyle, eds, *The Right Relationship: Reimagining the Implementation of Historical Treaties*. Toronto: University of Toronto Press.

Mills, Charles. 1997. *The Racial Contract*. Ithaca, NY: Cornell University Press.

Minsky, Amy. 2017. "Indigenous Communities Have to Lead before Ottawa Hands over Funding, Says Justin Trudeau." *Global News*, 27 June. https://globalnews.ca/news/3559832/liberals-indigenous-funding-justin-trudeau.

Moses, A. Dirk. 2000. "An Antipodean Genocide? The Origins of the Genocidal Moment in the Colonization of Australia." *Journal of Genocide Research* 2(1): 89–106.

Niskanen, William A., and Marian L. Tupy. 2005. "A Hard Look at the European Constitution." Cato Institute, 27 May. https://www.cato.org/publications/commentary/hard-look-european-constitution.

Preamble to the South African constitution passed in 1996. http://www.gov.za/documents/constitution-republic-south-africa-1996-preamble.

"Provincial Districts." In A.H. McLintock, ed., *An Encyclopedia of New Zealand*. Originally published in 1966. Accessed 18 April 2019. http://www.TeAra.govt.nz/en/1966/provinces-and-provincial-districts/page-5.

Riker, William. 1964. *Federalism: Origin, Operation, Significance*. Boston: Little, Brown.

Rodden, Jonathan. 2006. *Hamilton's Paradox: The Promise and Peril of Fiscal Federalism*. Cambridge: Cambridge University Press.

———, Gunnar Eskeland, and Jennie Litvack. 2003. *Fiscal Decentralization and the Challenge of Hard Budget Constraints*. Cambridge, MA: MIT Press.

Russell, Peter. 2017. *Canada's Odyssey: A Country Based on Incomplete Conquests*. Toronto: University of Toronto Press.

Sartori, Giovanni. 1994. *Comparative Constitutional Engineering: An Enquiry into Structures, Incentives, and Outcomes*. New York: New York University Press.

Schwartz, Daniel. 2013. "How does Native Funding Work?" CBC News, 6 February. http://www.cbc.ca/news/canada/how-does-native-funding-work-1.1301120.

Stepan, Alfred. 1999. "Federalism and Democracy: Beyond the U.S. Model." *Journal of Democracy* 10(4): 19–34.

Wibbels, Erik. 2005. *Federalism and the Market: Intergovernmental Conflict and Economic Reform in the Developing World*. Cambridge: Cambridge University Press.

Chapter 9

Cox, Gary, and Matthew McCubbins. 1993. *Legislative Leviathan: Party Government in the House*. Berkeley: University of California Press.

Duverger, Maurice. 1954. *Political Parties: Their Organization and Activity in the Modern State*. Trans. Barbara North and Robert North. London: Methuen.

Mayhew, David. 1974. *Congress: The Electoral Connection*. New Haven, CT: Yale University Press.

Mezey, Michael. 1979. *Comparative Legislatures*. Durham, NC: Duke University Press.

Morgenstern, Scott, and Benito Nacif, eds. 2002. *Legislative Politics in Latin America*. Cambridge: Cambridge University Press.

"NDP Announces BC Referendum on Proportional Representation." 2017. CBC News, 4 October. http://www.cbc.ca/news/canada/british-columbia/bc-referendum-proportional-representation-referendum-1.4329417.

"Parliament Prayer Changes—No More Queen or Jesus." 2017. *Stuff*, 10 November. https://www.stuff.co.nz/national/politics/98742522/parliament-prayer-changes--no-more-queen-or-jesus.

Shepsle, Kenneth, and Barry Weingast. 1981. "Structure-Induced Equilibrium and Legislative Choice." *Public Choice* 37: 509–19.

"Trump Declares a National Emergency, and Provokes a Constitutional Crisis." 2019. *New York Times*, 15 February. https://www.nytimes.com/2019/02/15/us/politics/national-emergency-trump.html.

Chapter 10

Aberbach, Joel, Robert Putnam, and Bert Rockman. 1981. *Bureaucrats and Politicians in Western Democracies*. Cambridge, MA: Harvard University Press.

Brownlee, Jason. 2007. *Authoritarianism in an Age of Democratization*. Cambridge: Cambridge University Press.

CBC Archives. "The Day Joe Clark's Short-Lived PC Government Came to an End." Posted 13 December 2018. https://www. cbc.ca/archives/the-day-joe-clark-s-short-lived-pc-government-came-to-an-end-1.4941568.

Furi, Megan. 2008. "Public Service Impartiality: Taking Stock." Public Service Commission of Canada, July. http://publications.gc.ca/collection_2008/psc-cfp/SC3-132-2008E.pdf.

Geddes, Barbara. 1990. "How the Cases You Choose Affect the Answers You Get: Selection Bias in Comparative Politics." *Political Analysis* 2(1): 131–50. https://www.google.ca/search?q=joe+clark+canaada+vote+of+non+confidence&ie=utf-8&oe=utf-8&client=firefox-b&gfe_rd=cr&dcr=0&ei=t2BqWvTfKIiR8QfdsJGICA.

———. 1994. *Politician's Dilemma: Building State Capacity in Latin America*. Berkeley: University of California Press.

Levitsky, Steven, and Lucan A. Way. 2010. *Competitive Authoritarianism: Hybrid Regimes after the Cold War*. New York: Cambridge University Press.

Lijphart, Arend. 1999. *Patterns of Democracy: Government Forms and Performance in Thirty-Six Democracies*. New Haven, CT: Yale University Press.

Neustadt, Richard. 1960. *Presidential Power*. New York: John Wiley and Sons.

Nordhaus, William. 1975. "The Political Business Cycle." *Review of Economic Studies* 42(2): 169–90.

Chapter 11

Associated Press. 2017. "Jimmy Carter Says US Has Become More an 'Oligarchy Than a Democracy' in Speech Critical of Trump." *The Telegraph*, 13 September. https://www.telegraph.co.uk/news/2017/09/13/jimmy-carter-says-us-has-become-oligarchy-democracy-speech-critical.

Collier, Ruth Berins, and David Collier. [1991] 2002. *Shaping the Political Arena: Critical Junctures, the Labor Movement, and Regime Dynamics in Latin America*. Notre Dame, IN: University of Notre Dame Press.

Dahl, Robert. 1989. *Democracy and Its Critics*. New Haven, CT: Yale University Press.

Evans, Peter. 1995. *Embedded Autonomy: States and Industrial Transformation*. Princeton, NJ: Princeton University Press.

Fukuyama, Francis. 1992. *The End of History and the Last Man*. New York: The Free Press.

Government of Nunavut. "Consensus Government." Accessed 18 April 2019. https://www.gov.nu.ca/consensus-government.

Katzenstein, Peter. 1985. *Small States in World Markets: Industrial Policy in Europe*. Ithaca, NY: Cornell University Press.

Kirchheimer, Otto. 1966. *The Transformation of Western European Party Systems*. Princeton, NJ: Princeton University Press.

Kitschelt, Herbert. 1994. *The Transformation of European Social Democracy*. Cambridge: Cambridge University Press.

Laakso, Markku, and Rein Taagepera. 1979. "'Effective' Number of Parties: A Measure with Application to West Europe." *Comparative Political Studies* 12(1): 3–27.

Lenin, Vladimir Il'ich. 1902. "What Is to Be Done? Burning Questions of Our Movement." https://www.marxists.org/archive/lenin/works/download/what-itd.pdf.

Lijphart, Arend. 1999. *Patterns of Democracy: Government Forms and Performance in Thirty-Six Countries*. New Haven, CT: Yale University Press.

Mainwaring, Scott, and Timothy Scully, eds. 1995. *Building Democratic Institutions: Party Systems in Latin America*. Cambridge: Cambridge University Press.

Marx, Karl, and Friedrich Engels. [1848] 1998. *The Communist Manifesto*. New York: Verso.

Mayhew, David. 1974. *Congress: The Electoral Connection*. New Haven, CT: Yale University Press.

Michels, Robert. [1911] 1962. *Political Parties: A Sociological Study of the Oligarchical Tendencies of Modern Democracy*. Trans. Eden Paul and Cedar Paul. New York: The Free Press.

Rae, Douglas. 1968. "A Note on the Fractionalization of Some European Party Systems." *Comparative Political Studies* 1(3): 413–18.

Sartori, Giovanni. 1976. *Parties and Party Systems: A Framework for Analysis*. New York: Cambridge University Press.

Schmitter, Philippe. 1974. "Still the Century of Corporatism?" *The Review of Politics* 36(1): 85–131.
Wiarda, Howard. 1997. *Corporatism and Comparative Politics: The Other Great "Ism."* New York: M.E. Sharpe.
Yarvin, Jessica. 2017. "Is Socialism in the United States Having a Moment?" *PBS News Hour*, 27 March. https://www.pbs.org/newshour/politics/socialism-united-states-moment.
Zakaria, Fareed. 1994. "Culture Is Destiny: A Conversation with Lee Kuan Yew." *Foreign Affairs* 73: 113.

Chapter 12

Alvarez, Sonia E., Evelina Dagnino, and Arturo Escobar. 1998. "Introduction: The Cultural and the Political in Latin American Social Movements." In Sonia E. Alvarez, Evelina Dagnino, and Arturo Escobar, eds, *Cultures of Politics, Politics of Cultures: Re-visioning Latin American Social Movements*, 1–32. Boulder, CO: Westview Press.
Arendt, Hannah. 1963. *On Revolution*. New York: Viking Press.
Belkin, Aaron, and Evan Schofer. 2003. "Toward a Structural Understanding of Coup Risk." *Journal of Conflict Resolution* 47(5): 594–620.
Benford, Robert D., and David A. Snow. 2000. "Framing Processes and Social Movements: An Overview and Assessment." *Annual Review of Sociology* 26: 611–39.
Bergesen, Albert J., and Omar Lizardo. 2004. "International Terrorism and the World System." *Sociological Theory* 22(1): 38–52.
Black, Donald. 2004. "The Geometry of Terrorism." *Sociological Theory* 22(1): 14–25.
Brinton, Crane. 1952. *The Anatomy of Revolution*. New York: Prentice-Hall.
Buechler, Steven M. 2004. "The Strange Career of Strain and Breakdown Theories of Collective Action." In David A. Snow, Sarah A. Soule, and Hanspeter Kriesi, eds, *The Blackwell Companion to Social Movements*, 47–66. Malden, MA: Blackwell.
Burns, Stewart, ed. 1997. *Daybreak of Freedom: The Montgomery Bus Boycott*. Chapel Hill: University of North Carolina Press.
Canadian Press. 2012. "Canada Froze $4.3B in Assets to Support Arab Spring." CBC News, 15 July. http://www.cbc.ca/news/canada/canada-froze-4-3b-in-assets-to-support-arab-spring-1.1175811.
Castells, Manuel. 2010. *The Power of Identity*. 2nd edn. Malden, MA: Wiley-Blackwell.
Centeno, Miguel A. 2002. *Blood and Debt: War and the Nation-State in Latin America*. University Park: Pennsylvania State University Press.
Coleman, James S. 1990. *Foundations of Social Theory*. Cambridge, MA: Belknap Press of Harvard University Press.
Finkel, Steven E., Edward N. Muller, and Karl-Dieter Opp. 1989. "Personal Influence, Collective Rationality, and Mass Political Action." *American Political Science Review* 83(3): 885–903.
Foran, John. 2005. *Taking Power: On the Origins of Third World Revolutions*. New York: Cambridge University Press.
Gamson, William A. 1992. *Talking Politics*. New York: Cambridge University Press.
Gibbs, Jack. 1989. "Conceptualization of Terrorism." *American Sociological Review* 54(3): 329–40.
Goffman, Erving. 1974. *Frame Analysis: An Essay on the Organization of Experience*. Cambridge, MA: Harvard University Press.
Goldstone, Jack. 1991. *Revolution and Rebellion in the Early Modern World*. Berkeley: University of California Press.
——— 2001. "Toward a Fourth Generation of Revolutionary Theory." *Annual Review of Political Science* 4: 139–87.
Greenfeld, Liah. 1995. "Russian Nationalism as a Medium of Revolution: An Exercise in Historical Sociology." *Qualitative Sociology* 18(2): 189–209.
Gurr, Ted. 1970. *Why Men Rebel*. Princeton, NJ: Princeton University Press.
Hobsbawm, Eric. 1981. *Bandits*. New York: Pantheon Books.
Hunt, Scott A., and Robert D. Benford. 2004. "Collective Identity, Solidarity, and Commitment." In David A. Snow, Sarah A. Soule, and Hanspeter Kriesi, eds, *The Blackwell Companion to Social Movements*, 433–57. Malden, MA: Blackwell.
Huntington, Samuel. 1968. *Political Order in Changing Societies*. New Haven, CT: Yale University Press.
Johnson, Thomas H., Robert O. Slater, and Pat McGowan. 1984. "Explaining African Military Coups d'État, 1960–1982." *American Political Science Review* 78(3): 622–40.
Kalyvas, Stathis. 2007. "Civil Wars." In Carles Boix and Susan C. Stokes, eds, *Oxford Handbook of Comparative Politics*, 416–34. New York: Oxford University Press.
Katz, Mark. 1999. *Revolutions and Revolutionary Waves*. New York: St Martin's Press.
Kumar, Krishan. 2005. "Revolution." In Maryanne Cline Horowitz, ed., *The New Dictionary of the History of Ideas*, vol. 5, 2112–21. Detroit: Charles Scribner's Sons.
Levitz, Stephanie. 2013. "Arab Spring Caught Canada by Surprise: Government Report." *Huffington Post*, 5 June. http://www.huffingtonpost.ca/2013/05/06/arab-spring-canada-government-report_n_3224719.html.
Lichbach, Mark Irving. 1995. *The Rebel's Dilemma*. Ann Arbor: University of Michigan Press.
——— 1998. "Contending Theories of Contentious Politics and the Structure-Action Problem of Social Order." *Annual Review of Political Science* 1: 401–24.
Lindholm, Charles, and José Pedro Zúquete. 2010. *The Struggle for the World: Liberation Movements for the 21st Century*. Stanford, CA: Stanford University Press.
McAdam, Doug. 1982. *Political Process and the Development of Black Insurgency, 1930–1970*. Chicago: University of Chicago Press.
——— 1996. "Conceptual Origins, Current Problems, Future Directions." In Doug McAdam, John D. McCarthy, and Mayer N. Zald, eds, *Comparative Perspectives on Social Movements: Political Opportunities, Mobilizing Structures, and Cultural Framings*, 23–37. New York: Cambridge University Press.
Martin, William G., ed. 2008. *Making Waves: Worldwide Social Movements, 1750–2005*. Boulder, CO: Paradigm Publishers.

Melucci, Alberto. 1989. *Nomads of the Present: Social Movements and Individual Needs in Contemporary Societies*. Philadelphia: Temple University Press.

Metelits, Claire. 2009. *Inside Insurgency: Violence, Civilians, and Revolutionary Group Behavior*. New York: New York University Press.

Meyer, David S., and Sidney Tarrow, eds. 1998. *The Social Movement Society: Contentious Politics for a New Century*. Lanham, MD: Rowman and Littlefield.

Michels, Robert. [1911] 1962. *Political Parties: A Sociological Study of the Oligarchical Tendencies of Modern Democracy*. Trans. Eden Paul and Cedar Paul. New York: The Free Press.

Oberschall, Anthony. 2004. "Explaining Terrorism: The Contribution of Collective Action Theory." *Sociological Theory* 22(1): 26–37.

O'Leary, Brendan, and Andrew Silke. 2007. "Conclusion: Understanding and Ending Persistent Conflicts: Bridging Research and Policy." In Marianne Heiberg, Brendan O'Leary, and John Tirman, eds, *Terror, Insurgency, and the State: Ending Protracted Conflicts*, 387–426. Philadelphia: University of Pennsylvania Press.

O'Leary, Brendan, and John Tirman. 2007. "Introduction: Thinking about Durable Political Violence." In Marianne Heiberg, Brendan O'Leary, and John Tirman, eds, *Terror, Insurgency, and the State: Ending Protracted Conflicts*, 1–17. Philadelphia: University of Pennsylvania Press.

Oliver, Pamela E., and Hank Johnston. 2000. "What a Good Idea! Ideologies and Frames in Social Movement Research." *Mobilization: An International Journal* 4(1): 37–54.

Olson, Mancur, Jr. 1965. *The Logic of Collective Action: Public Goods and the Theory of Groups*. Cambridge, MA: Harvard University Press.

Parsa, Misagh. 2000. *States, Ideologies, and Social Revolutions: A Comparative Analysis of Iran, Nicaragua, and the Philippines*. New York: Cambridge University Press.

Pérez Díaz, Victor. 2014. "Civil Society: A Multi-Layered Concept." *Current Sociology* 62(6): 812–30.

Pincus, Steven. 2007. "Rethinking Revolutions: A Neo-Tocquevillian Perspective." In Carles Boix and Susan C. Stokes, eds, *The Oxford Handbook of Comparative Politics*, 397–415. New York: Oxford University Press.

Podur, Justin. 2017. "Workers Strike against Poverty Wages at York University." *Ricochet*, 22 February. https://ricochet.media/en/1692/workers-strike-against-poverty-wages-at-york-university.

Powell, Jonathan, and Clayton Thyne. 2011. "Global Instances of Coups from 1950 to 2010: A New Dataset." *Journal of Peace Research* 48(2): 249–59.

Rummell, R.J. 1997. *Statistics of Democide: Genocide and Mass Murder since 1990*. Charlottesville, VA: Center for National Security Law, School of Law, University of Virginia.

Sanderson, Stephen K. 2010. *Revolutions: A Worldwide Introduction to Social and Political Contention*. 2nd edn. Boulder, CO: Paradigm Publishers.

Scott, James C. 1985. *Weapons of the Weak: Everyday Forms of Peasant Resistance*. New Haven, CT: Yale University Press.

Senechal de la Roche, Roberta. 2004. "Toward a Scientific Theory of Terrorism." *Sociological Theory* 22(1): 1–4.

Shils, Edward. 1997. *The Virtue of Civility: Selected Essays on Liberty, Tradition, and Civil Society*. Ed. Steven Grosby. Indianapolis: Liberty Fund.

Skocpol, Theda. 1979. *States and Social Revolutions: A Comparative Analysis of France, Russia, and China*. New York: Cambridge University Press.

——— 1994. *Social Revolutions in the Modern World*. New York: Cambridge University Press.

Smelser, Neil J. 1962. *Theory of Collective Behavior*. New York: The Free Press.

Tarrow, Sidney. 2005. *The New Transnational Activism*. New York: Cambridge University Press.

——— 2011. *Power in Movement: Social Movements, Collective Action, and Politics*. 3rd edn. New York: Cambridge University Press.

Tilly, Charles. 2004. "Terror, Terrorism, Terrorists." *Sociological Theory* 22(1): 5–13.

———. and Sidney Tarrow. 2007. *Contentious Politics*. Boulder, CO: Paradigm Publishers.

Toch, Hans. 1965. *The Social Psychology of Social Movements*. Indianapolis: Bobbs-Merrill.

Tullock, Gordon. 1971. "The Paradox of Revolution." *Public Choice* 11(1): 89–99.

Weber, Max. 1946. "Class, Status, and Party." In Hans H. Gerth and C. Wright Mills, eds and trans, *From Max Weber: Essays in Sociology*, 180–95. New York: Oxford University Press.

Chapter 13

Anderson, Benedict. [1983] 1991. *Imagined Communities: Reflections on the Origin and Spread of Nationalism*. New York: Verso.

Brewer, Marilynn B., and Wendi Gardner. 1996. "Who Is This 'We'? Levels of Collective Identity and Self Representations." *Journal of Personality and Social Psychology* 71(1): 83–93.

Brubaker, Rogers. 1992. *Citizenship and Nationhood in France and Germany*. Cambridge, MA: Harvard University Press.

——— 1999. "The Manichean Myth: Rethinking the Distinction between 'Civic' and 'Ethnic' Nationalism." In Hanspeter Kriesi, Klaus Armingeon, Hannes Siegrist, and Andreas Wimmer, eds, *Nation and National Identity: The European Experience in Perspective*, 55–71. Zurich: Verlag Ruller.

———, and David D. Laitin. 1998. "Ethnic and Nationalist Violence." *Annual Review of Sociology* 24: 423–52.

Calhoun, Craig. 1997. *Nationalism*. Minneapolis: University of Minnesota Press.

Cederman, Lars-Erik, Andreas Wimmer, and Brian Min. 2010. "Why Do Ethnic Groups Rebel? New Data and Analysis." *World Politics* 62(1): 87–119.

Chirot, Daniel. 2001. "Introduction." In Daniel Chirot and Martin Seligman, eds, *Ethnopolitical Warfare: Causes, Consequences, and Possible Solutions*, 3–26. Washington, DC: American Psychological Association.

Drumbl, Mark A. 2007. *Atrocity, Punishment, and International Law*. New York: Cambridge University Press.

Fearon, James D., and David D. Laitin. 1996. "Explaining Interethnic Cooperation." *American Political Science Review* 90(4): 715–35.

——— 2003. "Ethnicity, Insurgency, and Civil War." *American Political Science Review* 97(1): 75–90.

Garner, Robert, Peter Ferdinand, Stephanie Lawson, and David B. MacDonald. 2016. "The Academic Study of Nationalism." In Robert Garner, Peter Ferdinand, Stephanie Lawson, and David B. MacDonald, eds, *Introduction to Politics*, 2nd Canadian edn, 100–1. Toronto: Oxford University Press Canada.

Gellner, E. 1983. *Nations and Nationalism*. Oxford: Blackwell.

Greenfeld, Liah. 1992. *Nationalism: Five Roads to Modernity*. Cambridge, MA: Harvard University Press.

——— 2001. *The Spirit of Capitalism: Nationalism and Economic Growth*. Cambridge, MA: Harvard University Press.

———, and Daniel Chirot. 1994. "Nationalism and Aggression." *Theory and Society* 23: 79–130.

———, and Jonathan Eastwood. 2007. "National Identity." In Carles Boix and Susan C. Stokes, eds, *Oxford Handbook of Comparative Politics*, 256–73. New York: Oxford University Press.

Harff, Barbara. 2003. "No Lessons Learned from the Holocaust? Assessing Risks of Genocide and Political Mass Murder since 1955." *American Political Science Review* 97(1): 57–73.

———, and Ted Robert Gurr. 2004. *Ethnic Conflict in World Politics*. 2nd edn. Boulder, CO: Westview Press.

Hechter, Michael. 2000. *Containing Nationalism*. New York: Oxford University Press.

Horowitz, Donald L. 1985. *Ethnic Groups in Conflict*. Berkeley: University of California Press.

——— 2001. *The Deadly Ethnic Riot*. Berkeley: University of California Press.

Jowitt, Ken. 2001. "Ethnicity: Nice, Nasty, and Nihilistic." In Daniel Chirot and Martin Seligman, eds, *Ethno-Political Warfare: Causes, Consequences, and Possible Solutions*, 27–36. Washington, DC: American Psychological Association.

Kaufman, Stuart. 2001. *Modern Hatreds: The Symbolic Politics of Ethnic War*. Ithaca, NY: Cornell University Press.

Kohn, Hans. 1944. *The Idea of Nationalism: A Study in Its Origin and Background*. New York: MacMillan.

Laitin, David. 2007. *Nations, States, and Violence*. New York: Oxford University Press.

Lamont, Michele, and Virág Molnár. 2002. "The Study of Boundaries in the Social Sciences." *Annual Review of Sociology* 28: 167–95.

Lemarchand, René. 2007. "Consociationalism and Power Sharing in Africa: Rwanda, Burundi, and the Democratic Republic of the Congo." *African Affairs* 106(422): 1–20.

Lijphart, Arend. 1977. *Democracy in Plural Societies: A Comparative Exploration*. New Haven, CT: Yale University Press.

Marx, Anthony W. 2003. *Faith in Nation: Exclusionary Origins of Nationalism*. New York: Oxford University Press.

Özkirimli, Umut. 2000. *Theories of Nationalism: A Critical Introduction*. Basingstoke, UK: Palgrave Macmillan.

Petersen, Roger D. 2002. *Understanding Ethnic Violence: Fear, Hatred, and Resentment in Twentieth-Century Eastern Europe*. New York: Cambridge University Press.

Pettigrew, Thomas F., and Linda R. Tropp. 2011. *When Groups Meet: The Dynamics of Intergroup Contact*. London: Psychology Press.

Sikkink, Kathryn. 2011. *The Justice Cascade: How Human Rights Prosecutions Are Changing World Politics*. New York: W.W. Norton.

Smith, Anthony D. 1986. *The Ethnic Origins of Nations*. Malden, MA: Blackwell.

——— 1990. *National Identity*. London: Penguin.

——— 1996. "The 'Golden Age' and National Renewal." In G. Hosking and G. Schöpflin, eds, *Myths and Nationhood*, 36–59. London: C. Hurst.

——— 1998. *Nationalism and Modernism: A Critical Survey of Recent Theories of Nations and Nationalism*. London: Routledge.

——— 2010. *Nationalism*. Cambridge: Polity Press.

Snyder, Jack. 2000. *From Voting to Violence: Democratization and Nationalist Conflict*. New York: W.W. Norton.

Stets, Jan E., and Peter J. Burke. 2000. "Identity Theory and Social Identity Theory." *Social Psychology Quarterly* 63(3): 224–37.

Tajfel, Henri. 1981. *Human Groups and Social Categories: Studies in Social Psychology*. New York: Cambridge University Press.

Teitel, Ruti. 2011. *Humanity's Law*. New York: Oxford University Press.

Varshney, Ashutosh. 2002. *Ethnic Conflict and Civic Life: Hindus and Muslims in India*. New Haven, CT: Yale University Press.

Chapter 14

American Anthropological Association. *Race: Are We So Different?* (Project) Accessed 18 April 2019. http://www.understandingrace.org/home.html.

Barth, Fredrik, ed. 1969. *Ethnic Groups and Boundaries: The Social Organization of Culture Difference*. Boston: Little, Brown.

Blair-Loy, Mary. 2003. *Competing Devotions: Career and Family among Women Executives*. Cambridge, MA: Harvard University Press.

Blau, Francine D., and Lawrence M. Kahn. 1992. "The Gender Earnings Gap: Learning from International Comparisons." *American Economic Review* 82(2): 533–8.

Blumberg, Rae. 1984. "A General Theory of Gender Stratification." *Sociological Theory* 2: 23–101.

Brown, Michael K., Martin Carnoy, Elliott Currie, Troy Duster, David P. Oppenheimer, Marjorie M. Shultz, and David Wellman. 2003. *Whitewashing Race: The Myth of a Color-Blind Society*. Berkeley: University of California Press.

Cañizares-Esguerra, Jorge. 2009. "Demons, Stars, and the Imagination: The Early Modern Body in the Tropics." In Miriam Eliav-Feldon, Benjamin Isaac, and Joseph Ziegler, eds, *The Origins of Racism in the West*, 313–25. New York: Cambridge University Press.

Carbin, Maria, and Sara Edenheim. 2013. "The Intersectional Turn in Feminist Theory: A Dream of a Common Language?" *European Journal of Women's Studies* 20(3): 233–48.

Cornell, Stephen E., and Douglas Hartmann. 1998. *Ethnicity and Race: Making Identities in a Changing World*. Thousand Oaks, CA: Pine Forge Press.

Corrales, Javier, and Mario Pecheny, eds. 2010. *The Politics of Sexuality in Latin America: A Reader in Lesbian, Gay, Bisexual, and Transgender Rights*. Pittsburgh: University of Pittsburgh Press, 2010.

Costa, Paul T., Jr., Antonio Terracciano, and Robert R. McCrae. 2001. "Gender Differences in Personality Traits across Cultures: Robust and Surprising Findings." *Journal of Personality and Social Psychology* 81(2): 322–31.

Crenshaw, Kimberlé. 1989. "Demarginalizing the Intersection of Race and Sex: A Black Feminist Critique of Antidiscrimination Doctrine, Feminist Theory and Antiracist Politics." University of Chicago Legal Forum, vol. 1989: Iss. 1, Article 8. http://chicagounbound.uchicago.edu/uclf/vol1989/iss1.

de la Dehesa, Rafael. 2010. *Queering the Public Sphere in Mexico and Brazil: Sexual Rights Movements in Emerging Democracies*. Durham, NC: Duke University Press.

Dollar, David, and Roberta Gatti. 1999, May. "Gender Inequality, Income, and Growth: Are Good Times Good for Women?" World Bank Policy Research Report on Gender and Development, Working Paper Series, No. 1.

Dunning, Thad, and Lauren Harrison. 2010. "Cross-Cutting Cleavages and Ethnic Voting: An Experimental Study of Cousinage in Mali." *American Political Science Review* 104(1): 21–39.

Duster, Troy. 2005. "Race and Reification in Science." *Science* 307(5712): 1050–1.

Eccles, Jacquelynne. 1987. "Gender Roles and Women's Achievement-Related Decisions." *Psychology of Women Quarterly* 11(2): 135–72.

England, Paula, Melissa S. Herbert, Barbara Stanek Kilbourne, Lori L. Reid, and Lori McCreary Megdal. 1994. "The Gendered Valuation of Occupations and Skills: Earnings in 1980 Census Occupations." *Social Forces* 73(1): 65–100.

Franceschet, Susan, Mona Lena Krook, and Jennifer M. Piscopo, eds. 2012. *The Impact of Gender Quotas*. New York: Oxford University Press.

Fredrickson, George M. 2003. *Racism: A Short History*. Princeton, NJ: Princeton University Press.

Gans, Herbert J. 2005. "Race as Class." *Contexts* 4(4): 17–21.

Garcia, Y. Evie, and Annel Esparza. 2006. "Internalized Racism." In Yo Jackson, ed., *Encyclopedia of Multicultural Psychology*. Thousand Oaks, CA: Sage.

Garner, Robert, Peter Ferdinand, Stephanie Lawson, and David B. MacDonald. 2017. *Introduction to Politics*. 2nd Canadian edn. Toronto: Oxford University Press Canada.

Gold, Michael. 2018. "The ABC's of L.G.B.T.Q.I.A. +." *New York Times*, 21 June. https://www.nytimes.com/2018/06/21/style/lgbtq-gender-language.html.

Handa, Sudhanshu, and Benjamin Davis. 2006. "The Experience of Conditional Cash Transfers in Latin America and the Caribbean." *Development Policy Review* 5: 513–36.

Haveman, Heather A., and Lauren S. Beresford. 2012. "If You're So Smart, Why Aren't You the Boss? Explaining the Persistent Vertical Gender Gap in Management." *Annals of the American Academy of Political and Social Science* 639(1): 114–30.

Henderson, Sarah L., and Alana S. Jeydel. 2010. *Women and Politics in a Global World*. New York: Oxford University Press.

Herring, Cedric. 2002. "Is Job Discrimination Dead?" *Contexts* 1: 13–18.

Htun, Mala. 2004. "Is Gender Like Ethnicity? The Political Representation of Identity Groups." *Perspectives on Politics* 2(3): 439–58.

Izugbara, C. Otutubikey. 2004. "Gendered Micro-Lending Schemes and Sustainable Women's Empowerment in Nigeria." *Community Development Journal* 39(1): 72–84.

Jaschik, Scott. "Worldwide Paradox for Women." 2011. *Inside Higher Ed*, 15 March. http://www.insidehighered.com/news/2011/03/15/educators_consider_the_partial_progress_of_women_in_higher_education_around_the_world.

Katz, Jonathan Ned. 2007. *The Invention of Heterosexuality*. Chicago: University of Chicago Press.

Khagram, Sanjeev, and Peggy Levitt, eds. 2008. *The Transnational Studies Reader: Intersections and Innovations*. New York: Routledge.

Kimmel, Michael S. 2000. *The Gendered Society*. New York: Oxford University Press.

Krook, Mona Lena. 2009. *Quotas for Women in Politics: Gender and Candidate Selection Reform Worldwide*. New York: Oxford University Press.

Lijphart, Arend. 1977. *Democracy in Plural Societies: A Comparative Exploration*. New Haven, CT: Yale University Press.

Loveman, Mara. 2009. "The Race to Progress: Census Taking and Nation-Making in Brazil (1870–1920)." *Hispanic American Historical Review* 89(3): 435–70.

Lovenduski, Joni. 2005. "Introduction: State Feminism and the Political Representation of Women." In Joni Lovenduski, ed., *State Feminism and Political Representation*, 1–19. New York: Cambridge University Press.

Marx, Anthony. 1998. *Making Race and Nation: A Comparison of South Africa, the United States, and Brazil*. New York: Cambridge University Press.

Matland, Richard E. 1998. "Women's Representation in National Legislatures: Developed and Developing Countries." *Legislative Studies Quarterly* 23(1): 109–25.

Omi, Michael, and Howard Winant. 1994. *Racial Formation in the United States from the 1960s to the 1990s*. 2nd edn. New York: Routledge.

Ong, Aihwa. 1999. *Flexible Citizenship: The Cultural Logics of Trans-Nationality*. Durham, NC: Duke University Press.

Padavic, Irene, and Barbara Reskin. 2002. *Women and Men at Work*. 2nd edn. Thousand Oaks, CA: Pine Forge Press.

Pagden, Anthony. 2009. "The Peopling of the New World: Ethnos, Race, and Empire in the Early Modern World." In Miriam Eliav-Feldon, Benjamin Isaac, and Joseph Ziegler, eds, *The Origins of Racism in the West*, 292–312. New York: Cambridge University Press.

Pager, Devah, and Hana Shepherd. 2008. "The Sociology of Discrimination: Racial Discrimination in Employment, Housing, Credit, and Consumer Markets." *Annual Review of Sociology* 34: 181–209.

Pettit, Becky, and Bruce Western. 2004. "Mass Imprisonment and the Life Course: Race and Class Inequality in U.S. Incarceration." *American Sociological Review* 69(24): 151–69.

Posner, Daniel N. 2005. *Institutions and Ethnic Politics in Africa*. New York: Cambridge University Press.

Rawlings, Laura B., and Gloria M. Rubio. 2005. "Evaluating the Impact of Conditional Cash Transfer Programs." *The World Bank Research Observer* 20(1): 29–55.

Reynolds, Andrew. 2005. "Reserved Seats in National Legislatures: A Research Note." *Legislative Studies Quarterly* 30(2): 301–10.

Ridgeway, Cecilia L., and Shelley J. Correll. 2004. "Unpacking the Gender System: A Theoretical Perspective on Gender Beliefs and Social Relations." *Gender and Society* 18(4): 510–31.

Roediger, David R. 1999. *The Wages of Whiteness: Race and the Making of the American Working Class*. Revised edn. New York: Verso Press.

Roth, Louise Marie. 2006. *Selling Women Short: Gender and Inequality on Wall Street*. Princeton, NJ: Princeton University Press.

Sawer, Marian, Manon Tremblay, and Linda Trimble, eds. 2006. *Representing Women in Parliament: A Comparative Study*. New York: Routledge.

Smith, Anthony D. 1995. *Nations and Nationalism in a Global Era*. Malden, MA: Polity Press.

Sorenson, Aage. 2001. "The Basic Concepts of Stratification Research: Class, Status, and Power." In David B. Grusky, ed., *Social Stratification: Race, Class, and Gender in Sociological Perspective*, 287–300. Boulder, CO: Westview Press.

Squires, Judith. 2007. *The New Politics of Gender Equality*. New York: Palgrave Macmillan.

Stetson, Dorothy McBride, and Amy G. Mazur, eds. 1995. *Comparative State Feminism*. Thousand Oaks, CA: Sage Publications.

Van Cott, Donna Lena. 2005. *From Movements to Parties in Latin America*. New York: Cambridge University Press.

Weber, Max. 1946. "Class, Status, Party." In H.H. Gerth and C. Wright Mills, eds and trans, *From Max Weber: Essays in Sociology*, 180–95. New York: Oxford University Press.

Winn, Peter. 1992. *Americas: The Changing Face of Latin America and the Caribbean*. New York: Pantheon Books.

Yashar, Deborah J. 2005. *Contesting Citizenship in Latin America: The Rise of Indigenous Movements and the Postliberal Challenge*. New York: Cambridge University Press.

Zetterberg, Par. 2009. "Do Gender Quotas Foster Women's Political Engagement? Lessons from Latin America." *Political Research Quarterly* 62(4): 715–30.

Chapter 15

Appadurai, Arjun. 1996. *Modernity at Large: Cultural Dimensions of Globalization*. Minneapolis: University of Minnesota Press.

Asad, Talal. 2003. *Formations of the Secular: Christianity, Islam, Modernity*. Stanford, CA: Stanford University Press, 2003.

BBC. "Religions: Church of England." Last updated 30 June 2011. Accessed 18 April 2019. http://www.bbc.co.uk/religion/religions/christianity/cofe/cofe_1.shtml.

Bell, Daniel. [1960] 2000. *The End of Ideology: On the Exhaustion of Political Ideas in the Fifties*. Cambridge, MA: Harvard University Press.

———. 1977. "The Return of the Sacred? The Argument on the Future of Religion." *British Journal of Sociology* 28(4): 419–49.

Berger, Peter L. 1967. *The Sacred Canopy: Elements of a Sociological Theory of Religion*. New York: Anchor Books.

———. 1974. "Some Second Thoughts on Substantive versus Functional Definitions of Religion." *Journal for the Scientific Study of Religion* 13(2): 125–33.

———, ed. 1999. *The Desecularization of the World: Resurgent Religion and World Politics*. Grand Rapids, MI: William B. Eerdmans Publishing.

———, Brigitte Berger, and Hansfried Kellner. 1973. *The Homeless Mind: Modernization and Consciousness*. New York: Random House.

———, Grace Davie, and Effie Fokas. 2008. *Religious America, Secular Europe? A Theme and Variations*. Burlington, VT: Ashgate.

Blancarte, Roberto, ed. 2008. *Los retos de la laicidad y la secularización en el mundo contemporáneo*. Mexico, DF: El Colegio de México, Centro de Estudios Sociológicos.

Boli, John. 1981. "Marxism as World Religion." *Social Problems* 28(5): 510–13.

Bruce, Steve. 2002. *God is Dead: Secularization in the West*. Malden, MA: Blackwell.

Casanova, José. 1994. *Public Religions in the Modern World*. Chicago: University of Chicago Press.

———. 2007. "Immigration and the New Religious Pluralism: A European Union/United States Comparison." In Thomas Banchoff, ed., *Democracy and the New Religious Pluralism*, 59–84. New York: Oxford University Press.

Chatterjee, Partha. 1993. *The Nation and Its Fragments: Colonial and Postcolonial Histories*. Princeton, NJ: Princeton University Press.

———. 1997. *Our Modernity*. Rotterdam/Dakar: SEPHIS/CODESRIA.

Chaves, Mark. 1994. "Secularization as Declining Religious Authority." *Social Forces* 72(3): 749–74.
———, and Philip S. Gorski. 2001. "Religious Pluralism and Religious Participation." *Annual Review of Sociology* 27: 261–81.
Converse, Philip. 1964. "The Nature of Belief Systems in Mass Publics." In David E. Apter, ed., *Ideology and Discontent*, 206–61. New York: The Free Press.
Coronil, Fernando. 1997. *The Magical State: Nature, Money, and Modernity in Venezuela*. Chicago: University of Chicago Press.
Eisenstadt, Samuel N. 2000. "Multiple Modernities." *Daedalus* 129(1): 1–29.
Finke, Roger, and Laurence R. Iannaccone. 1993. "Supply Side Explanations for Religious Change." *Annals of the American Academy of Political and Social Science* 527: 27–39.
Fox, Jonathan. 2008. *A World Survey of Religion and the State*. New York: Cambridge University Press.
Freston, Paul, ed. 2008. *Evangelical Christianity and Democracy in Latin America*. New York: Oxford University Press.
Fukuyama, Francis. 1992. *The End of History and the Last Man*. New York: The Free Press.
Geertz, Clifford. 1973a. "Ideology as a Cultural System." In Clifford Geertz, ed., *The Interpretation of Cultures*, 193–233. New York: Basic Books.
———. 1973b. "Religion as a Cultural System." In Clifford Geertz, *The Interpretation of Cultures*, 87–125. New York: Basic Books.
Gerring, John. 1997. "Ideology: A Definitional Analysis." *Political Research Quarterly* 50(4): 957–94.
Gorski, Philip S., and Ates Altinordu. 2008. "After Secularization?" *Annual Review of Sociology* 34: 55–85.
Greenfeld, Liah. 1996. "The Modern Religion?" *Critical Review: A Journal of Politics and Society* 10(2): 169–91.
Hawkins, Kirk A. 2010. *Venezuela's Chavismo and Populism in Comparative Perspective*. New York: Cambridge University Press.
Hutchins, Aaron. 2015. "What Canadians Really Believe: A Surprising Poll." *Maclean's*, 26 March. http://www.macleans.ca/society/life/what-canadians-really-believe.
Inglehart, Ronald, and Christian Welzel. 2005. *Modernization, Cultural Change, and Democracy: The Human Development Sequence*. Cambridge: Cambridge University Press.
Inkeles, Alex, and David H. Smith. 1974. *Becoming Modern: Individual Change in Six Developing Countries*. Cambridge, MA: Harvard University Press.
James, William. 1902. *Varieties of Religious Experience: A Study in Human Nature*. New York: Longmans, Green.
Juergensmeyer, Mark. 1993. *The New Cold War? Religious Nationalism Confronts the Secular State*. Berkeley: University of California Press.
Kaufmann, Eric. 2010. *Shall the Religious Inherit the Earth? Demography and Politics in the Twenty-First Century*. London: Profile Books.
Kepel, Gilles. 1994. *The Revenge of God: The Resurgence of Islam, Christianity, and Judaism in the Modern World*. University Park: Pennsylvania State University Press.
Laclau, Ernesto. 2005. *On Populist Reason*. London: Polity Press.
Levitsky, Steven, and Kenneth M. Roberts, eds. 2011. *The Resurgence of the Latin American Left*. Baltimore, MD: Johns Hopkins University Press.
Lindholm, Charles, and Pedro Zúquete. 2010. *The Struggle for the World: Liberation Movements for the Twenty-First Century*. Stanford, CA: Stanford University Press.
Martin, David L. 2005. *On Secularization: Towards a Revised General Theory*. Burlington, VT: Ashgate.
Marx, Karl (with Friedrich Engels). 1978a. "Manifesto of the Communist Party." In Robert C. Tucker, ed., *The Marx-Engels Reader*, 469–500. New York: W.W. Norton.
Marx, Karl. 1978b. "On the Jewish Question." In Robert C. Tucker, ed., *The Marx-Engels Reader*, 26–52. New York: W.W. Norton.
Meyer, John W., John Boli, George M. Thomas, and Francisco O. Ramírez. 1997. "World Society and the Nation-State." *American Journal of Sociology* 103(1): 144–81.
Moaddel, Mansoor. 2005. *Islamic Modernism, Nationalism and Fundamentalism: Episode and Discourse*. Chicago: University of Chicago Press.
Mudde, Cas. 2004. "Populist Zeitgeist." *Government and Opposition* 39(4): 541–63. https://doi.org/10.1111/j.1477-7053.2004.00135.x.
———, and C. Rovira Kaltwasser. 2013. "Exclusionary vs. Inclusionary Populism: Comparing Contemporary Europe and Latin America." *Government and Opposition* 48(2): 147–74. doi:10.1017/gov.2012.11.
Müller, Jan-Werner. 2016. "What Is Populism?" Philadelphia: University of Pennsylvania Press
Niebuhr, H. Richard. 1929. *The Social Sources of Denominationalism*. New York: Henry Holt.
Norris, Pippa, and Ronald Inglehart. 2004. *Sacred and Secular: Religion and Politics Worldwide*. New York: Cambridge University Press.
Nye, Joseph. 1990. "Soft Power." *Foreign Policy* 80: 153–71.
Ostiguy, Pierre, and Kenneth M. Roberts. 2016. "Putting Trump in Comparative Perspective." *Journal of World Affairs* 23(1): 25–50.
Payne, Stanley. 1995. *A History of Fascism, 1914–1945*. Madison: University of Wisconsin Press.
Smilde, David, and Daniel Hellinger, eds. 2011. *Venezuela's Bolivarian Democracy: Participation, Politics, and Culture under Chávez*. Durham, NC: Duke University Press.
———, and Coraly Pagan. 2011. "Christianity and Politics in Venezuela's Bolivarian Democracy: Catholics, Evangelicals, and Political Polarization." In David Smilde and Daniel Hellinger, eds, *Venezuela's Bolivarian Democracy: Participation, Politics, and Culture under Chávez*, 315–39. Durham, NC: Duke University Press.
Smith, Christian, ed. 2003. *The Secular Revolution: Power, Interests, and Conflict in the Secularization of American Public Life*. Berkeley: University of California Press.
Stark, Rodney. 1999. "Secularization, R.I.P." *Sociology of Religion* 60(3): 249–73.

Stepan, Alfred C. 2000. "Religion, Democracy, and the 'Twin Tolerations.'" *Journal of Democracy* 11(4): 37–57.

Troeltsch, Ernst. 1969. "Three Types of Christian Community." In Norman Birnbaum and Gertrude Lenzer, eds, *Sociology of Religion: A Book of Readings*, 310–14. Englewood Cliffs, NJ: Prentice-Hall.

Voas, David, Alasdair Crockett, and Daniel V.A. Olson. 2002. "Religious Pluralism and Participation: Why Previous Research Is Wrong." *American Sociological Review* 67(2): 212–30.

Warner, R. Stephen. 1993. "Work in Progress toward a New Paradigm for the Sociological Study of Religion in the United States." *American Journal of Sociology* 98(5): 1044–93.

Weber, Max. 1958. "Science as a Vocation." In H.H. Gerth and C. Wright Mills, eds and trans., *From Max Weber: Essays in Sociology*, 129–156. New York: Oxford University Press.

———. 1969. "Church and Sect." In Norman Birnbaum and Gertrude Lenzer, eds, *Sociology of Religion: A Book of Readings*, 318–22. Englewood Cliffs, NJ: Prentice-Hall.

Weyland, Kurt. 2001. "Clarifying a Contested Concept: Populism in the Study of Latin American Politics." *Comparative Politics* 34(1): 1–22.

Woodberry, Robert D. 2011. "Religion and the Spread of Human Capital and Political Institutions: Christian Missions as a Quasi-Natural Experiment." In R. McCleary, ed., *The Oxford Handbook of the Economics of Religion*, 111–31. New York: Oxford University Press.

———, and Timothy S. Shah. 2004. "The Pioneering Protestants." *Journal of Democracy* 15(2): 47–61.

Chapter 16

Allison, Graham. 1971. *The Essence of Decision: Explaining the Cuban Missile Crisis*. Boston: Little, Brown.

Arms Control Association. "The Nuclear Testing Tally—Fact Sheets & Briefs." Updated February 2019. https://www.armscontrol.org/factsheets/nucleartesttally.

Axelrod, Robert, and William D. Hamilton. 1981. "The Evolution of Cooperation." *Science* 211: 1390–6.

Burke, Jason. "Al Qaeda." *Foreign Policy* 142: 18–26.

Doyle, Michael. 1983a. "Kant, Liberal Legacies, and Foreign Affairs." *Philosophy & Public Affairs* 12(3): 205–35.

———. 1983b. "Kant, Liberal Legacies, and Foreign Affairs, Part 2." *Philosophy & Public Affairs* 12(4): 323–53.

———. 1997. *Ways of War and Peace: Realism, Liberalism, and Socialism*. New York: W.W. Norton.

European Commission. "Countries and Regions: Canada." Accessed 18 April 2019. http://ec.europa.eu/trade/policy/countries-and-regions/countries/canada.

Friedman, Thomas. 2005. *The World Is Flat: A Brief History of the Twenty-First Century*. New York: Farrar, Strauss, and Giroux.

Gourevitch, Peter. 1978. "The Second Image Reversed: The International Sources of Domestic Politics." *International Organization* 32: 881–912.

Hobbes, Thomas. [1651] 1996. *Leviathan*. Cambridge: Cambridge University Press.

Huntington, Samuel. 2004. *Who Are We? The Challenges to America's National Identity*. New York: Simon and Schuster.

Intergovernmental Panel on Climate Change (IPCC). *Climate Change 2007: Synthesis Report*. Accessed 18 April 2019. http://www.ipcc.ch.

Jacobs, Ben. 2018. "Trump Defends Mexican Rapists Claim during Conspiracy-Laden Speech." *The Guardian*, 5 April. https://www.theguardian.com/us-news/2018/apr/05/trump-mexico-caravan-voter-claims-speech-west-virginia.

Johnston, Ian. 2017. "Brexit: Anti-Immigrant Prejudice Major Factor in Deciding Vote, Study Finds." *The Independent*, 22 June. https://www.independent.co.uk/news/uk/politics/brexit-racism-immigrant-prejudice-major-factor-leave-vote-win-study-a7801676.html.

Keck, Margaret, and Kathryn Sikkink. 1998. *Activists beyond Borders: Advocacy Networks in International Politics*. Ithaca, NY: Cornell University Press.

Keohane, Robert O. 1984. *After Hegemony: Cooperation and Discord in the World Political Economy*. Princeton, NJ: Princeton University Press.

———, and Joseph S. Nye. 1977. *Power and Interdependence: World Politics in Transition*. Boston: Little, Brown.

Lenin, Vladimir Il'ich. [1917] 1996. *Imperialism: The Highest Stage of Capitalism*. London: Pluto Press.

Machiavelli, Niccolò. [1532] 1984. *The Prince*. New York: Bantam Books.

McHugh, David. 2018. "Another Euro Crisis? Chaos Hits Italy's Financial Markets." *Huffington Post*, 29 May. https://www.huffingtonpost.ca/2018/05/29/italy-euro-crisis-italexit_a_23446021.

Mearsheimer, John. 2001. *The Tragedy of Great Power Politics*. New York: W.W. Norton.

Moravcsik, Andrew. 1997. "Taking Preferences Seriously: A Liberal Theory of International Politics." *International Organization* 51(4): 513–53.

Ostrom, Elinor. 1990. *Governing the Commons: The Evolution of Institutions for Collective Action*. Cambridge: Cambridge University Press.

Portes, Alejandro, and Rubén G. Rumbaut. 2006. *Immigrant America: A Portrait*. 3rd edn. Berkeley: University of California Press.

Putnam, Robert. 1988. "Diplomacy and Domestic Politics: The Logic of Two-Level Games." *International Organization* 42: 427–60.

Rogowski, Ronald. 1987. "Political Cleavages and Changing Exposure to Trade." *American Political Science Review* 81(4): 1121–37.

Said, Edward. 1978. *Orientalism*. New York: Vintage.

Scottish National Party (SNP). 2016. "Manifesto for the Islands." 4 April. https://www.snp.org/manifesto-for-the-islands.

———. "SNP Store." Accessed 18 April 2019. https://www.snpstore.org.

Singer, Peter. 2004. *One World: The Ethics of Globalization*. New Haven, CT: Yale University Press.

Statistics Canada. 2017. "Immigration and Ethnocultural Diversity: Key Results from the 2016 Census." Released on 25 October. https://www150.statcan.gc.ca/n1/daily-quotidien/171025/dq171025b-eng.htm.

Stiglitz, Joseph. 2002. *Globalization and Its Discontents*. New York: W.W. Norton.

———. 2007. *Making Globalization Work*. New York: W.W. Norton.

Stoett, Peter. 1999. *Human and Global Security: An Exploration of Terms*. Toronto: University of Toronto Press.

Thucydides. [n.d.] 1974. *History of the Peloponnesian Wars*. New York: Penguin Books.

US Department of State. "State Sponsors of Terrorism." Accessed 25 April 2019. https://www.state.gov/j/ct/list/c14151.htm.

Walt, Stephen. 1998. "International Relations: One World, Many Theories." *Foreign Policy* 110: 29–32, 34–46.

Waltz, Kenneth. 1954. *Man, the State, and War*. New York: Columbia University Press.

———. 1979. *Theory of International Politics*. Reading, MA: Addison-Wesley.

Wendt, Alexander. 1992. "Anarchy Is What States Make of It: The Social Construction of Power Politics." *International Organization* 46(2): 391–425.

———. *Social Theory of International Politics*. Cambridge: Cambridge University Press, 1999.

Wolf, Martin. 2004. *Why Globalization Works*. New Haven, CT: Yale University Press.

Note: Information for the country profiles comes from the following sources:

CIA World Factbook. https://www.cia.gov/library/publications/the-world-factbook/index.html. Accessed 2 March 2015.

United Nations. *Human Development Report 2016*. http://hdr.undp.org/sites/default/files/hdr16-report-en-1.pdf.

World Bank. *World Development Indicators*. http://data.worldbank.org/data-catalog/world-development-indicators. Accessed 2 March 2015.

Brazil

Barbara, Vanessa. 2017. "The Genocide of Brazil's Indians." *New York Times*, 29 May. https://www.nytimes.com/2017/05/29/opinion/the-genocide-of-brazils-indians.html.

Cardoso, Fernando Henrique, and Enzo Faletto. 1979. *Dependency and Development in Latin America*. Trans. Marjory Mattingly Urquidi. Berkeley: University of California Press.

dos Santos Carvalho Carinhanha, Ana Maria. 2018. "Assassination in Brazil Unmasks the Deadly Racism of a Country That Would Rather Ignore It." *The Conversation*, [12 April] 13 April. https://theconversation.com/assassination-in-brazil-unmasks-the-deadly-racism-of-a-country-that-would-rather-ignore-it-94389.

Evans, Peter. 1979. *Dependent Development: The Alliance of Multinational, State, and Local Capital in Brazil*. Princeton, NJ: Princeton University Press.

———. 1989. "Predatory, Developmental and Other Apparatuses: A Comparative Political Economy Perspective on the Third World State." *Sociological Forum* 4(4): 561–87.

Fausto, Boris. 1999. *A Concise History of Brazil*. New York: Cambridge University Press.

Graham, Richard. 1990. *Patronage and Politics in Nineteenth-Century Brazil*. Stanford, CA: Stanford University Press.

Haggard, Stephan, and Robert R. Kaufman. 1995. *The Political Economy of Democratic Transitions*. Princeton, NJ: Princeton University Press.

Htun, Mala. 2004. "Is Gender Like Ethnicity? The Political Representation of Gender Groups." *Perspectives on Politics* 2(3): 439–58.

———, and Timothy J. Power. 2006. "Gender, Parties, and Support for Equal Rights in the Brazilian Congress." *Latin American Politics and Society* 48(4): 83–104.

Macaulay, Fiona. 2006. *Gender Politics in Brazil and Chile: The Role of Parties in National and Local Policymaking*. New York: Palgrave Macmillan, in association with St Antony's College.

O'Donnell, Guillermo A. 1973. *Modernization and Bureaucratic-Authoritarianism: Studies in South American Politics*. Berkeley: Institute of International Studies, University of California.

———, Philippe Schmitter, and Laurence Whitehead, eds. [1986] 1993. *Transitions from Authoritarian Rule* (4 vols.). Baltimore, MD: Johns Hopkins University Press.

Roett, Riordan. 2011. *The New Brazil*. Washington, DC: Brookings Institution Press.

Skidmore, Thomas E. 2010. *Brazil: Five Centuries of Change*. 2nd edn. New York: Oxford University Press.

Stepan, Alfred C. 1971. *The Military in Politics: Changing Patterns in Brazil*. Princeton, NJ: Princeton University Press.

UNESCO (United Nations Educational, Scientific and Cultural Organization). "Indigenous Peoples in Brazil." Accessed 18 April 2019. http://www.unesco.org/new/en/brasilia/education/inclusive-education/indigenous-peoples.

Watts, Jonathan. 2016. "Dilma Rousseff Impeachment: What You Need to Know." *The Guardian*, 31 August. https://www.theguardian.com/news/2016/aug/31/dilma-rousseff-impeachment-brazil-what-you-need-to-know.

Zucco, Cesar. 2008. "The President's 'New' Constituency: Lula and the Pragmatic Vote in Brazil's 2006 Presidential Elections." *Journal of Latin American Studies* 40(1): 29–49.

Canada

BBC News: US & Canada. 2018. "Canada Profile—Timeline." 1 October. https://www.bbc.co.uk/news/world-us-canada-16841165.

"Bilingualism." [2006] 24 February 2015. *The Canadian Encyclopedia*. https://www.thecanadianencyclopedia.ca/en/article/bilingualism.

Burnet, Jean, and Leo Driedger. 27 June 2011. "Multiculturalism." *The Canadian Encyclopedia*. [Modified by Niko Block on 10 September 2014]. https://www.thecanadianencyclopedia.ca/en/article/multiculturalism.

CBC News. "50% Population, 25% Representation. Why the Parliamentary Gender Gap?" Accessed 18 April 2019. http://www.cbc.ca/news2/interactives/women-politics.

Daschuk, James. 2013. *Clearing the Plains: Disease, Politics of Starvation, and the Loss of Aboriginal Life*. Regina: University of Regina Press.

Everitt, Joanna. 2015. "Gender and Sexual Diversity in Provincial Election Campaigns." *Canadian Political Science Review* 9(1): 177–92.

Export Development Canada (EDC). "Trade Insights" page. Accessed 18 April 2019. https://edc.trade/trade-agreement-opportunities-for-canadian-companies.

Galloway, Gloria, and Dakshana Bascaramurty. 2017. "Census 2016: Canada Getting More Diverse as Immigration, Indigenous Population Increase." *Globe and Mail*, 25 October. https://beta.theglobeandmail.com/news/national/census-2016-highlights-diversity-housing-indigenous/article36711216/?ref=http://www.theglobeandmail.com&.

Global News. 2017. "Gender Equality in Canada: Where Do We Stand Today?" 5 July. https://globalnews.ca/news/3574060/gender-equality-in-canada-where-do-we-stand-today.

Granatstein, J.I. [7 February 2006] 29 April 2016. "Peacekeeping." *The Canadian Encyclopedia*. https://www.thecanadianencyclopedia.ca/en/article/peacekeeping.

Immigration, Refugees and Citizenship Canada. "Canada Welcomes More Privately Sponsored Refugees in 2019." Accessed 23 April 2019. https://www.canada.ca/en/immigration-refugees-citizenship/corporate/mandate/policies-operational-instructions-agreements/timely-protection-privately-sponsored-refugees.html.

Indigenous Foundation Arts. "Reserves." Accessed 23 April 2019. https://indigenousfoundations.arts.ubc.ca/reserves.

Jai, Julie. 2017. "Bargains Made in Bad Times: How Principles from Modern Treaties Can Reinvigorate Historic Treaties." In John Borrows and Michael Coyle, eds, *The Right Relationship: Reimagining the Implementation of Historical Treaties*, 105–48. Toronto: University of Toronto Press.

Jones, Richard, Donald B. Smith, and R. Douglas Francis. 2000. *Origins: Canadian History to Confederation*, 4th edn. Toronto: Harcourt Canada.

Lagace, Naithan, and Niigaanwewidam James Sinclair. 2015. "The White Paper, 1969." *The Canadian Encyclopedia*. https://www.thecanadianencyclopedia.ca/en/article/the-white-paper-1969.

Maracle, Lee. 2017. *My Conversations with Canadians*. Toronto: Book*hug Press.

Marshall, Tabitha, and David A. Cruikshank. [7 February 2006] 16 October 2015. "Persons Case." *The Canadian Encyclopedia*. https://www.thecanadianencyclopedia.ca/en/article/persons-case.

Miller, James R. 2010. "Reconciliation with Residential School Survivors: A Progress Report." In Jerry White, Julie Peters, and Dan Beavons, eds, *Aboriginal Policy Research: Voting, Governance, and Research Methodology*, 133–46. Toronto: Thompson Educational Publishing.

Moscovitch, Allan. [7 February 2006] 13 August 2015. "Welfare State." *The Canadian Encyclopedia*. https://www.thecanadianencyclopedia.ca/en/article/welfare-state.

Nagel, Jack H. 2012. "Evaluating Democracy in New Zealand under MMP." *Policy Quarterly* 8(2): 3–11.

Nossal, Kim Richard. 2005. "Anti-Americanism in Canada." CPS Working Papers. Center for Policy Studies, Central European University: 1–22.

O'Neill, Brenda. 2015. "Unpacking Gender's Role in Political Representation in Canada." *Canadian Parliamentary Review* (Summer): 22–30.

Palmater, Pamela D. 2011. *Beyond Blood: Rethinking Indigenous Identity*. Vancouver: UBC Press.

Perreaux, Les. 2017. "After Syria Initiative, UN Looks to Canada as a Refugee Haven." *Globe and Mail*, 3 November. https://www.theglobeandmail.com/news/politics/after-syria-initiative-un-looks-to-canada-as-a-refugee-haven/article36836631.

Statistics Canada. 2016. "National Household Survey, 2011." Table 4. Accessed 23 April 2019. https://www150.statcan.gc.ca/n1/pub/91-003-x/2014001/section03/33-eng.htm.

———. 2017. "Census in Brief: The Aboriginal Languages of First Nations People, Métis and Inuit." Accessed 3 April 2019. https://www12.statcan.gc.ca/census-recensement/2016/as-sa/98-200-x/2016022/98-200-x2016022-eng.cfm.

Trimble, Linda, Jane Arscott, and Manon Tremblay. 2014. *Stalled—The Representation of Women in Canadian Governments*. Vancouver: UBC Press.

Vowel, Chelsea. 2016. *Indigenous Writes: A Guide to First Nations, Metis and Inuit Issues in Canada*. Winnipeg: Portage and Main Press.

China

Averill, Stephen C. 1998. "Chinese Communist Revolution (1921–1949)." In Jack Goldstone, ed., *Encyclopedia of Political Revolutions*, 78–83. Washington, DC: Congressional Quarterly, Inc.

Edmonds, Richard Louis. 1997. "The State of Studies on Republican China." *The China Quarterly* 150: 255–59.

Epstein, Edward. 1984. "Legitimacy, Institutionalization, and Opposition in Exclusionary Bureaucratic-Authoritarian Regimes: The Situation of the 1980s." *Comparative Politics* 17(1): 37–54.

Fairbank, John King, and Merle Goldman. 2006. *China: A New History*. 2nd edn. Cambridge, MA: Belknap Press of Harvard University Press.

Gilley, Bruce. 2010. "Deng Ziaoping and His Successors: 1976 to the Present." In William A. Joseph, ed., *Politics in China*, 103–28. New York: Oxford University Press.

Harrison, Henrietta. 2001. *China: Inventing the Nation*. London: Arnold; New York: Oxford University Press.

Joseph, William A. 2010. "Ideology and Chinese Politics." In William A. Joseph, ed., *Politics in China: An Introduction*, 129–64. New York: Oxford University Press.

Perry, Elizabeth. 1998. "Chinese Cultural Revolutions (1966–1969)." In Jack Goldstone, ed., *Encyclopedia of Political Revolutions*, 83–5. Washington DC: Congressional Quarterly, Inc.

Pew Forum on Religion and Public Life. 2008. "Religion in China on the Eve of the 2008 Olympics." Accessed 23 April 2019. http://pewforum.org/Importance-of-Religion/Religion-in-China-on-the-Eve-of-the-2008-Beijing-Olympics.aspx.

Press Trust of India. 2017. "China Lifting 800 Million People out of Poverty Is Historic: World Bank." *Business Standard*, 13 October. https://www.business-standard.com/article/international/china-lifting-800-million-people-out-of-poverty-is-historic-world-bank-117101300027_1.html.

Schoppa, R. Keith. 2010. "From Empire to People's Republic." In William A. Joseph, ed., *Politics in China*, 37–62. New York: Oxford University Press.

Skocpol, Theda. 1979. *States and Social Revolutions: A Comparative Analysis of France, Russia, and China*. New York: Cambridge University Press.

Spence, Jonathan D. 1990. *The Search for Modern China*. New York: W.W. Norton.

Teiwes, Frederick C. 2010. "Mao Zedong in Power (1949–1976)." In William A. Joseph, ed., *Politics in China*, 63–102. New York: Oxford University Press.

Weiming, Tu. 1999. "The Quest for Meaning: Religion in the People's Republic of China." In Peter L. Berger, ed., *The Desecularization of the World: Resurgent Religion and World Politics*, 85–102. Grand Rapids, MI: William B. Eerdmans.

France

Arendt, Hannah. 1963. *On Revolution*. New York: Viking Press.

Bell, David A. 2001. *The Cult of the Nation in France: Inventing Nationalism, 1680–1800*. Cambridge, MA: Harvard University Press.

Doyle, William. 2003. *The Oxford History of the French Revolution*. 2nd edn. New York: Oxford University Press.

Furet, François. [1988] 1995. *Revolutionary France, 1770–1880*. Trans. Antonia Nevill. Oxford: Blackwell.

Greenfeld, Liah. 1992. *Nationalism: Five Roads to Modernity*. Cambridge, MA: Harvard University Press.

Kalman, Samuel. 2010. "Introduction: Colonial Violence." *Historical Reflections* 36(2): 1–6.

Kuru, Ahmet. 2009. *Secularism and State Policies toward Religion: The United States, France, and Turkey*. New York: Cambridge University Press.

Parry, D.L.L., and Pierre Girard. 2002. *France since 1800: Squaring the Hexagon*. New York: Oxford University Press.

Prasad, Monica. 2006. *The Politics of Free Markets: The Rise of Neoliberal Economic Policies in Britain, France, Germany, and the United States*. Chicago: University of Chicago Press.

Ramdani, Nabila. 2012. "Fifty Years after Algeria's Independence, France Is Still in Denial." *The Guardian: Opinion*, 5 July. https://www.theguardian.com/commentisfree/2012/jul/05/50-years-algeria-independence-france-denial.

Schwartz, Vanessa. 2011. *Modern France: A Very Short Introduction*. New York: Oxford University Press.

Germany

Berger, Stefan. 2004. *Germany: Inventing the Nation*. London: Arnold.

Browning, Christopher. 1992. *Ordinary Men: Reserve Police Battalion 101 and the Final Solution in Poland*. New York: HarperCollins.

Burke, Jason, and Philip Oltermann. 2016. "Germany Moves to Atone for 'Forgotten Genocide' in Namibia." *The Guardian*, 25 December. https://www.theguardian.com/world/2016/dec/25/germany-moves-to-atone-for-forgotten-genocide-in-namibia.

Davies, Norman. 1996. *Europe: A History*. New York: Harper Perennial.

Esping-Anderson, Gøsta. 1990. *The Three Worlds of Welfare Capitalism*. Princeton, NJ: Princeton University Press.

Fetzer, Joel S., and J. Christopher Soper. 2005. *Muslims and the State in Britain, France, and Germany*. New York: Cambridge University Press.

Fulbrook, Mary. 1990. *A Concise History of Germany*. New York: Cambridge University Press.

Goldhagen, Daniel. 1996. *Hitler's Willing Executioners: Ordinary Germans and the Holocaust*. New York: Knopf.

Greenfeld, Liah. 1992. *Nationalism: Five Roads to Modernity*. Cambridge, MA: Harvard University Press.

Hentschel, Volker. 2008. "German Economic and Social Policy, 1815–1939." In Peter Mathias and Sidney Pollard, eds, *The Cambridge Economic History of Europe*, vol. 8, 752–813. New York: Cambridge University Press (Cambridge Histories Online).

James, Harold. 2009. "The Weimar Economy." In Anthony McElligott, ed., *Weimar Germany (The Short Oxford History of Germany)*, 102–26. New York: Oxford University Press.

Kitchen, Martin. 2006. *A History of Modern Germany, 1800–2000*. Malden, MA: Blackwell.

McElligott, Anthony, ed. 2009. *Weimar Germany (The Short Oxford History of Germany)*. New York: Oxford University Press.

Mares, Isabela. 2001. "Strategic Bargaining and Social Policy Development: Unemployment Insurance in France and Germany." In Bernard Ebbinghaus and Philip Manow, eds, *Comparing Welfare Capitalism: Social Policy and Political Economy in Europe, Japan, and the USA*, 52–75. New York: Routledge.

Olson, Mancur. 1984. *The Rise and Decline of Nations: Economic Growth, Stagnation, and Social Rigidities*. New Haven, CT: Yale University Press.

Weber, Eugen. 1972. *Europe since 1715: A Modern Introduction*. New York: W.W. Norton.

India

Allen, Robert C. 2011. *Global Economic History: A Very Short Introduction*. New York: Oxford University Press.

Balakrishnan, Pulapre. 2010. *Economic Growth in India: History and Prospect*. New York: Oxford University Press.

Davis, Mike. 2000. *Late Victorian Holocausts: El Nino Famines and the Making of the Third World*. London: Verso Books.

Dirks, Nicholas B. 2001. *Castes of Mind: Colonialism and the Making of Modern India*. Princeton, NJ: Princeton University Press.

Dumont, Louis. [1966] 1981. *Homo Hierarchicus: The Caste System and Its Implications*. Chicago: University of Chicago Press.

Friedman, Thomas L. 2005. *The World Is Flat: A Brief History of the Twenty-First Century*. New York: Farrar, Strauss, and Giroux.

Kohli, Atul. 2004. *State-Directed Development: Political Power and Industrialization on the Global Periphery*. Cambridge: Cambridge University Press.

Mehta, Suketu. 2004. *Maximum City: Bombay Lost and Found*. New York: Alfred A. Knopf.

Metcalf, Barbara D., and Thomas R. Metcalf. 2006. *A Concise History of Modern India*. 2nd edn. New York: Cambridge University Press.

Pew Forum on Religion and Public Life. 2009. "Mapping the Global Muslim Population: A Report on the Size and Distribution of the World's Muslim Population." Pew Research Center, 7 October. http://www.pewforum.org/2009/10/07/mapping-the-global-muslim-population.

Sen, Amartya. 1999. *Development as Freedom*. New York: Alfred A. Knopf.

Iran

Arjomand, Said Amir. 2009. *After Khomeini: Iran under His Successors*. New York: Oxford University Press.

Foran, John. 2005. *Taking Power: On the Origins of Third World Revolutions*. New York: Cambridge University Press.

Hambly, Gavin R.G. [1991] 2008a. "The Pahlavī Autocracy: Riżā Shāh 1921–1941." In Peter Avery, Gavin Hambly, and Charles Melville, eds, *The Cambridge History of Iran*, vol. 7: *From Nadir Shah to the Islamic Republic*, online edn, 213–43. New York: Cambridge University Press.

——— [1991] 2008b. "The Pahlavī Autocracy: Muhammad Riżā Shāh 1941–1979." In Peter Avery, Gavin Hambly, and Charles Melville, eds, *The Cambridge History of Iran*, vol. 7: *From Nadir Shah to the Islamic Republic*, online edn, 244–93. New York: Cambridge University Press.

Hausmann, Ricardo, Laura D. Tyson, and Saadia Zahidi. "The Global Gender Gap Report 2010." World Economic Forum. Accessed 23 April 2019. http://www3.weforum.org/docs/WEF_GenderGap_Report_2010.pdf.

Keddie, Nikki. [1991] 2008. "Iran under the Later Qājārs, 1848–1922." In Peter Avery, Gavin Hambly, and Charles Melville, eds, *The Cambridge History of Iran*, vol. 7: *From Nadir Shah to the Islamic Republic*, online edn, 174–212. New York: Cambridge University Press.

Kurzman, Charles. 2004. *The Unthinkable Revolution in Iran*. Cambridge, MA: Harvard University Press.

Lowry, Rich. 2018. "The Real Conflict with Iran." *National Review*, 24 July. https://www.nationalreview.com/2018/07/iran-should-fear-financial-warfare-and-economic-crisis.

Mir-Hosseini, Ziba. 1999. *Islam and Gender: The Religious Debate in Contemporary Iran*. Princeton, NJ: Princeton University Press.

Moaddel, Mansoor. 2005. *Islamic Modernism, Nationalism, and Fundamentalism: Episode and Discourse*. Chicago: University of Chicago Press.

Parsa, Misagh. 2000. *States, Ideologies, and Social Revolutions: A Comparative Analysis of Iran, Nicaragua, and the Philippines*. New York: Cambridge University Press.

Sagan, Scott D. 1996. "Why Do States Build Nuclear Weapons? Three Models in Search of a Bomb." *International Security* 21(3): 54–86.

Salehi-Isfahani, Djavad. 2009. "Oil Wealth and Economic Growth in Iran." In Ali Gheissari, ed., *Contemporary Iran: Economy, Society, Politics*, 3–37. New York: Oxford University Press.

Takeyh, Ray. 2017. "Iran's President Isn't a Reformer. He's an Enabler." *Politico*, 22 May. https://www.politico.com/magazine/story/2017/05/22/irans-president-isnt-a-reformer-hes-an-enabler-215171.

World Bank. "Proportion of Seats Held by Women in National Parliaments (%)." Accessed 23 April 2019. https://data.worldbank.org/indicator/SG.GEN.PARL.ZS.

World Economic Forum. "The Global Gender Gap Report 2017." Accessed 23 April 2019. http://www3.weforum.org/docs/WEF_GGGR_2017.pdf.

Japan

Crawcour, E. Sydney. 2008. "Industrialization and Technological Change, 1885–1920." In Peter Duus, ed., *The Cambridge History of Japan*, vol. 6: *The Twentieth Century*, online edn, 385–450. New York: Cambridge University Press.

Eszter, Polyák. 2018. "Womenomics—Women at the Japanese Labour Market." *Geopolitika (Pallas Athene Geopolitical Research Institute)*, 18 February. http://www.geopolitika.hu/en/2018/02/13/womenomics-women-at-the-japanese-labour-market.

Evans, Peter B. 1989. "Predatory, Developmental, and Other Apparatuses: A Comparative Political Economy Perspective on the Third World State." *Sociological Forum* 4(4): 561–87.

Fukui, Haruhiro. [1988] 2008. "Postwar Politics: 1945–1973." In Peter Duus, ed., *The Cambridge History of Japan*, vol. 6: *The Twentieth Century*, online edn, 154–213. New York: Cambridge University Press.

Gordon, Andrew. 2009. *A Modern History of Japan: From Tokugawa Times to the Present*. 2nd edn. New York: Oxford University Press.

Horiuchi, Yusaku, and Jun Saito. 2003. "Reapportionment and Redistribution: Consequences of Electoral Reform in Japan." *American Journal of Political Science* 47(4): 669–82.

Inter-Parliamentary Union (IPU). "Women in National Parliaments." Accessed 23 April 2019. http://www.ipu.org/wmn-e/classif.htm.

Kabashima, Ikuo, and Gill Steel. 2010. *Changing Politics in Japan*. Ithaca, NY: Cornell University Press.

Kosai, Yutaka. 2008. "The Postwar Japanese Economy, 1945–1973." In Peter Duus, ed., *The Cambridge History of Japan*, vol. 6: *The Twentieth Century*, online edn, 494–537. New York: Cambridge University Press.

Kunio, Yoshihara. 2006. "Japanese Culture and Postwar Economic Growth." In Lawrence E. Harrison and Peter L. Berger, eds, *Developing Cultures: Case Studies*, 83–100. New York: Routledge.

Larmer, Brock. 2018. "Why Does Japan Make It So Hard for Working Women to Succeed?" *New York Times*, 17 October. https://www.nytimes.com/2018/10/17/magazine/why-does-japan-make-it-so-hard-for-working-women-to-succeed.html.

LeBlanc, Robin M. 1999. *Bicycle Citizens: The Political World of the Japanese Housewife*. Berkeley: University of California Press.

Manow, Philip. 2001. "Business Coordination, Wage Bargaining, and the Welfare State: Germany and Japan in Comparative Historical Perspective." In Bernhard Ebbinghaus and Philip Manow, eds, *Comparing Welfare Capitalism: Social Policy and Political Economy in Europe, Japan, and the USA*, 27–51. New York: Routledge.

Mitani, Taichiro. 2008. "The Establishment of Party Cabinets, 1898–1932." In Peter Duus, ed., *The Cambridge History of Japan*, vol. 6: *The Twentieth Century*, online edn, 55–96. New York: Cambridge University Press.

Murakami, Sakura. 2018. "Japan Fails to Shine in Annual Report on Women's Participation in Politics." *The Japan Times*, 7 March. https://www.japantimes.co.jp/news/2018/03/07/national/japan-fails-shine-annual-report-womens-participation-politics/#.XGIJKbjRWUk.

Nakamura, Takafusa. 2008. "Depression, Recovery, and War, 1920–1945." In Peter Duus, ed., *The Cambridge History of Japan*, vol. 6: *The Twentieth Century*, online edn, 451–93. New York: Cambridge University Press.

North, Douglass. 1990. *Institutions, Institutional Change, and Economic Performance*. New York: Cambridge University Press.

United Nations Development Programme (UNDP). "Human Development Reports Gender Equality Index 2018." Accessed 23 April 2019. http://hdr.undp.org/en/indicators/68606.

World Bank. "Proportion of Seats Held by Women in National Parliaments (%)." Accessed 23 April 2019. https://data.worldbank.org/indicator/SG.GEN.PARL.ZS?locations=JP.

Mexico

Anna, Timothy E. 1998. *Forging Mexico, 1821–1835*. Lincoln: University of Nebraska Press.

Basáñez, Miguel. 2006. "Mexico: The Camel and the Needle." In Lawrence E. Harrison and Peter L. Berger, eds, *Developing Cultures: Case Studies*, 287–303. New York: Routledge.

BBC News: Latin America. 2018. "Mexico Profile—Timeline." 3 December. https://www.bbc.co.uk/news/world-latin-america-19828041.

Blancarte, Roberto. 1992. *Historia de la Iglesia Católica en México* [History of the Catholic Church in Mexico]. *Mexico*, DF: El Colegio Mexiquense/Fondo de Cultura Económica.

Camp, Roderic Ai. 2007. *Politics in Mexico: The Democratic Consolidation*. New York: Oxford University Press.

CNN Library. 2018. "Andrés Manuel López Obrador Fast Facts." *CNN World*, 14 December. https://edition.cnn.com/2018/07/27/world/andrs-manuel-lpez-obrador-fast-facts/index.html.

Davis, Diane E. 2006. "Undermining the Rule of Law: Democratization and the Dark Side of Police Reform in Mexico." *Latin American Politics and Society* 48(1): 55–86.

Gill, Anthony. 2008. *The Political Origins of Religious Liberty*. New York: Cambridge University Press.

Halperín Donghi, Tulio. 1993. *The Contemporary History of Latin America*. Trans. John Charles Chasteen. Durham, NC: Duke University Press.

Hamnett, Brian. 1994. *Juárez*. New York: Longman.

Hernández Navarro, Luis, and Laura Carlsen. 2004. "Indigenous Rights: The Battle for Constitutional Reform in Mexico." In Kevin J. Middlebrook, ed., *Dilemmas of Political Change in Mexico*, 440–65. London: Institute of Latin American Studies.

Knight, Alan. 1990a. *The Mexican Revolution*, vol. 1: *Porfirians, Liberals, and Peasants*. Lincoln: University of Nebraska Press.

———. 1990b. *The Mexican Revolution*, vol. 2: *Counter-Revolution and Reconstruction*. Lincoln: University of Nebraska Press.

Krauze, Enrique. 1997. *Mexico, Biography of Power: A History of Modern Mexico*. Trans. Hank Heifetz. New York: Harper Perennial.

Lynch, John. 1973. *The Spanish-American Revolutions, 1808–1826*. New York: W.W. Norton.

———. 1986. "The Catholic Church in Latin America, 1830–1930." In Leslie Bethell, ed., *The Cambridge History of Latin America*, vol. 4: *c. 1870–1930*, 527–95. New York: Cambridge University Press.

Magaloni, Beatriz, and Guillermo Zepeda. 2004. "Democratization, Judicial and Law Enforcement Institutions, and the Rule of Law in Mexico." In Kevin J. Middlebrook, ed., *Dilemmas of Political Change in Mexico*, 168–97. London: Institute of Latin American Studies.

Mahoney, James. 2010. *Colonialism and Postcolonial Development: Spanish America in Comparative Perspective*. New York: Cambridge University Press.

Meyer, Michael C., and William L. Sherman. 1987. *The Course of Mexican History*. 3rd edn. New York: Oxford University Press.

Mörner, Magnus. 1993. *Region and State in Latin America's Past*. Baltimore, MD: Johns Hopkins University Press.

O'Neil, Shannon. 2009. "The Real War in Mexico: How Democracy Can Defeat the Drug Cartels." *Foreign Affairs* 88(4): 63–77.

Thomas, Hugh. 1993. *Conquest: Montezuma, Cortes, and the Fall of Old Mexico*. New York: Simon and Schuster.

Womack, John. 1968. *Zapata and the Mexican Revolution*. New York: Vintage.

Nigeria

BBC News: Africa. 2017. "Nigeria Profile—Media." 1 August. https://www.bbc.co.uk/news/world-africa-13949549.

———. 2019. "Nigeria Profile—Timeline." 18 February. https://www.bbc.co.uk/news/world-africa-13951696.

Bratton, Michael, and Nicolas van de Walle. 1997. *Democratic Experiments in Africa: Regime Transitions in Comparative Perspective*. Cambridge: Cambridge University Press.

Dorward, D.C. 1986. "British West Africa and Liberia." In A.D. Roberts, ed., *Cambridge History of Africa*, vol. 7: *From 1905 to 1940*, 399–459. New York: Cambridge University Press.

Dunning, Thad. 2008. *Crude Democracy: Natural Resource Wealth and Political Regimes*. Cambridge: Cambridge University Press.

Falola, Toyin, and Matthew M. Heaton. 2008. *A History of Nigeria*. New York: Cambridge University Press.

Herbst, Jeffrey. 2000. *States and Power in Africa: Comparative Lessons in Authority and Control*. Princeton, NJ: Princeton University Press.

Karl, Terry Lynn. 1997. *The Paradox of Plenty: Oil Booms and Petro States*. Berkeley: University of California Press.

Kohli, Atul. 2004. *State-Directed Development: Political Power and Industrialization in the Global Periphery*. Cambridge: Cambridge University Press.

Lange, Matthew. 2009. *Lineages of Despotism and Development: British Colonialism and State Power*. Chicago: University of Chicago Press.

Maclean, Ruth, and Eromo Egbejule. 2019. "Nigeria Election: 'Mr Honesty' Tainted by Failure to Tackle Corruption." *The Guardian*, 11 February. https://www.theguardian.com/world/2019/feb/11/nigeria-election-mr-honesty-muhammadu-buhari-tainted-by-failure-to-tackle-corruption.

Mamdani, Mahmood. 1996. *Citizen and Subject: Contemporary Africa and the Legacy of Late Colonialism*. Princeton, NJ: Princeton University Press.

Suberu, Rotimi T. 2001. *Federalism and Ethnic Conflict in Nigeria*. Washington, DC: United States Institute of Peace.

Williams, David. 1984. "English Speaking West Africa." In Michael Crowder, ed., *Cambridge History of Africa*, vol. 8: *From c. 1940 to c. 1975*, 331–82. New York: Cambridge University Press.

Russia

Ascher, Abraham. 2009. *Russia: A Short History*. New edn. Oxford: Oneworld Publications.

Ash, Timothy Garton. 2002. *The Polish Revolution: Solidarity*. 3rd edn. New Haven, CT: Yale University Press.

Brown, Archie. 2006. "Cultural Change and Continuity in the Transition from Communism: The Russian Case." In Lawrence E. Harrison and Peter L. Berger, eds, *Developing Cultures: Case Studies*, 387–405. New York: Routledge.

Bushkovitch, Paul. 2012. *A Concise History of Russia*. New York: Cambridge University Press.

Carr, E.H. [1979] 2004. *The Russian Revolution from Lenin to Stalin, 1917–1929*. New York: Palgrave Macmillan.

Colton, Timothy, and Michael McFaul. 2003. *Popular Choice and Managed Democracy: The Russian Elections of 1999 and 2000*. Washington, DC: The Brookings Institution Press.

Davies, Norman. 1996. *Europe: A History*. New York: Harper-Perennial.

Fitzpatrick, Sheila. 1994. *The Russian Revolution*. New York: Oxford University Press.

Greenfeld, Liah. 1992. *Nationalism: Five Roads to Modernity*. Cambridge, MA: Harvard University Press.

Goldman, Marshall I. 2004. "Putin and the Oligarchs." *Foreign Affairs* 83(6): 33–44.

Hanbury, Mary, and Áine Cain. 2018. "No One Knows Putin's Exact Net Worth, But Many Speculate He's the Wealthiest Person on the Planet—His $1 Billion Palace and $500 Million Yacht Explain Why." *Business Insider*, 16 July. https://www.businessinsider.com/how-putin-spends-his-mysterious-fortune-2017-6/?r=AU&IR=T/#the-repeated-rebuttals-have-done-nothing-to-dispel-the-scrutiny-on-putins-alleged-riches-in-a-country-where-20-million-people-can-barely-make-ends-meet-the-luxurious-life-of-the-president-is-a-brazen-and-cynical-challenge-to-society-from-a-high-handed-potentate-nemstov-wrote-in-one-2012-white-paper-the-politician-a-longtime-and-vocal-critic-of-putin-was-assassinated-in-2015-31.

Hughes, Lindsey. 2008. "Russian Culture in the Eighteenth Century." In Dominic Lieven, ed., *The Cambridge History of Russia*, vol. 2: *Imperial Russia, 1689–1917*, online edn, 67–91. New York: Cambridge University Press.

Kitchen, Martin. 2006. *A History of Modern Germany, 1800–2000*. Malden, MA: Blackwell.

Kottasová, Ivana. 2018. "How Rich Is Vladimir Putin?" *CNN Money*, 14 March. https://money.cnn.com/2018/03/14/news/putin-wealth-russia-election/index.html.

Levitsky, Steven, and Lucan A. Way. 2010. *Competitive Authoritarianism: Hybrid Regimes after the Cold War*. New York: Cambridge University Press.

McFaul, Michael. 2008. "The Russian Federation." In Ronald Grigor Suny, ed., *The Cambridge History of Russia*, vol. 3: *The Twentieth Century*, online edn, 352–80. New York: Cambridge University Press.

Mainwaring, Scott. 1998. "Party Systems in the Third Wave." *Journal of Democracy* 9(3): 67–81.

Rose, Richard, William Mishler, and Neil Munro. 2006. *Russia Transformed: Developing Popular Support for a New Regime*. New York: Cambridge University Press.

Service, Robert. 2009. *A History of Modern Russia: From Tsarism to the Twenty-First Century*. 3rd edn. Cambridge, MA: Harvard University Press.

Sharafutdinova, Gulnaz. 2011. *Political Consequences of Crony Capitalism inside Russia*. Notre Dame, IN: University of Notre Dame Press.

Stalin, Joseph.[1913] 1994. "The Nation." In John Hutchinson and Anthony D. Smith, eds, *Nationalism*, 18–20. New York: Oxford University Press.

Treisman, Daniel. 2011. *The Return: Russia's Journey from Gorbachev to Medvedev*. New York: The Free Press.

Saudi Arabia

Al Batati, Saeed. 2015. "Who are the Houthis in Yemen?" *Al Jazeera News*, 29 March. https://www.aljazeera.com/news/middleeast/2014/08/yemen-houthis-hadi-protests-201482132719818986.html.

Al Dabaan, Rasha. "Saudi Arabia History." http://www.sa.undp.org/content/saudi_arabia/en/home/countryinfo.html.

Al Jazeera News. 2017. "Beyond Oil: Saudi Arabia's 2030 Economic Vision." *Al Jazeera: Counting the Cost*, 4 November. https://www.aljazeera.com/programmes/countingthecost/2017/11/oil-saudi-arabia-2030-economic-vision-171104083501148.html.

———. 2019a. "EU Blacklists Saudi Arabia: What Does It Mean?" 13 February. https://www.aljazeera.com/news/2019/02/eu-blacklists-saudi-arabia-190213212736905.html.

———. 2019b. "Saudi Arabia: Corruption Crackdown Ends with $106bn Recovered." 31 January. https://www.aljazeera.com/news/2019/01/saudi-arabia-corruption-crackdown-ends-106bn-recovered-190131062458260.html.

———. 2019c. "Saudi Aramco: The Company and the State." 2 February. https://www.aljazeera.com/programmes/specialseries/2019/01/saudi-aramco-company-state-190126125553856.html.

Alyas, Fatimah. 2018. "U.S.–Saudi Arabia Relations." Council on Foreign Relations: Backgrounder, 7 December. https://www.cfr.org/backgrounder/us-saudi-arabia-relations.

Amnesty International. 2015. "Yemen War: The Forgotten War." 14 March. Accessed 23 April 2019. https://www.amnesty.org/en/latest/news/2015/09/yemen-the-forgotten-war.

BBC News: Middle East. 2017a. "Crown Prince Says Saudis Want Return to Moderate Islam." 25 October. https://www.bbc.com/news/world-middle-east-41747476.

———. 2017b. "Saudi Arabia Unveils Plans for 'Entertainment City' Near Riyadh." 8 April. https://www.bbc.com/news/world-middle-east-39538528.

———. 2018. "Saudi Arabia Profile—Timeline." 23 November. https://www.bbc.com/news/world-middle-east-14703523.

———. 2019. "Yemen Crisis: Why Is There a War?" 21 March. https://www.bbc.com/news/world-middle-east-29319423.

Blanchard, Christopher M. 2008. "The Islamic Traditions of Wahhabism and Salafiyya." *CRS Report for Congress*, 24 January. Library of Congress, Congressional Research Service. https://fas.org/sgp/crs/misc/RS21695.pdf.

Bleiker, Carla. 2019. "Women's Rights in Saudi Arabia: A Timeline." *Deutsche Welle*, 1 July. https://www.dw.com/en/womens-rights-in-saudi-arabia-a-timeline/g-40709135.

Bowen, Wayne H. 2008. *The History of Saudi Arabia.* Westport, CT: Greenwood Press.

Economist Intelligence Unit (EIU). 2018. "Democracy Index 2018: Me Too? Political Participation, Protest and Democracy." Accessed 23 April 2019. https://www.eiu.com/topic/democracy-index.

Hertog, Steffen. 2016. "Challenges to the Saudi Distributional State in the Age of Austerity." Presented at *Saudi Arabia: Domestic, Regional and International Challenges*, Middle East Institute, National University of Singapore, December. http://eprints.lse.ac.uk/68625.

Human Rights Watch. 2018. "Yemen: Houthi Hostage-Taking." 25 September. https://www.hrw.org/news/2018/09/25/yemen-houthi-hostage-taking.

———. 2019. "Saudi Arabia: 10 Reasons Why Women Flee." 30 January. https://www.hrw.org/news/2019/01/30/saudi-arabia-10-reasons-why-women-flee.

ICNL (International Center for Not-for-Profit Law). 2019. *Civic Freedom Monitor: Saudi Arabia.* Accessed 23 April 2019. http://www.icnl.org/research/monitor/saudiarabia.html.

Jay, Paul. 2014. "The Multiple Kingdoms of Saudi Arabia." *Truthout*, 9 April. https://truthout.org/video/the-multiple-kingdoms-of-saudi-arabia.

Krusch, David. "Islam: Wahhabism." *Jewish Virtual Library.* Accessed 23 April 2019. https://www.jewishvirtuallibrary.org/wahhabi-islam.

Lawson, Fred. 2017. "Modern Saudi Arabia." *Oxford Research Encyclopedias: Asian History*. DOI: 10.1093/acrefore/9780190277727.013.270; http://oxfordre.com/asianhistory/view/10.1093/acrefore/9780190277727.001.0001/acrefore-9780190277727-e-270.

Mahdawi, Arwa. 2018. "Saudi Arabia Is Not Driving Change—It Is Trying to Hoodwink the West." *The Guardian: Opinion*, 26 June. https://www.theguardian.com/world/2018/jun/26/saudi-arabia-is-not-driving-change-it-is-trying-to-hoodwink-the-west.

Malik, Adeel. 2018. "Can Saudi Arabia Diversify Its Economy without an Aramco IPO?" *Al Jazeera*, 4 September. https://www.aljazeera.com/indepth/opinion/saudi-arabia-diversify-economy-aramco-ipo-180904072248249.html.

Malik, Kenan. 2018. "Don't Be Deluded—Our Saudi 'Partners' Are Masters of Repression." *The Guardian: Opinion*, 26 August. https://www.theguardian.com/commentisfree/2018/aug/26/dont-be-deluded-our-saudi-partners-are-masters-of-repression.

Mazzetti, Mark, and Ben Hubbard. 2016. "Rise of Saudi Prince Shatters Decades of Royal Tradition." *New York Times*, 15 October. https://www.nytimes.com/2016/10/16/world/rise-of-saudi-prince-shatters-decades-of-royal-tradition.html.

Metz, Helen Chapin, ed. 1992. *Saudi Arabia: A Country Study.* Washington: GPO for the Library of Congress. http://countrystudies.us/saudi-arabia.

Montagu, Caroline. 2015. "Civil Society in Saudi Arabia: The Power and Challenges of Association." Chatham House Research Paper, March. https://www.chathamhouse.org/sites/default/files/field/field_document/20150331CivilSocietySaudiMontagu.pdf.

Saber, Israa, and Bruce Riedel. 2019. "Where is King Salman? The Saudi King Isn't Traveling Like He Used To." *Brookings: Order from Chaos* (blog), 9 January. https://www.brookings.edu/blog/order-from-chaos/2019/01/09/where-is-king-salman.

Sayigh, Yezid. 2018. "The Warrior Prince." Carnegie Middle East Center, 24 October. https://carnegie-mec.org/diwan/77570.

Stares, Paul B., and Helia Ighani. 2017. "How Stable Is Saudi Arabia?" Council on Foreign Relations: Expert Brief, 15 May. https://www.cfr.org/expert-brief/how-stable-saudi-arabia.

Umoh, Ruth. 2018. "This Royal Family's Wealth Could Be More Than $1 Trillion." CNBC, 18 August. https://www.cnbc.com/2018/08/18/this-royal-familys-wealth-could-be-more-than-1-trillion.html.

Vision 2030: Kingdom of Saudi Arabia. "Foreword: Our Vision: Saudi Arabia. The Heart of the Arab and Islamic Worlds, the Investment Powerhouse, and the Hub Connecting Three Continents." Accessed 23 April 2019. https://vision2030.gov.sa/en/foreword.

Wintour, Patrick. 2018. "Why Is Saudi Arabia in Yemen and What Does it Mean for Britain?" *The Guardian*, 8 March. https://www.theguardian.com/world/2018/mar/08/why-saudi-arabia-in-yemen-what-does-it-mean-for-britain.

United Kingdom

Berger, Peter, Grace Davie, and Effie Fokas. 2008. *Religious America, Secular Europe? A Theme and Variations*. Burlington VT: Ashgate.

Bruce, Steve. 2004. "The Strange Death of Protestant Britain." In Eric P. Kaufmann, ed., *Rethinking Ethnicity: Majority Groups and Dominant Minorities*, 116–35. New York: Routledge.

Clarke, Peter. 2004. *Hope and Glory: Britain 1900–2000*. 2nd edn. New York: Penguin Books.

Greenfeld, Liah. 1992. *Nationalism: Five Roads to Modernity*. Cambridge, MA: Harvard University Press.

———. 2001. *The Spirit of Capitalism: Nationalism and Economic Growth*. Cambridge, MA: Harvard University Press.

Habermas, Jurgen. 1989. *The Structural Transformation of the Public Sphere: An Inquiry into a Category of Bourgeois Society*. Trans. Thomas Burger. Cambridge, MA: MIT Press.

Harvie, Christopher. 2010. "Revolution and the Rule of Law (1789–1851)." In Kenneth O. Morgan, ed., *The Oxford History of Britain*, 470–517. New York: Oxford University Press.

Hastings, Adrian. 1997. *The Construction of Nationhood: Ethnicity, Religion, and Nationalism*. New York: Cambridge University Press.

Huber, Evelyne, and John D. Stephens. 2001. *Development and the Crisis of the Welfare State: Parties and Policies in Global Markets*. Chicago: University of Chicago Press.

Inglehart, Ronald, and Christian Welzel. 2005. *Modernization, Cultural Change, and Democracy: The Human Development Sequence*. New York: Cambridge University Press.

Kishlansky, Mark. 19976. *A Monarchy Transformed: Britain 1603–1714*. New York: Penguin Group.

Kohn, Hans. 1944. *The Idea of Nationalism*. New York: Macmillan.

Matthew, H.C.G. 2010. "The Liberal Age (1851–1914)." In Kenneth O. Morgan, ed., *The Oxford History of Britain*, 518–81. New York: Oxford University Press.

Modood, Tariq. 2007. *Multiculturalism: A Civic Idea*. Malden, MA: Polity Press.

Morgan, Kenneth O. 2010. "Epilogue (2000–2010)." In Kenneth O. Morgan, ed., *The Oxford History of Britain*, 677–710. New York: Oxford University Press.

Osborne, Samuel. 2016. "5 of the Worst Atrocities Carried out by the British Empire." *The Independent*, 19 January. https://www.independent.co.uk/news/uk/home-news/worst-atrocities-british-empire-amritsar-boer-war-concentration-camp-mau-mau-a6821756.html.

Parry, Marc. 2016. "Uncovering the Brutal Truth about the British Empire." *The Guardian: The Long Read*, 18 August. https://www.theguardian.com/news/2016/aug/18/uncovering-truth-british-empire-caroline-elkins-mau-mau.

Pincus, Steven. 2009. *1688: The First Modern Revolution*. New Haven, CT: Yale University Press.

Prasad, Monica. 2006. *The Politics of Free Markets: The Rise of Neoliberal Economic Policies in Britain, France, Germany, and the United States*. Chicago: University of Chicago Press.

Tharoor, Shashi. 2017. *Inglorious Empire: What the British Did to India*. London: Hurst Publishers.

Tilly, Charles. 1997. "Parliamentarization of Contention in Great Britain, 1758–1834." *Theory and Society* 26(2/3): 245–73.

United States

Bellah, Robert N., Richard Madsen, William M. Sullivan, Ann Swidler, and Steven M. Tipton. 1985. *Habits of the Heart: Individualism and Commitment in American Life*. Berkeley: University of California Press.

Brown, Michael K., Martin Carnoy, Elliott Currie, Troy Duster, David B. Oppenheimer, Marjorie M. Schultz, and David Wallman. 2003. *Whitewashing Race: The Myth of a Colorblind Society*. Berkeley: University of California Press.

"Democracy Continues Its Disturbing Retreat." 2018. *The Economist*, 31 January. https://www.economist.com/graphic-detail/2018/01/31/democracy-continues-its-disturbing-retreat.

Dunn, Richard S. [1972] 2000. *Sugar and Slaves: The Rise of the Planter Class in the English West Indies, 1624–1713*. Chapel Hill: University of North Carolina Press.

Economist Intelligence Unit (EIU). *Democracy Index 2018: Me Too? Political Participation, Protest and Democracy*. Accessed 23 April 2019. https://www.eiu.com/topic/democracy.

Fredericks, John, III. 1999. "America's First Nations: The Origins, History and Future of American Indian Sovereignty." *Journal of Law and Policy* 7(2): Article 1.

Hacker, Jacob, and Paul Pierson. 2010. *Winner-Take-All Politics: How Washington Made the Rich Richer—And Turned Its Back on the Middle Class*. New York: Simon and Schuster.

Iannaccone, Laurence R., Roger Finke, and Rodney Stark. 1997. "Deregulating Religion: The Economics of Church and State." *Economic Inquiry* 35: 350–64.

Kaufman, Jason. 2002. *For the Common Good? American Civic Life and the Golden Age of Fraternity*. New York: Oxford University Press.

Kennedy, David M. 1999. *Freedom from Fear: The American People in Depression and War, 1929–1945*. New York: Oxford University Press.

McPherson, James M. 1988. *Battle Cry of Freedom: The Civil War Era*. New York: Oxford University Press.

National Congress of American Indians (NCAI). [2017] 2019. *Tribal Nations & the United States: An Introduction*. March. Accessed 23 April 2019. http://www.ncai.org/about-tribes.

Niebuhr, H. Richard. 1929. *The Social Sources of Denominationalism*. New York: Henry Holt.

Norris, Pippa, and Ronald Inglehart. 2004. *Sacred and Secular: Religion and Politics Worldwide*. New York: Cambridge University Press.

Oxford Research Encyclopedias: Latin American History. https://oxfordre.com/latinamericanhistory/view/10.1093/acrefore/9780199366439.001.0001/acrefore-9780199366439-e-643.

Patterson, James T. 1996. *Grand Expectations: The United States, 1945–1974*. New York: Oxford University Press.

———. 2005. *Restless Giant: The United States from Watergate to* Bush v. Gore. New York: Oxford University Press.

Putnam, Robert D. 2000. *Bowling Alone: The Collapse and Revival of American Community*. New York: Simon and Schuster.

Schoultz, Lars. 1998. *Beneath the United States: A History of U.S. Policy toward Latin America*. Cambridge, MA: Harvard University Press.

Vicaire, Peter Scott. 2013. "Two Roads Diverged: A Comparative Analysis of Indigenous Rights in a North American Constitutional Context." *McGill Law Journal* 58(3): 607–62.

Wilkerson, Isabel. 2010. *The Warmth of Other Suns: The Epic Story of America's Great Migration*. New York: Random House.

Wood, Gordon. [1969] 1998. *The Creation of the American Republic, 1776–1787*. Chapel Hill: University of North Carolina Press.

Wuthnow, Robert. 2007. *After the Baby Boomers: How Twenty- and Thirty-Somethings Are Shaping the Future of American Religion*. Princeton, NJ: Princeton University Press.

Yakabuski, Konrad. 2019. "Democracy in America Is Down, but Not Out." *Globe and Mail*, 11 January. https://www.theglobeandmail.com/opinion/article-democracy-in-the-united-states-is-down-but-not-out.

INDEX